Microsoft

Windows® Internals, Sixth Edition, Part 2

Mark Russinovich
David A. Solomon
Alex Ionescu

D0730806

ANTARES TEAM

PUBLISHED BY
Microsoft Press
A Division of Microsoft Corporation
One Microsoft Way
Redmond, Washington 98052-6399

Library of Congress Control Number: 2012933511
ISBN: 978-0-7356-6587-3

Printed and bound in the United States of America.

First Printing

Microsoft Press books are available through booksellers and distributors worldwide. If you need support related to this book, email Microsoft Press Book Support at mspinput@microsoft.com. Please tell us what you think of this book at http://www.microsoft.com/learning/booksurvey.

Acquisitions Editor: Devon Musgrave
Developmental Editor: Devon Musgrave
Project Editor: Carol Dillingham
Editorial Production: Curtis Philips
Technical Reviewer: Christophe Nasarre; Technical Review services provided by Content Master, a member of CM Group, Ltd.
Copyeditor: John Pierce
Indexer: Jan Wright
Cover: Twist Creative • Seattle

To our parents, who guided and inspired us to follow our dreams

Contents at a Glance

Contents

What do you think of this book? We want to hear from you!

Microsoft is interested in hearing your feedback so we can continually improve our
books and learning resources for you. To participate in a brief online survey, please visit:

microsoft.com/learning/booksurvey

Chapter 10 Memory Management   187

Chapter 11 Cache Manager   355

Chapter 13   Startup and Shutdown   499

Chapter 14 Crash Dump Analysis 547

What do you think of this book? We want to hear from you!

Microsoft is interested in hearing your feedback so we can continually improve our
books and learning resources for you. To participate in a brief online survey, please visit:

microsoft.com/learning/booksurvey

Introduction

Windows Internals, Sixth Edition is intended for advanced computer professionals (both developers and system administrators) who want to understand how the core components of the Microsoft Windows 7 and Windows Server 2008 R2 operating systems work internally. With this knowledge, developers can better comprehend the rationale behind design choices when building applications specific to the Windows platform. Such knowledge can also help developers debug complex problems. System administrators can benefit from this information as well, because understanding how the operating system works "under the covers" facilitates understanding the performance behavior of the system and makes troubleshooting system problems much easier when things go wrong. After reading this book, you should have a better understanding of how Windows works and why it behaves as it does.

Structure of the Book

For the first time, the book has been divided in two parts. This was done to get the information out more quickly since it takes considerable time to update the book for each release of Windows.

Part 1 begins with two chapters that define key concepts, introduce the tools used in the book, and describe the overall system architecture and components. The next two chapters present key underlying system and management mechanisms. Part 1 wraps up by covering three core components of the operating system: processes, threads, and jobs; security; and networking.

Part 2 covers the remaining core subsystems: I/O, storage, memory management, the cache manager, and file systems. Part 2 concludes with a description of the startup and shutdown processes and a description of crash-dump analysis.

History of the Book

This is the sixth edition of a book that was originally called *Inside Windows NT* (Microsoft Press, 1992), written by Helen Custer (prior to the initial release of Microsoft Windows NT 3.1). *Inside Windows NT* was the first book ever published about Windows NT and provided key insights into the architecture and design of the system. *Inside Windows NT, Second Edition* (Microsoft Press, 1998) was written by David Solomon. It updated the original book to cover Windows NT 4.0 and had a greatly increased level of technical depth.

Inside Windows 2000, Third Edition (Microsoft Press, 2000) was authored by David Solomon and Mark Russinovich. It added many new topics, such as startup and shut-down, service internals, registry internals, file-system drivers, and networking. It also covered kernel changes in Windows 2000, such as the Windows Driver Model (WDM), Plug and Play, power management, Windows Management Instrumentation (WMI), encryption, the job object, and Terminal Services. *Windows Internals, Fourth Edition* was the Windows XP and Windows Server 2003 update and added more content focused on helping IT professionals make use of their knowledge of Windows internals, such as using key tools from Windows Sysinternals (*www.microsoft.com/technet/sysinternals*) and analyzing crash dumps. *Windows Internals, Fifth Edition* was the update for Windows Vista and Windows Server 2008. New content included the image loader, user-mode debugging facility, and Hyper-V.

Sixth Edition Changes

This latest edition has been updated to cover the kernel changes made in Windows 7 and Windows Server 2008 R2. Hands-on experiments have been updated to reflect changes in tools.

Hands-on Experiments

Even without access to the Windows source code, you can glean much about Windows internals from tools such as the kernel debugger and tools from Sysinternals and Winsider Seminars & Solutions. When a tool can be used to expose or demonstrate some aspect of the internal behavior of Windows, the steps for trying the tool yourself are listed in "EXPERIMENT" boxes. These appear throughout the book, and we encourage you to try these as you're reading—seeing visible proof of how Windows works internally will make much more of an impression on you than just reading about it will.

Topics Not Covered

Windows is a large and complex operating system. This book doesn't cover everything relevant to Windows internals but instead focuses on the base system components. For example, this book doesn't describe COM+, the Windows distributed object-oriented programming infrastructure, or the Microsoft .NET Framework, the foundation of managed code applications.

Because this is an internals book and not a user, programming, or system administration book, it doesn't describe how to use, program, or configure Windows.

A Warning and a Caveat

Because this book describes undocumented behavior of the internal architecture and the operation of the Windows operating system (such as internal kernel structures and functions), this content is subject to change between releases. (External interfaces, such as the Windows API, are not subject to incompatible changes.)

By "subject to change," we don't necessarily mean that details described in this book will change between releases, but you can't count on them not changing. Any software that uses these undocumented interfaces might not work on future releases of Windows. Even worse, software that runs in kernel mode (such as device drivers) and uses these undocumented interfaces might experience a system crash when running on a newer release of Windows.

Acknowledgments

First, thanks to Jamie Hanrahan and Brian Catlin of Azius, LLC for joining us on this project—the book would not have been finished without their help. They did the bulk of the updates on the "Security" and "Networking" chapters and contributed to the update of the "Management Mechanisms" and "Processes and Threads" chapters. Azius provides Windows-internals and device-driver training. See *www.azius.com* for more information.

We want to recognize Alex Ionescu, who for this edition is a full coauthor. This is a reflection of Alex's extensive work on the fifth edition, as well as his continuing work on this edition.

Also thanks to Daniel Pearson, who updated the "Crash Dump Analysis" chapter. His many years of dump analysis experience helped to make the information more practical.

Thanks to Eric Traut and Jon DeVaan for continuing to allow David Solomon access to the Windows source code for his work on this book as well as continued development of his Windows Internals courses.

Three key reviewers were not acknowledged for their review and contributions to the fifth edition: Arun Kishan, Landy Wang, and Aaron Margosis—thanks again to them! And thanks again to Arun and Landy for their detailed review and helpful input for this edition.

This book wouldn't contain the depth of technical detail or the level of accuracy it has without the review, input, and support of key members of the Microsoft Windows development team. Therefore, we want to thank the following people, who provided technical review and input to the book:

- Greg Cottingham

- Joe Hamburg

- Jeff Lambert

- Pavel Lebedinsky

- Joseph East

- Adi Oltean

- Alexey Pakhunov

- Valerie See

- Brad Waters

- Bruce Worthington

- Robin Alexander

- Bernard Ourghanlian

Also thanks to Scott Lee, Tim Shoultz, and Eric Kratzer for their assistance with the "Crash Dump Analysis" chapter.

For the "Networking" chapter, a special thanks to Gianluigi Nusca and Tom Jolly, who really went beyond the call of duty: Gianluigi for his extraordinary help with the BranchCache material and the amount of suggestions (and many paragraphs of material he wrote), and Tom Jolly not only for his own review and suggestions (which were excellent), but for getting many other developers to assist with the review. Here are all those who reviewed and contributed to the "Networking" chapter:

- Roopesh Battepati
- Molly Brown
- Greg Cottingham
- Dotan Elharrar
- Eric Hanson
- Tom Jolly
- Manoj Kadam
- Greg Kramer
- David Kruse
- Jeff Lambert
- Darene Lewis
- Dan Lovinger
- Gianluigi Nusca
- Amos Ortal
- Ivan Pashov
- Ganesh Prasad
- Paul Swan
- Shiva Kumar Thangapandi

Amos Ortal and Dotan Elharrar were extremely helpful on NAP, and Shiva Kumar Thangapandi helped extensively with EAP.

Thanks to Gerard Murphy for reviewing the shutdown mechanisms in Windows 7 and clarifying Group Policy behaviors.

Thanks to Tristan Brown from the Power Management team at Microsoft for spending a few late hours at the office with Alex going over core parking's algorithms and behaviors, as well as for the invaluable diagram he provided.

Thanks to Apurva Doshi for sending Alex a detailed document of cache manager changes in Windows 7, which was used to capture some of the new behaviors and changes described in the book.

Thanks to Matthieu Suiche for his kernel symbol file database, which allowed Alex to discover new and removed fields from core kernel data structures and led to the investigations to discover the underlying functionality changes.

Thanks to Cenk Ergan, Michel Fortin, and Mehmet Iyigun for their review and input on the Superfetch details.

The detailed checking Christophe Nasarre, overall technical reviewer, performed contributed greatly to the technical accuracy and consistency in the book.

We would like to again thank Ilfak Guilfanov of Hex-Rays (*www.hex-rays.com*) for the IDA Pro Advanced and Hex-Rays licenses they granted to Alex so that he could speed up his reverse engineering of the Windows kernel.

Finally, the authors would like to thank the great staff at Microsoft Press behind turning this book into a reality. Devon Musgrave served double duty as acquisitions editor and developmental editor, while Carol Dillingham oversaw the title as its project editor. Editorial and production manager Curtis Philips, copy editor John Pierce, proofreader Andrea Fox, and indexer Jan Wright also contributed to the quality of this book.

Last but not least, thanks to Ben Ryan, publisher of Microsoft Press, who continues to believe in the importance of continuing to provide this level of detail about Windows to their readers!

Errata & Book Support

We've made every effort to ensure the accuracy of this book and its companion content. Any errors that have been reported since this book was published are listed on our Microsoft Press site at oreilly.com:

http://go.microsoft.com/FWLink/?Linkid=258649

If you find an error that is not already listed, you can report it to us through the same page.

If you need additional support, email Microsoft Press Book Support at *mspinput@ microsoft.com*.

Please note that product support for Microsoft software is not offered through the addresses above.

We Want to Hear from You

At Microsoft Press, your satisfaction is our top priority, and your feedback our most valuable asset. Please tell us what you think of this book at:

http://www.microsoft.com/learning/booksurvey

The survey is short, and we read every one of your comments and ideas. Thanks in advance for your input!

Stay in Touch

Let's keep the conversation going! We're on Twitter: *http://twitter.com/MicrosoftPress*.

CHAPTER 8

I/O System

The Windows I/O system consists of several executive components that together manage hardware devices and provide interfaces to hardware devices for applications and the system. In this chapter, we'll first list the design goals of the I/O system, which have influenced its implementation. We'll then cover the components that make up the I/O system, including the I/O manager, Plug and Play (PnP) manager, and power manager. Then we'll examine the structure and components of the I/O system and the various types of device drivers. We'll look at the key data structures that describe devices, device drivers, and I/O requests, after which we'll describe the steps necessary to complete I/O requests as they move through the system. Finally, we'll present the way device detection, driver installation, and power management work.

I/O System Components

The design goals for the Windows I/O system are to provide an abstraction of devices, both hardware (physical) and software (virtual or logical), to applications with the following features:

- Uniform security and naming across devices to protect shareable resources. (See Chapter 6, "Security," in Part 1 for a description of the Windows security model.)

- High-performance asynchronous packet-based I/O to allow for the implementation of scalable applications.

- Services that allow drivers to be written in a high-level language and easily ported between different machine architectures.

- Layering and extensibility to allow for the addition of drivers that transparently modify the behavior of other drivers or devices, without requiring any changes to the driver whose behavior or device is modified.

- Dynamic loading and unloading of device drivers so that drivers can be loaded on demand and not consume system resources when unneeded.

- Support for Plug and Play, where the system locates and installs drivers for newly detected hardware, assigns them hardware resources they require, and also allows applications to discover and activate device interfaces.

- Support for power management so that the system or individual devices can enter low power states.

- Support for multiple installable file systems, including FAT, the CD-ROM file system (CDFS), the Universal Disk Format (UDF) file system, and the Windows file system (NTFS). (See Chapter 12, "File Systems," for more specific information on file system types and architecture.)

- Windows Management Instrumentation (WMI) support and diagnosability so that drivers can be managed and monitored through WMI applications and scripts. (WMI is described in Chapter 4, "Management Mechanisms," in Part 1.)

To implement these features the Windows I/O system consists of several executive components as well as device drivers, which are shown in Figure 8-1.

- The I/O manager is the heart of the I/O system. It connects applications and system components to virtual, logical, and physical devices, and it defines the infrastructure that supports device drivers.

- A device driver typically provides an I/O interface for a particular type of device. A driver is a software module that interprets high-level commands, such as read or write, and issues low-level, device-specific commands, such as writing to control registers. Device drivers receive commands routed to them by the I/O manager that are directed at the devices they manage, and they inform the I/O manager when those commands are complete. Device drivers often use the I/O manager to forward I/O commands to other device drivers that share in the implementation of a device's interface or control.

- The PnP manager works closely with the I/O manager and a type of device driver called a *bus driver* to guide the allocation of hardware resources as well as to detect and respond to the arrival and removal of hardware devices. The PnP manager and bus drivers are responsible for loading a device's driver when the device is detected. When a device is added to a system that doesn't have an appropriate device driver, the executive Plug and Play component calls on the device installation services of a user-mode PnP manager.

- The power manager also works closely with the I/O manager and the PnP manager to guide the system, as well as individual device drivers, through power-state transitions.

- Windows Management Instrumentation support routines, called the Windows Driver Model (WDM) WMI provider, allow device drivers to indirectly act as providers, using the WDM WMI provider as an intermediary to communicate with the WMI service in user mode. (For more information on WMI, see the section "Windows Management Instrumentation" in Chapter 4 in Part 1.)

- The registry serves as a database that stores a description of basic hardware devices attached to the system as well as driver initialization and configuration settings. (See "The Registry" section in Chapter 4 in Part 1 for more information.)

- INF files, which are designated by the .inf extension, are driver installation files. INF files are the link between a particular hardware device and the driver that assumes primary control of the device. They are made up of script-like instructions describing the device they correspond to, the source and target locations of driver files, required driver-installation registry modifications, and driver dependency information. Digital signatures that Windows uses to verify that a driver file has passed testing by the Microsoft Windows Hardware Quality Labs (WHQL) are stored in .cat files. Digital signatures are also used to prevent tampering of the driver or its INF file.

■ The hardware abstraction layer (HAL) insulates drivers from the specifics of the processor and interrupt controller by providing APIs that hide differences between platforms. In essence, the HAL is the bus driver for all the devices soldered onto the computer's motherboard that aren't controlled by other drivers.

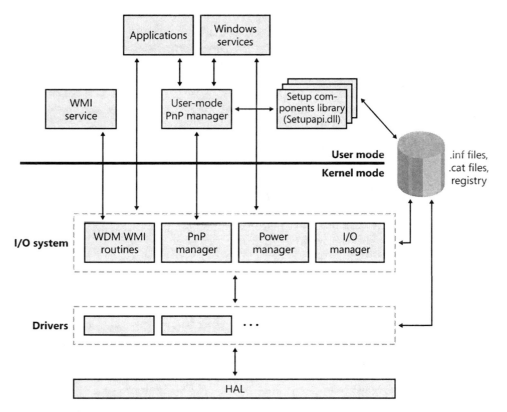

FIGURE 8-1 I/O system components

The I/O Manager

The *I/O manager* is the core of the I/O system because it defines the orderly framework, or model, within which I/O requests are delivered to device drivers. The I/O system is *packet driven*. Most I/O requests are represented by an *I/O request packet* (IRP), which travels from one I/O system component to another. (As you'll discover in the section "Fast I/O," fast I/O is the exception; it doesn't use IRPs.)

The design allows an individual application thread to manage multiple I/O requests concurrently. An IRP is a data structure that contains information completely describing an I/O request. (You'll find more information about IRPs in the section "I/O Request Packets" later in the chapter.)

The I/O manager creates an IRP in memory to represent an I/O operation, passing a pointer to the IRP to the correct driver and disposing of the packet when the I/O operation is complete. In contrast, a driver receives an IRP, performs the operation the IRP specifies, and passes the IRP back to the I/O manager, either because the requested I/O operation has been completed, or because it must be passed on to another driver for further processing.

In addition to creating and disposing of IRPs, the I/O manager supplies code that is common to different drivers and that the drivers can call to carry out their I/O processing. By consolidating common tasks in the I/O manager, individual drivers become simpler and more compact. For example, the I/O manager provides a function that allows one driver to call other drivers. It also manages buffers for I/O requests, provides timeout support for drivers, and records which installable file systems are loaded into the operating system. There are close to one hundred different routines in the I/O manager that can be called by device drivers.

The I/O manager also provides flexible I/O services that allow environment subsystems, such as Windows and POSIX, to implement their respective I/O functions. These services include sophisticated services for asynchronous I/O that allow developers to build scalable, high-performance server applications.

The uniform, modular interface that drivers present allows the I/O manager to call any driver without requiring any special knowledge of its structure or internal details. The operating system treats all I/O requests as if they were directed at a file; the driver converts the requests from requests made to a virtual file to hardware-specific requests. Drivers can also call each other (using the I/O manager) to achieve layered, independent processing of an I/O request.

Besides providing the normal open, close, read, and write functions, the Windows I/O system provides several advanced features, such as asynchronous, direct, buffered, and scatter/gather I/O, which are described in the "Types of I/O" section later in this chapter.

Typical I/O Processing

Most I/O operations don't involve all the components of the I/O system. A typical I/O request starts with an application executing an I/O-related function (for example, reading data from a device) that is processed by the I/O manager, one or more device drivers, and the HAL.

As just mentioned, in Windows, threads perform I/O on virtual files. A virtual file refers to any source or destination for I/O that is treated as if it were a file (such as files, directories, pipes, and mailslots). The operating system abstracts all I/O requests as operations on a virtual file, because the I/O manager has no knowledge of anything but files, therefore making it the responsibility of the driver to translate file-oriented comments (open, close, read, write) into device-specific commands. This abstraction thereby generalizes an application's interface to devices. User-mode applications (whether Windows or POSIX) call documented functions, which in turn call internal I/O system functions to read from a file, write to a file, and perform other operations. The I/O manager dynamically directs these virtual file requests to the appropriate device driver. Figure 8-2 illustrates the basic structure of a typical I/O request flow.

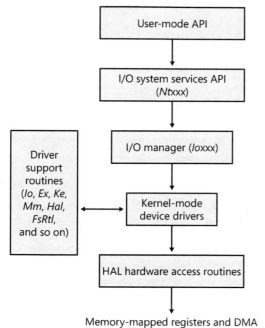

FIGURE 8-2 The flow of a typical I/O request

In the following sections, we'll look at these components more closely, covering the various types of device drivers, how they are structured, how they load and initialize, and how they process I/O requests. Then we'll cover the operation and roles of the PnP manager and the power manager.

Device Drivers

To integrate with the I/O manager and other I/O system components, a device driver must conform to implementation guidelines specific to the type of device it manages and the role it plays in managing the device. In this section, we'll look at the types of device drivers Windows supports as well as the internal structure of a device driver.

Types of Device Drivers

Windows supports a wide range of device driver types and programming environments. Even within a type of device driver, programming environments can differ, depending on the specific type of device for which a driver is intended. The broadest classification of a driver is whether it is a user-mode or kernel-mode driver. Windows supports a couple of types of user-mode drivers:

- Windows subsystem *printer drivers* translate device-independent graphics requests to printer-specific commands. These commands are then typically forwarded to a kernel-mode port driver such as the universal serial bus (USB) printer port driver (Usbprint.sys).

- User-Mode Driver Framework (UMDF) drivers are hardware device drivers that run in user mode. They communicate to the kernel-mode UMDF support library through ALPC. See the "User-Mode Driver Framework (UMDF)" section later in this chapter for more information.

In this chapter, the focus is on kernel-mode device drivers. There are many types of kernel-mode drivers, which can be divided into the following basic categories:

- *File system drivers* accept I/O requests to files and satisfy the requests by issuing their own, more explicit, requests to mass storage or network device drivers.

- *Plug and Play drivers* work with hardware and integrate with the Windows power manager and PnP manager. They include drivers for mass storage devices, video adapters, input devices, and network adapters.

- *Non–Plug and Play drivers*, which also include *kernel extensions*, are drivers or modules that extend the functionality of the system. They do not typically integrate with the PnP or power managers because they typically do not manage an actual piece of hardware. Examples include network API and protocol drivers. Process Monitor's driver, described in Chapter 4 in Part 1, is also an example.

Within the category of kernel-mode drivers are further classifications based on the driver model that the driver adheres to and its role in servicing device requests.

WDM Drivers

WDM drivers are device drivers that adhere to the Windows Driver Model (WDM). WDM includes support for Windows power management, Plug and Play, and WMI, and most Plug and Play drivers adhere to WDM. There are three types of WDM drivers:

- *Bus drivers* manage a logical or physical bus. Examples of buses include PCMCIA, PCI, USB, and IEEE 1394. A bus driver is responsible for detecting and informing the PnP manager of devices attached to the bus it controls as well as managing the power setting of the bus.

- *Function drivers* manage a particular type of device. Bus drivers present devices to function drivers via the PnP manager. The function driver is the driver that exports the operational interface of the device to the operating system. In general, it's the driver with the most knowledge about the operation of the device.

- *Filter drivers* logically layer either above or below function drivers (these are called *function filters*) or above the bus driver (these are called *bus filters*), augmenting or changing the behavior of a device or another driver. For example, a keyboard capture utility could be implemented with a keyboard filter driver that layers above the keyboard function driver.

In WDM, no one driver is responsible for controlling all aspects of a particular device. The bus driver is responsible for detecting bus membership changes (device addition or removal), assisting the PnP manager in enumerating the devices on the bus, accessing bus-specific configuration registers, and, in some cases, controlling power to devices on the bus. The function driver is generally the only driver that accesses the device's hardware.

Layered Drivers

Support for an individual piece of hardware is often divided among several drivers, each providing a part of the functionality required to make the device work properly. In addition to WDM bus drivers, function drivers, and filter drivers, hardware support might be split between the following components:

- *Class drivers* implement the I/O processing for a particular class of devices, such as disk, keyboard, or CD-ROM, where the hardware interfaces have been standardized, so one driver can serve devices from a wide variety of manufacturers.

- *Miniclass drivers* implement I/O processing that is vendor-defined for a particular class of devices. For example, although there is a standardized battery class driver written by Microsoft, both uninterruptible power supplies (UPS) and laptop batteries have highly specific interfaces that differ wildly between manufacturers, such that a miniclass is required from the vendor. Miniclass drivers are essentially kernel-mode DLLs and do not do IRP processing directly—the class driver calls into them, and they import functions from the class driver.

- *Port drivers* implement the processing of an I/O request specific to a type of I/O port, such as SATA, and are implemented as kernel-mode libraries of functions rather than actual device drivers. Port drivers are almost always written by Microsoft because the interfaces are typically standardized in such a way that different vendors can still share the same port driver. However, in certain cases, third parties may need to write their own for specialized hardware. In some cases, the concept of "I/O port" extends to cover logical ports as well. For example, NDIS is the network "port" driver, and Dxgport/Videoprt are the DirectX/video "port" drivers.

- *Miniport drivers* map a generic I/O request to a type of port into an adapter type, such as a specific network adapter. Miniport drivers are actual device drivers that import the functions supplied by a port driver. Miniport drivers are written by third parties, and they provide the interface for the port driver. Like miniclass drivers, they are kernel-mode DLLs and do not do IRP processing directly.

A simplified example for illustrative purposes will help demonstrate how device drivers work at a high level. A file system driver accepts a request to write data to a certain location within a particular file. It translates the request into a request to write a certain number of bytes to the disk at a particular (that is, the logical) location. It then passes this request (via the I/O manager) to a simple disk driver. The disk driver, in turn, translates the request into a physical location on the disk and communicates with the disk to write the data. This layering is illustrated in Figure 8-3.

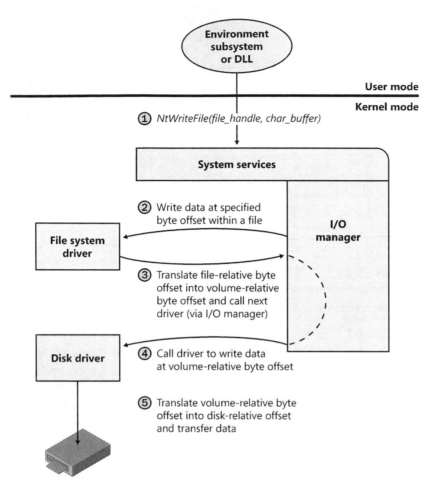

FIGURE 8-3 Layering of a file system driver and a disk driver

This figure illustrates the division of labor between two layered drivers. The I/O manager receives a write request that is relative to the beginning of a particular file. The I/O manager passes the request to the file system driver, which translates the write operation from a file-relative operation to a starting location (a sector boundary on the disk) and a number of bytes to write. The file system driver calls the I/O manager to pass the request to the disk driver, which translates the request to a physical disk location and transfers the data.

Because all drivers—both device drivers and file system drivers—present the same framework to the operating system, another driver can easily be inserted into the hierarchy without altering the existing drivers or the I/O system. For example, several disks can be made to seem like a very large single disk by adding a driver. This logical, volume manager driver is located between the file system and the disk drivers, as shown in the conceptual, simplified architectural diagram presented in Figure 8-4. (For the actual storage driver stack diagram, see Figure 9-3 in Chapter 9, "Storage Management"). Volume manager drivers are described in more detail in Chapter 9.

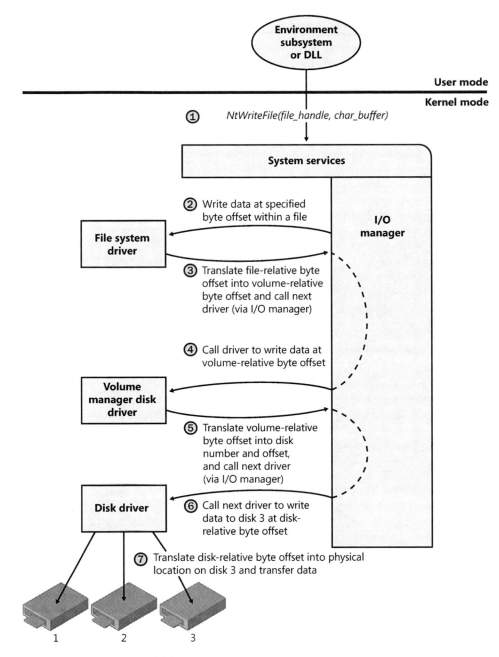

FIGURE 8-4 Adding a layered driver

EXPERIMENT: Viewing the Loaded Driver List

You can see a list of registered drivers by executing the Msinfo32.exe utility from the Run dialog box of the Start menu. Select the System Drivers entry under Software Environment to see the list of drivers configured on the system. Those that are loaded have the text "Yes" in the Started column, as shown here:

You can also view the list of loaded kernel-mode drivers with Process Explorer from Windows Sysinternals (*http://www.microsoft.com/technet/sysinternals*). Run Process Explorer, select the System process, and select DLLs from the Lower Pane View menu entry in the View menu:

Process Explorer lists the loaded drivers, their names, version information (including company and description), and load address (assuming you have configured Process Explorer to display the corresponding columns).

Finally, if you're looking at a crash dump (or live system) with the kernel debugger, you can get a similar display with the kernel debugger *lm kv* command:

```
lkd> lm kv
start    end        module name
82007000 823c0000   nt         (pdb symbols)
c:\programming\symbols\ntkrpamp.pdb\37D328E3BAE5460F8E662756ED80951D2\ntkrpamp.pdb
    Loaded symbol image file: ntkrpamp.exe
    Image path: ntkrpamp.exe
    Image name: ntkrpamp.exe
    Timestamp:        Fri Jan 18 21:30:58 2008 (47918B12)
    CheckSum:         00372038
    ImageSize:        003B9000
    File version:     6.0.6001.18000
    Product version:  6.0.6001.18000
    File flags:       0 (Mask 3F)
    File OS:          40004 NT Win32
    File type:        1.0 App
    File date:        00000000.00000000
    Translations:     0409.04b0
    CompanyName:      Microsoft Corporation
    ProductName:      Microsoft® Windows® Operating System
    InternalName:     ntkrpamp.exe
    OriginalFilename: ntkrpamp.exe
    ProductVersion:   6.0.6001.18000
    FileVersion:      6.0.6001.18000 (longhorn_rtm.080118-1840)
    FileDescription:  NT Kernel & System
    LegalCopyright:   © Microsoft Corporation. All rights reserved.
823c0000 823f3000   hal        (deferred)
    Image path: halmacpi.dll
    Image name: halmacpi.dll
    Timestamp:        Fri Jan 18 21:27:20 2008 (47918A38)
    CheckSum:         0003859F
    ImageSize:        00033000
    Translations:     0000.04b0 0000.04e0 0409.04b0 0409.04e0
82600000 82671000   ksecdd     (deferred)
    Image path: \SystemRoot\System32\Drivers\ksecdd.sys
    Image name: ksecdd.sys
    Timestamp:        Fri Jan 18 21:41:20 2008 (47918D80)
    CheckSum:         0006E742
    ImageSize:        00071000
    Translations:     0000.04b0 0000.04e0 0409.04b0 0409.04e0
```

Structure of a Driver

The I/O system drives the execution of device drivers. Device drivers consist of a set of routines that are called to process the various stages of an I/O request. Figure 8-5 illustrates the key driver-function routines.

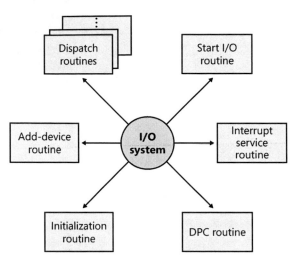

FIGURE 8-5 Primary device driver routines

- **An initialization routine** The I/O manager executes a driver's initialization routine, which is set by the WDK to *GSDriverEntry*, when it loads the driver into the operating system. *GSDriverEntry* initializes the compiler's protection against stack-overflow errors (called a *cookie*) and then calls *DriverEntry,* which is what the driver writer must implement. The routine fills in system data structures to register the rest of the driver's routines with the I/O manager and performs any global driver initialization that's necessary.

- **An add-device routine** A driver that supports Plug and Play implements an add-device routine. The PnP manager sends a notification to the driver via this routine whenever a device for which the driver is responsible is detected. In this routine, a driver typically creates a device object (described later in this chapter) to represent the device.

- **A set of dispatch routines** Dispatch routines are the main entry points that a device driver provides. Some examples are open, close, read, and write and any other capabilities the device, file system, or network supports. When called on to perform an I/O operation, the I/O manager generates an IRP and calls a driver through one of the driver's dispatch routines.

- **A start I/O routine** A driver can use a start I/O routine to initiate a data transfer to or from a device. This routine is defined only in drivers that rely on the I/O manager to queue their incoming I/O requests. The I/O manager serializes IRPs for a driver by ensuring that the driver processes only one IRP at a time. Drivers can process multiple IRPs concurrently, but serialization is usually required for most devices because they cannot concurrently handle multiple I/O requests.

- **An interrupt service routine (ISR)** When a device interrupts, the kernel's interrupt dispatcher transfers control to this routine. In the Windows I/O model, ISRs run at device interrupt request level (DIRQL), so they perform as little work as possible to avoid blocking lower IRQL interrupts. (See Chapter 3, "System Mechanisms," in Part 1 for more information on IRQLs.) An ISR usually queues a deferred procedure call (DPC), which runs at a lower IRQL (DPC/dispatch level), to execute the remainder of interrupt processing. (Only drivers for interrupt-driven devices have ISRs; a file system driver, for example, doesn't have one.)

- **An interrupt-servicing DPC routine** A DPC routine performs most of the work involved in handling a device interrupt after the ISR executes. The DPC routine executes at a lower IRQL (DPC/dispatch level) than that of the ISR, which runs at device level, to avoid blocking other interrupts. A DPC routine initiates I/O completion and starts the next queued I/O operation on a device.

Although the following routines aren't shown in Figure 8-5, they're found in many types of device drivers:

- **One or more I/O completion routines** A layered driver might have I/O completion routines that will notify it when a lower-level driver finishes processing an IRP. For example, the I/O manager calls a file system driver's I/O completion routine after a device driver finishes transferring data to or from a file. The completion routine notifies the file system driver about the operation's success, failure, or cancellation, and it allows the file system driver to perform cleanup operations.

- **A cancel I/O routine** If an I/O operation can be canceled, a driver can define one or more cancel I/O routines. When the driver receives an IRP for an I/O request that can be canceled, it assigns a cancel routine to the IRP, and as the IRP goes through various stages of processing, this routine can change, or outright disappear, if the current operation is not cancellable. If a thread that issues an I/O request exits before the request is completed or cancels the operation (with the *CancelIo* Windows function, for example), the I/O manager executes the IRP's cancel routine if one is assigned to it. A cancel routine is responsible for performing whatever steps are necessary to release any resources acquired during the processing that has already taken place for the IRP as well as for completing the IRP with a canceled status.

- **Fast dispatch routines** Drivers that make use of the cache manager in Windows (see Chapter 11, "Cache Manager," for more information on the cache manager), such as file system drivers, typically provide these routines to allow the kernel to bypass typical I/O processing when accessing the driver. For example, operations such as reading or writing can be quickly performed by accessing the cached data directly, instead of taking the I/O manager's usual path that generates discrete I/O operations. Fast dispatch routines are also used as a mechanism for callbacks from the memory manager and cache manager to file system drivers. For instance, when creating a section, the memory manager calls back into the file system driver to acquire the file exclusively.

- **An unload routine** An unload routine releases any system resources a driver is using so that the I/O manager can remove the driver from memory. Any resources acquired in the initialization routine (*DriverEntry*) are usually released in the unload routine. A driver can be loaded and unloaded while the system is running if the driver supports it, but the unload routine will be called only after all file handles to the device are closed.

- **A system shutdown notification routine**   This routine allows driver cleanup on system shutdown.

- **Error-logging routines**   When unexpected errors occur (for example, when a disk block goes bad), a driver's error-logging routines note the occurrence and notify the I/O manager. The I/O manager writes this information to an error log file.

> **Note** Most kernel-mode device drivers are written in C. Starting with the Windows Driver Kit 8.0, drivers can also be safely written in C++ due to specific support for kernel-mode C++ in the new compilers. Use of assembly language is highly discouraged because of the complexity it introduces and its effect of making a driver difficult to port between hardware architectures such as the x86, x64, and IA64.

Driver Objects and Device Objects

When a thread opens a handle to a file object (described in the "I/O Processing" section later in this chapter), the I/O manager must determine from the file object's name which driver it should call to process the request. Furthermore, the I/O manager must be able to locate this information the next time a thread uses the same file handle. The following system objects fill this need:

- A *driver object* represents an individual driver in the system. The I/O manager obtains the address of each of the driver's dispatch routines (entry points) from the driver object.

- A *device object* represents a physical or logical device on the system and describes its characteristics, such as the alignment it requires for buffers and the location of its device queue to hold incoming IRPs. It is the target for all I/O operations because this object is what the handle communicates with.

The I/O manager creates a driver object when a driver is loaded into the system, and it then calls the driver's initialization routine (*DriverEntry*), which fills in the object attributes with the driver's entry points.

At any time after loading, a driver creates device objects to represent logical or physical devices, or even a logical interface or endpoint to the driver, by calling *IoCreateDevice* or *IoCreateDeviceSecure*. However, most Plug and Play drivers create devices with their add-device routine when the PnP manager informs them of the presence of a device for them to manage. Non–Plug and Play drivers, on the other hand, usually create device objects when the I/O manager invokes their initialization routine. The I/O manager unloads a driver when the driver's last device object has been deleted and no references to the driver remain.

When a driver creates a device object, the driver can optionally assign the device a name. A name places the device object in the object manager namespace, and a driver can either explicitly define a name or let the I/O manager autogenerate one. (The object manager namespace is described in Chapter 3 in Part 1.) By convention, device objects are placed in the \Device directory in the namespace, which is inaccessible by applications using the Windows API.

> **Note** Some drivers place device objects in directories other than \Device. For example, the IDE driver creates the device objects that represent IDE ports and channels in the \Device\ Ide directory. See Chapter 9 for a description of storage architecture, including the way storage drivers use device objects.

If a driver needs to make it possible for applications to open the device object, it must create a symbolic link in the \Global?? directory to the device object's name in the \Device directory. (See Chapter 3 in Part 1 for more information on \??.) Non–Plug and Play and file system drivers typically create a symbolic link with a well-known name (for example, \Device\Hardware2). Because well-known names don't work well in an environment in which hardware appears and disappears dynami-cally, PnP drivers expose one or more interfaces by calling the *IoRegisterDeviceInterface* function, specifying a GUID (globally unique identifier) that represents the type of functionality exposed. GUIDs are 128-bit values that you can generate by using a tool called Uuidgen, which is included with the WDK and the Windows SDK. Given the range of values that 128 bits represents, it's statistically almost certain that each GUID that Uuidgen creates will be forever and globally unique.

IoRegisterDeviceInterface generates the symbolic link associated with a device instance; however, a driver must call *IoSetDeviceInterfaceState* to enable the interface to the device before the I/O man-ager actually creates the link. Drivers usually do this when the PnP manager starts the device by send-ing the driver a *start-device* IRP—in this case, IRP_MJ_PNP, IRP_MN_START_DEVICE.

An application wanting to open a device object whose interfaces are represented with a GUID can call Plug and Play setup functions in user space, such as *SetupDiEnumDeviceInterfaces*, to enumerate the interfaces present for a particular GUID and to obtain the names of the symbolic links it can use to open the device objects. For each device reported by *SetupDiEnumDeviceInterfaces*, an application executes *SetupDiGetDeviceInterfaceDetail* to obtain additional information about the device, such as its autogenerated name. After obtaining a device's name from *SetupDiGetDeviceInterfaceDetail*, the application can execute the Windows function *CreateFile* to open the device and obtain a handle.

EXPERIMENT: Looking at Device Objects

You can use the WinObj tool from Sysinternals or the *!object* kernel debugger command to view the device names under \Device in the object manager namespace. The following screen shot shows an I/O manager–assigned symbolic link that points to a device object in \Device with an autogenerated name:

When you run the *!object* kernel debugger command and specify the \Device directory, you should see output similar to the following:

```
lkd> !object \Device
Object: 8b611b88  Type: (84d10d40) Directory
    ObjectHeader: 8b611b70 (old version)
    HandleCount: 0  PointerCount: 365
    Directory Object: 8b602470  Name: Device

    Hash Address  Type          Name
    ---- -------  ----          ----
     00  85557a00 Device        KsecDD
         855589d8 Device        Ndis
         8b6151b0 SymbolicLink  {941D252A-0BDA-4772-B3CB-30697579BD4A}
         86859030 Device        0000009b
         88c92da8 Device        SrvNet
         886723f0 Device        Beep
         8b71fb90 SymbolicLink  ScsiPort2
         84d17a98 Device        00000032
         84d15f00 Device        00000025
         84d13030 Device        00000019
     01  86d44030 Device        NDMP10
         8d291eb0 SymbolicLink  {E85EEE75-32E3-4A94-8905-52709C2C9BCC}
         886da3c8 Device        Netbios
         86862030 Device        0000009c
         84d177c8 Device        00000033
         84d15c70 Device        00000026
     02  86de9030 Device        NDMP11
         84d19320 Device        00000040
```

```
        88633ca0  Device        NetBT_Tcpip_{033C65A4-C1D6-4824-B420-DDAEADFF873E}
        8b7dcdd0  SymbolicLink  Ip
        84d17500  Device        00000034
        84d159a8  Device        00000027
    03  86df3380  Device        NDMP12
        8515ede0  Device        WMIAdminDevice
        84d1a030  Device        00000041
        8862e040  Device        Video0
        86eaec28  Device        KeyboardClass0
        84d03b00  Device        KMDF0
        84d17230  Device        00000035
        84d156e0  Device        00000028
    04  86e0d030  Device        NDMP13
        86e65030  Device        NDMP20
        85541030  Device        VolMgrControl
        86e6c358  Device        Tun0
        84d1ad68  Device        00000042
        8862ec48  Device        Video1
        88e15158  Device        0000009f
        9badd848  SymbolicLink  MailslotRedirector
        86e1d488  Device        KeyboardClass1
    ...
```

When you enter the *!object* command and specify an object manager directory object, the kernel debugger dumps the contents of the directory according to the way the object manager organizes it internally. For fast lookups, a directory stores objects in a hash table based on a hash of the object names, so the output shows the objects stored in each bucket of the directory's hash table.

As Figure 8-6 illustrates, a device object points back to its driver object, which is how the I/O manager knows which driver routine to call when it receives an I/O request. It uses the device object to find the driver object representing the driver that services the device. It then indexes into the driver object by using the function code supplied in the original request; each function code corresponds to a driver entry point. (The function codes shown in Figure 8-6 are described in the section "IRP Stack Locations" later in this chapter.)

A driver object often has multiple device objects associated with it. The list of device objects represents the physical or logical devices that the driver controls. For example, each partition of a hard disk has a separate device object that contains partition-specific information. However, the same hard disk driver is used to access all partitions. When a driver is unloaded from the system, the I/O manager uses the queue of device objects to determine which devices will be affected by the removal of the driver.

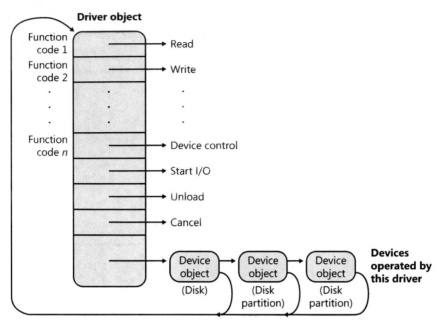

FIGURE 8-6 The driver object

EXPERIMENT: Displaying Driver and Device Objects

You can display driver and device objects with the kernel debugger *!drvobj* and *!devobj* commands, respectively. In the following example, the driver object for the keyboard class driver is examined, and its lone device object viewed:

```
lkd> !drvobj kbdclass
Driver object (86e379a0) is for:
 \Driver\kbdclass
Driver Extension List: (id , addr)

Device Object list:
86e1d488   86eaec28

lkd> !devobj 86eaec28
Device object (86eaec28) is for:
 KeyboardClass0 \Driver\kbdclass DriverObject 86e379a0
Current Irp 00000000 RefCount 0 Type 0000000b Flags 00002044
DevExt 86eaece0 DevObjExt 86eaedc0
ExtensionFlags (0x00000800)
                         Unknown flags 0x00000800
AttachedDevice (Upper) 86e15a40 \Driver\ctrl2cap
AttachedTo (Lower) 86e15020 \Driver\i8042prt
Device queue is not busy
```

Notice that the *!devobj* command also shows you the addresses and names of any device objects that the object you're viewing is layered over (the *AttachedTo* line) as well as the device objects layered on top of the object specified (the *AttachedDevice* line).

Using objects to record information about drivers means that the I/O manager doesn't need to know details about individual drivers. The I/O manager merely follows a pointer to locate a driver, thereby providing a layer of portability and allowing new drivers to be loaded easily.

Opening Devices

A file object is a kernel-mode data structure that represents a handle to a device. File objects clearly fit the criteria for objects in Windows: they are system resources that two or more user-mode processes can share, they can have names, they are protected by object-based security, and they support synchronization. Shared resources in the I/O system, like those in other components of the Windows executive, are manipulated as objects. (See Chapter 3 in Part 1 for a description of the object manager and Chapter 6 in Part 1 for information on object security.)

File objects provide a memory-based representation of resources that conform to an I/O-centric interface, in which they can be read from or written to. Table 8-1 lists some of the file object's attributes. For specific field declarations and sizes, see the structure definition for FILE_OBJECT in WDM.h.

TABLE 8-1 File Object Attributes

Attribute	Purpose
File name	Identifies the physical file that the file object refers to, which was passed in to the *CreateFile* API.
Current byte offset	Identifies the current location in the file (valid only for synchronous I/O).
Share modes	Indicate whether other callers can open the file for read, write, or delete operations while the current caller is using it.
Open mode flags	Indicate whether I/O will be synchronous or asynchronous, cached or noncached, sequential or random, and so on.
Pointer to device object	Indicates the type of device the file resides on.
Pointer to the volume parameter block (VPB)	Indicates the volume, or partition, that the file resides on.
Pointer to section object pointers	Indicates a root structure that describes a mapped/cached file. This structure also contains the shared cache map, which identifies which parts of the file are cached (or rather mapped) by the cache manager and where they reside in the cache.
Pointer to private cache map	Used to store per-handle caching information such as the read patterns for this handle or the page priority for the process. See Chapter 10, "Memory Management," for more information on page priority.
List of I/O request packets (IRPs)	If thread-agnostic I/O is used (to be described later) and the file object is associated with a completion port (also described later), this is a list of all the I/O operations that are associated with this file object.
I/O completion context	Context information for the current I/O completion port, if one is active.
File object extension	Stores the I/O priority (explained later in this chapter) for the file and whether share-access checks should be performed on the file object, and contains optional file object extensions that store context-specific information.

To maintain some level of opacity toward driver code that uses the file object, as well as to enable extending the file object functionality without enlarging the structure, the file object also contains an extension field, which allows for up to six different kinds of additional attributes. These are described in Table 8-2.

TABLE 8-2 File Object Extensions

Extension	Purpose
Transaction parameters	Contains the transaction parameter block, which contains information about a transacted file operation. Returned by *IoGetTransactionParameterBlock*.
Device object hint	Identifies the device object of the filter driver with which this file should be associated. Set with *IoCreateFileEx* or *IoCreateFileSpecifyDeviceObjectHint*.
I/O status block range	Allows applications to lock a user-mode buffer into kernel-mode memory to optimize asynchronous I/Os. See the section on I/O completion port optimizations later in this chapter. Set with *SetFileIoOverlappedRange*.
Generic	Contains filter-driver-specific information, as well as extended create parameters (ECP) that were added by the caller. Set with *IoCreateFileEx*.
Scheduled file I/O	Stores a file's bandwidth reservation information, which is used by the storage system to optimize and guarantee throughput for multimedia applications. See the section on bandwidth reservation later in this chapter. Set with *SetFileBandwidthReservation*.
Symbolic link	Added to the file object upon creation, when a mount point or directory junction is traversed (or a filter explicitly reparses the path). It stores the caller-supplied path, including information about any intermediate junctions, so that if a relative symbolic link is hit, it can walk back through the junctions. See Chapter 12 for more information on NTFS symbolic links, mount points, and directory junctions.

When a caller opens a file or a simple device, the I/O manager returns a handle to a file object. Figure 8-7 illustrates what occurs when a file is opened.

In this example, (1) a C program calls the run-time library function *fopen*, which in turn (2) calls the Windows *CreateFile* function. The Windows subsystem DLL (in this case, Kernel32.dll) then (3) calls the native *NtCreateFile* function in Ntdll.dll. The routine in Ntdll.dll contains the appropriate instruction to cause a transition into kernel mode to the system service dispatcher, which then (4) calls the real *NtCreateFile* routine in Ntoskrnl.exe. (See Chapter 3 in Part 1 for more information about system service dispatching.) Finally, this routine wraps the parameters and flags in such a way that the I/O manager function *IoCreateFile* can actually perform the operation.

> **Note** File objects represent open instances of files, not files themselves. Unlike UNIX systems, which use *vnodes*, Windows does not define the representation of a file; Windows file system drivers define their own representations.

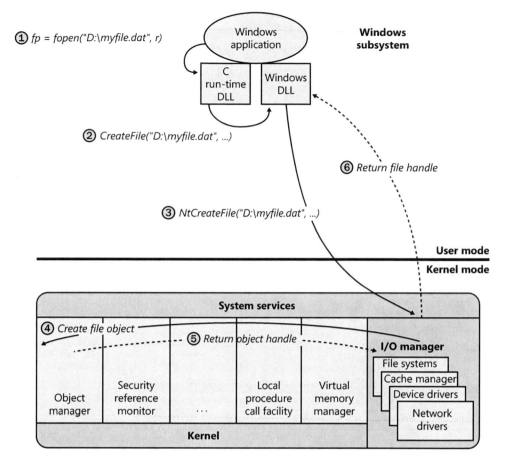

FIGURE 8-7 Opening a file object

Similar to executive objects, files are protected by a security descriptor that contains an access control list (ACL). The I/O manager consults the security subsystem to determine whether a file's ACL allows the process to access the file in the way its thread is requesting. If it does (5, 6), the object manager grants the access and associates the granted access rights with the file handle that it returns. If this thread or another thread in the process needs to perform additional operations not specified in the original request, the thread must open the same file again with a different request to get another handle, which prompts another security check. (See Chapter 6 in Part 1 for more information about object protection.)

EXPERIMENT: Viewing Device Handles

Any process that has an open handle to a device will have a file object in its handle table corresponding to the open instance. You can view these handles with Process Explorer by selecting a process and checking Handles in the Lower Pane View submenu of the View menu. Sort by the Type column and scroll to where you see the handles that represent file objects, which are labeled as File.

In this example, the Csrss process has a handle open to a device created by the kernel security device driver (Ksecdd.sys). You can look at the specific file object in the kernel debugger by first identifying the address of the object. The following command reports information on the highlighted handle (handle value 0xD4) in the preceding screen shot, which is in the Csrss.exe process that has a process ID of 512 (0x200):

```
lkd> !handle d4 f 200

Searching for Process with Cid == 200
PROCESS fffffa800bf35b30
    SessionId: 0  Cid: 0200    Peb: 7fffffd8000  ParentCid: 0188
    DirBase: 1dba50000  ObjectTable: fffff8a000f28d80  HandleCount: 630.
    Image: csrss.exe

Handle table at fffff8a000f28d80 with 630 entries in use

00d4: Object: fffffa800c9cc9f0  GrantedAccess: 00100001 Entry: fffff8a001409350
Object: fffffa800c9cc9f0  Type: (fffffa800737a080) File
    ObjectHeader: fffffa800c9cc9c0 (new version)
        HandleCount: 1  PointerCount: 1
```

Because the object is a file object, you can get information about it with the *!fileobj* command:

```
lkd> !fileobj fffffa800c9cc9f0

Device Object: 0xfffffa8007da1550   \Driver\KSecDD
Vpb is NULL
Event signalled

Flags:  0x40002
        Synchronous IO
        Handle Created
CurrentByteOffset: 0
```

Because a file object is a memory-based representation of a shareable resource and not the re-source itself, it's different from other executive objects. A file object contains only data that is unique to an object handle, whereas the file itself contains the data or text to be shared. Each time a thread opens a file, a new file object is created with a new set of handle-specific attributes. For example, for files opened synchronously, the current byte offset attribute refers to the location in the file at which the next read or write operation using that handle will occur. Each handle to a file has a private byte offset even though the underlying file is shared. A file object is also unique to a process, except when a process duplicates a file handle to another process (by using the Windows *DuplicateHandle* func-tion) or when a child process inherits a file handle from a parent process. In these situations, the two processes have separate handles that refer to the same file object.

Although a file handle is unique to a process, the underlying physical resource is not. Therefore, as with any shared resource, threads must synchronize their access to shareable resources such as files, file directories, and devices. If a thread is writing to a file, for example, it should specify exclusive write access when opening the file to prevent other threads from writing to the file at the same time. Alternatively, by using the Windows *LockFile* function, the thread could lock a portion of the file while writing to it when exclusive access is required.

When a file is opened, the file name includes the name of the device object on which the file re-sides. For example, the name \Device\HarddiskVolume1\Myfile.dat refers to the file Myfile.dat on the C: volume. The substring \Device\HarddiskVolume1 is the name of the internal Windows device object representing that volume. When opening Myfile.dat, the I/O manager creates a file object and stores a pointer to the HarddiskVolume1 device object in the file object and then returns a file handle to the caller. Thereafter, when the caller uses the file handle, the I/O manager can find the HarddiskVolume1 device object directly. Keep in mind that internal Windows device names can't be used in Windows applications—instead, the device name must appear in a special directory in the object manager's namespace, which is \Global??. This directory contains symbolic links to the real, internal Windows device names. As was described earlier, device drivers are responsible for creating links in this direc-tory so that their devices will be accessible to Windows applications. You can examine or even change these links programmatically with the Windows *QueryDosDevice* and *DefineDosDevice* functions.

EXPERIMENT: Viewing Windows Device Name to Windows Device Name Mappings

You can examine the symbolic links that define the Windows device namespace with the WinObj utility from Sysinternals. Run WinObj, and click on the \Global?? directory, as shown here:

Name	Type	SymLink
Global	SymbolicLink	\GLOBAL??
ACPI#GenuineIntel_-_x86_Family_6_Model_15#_0#{97fadb10-4e33-40ae-359...	SymbolicLink	\Device\00000051
ACPI#GenuineIntel_-_x86_Family_6_Model_15#_1#{97fadb10-4e33-40ae-359...	SymbolicLink	\Device\00000052
ACPI#PNP0303#4&2e9ee815&0#{884b96c3-56ef-11d1-bc8c-00a0c91405dd}	SymbolicLink	\Device\00000060
ACPI#PNP0C0A#1#{72631e54-78a4-11d0-bcf7-00aa00b7b32a}	SymbolicLink	\Device\00000056
ACPI#PNP0C0C#2&daba3ff&2#{4afa3d53-74a7-11d0-be5e-00a0c9062857}	SymbolicLink	\Device\00000058
ACPI#PNP0C0D#2&daba3ff&2#{4afa3d53-74a7-11d0-be5e-00a0c9062857}	SymbolicLink	\Device\00000057
ACPI#PNP0C0E#2&daba3ff&2#{4afa3d53-74a7-11d0-be5e-00a0c9062857}	SymbolicLink	\Device\00000059
ACPI#PNP0C32#0#{629758ee-986e-4d9e-8e47-de27f8ab054d}	SymbolicLink	\Device\0000005a
ACPI#PNP0F13#4&2e9ee815&0#{378de44c-56ef-11d1-bc8c-00a0c91405dd}	SymbolicLink	\Device\0000005f
ACPI#ThermalZone#THM_#{4afa3d51-74a7-11d0-be5e-00a0c9062857}	SymbolicLink	\Device\00000053
AscKmd	SymbolicLink	\Device\AscKmd
AUX	SymbolicLink	\DosDevices\COM1
C:	SymbolicLink	\Device\HarddiskVolum...
CdRom0	SymbolicLink	\Device\CdRom0
COM10	SymbolicLink	\Device\VCom10
COM11	SymbolicLink	\Device\VCom11

Notice the symbolic links on the right. Try right-clicking on the device C: and selecting Properties. You should see something like this:

C: is a symbolic link to the internal device named \Device\HarddiskVolume3, or the first volume on the first hard drive in the system. The COM1 entry in WinObj is a symbolic link to \Device\Serial0, and so forth. Try creating your own links with the *subst* command at a command prompt.

I/O Processing

Now that we've covered the structure and types of drivers and the data structures that support them, let's look at how I/O requests flow through the system. I/O requests pass through several predictable stages of processing. The stages vary depending on whether the request is destined for a device operated by a single-layered driver or for a device reached through a multilayered driver. Processing varies further depending on whether the caller specified synchronous or asynchronous I/O, so we'll begin our discussion of I/O types with these two and then move on to others.

Types of I/O

Applications have several options for the I/O requests they issue. Furthermore, the I/O manager gives drivers the choice of implementing a shortcut I/O interface that can often mitigate IRP allocation for I/O processing. In this section, we'll explain these options for I/O requests.

Synchronous and Asynchronous I/O

Most I/O operations that applications issue are *synchronous* (which is the default); that is, the application thread waits while the device performs the data operation and returns a status code when the I/O is complete. The program can then continue and access the transferred data immediately. When used in their simplest form, the Windows *ReadFile* and *WriteFile* functions are executed synchronously. They complete the I/O operation before returning control to the caller.

Asynchronous I/O allows an application to issue multiple I/O requests and continue executing while the device performs the I/O operation. This type of I/O can improve an application's throughput because it allows the application thread to continue with other work while an I/O operation is in progress. To use asynchronous I/O, you must specify the FILE_FLAG_OVERLAPPED flag when you call the Windows *CreateFile* function. Of course, after issuing an asynchronous I/O operation, the thread must be careful not to access any data from the I/O operation until the device driver has finished the data operation. The thread must synchronize its execution with the completion of the I/O request by monitoring a handle of a synchronization object (whether that's an event object, an I/O completion port, or the file object itself) that will be signaled when the I/O is complete.

Regardless of the type of I/O request, internally I/O operations issued to a driver on behalf of the application are performed asynchronously; that is, once an I/O request has been initiated, the device driver returns to the I/O system. Whether or not the I/O system returns immediately to the caller depends on whether the handle was opened for synchronous or asynchronous I/O. Figure 8-8 illustrates the flow of control when a read operation is initiated. Notice that if a wait is done, which depends on the overlapped flag in the file object, it is done in kernel mode by the *NtReadFile* function.

You can test the status of a pending asynchronous I/O operation with the Windows *HasOverlappedIoCompleted* macro. If you're using I/O completion ports (described in the "I/O Completion Ports" section later in this chapter), you can use the *GetQueuedCompletionStatus(Ex)* function(s).

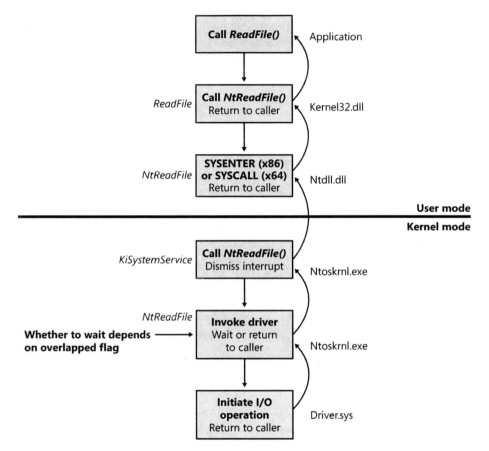

FIGURE 8-8 Control flow for an I/O operation

Fast I/O

Fast I/O is a special mechanism that allows the I/O system to bypass generating an IRP and instead go directly to the driver stack to complete an I/O request. (Fast I/O is described in detail in Chapters 11 and 12.) A driver registers its fast I/O entry points by entering them in a structure pointed to by the PFAST_IO_DISPATCH pointer in its driver object.

EXPERIMENT: Looking at a Driver's Registered Fast I/O Routines

The *!drvobj* kernel debugger command can list the fast I/O routines that a driver registers in its driver object. However, typically only file system drivers have any use for fast I/O routines, although there are exceptions, such as network protocol drivers and bus filter drivers. The following output shows the fast I/O table for the NTFS file system driver object:

```
lkd> !drvobj \FileSystem\Ntfs 2
Driver object (fffffa8007d9fbe0) is for:
 \FileSystem\Ntfs
DriverEntry:   fffff880017d406c      Ntfs!GsDriverEntry
DriverStartIo: 00000000
DriverUnload:  00000000
AddDevice:     00000000

Dispatch routines:
...

Fast I/O routines:
FastIoCheckIfPossible     fffff88001782230      Ntfs!NtfsFastIoCheckIfPossible
FastIoRead                fffff880016efd60      Ntfs!NtfsCopyReadA
FastIoWrite               fffff880016f2a10      Ntfs!NtfsCopyWriteA
FastIoQueryBasicInfo      fffff880016e42e8      Ntfs!NtfsFastQueryBasicInfo
...
ReleaseForModWrite        fffff8800166fee4      Ntfs!NtfsReleaseFileForModWrite
AcquireForCcFlush         fffff8800167133c      Ntfs!NtfsAcquireFileForCcFlush
ReleaseForCcFlush         fffff880016713a0      Ntfs!NtfsReleaseFileForCcFlush
```

The output shows that NTFS has registered its *NtfsCopyReadA* routine as the fast I/O table's *FastIoRead* entry. As the name of this fast I/O entry implies, the I/O manager calls this function when issuing a read I/O request if the file is cached. If the call doesn't succeed, the standard IRP path is selected.

Mapped File I/O and File Caching

Mapped file I/O is an important feature of the I/O system, one that the I/O system and the memory manager produce jointly. (See Chapter 10 for details on how mapped files are implemented.) *Mapped file I/O* refers to the ability to view a file residing on disk as part of a process's virtual memory. A program can access the file as a large array without buffering data or performing disk I/O. The program accesses memory, and the memory manager uses its paging mechanism to load the correct page from the disk file. If the application writes to its virtual address space, the memory manager writes the changes back to the file as part of normal paging.

Mapped file I/O is available in user mode through the Windows *CreateFileMapping* and *MapViewOfFile* functions. Within the operating system, mapped file I/O is used for important operations such as file caching and image activation (loading and running executable programs). The other major consumer of mapped file I/O is the cache manager. File systems use the cache manager to map file data in virtual memory to provide better response time for I/O-bound programs. As the caller uses the file, the memory manager brings accessed pages into memory. Whereas most caching systems allocate a fixed number of bytes for caching files in memory, the Windows cache grows or shrinks depending on how much memory is available. This size variability is possible because the cache manager relies on the memory manager to automatically expand (or shrink) the size of the cache, using the normal working set mechanisms explained in Chapter 10, in this case applied to the system working set. By taking advantage of the memory manager's paging system, the cache manager avoids duplicating the work that the memory manager already performs. (The workings of the cache manager are explained in detail in Chapter 11.)

Scatter/Gather I/O

Windows also supports a special kind of high-performance I/O that is called *scatter/gather*, available via the Windows *ReadFileScatter* and *WriteFileGather* functions. These functions allow an application to issue a single read or write from more than one buffer in virtual memory to a contiguous area of a file on disk instead of issuing a separate I/O request for each buffer. To use scatter/gather I/O, the file must be opened for noncached I/O, the user buffers being used have to be page-aligned, and the I/Os must be asynchronous (overlapped). Furthermore, if the I/O is directed at a mass storage device, the I/O must be aligned on a device sector boundary and have a length that is a multiple of the sector size.

I/O Request Packets

The I/O request packet (IRP) is where the I/O system stores information it needs to process an I/O request. When a thread calls an I/O API, the I/O manager constructs an IRP to represent the operation as it progresses through the I/O system. If possible, the I/O manager allocates IRPs from one of three per-processor IRP nonpaged look-aside lists: the small-IRP look-aside list stores IRPs with one stack location (IRP stack locations are described shortly), the medium-IRP look-aside list contains IRPs with 4 stack locations (which can also be used for IRPs that require only 2 or 3 stack locations), and the large-IRP look-aside list contains IRPs with more than 4 stack locations—by default, the system stores IRPs with 10 stack locations on the large-IRP look-aside list, but once per minute the system adjusts the number of stack locations allocated and can increase it up to a maximum of 20, based on how many stack locations have been recently required. Additionally, these lists are backed by global look-aside lists as well, allowing efficient cross-CPU IRP flow. If an IRP requires more stack locations than are contained in the IRPs on the large-IRP look-aside list, the I/O manager allocates IRPs from nonpaged pool. After allocating and initializing an IRP, the I/O manager stores a pointer to the caller's file object in the IRP.

> **Note** If defined, the DWORD registry value HKLM\System\CurrentControlSet\Session Manager\I/O System\LargeIrpStackLocations specifies how many stack locations are contained in IRPs stored on the large-IRP look-aside list.

Figure 8-9 shows a sample I/O request that demonstrates the relationship between an IRP and the file, device, and driver objects described in the preceding sections. Although this example shows an I/O request to a single-layered device driver, most I/O operations aren't this direct; they involve one or more layered drivers. (This case will be shown later in this section.)

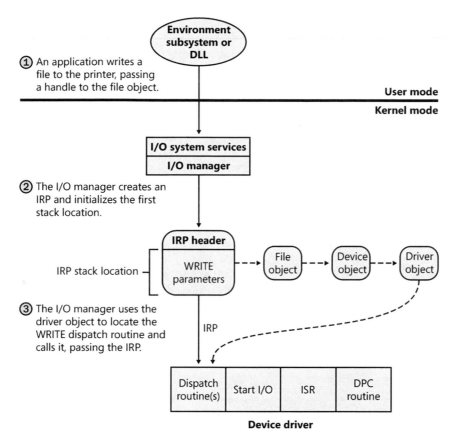

① An application writes a file to the printer, passing a handle to the file object.

② The I/O manager creates an IRP and initializes the first stack location.

IRP stack location —

③ The I/O manager uses the driver object to locate the WRITE dispatch routine and calls it, passing the IRP.

FIGURE 8-9 Data structures involved in a single-layered driver I/O request

IRP Stack Locations

An IRP consists of two parts: a fixed header (often referred to as the IRP's *body*) and one or more stack locations. The fixed portion contains information such as the type and size of the request, whether the request is synchronous or asynchronous, a pointer to a buffer for buffered I/O, and state information that changes as the request progresses. An IRP stack location contains a function code (consisting of a major code and a minor code), function-specific parameters, and a pointer to the caller's file object. The *major function code* identifies which of a driver's dispatch routines the I/O manager invokes when passing an IRP to a driver. An optional *minor function code* sometimes serves as a modifier of the major function code. Power and Plug and Play commands always have minor function codes.

Most drivers specify dispatch routines to handle only a subset of possible major function codes, including create (open), read, write, device I/O control, power, Plug and Play, system control (for WMI commands), cleanup, and close. (See the following experiment for a complete listing of major function codes.) File system drivers are an example of a driver type that often fills in most or all of its dispatch entry points with functions. In contrast, a driver for a simple USB device would probably fill in only the routines needed for open, close, read, write, and sending I/O control codes. The I/O manager sets any dispatch entry points that a driver doesn't fill to point to its own *IopInvalidDeviceRequest*, which completes the IRP with an error status indicating that the major function specified in the IRP is invalid for that device.

EXPERIMENT: Looking at Driver Dispatch Routines

You can obtain a listing of the functions a driver has defined for its dispatch routines by entering a **7** after the driver object's name (or address) in the *!drvobj* kernel debugger command. The following output shows that drivers support 28 IRP types.

```
lkd> !drvobj \Driver\kbdclass 7
Driver object (fffffa800adc2e70) is for:
 \Driver\kbdclass
Driver Extension List: (id , addr)

Device Object list:
fffffa800b04fce0  fffffa800abde560

DriverEntry:   fffff880071c8ecc  kbdclass!GsDriverEntry
DriverStartIo: 00000000
DriverUnload:  00000000
AddDevice:     fffff880071c53b4  kbdclass!KeyboardAddDevice

Dispatch routines:
[00] IRP_MJ_CREATE                 fffff880071bedd4  kbdclass!KeyboardClassCreate
[01] IRP_MJ_CREATE_NAMED_PIPE      fffff800036abc0c  nt!IopInvalidDeviceRequest
[02] IRP_MJ_CLOSE                  fffff880071bf17c  kbdclass!KeyboardClassClose
[03] IRP_MJ_READ                   fffff880071bf804  kbdclass!KeyboardClassRead
...
[19] IRP_MJ_QUERY_QUOTA            fffff800036abc0c  nt!IopInvalidDeviceRequest
[1a] IRP_MJ_SET_QUOTA              fffff800036abc0c  nt!IopInvalidDeviceRequest
[1b] IRP_MJ_PNP                    fffff880071c0368  kbdclass!KeyboardPnP
```

While active, each IRP is usually queued in an IRP list associated with the thread that requested the I/O. (Otherwise, it is stored in the file object when performing thread-agnostic I/O, which is described earlier in this chapter.) This allows the I/O system to find and cancel any outstanding IRPs if a thread terminates with I/O requests that have not been completed. Additionally, paging I/O IRPs are also associated with the faulting thread (although they are not cancellable). This allows Windows to use the thread-agnostic I/O optimization —when an APC is not used to complete I/O if the current thread is the initiating thread. This means that page faults occur inline, instead of requiring APC delivery.

EXPERIMENT: Looking at a Thread's Outstanding IRPs

When you use the *!thread* command, it prints any IRPs associated with the thread. Run the kernel debugger with live debugging, and locate the service control manager process (Services.exe) in the output generated by the *!process* command:

```
lkd> !process 0 0
**** NT ACTIVE PROCESS DUMP ****
...
PROCESS 8623b840  SessionId: 0  Cid: 0270    Peb: 7ffd6000  ParentCid: 0210
    DirBase: ce21e080  ObjectTable: 964c06a0  HandleCount: 198.
    Image: services.exe
...
```

Then dump the threads for the process by executing the *!process* command on the process object. You should see many threads, with most of them having IRPs reported in the IRP List area of the thread information (note that the debugger will show only the first 17 IRPs for a thread that has more than 17 outstanding I/O requests):

```
lkd> !process 8623b840
PROCESS 8623b840  SessionId: 0  Cid: 0270    Peb: 7ffd6000  ParentCid: 0210
    DirBase: ce21e080  ObjectTable: 964c06a0  HandleCount: 198.
    Image: services.exe
    VadRoot 862b1358 Vads 71 Clone 0 Private 466. Modified 14. Locked 2.
    DeviceMap 8b0087d8
...
    THREAD 86a1d248  Cid 0270.053c  Teb: 7ffdc000 Win32Thread: 00000000
            WAIT: (UserRequest) UserMode Alertable
        86a40ca0  NotificationEvent
        86a40490  NotificationEvent
      IRP List:
        86a81190: (0006,0094) Flags: 00060900  Mdl: 00000000
...
```

Choose an IRP, and examine it with the *!irp* command:

```
lkd> !irp 86a81190
Irp is active with 1 stacks 1 is current (= 0x86a81200)
 No Mdl: No System Buffer: Thread 86a1d248:  Irp stack trace.
    cmd  flg cl Device   File      Completion-Context
>[ 3, 0]   0  1 86156328 86a4e7a0 00000000-00000000    pending
        \FileSystem\Npfs
            Args: 00000800 00000000 00000000 00000000
```

This IRP has a major function of 3, which corresponds to IRP_MJ_READ, which can be found in WDM.h. It has one stack location and is targeted at a device owned by the Npfs driver (the Named Pipe File System driver). (Npfs is described in Chapter 7, "Networking," in Part 1.)

IRP Buffer Management

When an application or a device driver indirectly creates an IRP by using the *NtReadFile, NtWriteFile*, or *NtDeviceIoControlFile* system services (or the Windows API functions corresponding to these services, which are *ReadFile, WriteFile*, and *DeviceIoControl*), the I/O manager determines whether it needs to participate in the management of the caller's input or output buffers. The I/O manager performs three types of buffer management:

- **Buffered I/O**   The I/O manager allocates a buffer in nonpaged pool of equal size to the caller's buffer. For write operations, the I/O manager copies the caller's buffer data into the allocated buffer when creating the IRP. For read operations, the I/O manager copies data from the allocated buffer to the user's buffer when the IRP completes and then frees the allocated buffer. The nonpaged pool buffer is pointed to by the IRP's *AssociatedIrp.SystemBuffer* field.

- **Direct I/O**   When the I/O manager creates the IRP, it locks the user's buffer into memory (that is, makes it nonpaged). When the I/O manager has finished using the IRP, it unlocks the buffer. The I/O manager stores a description of the memory in the form of a *memory descriptor list* (MDL). An MDL specifies the physical memory occupied by a buffer. (See the WDK for more information on MDLs.) Devices that perform direct memory access (DMA) require only physical descriptions of buffers, so an MDL is sufficient for the operation of such devices. (Devices that support DMA transfer data directly between the device and the computer's memory by using a DMA controller, not the CPU.) If a driver must access the contents of a buffer, however, it can map the buffer into the system's address space.

- **Neither I/O**   The I/O manager doesn't perform any buffer management. Instead, buffer management is left to the discretion of the device driver, which can choose to manually perform the steps the I/O manager performs with the other buffer management types.

For each type of buffer management, the I/O manager places applicable references in the IRP to the locations of the input and output buffers. The type of buffer management the I/O manager performs depends on the type of buffer management a driver requests for each type of operation. A driver registers the type of buffer management it desires for read and write operations in the device object that represents the device. Device I/O control operations (those requested by calling *NtDeviceIoControlFile*) are specified with driver-defined I/O control codes, and a control code contains bits specifying the buffer management the I/O manager should use when issuing IRPs that contain that code.

Drivers commonly use buffered I/O when callers transfer requests smaller than one page (4 KB on x86 processors) or when the device does not support DMA. They use direct I/O for larger requests on DMA-aware devices. File system drivers commonly use neither I/O because no buffer management overhead is incurred when data can be copied from the file system cache into the caller's original buffer. The reason that most drivers don't use neither I/O is that a pointer to a caller's buffer is valid only while a thread of the caller's process is executing.

Drivers that use neither I/O to access buffers that might be located in user space must take special care to ensure that buffer addresses are both valid and do not reference kernel-mode memory. Scalar values, however, are perfectly safe to pass, although a few drivers have only a scalar value to pass around. Failure to do so could result in crashes or in security vulnerabilities, where applications have access to kernel-mode memory or can inject code into the kernel. The *ProbeForRead* and *ProbeFor-Write* functions that the kernel makes available to drivers verify that a buffer resides entirely in the user-mode portion of the address space. To avoid a crash from referencing an invalid user-mode address, drivers can access user-mode buffers from within exception-handling code (called try/except blocks in C) that catch any invalid memory faults and translate them into error codes to return to the application. Additionally, drivers should also capture all input data into a kernel buffer instead of relying on user-mode addresses, since the caller could always modify the data behind the driver's back, even if the memory address itself is still valid.

I/O Request to a Single-Layered Driver

This section traces a synchronous I/O request to a single-layered kernel-mode device driver. In its most simplified form, handling a synchronous I/O to a single-layered driver consists of seven steps:

1. The I/O request passes through a subsystem DLL.

2. The subsystem DLL calls the I/O manager's *NtWriteFile* service.

3. The I/O manager allocates an IRP describing the request and sends it to the driver (a device driver in this case) by calling its own *IoCallDriver* function.

4. The driver transfers the data in the IRP to the device and starts the I/O operation.

5. The device signals I/O completion by interrupting the CPU.

6. The device driver services the interrupt.

7. The driver calls the I/O manager's *IoCompleteRequest* function to inform it that it has finished processing the IRP's request, and the I/O manager completes the I/O request.

These seven steps are illustrated in Figure 8-10.

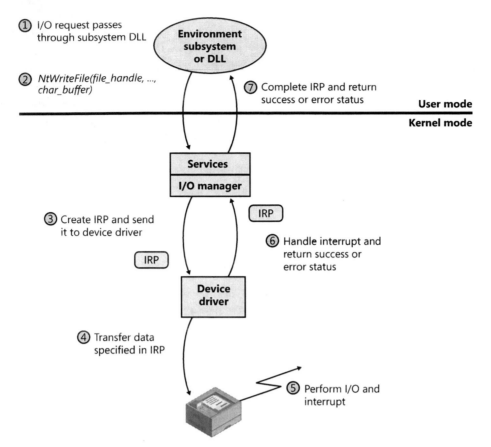

① I/O request passes
   through subsystem DLL

② NtWriteFile(file_handle, ...,
   char_buffer)

⑦ Complete IRP and return
   success or error status

User mode

Kernel mode

③ Create IRP and send
   it to device driver

⑥ Handle interrupt and
   return success or
   error status

④ Transfer data
   specified in IRP

⑤ Perform I/O and
   interrupt

FIGURE 8-10 Issuing and completing a synchronous I/O request

Now that we've seen how an I/O is initiated, let's take a closer look at interrupt processing and I/O completion.

Servicing an Interrupt

After an I/O device completes a data transfer, it interrupts for service, and the Windows kernel, I/O manager, and device driver are called into action. Figure 8-11 illustrates the first phase of the process. (Chapter 3 in Part 1 describes the interrupt dispatching mechanism, including DPCs. We've included a brief recap here because DPCs are key to I/O processing on interrupt-driven devices.)

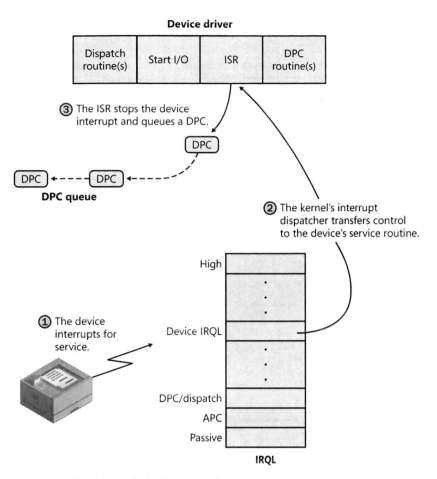

Device driver

Dispatch routine(s)	Start I/O	ISR	DPC routine(s)

③ The ISR stops the device interrupt and queues a DPC.

DPC

DPC ◄----DPC ◄-------

DPC queue

② The kernel's interrupt dispatcher transfers control to the device's service routine.

High

Device IRQL

① The device interrupts for service.

DPC/dispatch

APC

Passive

IRQL

FIGURE 8-11 Servicing a device interrupt (phase 1)

When a device interrupt occurs, the processor transfers control to the kernel trap handler, which indexes into its interrupt dispatch table to locate the ISR for the device. ISRs in Windows typically handle device interrupts in two steps. When an ISR is first invoked, it usually remains at device IRQL only long enough to capture the device status and then stop the device's interrupt. It then queues a DPC and exits, dismissing the interrupt. Later, when the DPC routine is called at IRQL 2, the device finishes processing the interrupt. When that's done, the device calls the I/O manager to complete the I/O and dispose of the IRP. It will also start the next I/O request that is waiting in the device queue.

The advantage of using a DPC to perform most of the device servicing is that any blocked interrupt whose IRQL lies between the device IRQL and the DPC/dispatch IRQL (2) is allowed to occur before the lower-priority DPC processing occurs. Intermediate-level interrupts are thus serviced more promptly than they otherwise would be, and this reduces latency on the system. This second phase of an I/O (the DPC processing) is illustrated in Figure 8-12.

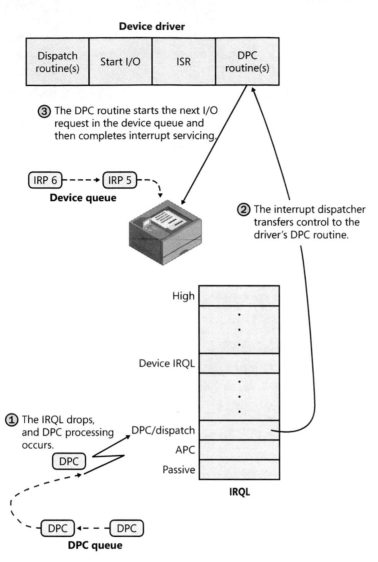

Device driver

Dispatch routine(s)	Start I/O	ISR	DPC routine(s)

③ The DPC routine starts the next I/O request in the device queue and then completes interrupt servicing.

IRP 6 ----▶ IRP 5 ----
Device queue

② The interrupt dispatcher transfers control to the driver's DPC routine.

High

Device IRQL

① The IRQL drops, and DPC processing occurs.

DPC

DPC/dispatch
APC
Passive

IRQL

DPC ◀- - DPC
DPC queue

FIGURE 8-12 Servicing a device interrupt (phase 2)

Completing an I/O Request

After a device driver's DPC routine has executed, some work still remains before the I/O request can be considered finished. This third stage of I/O processing is called *I/O completion* and is initiated when a driver calls *IoCompleteRequest* to inform the I/O manager that it has completed processing the request specified in the IRP (and the stack location that it owns). The steps I/O completion entails vary with different I/O operations. For example, all the I/O drivers record the outcome of the operation in an *I/O status block*, a data structure stored in the IRP and then copied back into a caller-supplied buffer during I/O completion. Similarly, some drivers that perform buffered I/O require the I/O system to return data to the calling thread.

In both cases, the I/O system must copy data that is stored in system memory into the caller's virtual address space. If the IRP completed synchronously, the caller's address space is current and directly accessible, but if the IRP completed asynchronously, the I/O manager must delay IRP completion until it can access the caller's address space. To gain access to the caller's virtual address space, the I/O manager must transfer the data "in the context of the caller's thread"—that is, while the caller's thread is executing (which implies that the caller's process is the current process and its address space is mapped on the processor). It does so by queuing a special kernel-mode asynchronous procedure call (APC) to the thread. This process is illustrated in Figure 8-13.

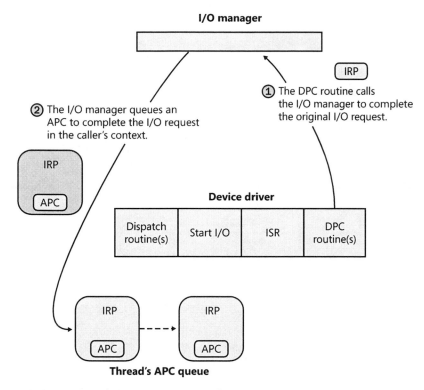

FIGURE 8-13 Completing an I/O request (phase 1)

As explained in Chapter 3 in Part 1, APCs execute in the context of a particular thread, whereas a DPC executes in arbitrary thread context, meaning that the DPC routine can't touch the user-mode process address space. Remember too that DPCs have a higher IRQL than APCs.

The next time that the thread begins to execute at low IRQL (below DISPATCH_LEVEL), the pending APC is delivered. The kernel transfers control to the I/O manager's APC routine, which copies the data (for a read request) and the return status into the original caller's address space, frees the IRP representing the I/O operation, and either sets the caller's file handle (and any caller-supplied event) to the signaled state for synchronous I/O or queues an entry to the caller's I/O completion port. The I/O is now considered complete. The original caller or any other threads that are waiting on the file (or other object) handle are released from their waiting state and readied for execution. Figure 8-14 illustrates the second stage of I/O completion.

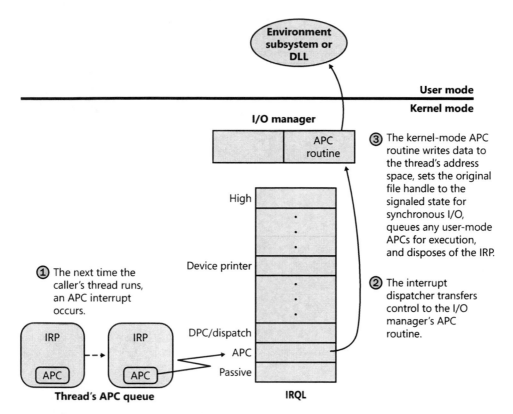

FIGURE 8-14 Completing an I/O request (phase 2)

Although this is the normal path through which I/O completion occurs, Windows can take a short-cut if the I/O happens to be completed in the same thread that issued the I/O request. In this situation, as long as APC delivery was not disabled (in order to maintain compatibility with legacy versions of Windows, which always used an APC, even in this situation), the phase 2 I/O completion mechanism is called inline.

A final note about I/O completion: the asynchronous I/O functions *ReadFileEx* and *WriteFileEx* allow a caller to supply a user-mode APC as a parameter. If the caller does so, the I/O manager queues this APC to the caller's thread APC queue as the last step of I/O completion. This feature allows a caller to specify a subroutine to be called when an I/O request is completed or canceled. User-mode APC completion routines execute in the context of the requesting thread and are delivered only when the thread enters an alertable wait state (such as calling the Windows *SleepEx*, *WaitForSingleObjectEx*, or *WaitForMultipleObjectsEx* function).

Synchronization

Drivers must synchronize their access to global driver data and hardware registers for two reasons:

- The execution of a driver can be preempted by higher-priority threads and time-slice (or quantum) expiration or can be interrupted by higher IRQL interrupts.

- On multiprocessor systems, Windows can run driver code simultaneously on more than one processor.

Without synchronization, corruption could occur—for example, because device driver code running at passive IRQL (0) when a caller initiates an I/O operation can be interrupted by a device interrupt, causing the device driver's ISR to execute while its own device driver is already running. If the device driver was modifying data that its ISR also modifies, such as device registers, heap storage, or static data, the data can become corrupted when the ISR executes. Figure 8-15 illustrates this problem.

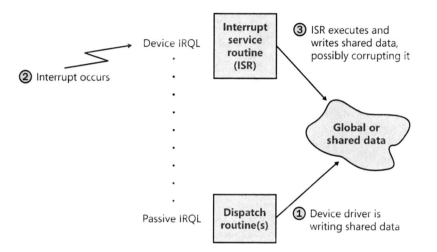

FIGURE 8-15 Concurrent access to shared data by a device driver dispatch routine and ISR

To avoid this situation, a device driver written for Windows must synchronize its access to any data that can be accessed at more than one IRQL. Before attempting to update shared data, the device driver must lock out all other threads (or CPUs, in the case of a multiprocessor system) to prevent them from updating the same data structure.

The Windows kernel provides a special synchronization routine called *KeSynchronizeExecution* that device drivers call when they access data that their ISRs also access. This kernel synchronization routine keeps the ISR from executing while the shared data is being accessed. A driver can also use *KeAcquireInterruptSpinLock* to access an interrupt object's spinlock directly, although drivers can generally behave better by relying on *KeSynchronizeExecution* for synchronization with an ISR because calling this function at PASSIVE_LEVEL will synchronize with a KEVENT in the interrupt object structure instead of raising IRQL.

By now, you should realize that although ISRs require special attention, any data that a device driver uses is subject to being accessed by the same device driver running on another processor. Therefore, it's critical for device driver code to synchronize its use of any global or shared data (or any accesses to the physical device itself). If the ISR uses that data, the device driver must use *KeSynchronizeExecution* or *KeAcquireInterruptSpinLock*; otherwise, the device driver can use standard kernel spinlocks (which are acquired at DISPATCH_LEVEL (IRQL 2).

I/O Requests to Layered Drivers

The preceding section showed how an I/O request to a simple device controlled by a single device driver is handled. I/O processing for file-based devices or for requests to other layered drivers happens in much the same way. The major difference is, obviously, that one or more additional layers of processing are added to the model.

Figure 8-16 shows a very simplified, illustrative example of how an asynchronous I/O request might travel through layered drivers. It uses as an example a disk controlled by a file system.

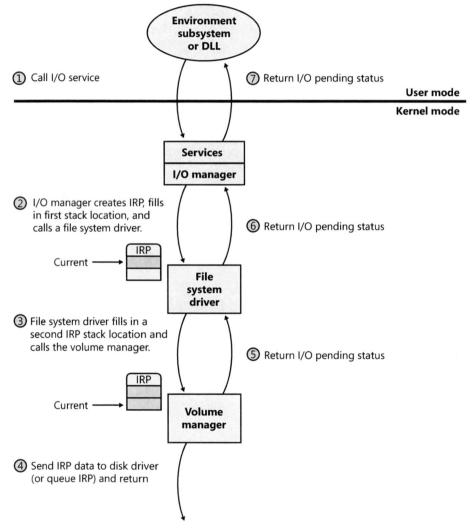

FIGURE 8-16 Queuing an asynchronous request to layered drivers

Once again, the I/O manager receives the request and creates an I/O request packet to represent it. This time, however, it delivers the packet to a file system driver. The file system driver exercises great control over the I/O operation at that point. Depending on the type of request the caller made, the file system can send the same IRP to the disk driver or it can generate additional IRPs and send them separately to the disk driver.

EXPERIMENT: Viewing a Device Stack

The kernel debugger command *!devstack* shows you the device stack of layered device objects associated with a specified device object. This example shows the device stack associated with a device object, \device\keyboardclass0, which is owned by the keyboard class driver:

```
lkd> !devstack keyboardclass0
  !DevObj           !DrvObj              !DevExt          ObjectName
  ffffffa800a5e2040  \Driver\Ctrl2cap    ffffffa800a5e2190
> ffffffa800a612ce0  \Driver\kbdclass    ffffffa800a612e30  KeyboardClass0
  ffffffa800a612040  \Driver\i8042prt    ffffffa800a612190
  ffffffa80076e0a00  \Driver\ACPI        ffffffa80076f3a90  0000005c
!DevNode ffffffa800770f750 :
  DeviceInst is "ACPI\PNP0303\4&b0a2531&0"
  ServiceName is "i8042prt"
```

The output highlights the entry associated with KeyboardClass0 with the ">" character in column one. The entries above that line are drivers layered above the keyboard class driver, and those below are layered beneath it. In general, IRPs flow from the top of the stack to the bottom.

The file system is most likely to reuse an IRP if the request it receives translates into a single straightforward request to a device. For example, if an application issues a read request for the first 512 bytes in a file stored on a volume, the NTFS file system would simply call the volume manager driver, asking it to read one sector from the volume, beginning at the file's starting location.

To accommodate its reuse by multiple drivers in a request to layered drivers, an IRP contains a series of *IRP stack locations* (not to be confused with the CPU stack used by threads to store function parameters and return addresses). These data areas, one for every driver that will be called, contain the information that each driver needs to execute its part of the request—for example, function code, parameters, and driver context information. As Figure 8-16 illustrates, additional stack locations are filled in as the IRP passes from one driver to the next. You can think of an IRP as being similar to a stack in the way data is added to it and removed from it during its lifetime. However, an IRP isn't associated with any particular process, and its allocated size doesn't grow or shrink. The I/O manager allocates an IRP from one of its IRP look-aside lists or nonpaged system memory at the beginning of the I/O operation.

Note Since the number of devices on a given stack is known in advance, the I/O manager allocates one stack location per device driver on the stack. However, there are situations in which an IRP might be directed into a new driver stack, as can happen in scenarios involving the Filter Manager, which allows one filter to redirect an IRP to another filter (going from a local file system to a network file system, for example). The I/O manager exposes an API, *IoAdjustStackSizeForRedirection*, that enables this functionality by adding the required stack locations because of devices present on the redirected stack.

EXPERIMENT: Examining IRPs

In this experiment, you'll find an uncompleted IRP on the system, and you'll determine the IRP type, the device at which it's directed, the driver that manages the device, the thread that issued the IRP, and what process the thread belongs to.

At any point in time, there are at least a few uncompleted IRPs on a system. This occurs because there are many devices to which applications can issue IRPs that a driver will complete only when a particular event occurs, such as data becoming available. One example is a blocking read from a network endpoint. You can see the outstanding IRPs on a system with the *!irpfind* kernel debugger command:

```
lkd> !irpfind

Scanning large pool allocation table for Tag: Irp? (86c16000 : 86d16000)
Searching NonPaged pool (80000000 : ffc00000) for Tag: Irp?

  Irp     [ Thread ] irpStack: (Mj,Mn)   DevObj  [Driver]        MDL Process
862d2380 [8666dc68] irpStack: ( c, 2)  84a6f020 [ \FileSystem\Ntfs]
862d2bb0 [864e3d78] irpStack: ( e,20)  86171348 [ \Driver\AFD] 0x864dbd90
862d4518 [865f7600] irpStack: ( d, 0)  86156328 [ \FileSystem\Npfs]
862d4688 [867133f0] irpStack: ( 3, 0)  86156328 [ \FileSystem\Npfs]
862dd008 [00000000] Irp is complete (CurrentLocation 4 > StackCount 3) 0x00420000
862dee28 [864fc030] irpStack: ( 3, 0)  84baf030 [ \Driver\kbdclass]
```

The entry in bold in the output describes an IRP that is directed at the Kbdclass driver, so it is likely that the IRP was issued by the Windows subsystem raw input thread that reads keyboard input. Examining the IRP with the *!irp* command reveals the following:

```
lkd> !irp 862dee28
Irp is active with 3 stacks 3 is current (= 0x862deee0)
 No Mdl: System buffer=864f5108: Thread 864fc030:  Irp stack trace.
    cmd  flg cl Device   File     Completion-Context
[ 0, 0]   0  0 00000000 00000000 00000000-00000000

          Args: 00000000 00000000 00000000 00000000
[ 0, 0]   0  0 00000000 00000000 00000000-00000000
```

```
                  Args: 00000000 00000000 00000000 00000000
>[  3,  0]    0  1 84baf030 864f52f8 00000000-00000000     pending
              \Driver\kbdclass
              Args: 00000078 00000000 00000000 00000000
```

The active stack location is at the bottom. (The debugger shows the active location with a ">" character in column one.) It has a major function of 3, which corresponds to IRP_MJ_READ.

The next step is to see what device object the IRP is targeting by executing the *!devobj* command on the device object address in the active stack location.

```
lkd> !devobj 84baf030
Device object (84baf030) is for:
 KeyboardClass1 \Driver\kbdclass DriverObject 84b706b8
Current Irp 00000000 RefCount 0 Type 0000000b Flags 00002044
Dacl 8b0538b8 DevExt 84baf0e8 DevObjExt 84baf1c8
ExtensionFlags (0x00000800)
                                Unknown flags 0x00000800
AttachedTo (Lower) 84badaa0 \Driver\TermDD
Device queue is not busy.
```

The device at which the IRP is targeted is KeyboardClass1. The presence of a device object owned by the Termdd driver attached beneath it reveals that it is the device that represents keyboard input from a Terminal Server client, not the physical keyboard.

We can see details about the thread and process that issued the IRP by using the *!thread* and *!process* commands:

```
lkd> !thread 864fc030
THREAD 864fc030  Cid 01d4.0234  Teb: 7ffd9000 Win32Thread: ffac4008
              WAIT: (WrUserRequest) KernelMode Alertable
    8623c620  SynchronizationEvent
    864fc3a8  NotificationTimer
    864fc378  SynchronizationTimer
    864fc360  SynchronizationEvent
IRP List:
    86af0e28: (0006,01d8) Flags: 00060970  Mdl: 00000000
    86503958: (0006,0268) Flags: 00060970  Mdl: 00000000
    862dee28: (0006,01d8) Flags: 00060970  Mdl: 00000000
Not impersonating
DeviceMap                 8b0087d8
Owning Process            0       Image:        <Unknown>
Attached Process          864d2d90      Image:        csrss.exe
Wait Start TickCount      171909        Ticks: 29 (0:00:00:00.452)
Context Switch Count      121222
UserTime                  00:00:00.000
KernelTime                00:00:00.717
Win32 Start Address 0x764d9a30
Stack Init 96f46000 Current 96f45c28 Base 96f46000 Limit 96f43000 Call 0
Priority 15 BasePriority 13 PriorityDecrement 0 IoPriority 2 PagePriority 5

lkd> !process 864d2d90
PROCESS 864d2d90  SessionId: 1  Cid: 0208    Peb: 7ffdf000  ParentCid: 0200
    DirBase: ce21e0a0  ObjectTable: 964a6e68  HandleCount: 284.
    Image: csrss.exe
```

Locating the thread in Process Explorer by opening the Properties dialog box for Csrss.exe and going to the Threads tab confirms, through the names of the functions on its stack, the role of the thread as a raw input thread for the Windows subsystem:

After the disk controller's DMA adapter finishes a data transfer, the disk controller interrupts the host, causing the ISR for the disk controller to run, which requests a DPC callback completing the IRP, as shown in Figure 8-17.

As an alternative to reusing a single IRP, a file system can establish a group of *associated* IRPs that work in parallel on a single I/O request. For example, if the data to be read from a file is dispersed across the disk, the file system driver might create several IRPs, each of which reads some portion of the request from a different sector. This queuing is illustrated in Figure 8-18.

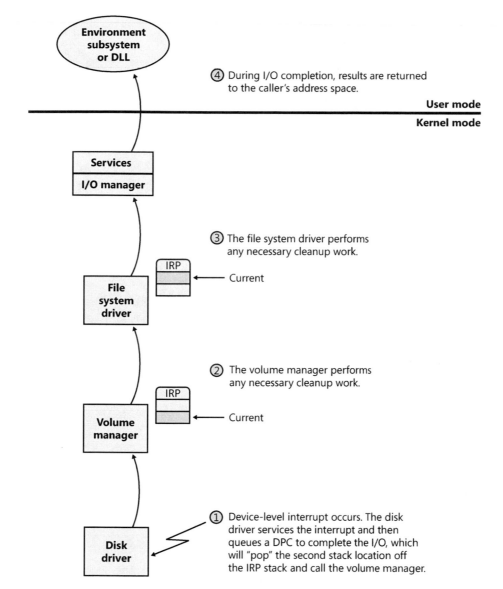

FIGURE 8-17 Completing a layered I/O request

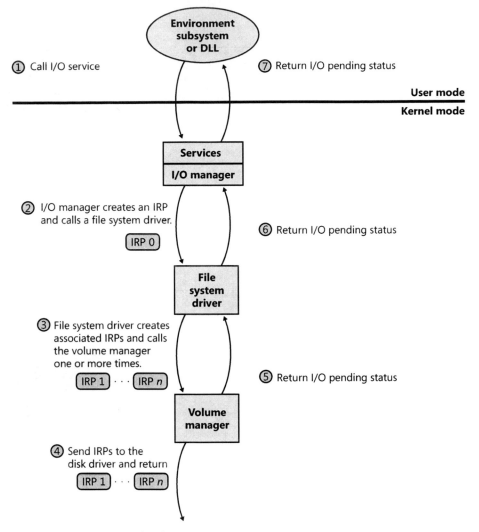

FIGURE 8-18 Queuing associated IRPs

The file system driver delivers the associated IRPs to the volume manager, which in turn sends them to the disk device driver, which queues them to the disk device. They are processed one at a time, and the file system driver keeps track of the returned data. When all the associated IRPs complete, the I/O system completes the original IRP and returns to the caller, as shown in Figure 8-19.

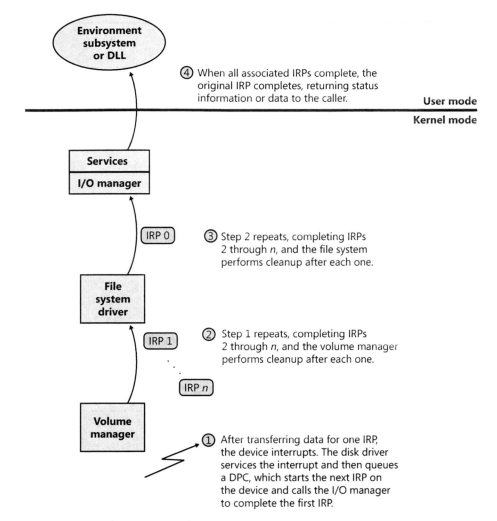

FIGURE 8-19 Completing associated IRPs

Note All Windows file system drivers that manage disk-based file systems are part of a stack of drivers that is at least three layers deep: the file system driver sits at the top, a volume manager in the middle, and a disk driver at the bottom. In addition, any number of filter drivers can be interspersed above and below these drivers. For clarity, the preceding example of layered I/O requests includes only a file system driver and the volume manager driver. See Chapter 9, on storage management, for more information.

Thread Agnostic I/O

In the I/O models described thus far, IRPs are queued to the thread that initiated the I/O and are completed by the I/O manager issuing an APC to that thread so that process-specific and thread-specific context is accessible by completion processing. Thread-specific I/O processing is usually sufficient for the performance and scalability needs of most applications, but Windows also includes support for *thread agnostic I/O* via two mechanisms:

- I/O completion ports, which are described at length later in this chapter

- Locking the user buffer into memory and mapping it into the system address space

With I/O completion ports, the application decides when it wants to check for the completion of I/O, so the thread that happens to have issued an I/O request is not necessarily relevant because any other thread can perform the completion request. As such, instead of completing the IRP inside the specific thread's context, it can be completed in the context of any thread that has access to the completion port.

Likewise, with a locked and kernel-mapped version of the user buffer, there's no need to be in the same memory address space as the issuing thread because the kernel can access the memory from arbitrary contexts. Applications can enable this mechanism by using *SetFileIoOverlappedRange* as long as they have the SE_LOCK_MEMORY privilege.

With both completion port I/O and I/O on file buffers set by *SetFileIoOverlappedRange*, the I/O manager associates the IRPs with the file object to which they have been issued instead of with the issuing thread. The *!fileobj* extension in WinDbg will show an IRP list for file objects that are used with these mechanisms.

In the next sections, we'll see how thread agnostic I/O increases the reliability and performance of applications on Windows.

I/O Cancellation

While there are many ways in which IRP processing occurs and various methods to complete an I/O request, a great many I/O processing operations actually end in cancellation rather than completion. For example, a device may require removal while IRPs are still active, or the user might cancel a long-running operation to a device—for example, a network operation. Another situation requiring I/O cancellation support is thread and process termination. When a thread exits, the I/Os associated with the thread must be cancelled because the I/O operations are no longer relevant, and the thread cannot be deleted until the outstanding I/Os have completed.

The Windows I/O manager, working with drivers, must deal with these requests efficiently and reliably to provide a smooth user experience. Drivers manage this need by registering a *cancel routine* for their cancellable I/O operations (typically, those operations that are still enqueued and not yet in progress), which is invoked by the I/O manager to cancel an I/O operation. When drivers fail to play their role in these scenarios, users may experience unkillable processes, which have disappeared visually but linger and still appear in Task Manager or Process Explorer. (See Chapter 5, "Processes, Threads, and Jobs" in Part 1 for more information on processes and threads.)

User-Initiated I/O Cancellation

Most software uses one thread to handle user interface (UI) input and one or more threads to perform work, including I/O. In some cases, when a user wants to abort an operation that was initiated in the UI, an application might need to cancel outstanding I/O operations. Operations that complete quickly might not require cancellation, but for operations that take arbitrary amounts of time—like large data transfers or network operations— Windows provides support for cancelling both synchronous operations and asynchronous operations. A thread can cancel its own outstanding asynchronous I/Os by calling *CancelIo*. It can cancel all asynchronous I/Os issued to a specific file handle, regardless of by which thread, in the same process with *CancelIoEx*. *CancelIoEx* also works on operations associated with I/O completion ports through the thread-agnostic support in Windows that was mentioned earlier because the I/O system keeps track of a completion port's outstanding I/Os by linking them with the completion port.

For cancelling synchronous I/Os, a thread can call *CancelSynchronousIo*. *CancelSynchronousIo* enables even create (open) operations to be cancelled when supported by a device driver, and several drivers in Windows support this functionality, including the drivers that manage network file systems (for example, MUP, DFS, and SMB), which can cancel open operations to network paths. Figures 8-20 and 8-21 show synchronous and asynchronous I/O cancellation. (To a driver, all cancel processing looks the same.)

Synchronous I/O Cancellation

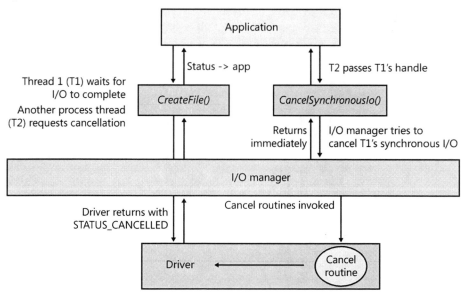

FIGURE 8-20 Synchronous I/O cancellation

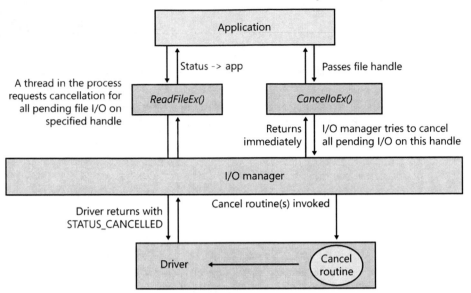

FIGURE 8-21 Asynchronous I/O cancellation

I/O Cancellation for Thread Termination

The other scenario in which I/Os must be cancelled is when a thread exits, either directly or as the result of its process terminating (which causes the threads of the process to terminate). Because every thread has a list of IRPs associated with it, the I/O manager can walk this list, look for cancellable IRPs, and cancel them. Unlike *CancelIoEx*, which does not wait for an IRP to be cancelled before returning, the process manager will not allow thread termination to proceed until all I/Os have been cancelled. As a result, if a driver fails to cancel an IRP, the process and thread object will remain allocated until the system shuts down. Figure 8-22 illustrates the process termination scenario.

Process Termination Example

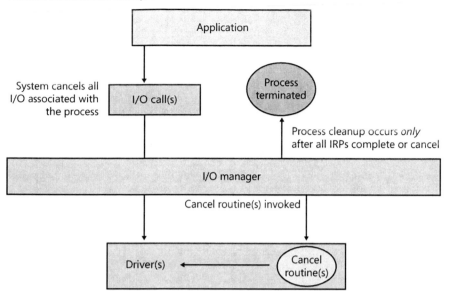

FIGURE 8-22 Cancellation during process termination

Note Only IRPs for which a driver sets a cancel routine are cancellable. The process manager waits until all I/Os associated with a thread are either cancelled or completed before deleting the thread.

EXPERIMENT: Debugging an Unkillable Process

In this experiment, we'll use Notmyfault from Sysinternals (we'll cover Notmyfault heavily in the "Crash Dump Analysis" section in Chapter 14, "Crash Dump Analysis") to force the unkillable process problem to exhibit itself by causing the Myfault.sys driver (which Notmyfault.exe uses) to indefinitely hold an IRP without having registered a cancel routine for it.

To start, run Notmyfault.exe, select Hang With IRP from the list of options on the Hang tab, and then click the Hang button. The dialog box should look like the following when properly configured.

You shouldn't see anything happen, and you should be able to click the Cancel button to quit the application. However, you should still see the Notmyfault process in Task Manager or Process Explorer. Attempts to terminate the process will fail because Windows will wait forever for the IRP to complete given that the Myfault driver doesn't register a cancel routine.

To debug an issue such as this, you can use WinDbg to look at what the thread is currently doing. Open a local kernel debugger session, and start by listing the information about the Notmyfault.exe process with the *!process* command:

```
lkd> !process 0 7 notmyfault.exe
PROCESS 86843ab0  SessionId: 1  Cid: 0594    Peb: 7ffd8000  ParentCid: 05c8
    DirBase: ce21f380  ObjectTable: 9cfb5070  HandleCount:  33.
    Image: NotMyfault.exe
    VadRoot 86658138 Vads 44 Clone 0 Private 210. Modified 5. Locked 0.
    DeviceMap 987545a8
...
    THREAD 868139b8  Cid 0594.0230  Teb: 7ffde000 Win32Thread: 00000000
                    WAIT: (Executive) KernelMode Non-Alertable
        86797c64  NotificationEvent
    IRP List:
        86a51228: (0006,0094) Flags: 00060000  Mdl: 00000000
...

        ChildEBP RetAddr  Args to Child
        88ae4b78 81cf23bf 868139b8 86813a40 00000000 nt!KiSwapContext+0x26
        88ae4bbc 81c8fcf8 868139b8 86797c08 86797c64 nt!KiSwapThread+0x44f
        88ae4c14 81e8a356 86797c64 00000000 00000000 nt!KeWaitForSingleObject+0x492
        88ae4c40 81e875a3 86a51228 86797c08 86a51228 nt!IopCancelAlertedRequest+0x6d
        88ae4c64 81e87cba 00000103 86797c08 00000000 nt!IopSynchronousServiceTail+0x267
        88ae4d00 81e7198e 86727920 86a51228 00000000 nt!IopXxxControlFile+0x6b7
        88ae4d34 81c92a7a 0000007c 00000000 00000000 nt!NtDeviceIoControlFile+0x2a
```

```
        88ae4d34 77139a94 0000007c 00000000 00000000 nt!KiFastCallEntry+0x12a
        01d5fecc 00000000 00000000 00000000 00000000 ntdll!KiFastSystemCallRet
...
```

From the stack trace, you can see that the thread that initiated the I/O realized that the IRP had been cancelled (*IopSynchronousServiceTail* called *IopCancelAlertedRequest*) and is now waiting for the cancellation or completion. The next step is to use the same debugger extension command used in the previous experiments, *!irp*, and attempt to analyze the problem. Copy the IRP pointer, and examine it with *!irp*:

```
lkd> !irp 86a51228
Irp is active with 1 stacks 1 is current (= 0x86a51298)
 No Mdl: No System Buffer: Thread 868139b8:  Irp stack trace.
    cmd  flg cl Device   File     Completion-Context
>[  e, 0]   5  0 86727920 86797c08 00000000-00000000
         \Driver\MYFAULT
         Args: 00000000 00000000 83360020 00000000
```

From this output, it is obvious who the culprit driver is: \Driver\MYFAULT, or Myfault.sys. The name of the driver emphasizes that the only way this situation can happen is through a driver problem and not a buggy application. Unfortunately, now that you know which driver caused this issue, there isn't much you can do—a system reboot is necessary because Windows can never safely assume it is okay to ignore the fact that cancellation hasn't occurred yet. The IRP could return at any time and cause corruption of system memory. If you encounter this situation in practice, you should check for a newer version of the driver, which might include a fix for the bug.

I/O Completion Ports

Writing a high-performance server application requires implementing an efficient threading model. Having either too few or too many server threads to process client requests can lead to performance problems. For example, if a server creates a single thread to handle all requests, clients can become starved because the server will be tied up processing one request at a time. A single thread could simultaneously process multiple requests, switching from one to another as I/O operations are started, but this architecture introduces significant complexity and can't take advantage of systems with more than one logical processor. At the other extreme, a server could create a big pool of threads so that virtually every client request is processed by a dedicated thread. This scenario usually leads to thread-thrashing, in which lots of threads wake up, perform some CPU processing, block while waiting for I/O, and then, after request processing is completed, block again waiting for a new request. If nothing else, having too many threads results in excessive context switching, caused by the scheduler having to divide processor time among multiple active threads.

The goal of a server is to incur as few context switches as possible by having its threads avoid unnecessary blocking, while at the same time maximizing parallelism by using multiple threads. The ideal is for there to be a thread actively servicing a client request on every processor and for those threads not to block when they complete a request if additional requests are waiting. For this optimal process to work correctly, however, the application must have a way to activate another thread when a thread processing a client request blocks on I/O (such as when it reads from a file as part of the processing).

The *IoCompletion* Object

Applications use the *IoCompletion* executive object, which is exported to the Windows API as a *completion port*, as the focal point for the completion of I/O associated with multiple file handles. Once a file is associated with a completion port, any asynchronous I/O operations that complete on the file result in a completion packet being queued to the completion port. A thread can wait for any outstanding I/Os to complete on multiple files simply by waiting for a completion packet to be queued to the completion port. The Windows API provides similar functionality with the *WaitFor-MultipleObjects* API function, but the advantage that completion ports have is that *concurrency*, or the number of threads that an application has actively servicing client requests, is controlled with the aid of the system.

When an application creates a completion port, it specifies a concurrency value. This value indicates the maximum number of threads associated with the port that should be running at any given time. As stated earlier, the ideal is to have one thread active at any given time for every processor in the system. Windows uses the concurrency value associated with a port to control how many threads an application has active. If the number of active threads associated with a port equals the concurrency value, a thread that is waiting on the completion port won't be allowed to run. Instead, it is expected that one of the active threads will finish processing its current request and check to see whether another packet is waiting at the port. If one is, the thread simply grabs the packet and goes off to process it. When this happens, there is no context switch, and the CPUs are utilized nearly to their full capacity.

Using Completion Ports

Figure 8-23 shows a high-level illustration of completion port operation. A completion port is created with a call to the Windows API function *CreateIoCompletionPort*. Threads that block on a completion port become associated with the port and are awakened in last in, first out (LIFO) order so that the thread that blocked most recently is the one that is given the next packet. Threads that block for long periods of time can have their stacks swapped out to disk, so if there are more threads associated with a port than there is work to process, the in-memory footprints of threads blocked the longest are minimized.

A server application will usually receive client requests via network endpoints that are identified by file handles. Examples include Windows Sockets 2 (Winsock2) sockets or named pipes. As the server creates its communications endpoints, it associates them with a completion port and its threads wait for incoming requests by calling *GetQueuedCompletionStatus* on the port. When a thread is given a packet from the completion port, it will go off and start processing the request, becoming an active thread. A thread will block many times during its processing, such as when it needs to read or write data to a file on disk or when it synchronizes with other threads. Windows detects this activity and recognizes that the completion port has one less active thread. Therefore, when a thread becomes inactive because it blocks, a thread waiting on the completion port will be awakened if there is a packet in the queue.

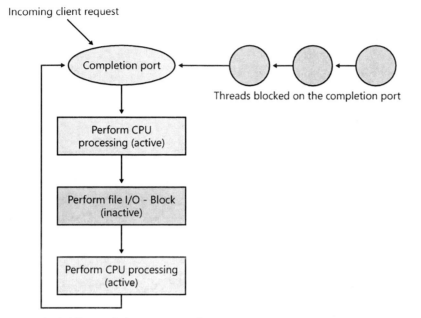

Incoming client request

FIGURE 8-23 I/O completion port operation

Microsoft's guidelines are to set the concurrency value roughly equal to the number of processors in a system. Keep in mind that it's possible for the number of active threads for a completion port to exceed the concurrency limit. Consider a case in which the limit is specified as 1. A client request comes in, and a thread is dispatched to process the request, becoming active. A second request arrives, but a second thread waiting on the port isn't allowed to proceed because the concurrency limit has been reached. Then the first thread blocks waiting for a file I/O, so it becomes inactive. The second thread is then released, and while it's still active, the first thread's file I/O is completed, making it active again. At that point—and until one of the threads blocks—the concurrency value is 2, which is higher than the limit of 1. Most of the time, the count of active threads will remain at or just above the concurrency limit.

The completion port API also makes it possible for a server application to queue privately defined completion packets to a completion port by using the *PostQueuedCompletionStatus* function. A server typically uses this function to inform its threads of external events, such as the need to shut down gracefully.

Applications can use thread agnostic I/O, described earlier, with I/O completion ports to avoid associating threads with their own I/Os and associating them with a completion port object instead. In addition to the other scalability benefits of I/O completion ports, their use can minimize context switches. Standard I/O completions must be executed by the thread that initiated the I/O, but when an I/O associated with an I/O completion port completes, the I/O manager uses any waiting thread to perform the completion operation.

I/O Completion Port Operation

Windows applications create completion ports by calling the Windows API *CreateIoCompletionPort* and specifying a NULL completion port handle. This results in the execution of the *NtCreateIo-Completion* system service. The executive's *IoCompletion* object contains a kernel synchronization object called a *kernel queue*. Thus, the system service creates a completion port object and initializes a queue object in the port's allocated memory. (A pointer to the port also points to the queue object because the queue is at the start of the port memory.) A kernel queue object has a concurrency value that is specified when a thread initializes it, and in this case the value that is used is the one that was passed to *CreateIoCompletionPort*. *KeInitializeQueue* is the function that *NtCreateIoCompletion* calls to initialize a port's queue object.

When an application calls *CreateIoCompletionPort* to associate a file handle with a port, the *NtSetInformationFile* system service is executed with the file handle as the primary parameter. The information class that is set is *FileCompletionInformation*, and the completion port's handle and the *CompletionKey* parameter from *CreateIoCompletionPort* are the data values. *NtSetInformationFile* dereferences the file handle to obtain the file object and allocates a completion context data structure.

Finally, *NtSetInformationFile* sets the *CompletionContext* field in the file object to point at the context structure. When an asynchronous I/O operation completes on a file object, the I/O manager checks to see whether the *CompletionContext* field in the file object is non-NULL. If it is, the I/O manager allocates a completion packet and queues it to the completion port by calling *KeInsertQueue* with the port as the queue on which to insert the packet. (Remember that the completion port object and queue object have the same address.)

When a server thread invokes *GetQueuedCompletionStatus*, the system service *NtRemoveIoCompletion* is executed. After validating parameters and translating the completion port handle to a pointer to the port, *NtRemoveIoCompletion* calls *IoRemoveIoCompletion*, which eventually calls *KeRemoveQueueEx*. For high-performance scenarios, it's possible that multiple I/Os may have been completed, and although the thread will not block, it will still call into the kernel each time to get one item. The *GetQueuedCompletionStatus* or *GetQueuedCompletionStatusEx* API allows applications to retrieve more than one I/O completion status at the same time, reducing the number of user-to-kernel roundtrips and maintaining peak efficiency. Internally, this is implemented through the *NtRemoveIoCompletionEx* function, which calls *IoRemoveIoCompletion* with a count of queued items, which is passed on to *KeRemoveQueueEx*.

As you can see, *KeRemoveQueueEx* and *KeInsertQueue* are the engines behind completion ports. They are the functions that determine whether a thread waiting for an I/O completion packet should be activated. Internally, a queue object maintains a count of the current number of active threads and the maximum number of active threads. If the current number equals or exceeds the maximum when a thread calls *KeRemoveQueueEx*, the thread will be put (in LIFO order) onto a list of threads waiting for a turn to process a completion packet. The list of threads hangs off the queue object. A thread's control block data structure (KTHREAD) has a pointer in it that references the queue object of a queue that it's associated with; if the pointer is NULL, the thread isn't associated with a queue.

Windows keeps track of threads that become inactive because they block on something other than the completion port by relying on the queue pointer in a thread's control block. The scheduler routines that possibly result in a thread blocking (such as *KeWaitForSingleObject*, *KeDelayExecution-Thread*, and so on) check the thread's queue pointer. If the pointer isn't NULL, the functions call *KiActivateWaiterQueue*, a queue-related function that decrements the count of active threads associated with the queue. If the resultant number is less than the maximum and at least one completion packet is in the queue, the thread at the front of the queue's thread list is awakened and given the oldest packet. Conversely, whenever a thread that is associated with a queue wakes up after blocking, the scheduler executes the function *KiUnwaitThread*, which increments the queue's active count.

Finally, the *PostQueuedCompletionStatus* Windows API function results in the execution of the *NtSetIoCompletion* system service. This function simply inserts the specified packet onto the completion port's queue by using *KeInsertQueue*.

Figure 8-24 shows an example of a completion port object in operation. Even though two threads are ready to process completion packets, the concurrency value of 1 allows only one thread associated with the completion port to be active, and so the two threads are blocked on the completion port.

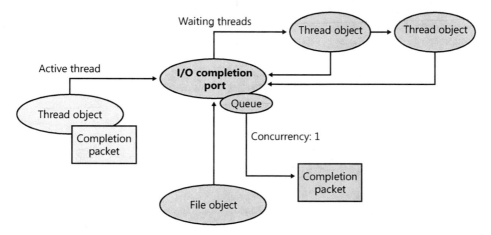

FIGURE 8-24 I/O completion port operation

Finally, the exact notification model of the I/O completion port can be fine-tuned through the *SetFileCompletionNotificationModes* API, which allows application developers to take advantage of additional, specific improvements that usually require code changes but can offer even more throughput. Three notification-mode optimizations are supported, which are listed in Table 8-3. Note that these modes are per file handle and permanent.

TABLE 8-3 I/O Completion Port Notification Modes

Notification Mode	Meaning
Skip completion port on success	If the following three conditions are true, the I/O manager does not queue a completion entry to the port when it would ordinarily do so. First, a completion port must be associated with the file handle; second, the file must be opened for asynchronous I/O; third, the request must return success immediately without returning ERROR_PENDING.
Skip set event on handle	The I/O manager does not set the event for the file object if a request returns with a success code or the error returned is ERROR_PENDING and the function that is called is not a synchronous function. If an explicit event is provided for the request, it is still signaled.
Skip set user event on fast I/O	The I/O manager does not set the explicit event provided for the request if a request takes the fast I/O path and returns with a success code or the error returned is ERROR_PENDING and the function that is called is not a synchronous function.

I/O Prioritization

Without I/O priority, background activities like search indexing, virus scanning, and disk defragmenting can severely impact the responsiveness of foreground operations. A user launching an application or opening a document while another process is performing disk I/O, for example, experiences delays as the foreground task waits for disk access. The same interference also affects the streaming playback of multimedia content like music from a disk.

Windows includes two types of I/O prioritization to help foreground I/O operations get preference: priority on individual I/O operations and I/O bandwidth reservations.

I/O Priorities

The Windows I/O manager internally includes support for five I/O priorities, as shown in Table 8-4, but only three of the priorities are used. (Future versions of Windows may support High and Low.)

TABLE 8-4 I/O Priorities

I/O Priority	Usage
Critical	Memory manager
High	Not used
Normal	Normal application I/O
Low	Not used
Very Low	Scheduled tasks, Superfetch, defragmenting, content indexing, background activities

I/O has a default priority of Normal, and the memory manager uses Critical when it wants to write dirty memory data out to disk under low-memory situations to make room in RAM for other data and code. The Windows Task Scheduler sets the I/O priority for tasks that have the default task priority to Very Low. The priority specified by applications that perform background processing is Very Low. All of the Windows background operations, including Windows Defender scanning and desktop search indexing, use Very Low I/O priority.

Prioritization Strategies

Internally, these five I/O priorities are divided into two I/O prioritization modes, called *strategies*. These are the *hierarchy prioritization* and the *idle prioritization* strategies. Hierarchy prioritization deals with all the I/O priorities except Very Low. It implements the following strategy:

- All critical-priority I/O must be processed before any high-priority I/O.

- All high-priority I/O must be processed before any normal-priority I/O.

- All normal-priority I/O must be processed before any low-priority I/O.

- All low-priority I/O is processed after any higher-priority I/O.

As each application generates I/Os, IRPs are put on different I/O queues based on their priority, and the hierarchy strategy decides the ordering of the operations.

The idle prioritization strategy, on the other hand, uses a separate queue for non-idle priority I/O. Because the system processes all hierarchy prioritized I/O before idle I/O, it's possible for the I/Os in this queue to be starved, as long as there's even a single non-idle I/O on the system in the hierarchy priority strategy queue.

To avoid this situation, as well as to control backoff (the sending rate of I/O transfers), the idle strategy uses a timer to monitor the queue and guarantee that at least one I/O is processed per unit of time (typically, half a second). Data written using non-idle I/O priority also causes the cache manager to write modifications to disk immediately instead of doing it later and to bypass its read-ahead logic for read operations that would otherwise preemptively read from the file being accessed. The prioritization strategy also waits for 50 milliseconds after the completion of the last non-idle I/O in order to issue the next idle I/O. Otherwise, idle I/Os would occur in the middle of non-idle streams, causing costly seeks.

Combining these strategies into a virtual global I/O queue for demonstration purposes, a snapshot of this queue might look similar to Figure 8-25. Note that within each queue, the ordering is first-in, first-out (FIFO). The order in the figure is shown only as an example.

I/O Queue

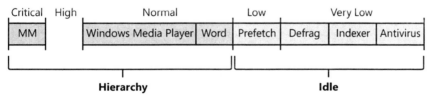

FIGURE 8-25 Sample entries in a global I/O queue

User-mode applications can set I/O priority on three different objects. *SetPriorityClass* and *SetThreadPriority* set the priority for all the I/Os that either the entire process or specific threads will generate (the priority is stored in the IRP of each request). *SetFileInformationByHandle* can set the priority for a specific file object (the priority is stored in the file object). Drivers can also set I/O priority directly on an IRP by using the *IoSetIoPriorityHint* API.

> **Note** The I/O priority field in the IRP and/or file object is a *hint*. There is no guarantee that the I/O priority will be respected or even supported by the different drivers that are part of the storage stack.

The two prioritization strategies are implemented by two different types of drivers. The hierarchy strategy is implemented by the storage *port* drivers, which are responsible for all I/Os on a specific port, such as ATA, SCSI, or USB. Only the ATA port driver (%SystemRoot%\System32\Ataport.sys) and USB port driver (%SystemRoot%\System32\Usbstor.sys) implement this strategy, while the SCSI and storage port drivers (%SystemRoot%\System32\Scsiport.sys and %SystemRoot%\System32\Storport.sys) do not.

> **Note** All port drivers check specifically for Critical priority I/Os and move them ahead of their queues, even if they do not support the full hierarchy mechanism. This mechanism is in place to support critical memory manager paging I/Os to ensure system reliability.

This means that consumer mass storage devices such as IDE or SATA hard drives and USB flash disks will take advantage of I/O prioritization, while devices based on SCSI, Fibre Channel, and iSCSI will not.

On the other hand, it is the system storage class device driver (%SystemRoot%\System32\Classpnp.sys) that enforces the idle strategy, so it automatically applies to I/Os directed at all storage devices, including SCSI drives. This separation ensures that idle I/Os will be subject to back-off algorithms to ensure a reliable system during operation under high idle I/O usage and so that applications that use them can make forward progress. Placing support for this strategy in the Microsoft-provided class driver avoids performance problems that would have been caused by lack of support for it in legacy third-party port drivers.

Figure 8-26 displays a simplified view of the storage stack and where each strategy is implemented. See Chapter 9 for more information on the storage stack.

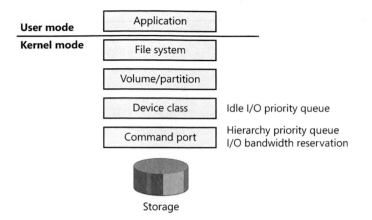

User mode | Application
Kernel mode | File system
Volume/partition
Device class — Idle I/O priority queue
Command port — Hierarchy priority queue / I/O bandwidth reservation

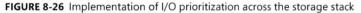

Storage

FIGURE 8-26 Implementation of I/O prioritization across the storage stack

I/O Priority Inversion Avoidance (I/O Priority Inheritance)

To avoid I/O priority inversion (in which a high-I/O-priority thread can be starved by a low-I/O-priority thread), the executive resource (ERESOURCE) locking functionality utilizes several strategies. The ERESOURCE was picked for the implementation of I/O priority inheritance particularly because of its heavy use in file system and storage drivers, where most I/O priority inversion issues can appear.

If an ERESOURCE is being acquired by a thread with low I/O priority, and there are currently waiters on the ERESOURCE with normal or higher priority, the current thread is temporarily boosted to normal I/O priority by using the *PsBoostThreadIo* API, which increments the *IoBoostCount* in the ETHREAD structure.

It then calls the *IoBoostThreadIoPriority* API, which enumerates all the IRPs queued to the target thread (recall that each thread has a list of pending IRPs) and checks which ones have a lower priority than the target priority (normal in this case), thus identifying pending idle I/O priority IRPs. In turn, the device object responsible for each of those IRPs is identified, and the I/O manager checks whether a priority callback has been registered, which driver developers can do through the *IoRegister-PriorityCallback* API and by setting the DO_PRIORITY_CALLBACK_ENABLED flag on their device object. Depending on whether the IRP was a paging I/O, this mechanism is called the *threaded boost* or the *paging boost*.

Finally, if no matching IRPs were found, but the thread has at least some pending IRPs, all are boosted regardless of device object or priority, which is called *blanket boosting*.

I/O Priority Boosts and Bumps

A few other subtle modifications to normal I/O paths are used by Windows to avoid starvation, inversion, or otherwise unwanted scenarios when I/O priority is being used. Typically, these modifications are done by boosting I/O priority when needed. The following scenarios exhibit this behavior.

- When a driver is being called with an IRP targeted to a particular file object, Windows makes sure that if the request comes from kernel mode, the IRP uses normal priority even if the file object has a lower I/O priority hint. This is called the *kernel bump*.

- When reads or writes to the paging file are occurring (through *IoPageRead* and *IoPageWrite*), Windows checks whether the request comes from kernel mode and is not being performed on behalf of Superfetch (which always uses idle I/O). In this case, the IRP uses normal priority even if the current thread has a lower I/O priority. This is called the *paging bump*.

The following experiment will show you an example of Very Low I/O priority and how you can use Process Monitor to look at I/O priorities on different requests.

EXPERIMENT: Very Low vs. Normal I/O Throughput

You can use the IO Priority sample application (included in the book's utilities) to look at the throughput difference between two threads with different I/O priorities. Launch IoPriority.exe, make sure Thread 1 is checked to use Low priority, and then click the Start IO button. You should notice a significant difference in speed between the two threads, as shown in the following screen.

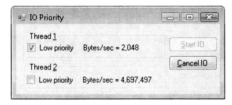

You should also notice that Thread 1's throughput remains fairly constant, around 2 KB/s. This can easily be explained by the fact that IO Priority performs its I/Os at 2 KB/s, which means that the idle prioritization strategy is kicking in and guaranteeing at least one I/O each half-second. Otherwise, Thread 2 would starve any I/O that Thread 1 is attempting to make.

Note that if both threads run at low priority and the system is relatively idle, their throughput will be roughly equal to the throughput of a single normal I/O priority in the example. This is because low priority I/Os are not artificially throttled or otherwise hindered if there isn't any competition from higher priority I/O.

You can also use Process Monitor to trace IO Priority's I/Os and look at their I/O priority hint. Launch Process Monitor, configure a filter for IoPriority.exe, and repeat the experiment. In this application, Thread 1 writes to File_1, and Thread 2 writes to File_2. Scroll down until you see a write to File_1, and you should see output similar to that shown next.

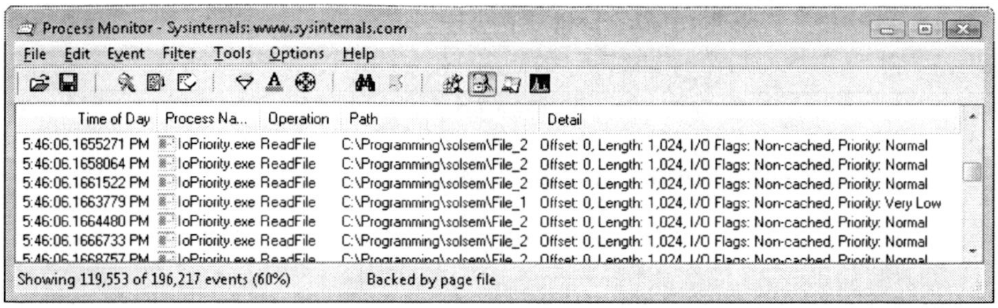

You can see that I/Os directed at File_1 have a priority of Very Low. By looking at the Time Of Day column, you'll also notice that the I/Os are spaced 0.5 second from each other—another sign of the idle strategy in action.

Finally, by using Process Explorer, you can identify Thread 1 in the IoPriority process by looking at the I/O priority for each of its threads on the Threads tab of its process Properties dialog box. You can also see that the priority for the thread is lower than the default of 8 (normal), which indicates that the thread is probably running in *background priority mode*. The following screen shot shows what you should expect to see.

Note that if IO Priority sets the priority on File_1 instead of on the issuing thread, both threads would look the same. Only Process Monitor could show you the difference in I/O priorities.

The kernel exposes several internal variables that can be queried through the undocumented *SystemLowPriorityIoInformation* system class available in *NtQuerySystemInformation*. However, even without writing or relying on such an application, you can use the local kernel debugger for viewing these numbers on your system. The following variables are available:

- *IoLowPriorityReadOperationCount* and *IoLowPriorityWriteOperationCount*

- *IoKernelIssuedIoBoostedCount*

- *IoPagingReadLowPriorityCount* and *IoPagingWriteLowPriorityCount*

- *IoPagingReadLowPriorityBumpedCount* and *IoPagingWriteHighPriorityBumpedCount*

- *IoBoostedThreadedIrpCount* and *IoBoostedPagingIrpCount*

- *IoBlanketBoostCount*

You can use the *dd* memory-dumping command in the kernel debugger to see the values of these variables.

Bandwidth Reservation (Scheduled File I/O)

Windows I/O bandwidth reservation support is useful for applications that desire consistent I/O throughput. Using the *SetFileBandwidthReservation* call, a media player application asks the I/O system to guarantee it the ability to read data from a device at a specified rate. If the device can deliver data at the requested rate and existing reservations allow it, the I/O system gives the application guidance as to how fast it should issue I/Os and how large the I/Os should be.

The I/O system won't service other I/Os unless it can satisfy the requirements of applications that have made reservations on the target storage device. Figure 8-27 shows a conceptual timeline of I/Os issued on the same file. The shaded regions are the only ones that will be available to other applications. If I/O bandwidth is already taken, new I/Os will have to wait until the next cycle.

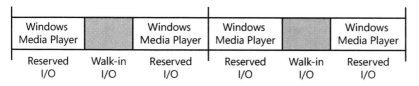

Windows Media Player		Windows Media Player	Windows Media Player		Windows Media Player
Reserved I/O	Walk-in I/O	Reserved I/O	Reserved I/O	Walk-in I/O	Reserved I/O

FIGURE 8-27 Effect of I/O requests during bandwidth reservation

Like the hierarchy prioritization strategy, bandwidth reservation is implemented at the port driver level, which means it is available only for IDE, SATA, or USB-based mass-storage devices.

Container Notifications

Container notifications are specific classes of events that drivers can register for through an asynchronous callback mechanism by using the *IoRegisterContainerNotification* API and selecting the notification class that interests them. Thus far, one class is implemented in Windows, which is the *IoSessionStateNotification* class. This class allows drivers to have their registered callback invoked whenever a change in the state of a given session is registered. The following changes are supported:

- A session is created or terminated

- A user connects to or disconnects from a session

- A user logs on to or logs off from a session

By specifying a device object that belongs to a specific session, the driver callback will be active only for that session, while by specifying a global device object (or no device object at all), the driver will receive notifications for all events on a system. This feature is particularly useful for devices that participate in the Plug and Play device redirection functionality that is provided through Terminal Services, which allows a remote device to be visible on the connecting host's Plug and Play manager bus as well (such as audio or printer device redirection). Once the user disconnects from a session with audio playback, for example, the device driver needs a notification in order to stop redirecting the source audio stream.

Driver Verifier

Driver Verifier is a mechanism that can be used to help find and isolate common bugs in device drivers or other kernel-mode system code. Microsoft uses Driver Verifier to check its own device drivers as well as all device drivers that vendors submit for Windows Hardware Quality Labs (WHQL) testing. Doing so ensures that the drivers submitted are compatible with Windows and free from common driver errors. (Although not described in this book, there is also a corresponding Application Verifier tool that has resulted in quality improvements for user-mode code in Windows.)

Also, although Driver Verifier serves primarily as a tool to help device driver developers discover bugs in their code, it is also a powerful tool for system administrators experiencing crashes. Chapter 14 describes its role in crash analysis troubleshooting.

Driver Verifier consists of support in several system components: the memory manager, I/O manager, and HAL all have driver verification options that can be enabled. These options are configured using the Driver Verifier Manager (%SystemRoot%\System32\Verifier.exe). When you run Driver Verifier with no command-line arguments, it presents a wizard-style interface, as shown in Figure 8-28.

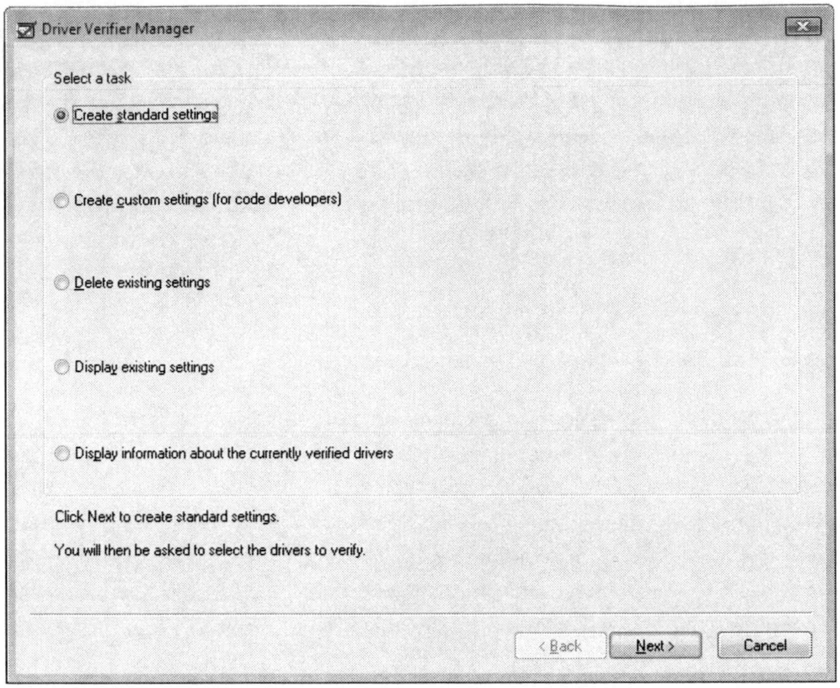

FIGURE 8-28 Driver Verifier Manager

You can also enable and disable Driver Verifier, as well as display current settings, by using its command-line interface. From a command prompt, type **verifier /?** to see the switches.

Even when you don't select any options, Driver Verifier monitors drivers selected for verification, looking for a number of illegal and boundary operations, including calling kernel-memory pool functions at invalid IRQL, double-freeing memory, allocating synchronization objects from NonPaged-PoolSession memory, referencing a freed object, delaying shutdown for longer than 20 minutes, and requesting a zero-size memory allocation.

What follows is a description of the I/O-related verification options (shown in Figure 8-29). The options related to memory management are described in Chapter 10, along with how the memory manager redirects a driver's operating system calls to special verifier versions.

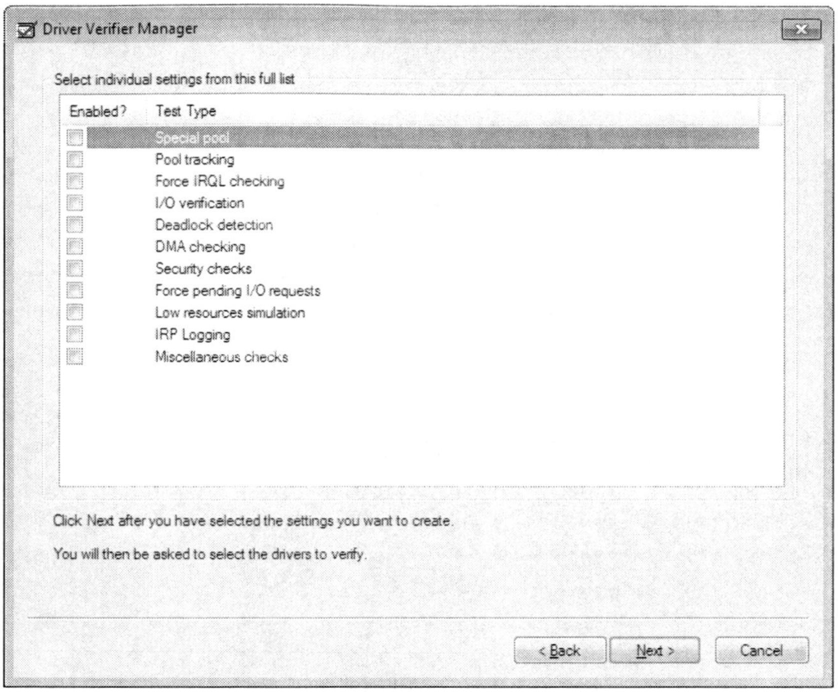

FIGURE 8-29 Driver Verifier I/O-related options

These options have the following effects:

- **I/O Verification** When this option is selected, the I/O manager allocates IRPs for verified drivers from a special pool and their usage is tracked. In addition, the Verifier crashes the system when an IRP is completed that contains an invalid status or when an invalid device object is passed to the I/O manager. This option also monitors all IRPs to ensure that drivers mark them correctly when completing them asynchronously, that they manage device-stack locations correctly, and that they delete device objects only once. In addition, the Verifier randomly stresses drivers by sending them fake power management and WMI IRPs, changing the order in which devices are enumerated, and adjusting the status of PnP and power IRPs when they complete to test for drivers that return incorrect status from their dispatch routines. Finally, Verifier also detects incorrect re-initialization of remove locks while they are still being held due to pending device removal.

- **DMA Checking** DMA (direct access memory) is a hardware-supported mechanism that allows devices to transfer data to or from physical memory without involving the CPU. The I/O manager provides a number of functions that drivers use to initiate and control DMA operations, and this option enables checks for correct use of the functions and buffers that the I/O manager supplies for DMA operations.

- **Force Pending I/O Requests** For many devices, asynchronous I/Os complete immediately, so drivers may not be coded to properly handle the occasional asynchronous I/O. When this option is enabled, the I/O manager will randomly return STATUS_PENDING in response to a driver's calls to *IoCallDriver*, which simulates the asynchronous completion of an I/O.

- **IRP Logging** This option monitors a driver's use of IRPs and makes a record of IRP usage, which is stored as WMI information. You can then use the Dc2wmiparser.exe utility in the WDK to convert these WMI records to a text file. Note that only 20 IRPs for each device will be recorded—each subsequent IRP will overwrite the entry added least recently. After a reboot, this information is discarded, so Dc2wmiparser.exe should be run if the contents of the trace are to be analyzed later.

Kernel-Mode Driver Framework (KMDF)

We've already discussed some details about the Windows Driver Foundation (WDF) in Chapter 2, "System Architecture," in Part 1. In this section, we'll take a deeper look at the components and functionality provided by the kernel-mode part of the framework, KMDF. Note that this section will only briefly touch on some of the core architecture of KMDF. For a much more complete overview on the subject, please refer to *http://msdn.microsoft.com/en-us/library/windows/hardware/gg463370.aspx*.

Structure and Operation of a KMDF Driver

First, let's take a look at which kinds of drivers or devices are supported by KMDF. In general, any WDM-conformant driver should be supported by KMDF, as long as it performs standard I/O processing and IRP manipulation. KMDF is not suitable for drivers that don't use the Windows kernel API directly but instead perform library calls into existing port and class drivers. These types of drivers cannot use KMDF because they only provide callbacks for the actual WDM drivers that do the I/O processing. Additionally, if a driver provides its own dispatch functions instead of relying on a port or class driver, IEEE 1394 and ISA, PCI, PCMCIA, and SD Client (for Secure Digital storage devices) drivers can also make use of KMDF.

Although KMDF provides an abstraction on top of WDM, the basic driver structure shown earlier also generally applies to KMDF drivers. At their core, KMDF drivers must have the following functions:

- **An initialization routine** Just like any other driver, a KMDF driver has a *DriverEntry* function that initializes the driver. KMDF drivers will initiate the framework at this point and perform any configuration and initialization steps that are part of the driver or part of describing the driver to the framework. For non–Plug and Play drivers, this is where the first device object should be created.

- **An *add-device routine*** KMDF driver operation is based on events and callbacks (described shortly), and the *EvtDriverDeviceAdd* callback is the single most important one for PnP devices because it receives notifications when the PnP manager in the kernel enumerates one of the driver's devices.

- **One or more *EvtIo* routines*** Just like a WDM driver's dispatch routines, these callback routines handle specific types of I/O requests from a particular device queue. A driver typically creates one or more queues in which KMDF places I/O requests for the driver's devices. These queues can be configured by request type and dispatching type.

The simplest KMDF driver might need to have only an initialization and add-device routine because the framework will provide the default, generic functionality that's required for most types of I/O processing, including power and Plug and Play events. In the KMDF model, *events* refer to runtime states to which a driver can respond or during which a driver can participate. These events are not related to the synchronization primitives (synchronization is discussed in Chapter 3 in Part 1), but are internal to the framework.

For events that are critical to a driver's operation, or which need specialized processing, the driver registers a given callback routine to handle this event. In other cases, a driver can allow KMDF to perform a default, generic action instead. For example, during an eject event (*EvtDeviceEject*), a driver can choose to support ejection and supply a callback or to fall back to the default KMDF code that will tell the user that the device is not ejectable. Not all events have a default behavior, however, and callbacks must be provided by the driver. One notable example is the *EvtDriverDeviceAdd* event that is at the core of any Plug and Play driver.

EXPERIMENT: Displaying KMDF Drivers

The Wdfkd.dll extension that ships with the Debugging Tools for Windows package provides many commands that can be used to debug and analyze KMDF drivers and devices (instead of using the built-in WDM-style debugging extension that may not offer the same kind of WDF-specific information). You can display installed KMDF drivers with the *!wdfkd.wdfldr* debugger command. In the following example, the output from a typical Windows computer is shown, displaying the built-in drivers that are installed.

```
lkd> !wdfkd.wdfldr
 LoadedModuleList        0xfffff880010682d8
---------------------------------
LIBRARY_MODULE  fffffa8002776120
  Version        v1.9 build(7600)
  Service        \Registry\Machine\System\CurrentControlSet\Services\Wdf01000
  ImageName      Wdf01000.sys
  ImageAddress   0xfffff88000c00000
  ImageSize      0xa4000
  Associated Clients: 16
```

```
ImageName           Version     WdfGlobals           FxGlobals            ImageAddress
                    ImageSize
peauth.sys          v1.7(6001)  0xfffffa8004754210   0xfffffa80047540c0   0xfffff880074cc000
                    0x000a6000
scfilter.sys        v1.5(6000)  0xfffffa8002ef34e0   0xfffffa8002ef3390   0xfffff880040b3000
                    0x0000e000
WinUSB.sys          v1.9(7600)  0xfffffa8002eefd20   0xfffffa8002eefbd0   0xfffff88004000000
                    0x00011000
monitor.sys         v1.9(7600)  0xfffffa8004854a10   0xfffffa80048548c0   0xfffff8800412a000
                    0x0000e000
vmswitch.sys        v1.5(6000)  0xfffffa8002de5d60   0xfffffa8002de5c10   0xfffff88003e9b000
                    0x00068000
vmbus.sys           v1.5(6000)  0xfffffa8002d7fcf0   0xfffffa8002d7fba0   0xfffff88003e5f000
                    0x0003c000
Vid.sys             v1.5(6000)  0xfffffa8002ddacf0   0xfffffa8002ddaba0   0xfffff88002a00000
                    0x00033000
umbus.sys           v1.9(7600)  0xfffffa8002e57e70   0xfffffa8002e57d20   0xfffff880035db000
                    0x00012000
storvsp.sys         v1.5(6000)  0xfffffa8002e48b10   0xfffffa8002e489c0   0xfffff88003575000
                    0x00023000
CompositeBus.sys    v1.9(7600)  0xfffffa8002d79160   0xfffffa8002d79010   0xfffff88002936000
                    0x00010000
HDAudBus.sys        v1.7(6001)  0xfffffa8002e357f0   0xfffffa8002e356a0   0xfffff880037a9000
                    0x00024000
intelppm.sys        v1.9(7600)  0xfffffa8002c518f0   0xfffffa8002c517a0   0xfffff880027e7000
                    0x00016000
cdrom.sys           v1.9(7600)  0xfffffa80028bf8f0   0xfffffa80028bf7a0   0xfffff880011c4000
                    0x0002a000
vmstorfl.sys        v1.5(6000)  0xfffffa8002b2cdd0   0xfffffa8002b2cc80   0xfffff8800144a000
                    0x00010000
vdrvroot.sys        v1.9(7600)  0xfffffa80027887c0   0xfffffa8002788670   0xfffff8800139c000
                    0x0000d000
msisadrv.sys        v1.9(7600)  0xfffffa80029c5430   0xfffffa80029c52e0   0xfffff8800135f000
                    0x0000a000
----------------------------------
Total:  1  library  loaded
```

KMDF Data Model

The KMDF data model is object-based, much like the model for the kernel, but it does not make use of the object manager. Instead, KMDF manages its own objects internally, exposing them as handles to drivers and keeping the actual data structures opaque. For each object type, the framework provides routines to perform operations on the object, such as *WdfDeviceCreate*, which creates a device. Additionally, objects can have specific data fields or members that can be accessed by *Get/Set* (used for modifications that should never fail) or *Assign/Retrieve* APIs (used for modifications that can fail). For example, the *WdfInterruptGetInfo* function returns information on a given interrupt object (WDFINTERRUPT).

Also unlike the implementation of kernel objects, which all refer to distinct and isolated object types, KMDF objects are all part of a hierarchy—most object types are bound to a parent. The root object is the WDFDRIVER structure, which describes the actual driver. The structure and meaning is analogous to the DRIVER_OBJECT structure provided by the I/O manager, and all other KMDF structures are children of it. The next most important object is WDFDEVICE, which refers to a given instance of a detected device on the system, which must have been created with *WdfDeviceCreate*. Again, this is analogous to the DEVICE_OBJECT structure that's used in the WDM model and by the I/O manager. Table 8-5 lists the object types supported by KMDF.

TABLE 8-5 KMDF Object Types

Object	Type	Description
Child List	WDFCHILDLIST	List of child WDFDEVICE objects associated with the device. Only used by bus drivers.
Collection	WDFCOLLECTION	List of objects of a similar type, such as a group of WDFDEVICE objects being filtered.
Deferred Procedure Call	WDFDPC	Instance of a DPC object (see Chapter 3 in Part 1 for more information on DPCs).
Device	WDFDEVICE	Instance of a device.
DMA Common Buffer	WDFCOMMONBUFFER	Region of memory that a device and driver can access for direct memory access (DMA).
DMA Enabler	WDFDMAENABLER	Enables DMA on a given channel for a driver.
DMA Transaction	WDFDMATRANSACTION	Instance of a DMA transaction.
Driver	WDFDRIVER	Root object for the driver; represents the driver, its parameters, and its callbacks, among other items.
File	WDFFILEOBJECT	Instance of a file object that can be used as a channel for communication between an application and the driver.
Generic Object	WDFOBJECT	Allows driver-defined custom data to be wrapped inside the framework's object data model as an object.
Interrupt	WDFINTERRUPT	Instance of an interrupt that the driver must handle.
I/O Queue	WDFQUEUE	Represents a given I/O queue.
I/O Request	WDFREQUEST	Represents a given request on a WDFQUEUE.
I/O Target	WDFIOTARGET	Represents the device stack being targeted by a given WDFREQUEST.
Look-Aside List	WDFLOOKASIDE	Describes an executive look-aside list.
Memory	WDFMEMORY	Describes a region of paged or nonpaged pool.
Registry Key	WDFKEY	Describes a registry key.
Resource List	WDFCMRESLIST	Identifies the hardware resources assigned to a WDFDEVICE.

Object	Type	Description
Resource Range List	WDFIORESLIST	Identifies a given possible hardware resource range for a WDFDEVICE.
Resource Requirements List	WDFIORESREQLIST	Contains an array of WDFIORESLIST objects describing all possible resource ranges for a WDFDEVICE.
Spinlock	WDFSPINLOCK	Describes a spinlock (see Chapter 3 in Part 1 for more information).
String	WDFSTRING	Describes a Unicode string structure.
Timer	WDFTIMER	Describes an executive timer (see Chapter 3 in Part 1 for more information).
USB Device	WDFUSBDEVICE	Identifies the one instance of a USB device.
USB Interface	WDFUSBINTERFACE	Identifies one interface on the given WDFUSBDEVICE.
USB Pipe	WDFUSBPIPE	Identifies a pipe to an endpoint on a given WDFUSBINTERFACE.
Wait Lock	WDFWAITLOCK	Represents a kernel dispatcher event object.
WMI Instance	WDFWMIINSTANCE	Represents a WMI data block for a given WDFWMIPROVIDER.
WMI Provider	WDFWMIPROVIDER	Describes the WMI schema for all the WDFWMIINSTANCE objects supported by the driver.
Work Item	WDFWORKITEM	Describes an executive work item.

For each of these objects, other KMDF objects can be attached as children—some objects have only one or two valid parents, while other objects can be attached to any parent. For example, a WDFINTERRUPT object must be associated with a given WDFDEVICE, but a WDFSPINLOCK or WDFSTRING can have any object as a parent, allowing fine-grained control over their validity and usage and reducing global state variables. Figure 8-30 shows the entire KMDF object hierarchy.

Note that the associations mentioned earlier and shown in the figure are not necessarily immediate. The parent must simply be on the *hierarchy chain*, meaning one of the ancestor nodes must be of this type. This relationship is useful to implement because object hierarchies affect not only the objects' locality but also their lifetime. Each time a child object is created, a reference count is added to it by its link to its parent. Therefore, when a parent object is destroyed, all the child objects are also destroyed, which is why associating objects such as WDFSTRING or WDFMEMORY with a given object, instead of the default WDFDRIVER object, can automatically free up memory and state information when the parent object is destroyed.

Closely related to the concept hierarchy is KMDF's notion of *object context*. Because KMDF objects are opaque, as discussed, and are associated with a parent object for locality, it becomes important to allow drivers to attach their own data to an object in order to track certain specific information outside the framework's capabilities or support.

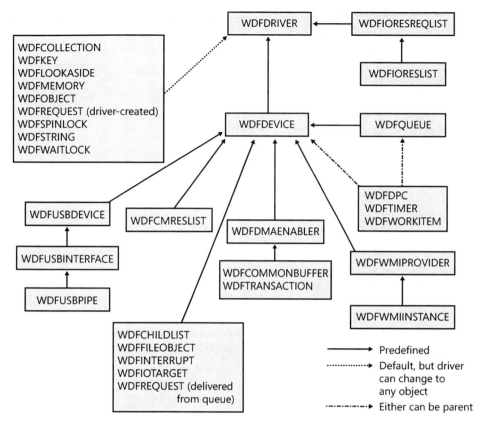

FIGURE 8-30 KMDF object hierarchy

Object contexts allow all KMDF objects to contain such information, and they additionally allow multiple *object context areas*, which permit multiple layers of code inside the same driver to interact with the same object in different ways. In the WDM model, the *device extension* data structure allows such information to be associated with a given device, but with KMDF even a spinlock or string can contain context areas. This extensibility allows each library or layer of code responsible for processing an I/O to interact independently of other code, based on the context area that it works with, and allows a mechanism similar to inheritance.

Finally, KMDF objects are also associated with a set of attributes that are shown in Table 8-6. These attributes are usually configured to their defaults, but the values can be overridden by the driver when creating the object by specifying a WDF_OBJECT_ATTRIBUTES structure (similar to the object manager's OBJECT_ATTRIBUTES structure that's used when creating a kernel object).

TABLE 8-6 KMDF Object Attributes

Attribute	Description
ContextSizeOverride	Size of the object context area.
ContextTypeInfo	Type of the object context area.
EvtCleanupCallback	Callback to notify the driver of the object's cleanup before deletion (references may still exist).
EvtDestroyCallback	Callback to notify the driver of the object's imminent deletion (reference count will be 0).
ExecutionLevel	Describes the maximum IRQL at which the callbacks may be invoked by KMDF.
ParentObject	Identifies the parent of this object.
Size	Size of the object.
SynchronizationScope	Specifies whether callbacks should be synchronized with the parent, a queue or device, or nothing.

KMDF I/O Model

The KMDF I/O model follows the WDM mechanisms discussed earlier in the chapter. In fact, one can even think of the framework itself as a WDM driver, since it uses kernel APIs and WDM behavior to abstract KMDF and make it functional. Under KMDF, the framework driver sets its own WDM-style IRP dispatch routines and takes control over all IRPs sent to the driver. After being handled by one of three KMDF I/O handlers (which we'll describe shortly), it then packages these requests in the appropriate KMDF objects, inserts them in the appropriate queues if required, and performs driver callback if the driver is interested in those events. Figure 8-31 describes the flow of I/O in the framework.

Based on the IRP processing discussed for WDM drivers earlier, KMDF performs one of the following three actions:

- Sends the IRP to the I/O handler, which processes standard device operations

- Sends the IRP to the PnP and power handler that processes these kinds of events and notifies other drivers if the state has changed

- Sends the IRP to the WMI handler, which handles tracing and logging.

These components will then notify the driver of any events it registered for, potentially forward the request to another handler for further processing, and then complete the request based on an internal handler action or as the result of a driver call. If KMDF has finished processing the IRP but the request itself has still not been fully processed, KMDF will take one of the following actions:

- For bus drivers and function drivers, complete the IRP with STATUS_INVALID_DEVICE_REQUEST

- For filter drivers, forward the request to the next lower driver

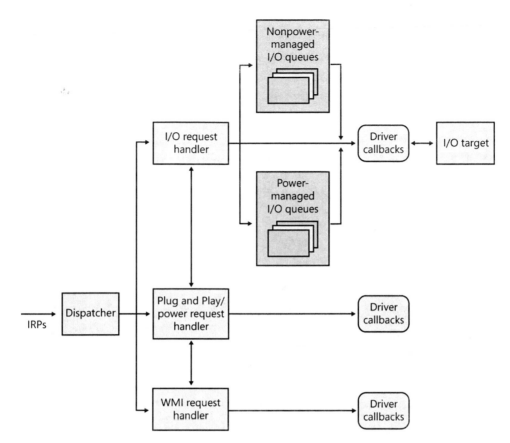

FIGURE 8-31 KMDF I/O flow and IRP processing

I/O processing by KMDF is based on the mechanism of *queues* (WDFQUEUE, not the KQUEUE object discussed in the earlier section on I/O completion and in Chapter 3 in Part 1). KMDF queues are highly scalable containers of I/O requests (packaged as WDFREQUEST objects) and provide a rich feature set beyond merely sorting the pending I/Os for a given device. For example, queues also track currently active requests and support I/O cancellation, I/O concurrency (the ability to perform and complete more than one I/O request at a time), and I/O synchronization (as noted in the list of object attributes in Table 8-6). A typical KMDF driver creates at least one queue (if not more) and associates one or more events with each queue, as well as some of the following options:

- The callbacks registered with the events associated with this queue.

- The power management state for the queue. KMDF supports both power-managed and nonpower-managed queues. For the former, the I/O handler will handle waking up the device when required (and when possible), arm the idle timer when the device has no I/Os queued up, and call the driver's I/O cancellation routines when the system is switching away from a working state.

- The dispatch method for the queue. KMDF can deliver I/Os from a queue either in a sequential, parallel, or manual mode. Sequential I/Os are delivered one at a time (KMDF waits for the driver to complete the previous request), while parallel I/Os are delivered to the driver as soon as possible. In manual mode, the driver must manually retrieve I/Os from the queue.

- Whether or not the queue can accept zero-length buffers, such as incoming requests that don't actually contain any data.

> **Note** The dispatch method affects solely the number of requests that are allowed to be active inside a driver's queue at one time. It does not determine whether the event callbacks themselves will be called concurrently or serially. That behavior is determined through the synchronization scope object attribute described earlier. Therefore, it is possible for a parallel queue to have concurrency disabled but still have multiple incoming requests.

Based on the mechanism of queues, the KMDF I/O handler can perform several possible tasks upon receiving either a create, close, cleanup, write, read, or device control (IOCTL) request:

- For create requests, the driver can request to be immediately notified through *EvtDeviceFile-Create*, or it can create a nonmanual queue to receive create requests. It must then register an *EvtIoDefault* callback to receive the notifications. Finally, if none of these methods are used, KMDF will simply complete the request with a success code, meaning that by default, applications will be able to open handles to KMDF drivers that don't supply their own code.

- For cleanup and close requests, the driver will be immediately notified through *EvtFileCleanup* and *EvtFileClose* callbacks, if registered. Otherwise, the framework will simply complete with a success code.

- Finally, Figure 8-32 illustrates the flow of an I/O request to a KMDF driver for the most common driver operations (read, write, and I/O control codes).

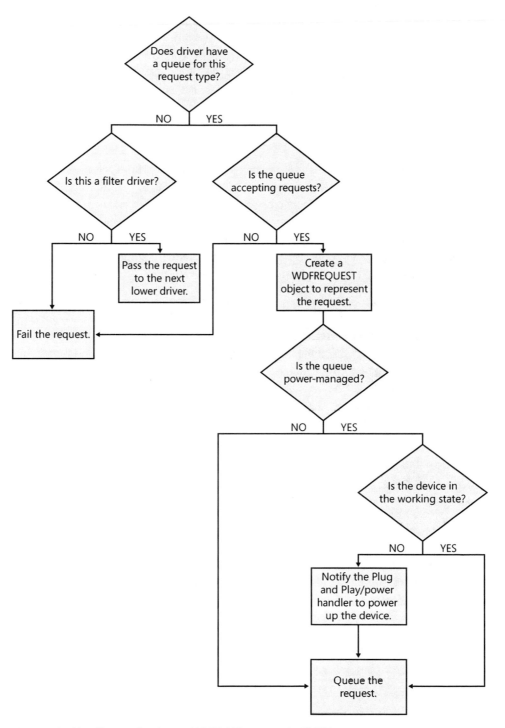

FIGURE 8-32 Handling read, write, and IOCTL I/O requests by KMDF

User-Mode Driver Framework (UMDF)

Although this chapter focuses on kernel-mode drivers, Windows includes a growing number of drivers that actually run in user mode, as previously described, using the User-Mode Driver Framework (UMDF) that is part of the WDF. Before finishing our discussion on drivers, we'll take a quick look at the architecture of UMDF and what it offers. Once again, for a much more complete overview on the subject, please refer to *http://msdn.microsoft.com/en-us/library/windows/hardware/gg463370.aspx*.

UMDF is designed specifically to support what are called *protocol device classes*, which refers to devices that all use the same standardized, generic protocol and offer specialized functionality on top of it. These protocols currently include IEEE 1394 (FireWire), USB, Bluetooth, and TCP/IP. Any device running on top of these buses (or connected to a network) is a potential candidate for UMDF—examples include portable music players, PDAs, cell phones, cameras and webcams, and so on. Two other large users of UMDF are SideShow-compatible devices (auxiliary displays) and the Windows Portable Device (WPD) Framework, which supports USB removable storage (USB bulk transfer devices). Finally, as with KMDF, it's possible to implement software-only drivers, such as for a virtual device, in UMDF.

To make porting code easier from kernel mode to user mode, and to keep a consistent architecture, UMDF uses the same conceptual driver programming model as KMDF, but it uses different components, interfaces, and data structures. For example, KMDF includes objects unique to kernel mode, while UMDF includes some objects unique to user mode. Objects and functionality that can't be accessed through UMDF include direct handling of interrupts, DMA, nonpaged pool, and strict timing requirements. Furthermore, a UMDF driver can't be on any kernel driver stack or be a client of another driver or the kernel itself.

Unlike KMDF drivers, which run as driver objects representing a .sys image file, UMDF drivers run in a *driver host process*, similar to a service-hosting process. The host process contains the driver itself (which is implemented as an in-process COM component), the user-mode driver framework (implemented as a DLL containing COM-like components for each UMDF object), and a run-time environment (responsible for I/O dispatching, driver loading, device-stack management, communication with the kernel, and a thread pool).

Just like in the kernel, each UMDF driver runs as part of a stack, which can contain multiple drivers that are responsible for managing a device. Naturally, since user-mode code can't access the kernel address space, UMDF also includes some components that allow this access to occur through a specialized interface to the kernel. This is implemented by a kernel-mode side of UMDF that uses ALPC (see Chapter 3 in Part 1 for more information on advanced local procedure call) to talk to the run-time environment in the user-mode driver host processes. Figure 8-33 displays the architecture of the UMDF driver model.

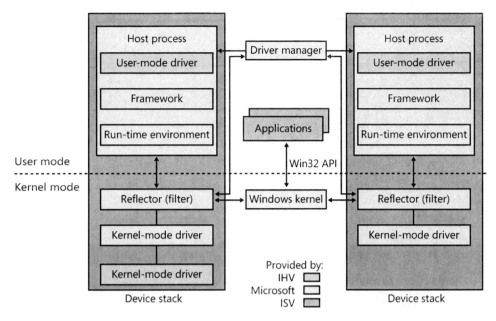

FIGURE 8-33 UMDF architecture

Figure 8-33 shows two different device stacks that manage two different hardware devices, each with a UMDF driver running inside its own driver host process. From the diagram, you can see that the following components take part in the architecture:

- **Applications** Applications are the clients of the drivers. These are standard Windows applications that use the same APIs to perform I/Os as they would with a KMDF-managed or a WDM-managed device. Applications don't know that they're talking to a UMDF-based device, and the calls are still sent to the kernel's I/O manager.

- **Windows kernel (I/O manager)** Based on the application I/O APIs, the I/O manager builds the IRPs for the operations, just like for any other standard device.

- **Reflector** The reflector is what makes UMDF "tick." It is a standard WDM filter driver that sits at the top of the device stack of each device that is being managed by a UMDF driver. The reflector is responsible for managing the communication between the kernel and the user-mode driver host process. IRPs related to power management, Plug and Play, and standard I/O are redirected to the host process through ALPC. This lets the UMDF driver respond to the I/Os and perform work, as well as be involved in the Plug and Play model, by providing enumeration, installation, and management of its devices. The reflector is also responsible for keeping an eye on the driver host processes by making sure that they remain responsive to requests within an adequate time to prevent drivers and applications from hanging.

- **Driver manager** The driver manager is responsible for starting and quitting the driver host processes, based on which UMDF-managed devices are present, and also for managing information on them. It is also responsible for responding to messages coming from the reflector and applying them to the appropriate host process (such as reacting to device installation). The driver manager runs as a standard Windows service and is configured for automatic startup as soon as the first UMDF driver for a device is installed. Only one instance of the driver manager runs for all driver host processes, and it must always be running to allow UMDF drivers to work.

- **Host process** The host process provides the address space and run-time environment for the actual driver. Although it runs in the local service account, it is not actually a Windows service and is not managed by the SCM—only by the driver manager. The host process is also responsible for providing the user-mode device stack for the actual hardware, which is visible to all applications on the system. In the current UMDF release, each device instance has its own device stack, which runs in a separate host process. In the future, multiple instances may share the same host process. Host processes are child processes of the driver manager.

- **Kernel-mode drivers** If specific kernel support for a device that is managed by a UMDF driver is needed, it is also possible to write a companion kernel-mode driver that fills that role. In this way, it is possible for a device to be managed both by a UMDF and a KMDF (or WDM) driver.

You can easily see UMDF in action on your system by inserting a USB flash drive with some content on it. Run Process Explorer, and you should see a WUDFHost.exe process that corresponds to a driver host process. Switch to DLL view and scroll down until you see DLLs similar to the ones shown in Figure 8-34.

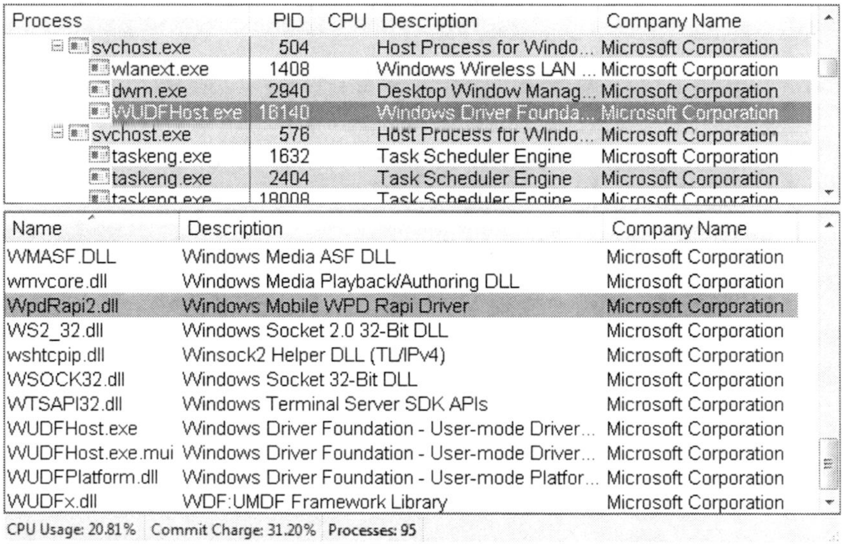

Process	PID	CPU	Description	Company Name
⊟ 📁 svchost.exe	504		Host Process for Windo...	Microsoft Corporation
📁 wlanext.exe	1408		Windows Wireless LAN ...	Microsoft Corporation
📁 dwm.exe	2940		Desktop Window Manag...	Microsoft Corporation
📁 WUDFHost.exe	16140		Windows Driver Founda...	Microsoft Corporation
⊟ 📁 svchost.exe	576		Host Process for Windo...	Microsoft Corporation
📁 taskeng.exe	1632		Task Scheduler Engine	Microsoft Corporation
📁 taskeng.exe	2404		Task Scheduler Engine	Microsoft Corporation
📁 taskeng.exe	18008		Task Scheduler Engine	Microsoft Corporation

Name	Description	Company Name
WMASF.DLL	Windows Media ASF DLL	Microsoft Corporation
wmvcore.dll	Windows Media Playback/Authoring DLL	Microsoft Corporation
WpdRapi2.dll	Windows Mobile WPD Rapi Driver	Microsoft Corporation
WS2_32.dll	Windows Socket 2.0 32-Bit DLL	Microsoft Corporation
wshtcpip.dll	Winsock2 Helper DLL (TL/IPv4)	Microsoft Corporation
WSOCK32.dll	Windows Socket 32-Bit DLL	Microsoft Corporation
WTSAPI32.dll	Windows Terminal Server SDK APIs	Microsoft Corporation
WUDFHost.exe	Windows Driver Foundation - User-mode Driver...	Microsoft Corporation
WUDFHost.exe.mui	Windows Driver Foundation - User-mode Driver...	Microsoft Corporation
WUDFPlatform.dll	Windows Driver Foundation - User-mode Platfor...	Microsoft Corporation
WUDFx.dll	WDF:UMDF Framework Library	Microsoft Corporation

CPU Usage: 20.81%   Commit Charge: 31.20%   Processes: 95

FIGURE 8-34 DLL in UMDF host process

You can identify three main components, which match the architectural overview described earlier:

- WUDFx.dll, the framework itself

- WUDFPlatform.dll, the run-time environment

- WpdRapi2.dll, the COM component representing the WPD driver, exposing contents of USB storage devices to Windows shell and media applications

The Plug and Play (PnP) Manager

The PnP manager is the primary component involved in supporting the ability of Windows to recognize and adapt to changing hardware configurations. A user doesn't need to understand the intricacies of hardware or manual configuration to install and remove devices. For example, it's the PnP manager that enables a running Windows laptop that is placed on a docking station to automatically detect additional devices located in the docking station and make them available to the user.

Plug and Play support requires cooperation at the hardware, device driver, and operating system levels. Industry standards for the enumeration and identification of devices attached to buses are the foundation of Windows Plug and Play support. For example, the USB standard defines the way that devices on a USB bus identify themselves. With this foundation in place, Windows Plug and Play support provides the following capabilities:

- The PnP manager automatically recognizes installed devices, a process that includes enumerating devices attached to the system during a boot and detecting the addition and removal of devices as the system executes.

- Hardware resource allocation is a role the PnP manager fills by gathering the hardware resource requirements (interrupts, I/O memory, I/O registers, or bus-specific resources) of the devices attached to a system and, in a process called *resource arbitration*, optimally assigning resources so that each device meets the requirements necessary for its operation. Because hardware devices can be added to the system after boot-time resource assignment, the PnP manager must also be able to reassign resources to accommodate the needs of dynamically added devices.

- Loading appropriate drivers is another responsibility of the PnP manager. The PnP manager determines, based on the identification of a device, whether a driver capable of managing the device is installed on the system, and if one is, it instructs the I/O manager to load it. If a suitable driver isn't installed, the kernel-mode PnP manager communicates with the user-mode PnP manager to install the device, possibly requesting the user's assistance in locating a suitable set of drivers.

- The PnP manager also implements application and driver mechanisms for the detection of hardware configuration changes. Applications or drivers sometimes require a specific hardware device to function, so Windows includes a means for them to request notification of the presence, addition, or removal of devices.

- It also provides a place for storage device state, and it participates in system setup, upgrade, migration, and offline image management.

- In addition, it supports network connected devices, such as network projectors and printers, by allowing specialized bus drivers to detect the network as a bus and create device nodes for the devices running on it.

Level of Plug and Play Support

Windows aims to provide full support for Plug and Play, but the level of support possible depends on the attached devices and installed drivers. If a single device or driver doesn't support Plug and Play, the extent of Plug and Play support for the system can be compromised. In addition, a driver that doesn't support Plug and Play might prevent other devices from being usable by the system. Table 8-7 shows the outcome of various combinations of devices and drivers that can and can't support Plug and Play.

TABLE 8-7 Device and Driver Plug and Play Capability

	Type of Driver	
Type of Device	Plug and Play	Non–Plug and Play
Plug and Play	Full Plug and Play	No Plug and Play
Non–Plug and Play	Possible partial Plug and Play	No Plug and Play

A device that isn't Plug and Play–compatible is one that doesn't support automatic detection, such as a legacy ISA sound card. Because the operating system doesn't know where the hardware physically lies, certain operations—such as laptop undocking, sleep, and hibernation—are disallowed. However, if a Plug and Play driver is manually installed for the device, the driver can at least implement PnP manager–directed resource assignment for the device.

Drivers that aren't Plug and Play–compatible include legacy drivers, such as those that ran on Windows NT 4. Although these drivers might continue to function on later versions of Windows, the PnP manager can't reconfigure the resources assigned to such devices in the event that resource reallocation is necessary to accommodate the needs of a dynamically added device. For example, a device might be able to use I/O memory ranges A and B, and during the boot the PnP manager assigns it range A. If a device that can use only A is attached to the system later, the PnP manager can't direct the first device's driver to reconfigure itself to use range B. This prevents the second device from obtaining required resources, which results in the device being unavailable for use by the system. Legacy drivers also impair a machine's ability to sleep or hibernate. (See the section "The Power Manager" later in this chapter for more details.)

Driver Support for Plug and Play

To support Plug and Play, a driver must implement a Plug and Play dispatch routine, a power management dispatch routine (described in the section "The Power Manager" later in this chapter), and an add-device routine. Bus drivers must support different types of Plug and Play requests than function or filter drivers do, however. For example, when the PnP manager is guiding device enumeration during the system boot (described in detail later in this chapter), it asks bus drivers for a description of the devices that they find on their respective buses. The description includes data that uniquely identifies each device as well as the resource requirements of the devices. The PnP manager takes this information and loads any function or filter drivers that have been installed for the detected devices. It then calls the add-device routine of each driver for every installed device the drivers are responsible for.

Function and filter drivers prepare to begin managing their devices in their *add-device* routines, but they don't actually communicate with the device hardware. Instead, they wait for the PnP manager to send a *start-device* command for the device to their Plug and Play dispatch routine. Prior to sending the *start-device* command the PnP manager performs resource arbitration to decide what resources to assign the device. The *start-device* command includes the resource assignment that the PnP manager determines during resource arbitration. When a driver receives a *start-device* command, it can configure its device to use the specified resources. If an application tries to open a device that hasn't finished starting, it receives an error indicating that the device does not exist.

After a device has started, the PnP manager can send the driver additional Plug and Play commands, including ones related to a device's removal from the system or to resource reassignment. For example, when the user invokes the remove/eject device utility, shown in Figure 8-35 (accessible by right-clicking on the USB connector icon in the taskbar and selecting Eject USB Mass Storage Device), to tell Windows to eject a USB flash drive, the PnP manager sends a *query-remove* notification to any applications that have registered for Plug and Play notifications for the device. Applications typically register for notification on their handles, which they close during a query-remove notification. If no applications veto the query-remove request, the PnP manager sends a *query-remove* command to the driver that owns the device being ejected. At that point, the driver has a chance to deny the removal or to ensure that any pending I/O operations involving the device have completed and to begin rejecting further I/O requests aimed at the device. If the driver agrees to the remove request and no open handles to the device remain, the PnP manager next sends a *remove* command to the driver to request that the driver discontinue accessing the device and release any resources the driver has allocated on behalf of the device.

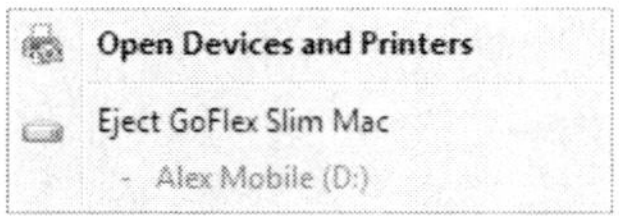

Open Devices and Printers

Eject GoFlex Slim Mac

- Alex Mobile (D:)

FIGURE 8-35 Remove/eject utility

When the PnP manager needs to reassign a device's resources, it first asks the driver whether it can temporarily suspend further activity on the device by sending the driver a *query-stop* command. The driver either agrees to the request, if doing so wouldn't cause data loss or corruption, or denies the request. As with a *query-remove* command, if the driver agrees to the request, the driver completes pending I/O operations and won't initiate further I/O requests for the device that can't be aborted and subsequently restarted. The driver typically queues new I/O requests so that the resource reshuffling is transparent to applications currently accessing the device. The PnP manager then sends the driver a *stop* command. At that point, the PnP manager can direct the driver to assign different resources to the device and once again send the driver a *start-device* command for the device.

The various Plug and Play commands essentially guide a device through an assortment of operational states, forming a well-defined state-transition table, which is shown in simplified form in Figure 8-36. (Several possible transitions and Plug and Play commands have been omitted for clarity. Also, the state diagram depicted is that implemented by function drivers. Bus drivers implement a more complex state diagram.) A state shown in the figure that we haven't discussed is the one that results from the PnP manager's *surprise-remove* command. This command results when either a user removes a device without warning, as when the user ejects a PCMCIA card without using the remove/eject utility, or the device fails. The *surprise-remove* command tells the driver to immediately cease all interaction with the device because the device is no longer attached to the system and to cancel any pending I/O requests.

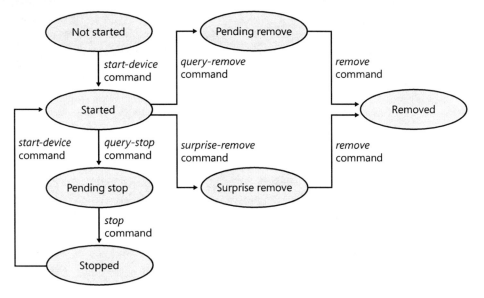

FIGURE 8-36 Device Plug and Play state transitions

Driver Loading, Initialization, and Installation

Driver loading and initialization on Windows consists of two types of loading: explicit loading and enumeration-based loading. Explicit loading is guided by the HKLM\SYSTEM\CurrentControlSet\Services branch of the registry, as described in the section "Service Applications" in Chapter 4 in Part 1. Enumeration-based loading results when the PnP manager dynamically loads drivers for the devices that a bus driver reports during bus enumeration.

The Start Value

In Chapter 4 in Part 1, we explained that every driver and Windows service has a registry key under the Services branch of the current control set. The key includes values that specify the type of the image (for example, Windows service, driver, and file system), the path to the driver or service's image file, and values that control the driver or service's load ordering. There are two main differences between explicit device driver loading and Windows service loading:

- Only device drivers can specify Start values of boot-start (0) or system-start (1).

- Device drivers can use the Group and Tag values to control the order of loading within a phase of the boot, but unlike services, they can't specify DependOnGroup or DependOnService values.

Chapter 13, "Startup and Shutdown," describes the phases of the boot process and explains that a driver Start value of 0 means that the operating system loader loads the driver. A Start value of 1 means that the I/O manager loads the driver after the executive subsystems have finished initializing. The I/O manager calls driver initialization routines in the order that the drivers load within a boot phase. Like Windows services, drivers use the Group value in their registry key to specify which group they belong to; the registry value HKLM\SYSTEM\CurrentControlSet\Control\ServiceGroupOrder\List determines the order that groups are loaded within a boot phase.

A driver can further refine its load order by including a Tag value to control its order within a group. The I/O manager sorts the drivers within each group according to the Tag values defined in the drivers' registry keys. Drivers without a tag go to the end of the list in their group. You might assume that the I/O manager initializes drivers with lower-number tags before it initializes drivers with higher-number tags, but such isn't necessarily the case. The registry key HKLM\SYSTEM\Current-ControlSet\Control\GroupOrderList defines tag precedence within a group; with this key, Microsoft and device driver developers can take liberties with redefining the integer number system.

Here are the guidelines by which drivers set their Start value:

- Non–Plug and Play drivers set their Start value to reflect the boot phase they want to load in.

- Drivers, including both Plug and Play and non–Plug and Play drivers, that must be loaded by the boot loader during the system boot specify a Start value of boot-start (0). Examples include system bus drivers and the boot file system driver.

- A driver that isn't required for booting the system and that detects a device that a system bus driver can't enumerate specifies a Start value of system-start (1). An example is the serial port driver, which informs the PnP manager of the presence of standard PC serial ports that were detected by Setup and recorded in the registry.

- A non–Plug and Play driver or file system driver that doesn't have to be present when the system boots specifies a Start value of auto-start (2). An example is the Multiple Universal Naming Convention (UNC) Provider (MUP) driver, which provides support for UNC-based path names to remote resources (for example, \\REMOTECOMPUTERNAME\SHARE).

- Plug and Play drivers that aren't required to boot the system specify a Start value of demand-start (3). Examples include network adapter drivers.

The only purpose that the Start values for Plug and Play drivers and drivers for enumerable devices have is to ensure that the operating system loader loads the driver—if the driver is required for the system to boot successfully. Beyond that, the PnP manager's device enumeration process, described next, determines the load order for Plug and Play drivers.

Device Enumeration

The PnP manager begins device enumeration with a virtual bus driver called Root, which represents the entire computer system and acts as the bus driver for non–Plug and Play drivers and for the HAL. The HAL acts as a bus driver that enumerates devices directly attached to the motherboard as well as system components such as batteries. Instead of actually enumerating, the HAL relies on the hardware description the Setup process recorded in the registry to detect the primary bus (a PCI bus in most cases) and devices such as batteries and fans.

The primary bus driver enumerates the devices on its bus, possibly finding other buses, for which the PnP manager initializes drivers. Those drivers in turn can detect other devices, including other subsidiary buses. This recursive process of enumeration, driver loading (if the driver isn't already loaded), and further enumeration proceeds until all the devices on the system have been detected and configured.

As the bus drivers report detected devices to the PnP manager, the PnP manager creates an internal tree called the *device tree* that represents the relationships between devices. Nodes in the tree are called *devnodes*, and a devnode contains information about the device objects that represent the device as well as other Plug and Play–related information stored in the devnode by the PnP manager. Figure 8-37 shows an example of a simplified device tree. This system is ACPI-compliant, so an ACPI-compliant HAL serves as the primary bus enumerator. A PCI bus serves as the system's primary bus, which USB, ISA, and SCSI buses are connected to.

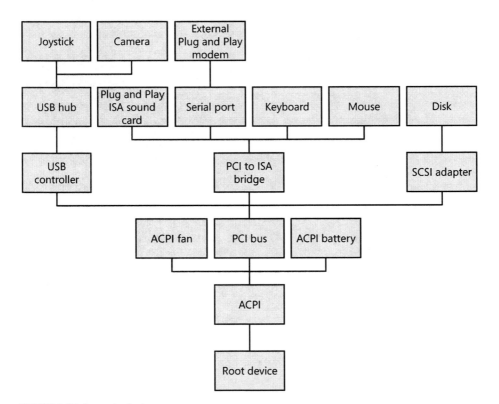

FIGURE 8-37 Example device tree

The Device Manager utility, which is accessible from the Computer Management snap-in in the Programs/Administrative Tools folder of the Start menu (and also from the Device Manager link of the System utility in Control Panel), shows a simple list of devices present on a system in its default configuration. You can also select the Devices By Connection option from the Device Manager's View menu to see the devices as they relate to the device tree. Figure 8-38 shows an example of the Device Manager's Devices By Connection view.

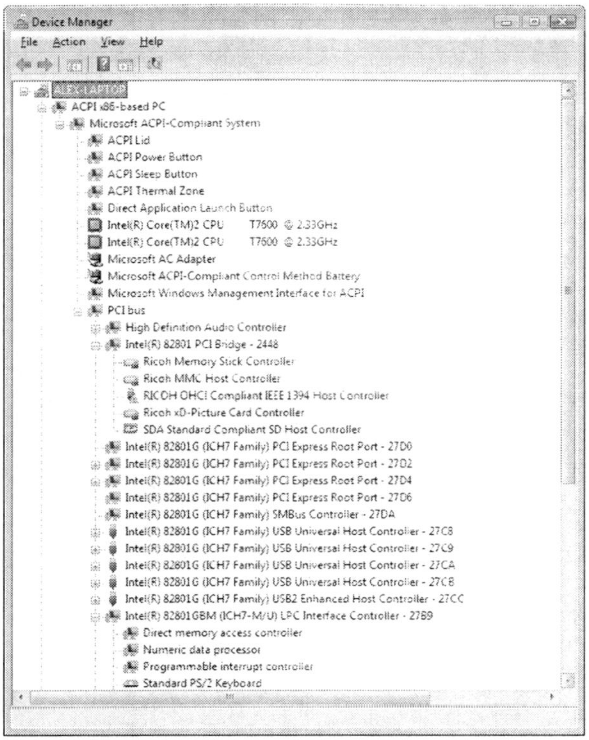

FIGURE 8-38 Device Manager showing the device tree

Taking device enumeration into account, the load and initialization order of drivers is as follows:

1. The I/O manager invokes the driver entry routine of each boot-start driver. If a boot driver has child devices, the I/O manager enumerates those devices, reporting their presence to the PnP manager. The child devices are configured and started if their drivers are boot-start drivers. If a device has a driver that isn't a boot-start driver, the PnP manager creates a devnode for the device but doesn't start it or load its driver.

2. After the boot-start drivers are initialized, the PnP manager walks the device tree, loading the drivers for devnodes that weren't loaded in step 1 and starting their devices. As each device starts, the PnP manager enumerates related child devices, if a device has any, starting those devices' drivers and performing enumeration of their children as required. The PnP manager loads the drivers for detected devices in this step *regardless of the driver's Start value.* (The one exception is if the Start value is set to disabled.) At the end of this step, all Plug and Play devices have their drivers loaded and are started, except devices that aren't enumerable and the children of those devices.

3. The PnP manager loads any drivers with a Start value of system-start that aren't yet loaded. Those drivers detect and report their nonenumerable devices. The PnP manager loads drivers for those devices until all enumerated devices are configured and started.

4. The service control manager loads drivers marked as auto-start.

The device tree serves to guide both the PnP manager and the power manager as they issue Plug and Play and power IRPs to devices. In general, IRPs flow from the top of a devnode to the bottom, and in some cases a driver in one devnode creates new IRPs to send to other devnodes, always moving toward the root. The flow of Plug and Play and power IRPs is further described later in this chapter.

EXPERIMENT: Dumping the Device Tree

A more detailed way to view the device tree than using Device Manager is to use the *!devnode* kernel debugger command. Specifying *0 1* as command options dumps the internal device tree devnode structures, indenting entries to show their hierarchical relationships, as shown here:

```
lkd> !devnode 0 1
Dumping IopRootDeviceNode (= 0x85161a98)
DevNode 0x85161a98 for PDO 0x84d10390
  InstancePath is "HTREE\ROOT\0"
  State = DeviceNodeStarted (0x308)
  Previous State = DeviceNodeEnumerateCompletion (0x30d)
  DevNode 0x8515bea8 for PDO 0x8515b030
  DevNode 0x8515c698 for PDO 0x8515c820
    InstancePath is "Root\ACPI_HAL\0000"
    State = DeviceNodeStarted (0x308)
    Previous State = DeviceNodeEnumerateCompletion (0x30d)
    DevNode 0x84d1c5b0 for PDO 0x84d1c738
      InstancePath is "ACPI_HAL\PNP0C08\0"
      ServiceName is "ACPI"
      State = DeviceNodeStarted (0x308)
      Previous State = DeviceNodeEnumerateCompletion (0x30d)
      DevNode 0x85ebf1b0 for PDO 0x85ec0210
        InstancePath is "ACPI\GenuineIntel_-_x86_Family_6_Model_15\_0"
        ServiceName is "intelppm"
        State = DeviceNodeStarted (0x308)
        Previous State = DeviceNodeEnumerateCompletion (0x30d)
      DevNode 0x85ed6970 for PDO 0x8515e618
        InstancePath is "ACPI\GenuineIntel_-_x86_Family_6_Model_15\_1"
        ServiceName is "intelppm"
        State = DeviceNodeStarted (0x308)
        Previous State = DeviceNodeEnumerateCompletion (0x30d)
      DevNode 0x85ed75c8 for PDO 0x85ed79e8
        InstancePath is "ACPI\ThermalZone\THM_"
        State = DeviceNodeStarted (0x308)
        Previous State = DeviceNodeEnumerateCompletion (0x30d)
      DevNode 0x85ed6cd8 for PDO 0x85ed6858
        InstancePath is "ACPI\pnp0c14\0"
        ServiceName is "WmiAcpi"
        State = DeviceNodeStarted (0x308)
        Previous State = DeviceNodeEnumerateCompletion (0x30d)
```

```
DevNode 0x85ed7008 for PDO 0x85ed6730
  InstancePath is "ACPI\ACPI0003\2&daba3ff&2"
  ServiceName is "CmBatt"
  State = DeviceNodeStarted (0x308)
  Previous State = DeviceNodeEnumerateCompletion (0x30d)
DevNode 0x85ed7e60 for PDO 0x84d2e030
  InstancePath is "ACPI\PNP0C0A\1"
  ServiceName is "CmBatt"
...
```

Information shown for each devnode includes the InstancePath, which is the name of the device's enumeration registry key stored under HKLM\SYSTEM\CurrentControlSet\Enum, and the ServiceName, which corresponds to the device's driver registry key under HKLM\SYSTEM\CurrentControlSet\Services. To see the resources, such as interrupts, ports, and memory, assigned to each devnode, specify *0 3* as the command options for the *!devnode* command.

A record of all the devices detected since the system was installed is recorded under the HKLM\SYSTEM\CurrentControlSet\Enum registry key. Subkeys are in the form <Enumerator>\<Device ID>\<Instance ID>, where the enumerator is a bus driver, the device ID is a unique identifier for a type of device, and the instance ID uniquely identifies different instances of the same hardware.

Device Stacks

As the devnodes are created by the PnP manager, driver objects and device objects are created to manage and logically represent the linkage between the devnodes. This linkage is called a *device stack*, and it can be thought of as an ordered list of device object/driver pairs. Each device stack has a bottom and top, and Figure 8-39 shows that a device stack is made up of at least two, and sometimes more, device objects:

- A *physical device object* (PDO) that the PnP manager instructs a bus driver to create when the bus driver reports the presence of a device on its bus during enumeration. The PDO represents the physical interface to the device and is always on the bottom of the device stack.

- One or more optional filter device objects (FiDOs) that layer between the PDO and the functional device object (FDO; described later in this list) and that are created by bus filter drivers.

- One or more optional FiDOs that layer between the PDO and the FDO (and that layer above any FiDOs created by bus filter drivers) that are created by lower-level filter drivers.

- One (and only one) functional device object (FDO) that is created by the driver, which is called a function driver, that the PnP manager loads to manage a detected device. An FDO represents the logical interface to a device. A function driver can also act as a bus driver if devices are attached to the device represented by the FDO. The function driver often creates an interface (described earlier) to the FDO's corresponding PDO so that applications and other drivers can open the device and interact with it. Sometimes function drivers are divided into a separate class/port driver and miniport driver that work together to manage I/O for the FDO.

- One or more optional FiDOs that layer above the FDO and that are created by upper-level filter drivers.

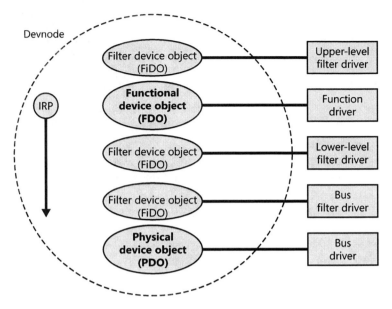

FIGURE 8-39 Device stack internals

Device stacks are built from the bottom up and rely on the I/O manager's layering functionality, so IRPs flow from the top of a device stack toward the bottom. However, any level in the device stack can choose to complete an IRP. For example, the function driver can handle a read request without passing the IRP to the bus driver. Only when the function driver requires the help of a bus driver to perform bus-specific processing does the IRP flow all the way to the bottom and then into the device stack containing the bus driver.

Device Stack Driver Loading

So far, we've avoided answering two important questions: "How does the PnP manager determine what function driver to load for a particular device?" and "How do filter drivers register their presence so that they are loaded at appropriate times in the creation of a device stack?"

The answer to both these questions lies in the registry. When a bus driver performs device enumeration, it reports device identifiers for the devices it detects back to the PnP manager. The identifiers are bus-specific; for a USB bus, an identifier consists of a *vendor ID* (VID) for the hardware vendor that made the device and a *product ID* (PID) that the vendor assigned to the device. (See the WDK for more information on device ID formats.) Together these IDs form what Plug and Play calls a *device ID*. The PnP manager also queries the bus driver for an *instance ID* to help it distinguish different instances of the same hardware. The instance ID can describe either a bus-relative location (for example, the USB port) or a globally unique descriptor (for example, a serial number).

The device ID and instance ID are combined to form a *device instance ID* (DIID), which the PnP manager uses to locate the device's key in the enumeration branch of the registry (HKLM\SYSTEM\CurrentControlSet\Enum). Figure 8-40 presents an example of a keyboard's enumeration subkey. The device's key contains descriptive data and includes values named Service and ClassGUID (which are obtained from a driver's INF file) that help the PnP manager locate the device's drivers.

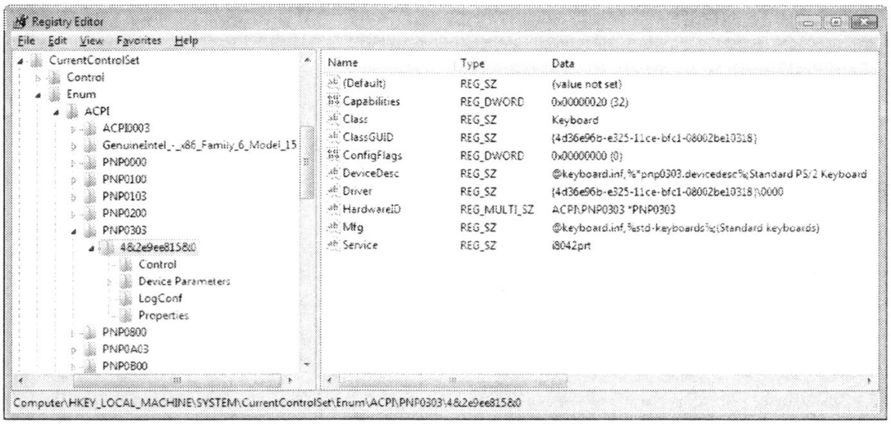

FIGURE 8-40 Keyboard enumeration key

To deal with multifunction devices (such as all-in-one printers or cell phones with integrated camera and music player functionalities), Windows also supports a container ID property that can be associated with a devnode. The container ID is a globally unique identifier (GUID) that is unique to a single instance of a physical device and shared between all the function devnodes that belong to it, as shown in Figure 8-41.

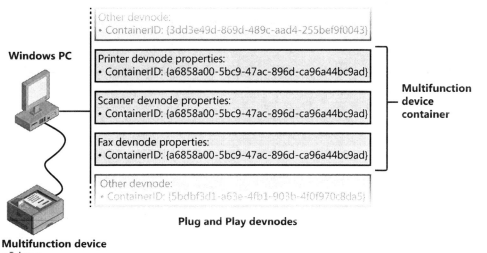

FIGURE 8-41: All-in-one printer with a unique ID as seen by the PnP manager

The container ID is a property that, similar to the instance ID, is reported back by the bus driver of the corresponding hardware. Then, when the device is being enumerated, all devnodes associated with the same PDO share the container ID. Because Windows already supports many buses out of the box—such as PnP-X, Bluetooth, and USB—most device drivers can simply return the bus-specific ID, from which Windows will generate the corresponding container ID. For other kinds of devices or buses, the driver can generate its own unique ID through software.

Finally, when device drivers do not supply a container ID, Windows can make educated guesses by querying the topology for the bus, when that's available, through mechanisms such as ACPI. By understanding whether a certain device is a child of another, and whether it is removable, hot-pluggable, or user-reachable (as opposed to an internal motherboard component), Windows is able to assign container IDs to device nodes that reflect multifunction devices correctly.

The final end-user benefit of grouping devices by container IDs is visible in the Devices And Printers UI present in modern versions of Windows. This feature is able to display the scanner, printer, and faxing components of an all-in-one printer as a single graphical element instead of as three distinct devices. For example, in Figure 8-42, the HP PSC 1500 series is identified as a single device.

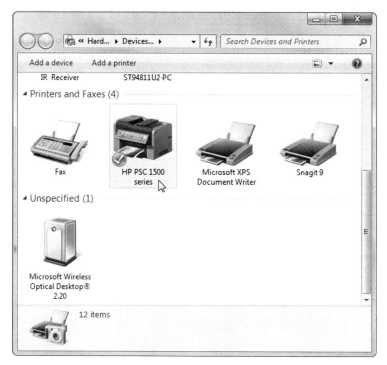

FIGURE 8-42 Devices And Printers

EXPERIMENT: Viewing Detailed Devnode Information in Device Manager

The Device Manager applet that you can access from the Hardware link of the System Control Panel application shows detailed information about a device node on its Details tab. The tab allows you to view an assortment of fields, including the devnode's device instance ID, hardware ID, service name, filters, and power capabilities.

The following screen shows the selection combo box of the Details tab expanded to reveal the types of information you can access:

Using the ClassGUID value, the PnP manager locates the device's class key under HKLM\SYSTEM\ CurrentControlSet\Control\Class. The keyboard class key is shown in Figure 8-43. The enumeration key and class key supply the PnP manager with the information it needs to load the drivers necessary for the device's devnode. Drivers are loaded in the following order:

1. Any lower-level filter drivers specified in the LowerFilters value of the device's enumeration key.

2. Any lower-level filter drivers specified in the LowerFilters value of the device's class key.

3. The function driver specified by the Service value in the device's enumeration key. This value is interpreted as the driver's key under HKLM\SYSTEM\CurrentControlSet\Services.

4. Any upper-level filter drivers specified in the UpperFilters value of the device's enumeration key.

5. Any upper-level filter drivers specified in the UpperFilters value of the device's class key.

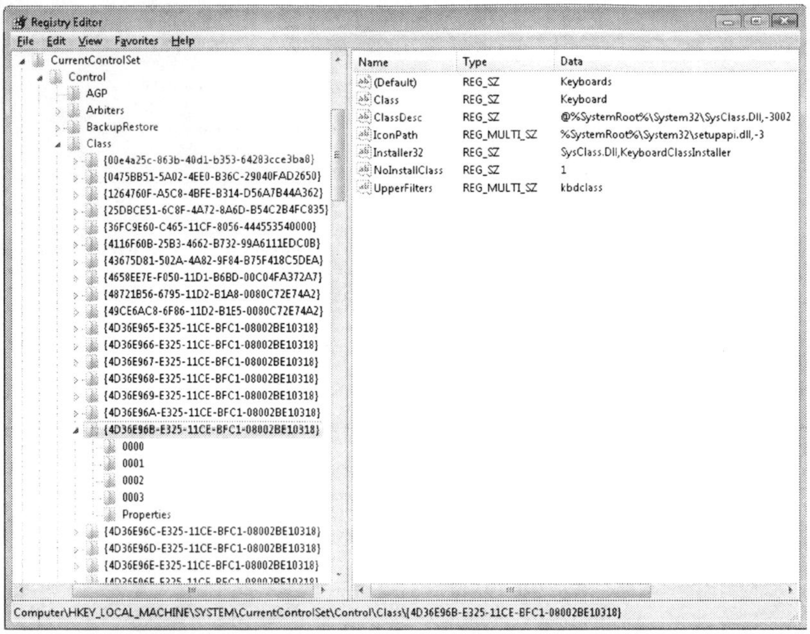

FIGURE 8-43 Keyboard class key

In all cases, drivers are referenced by the name of their key under HKLM\SYSTEM\CurrentControl-Set\Services.

> **Note** The WDK refers to a device's enumeration key as its *hardware key* and to the class key as the *software key*.

The keyboard device shown in Figure 8-40 and Figure 8-43 has no lower-level filter drivers. The function driver is the i8042prt driver, and there are two upper-level filter drivers specified in the keyboard's class key: kbdclass and vmkbd2.

Driver Installation

If the PnP manager encounters a device for which no driver is installed, it relies on the user-mode PnP manager to guide the installation process. If the device is detected during the system boot, a devnode is defined for the device, but the loading process is postponed until the user-mode PnP manager starts. (The user-mode PnP manager is implemented in %SystemRoot%\System32\Umpnpmgr.dll and runs in a service hosting process (Svchost.exe).)

The components involved in a driver's installation are shown in Figure 8-44. Dark-shaded objects in the figure correspond to components generally supplied by the system, whereas lighter-shaded objects are those included in a driver's installation files. First, a bus driver informs the PnP manager of a device it enumerates using a DIID (1). The PnP manager checks the registry for the presence of a corresponding function driver, and when it doesn't find one, it informs the user-mode PnP manager

(2) of the new device by its DIID. The user-mode PnP manager first tries to perform an automatic install without user intervention. If the installation process involves the posting of dialog boxes that require user interaction and the currently logged-on user has administrator privileges, (3) the user-mode PnP manager launches the Rundll32.exe application (the same application that hosts Control Panel utilities) to execute the Hardware Installation Wizard (%SystemRoot%\System32\Newdev.dll). If the currently logged-on user doesn't have administrator privileges (or if no user is logged on) and the installation of the device requires user interaction, the user-mode PnP manager defers the installation until a privileged user logs on. The Hardware Installation Wizard uses Setupapi.dll and CfgMgr32.dll (configuration manager) API functions to locate INF files that correspond to drivers that are compatible with the detected device. This process might involve having the user insert installation media containing a vendor's INF files, or the wizard might locate a suitable INF file in the driver store (%SystemRoot%\System32\DriverStore) that contains drivers that ship with Windows or others that are downloaded through Windows Update. Installation is performed in two steps. In the first, the third-party driver developer imports the driver package into the driver store, and in the second step, the system performs the actual installation, which is always done through the %SystemRoot%\System32\Drvinst.exe process.

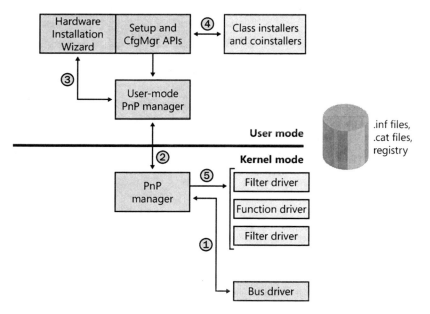

FIGURE 8-44 Driver installation components

To find drivers for the new device, the installation process gets a list of *hardware IDs* and *compatible IDs* from the bus driver. These IDs describe all the various ways the hardware might be identified in a driver installation file (.inf). The lists are ordered so that the most specific description of the hardware is listed first. If matches are found in multiple INFs, more precise matches are preferred over less precise matches, digitally signed INFs are preferred over unsigned ones, and newer signed INFs are preferred over older signed ones. If a match is found based on a compatible ID, the Hardware

Installation Wizard can choose to prompt for media in case a more up-to-date driver came with the hardware.

The INF file locates the function driver's files and contains commands that fill in the driver's enumeration and class keys, and the INF file might direct the Hardware Installation Wizard to (4) launch class or device coinstaller DLLs that perform class-specific or device-specific installation steps, such as displaying configuration dialog boxes that let the user specify settings for a device.

EXPERIMENT: Looking at a Driver's INF File

When a driver or other software that has an INF file is installed, the system copies its INF file to the %SystemRoot%\Inf directory. One file that will always be there is Keyboard.inf because it's the INF file for the keyboard class driver. View its contents by opening it in Notepad and you should see something like this:

```
; Copyright (c) Microsoft Corporation.  All rights reserved.

[Version]
Signature="$Windows NT$"
Class=Keyboard
ClassGUID={4D36E96B-E325-11CE-BFC1-08002BE10318}
Provider=%MS%
DriverVer=06/21/2006,6.1.7601.17514

[SourceDisksNames]
3426=windows cd
...
```

If you search the file for ".sys", you'll come across the entry that directs the user-mode PnP manager to install the i8042prt.sys and kbdclass.sys drivers:

```
...

[STANDARD_CopyFiles]
i8042prt.sys,,,0x100
kbdclass.sys,,,0x100
...
```

Before actually installing a driver, the user-mode PnP manager checks the system's driver-signing policy. If the settings specify that the system should block or warn of the installation of unsigned drivers, the user-mode PnP manager checks the driver's INF file for an entry that locates a catalog (a file that ends with the .cat extension) containing the driver's digital signature.

Microsoft's WHQL tests the drivers included with Windows and those submitted by hardware vendors. When a driver passes the WHQL tests, it is "signed" by Microsoft. This means that WHQL obtains a *hash*, or unique value representing the driver's files, including its image file, and then cryptographically signs it with Microsoft's private driver-signing key. The signed hash is stored in a catalog file and included on the Windows installation media or returned to the vendor that submitted the driver for inclusion with its driver.

EXPERIMENT: Viewing Catalog Files

When you install a component such as a driver that includes a catalog file, Windows copies the catalog file to a directory under %SystemRoot%\System32\Catroot. Navigate to that directory in Explorer and you find the subdirectory that contains .cat files. Nt5.cat and Nt5ph.cat store the signatures and page hashes for Windows system files, for example.

If you open one of the catalog files, a dialog box appears with two pages. The page labeled General shows information about the signature on the catalog file, and the Security Catalog page has the hashes of the components that are signed with the catalog file. This screen shot of a catalog file for NVIDIA video drivers shows the hash for the video adapter's kernel miniport driver. Other hashes in the catalog are associated with the various support DLLs that ship with the driver.

As it is installing a driver, the user-mode PnP manager extracts the driver's signature from its catalog file, decrypts the signature using the public half of Microsoft's driver-signing private/public key pair, and compares the resulting hash with a hash of the driver file it's about to install. If the hashes match, the driver is verified as having passed WHQL testing. If a driver fails the signature verification, the user-mode PnP manager acts according to the settings of the system driver-signing policy, either failing the installation attempt, warning the user that the driver is unsigned, or silently installing the driver.

> **Note** Drivers installed using setup programs that manually configure the registry and copy driver files to a system and driver files that are dynamically loaded by applications aren't checked for signatures by the PnP manager's signing policy. Instead, they are checked by the Kernel Mode Code Signing policy described in Chapter 3 in Part 1. Only drivers installed using INF files are validated against the PnP manager's driver-signing policy.

After a driver is installed, the kernel-mode PnP manager (step 5 in Figure 8-44) starts the driver and calls its add-device routine to inform the driver of the presence of the device it was loaded for. The construction of the device stack then continues as described earlier.

> **Note** The user-mode PnP manager also checks to see whether the driver it's about to install is on the *protected driver list* maintained by Windows Update and, if so, blocks the installation with a warning to the user. Drivers that are known to have incompatibilities or bugs are added to the list and blocked from installation.

The Power Manager

Just as Windows Plug and Play features require support from a system's hardware, its power-management capabilities require hardware that complies with the Advanced Configuration and Power Interface (ACPI) specification (available at *http://www.acpi.info*).

The ACPI standard defines various power levels for a system and for devices. The six system power states are described in Table 8-8. They are referred to as S0 (*fully on* or *working*) through S5 (*fully off*). Each state has the following characteristics:

- **Power consumption** The amount of power the computer consumes
- **Software resumption** The software state from which the computer resumes when moving to a "more on" state
- **Hardware latency** The length of time it takes to return the computer to the fully on state

States S1 through S4 are sleeping states, in which the computer appears to be off because of reduced power consumption. However, the computer retains enough information, either in memory or on disk, to move to S0. For states S1 through S3, enough power is required to preserve the contents of the computer's memory so that when the transition is made to S0 (when the user or a device wakes up the computer), the power manager continues executing where it left off before the suspend.

TABLE 8-8 System Power-State Definitions

State	Power Consumption	Software Resumption	Hardware Latency
S0 (fully on)	Maximum	Not applicable	None
S1 (sleeping)	Less than S0, more than S2	System resumes where it left off (returns to S0)	Less than 2 seconds
S2 (sleeping)	Less than S1, more than S3	System resumes where it left off (returns to S0)	2 or more seconds
S3 (sleeping)	Less than S2; processor is off	System resumes where it left off (returns to S0)	Same as S2
S4 (hibernating)	Trickle current to power button and wake circuitry	System restarts from saved hibernatation file and resumes where it left off prior to hibernation (returns to S0)	Long and undefined
S5 (fully off)	Trickle current to power button	System boot	Long and undefined

When the system moves to S4, the power manager saves the compressed contents of memory to a hibernation file named Hiberfil.sys, which is large enough to hold the uncompressed contents of memory, in the root directory of the system volume. (Compression is used to minimize disk I/O and to improve hibernation and resume-from-hibernation performance.) After it finishes saving memory, the power manager shuts off the computer. When a user subsequently turns on the computer, a normal boot process occurs, except that Bootmgr checks for and detects a valid memory image stored in the hibernation file. If the hibernation file contains saved system state, Bootmgr launches Winresume, which reads the contents of the file into memory, and then resumes execution at the point in memory that is recorded in the hibernation file.

On systems with hybrid sleep enabled (by default, only desktop computers), a user request to put the computer to sleep will actually be a combination of both the S3 state and the S4 state: while the computer is put to sleep, an emergency hibernation file will also be written to disk. Unlike typical hibernation files, which contain almost all active memory, the emergency hibernation file includes only data that could not be paged in at a later time, making the suspend operation faster than a typical hibernation (because less data is written to disk). Drivers will then be notified that an S4 transition is occurring, allowing them to configure themselves and save state just as if an actual hibernation request had been initiated. After this point, the system is put in the normal sleep state just like during a standard sleep transition. However, if the power goes out, the system is now essentially in an S4 state—the user can power on the machine, and Windows will resume from the emergency hibernation file.

The computer never directly transitions between states S1 and S4; instead, it must move to state S0 first. As illustrated in Figure 8-45, when the system is moving from any of states S1 through S5 to state S0, it's said to be *waking*, and when it's transitioning from state S0 to any of states S1 through S5, it's said to be *sleeping*.

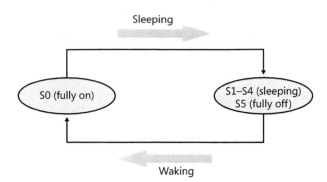

FIGURE 8-45 System power-state transitions

Although the system can be in one of six power states, ACPI defines devices as being in one of four power states, D0 through D3. State D0 is *fully on*, and state D3 is *fully off*. The ACPI standard leaves it to individual drivers and devices to define the meanings of states D1 and D2, except that state D1 must consume an amount of power less than or equal to that consumed in state D0, and when the device is in state D2, it must consume power less than or equal to that consumed in D1. Microsoft, in conjunction with the major hardware OEMs, has defined a series of power management reference specifications that specify the device power states that are required for all devices in a particular class (for the major device classes: display, network, SCSI, and so on). For some devices, there's no intermediate power state between fully on and fully off, which results in these states being undefined.

Power Manager Operation

Power management policy in Windows is split between the power manager and the individual device drivers. The power manager is the owner of the system power policy. This ownership means that the power manager decides which system power state is appropriate at any given point, and when a sleep, hibernation, or shutdown is required, the power manager instructs the power-capable devices in the system to perform appropriate system power-state transitions. The power manager decides when a system power-state transition is necessary by considering a number of factors:

- System activity level

- System battery level

- Shutdown, hibernate, or sleep requests from applications

- User actions, such as pressing the power button

- Control Panel power settings

When the PnP manager performs device enumeration, part of the information it receives about a device is its power-management capabilities. A driver reports whether or not its devices support device states D1 and D2 and, optionally, the latencies, or times required, to move from states D1 through D3 to D0. To help the power manager determine when to make system power-state transitions, bus drivers also return a table that implements a mapping between each of the system power states (S0 through S5) and the device power states that a device supports.

The table lists the lowest possible device power state for each system state and directly reflects the state of various power planes when the machine sleeps or hibernates. For example, a bus that supports all four device power states might return the mapping table shown in Table 8-9. Most device drivers turn their devices completely off (D3) when leaving S0 to minimize power consumption when the machine isn't in use. Some devices, however, such as network adapter cards, support the ability to wake up the system from a sleeping state. This ability, along with the lowest device power state in which the capability is present, is also reported during device enumeration.

TABLE 8-9 Example System-to-Device Power Mappings

System Power State	Device Power State
S0 (fully on)	D0 (fully on)
S1 (sleeping)	D1
S2 (sleeping)	D2
S3 (sleeping)	D2
S4 (hibernating)	D3 (fully off)
S5 (fully off)	D3 (fully off)

Driver Power Operation

When the power manager decides to make a transition between system power states, it sends power commands to a driver's power dispatch routine. More than one driver can be responsible for managing a device, but only one of the drivers is designated as the device power-policy owner. This driver determines, based on the system state, a device's power state. For example, if the system transitions between state S0 and S1, a driver might decide to move a device's power state from D0 to D1.

Instead of directly informing the other drivers that share the management of the device of its decision, the device power-policy owner asks the power manager, via the *PoRequestPowerIrp* function, to tell the other drivers by issuing a device power command to their power dispatch routines. This behavior allows the power manager to control the number of power commands that are active on a system at any given time. For example, some devices in the system might require a significant amount of current to power up. The power manager ensures that such devices aren't powered up simultaneously.

EXPERIMENT: Viewing a Driver's Power Mappings

You can see a driver's system power state to driver power state mappings with Device Manager. Open the Properties dialog box for a device, and choose the Power Data entry in the drop-down list on the Details tab to see the mappings.

The dialog box also displays the current power state of the device, the device-specific power capabilities that it provides, and the power states from which it is able to wake the system.

Many power commands have corresponding query commands. For example, when the system is moving to a sleep state, the power manager will first ask the devices on the system whether the transition is acceptable. A device that is busy performing time-critical operations or interacting with device hardware might reject the command, which results in the system maintaining its current system power-state setting.

EXPERIMENT: Viewing the System Power Capabilities and Policy

You can view a computer's system power capabilities by using the *!pocaps* kernel debugger command. Here's the output of the command when run on an ACPI-compliant laptop:

```
lkd> !pocaps
PopCapabilities @ 0x82114d80
  Misc Supported Features:   PwrButton SlpButton Lid S3 S4 S5 HiberFile FullWake
                             VideoDim
  Processor Features:        Thermal
  Disk Features:             SpinDown
  Battery Features:          BatteriesPresent
    Battery 0 - Capacity:        0  Granularity:        0
    Battery 1 - Capacity:        0  Granularity:        0
    Battery 2 - Capacity:        0  Granularity:        0
  Wake Caps
    Ac OnLine Wake:        Sx
    Soft Lid Wake:        Sx
    RTC Wake:        S4
    Min Device Wake:        Sx
    Default Wake:        Sx
```

The Misc Supported Features line reports that, in addition to S0 (fully on), the system supports system power states S1, S3, S4, and S5 (it doesn't implement S2) and has a valid hibernation file to which it can save system memory when it hibernates (state S4).

The Power Options page, shown here (available by selecting Power Options in Control Panel), lets you configure various aspects of the system's power policy. The exact properties you can configure depend on the system's power capabilities, which we just examined.

By changing any of the preconfigured plan settings, you can set the idle detection timeouts that control when the system turns off the monitor, spins down hard disks, goes to standby mode (moves to system power state S1), and hibernates (moves the system to power state S4). In addition, selecting the Change Plan Settings option lets you specify the power-related behavior of the system when you press the power or sleep buttons or close a laptop's lid.

The settings you configure by clicking the Change Advanced Power Settings link directly affect values in the system's power policy, which you can display with the *!popolicy* debugger command. Here's the output of the command on the same system:

```
lkd> !popolicy
SYSTEM_POWER_POLICY (R.1) @ 0x82107994
    PowerButton:        Sleep   Flags: 00000000   Event: 00000000
    SleepButton:        Sleep   Flags: 00000000   Event: 00000000
    LidClose:           Sleep   Flags: 00000000   Event: 00000000
    Idle:               Sleep   Flags: 00000000   Event: 00000000
    OverThrottled:      None    Flags: 00000000   Event: 00000000
    IdleTimeout:          384   IdleSensitivity:      90%
    MinSleep:              S3   MaxSleep:             S3
    LidOpenWake:           S0   FastSleep:            S0
    WinLogonFlags:          1   S4Timeout:            fd20
    VideoTimeout:         300   VideoDim:              0
    SpinTimeout:          258   OptForPower:           0
    FanTolerance:          0%   ForcedThrottle:        0%

    SpinTimeout:          258   OptForPower:           0
    MinThrottle:           0%   DyanmicThrottle:     None
```

The first lines of the display correspond to the button behaviors specified on the Advanced Settings tab of Power Options, and on this system both the power and the sleep buttons put the computer in a sleep state, just as closing the lid does.

The timeout values shown at the end of the output are expressed in seconds and displayed in hexadecimal notation. The values reported here directly correspond to the settings you can see configured on the Power Options page. (The laptop is on battery.) For example, the video timeout is 300, meaning the monitor turns off after 300 seconds, or 5 minutes, and the hard disk spin-down timeout is 0x258, which corresponds to 600 seconds, or 10 minutes.

Driver and Application Control of Device Power

Besides responding to power manager commands related to system power-state transitions, a driver can unilaterally control the device power state of its devices. In some cases, a driver might want to reduce the power consumption of a device it controls when the device is left inactive for a period of time. Examples include monitors that support a dimmed mode and disks that support spin-down. A driver can either detect an idle device itself or use facilities provided by the power manager. If the device uses the power manager, it registers the device with the power manager by calling the *PoRegisterDeviceForIdleDetection* function.

This function informs the power manager of the timeout values to use to detect a device as idle and of the device power state that the power manager should apply when it detects the device as being idle. The driver specifies two timeouts: one to use when the user has configured the computer to conserve energy and the other to use when the user has configured the computer for optimum performance. After calling *PoRegisterDeviceForIdleDetection*, the driver must inform the power manager, by calling the *PoSetDeviceBusy* or *PoSetDeviceBusyEx* functions, whenever the device is active, and then register for idle detection again to disable and re-enable it as needed. The *PoStartDeviceBusy* and *PoEndDeviceBusy* APIs are available in newer versions of Windows as well, which simplify the programming logic required to achieve the behavior that's desired.

Although a device has control over its own power state, it does not have the ability to manipulate the system power state or to prevent system power transitions from occurring. For example, if a badly designed driver doesn't support any low-power states, it can choose to remain on or turn itself completely off without hindering the system's overall ability to enter a low-power state—this is because the power manager only *notifies* the driver of a transition and doesn't ask for *consent*.

Although drivers and the kernel are chiefly responsible for power management, applications are also allowed to provide their input. User-mode processes can register for a variety of power notifications, such as when the battery is low or critically low, when the laptop has switched from DC (battery) to AC (adapter/charger) power, or when the system is initiating a power transition. Just like drivers, however, applications cannot veto these operations, and they can have up to two seconds to clean up any state necessary before a sleep transition.

Power Availability Requests

Even though applications and drivers cannot veto sleep transitions that are already initiated, certain scenarios demand a mechanism for disabling the ability to initiate sleep transitions when a user is interacting with the system in certain ways. For example, if the user is currently watching a movie and the machine would normally go idle (based on a lack of mouse or keyboard input after 15 minutes), the media player application should have the capability to temporarily disable idle transitions as long as the movie is playing. You can probably imagine other power-saving measures that the system would normally undertake, such as turning off or even just dimming the screen, that would also limit your enjoyment of visual media. In legacy versions of Windows, *SetThreadExecutionState* was a user-mode API capable of controlling system and display idle transitions by informing the power manager that a user was still present on the machine, but this API did not provide any sort of diagnostic capabilities, nor did it allow sufficient granularity for defining the availability request. Also, drivers were not able to issue their own requests, and even user applications had to correctly manage their threading model, because these requests were at the thread level, not at the process or system level.

Windows now supports power request objects, which are implemented by the kernel and are bona-fide object manager–defined objects. You can use the WinObj utility that was introduced in Chapter 3 in Part 1 and see the PowerRequest object type in the \ObjectTypes directory, or use the *!object* kernel debugger command on the \ObjectTypes\PowerRequest object type, to validate this. Power availability requests are generated by user-mode applications through the *PowerCreateRequest* API and then enabled or disabled with the *PowerSetRequest* and *PowerClearRequest* APIs, respectively. In the kernel, drivers use *PoCreatePowerRequest*, *PoSetPowerRequest,* and *PoClearPowerRequest*. Because no handles are used, *PoDeletePowerRequest* is implemented to remove the reference on the object (while user mode can simply use *CloseHandle*).

There are three kinds of requests that can be used through the Power Request API: a system request, a display request, and an "away-mode" request. The first type requests that the system not automatically go to sleep due to the idle timer (although the user can still close the lid to enter sleep, for example), while the second does the same for the display. "Away-mode" is a modification to the normal sleep (S3 state) behavior of Windows, which is used to keep the computer in full powered-on mode but with the display and sound card turned off, making it appear to the user as though the machine is really sleeping. This behavior is normally used only by specialized set-top boxes or media center devices when media delivery must continue even though the user has pressed a physical sleep button, for example. In the future, Windows may support other requests as well.

EXPERIMENT: Viewing a Power Availability Request in the Debugger

Because power availability requests are objects managed by the object manager, applications have handles open to them when calling the *PowerCreateRequest* API, and Process Explorer is able to find these handles by using the Search DLL/Handle functionality that was introduced in previous chapters.

You can search for "PowerRequest" and find certain services and applications on your machine that have made availability requests. (Drivers will not show up because the kernel API does not use handles.) For example, the Print Spooler (Spoolsvc.exe) and Windows Media Player Network Sharing Service (Wmpntwk.exe) are two Windows services that have availability request objects.

By launching the Poavltst.exe test utility from the Book Tools and searching with Process Explorer, you will also find that it too has a handle open. Use the handle lower-pane view to obtain the kernel address of the object, in this case 0x8544ABF8.

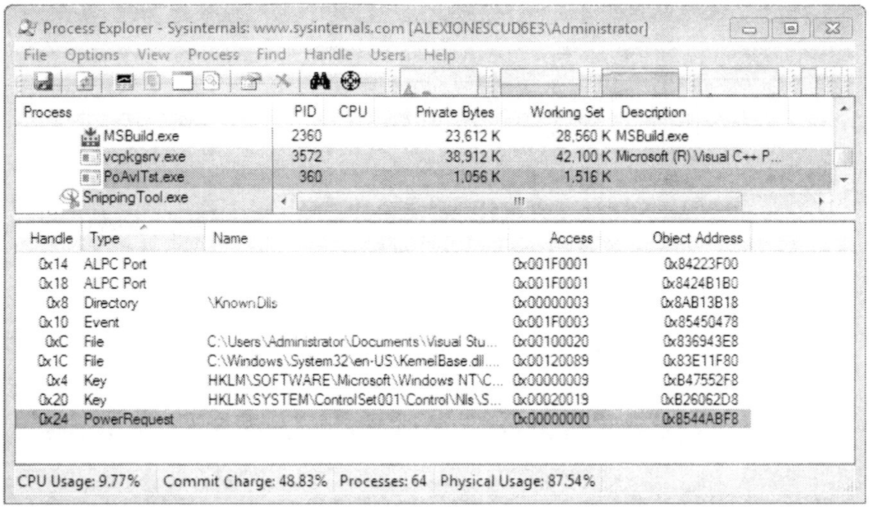

You can then use local kernel debugging to dump the power request object as shown next. Unfortunately, the underlying kernel data structure is not present in the symbol files, so only a hex dump is possible. Nevertheless, the layout of the object is easy to understand: a doubly linked list (the first two pointers), some flags, and then a pointer to the actual request information that the test application supplied, which is highlighted in bold.

```
kd> dc 8544ABF8
855d01a8  819586c0 85448ea0 00000001 00000007  ......D.........
855d01b8  00000000 00000000 00000000 00000000  ................
855d01c8  b13e9b50
```

By using the same dump command on the pointer, the power request's diagnostic reason is visible: "Computation in progress."

```
kd> dc b13e9b50
b13e9b50  00000001 8556b030 00000000 00000044  ....0.V.....D...
b13e9b60  00000001 00000014 00000000 80080001  ................
b13e9b70  00000000 006f0043 0070006d 00740075  ....C.o.m.p.u.t.
b13e9b80  00740061 006f0069 0020006e 006e0069  a.t.i.o.n. .i.n.
b13e9b90  00700020 006f0072 00720067 00730065  .p.r.o.g.r.e.s
```

You can also use the *dl* (dump list) command on the first pointer in the object's dump to dump a list of all the power requests on the system, which are linked by the *PopPowerRequestObjectList* symbol in the kernel. This will let you see power requests that Process Explorer cannot locate, such as those created by drivers.

Processor Power Management (PPM)

So far, this section has only described the power manager's control over device (D) and system (S) states, but another important state management must also be performed on a modern operating system: that of the processor (P and C states). Windows implements a processor power manager (PPM) that is responsible for controlling both C states (the idle states of the processor) and P states (the package states of the processor) and for interacting with ACPI firmware as well as a vendor-supplied power management driver, as needed (Intelppm.sys for Intel CPUs, for example). Which states are chosen is usually determined by a combination of internal algorithms and settings that ship in the Windows registry, most of which are tunable by OEMs and administrators. We will show all these tunable policy values later in this section.

Although the exact specifics of PPM are outside the scope of this book and are often hardware-specific, it is worth going into detail about one particular technology that is unique to Windows: core parking. At its essence, core parking is a load-based engine running inside the PPM that makes two sets of decisions:

- Which particular P states should be entered for a given processor, and how power should be managed across a power domain. A domain is the set of functional units associated with a given processor core (including the core itself), which are all sharing the same clock generator crystal with the same divider, and thus the same frequency. This could be an entire package, half a package, or even just one SMT core with multiple logical processors.

- Which particular cores should be made unavailable to the scheduler engine (see Chapter 5 in Part 1 for more information on scheduling) in order to reduce attempts to make those selected cores busy again. These selected cores are called *parked cores.* Note that hard affinity settings will still force the scheduler to pick one of these "unavailable" cores, as described later.

> **Note** In its current implementation, core parking does not rebalance interrupts or shift software timers away from parked cores, but it may do so in the future.

To summarize, core parking aggressively puts processors in their deepest idle (C) states (not necessarily P states) and tries to keep them that way.

Core Parking Policies

Because the power requirements and usage models of desktop machines vary from those of server machines, core parking implements two internal policies for managing processor cores. The first policy, called *core parking override,* is used by default on client systems. This policy has lower idle thresholds for when to begin parking (that is, it parks more aggressively) and, most importantly, always leaves one thread in an SMT package unparked—in other words, it is responsible for essentially disabling the Hyper-Threading feature found on Intel CPUs until load warrants it. This effect is shown in Figure 8-46: CPU 1 and CPU 3 are parked because they correspond to the second thread of CPU 0's and CPU 2's SMT sets.

The second core parking policy is the default behavior, which is to say that it does not make any special considerations for SMT cores. This policy is also paired with less aggressive threshold parameters that are more suitable for server workloads, in which load is usually low during the majority of the time but all processors should be readily available when peaks are hit.

Additionally, the engine is tuned to avoid coalescing processing too much to a single node or subset of nodes. Although consolidating work has energy benefits because less power is distributed or wasted across the system, it now adds significant contention to the memory controller(s), which on a distributed NUMA system would have been less busy because of the scheduler's ideal node and process-seed selection algorithms. (See Chapter 5 in Part 1 for more information.) Therefore, core parking has to walk an interesting tightrope between reducing power, increasing cache and memory access effectiveness, and reducing contention on node-local resources. An example of this balancing act is that the core parking engine will always keep at least one core available per NUMA node to keep the scheduler's spreading efforts useful and to help support applications that specifically partition their workloads across nodes through NUMA-aware thread affinity and memory allocation.

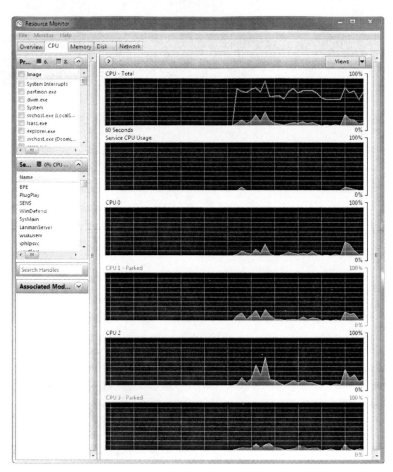

FIGURE 8-46 Resource Monitor showing core parking effects on SMT systems

Utility Function

Decisions taken by the PPM engine as to whether to modify the power state of a core, as well as which cores to park or unpark, are gated by one primal metric: utility. The utility of a processor represents, in the engine's view, the load of a given core and is computed by multiplying the average frequency of a core (expressed as a percentage of its maximum) by the busy period of the core (expressed as a percentage of non-idle time). Because two percentages are being multiplied, the maximum utility is 10,000, and almost all the engine's calculations are done by comparing utility (actually, as we show later, a value derived from utility) with some threshold or average.

> **Note** On modern processors, the average frequency is obtained by invoking the feedback handler associated with the current power domain, which is managed by the vendor-supplied power management driver (such as Intelppm.sys). If a feedback mechanism is not available, the current domain's frequency is used instead.

Because the utility of a processor can, obviously, change rapidly over time, the engine builds a history of the utilities of each core, as well as a core's average frequency. It also keeps a running sum of the utilities added up over time, such that the final averaged utility is calculated as the running sum divided by the number of history entries.

EXPERIMENT: Viewing Utility and Frequency Information

As with most other PPM-related information, the KPRCB stores information on the current utility as well as the utility history. Furthermore, a few debugger extensions are also available to easily visualize PPM utility information.

When you run the *!ppm* kernel debugger command, you should see output similar to the following, which shows information for LP 0:

```
lkd> !ppm

Processor 0

  Idle States (3)
    0: C1 - intelppm
    1: C2 - intelppm
    2: C3 - intelppm
  Last Used Idle State:    2

  Current Frequency:    100%
  HardwareFeedback:     55%
  Maximum Policy:       100%
  Platform Cap:         100%
  Minimum Policy:       5%
  Minimum Performace:   44%
  Minimum Throttle:     5%

  Utility:              5400
```

Highlighted in bold are the three values that were described earlier. The utility of this processor is 5400, and it is currently running at 100 percent of its maximum frequency. The hardware feedback is the average frequency from the feedback handler described previously, which the Intelppm.sys vendor-supplied PPM driver has calculated as 55 percent on this processor.

You can also look at the PPM information for other processors while in a remote debugging session by using the ~ (tilde) command to switch processors. When using the local kernel debugger, you have to dump the KPRCB structure manually and list the *.PowerState* substructure, as shown in the following output. In this example, the PPM state for LP 1 is dumped.

```
lkd> !running -i

System Processors:   (0000000f)
  Idle Processors:   (0000000a)

     Prcbs     Current (pri) Next    (pri) Idle
  0  8376cd20  87f0b030 (12)                83776380   . . . . . . . . . . . . . . .
  1  8b404120  8b409800 ( 0)                8b409800   . . . . . . . . . . . . . . .
```

```
2    8b43a120  86e6ed48 (11)              8b43f800  . . . . . . . . . . . . . .
3    8b470120  8b475800 ( 0)              8b475800  . . . . . . . . . . . . . .

lkd> dt nt!_KPRCB 8b404120    PowerState.
  +0x33a0 PowerState  :
      +0x000 IdleStates   : 0x877ff890 _PPM_IDLE_STATES
      +0x008 IdleTimeLast : 0xed
      +0x010 IdleTimeTotal : 0xadae7baa
...
```

EXPERIMENT: Viewing Utility and Frequency History

If the current core parking policy enables history tracking (which is normally disabled on client systems), you can also see the utility function over time, as well as the frequency. To do so, a different kernel extension has to used, *!ppmstate*.

Here's the output of *!ppmstate* on a server system with core parking enabled:

```
lkd> !ppmstate


Prcb.PowerState - 0x837700c0

  IdleStates:            0x877fe1b0
  IdleTimeLast:          0.000.006us (0x860 )
  IdleTimeTotal:         11:35.968.474us (0x6bc4ae5f )
  IdleAccounting:        0x874d8008

  Hypervisor State:      0x0
  LastPerfCheck:         13:20.311.497us (0x7becdf55)
  PerfDomain:            0x874d9c50
  PerfConstraint:        0x874d9cc8
  Utility:               0xf6c

  PerfHistory:           0x88604300
  PerfHistory contents   (3 slots, oldest to newest)

    Slot    Utility    Frequency
       0       3435          82%
       1      10800         108%
       2      10900         109%

  ThermalConstraint:     100%
  PerfActionDPC:         0x83770120
  PerfActionMask:        0x0
  WmiDispatchPtr:        nt!PpmWmiDispatch
  WmiInterfaceEnabled:   0x1

  CurrentKernelUserTime:   0xc59e
  CurrentIdleThreadKTime:  0xb556
```

Unlike with *!ppm*, you can also easily use *!ppmstate* during local kernel debugging because the extension accepts the address of the *PowerState* field of any KPRCB as a parameter.

When parking and unparking cores, the engine also uses a secondary metric called *generic utility*. Generic utility is the sum of all the utility functions across all the processors involved in the core parking algorithm. This value is used to gauge the overall activity level of the system and is later converted into a percentage (this will be described later in the algorithm section). Thus, because administrators and users set power policies on a systemwide basis and not on a processor basis (while core parking works at the processor level), generic utility is needed to convert the per-processor utility function into a systemwide representation of utility.

Algorithm Overrides

Since core parking is decoupled from the scheduler (which is what developers have some control over), there are a few scenarios in which the scheduler's goals must override those of the core parking engine. The first scenario is forced affinitization. When discussing the scheduler's algorithms in Chapter 5 in Part 1, we noted that the scheduler will sometimes forcefully pick a parked core if it is the ideal processor of a thread and when no unparked cores are available. When this happens, the core parking engine is made aware because the affinity count in the KPRCB's power state is incremented. Over time, the engine builds a weighted history (as configured by policy) of cores that are repeatedly targeted by hard-affinitized policy and, past a certain threshold, also configured by policy, will cause the engine to react appropriately (this will be described in the algorithm outlined later in this section).

A second override occurs whenever a core is parked (which means that a low, or zero, utility function is expected), yet the calculated utility is past the configured threshold. This override is not controllable through scheduling—in fact, it means that software timer expirations, DPCs, interrupts, and other similar scenarios have caused a parked core to run code outside the scheduler's purview. When such a situation is detected, the engine reacts differently, as described by the algorithm. Additionally, a history of such "overutilization" is kept, weighted according to the current policy, and it too will cause changes in the algorithm if it reaches a certain policy-configurable threshold.

Look back at Figure 8-46, which showed the Resource Monitor, and notice how CPU 1 and 3, even though parked, still had accumulated some CPU time. Depending on the current policy, one or more of those CPUs could have been considered overutilized.

Increase/Decrease Actions

Whenever the PPM engine is in a situation in which it must increase or decrease the amount of parked cores, or increase or decrease a given core's performance state, it can apply one of three different actions:

- **Ideal** In the ideal model, the engine tries to achieve a performance (frequency) midpoint between the decrease and increase thresholds when choosing a performance state (PERF-STATE_POLICY_CHANGE_IDEAL). When parking or unparking cores, it modifies the parked state of as many cores as needed until the generic utility distribution across unparked cores reaches a value that is just below or above the increase or decrease threshold, respectively (CORE_PARKING_POLICY_CHANGE_IDEAL).

- **Step** In the step model, the engine increases or decreases performance (frequency) by one frequency step (if specific frequency steps are exposed through ACPI) or by 5 percent as needed (PERFSTATE_POLICY_CHANGE_STEP). When parking or unparking cores, it always picks just one more core to park or unpark (CORE_PARKING_POLICY_CHANGE_STEP).

- **Rocket** In the rocket model, the engine sets the core to its maximum or minimum performance (frequency) state (PERFSTATE_POLICY_CHANGE_ROCKET). When parking, it parks all cores (except one per node, or whatever the current policy specifies), and when unparking, it unparks all cores (CORE_PARKING_POLICY_CHANGE_ROCKET).

Later in this section, when we look at the actual core parking algorithm, we'll see when these increase and decrease actions are taken.

Thresholds and Policy Settings

Ultimately, what determines whether performance states will be pushed up or down and whether cores will be parked or unparked depends on the thresholds and policy settings that have been set in the registry, configured in particular for each processor vendor and type as well as across client and server systems, AC versus DC power, and different power plans (for example, High Performance, Balanced, or Low Power). Core parking uses the policy settings and thresholds shown in Table 8-10 through Table 8-14.

TABLE 8-10 Processor Performance Policies (GUID_PROCESSOR_PERF)

Policy GUID	Policy Meaning
INCREASE/DECREASE_THRESHOLD	Specifies the busy threshold that must be met before changing the processor's performance state
INCREASE/DECREASE_POLICY	Specifies the algorithm used to select a new performance state when the ideal performance state does not match the current performance state
INCREASE/DECREASE_TIME	Specifies the minimum number of performance check intervals since the last performance state change before the performance state can be changed
TIME_CHECK	Specifies the amount of time that must expire before processor performance states and parked cores may be reevaluated (in milliseconds)
BOOST_POLICY	Specifies how much processors may opportunistically increase frequency above maximum when allowed by current operating conditions
ALLOW_THROTTLING	Allows processors to use throttle states (T states) in addition to performance states.
HISTORY	Specifies the number of processor-performance time-check intervals to use when calculating the average utility

TABLE 8-11 Idle State Management Policies (GUID_PROCESSOR_IDLE)

Policy GUID	Policy Meaning
ALLOW_SCALING	Specifies whether the idle state promotion and demotion values should be scaled based on the current performance state
DISABLE	Specifies whether idle states should be disabled
TIME_CHECK	Specifies the time that must elapse since the last idle state promotion or demotion before idle states may be promoted or demoted again (in microseconds)
DEMOTE/PROMOTE_THRESHOLD	Specifies the busy threshold that must be met before changing the idle state of the processor

TABLE 8-12 Core Parking Policies (GUID_PROCESSOR_CORE_PARKING)

Policy GUID	Policy Meaning
INCREASE/DECREASE_THRESHOLD	Specifies the busy threshold that must be met before changing the number of cores that are unparked
INCREASE/DECREASE_POLICY	Specifies the algorithm used to select the number of cores to park or unpark when required
MAX/MIN_CORES	Specifies the number of unparked cores allowed (in a percentage)
INCREASE/DECREASE_TIME	Specifies the minimum number of performance-check intervals that must elapse before more cores can be parked or unparked
CORE_OVERRIDE	Ensures that at least one processor remains unparked per core
PERF_STATE	Specifies what performance state a processor enters when parked

TABLE 8-13 Affinity History Policies (GUID_PROCESSOR_CORE_PARKING_AFFINITY_HISTORY)

Policy GUID	Policy Meaning
DECREASE_FACTOR	Specifies the factor by which to decrease affinity history on each core after the current performance check
THRESHOLD	Specifies the threshold above which a core is considered to have had significant affinitized work scheduled to it while parked
WEIGHTING	Specifies the weighting given to each occurrence where affinitized work was scheduled to a parked core

TABLE 8-14 Overutilization Policies (GUID_PROCESSOR_CORE_PARKING_OVER_UTILIZATION)

Policy GUID	Policy Meaning
HISTORY_DECREASE_FACTOR	Specifies the factor by which to decrease the overutilization history on each core after the current performance check
HISTORY_THRESHOLD	Specifies the threshold above which a core is considered to have been recently overutilized while parked
WEIGHTING	Specifies the weighting given to each occurrence when a parked core is found to be overutilized
THRESHOLD	Specifies the busy threshold that must be met before a parked core is considered overutilized

EXPERIMENT: Viewing Current Core Parking Policy

When the *!popolicy* experiment was used in an earlier part of this chapter, it showed you only the system power policy, not the entire policy, which also covers PPM. By using the *dt* command with the correct structure type, you are also able to see the PPM policy, which covers the policy GUIDs that were shown in the preceding tables. Because the system power policy starts at offset 4, simply subtract 4 from the pointer returned by *!popolicy*.

```
lkd> !popolicy
SYSTEM_POWER_POLICY (R.1) @ 0x8377a6c4

lkd> dt nt!_POP_POWER_SETTING_VALUES 8377a6c0
...
```

```
  +0x10c AllowThrottling   : 0 ''
  +0x10d PerfHistoryCount  : 0x20 ' '
  +0x110 PerfTimeCheck     : 0xf
  +0x114 PerfIncreaseTime  : 1
  +0x118 PerfDecreaseTime  : 1
  +0x11c PerfIncreaseThreshold : 0x1e ''
  +0x11d PerfDecreaseThreshold : 0xa ''
  +0x11e PerfIncreasePolicy : 0x2 ''
  +0x11f PerfDecreasePolicy : 0x1 ''
  +0x120 PerfMinPolicy     : 0x5 ''
  +0x121 PerfMaxPolicy     : 0x64 'd'
  +0x124 PerfBoostPolicy   : 0x64
  +0x128 CoreParkingIncreaseThreshold : 0x55 'U'
  +0x129 CoreParkingDecreaseThreshold : 0x32 '2'
  +0x12a CoreParkingMaxCores : 0x64 'd'
  +0x12b CoreParkingMinCores : 0xa ''
  +0x12c CoreParkingIncreasePolicy : 0 ''
  +0x12d CoreParkingDecreasePolicy : 0 ''
  +0x130 CoreParkingIncreaseTime : 7
  +0x134 CoreParkingDecreaseTime : 0x14
  +0x138 CoreParkingAffinityHistoryDecreaseFactor : 0x2 ''
  +0x13a CoreParkingAffinityHistoryThreshold : 0x96
  +0x13c CoreParkingAffinityWeighting : 0x64
  +0x13e CoreParkingOverUtilizationHistoryDecreaseFactor : 0x2 ''
  +0x140 CoreParkingOverUtilizationHistoryThreshold : 0x28
  +0x142 CoreParkingOverUtilizationWeighting : 0x64
  +0x144 CoreParkingOverUtilizationThreshold : 0x3c '<'
  +0x145 ParkingCoreOverride : 0x1 ''
  +0x146 ParkingPerfState : 0 ''
```

Another way to see a more limited set of the current policy is to use the *!ppmperfpolicy* extension, which displays a few of the core policy settings:

```
lkd> !ppmperfpolicy

  MaxPerf:           100%
  MinPerf:           5%
  TimeCheck:         15 ms
  IncreaseTime:      1 time check period(s)
  DecreaseTime:      1 time check period(s)
  IncreaseThreshold: 30%
  DecreaseThreshold: 10%
  IncreasePolicy:    2
  DecreasePolicy:    1
  HistoryCount:      1
  BoostPolicy:       100
```

Performance Check

The algorithm that powers the PPM engine is called the *performance check*. It is executed by the *PpmCheckStart* timer callback, which runs periodically based on the current policy's performance-check interval. The callback acquires the policy lock and sets the initial phase to *PpmCheckPhase-Initiate*. It calls *PpmCheckRun*, which runs the algorithm illustrated in the following diagram.

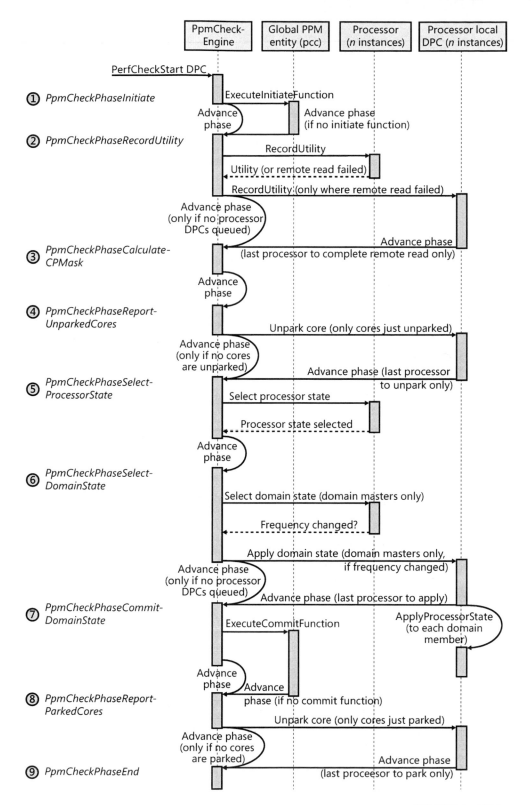

| | PpmCheck-Engine | Global PPM entity (pcc) | Processor (n instances) | Processor local DPC (n instances) |

PerfCheckStart DPC

① *PpmCheckPhaseInitiate*

ExecuteInitiateFunction

Advance phase

Advance phase (if no initiate function)

② *PpmCheckPhaseRecordUtility*

RecordUtility

Utility (or remote read failed)

RecordUtility (only where remote read failed)

Advance phase (only if no processor DPCs queued)

Advance phase (last processor to complete remote read only)

③ *PpmCheckPhaseCalculate-CPMask*

Advance phase

④ *PpmCheckPhaseReport-UnparkedCores*

Unpark core (only cores just unparked)

Advance phase (only if no cores are unparked)

Advance phase (last processor to unpark only)

⑤ *PpmCheckPhaseSelect-ProcessorState*

Select processor state

Processor state selected

Advance phase

⑥ *PpmCheckPhaseSelect-DomainState*

Select domain state (domain masters only)

Frequency changed?

Apply domain state (domain masters only, if frequency changed)

Advance phase (only if no processor DPCs queued)

Advance phase (last processor to apply)

⑦ *PpmCheckPhaseCommit-DomainState*

ApplyProcessorState (to each domain member)

ExecuteCommitFunction

Advance phase

Advance phase (if no commit function)

⑧ *PpmCheckPhaseReport-ParkedCores*

Unpark core (only cores just parked)

Advance phase (only if no cores are parked)

Advance phase (last processor to park only)

⑨ *PpmCheckPhaseEnd*

The steps shown in the diagram line up with the PPM_CHECK_PHASE enumeration described in Table 8-15.

TABLE 8-15 PPM Check Phases

Phase Name	Phase Meaning
PpmCheckPhaseInitiate	Notifies the vendor-supplied processor power driver that the core parking engine is about to start its performance check
PpmCheckPhaseRecordUtility	Runs on each processor to calculate the utility function for each core
PpmCheckPhaseCalculateCoreParkingMask	Using the utility function, current core parking status, affinitization, and overutilization history, organizes all the cores in different sets that are used to determine the best cores to unpark or park. It then performs the unparking of cores
PpmCheckPhaseReportUnparkedCores	Runs on each unparked processor to notify the scheduler that the core has been unparked
PpmCheckPhaseSelectProcessorState	Computes the new performance state (target frequency) for each processor based on its parking state and utility
PpmCheckPhaseSelectDomainState	Selects the best performance state for all the processors in a given domain based on the constraints, and switches to the new processor performance state
PpmCheckPhaseCommitDomainState	Calls the vendor-supplied processor power driver to commit the new processor performance states
PpmCheckPhaseReportParkedCores	Runs on each parked processor to notify the scheduler that the core has been unparked. Any ongoing or queued thread activity is moved off the core.
PpmCheckPhaseEnd	Releases the policy lock and switches the phase to the not-running phase
PpmCheckPhaseNotRunning	Indicates that the performance check is not running

Some of the steps in Table 8-15 require a bit more discussion than just a single line. Here are extended details.

Step 2: Recording utility   *PpmCheckRecordAllUtility* enumerates all processors that are part of the core parking engine's current registered set and determines which ones it will query for utility remotely (that is, from the current core running the check algorithm) or whether it will force a targeted DPC to query utility locally. This determination is made by calling *PpmPerfRecordUtility* and hinges on the idleness of the core and its current utility value. Because these numbers end up multiplied together, the busier a core becomes (higher utility), the greater the inaccuracy of not having precise frequency measurements becomes, the latter being a side effect of running the check on a remote instead of a local core.

Additionally, while running locally, the function can also check whether the CPU was throttled outside the PPM's purview, usually indicating broken firmware or drivers (or the existence of a power management strategy that is outside the OS's view and/or control).

Other than those checks, recording the utility is ultimately about computing the value described earlier in the "Utility Function" section and keeping track of its history, if the policy enables it.

Step 4: Choosing which cores to unpark The work in this step is done by two functions. The first, *PpmPerfCalculateCoreParkingMask*, computes how many cores should be unparked and builds a variety of sets that can be used to prioritize unparking:

- **Overutilized cores** Those whose utility is higher than the policy threshold, as described in the "Algorithm Overrides" section.

- **Previously overutilized cores** Cores that were overutilized during the previous performance check, as described in the "Algorithms Overrides" section.

- **Affinitized cores** Cores that have been forcefully chosen by the scheduler because of affinitization overrides, also described in the "Algorithms Overrides" section.

- **Unparked cores** Cores that are already unparked.

- **Highly utilized unparked codes** Unparked cores with a high utility function.

The function then computes the generic utility (described in the "Utility Function" section) and determines whether the generic utility percentage (defined as the generic utility divided by the sum of busy frequencies across all cores) is above or below the thresholds specified in the policy. Based on which threshold is crossed, if any, the policy-defined increase/decrease action (described in the "Increase/Decrease Actions" section earlier) is performed, which results in a count of cores to unpark.

This number, the generic utility, and the sets described earlier are sent to *PpmPerfChooseCoresToUnpark*, which is responsible for picking which processors should be unparked based on how to spread the generic utility. The algorithm first checks whether the target count is already covered by the already unparked cores, and if so, exits. Otherwise, it keeps unparking cores until the overutilized group is enough to handle the remaining unpark requests. In other words, overutilized cores always become unparked, and the algorithm must pick which other, nonoverutilized cores, should also be unparked.

To do so, it runs the following elimination round in the specified order. Each step is taken only if it results in a nonzero intersection (if other candidates exist):

- Remove any processors that are not already overutilized

- Remove any processors that are not already highly utilized

- Remove any processors that are not already unparked

- Remove any processors that were not previously overutilized

- Remove any processors that do not have forced affinitized threads

In the most optimistic scenario, this results in a set of overutilized, highly utilized, previously overutilized, and forced-affinitized processors. In other words, this set contains the processors least likely to benefit from parking in the first place. From this set, the core parking engine picks the lowest processor number and then enters a new round of elimination until the conditions specified earlier match.

At the end of the algorithm, after all overutilized cores and noneliminated cores have been un-parked, the generic utility is balanced (distributed equally) across all the newly unparked processors.

Step 5: Selecting processor state *PpmPerfSelectProcessorStates* enumerates each processor that's part of this run and calls *PpmPerfSelectProcessorState* for each one. In this case, the algorithm can run remotely (without requiring a local DPC callback on the core) because all the data is available from the KPRCB. The purpose of this function is to decide which processor state makes the most sense for the given processor, based on its expected utility function.

The first check is to verify whether this processor has been selected for parking in step 3. If it was selected, the target power state for parked cores, based on policy, is selected. Three possibilities exist:

- **Lightest**   The parked processor is targeted to run at 100 percent of its frequency.

- **Deepest**   The parked processor is targeted to run at 1 percent of its frequency.

- **No Preference**   The parked processor will be treated just like any other processor and continue the regular algorithm.

Assuming that the algorithm does continue, the next step is to compute the busyness of the processor. Since the utility function is equal to the busyness percentage multiplied by the average frequency, this means that the busyness of the processor is its utility divided by its average frequency. This busyness is then compared with the increase and/or decrease thresholds specified by policy, and one of the three possible actions are taken (ideal, step, or rocket, described earlier in "Increase/Decrease Actions").

The domain performance handler callback (owned by the vendor-supplied processor driver) is then called with the new target frequencies and with whether throttling was allowed by the policy.

Step 6: Selecting domain state As shown in the previous illustration, this step is also composed of a few substeps. The first, done remotely, is performed by *PpmPerfSelectDomainStates*, which picks the domain masters and calls *PpmPerfSelectDomainState* to run on them. This function iterates over all the processors in the domain and picks the one with the highest performance state (the highest desired frequency). It then sets this as the desired frequency for the entire domain.

Now that each domain master has selected its domain state, control returns to *PpmPerfSelect-DomainStates*, which queues a local DPC for all of the domain masters that is implemented by *PpmPerfApplyDomainState*. This is the second step. This function takes into consideration the valid P states (and T states, if throttling is enabled by policy) and trims any states outside the current processor constraints, which include percentage caps and thermal caps. When it has picked the best target frequency (and consulted with the domain performance handler callback), it queues a DPC to all the processors in each domain to apply the selected performance state to each core.

In this third step, implemented by the *PpmPerfApplyProcessorState* DPC routine, the domain's performance handler callback is called to switch states. Finally, *PpmScaleIdleStateValues* is called. If idle scaling is enabled by policy, this function scales the processor's C states (idle states) according to the promotion/demotion percentages specified in the policy.

EXPERIMENT: Viewing Current PPM Check Information

The kernel debugger includes an extension, *!ppmcheck,* which you can use to check whether core parking is enabled and which cores are currently parked, as well as the internal performance checking algorithm state. Here's a sample output of the extension:

```
lkd> !ppmcheck
        PpmCheckArmed:          TRUE
        PpmCheckStartDpc:       0x8377aa58
        PpmCheckDpc:            0x8377aa78
        PpmCheckTimer:          0x8377aa30
        PpmCheckMakeupCount:    -
        PpmCheckLastExecutionTime: -
        PpmCheckTime:           08:40.738.783us (0x50a26d3d)
        PpmCheckPhase:          9
        PpmCheckRegistered:     0x8376b408
          {[0000000F]}
        PpmPerfStatesRegistered: 0x8376b390
          {[0000000F]}
        CoreParkingEnabled:     TRUE
        CoreParkingMask:        0x8376b35c
          {[0000000A]}
```

You can also see the complete PPM information for a given processor by looking at the PRCB's *PowerState* field and further drilling down into the *Domain* and *PerfConstraint* members. This will show you the selected domain performance state, the constraints (thermal and frequency caps), and other accounting information. You can use *dt nt!_KPRCB @$prcb PowerState* to see this information for the current PRCB:

```
+0x33a0 PowerState  :
    +0x000 IdleStates  : 0x877fe1b0 _PPM_IDLE_STATES
    +0x008 IdleTimeLast : 0xa6
    +0x010 IdleTimeTotal : 0x97789fc9
    +0x018 IdleTimeEntry : 0
    +0x020 IdleAccounting : 0x874d8008 _PROC_IDLE_ACCOUNTING
    +0x024 Hypervisor  : 0 ( ProcHypervisorNone )
    +0x028 PerfHistoryTotal : 0
    +0x02c ThermalConstraint : 0x64 'd'
    +0x02d PerfHistoryCount : 0x1 ''
    +0x02e PerfHistorySlot : 0 ''
    +0x02f Reserved    : 0 ''
    +0x030 LastSysTime : 0xfa86
    +0x034 WmiDispatchPtr : 0x837c5464
    +0x038 WmiInterfaceEnabled : 0n1
    +0x040 FFHThrottleStateInfo : _PPM_FFH_THROTTLE_STATE_INFO
    +0x060 PerfActionDpc : _KDPC
    +0x080 PerfActionMask : 0n0
    +0x088 IdleCheck   : _PROC_IDLE_SNAP
    +0x098 PerfCheck   : _PROC_IDLE_SNAP
    +0x0a8 Domain      : 0x874d9c50 _PROC_PERF_DOMAIN
    +0x0ac PerfConstraint : 0x874d9cc8 _PROC_PERF_CONSTRAINT
    +0x0b0 Load        : (null)
```

```
       +0x0b4 PerfHistory : (null)
       +0x0b8 Utility      : 0xba8
       +0x0bc OverUtilizedHistory : 0
       +0x0c0 AffinityCount : 0
       +0x0c4 AffinityHistory : 0

lkd> dt  0x874d9c50 _PROC_PERF_DOMAIN
nt!_PROC_PERF_DOMAIN
   +0x000 Link             : _LIST_ENTRY [ 0x8376b39c - 0x8376b39c ]
   +0x008 Master           : 0x8b470120 _KPRCB
   +0x00c Members          : _KAFFINITY_EX
   +0x018 FeedbackHandler  : 0x93d19d08     unsigned char  +0
   +0x01c GetFFHThrottleState : 0x93d1804e     void  +0
   +0x020 BoostPolicyHandler : 0x93d18104     void  +0
   +0x024 PerfSelectionHandler : 0x93d19bee     unsigned long  +0
   +0x028 PerfHandler      : 0x93d19d40     void  +0
   +0x02c Processors       : 0x874d9cc8 _PROC_PERF_CONSTRAINT
   +0x030 PerfChangeTime   : 0xaa90c1ed
   +0x038 ProcessorCount   : 4
   +0x03c PreviousFrequencyMhz : 0x532
   +0x040 CurrentFrequencyMhz : 0xa65
   +0x044 PreviousFrequency : 0x31
   +0x048 CurrentFrequency : 0x64
   +0x04c CurrentPerfContext : 0
   +0x050 DesiredFrequency : 0x64
   +0x054 MaxFrequency     : 0xa65
   +0x058 MinPerfPercent   : 0x2c
   +0x05c MinThrottlePercent : 5
   +0x060 MaxPercent       : 0x64
   +0x064 MinPercent       : 5
   +0x068 ConstrainedMaxPercent : 0x64
   +0x06c ConstrainedMinPercent : 0x2c
   +0x070 Coordination     : 0x1 ''
   +0x074 PerfChangeIntervalCount : 0n0

lkd> dt 0x874d9cc8 _PROC_PERF_CONSTRAINT
ntdll!_PROC_PERF_CONSTRAINT
   +0x000 Prcb             : 0x8376cd20 _KPRCB
   +0x004 PerfContext      : 0x877febe0
   +0x008 PercentageCap    : 0x64
   +0x00c ThermalCap       : 0x64
   +0x010 TargetFrequency  : 0x36
   +0x014 AcumulatedFullFrequency : 0x46c3df
   +0x018 AcumulatedZeroFrequency : 0xd51828
   +0x01c FrequencyHistoryTotal : 0
   +0x020 AverageFrequency : 0x36
```

Conclusion

The I/O system defines the model of I/O processing on Windows and performs functions that are common to or required by more than one driver. Its chief responsibility is to create IRPs representing I/O requests and to shepherd the packets through various drivers, returning results to the caller when an I/O is complete. The I/O manager locates various drivers and devices by using I/O system objects, including driver and device objects. Internally, the Windows I/O system operates asynchronously to achieve high performance and provides both synchronous and asynchronous I/O capabilities to user-mode applications.

Device drivers include not only traditional hardware device drivers but also file system, network, and layered filter drivers. All drivers have a common structure and communicate with one another and the I/O manager by using common mechanisms. The I/O system interfaces allow drivers to be written in a high-level language to lessen development time and to enhance their portability. Because drivers present a common structure to the operating system, they can be layered one on top of another to achieve modularity and reduce duplication between drivers. Also, all Windows device drivers should be designed to work correctly on multiprocessor systems.

Finally, the role of the PnP manager is to work with device drivers to dynamically detect hardware devices and to build an internal device tree that guides hardware device enumeration and driver installation. The power manager works with device drivers to move devices into low-power states when applicable to conserve energy and prolong battery life.

Three more upcoming chapters will cover additional topics related to the I/O system: storage management, file systems (including details on the NTFS file system), and the cache manager.

CHAPTER 9

Storage Management

Storage management defines the way that an operating system interfaces with nonvolatile storage devices and media. The term *storage* encompasses many different devices, including optical media, USB flash drives, floppy disks, hard disks, solid state disks (SSDs), network storage such as iSCSI, storage area networks (SANs), and virtual storage such as VHDs (virtual hard disks). Windows provides specialized support for each of these classes of storage media. Because our focus in this book is on the kernel components of Windows, in this chapter we'll concentrate on just the fundamentals of the hard disk storage subsystem in Windows, which includes support for external disks and flash drives. Significant portions of the support Windows provides for removable media and remote storage (offline archiving) are implemented in user mode.

In this chapter, we'll examine how kernel-mode device drivers interface file system drivers to disk media, discuss how disks are partitioned, describe the way volume managers abstract and manage volumes, and present the implementation of multipartition disk-management features in Windows, including replicating and dividing file system data across physical disks for reliability and for performance enhancement. We'll also describe how file system drivers mount volumes they are responsible for managing, and we'll conclude by discussing drive encryption technology in Windows and support for automatic backups and recovery.

Storage Terminology

To fully understand the rest of this chapter, you need to be familiar with some basic terminology:

- *Disks* are physical storage devices such as a hard disk, CD-ROM, DVD, Blu-ray, solid state disk (SSD), or flash.

- A disk is divided into *sectors*, which are addressable blocks of fixed size. Sector sizes are determined by hardware. Most hard disk sectors are 512 bytes (but are moving to 4,096 bytes), and CD-ROM sectors are typically 2,048 bytes. For more information on moving to 4,096-byte sectors, see *http://support.microsoft.com/kb/2510009*.

- *Partitions* are collections of contiguous sectors on a disk. A partition table or other disk-management database stores a partition's starting sector, size, and other characteristics and is located on the same disk as the partition.

- *Simple volumes* are objects that represent sectors from a single partition that file system drivers manage as a single unit.

- *Multipartition volumes* are objects that represent sectors from multiple partitions and that file system drivers manage as a single unit. Multipartition volumes offer performance, reliability, and sizing features that simple volumes do not.

Disk Devices

From the perspective of Windows, a disk is a device that provides addressable long-term storage for blocks of data, which are accessed using file system drivers. In other words, each byte on the disk does not have its own address, but each block does have an address. These blocks are known as *sectors* and are the basic unit of storage and transfer to and from the device (in other words, all transfers must be a multiple of the sector size). Whether the device is implemented using rotating magnetic media (hard disk or floppy disk) or solid state memory (flash disk or thumb drive) is irrelevant.

Windows supports a wide variety of interconnect mechanisms for attaching a disk to a system, including SCSI, SAS (Serial Attached SCSI), SATA (Serial Advanced Technology Attachment), USB, SD/MMC, and iSCSI.

Rotating Magnetic Disks

The typical disk drive (often referred to as a *hard disk*) is built using one or more rigid rotating platters covered in a magnetic material. An arm containing a *head* moves back and forth across the surface of the platter reading and writing bits that are stored magnetically.

Disk Sector Format

While the disk interconnect mechanisms have been evolving since IBM introduced hard disks in 1956 and have become faster and more intelligent, the underlying disk format has changed very little, except for annual increases in areal density (the number of bits per square inch). Since the inception of disk drives, the data portion of a disk sector has typically been 512 bytes.

Disk storage areal density has increased from 2,000 bits per square inch in 1956 to over 650 billion bits per square inch in 2011, with most of that gain coming in the last 15 years. Disk manufacturers are reaching the physical limits of current magnetic disk technology, so they are changing the format of the disks: increasing the sector size from 512 bytes to 4,096 bytes, and changing the size of the error correcting code (ECC) from 50 bytes to 100 bytes. This new disk format is known as the *advanced format*. The size of the advanced format sector was chosen because it matches the x86 page size and the NTFS cluster size. The advanced format provides about 10 percent greater capacity by reducing the amount of overhead per sector (everything except the data area is overhead) and through better error correcting capabilities. (A single 100-byte ECC is better than eight 50-byte ECCs). The downside to advanced format disks is potentially wasted space for small files, but as you'll see in Chapter 12, "File Systems," NTFS has a mechanism for efficiently storing small files.

Advanced format disks provide an emulation mechanism (known as 512e) for legacy operating systems that understand only 512-byte sectors. With 512e, the host does not know that the disk supports 4,096-byte sectors; it continues to read and write 512-byte sectors (called *logical blocks*). The disk's controller will translate a logical block number into the correct physical sector. For example, if the host issues a read request for logical block number 6, then the disk controller will read physical sector number 0 into its internal buffer and return only the 512-byte portion corresponding to logical block 6 to the host, as shown in Figure 9-1.

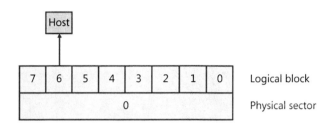

FIGURE 9-1 Advanced format sector with 512e

Writes are a little more complicated in that they require the disk's controller to perform a read-modify-write operation, as shown in Figure 9-2.

1. The host writes logical block 6 to the controller.

2. The controller maps logical block 6 to physical sector 0 and reads the entire sector into the controller's memory.

3. The controller copies logical block 6 into its position within the copy of the physical sector in the controller's memory.

4. The controller writes the 4,096-byte physical sector from memory back to the disk.

Obviously, there is a performance penalty associated with using 512e, but advanced format disks will still work with legacy operating systems.

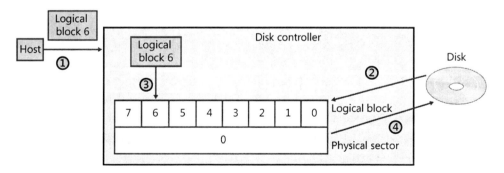

FIGURE 9-2 512e read-modify-write operation

Windows supports native 4,096-byte advance format sectors, so there is no additional read-modify-write overhead. As you will see in Chapter 12, NTFS was written to support sectors of more than 512 bytes and by default issues disk I/Os using a 4,096-byte *cluster*. The Windows cache manager (see Chapter 11) will attempt to reduce the penalty of applications assuming 512-byte sectors; however, applications should be upgraded to query the size of a disk's sectors (by issuing an IOCTL_STORAGE_QUERY_PROPERTY I/O request and examining the returned *BytesPerPhysicalSector* value) and not assume 512-byte sectors when performing sector I/O. It is very important that partitioning tools understand the size of a disk's physical sectors and align partitions to physical sector boundaries because partitions must be an integral number of physical sectors.

Solid State Disks

Recently, the cost of manufacturing flash memory has decreased to the point where manufacturers are building storage subsystems with a disk-type interface, calling the device a *solid state disk* (SSD) or *flash disk*. As far as Windows is concerned, an SSD is a disk, but there are some important differences between a rotating disk and an SSD that Windows has to support. Before getting into the details of how Windows supports SSDs, let's look at how an SSD is implemented.

Flash memory in some respects is very similar to a computer's RAM (random access memory), except that flash memory does not lose its contents when the power is removed, which means that flash memory is nonvolatile. The most common types of flash memory are NOR and NAND. NOR flash memory is operationally the closest to RAM in that each byte is individually addressable, while NAND flash memory is organized into blocks, like a disk. Typically, NOR-type flash memory is used to hold the BIOS on your computer's motherboard, and NAND-type flash memory is used in SSDs.

The most important difference between flash memory and RAM is that RAM can be read and written an almost infinite number of times, while flash memory can be overwritten something less than 100,000 times. (Depending on the type of flash memory, it may be as few as 1,000 times). In effect, flash memory wears out, so flash memory should be treated more like media with a limited lifetime (such as a floppy disk) than RAM or a magnetic disk. Another major difference between flash memory and RAM is that flash memory cannot be updated in place; a block must be erased before it can be written (even for NOR-type flash memory). Flash memory is significantly faster than magnetic disks (usually by a factor of 100,000, or so; access time: 50 nanoseconds versus 5 milliseconds), but it is slower than RAM (usually by a factor of 50). From a practical perspective, memory access time is not the whole story because flash memory is not on the system memory bus. Instead, it sits behind a disk-type controller interface on an I/O bus, so in reality the difference between flash and magnetic disks may be on the order of only 1,000 times faster, and in some workloads a rotating magnetic disk can outperform a low-end SSD.

NAND-Type Flash Memory

NAND-type flash memory is most commonly used in SSDs, so that is what we will examine in detail. NAND-type flash comes in two types:

- Single-level cell (SLC) stores 1 bit per internal cell, has a higher number of program/erase cycles (on the order of 100,000), and is significantly faster than multilevel cell (MLC), but it is much more expensive than MLC.

- Multilevel cell (MLC) stores multiple bits per internal cell and is significantly cheaper than SLC. MLC needs more ECC bits than SLC, has fewer erase cycles (~5,000), and consumes more power than SLC.

NAND-type flash is typically organized into 4,096-byte pages (which may be exposed as eight 512-byte sectors or a single 4,096-byte sector), which are the smallest readable or writable units, and the pages are grouped into blocks of 64 to 1,024 pages, with thousands of blocks per chip. As with a magnetic disk, there is overhead on each page, with ECC, page health, and spare bits. The block is the smallest erasable unit, so to change a single sector within a page requires that the entire block be erased and then rewritten. (Flash cells can be written only after they have been erased.) This means that writing a sector to an empty block is very fast, but if there is not an available empty block, the controller has to perform the following actions:

1. Read the entire block into the controller's internal RAM.

2. Erase the block in the flash memory.

3. Update the block in RAM with the contents of the new sector.

4. Write the entire block to the flash memory.

Notice that what started as a write to a sector (512 bytes) became a write of an entire block. For this example, if we assume 128 pages in a block and a completely full block, then the write would take 1,023 times longer (the block contains 1,024 sectors) than the write of a single sector to an empty block. This example is a worst case and is decidedly not the norm, but it illustrates an important aspect of SSDs: as more and more of the SSD's memory is consumed, it will have to rewrite substantially more data than a single sector. In effect, SSDs slow down as they fill up. This has important implications that are addressed in the next section, "File Deletion and the Trim Command."

As a block wears out, eventually it will fail to erase. Also, the more a block is erased and rewritten, the slower it becomes (a result of the physics behind how flash memory is implemented). This means that an SSD will only get slower as you use it—even on an empty block. For example, on a 1-GB USB MLC flash disk with 128 pages per block (giving us 2,048 blocks), erasing and writing one block per second would wear out all the blocks in 23.7 days (assuming a maximum of 1,000 erase cycles per block, which is typical for the cheaper flash disks). Erasing and writing the same block once per second will wear out that block in only 16.6 minutes! SSDs typically have spare blocks held in reserve (often 20 percent of the SSD's capacity) so that if a block wears out, the data is moved to a spare block. Clearly, flash memory cannot be used the same way as RAM or a magnetic disk.

The flash memory controller implements a technique called *wear-leveling* to spread the wear (erases) across the SSD. Wear-leveling depends on the fact that most of the data that you write to a disk is static; that is, it does not change often (it is usually read frequently, but that doesn't cause wear). Of course, there is also dynamic data (such as log files) that changes frequently. There are many different types of wear-leveling algorithms, but describing them is beyond the scope of this book. The important concept to understand about wear-leveling is that the controller will move data around within the flash memory in an attempt to spread writes across all the flash memory, thus prolonging the overall life of the SSD. An implication of wear-leveling is that more blocks are subjected to more frequent program/erase cycles in an attempt to extend the overall life of the flash memory, but when the drive fails (as they all do), then more blocks will fail at the same time. Keep in mind that the SSD industry is moving toward the point where SSDs will advertise their health more explicitly, and at the point of impending write failure they will become read-only drives.

File Deletion and the Trim Command

The file system keeps track of which areas of a disk are currently in use for each file, and when a file is deleted it does not zero all the areas on the disk that contained the file—if it did, then deleting a large file would take longer than deleting a small file, and file undelete utilities would not work. Instead, the file system driver will mark those areas of the disk as available in its data structures (usually referred to as *metadata*; see Chapter 12 for more information). This is not a problem for magnetic disks because they read and write sectors natively, but SSDs do not read and write sectors natively (recall that the size of the writable unit, the page, is much smaller than the size of the erasable unit, the block).

SSDs have to manage the contents of pages and blocks when updating a sector. This becomes a huge problem because the SSD does not know that the contents of a page are free unless it has been erased. The SSD would continue to preserve "deleted" data when updating a sector or during wear-leveling, reducing the amount of free space available to the SSD controller. The end result would be that the speed of the SSD would degrade up to the point at which all sectors have been accessed (at least once), and the only way to speed it up again would be to erase the entire drive. This is exactly the behavior that existed in early SSDs.

The solution to this problem was the introduction of the *trim* command to the SSD's controller. The file system detects that the SSD supports the trim command by sending the I/O request IOCTL_STORAGE_QUERY_PROPERTY with the property ID *StorageDeviceTrimProperty* down the storage stack (covered later in this chapter). When a file is deleted or truncated on a disk that supports the trim command, the file system sends the list of sectors that the file occupied to the disk driver, using the I/O request IOCTL_STORAGE_MANAGE_DATA_SET_ATTRIBUTES with the action parameter *DeviceDsmAction_Trim*. When the disk driver receives this I/O request, it sends a trim command to the SSD, notifying the SSD that those sectors are now free and may be erased and repurposed at the SSD's convenience. This lets the SSD reclaim those sectors during an update or wear-leveling operation, thereby improving the performance of the SSD. Note that the trim command cannot be queued internally within the SSD's controller and executes synchronously, which may manifest as a noticeable pause when a large file is being deleted.

While Windows does support SSDs, Microsoft recommends that they be backed up frequently if they are being used for important data. A standard disk defragmenter should never be used on an SSD because it will wear out the flash very quickly. The Windows defragmenter will not attempt to defragment an SSD. (Defragmenting an SSD isn't generally useful because file fragmentation does not slow down access to a file on an SSD in the same way that it does on a magnetic disk.) As we'll see in Chapter 12, NTFS was not designed with short-lived (flash memory) disks in mind, and it frequently issues lots of small writes to its transaction log, which is important for increasing reliability but causes additional wear to the flash memory. Using an SSD as your C: drive may drastically increase the speed of your system, but understand that the SSD will wear out before a magnetic disk would.

Note High-end magnetic disks can outperform low-end SSDs in some cases because many low-end SSDs perform poorly for small, random writes, which is a characteristic of the typical Windows workload.

Disk Drivers

The device drivers involved in managing a particular storage device are collectively known as a *storage stack*. Figure 9-3 shows each type of driver that might be present in a stack and includes a brief description of its purpose. This chapter describes the behavior of device drivers below the file system layer in the stack. (The file system driver operation is described in Chapter 12.)

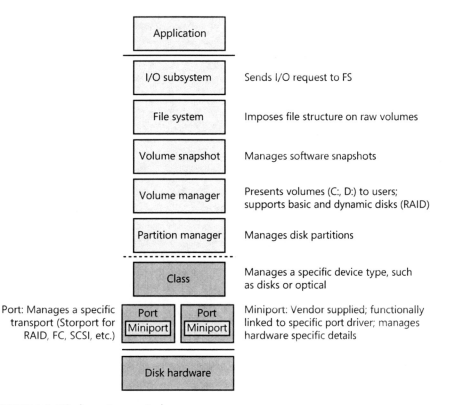

FIGURE 9-3 Windows storage stack

Winload

As you saw in Chapter 4, "Management Mechanisms," in Part 1, Winload is the Windows operating system file that conducts the first portion of the Windows boot process. Although Winload isn't technically part of the storage stack, it is involved with storage management because it includes support for accessing disk devices before the Windows I/O system is operational. Winload resides on the boot volume; the boot-sector code on the system volume executes Bootmgr. Bootmgr reads the Boot Configuration Database (BCD) from the system volume or EFI firmware and presents the computer's boot choices to the user. Bootmgr translates the name of the BCD boot entry that a user selects to the appropriate boot partition and then runs Winload to load the Windows system files (starting with the registry, Ntoskrnl.exe and its dependencies, and the boot drivers) into memory to continue the boot process. In all cases, Winload uses the computer firmware to read the disk containing the system volume.

Disk Class, Port, and Miniport Drivers

During initialization, the Windows I/O manager starts the disk storage drivers. Storage drivers in Windows follow a class/port/miniport architecture, in which Microsoft supplies a storage class driver that implements functionality common to all storage devices and a storage port driver that implements class-specific functionality common to a particular bus—such as SATA (Serial Advanced Technology Attachment), SAS (Serial Attached SCSI), or Fibre Channel—and OEMs supply miniport drivers that plug into the port driver to interface Windows to a particular controller implementation.

In the disk storage driver architecture, only class drivers conform to the standard Windows device driver interfaces. Miniport drivers use a port driver interface instead of the device driver interface, and the port driver simply implements a collection of device driver support routines that interface miniport drivers to Windows. This approach simplifies the role of miniport driver developers and, because Microsoft supplies operating system–specific port drivers, allows driver developers to focus on hardware-specific driver logic. Windows includes Disk (%SystemRoot%\System32\Drivers\ Disk.sys), a class driver that implements functionality common to all disks. Windows also provides a handful of disk port drivers. For example, %SystemRoot%\System32\Drivers\Scsiport.sys is the legacy port driver for disks on SCSI buses (Scsiport is now deprecated and should no longer be used), and %SystemRoot%\System32\Drivers\Ataport.sys is a port driver for IDE-based systems. Most newer drivers use the %SystemRoot%\System32\Drivers\Storport.sys port driver as a replacement for Scsiport.sys. Storport.sys is designed to realize the high performance capabilities of hardware RAID and Fibre Channel adapters. The Storport model is similar to Scsiport, making it easy for vendors to migrate existing Scsiport miniport drivers to Storport. Miniport drivers that developers write to use Storport take advantage of several of Storport's performance enhancing features, including support for the parallel execution of I/O initiation and completion on multiprocessor systems, a more controllable I/O request-queue architecture, and execution of more code at lower IRQL to minimize the duration of hardware interrupt masking. Storport also includes support for dynamic redirection of interrupts and DPCs to the best (most local) NUMA node (often referred to as *NUMA I/O*) on systems that support it.

Both the Scsiport.sys and Ataport.sys drivers implement a version of the disk scheduling algorithm known as C-LOOK. The drivers place disk I/O requests in lists sorted by the first sector (also known as the *logical block address,* or LBA) at which an I/O request is directed. They use the *KeInsertByKey-DeviceQueue* and *KeRemoveByKeyDeviceQueue* functions (documented in the Windows Driver Kit) representing I/O requests as items and using a request's starting sector as the key required by the functions. When servicing requests, the drivers proceed through the list from lowest sector to highest. When they reach the end of the list the drivers start back at the beginning, since new requests might have been inserted in the meantime. If disk requests are spread throughout a disk this approach results in the disk head continuously moving from near the outermost cylinders of the disk toward the innermost cylinders. Storport.sys does not implement disk scheduling because it is commonly used for managing I/Os directed at storage arrays where there is no clearly defined notion of a disk start and end.

Windows ships with several miniport drivers. On systems that have at least one ATAPI-based IDE device, %SystemRoot%\System32\Drivers\Atapi.sys, %SystemRoot%\System32\Drivers\Pciidex.sys, and %SystemRoot%\System32\Drivers\Pciide.sys together provide miniport functionality. Most Windows installations include one or more of the drivers mentioned.

iSCSI Drivers

The development of iSCSI as a disk transport protocol integrates the SCSI protocol with TCP/IP networking so that computers can communicate with block-storage devices, including disks, over IP networks. Storage area networking (SAN) is usually architected on Fibre Channel networking, but administrators can leverage iSCSI to create relatively inexpensive SANs from networking technology such as Gigabit Ethernet to provide scalability, disaster protection, efficient backup, and data protection. Windows support for iSCSI comes in the form of the Microsoft iSCSI Software Initiator, which is available on all editions of Windows.

The Microsoft iSCSI Software Initiator includes several components:

- **Initiator** This optional component, which consists of the Storport port driver and the iSCSI miniport driver (%SystemRoot%\System32\Drivers\Msiscsi.sys), uses the TCP/IP driver to implement software iSCSI over standard Ethernet adapters and TCP/IP offloaded network adapters.

- **Initiator service** This service, implemented in %SystemRoot%\System32\Iscsicli.exe, manages the discovery and security of all iSCSI initiators as well as session initiation and termination. iSCSI device discovery functionality is implemented in %SystemRoot%\System32\Iscsium.dll. An important goal of the iSCSI service is to provide a common discovery/management infrastructure irrespective of the protocol driver being used, which could be the Microsoft software initiator driver or an HBA driver (host bus adapter; iSCSI protocol handling offloaded to hardware, which is generally Storport miniports). In this context, iSCSI also provides Win32 and WMI interfaces for management and configuration. The iSCSI initiator service supports four discovery mechanisms:

  - **iSNS (Internet Storage Name Service)** The addresses of the iSNS servers that the iSCSI initiator service will use are statically configured using the *iscsicli AddiSNSServer* command.

- **SendTargets**   The SendTarget portals are statically configured using the *iscsicli AddTarget-Portal* command.

- **Host Bus Adapter Discovery**   iSCSI HBAs that conform to the iSCSI initiator service interfaces can participate in target discovery by means of an interface between the HBA and the iSCSI initiator service.

- **Manually Configured Targets**   iSCSI targets can be manually configured using the *iscsicli AddTarget* command or with the iSCSI Control Panel applet.

- **Management applications**   These include Iscsicli.exe, a command-line tool for managing iSCSI device connections and security, and the corresponding Control Panel application.

Some vendors produce iSCSI adapters that offload the iSCSI protocol to hardware. The initiator service works with these adapters, which must support the iSNS protocol (RFC 4171), so that all iSCSI devices, including those discovered by the initiator service and those discovered by iSCSI hardware, are recognized and managed through standard Windows interfaces.

Multipath I/O (MPIO) Drivers

Most disk devices have one *path*—or series of adapters, cables, and switches—between them and a computer. Servers requiring high levels of availability use *multipathing* solutions, where more than one set of connection hardware exists between the computer and a disk so that if a path fails, the system can still access the disk via an alternate path. Without support from the operating system or disk drivers, however, a disk with two paths, for example, appears as two different disks. Windows includes multipath I/O support to manage multipath disks as a single disk. This support relies on built-in or third-party drivers called *device-specific modules* (DSMs) to manage details of the path management—for example, load balancing policies that choose which path to use for routing requests and error detection mechanisms to inform Windows when a path fails. Built into Windows is a DSM (%SystemRoot%\System32\Drivers\Msdsm.sys) that works with all storage arrays that conform to the industry standard (T10 SPC4 specification) definition of asymmetric logical unit arrays (ALUA). Storage array vendors must write their own DSM if the modules are not ALUA-compliant. Support for writing a DSM is now part of the Windows Driver Kit. MPIO support is available as an optional feature for Windows Server 2008/R2, which must be installed via Server Manager. MPIO is not available on client editions of Windows.

In a Windows MPIO storage stack, shown in Figure 9-4, the disk driver includes functionality for MPIO devices, which in older versions of Windows was a separate driver (Mpdev.sys). Disk.sys is responsible for claiming ownership of device objects representing multipath disks—so that it can ensure that only one device object is created to represent those disks—and for locating the appropriate DSM to manage the paths to the device. The Multipath Bus Driver (%SystemRoot%\System32\Drivers\Mpio.sys) manages connections between the computer and the device, including power management for the device. Disk.sys informs Mpio.sys of the presence of the devices for it to manage. The port driver (and the miniport drivers beneath it) for a multipath disk is not MPIO-aware and does not participate in anything related to handling multiple paths. There are a total of three disk device stacks, two representing the physical paths (children of the adapter device stacks) and one representing the disk (child of the MPIO adapter device stack). When the latter receives a request, it uses the DSM to determine which path to forward that request to. The DSM makes the selection based on policy, and the request is sent to the corresponding disk device stack, which in turn forwards it to the device via the corresponding adapter.

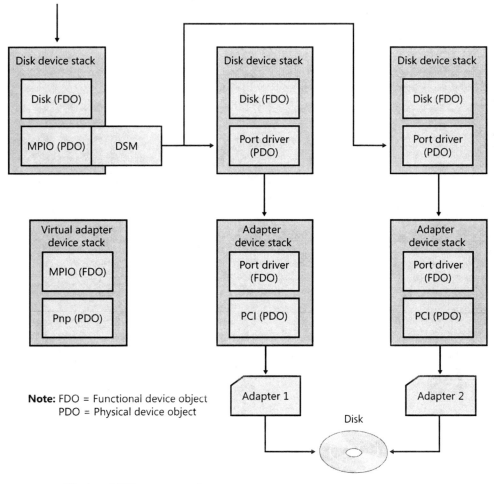

FIGURE 9-4 Windows MPIO storage stack

The system crash dump and hibernation mechanisms operate in a very restricted environment (very little operating system and device driver support). Drivers operating in this environment have some knowledge of MPIO, but there are limits as to what can be supported. For example, if one path to a disk is down, Windows can failover only to another disk that is controlled by the same miniport driver.

MPIO configuration management is provided through MPClaim (%SystemRoot%\System32\ Mpclaim.exe) and a disk properties tab in Explorer.

EXPERIMENT: Watching Physical Disk I/O

Diskmon from Windows Sysinternals (*www.microsoft.com/technet/sysinternals*) uses the disk class driver's Event Tracing for Windows (or ETW, which is described in Chapter 3, "System Mechanisms," in Part 1) instrumentation to monitor I/O activity to physical disks and display it in a window. Diskmon updates once a second with new data. For each operation, Diskmon shows the time, duration, target disk number, type and offset, and length, as you can see in the screen shown here.

#	Time	Duration (s)	Disk	Request	Sector	Length
21	5.034749	0.00643730	0	Write	222408832	8
22	5.035441	0.00643730	0	Write	27244544	8
23	5.072749	0.00643730	0	Write	27244544	8
24	5.073164	0.00643730	0	Write	258235032	32
25	5.074025	0.00643730	0	Write	222408840	24
26	5.074473	0.00643730	0	Write	258235064	32
27	5.074910	0.00643730	0	Write	256123320	32
28	5.075335	0.00643730	0	Write	256123224	32
29	5.075825	0.00643730	0	Write	31155656	8
30	5.136805	0.00643730	0	Write	31155656	8
31	5.137212	0.00643730	0	Write	222408832	8
32	5.137901	0.00643730	0	Write	27244552	8

Disk Device Objects

The Windows disk class driver creates device objects that represent disks. Device objects that represent disks have names of the form \Device\Harddisk*X*\DR*X*; the number that identifies the disk replaces both *X*s. To maintain compatibility with applications that use older naming conventions, the disk class driver creates symbolic links with Windows NT 4–formatted names that refer to the device objects the driver created. For example, the volume manager driver creates the link \Device\Harddisk0\Partition0 to refer to \Device\Harddisk0\DR0, and \Device\Harddisk0\Partition1 to refer to the first partition device object of the first disk. For backward compatibility with applications that expect legacy names, the disk class driver also creates the same symbolic links in Windows that represent physical drives that it would have created on Windows NT 4 systems. Thus, for example, the link \GLOBAL??\PhysicalDrive0 references \Device\Harddisk0\DR0. Figure 9-5 shows the WinObj utility from Sysinternals displaying the contents of a Harddisk directory for a basic disk. You can see the physical disk and partition device objects in the pane at the right.

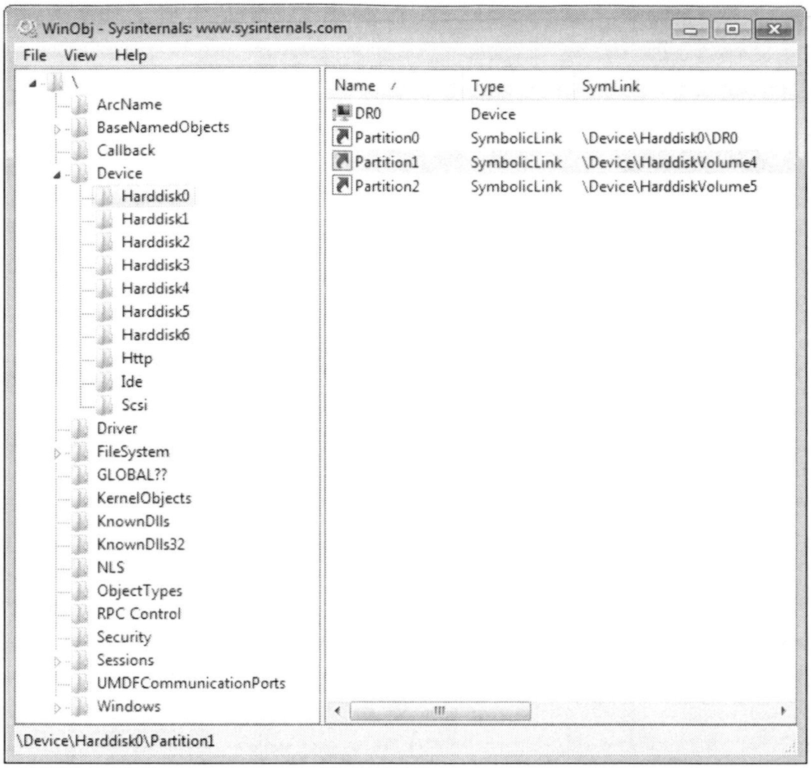

FIGURE 9-5 WinObj showing a Harddisk directory of a basic disk

As you saw in Chapter 3 in Part 1, the Windows API is unaware of the Windows object manager namespace. Windows reserves two groups of namespace subdirectories to use, one of which is the \Global?? subdirectory. (The other group is the collection of per-session \BaseNamedObjects subdirectories, which are covered in Chapter 3.) In this subdirectory, Windows makes available device objects that Windows applications interact with—including COM and parallel ports—as well as disks. Because disk objects actually reside in other subdirectories, Windows uses symbolic links to connect names under \Global?? to objects located elsewhere in the namespace. For each physical disk on a system, the I/O manager creates a \Global??\PhysicalDrive*X* link that points to \Device\Harddisk*X*\DR*X*. (Numbers, starting from 0, replace *X*.) Windows applications that directly interact with the sectors on a disk open the disk by calling the Windows *CreateFile* function and specifying the name \\.\PhysicalDrive*X* (in which *X* is the disk number) as a parameter. (Note that directly accessing a mounted disk's sectors requires administrator privileges.) The Windows application layer converts the name to \Global??\PhysicalDrive*X* before handing the name to the Windows object manager.

Partition Manager

The partition manager, %SystemRoot%\System32\Drivers\Partmgr.sys, is responsible for discovering, creating, deleting, and managing partitions. To become aware of partitions, the partition manager acts as the function driver for disk device objects created by disk class drivers. The partition manager uses the I/O manager's *IoReadPartitionTableEx* function to identify partitions and create device objects that represent them. As miniport drivers present the disks that they identify early in the boot process to the disk class driver, the disk class driver invokes the *IoReadPartitionTableEx* function for each disk. This function invokes sector-level disk I/O that the class, port, and miniport drivers provide to read a disk's MBR (Master Boot Record) or GPT (GUID Partition Table; described later in this chapter), constructs an internal representation of the disk's partitioning, and returns a PDRIVE_LAYOUT_INFORMATION_EX structure. The partition manager driver creates device objects to represent each primary partition (including logical drives within extended partitions) that the driver obtains from *IoReadPartitionTableEx*. These names have the form \Device\HarddiskVolume*Y*, where *Y* represents the partition number.

The partition manager is also responsible for ensuring that all disks and partitions have a unique ID (a signature for MBR and a GUID for GPT). If it encounters two disks with the same ID, it tries to determine (by writing to one disk and reading from the other) whether they are two different disks or the same disk being viewed via two different paths (this can happen if the MPIO software isn't present or isn't working correctly). If the two disks are different, the partition manager makes only one available for use by the upper layers of the storage stack, bringing them online and keeping the others offline. Disk-management utilities and storage APIs can force an offline disk online, however the partition manager will change the ID in doing so to prevent conflicts.

By managing disk attributes that are persisted in the registry (such as *read-only* and *offline*), the partition manager can perform actions such as hiding partitions from the volume manager, which inhibits the volumes from manifesting on the system. Clustering and Hyper-V use these attributes. The partition manager also redirects write operations that are sent directly to the disk but fall within a partition space to the corresponding volume manager. The volume manager determines whether to allow the write operation based on whether the volume is dismounted or not.

Volume Management

Windows has the concept of *basic* and *dynamic* disks. Windows calls disks that rely exclusively on the MBR-style or GPT partitioning scheme *basic disks*. Dynamic disks implement a more flexible partitioning scheme than that of basic disks. The fundamental difference between basic and dynamic disks is that dynamic disks support the creation of new multipartition volumes. Recall from the list of terms earlier in the chapter that multipartition volumes provide performance, sizing, and reliability features not supported by simple volumes. Windows manages all disks as basic disks unless you manually create dynamic disks or convert existing basic disks (with enough free space) to dynamic disks. Microsoft recommends that you use basic disks unless you require the multipartition functionality of dynamic disks.

> **Note** Windows does not support multipartition volumes on basic disks. For a number of reasons, including the fact that laptops usually have only one disk and laptop disks typically don't move easily between computers, Windows uses only basic disks on laptops. In addition, only fixed disks can be dynamic, and disks located on IEEE 1394 or USB buses or on shared cluster server disks are by default basic disks.

Basic Disks

This section describes the two types of partitioning, MBR-style and GPT, that Windows uses to define volumes on basic disks and the volume manager driver that presents the volumes to file system drivers. Windows silently defaults to defining all disks as basic disks.

MBR-Style Partitioning

The standard BIOS implementations that BIOS-based (non-EFI) x86 (and x64) hardware uses dictate one requirement of the partitioning format in Windows—that the first sector of the primary disk contains the Master Boot Record (MBR). When a BIOS-based x86 system boots, the computer's BIOS reads the MBR and treats part of the MBR's contents as executable code. The BIOS invokes the MBR code to initiate an operating system boot process after the BIOS performs preliminary configuration of the computer's hardware. In Microsoft operating systems such as Windows, the MBR also contains a *partition table*. A partition table consists of four entries that define the locations of as many as four *primary partitions* on a disk. The partition table also records a partition's type. Numerous predefined partition types exist, and a partition's type specifies which file system the partition includes. For example, partition types exist for FAT32 and NTFS.

A special partition type, an *extended partition*, contains another MBR with its own partition table. The equivalent of a primary partition in an extended partition is called a *logical drive*. By using extended partitions, Microsoft's operating systems overcome the apparent limit of four partitions per disk. In general, the recursion that extended partitions permit can continue indefinitely, which means that no upper limit exists to the number of possible partitions on a disk. The Windows boot process makes evident the distinction between primary and logical drives. The system must mark one primary partition of the primary disk as active (bootable). The Windows code in the MBR loads the code stored in the first sector of the active partition (the system volume) into memory and then transfers control to that code. Because of the role in the boot process played by this first sector in the primary partition, Windows designates the first sector of any partition as the boot sector. As you will see in Chapter 13, "Startup and Shutdown," every partition formatted with a file system has a boot sector that stores information about the structure of the file system on that partition.

GUID Partition Table Partitioning

As part of an initiative to provide a standardized and extensible firmware platform for operating systems to use during their boot process, Intel designed the Extensible Firmware Interface (EFI) specification, originally for the Itanium processor. Intel donated EFI to the Unified EFI Forum, which has continued to evolve UEFI for x86, x64, and ARM CPUs. UEFI includes a mini–operating system environment implemented in firmware (typically flash memory) that operating systems use early in the system boot process to load system diagnostics and their boot code. UEFI defines a partitioning scheme, called the GUID (globally unique identifier) Partition Table (GPT) that addresses some of the shortcomings of MBR-style partitioning. For example, the sector addresses that the GPT structures use are 64 bits wide instead of 32 bits. A 32-bit sector address is sufficient to access only 2 terabytes (TB) of storage, while a GPT allows the addressing of disk sizes into the foreseeable future. Other advantages of the GPT scheme include the fact that it uses cyclic redundancy checksums (CRC) to ensure the integrity of the partition table, and it maintains a backup copy of the partition table. GPT takes its name from the fact that in addition to storing a 36-byte Unicode partition name for each partition, it assigns each partition a GUID.

Figure 9-6 shows a sample GPT partition layout. As in MBR-style partitioning, the first sector of a GPT disk is an MBR (*protective MBR*) that serves to protect the GPT partitioning in case the disk is accessed from a non-GPT-aware operating system. However, the second and last sectors of the disk store the GPT headers with the actual partition table following the second sector and preceding the last sector. With its extensible list of partitions, GPT partitioning doesn't require nested partitions, as MBR partitions do.

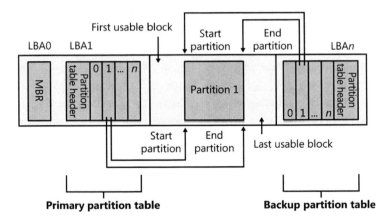

Note: LBA = Logical block address

FIGURE 9-6 Example GPT partition layout

> **Note** Because Windows doesn't support the creation of multipartition volumes on basic disks, a new basic disk partition is the equivalent of a volume. For this reason, the Disk Management MMC snap-in uses the term *partition* when you create a volume on a basic disk.

Basic Disk Volume Manager

The volume manager driver (%SystemRoot%\System32\Drivers\Volmgr.sys) creates disk device objects that represent volumes on basic disks and plays an integral role in managing all basic disk volumes, including simple volumes. For each volume, the volume manager creates a device object of the form \Device\HarddiskVolume*X*, in which *X* is a number (starting from 1) that identifies the volume.

The volume manager is actually a bus driver because it's responsible for enumerating basic disks to detect the presence of basic volumes and report them to the Windows Plug and Play (PnP) manager. To implement this enumeration, the volume manager leverages the PnP manager, with the aid of the partition manager (Partmgr.sys) driver to determine what basic disk partitions exist. The partition manager registers with the PnP manager so that Windows can inform the partition manager whenever the disk class driver creates a partition device object. The partition manager informs the volume manager about new partition objects through a private interface and creates filter device objects that the partition manager then attaches to the partition objects. The existence of the filter objects prompts Windows to inform the partition manager whenever a partition device object is deleted so that the partition manager can update the volume manager. The disk class driver deletes a partition device object when a partition in the Disk Management MMC snap-in is deleted. As the volume manager becomes aware of partitions, it uses the basic disk configuration information to determine the correspondence of partitions to volumes and creates a volume device object when it has been informed of the presence of all the partitions in a volume's description.

Windows volume drive-letter assignment, a process described shortly, creates drive-letter symbolic links under the \Global?? object manager directory that point to the volume device objects that the volume manager creates. When the system or an application accesses a volume for the first time, Windows performs a *mount* operation that gives file system drivers the opportunity to recognize and claim ownership for volumes formatted with a file system type they manage. (Mount operations are described in the section "Volume Mounting" later in this chapter.)

Dynamic Disks

As we've stated, dynamic disks are the disk format in Windows necessary for creating multipartition volumes such as mirrors, striped arrays, and RAID-5 arrays (described later in the chapter). Dynamic disks are partitioned using Logical Disk Manager (LDM) partitioning. LDM is part of the Virtual Disk Service (VDS) subsystem in Windows, which consists of user-mode and device driver components and oversees dynamic disks. A major difference between LDM's partitioning and MBR-style and GPT partitioning is that LDM maintains one unified database that stores partitioning information for all the dynamic disks on a system—including multipartition-volume configuration.

The LDM Database

The LDM database resides in a 1-MB reserved space at the end of each dynamic disk. The need for this space is the reason Windows requires free space at the end of a basic disk before you can convert it to a dynamic disk. The LDM database consists of four regions, which Figure 9-7 shows: a header sector that LDM calls the Private Header, a table of contents area, a database records area, and a transactional log area. (The fifth region shown in Figure 9-7 is simply a copy of the Private Header.) The Private Header sector resides 1 MB before the end of a dynamic disk and anchors the database. As you spend time with Windows, you'll quickly notice that it uses GUIDs to identify just about everything, and disks are no exception. A GUID (globally unique identifier) is a 128-bit value that various components in Windows use to uniquely identify objects. LDM assigns each dynamic disk a GUID, and the Private Header sector notes the GUID of the dynamic disk on which it resides—hence the Private Header's designation as information that is private to the disk. The Private Header also stores the name of the disk group, which is the name of the computer concatenated with Dg0 (for example, Daryl-Dg0 if the computer's name is Daryl), and a pointer to the beginning of the database table of contents. For reliability, LDM keeps a copy of the Private Header in the disk's last sector.

The database table of contents is 16 sectors in size and contains information regarding the database's layout. LDM begins the database record area immediately following the table of contents with a sector that serves as the database record header. This sector stores information about the database record area, including the number of records it contains, the name and GUID of the disk group the database relates to, and a sequence number identifier that LDM uses for the next entry it creates in the database. Sectors following the database record header contain 128-byte fixed-size records that store entries that describe the disk group's partitions and volumes.

A database entry can be one of four types: partition, disk, component, and volume. LDM uses the database entry types to identify three levels that describe volumes. LDM connects entries with internal object identifiers. At the lowest level, *partition entries* describe soft partitions (hard partitions are described later in this chapter), which are contiguous regions on a disk; identifiers stored in a partition entry link the entry to a component and disk entry. A *disk entry* represents a dynamic disk that is part of the disk group and includes the disk's GUID. A *component entry* serves as a connector between one or more partition entries and the volume entry each partition is associated with. A *volume entry* stores the GUID of the volume, the volume's total size and state, and a drive-letter hint. Disk entries that are larger than a database record span multiple records; partition, component, and volume entries rarely span multiple records.

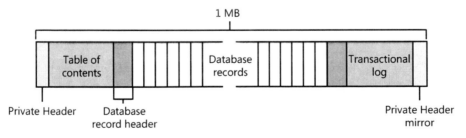

FIGURE 9-7 LDM database layout

LDM requires three entries to describe a simple volume: a partition, component, and volume entry. The following listing shows the contents of a simple LDM database that defines one 200-MB volume that consists of one partition:

```
Disk Entry          Volume Entry      Component Entry       Partition Entry
Name: Disk1         Name: Volume1     Name: Volume1-01      Name: Disk1-01
GUID: XXX-XX...     ID: 0x408         ID: 0x409             ID: 0x407
Disk ID: 0x404      State: ACTIVE     Parent ID: 0x408      Parent ID: 0x409
                    Size: 200MB                             Disk ID: 0x404
                    GUID: XXX-XX...                         Start: 300MB
                    Drive Hint: H:                          Size: 200MB
```

The partition entry describes the area on a disk that the system assigned to the volume, the component entry connects the partition entry with the volume entry, and the volume entry contains the GUID that Windows uses internally to identify the volume. Multipartition volumes require more than three entries. For example, a striped volume (which is described later in the chapter) consists of at least two partition entries, a component entry, and a volume entry. The only volume type that has more than one component entry is a mirror; mirrors have two component entries, each of which represents one half of the mirror. LDM uses two component entries for mirrors so that when you break a mirror, LDM can split it at the component level, creating two volumes with one component entry each.

The final area of the LDM database is the transactional log area, which consists of a few sectors for storing backup database information as the information is modified. This setup safeguards the database in case of a crash or power failure because LDM can use the log to return the database to a consistent state.

EXPERIMENT: Using LDMDump to View the LDM Database

You can use LDMDump from Sysinternals to view detailed information about the contents of the LDM database. LDMDump takes a disk number as a command-line argument, and its output is usually more than a few screens in size, so you should pipe its output to a file for viewing in a text editor—for example, *ldmdump /d0 > disk.txt*. The following example shows excerpts of LDMDump output. The LDM database header displays first, followed by the LDM database records that describe a 12-GB disk with three 4-GB dynamic volumes. The volume's database entry is listed as Volume1. At the end of the output, LDMDump lists the soft partitions and definitions of volumes it locates in the database.

```
C:\>ldmdump /d0
Logical Disk Manager Configuration Dump v1.03
Copyright (C) 2000-2002 Mark Russinovich

PRIVATE HEAD:
Signature           : PRIVHEAD
Version             : 2.12
Disk Id             : b5f4a801-758d-11dd-b7f0-000c297f0108
Host Id             : 1b77da20-c717-11d0-a5be-00a0c91db73c
Disk Group Id       : b5f4a7fd-758d-11dd-b7f0-000c297f0108
Disk Group Name     : WIN-SL5V78KD01W-Dg0
Logical disk start  : 3F
Logical disk size   : 7FF7C1 (4094 MB)
Configuration start : 7FF800
Configuration size  : 800 (1 MB)
```

```
Number of TOCs     : 2
TOC size           : 7FD (1022 KB)
Number of Configs  : 1
Config size        : 5C9 (740 KB)
Number of Logs     : 1
Log size           : E0 (112 KB)

TOC 1:
Signature          : TOCBLOCK
Sequence           : 0x1
Config bitmap start: 0x11
Config bitmap size : 0x5C9
Log bitmap start   : 0x5DA
Log bitmap size    : 0xE0
...
VBLK DATABASE:
0x000004: [000001] <DiskGroup>
        Name       : WIN-SL5V78KD01W-Dg0
        Object Id  : 0x0001
        GUID       : b5f4a7fd-758d-11dd-b7f0-000c297f010
0x000006: [000003] <Disk>
        Name       : Disk1
        Object Id  : 0x0002
        Disk Id    : b5f4a7fe-758d-11dd-b7f0-000c297f010

0x000007: [000005] <Disk>
        Name       : Disk2
        Object Id  : 0x0003
        Disk Id    : b5f4a801-758d-11dd-b7f0-000c297f010

0x000008: [000007] <Disk>
        Name       : Disk3
        Object Id  : 0x0004
        Disk Id    : b5f4a804-758d-11dd-b7f0-000c297f010

0x000009: [000009] <Component>
        Name       : Volume1-01
        Object Id  : 0x0006
        Parent Id  : 0x0005

0x00000A: [00000A] <Partition>
        Name       : Disk1-01
        Object Id  : 0x0007
        Parent Id  : 0x3157
        Disk Id    : 0x0000
        Start      : 0x7C100
        Size       : 0x0 (0 MB)
        Volume Off : 0x3 (0 MB)

0x00000B: [00000B] <Partition>
        Name       : Disk2-01
        Object Id  : 0x0008
        Parent Id  : 0x3157
        Disk Id    : 0x0000
        Start      : 0x7C100
```

```
        Size        : 0x0 (0 MB)
        Volume Off  : 0x7FE80003 (1047808 MB)

0x00000C: [00000C] <Partition>
        Name        : Disk3-01
        Object Id   : 0x0009
        Parent Id   : 0x3157
        Disk Id     : 0x0000
        Start       : 0x7C100
        Size        : 0x0 (0 MB)
        Volume Off  : 0xFFD00003 (2095616 MB)

0x00000D: [00000F] <Volume>
        Name        : Volume1
        Object Id   : 0x0005
        Volume state: ACTIVE
        Size        : 0x017FB800 (12279 MB)
        GUID        : b5f4a806-758d-11dd-b7f0-c297f0108
        Drive Hint  : E:
```

LDM and GPT or MBR-Style Partitioning

When you install Windows on a computer, one of the first things it requires you to do is to create a partition on the system's primary physical disk (specified in the BIOS or UEFI as the disk from which to boot the system). To make enabling BitLocker easier, Windows Setup will create a small (100 MB) unencrypted partition known as the *system volume*, containing the Boot Manager (Bootmgr), Boot Configuration Database (BCD), and other early boot files. (By default, this volume does not have a drive letter assigned to it, but you can assign one using the Disk Management MMC snap-in, at %SystemRoot%\System32\Diskmgmt.msc, if you want to examine the contents of the volume with Windows Explorer). In addition, Windows Setup requires you to create a partition that serves as the home for the boot volume, onto which the setup program installs the Windows system files and creates the system directory (\Windows). The nomenclature that Microsoft defines for system and boot volumes is somewhat confusing. The system volume is where Windows places boot files, such as the Boot Manager, and the boot volume is where Windows stores the rest of the operating system files, such as Ntoskrnl.exe, the core kernel file.

> **Note** If the system has BitLocker enabled, the boot volume will be encrypted, but the system volume is never encrypted.

Although the partitioning data of a dynamic disk resides in the LDM database, LDM implements MBR-style partitioning or GPT partitioning so that the Windows boot code can find the system and boot volumes when the volumes are on dynamic disks. (Winload and the Itanium firmware, for example, know nothing about LDM partitioning.) If a disk contains the system or boot volumes, partitions in the MBR or GPT describe the location of those volumes. Otherwise, one partition encompasses the entire usable area of the disk. LDM marks this partition as type "LDM". The region encompassed by this place-holding MBR-style or GPT partition is where LDM creates partitions that the LDM database organizes. On MBR-partitioned disks the LDM database resides in hidden sectors at the end of the disk, and on GPT-partitioned disks there exists an LDM metadata partition that contains the LDM database near the beginning of the disk.

Another reason LDM creates an MBR or a GPT is so that legacy disk-management utilities, including those that run under Windows and under other operating systems in dual-boot environments, don't mistakenly believe a dynamic disk is unpartitioned.

Because LDM partitions aren't described in the MBR or GPT of a disk, they are called *soft partitions*; MBR-style and GPT partitions are called *hard partitions*. Figure 9-8 illustrates this dynamic disk layout on an MBR-style partitioned disk.

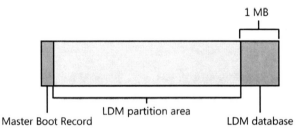

1 MB

Master Boot Record   LDM partition area   LDM database

FIGURE 9-8 Internal dynamic disk organization

Dynamic Disk Volume Manager

The Disk Management MMC snap-in DLL (DMDiskManager, located in %SystemRoot%\System32\Dmdskmgr.dll), shown in Figure 9-9, is used to create and change the contents of the LDM database. When you launch the Disk Management MMC snap-in, DMDiskManager loads into memory and reads the LDM database from each disk and returns the information it obtains to the user. If it detects a database from another computer's disk group, it notes that the volumes on the disk are foreign and lets you import them into the current computer's database if you want to use them. As you change the configuration of dynamic disks, DMDiskManager updates its in-memory copy of the database. When DMDiskManager commits changes, it passes the updated database to the VolMgrX driver (%SystemRoot%\System32\Drivers\Volmgrx.sys). VolMgrX is a kernel-mode DLL that provides dynamic disk functionality for VolMgr, so it controls access to the on-disk database and creates device objects that represent the volumes on dynamic disks. When you exit Disk Management, DMDisk-Manager stops.

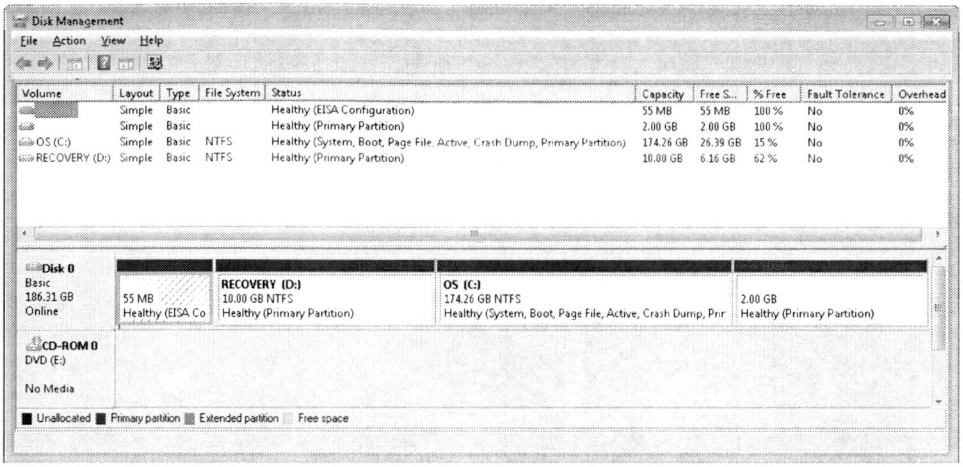

FIGURE 9-9 Disk Management MMC snap-in

Multipartition Volume Management

VolMgr is responsible for presenting volumes that file system drivers manage and for mapping I/O directed at volumes to the underlying partitions that they're part of. For simple volumes, this process is straightforward: the volume manager ensures that volume-relative offsets are translated to disk-relative offsets by adding the volume-relative offset to the volume's starting disk offset.

Multipartition volumes are more complex because the partitions that make up a volume can be located on discontiguous partitions or even on different disks. Some types of multipartition volumes use data redundancy, so they require more involved volume-to-disk–offset translation. Thus, VolMgr uses VolMgrX to process all I/O requests aimed at the multipartition volumes they manage by determining which partitions the I/O ultimately affects.

The following types of multipartition volumes are available in Windows:

- Spanned volumes

- Mirrored volumes

- Striped volumes

- RAID-5 volumes

After describing multipartition-volume partition configuration and logical operation for each of the multipartition-volume types, we'll cover the way that the VolMgr driver handles IRPs that a file system driver sends to multipartition volumes. The term *volume manager* is used to represent VolMgr and the VolMgrX extension DLL throughout the explanation of multipartition volumes.

Spanned Volumes

A *spanned volume* is a single logical volume composed of a maximum of 32 free partitions on one or more disks. The Disk Management MMC snap-in combines the partitions into a spanned volume, which can then be formatted for any of the Windows-supported file systems. Figure 9-10 shows a 100-GB spanned volume identified by drive letter D that has been created from the last third of the first disk and the first third of the second. Spanned volumes were called *volume sets* in Windows NT 4.

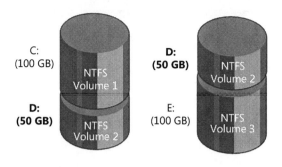

FIGURE 9-10 Spanned volume

A spanned volume is useful for consolidating small areas of free disk space into one larger volume or for creating a single large volume out of two or more small disks. If the spanned volume has been formatted for NTFS, it can be extended to include additional free areas or additional disks without affecting the data already stored on the volume. This extensibility is one of the biggest benefits of describing all data on an NTFS volume as a file. NTFS can dynamically increase the size of a logical volume because the bitmap that records the allocation status of the volume is just another file—the bitmap file. The bitmap file can be extended to include any space added to the volume. Dynamically extending a FAT volume, on the other hand, would require the FAT itself to be extended, which would dislocate everything else on the disk.

A volume manager hides the physical configuration of disks from the file systems installed on Windows. NTFS, for example, views volume D: in Figure 9-10 as an ordinary 100-GB volume. NTFS consults its bitmap to determine what space in the volume is free for allocation. After translating a byte offset to a cluster offset, it then calls the volume manager to read or write data beginning at a particular cluster offset on the volume. The volume manager views the physical sectors in the spanned volume as numbered sequentially from the first free area on the first disk to the last free area on the last disk. It determines which physical sector on which disk corresponds to the supplied cluster offset.

Striped Volumes

A *striped volume* is a series of up to 32 partitions, one partition per disk, that gets combined into a single logical volume. Striped volumes are also known as *RAID level 0* (RAID-0) volumes. Figure 9-11 shows a striped volume consisting of three partitions, one on each of three disks. (A partition in a striped volume need not span an entire disk; the only restriction is that the partitions on each disk be the same size.)

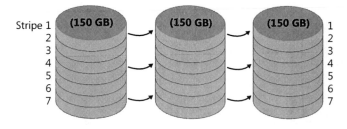

FIGURE 9-11 Striped volume

To a file system, this striped volume appears to be a single 450-GB volume, but the volume manager optimizes data storage and retrieval times on the striped volume by distributing the volume's data among the physical disks. The volume manager accesses the physical sectors of the disks as if they were numbered sequentially in stripes across the disks, as illustrated in Figure 9-12.

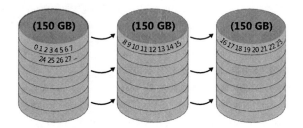

FIGURE 9-12 Logical numbering of physical sectors on a striped volume

Because each stripe unit is a relatively narrow 64 KB (a value chosen to prevent small individual reads and writes from accessing two disks), the data tends to be distributed evenly among the disks. Striping thus increases the probability that multiple pending read and write operations will be bound for different disks. And because data on all three disks can be accessed simultaneously, latency time for disk I/O is often reduced, particularly on heavily loaded systems.

Spanned volumes make managing disk volumes more convenient, and striped volumes spread the I/O load over multiple disks. These two volume-management features don't provide the ability to recover data if a disk fails, however. For data recovery, the volume manager implements two redundant storage schemes: mirrored volumes and RAID-5 volumes. These features are created with the Windows Disk Management administrative tool.

Mirrored Volumes

In a *mirrored volume*, the contents of a partition on one disk are duplicated in an equal-sized partition on another disk. Mirrored volumes are sometimes referred to as *RAID level 1* (RAID-1). A mirrored volume is shown in Figure 9-13.

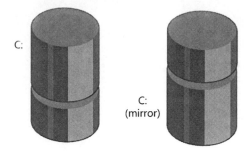

FIGURE 9-13 Mirrored volume

When a program writes to drive C:, the volume manager writes the same data to the same location on the mirror partition. If the first disk or any of the data on its C: partition becomes unreadable because of a hardware or software failure, the volume manager automatically accesses the data from the mirror partition. A mirror volume can be formatted for any of the Windows-supported file systems. The file system drivers remain independent and are not affected by the volume manager's mirroring activity.

Mirrored volumes can aid in read I/O throughput on heavily loaded systems. When I/O activity is high, the volume manager balances its read operations between the primary partition and the mirror partition (accounting for the number of unfinished I/O requests pending from each disk). Two read operations can proceed simultaneously and thus theoretically finish in half the time. When a file is modified, both partitions of the mirror set must be written, but disk writes are performed in parallel, so the performance of user-mode programs is generally not affected by the extra disk update.

Mirrored volumes are the only multipartition volume type supported for system and boot volumes. The reason for this is that the Windows boot code, including the MBR code and Winload, don't have the sophistication required to understand multipartition volumes—mirrored volumes are the exception because the boot code treats them as simple volumes, reading from the half of the mirror marked as the boot or system drive in the MBR-style partition table. Because the boot code doesn't modify the disk metadata and will read or write to the same half of the mirrored set, it can safely ignore the other half of the mirror; however, the Boot Manager and OS loader will update the file \Boot\BootStat.dat on the system volume. This file is used only to communicate status between the various phases of booting, so, again, it does not need to be written to the other half of the mirror.

EXPERIMENT: Watching Mirrored Volume I/O Operations

Using the Performance Monitor, you can verify that write operations directed at mirrored volumes copy to both disks that make up the mirror and that read operations, if relatively infrequent, occur primarily from one half of the volume. This experiment requires three hard disks. If you don't have three disks, you can skip the experiment setup instructions and view the Performance tool screen shot in this experiment that demonstrates the experiment's results.

Use the Disk Management MMC snap-in to create a mirrored volume. To do this, perform the following steps:

1. Run Disk Management by starting Computer Management, expanding the Storage tree, and clicking Disk Management (or by inserting Disk Management as a snap-in in an MMC console).

2. Right-click on an unallocated space of a drive, and then click New Simple Volume.

3. Follow the instructions in the New Simple Volume Wizard to create a simple volume. (Make sure there's enough room on another disk for a volume of the same size as the one you're creating.)

4. Right-click on the new volume, and then click Add Mirror on the context menu.

Once you have a mirrored volume, run the Performance Monitor tool and add counters for the PhysicalDisk performance object for both disk instances that contain a partition belonging to the mirror. Select the Disk Writes/sec counters for each instance. Select a large directory from the third disk (the one that isn't part of the mirrored volume), and copy it to the mirrored volume. The Performance Monitor tool output window should look something like the following screen shot as the copy operation progresses.

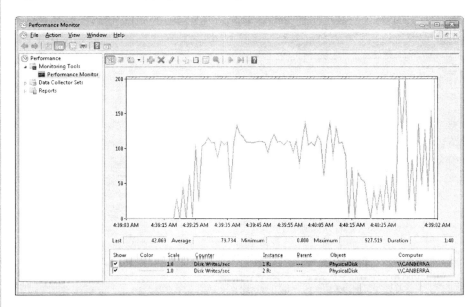

The top two lines, which overlap throughout the timeline, are the Disk Writes/sec counters for each disk. The screen shot reveals that the volume manager (in this case VolMgr) is writing the copied file data to both halves of the volume.

RAID-5 Volumes

A *RAID-5 volume* is a fault tolerant variant of a regular striped volume. RAID-5 volumes implement *RAID level 5*. They are also known as *striped volumes with rotated parity* because they are based on the striping approach taken by striped volumes. Fault tolerance is achieved by reserving the equivalent of one disk for storing parity for each stripe. Figure 9-14 is a visual representation of a RAID-5 volume.

In Figure 9-14, the parity for stripe 1 is stored on disk 1. It contains a byte-for-byte logical sum (XOR) of the first stripe units on disks 2 and 3. The parity for stripe 2 is stored on disk 2, and the parity for stripe 3 is stored on disk 3. Rotating the parity across the disks in this way is an I/O optimization technique. Each time data is written to a disk, the parity bytes corresponding to the modified bytes must be recalculated and rewritten. If the parity were always written to the same disk, that disk would be busy continually and could become an I/O bottleneck.

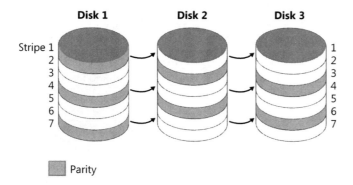

 Parity

FIGURE 9-14 RAID-5 volume

Recovering a failed disk in a RAID-5 volume relies on a simple arithmetic principle: in an equation with n variables, if you know the value of $n - 1$ of the variables, you can determine the value of the missing variable by subtraction. For example, in the equation $x + y = z$, where z represents the parity stripe unit, the volume manager computes $z - y$ to determine the contents of x; to find y, it computes $z - x$. The volume manager uses similar logic to recover lost data. If a disk in a RAID-5 volume fails or if data on one disk becomes unreadable, the volume manager reconstructs the missing data by using the XOR operation (bitwise logical addition).

If disk 1 in Figure 9-14 fails, the contents of its stripe units 2 and 5 are calculated by XOR-ing the corresponding stripe units of disk 3 with the parity stripe units on disk 2. The contents of stripes 3 and 6 on disk 1 are similarly determined by XOR-ing the corresponding stripe units of disk 2 with the parity stripe units on disk 3. At least three disks (or, rather, three same-sized partitions on three disks) are required to create a RAID-5 volume.

The Volume Namespace

The volume namespace mechanism handles the assignment of drive letters to device objects that represent actual volumes, which lets Windows applications access these drives through familiar means, and also provides mount and dismount functionality.

The Mount Manager

The Mount Manager device driver (%SystemRoot%\System32\Drivers\Mountmgr.sys) assigns drive letters for dynamic disk volumes and basic disk volumes created after Windows is installed, CD-ROMs, floppies, and removable devices. Windows stores all drive-letter assignments under HKLM\SYSTEM\MountedDevices. If you look in the registry under that key, you'll see values with names such as \??\Volume{X} (where X is a GUID) and values such as \DosDevices\C:. Every volume has a volume name entry, but a volume doesn't necessarily have an assigned drive letter (for example, the system volume). Figure 9-15 shows the contents of an example Mount Manager registry key. Note that the MountedDevices key isn't included in a control set and so isn't protected by the last known good boot option. (See the section "Last Known Good" in Chapter 13 for more information on control sets and the last known good boot option.)

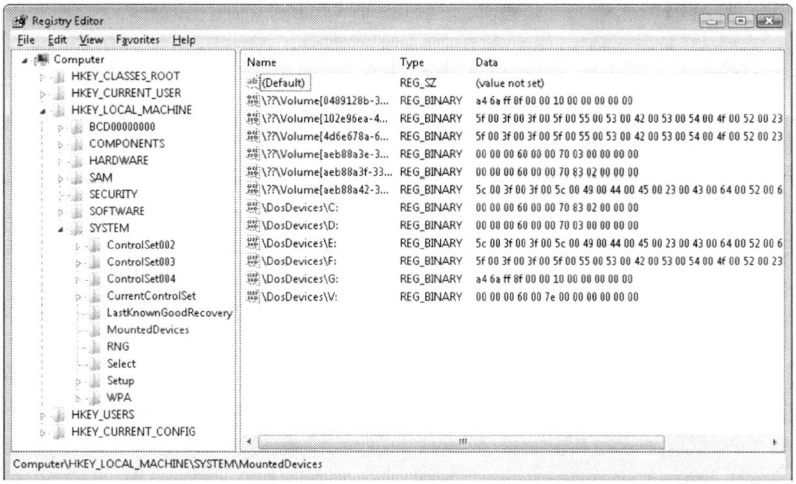

FIGURE 9-15 Mounted devices listed in the Mount Manager's registry key

The data that the registry stores in values for basic disk volume drive letters and volume names is the disk signature and the starting offset of the first partition associated with the volume. The data that the registry stores in values for dynamic disk volumes includes the volume's VolMgr-internal GUID. When the Mount Manager initializes during the boot process, it registers with the Windows Plug and Play subsystem so that it receives notification whenever a device identifies itself as a volume. When the Mount Manager receives such a notification, it determines the new volume's GUID or disk signature and uses the GUID or signature as a guide to look in its internal database, which reflects the contents of the MountedDevices registry key. The Mount Manager then determines whether its internal database contains the drive-letter assignment. If the volume has no entry in the database, the Mount Manager asks VolMgr for a suggested drive-letter assignment and stores that in the database.

VolMgr doesn't return suggestions for simple volumes, but it looks at the drive-letter hint in the volume's database entry for dynamic volumes.

If no suggested drive-letter assignment exists for a dynamic volume, the Mount Manager uses the first unassigned drive letter (if one exists), defines a new assignment, creates a symbolic link for the assignment (for example, \Global??\D:), and updates the MountedDevices registry key. If there are no available drive letters, no drive-letter assignment is made. At the same time, the Mount Manager creates a volume symbolic link (that is, \Global??\Volume{*X*}) that defines a new volume GUID if the volume doesn't already have one. This GUID is different from the volume GUIDs that VolMgr uses internally.

Mount Points

Mount points let you link volumes through directories on NTFS volumes, which makes volumes with no drive-letter assignment accessible. For example, an NTFS directory that you've named C:\Projects could mount another volume (NTFS or FAT) that contains your project directories and files. If your project volume had a file you named \CurrentProject\Description.txt, you could access the file through the path C:\Projects\CurrentProject\Description.txt. What makes mount points possible is *reparse point* technology. (Reparse points are discussed in more detail in Chapter 12.)

A reparse point is a block of arbitrary data with some fixed header data that Windows associates with an NTFS file or directory. An application or the system defines the format and behavior of a reparse point, including the value of the unique reparse point tag that identifies reparse points belonging to the application or system and specifies the size and meaning of the data portion of a reparse point. (The data portion can be as large as 16 KB.) Any application that implements a reparse point must supply a file system filter driver to watch for reparse-related return codes for file operations that execute on NTFS volumes, and the driver must take appropriate action when it detects the codes. NTFS returns a reparse status code whenever it processes a file operation and encounters a file or directory with an associated reparse point.

The Windows NTFS file system driver, the I/O manager, and the object manager all partly implement reparse point functionality. The object manager initiates pathname parsing operations by using the I/O manager to interface with file system drivers. Therefore, the object manager must retry operations for which the I/O manager returns a reparse status code. The I/O manager implements pathname modification that mount points and other reparse points might require, and the NTFS file system driver must associate and identify reparse point data with files and directories. You can therefore think of the I/O manager as the reparse point file system filter driver for many Microsoft-defined reparse points.

One common use of reparse points is the symbolic link functionality offered on Windows by NTFS (see Chapter 12 for more information on NTFS symbolic links). If the I/O manager receives a reparse status code from NTFS and the file or directory for which NTFS returned the code isn't associated with one of a handful of built-in Windows reparse points, no filter driver claimed the reparse point. The I/O manager then returns an error to the object manager that propagates as a "file cannot be accessed by the system" error to the application making the file or directory access.

Mount points are reparse points that store a volume name (\Global??\Volume{X}) as the reparse data. When you use the Disk Management MMC snap-in to assign or remove path assignments for volumes, you're creating mount points. You can also create and display mount points by using the built-in command-line tool *Mountvol.exe* (%SystemRoot%\System32\Mountvol.exe).

The Mount Manager maintains the Mount Manager remote database on every NTFS volume in which the Mount Manager records any mount points defined for that volume. The database file resides in the directory System Volume Information on the NTFS volume. Mount points move when a disk moves from one system to another and in dual-boot environments—that is, when booting between multiple Windows installations—because of the existence of the Mount Manager remote database. NTFS also keeps track of reparse points in the NTFS metadata file \$Extend\$Reparse. (NTFS doesn't make any of its metadata files available for viewing by applications.) NTFS stores reparse point information in the metadata file so that Windows can, for example, easily enumerate the mount points (which are reparse points) defined for a volume when a Windows application, such as Disk Management, requests mount-point definitions.

Volume Mounting

Because Windows assigns a drive letter to a volume doesn't mean that the volume contains data that has been organized in a file system format that Windows recognizes. The volume-recognition process consists of a file system claiming ownership for a partition; the process takes place the first time the kernel, a device driver, or an application accesses a file or directory on a volume. After a file system driver signals its responsibility for a partition, the I/O manager directs all IRPs aimed at the volume to the owning driver. Mount operations in Windows consist of three components: file system driver registration, volume parameter blocks (VPBs), and mount requests.

> **Note** The partition manager honors the system SAN policy, which can be set with the Windows DiskPart utility, that specifies whether it should surface disks for visibility to the volume manager. The default policy in Windows Server 2008 Enterprise and Datacenter editions is to not make SAN disks visible, which prevents the system from aggressively mounting their volumes.

The I/O manager oversees the mount process and is aware of available file system drivers because all file system drivers register with the I/O manager when they initialize. The I/O manager provides the *IoRegisterFileSystem* function to local disk (rather than network) file system drivers for this registration. When a file system driver registers, the I/O manager stores a reference to the driver in a list that the I/O manager uses during mount operations.

Every device object contains a VPB data structure, but the I/O manager treats VPBs as meaningful only for volume device objects. A VPB serves as the link between a volume device object and the device object that a file system driver creates to represent a mounted file system instance for that volume. If a VPB's file system reference is empty (*VPB->DeviceObject == NULL*), no file system has mounted the volume. The I/O manager checks a volume device object's VPB whenever an open API that specifies a file name or a directory name on a volume device object executes.

For example, if the Mount Manager assigns drive letter D to the second volume on a system, it creates a \Global??\D: symbolic link that resolves to the device object \Device\HarddiskVolume2. A Windows application that attempts to open the \Temp\Test.txt file on the D: drive specifies the name D:\Temp\Test.txt, which the Windows subsystem converts to \Global??\D:\Temp\Test.txt before invoking *NtCreateFile*, the kernel's file-open routine. *NtCreateFile* uses the object manager to parse the name, and the object manager encounters the \Device\HarddiskVolume2 device object with the path \Temp\Test.txt still unresolved. At that point, the I/O manager checks to see whether \Device\HarddiskVolume2's VPB references a file system. If it doesn't, the I/O manager asks each registered file system driver via a mount request whether the driver recognizes the format of the volume in question as the driver's own.

EXPERIMENT: Looking at VPBs

You can look at the contents of a VPB by using the *!vpb* kernel debugger command. Because the VPB is pointed to by the device object for a volume, you must first locate a volume device object. To do this, you must dump the volume manager's driver object, locate a device object that represents a volume, and display the device object, which reveals its *Vpb* field.

```
lkd> !drvobj volmgr
Driver object (84905030) is for:
 \Driver\volmgr
Driver Extension List: (id , addr)

Device Object list:
84a64780  849d5b28  84a64518  84a64030
84905e00
```

The *!drvobj* command lists the addresses of the device objects a driver owns. In this example, there are five device objects. One of them represents the programmatic (control) interface to the device driver, and the rest are volume device objects. Because the objects are listed in reverse order from the way that they were created and the driver creates the control device object first, the first device object listed is that of a volume. Now execute the *!devobj* kernel debugger command on the volume device object address:

```
lkd> !devobj 84a64780
Device object (84a64780) is for:
 HarddiskVolume4 \Driver\volmgr DriverObject 84905030
Current Irp 00000000 RefCount 0 Type 00000007 Flags 00001050
Vpb 84a64228 Dacl 8b1a8674 DevExt 84a64838 DevObjExt 84a64930 Dope 849fd838 DevNode
    849d5938
ExtensionFlags (0x00000800)
                              Unknown flags 0x00000800
AttachedDevice (Upper) 84a66020 \Driver\volsnap
Device queue is not busy
```

The *!devobj* command shows the *Vpb* field for the volume device object. (The device object shown is named HarddiskVolume4.) Now you're ready to execute the *!vpb* command:

```
lkd> !vpb 84a64228
Vpb at 0x84a64228
```

```
Flags: 0x1 mounted
DeviceObject: 0x84a6b020
RealDevice:   0x849d5b28
RefCount: 4311
Volume Label:   OS
```

The command reveals that the volume device object is mounted by a file system driver that has assigned the volume the name OS. The *RealDevice* field in the VPB points back to the volume device object, and the *DeviceObject* field points to the mounted file system device object. You can use *!devobj* on this address to get more information on the mounted file system, as seen in the following output, which shows that NTFS has mounted the volume:

```
lkd> !devobj 0x84a6b020
Device object (84a6b020) is for:
  \FileSystem\Ntfs DriverObject 84a02ad0
Current Irp 00000000 RefCount 0 Type 00000008 Flags 00040000
DevExt 84a6b0d8 DevObjExt 84a6bc00
ExtensionFlags (0x00000800)
                              Unknown flags 0x00000800
AttachedDevice (Upper) 84a63ac0 \FileSystem\FltMgr
Device queue is not busy
```

The convention followed by file system drivers for recognizing volumes mounted with their format is to examine the volume's boot record (VBR), which is stored in the first sector of the volume. Boot records for Microsoft file systems contain a field that stores a file system format type. File system drivers usually examine this field, and if it indicates a format they manage, they look at other information stored in the boot record. This information usually includes a file system name field and enough data for the file system driver to locate critical metadata files on the volume. NTFS, for example, will recognize a volume only if the MBR partition *Type* field is NTFS (0x07), the *Name* field is "NTFS," and the critical metadata files described by the boot record are consistent.

If a file system driver signals affirmatively, the I/O manager fills in the VPB and passes the open request with the remaining path (that is, \Temp\Test.txt) to the file system driver. The file system driver completes the request by using its file system format to interpret the data that the volume stores. After a mount fills in a volume device object's VPB, the I/O manager hands subsequent open requests aimed at the volume to the mounted file system driver. If no file system driver claims a volume, Raw— a file system driver built into Ntoskrnl.exe—claims the volume and fails all requests to open files on that partition; however, Raw does allow sector I/O to the partition for applications with administrator privileges, but even an administrator cannot write to sectors of a mounted volume, except for the boot sectors. Figure 9-16 shows a simplified example (that is, the figure omits the file system driver's interactions with the Windows cache and memory managers) of the path that I/O directed at a mounted volume follows.

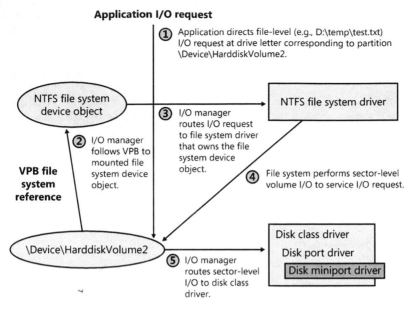

Application I/O request

① Application directs file-level (e.g., D:\temp\test.txt) I/O request at drive letter corresponding to partition \Device\HarddiskVolume2.

NTFS file system device object

② I/O manager follows VPB to mounted file system device object.

VPB file system reference

③ I/O manager routes I/O request to file system driver that owns the file system device object.

NTFS file system driver

④ File system performs sector-level volume I/O to service I/O request.

\Device\HarddiskVolume2

⑤ I/O manager routes sector-level I/O to disk class driver.

Disk class driver
Disk port driver
Disk miniport driver

FIGURE 9-16 Mounted volume I/O flow

Instead of having every file system driver loaded, regardless of whether they have any volumes to manage, Windows tries to minimize memory usage by using a surrogate driver named File System Recognizer (%SystemRoot%\System32\Drivers\Fs_rec.sys) to perform preliminary file system recognition. File System Recognizer knows enough about each file system format that Windows supports to be able to examine a boot record and determine whether it's associated with a Windows file system driver. When the system boots, File System Recognizer registers as a file system driver, and when the I/O manager calls it during a file system mount operation for a new volume, File System Recognizer loads the appropriate file system driver if the VBR describes a file system that isn't loaded. After loading a file system driver, File System Recognizer forwards the mount IRP to the file system driver and lets it claim ownership of the volume.

Aside from the boot volume, which a driver mounts while the kernel is initializing, file system drivers mount most volumes when the Chkdsk file system consistency-checking application runs during a boot sequence. The boot-time version of Chkdsk is a native application (as opposed to a Win32 application) named Autochk.exe (%SystemRoot%\System32\Autochk.exe), and the Session Manager (%SystemRoot%\System32\Smss.exe) runs it because it is specified as a boot-run program in the HKLM\SYSTEM\CurrentControlSet\Control\Session Manager\BootExecute value. Autochk accesses each drive letter to see whether the volume associated with the letter requires a consistency check.

One place in which mounting can occur more than once for the same disk is with removable media. Windows file system drivers respond to media changes by querying the disk's volume identifier. If they see the volume identifier change, the driver dismounts the disk and attempts to remount it.

Volume I/O Operations

File system drivers manage data stored on volumes but rely on the volume manager to interact with storage drivers to transfer data to and from the disk or disks on which a volume resides. File system drivers obtain references to the volume manager's volume objects through the mount process and then send the volume manager requests via the volume objects. Applications can also send the volume manager requests, bypassing file system drivers, when they want to directly manipulate a volume's data. File-undelete programs are an example of applications that do this.

Whenever a file system driver or an application sends an I/O request to a device object that represents a volume, the Windows I/O manager routes the request (which comes in an IRP—a self-contained package, described in Chapter 8, "I/O System") to the volume manager that created the target device object. Thus, if an application (running with administrator privileges) wants to read the boot sector of the second volume on the system (which is a simple volume in this example), it opens a handle to \\.\HarddiskVolume2 and then calls *ReadFile* to read 512 bytes starting at offset zero on the device. (Both the starting byte offset and length must be a multiple of the sector size.) The I/O manager sends the application's request in the form of an IRP to the volume manager that owns the device object, notifying it that the IRP is directed at the HarddiskVolume2 device.

Because volumes are logical conveniences that Windows uses to represent contiguous areas on one or more physical disks, the volume manager must translate offsets that are relative to a volume to offsets that are relative to the beginning of a disk. If volume 2 consists of one partition that begins 4,096 sectors into the disk, the partition manager would adjust the IRP's parameters to designate an offset with that value before passing the request to the disk class driver. The disk class driver uses a miniport driver to carry out physical disk I/O, and reads the requested data into an application buffer designated in the IRP.

Some examples of a volume manager's operations will help clarify its role when it handles requests aimed at multipartition volumes. If a striped volume consists of two partitions, partition 1 and partition 2, the VolMgr device object intercepts file system disk I/O aimed at the device object for the volume, and the VolMgr driver adjusts the request before passing it to the disk class driver. The adjustment that VolMgr makes configures the request to refer to the correct offset of the request's target stripe on either partition 1 or partition 2. If the I/O spans both partitions of the volume, VolMgr must issue two *associated* I/O requests, one aimed at each disk. This is shown in Figure 9-17.

In the case of writes to a mirrored volume, VolMgr splits each request so that each half of the mirror receives the write operation. For mirrored reads, VolMgr performs a read from half of a mirror, relying on the other half when a read operation fails.

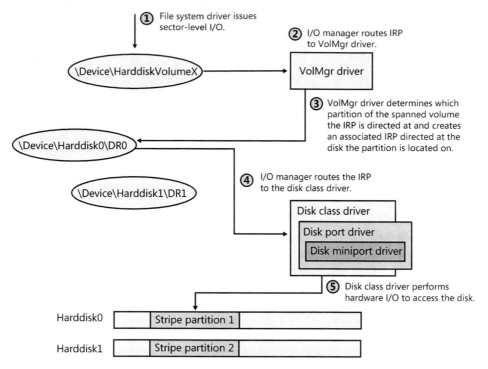

FIGURE 9-17 VolMgr I/O operations

Virtual Disk Service

A company that makes storage products such as RAID adapters, hard disks, or storage arrays has to implement custom applications for installing and managing their devices. The use of different management applications for different storage devices has obvious drawbacks from the perspective of system administration. These drawbacks include learning multiple interfaces and the inability to use standard Windows storage management tools to manage third-party storage devices.

Windows includes the Virtual Disk Service (or VDS, located at %SystemRoot%\System32\Vds.exe), which provides a unified high-level storage interface so that administrators can manage storage devices from different vendors using the same user interfaces. VDS is shown in Figure 9-18. VDS exports a COM-based API that allows applications to create and format disks and to view and manage hardware RAID adapters. For example, a utility can use the VDS API to query the list of physical disks that map to a RAID logical unit number (LUN). Windows disk-management utilities, including the Disk Management MMC snap-in and the DiskPart and DiskRAID command-line tools, use VDS APIs.

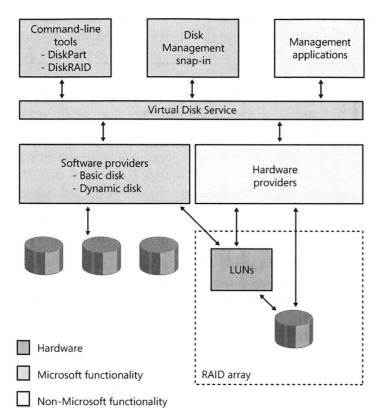

Hardware

Microsoft functionality

Non-Microsoft functionality

FIGURE 9-18 VDS service architecture

VDS supplies two interfaces, one for software providers and one for hardware providers:

■ Software providers implement interfaces to high-level storage abstractions such as disks, disk partitions, and volumes. Examples of operations supported by these interfaces include creating, extending, and deleting volumes; adding or breaking mirrors; and formatting and assigning drive letters. VDS looks for registered software providers in HKLM\SYSTEM\Current-ControlSet\Services\Vds\SoftwareProviders, which contains subkeys whose names are GUIDs. Within each subkey is a value named ClsId, which specifies the COM class ID, and these are listed in HKEY_CLASSES_ROOT\CLSID\<ClsId>. Windows includes the VDS Dynamic Provider (%SystemRoot%\System32\Vdsdyn.dll) for interfacing to dynamic disks and the VDS Basic Provider (%SystemRoot%\System32\Vdsbas.dll) for interfacing to basic disks.

■ Hardware vendors implement VDS hardware providers as DLLs that register under HKLM\SYSTEM\CurrentControlSet\Services\Vds\HardwareProviders and that translate device-independent VDS commands into commands for their hardware. The hardware provider allows for management of a storage subsystem such as a hardware RAID array or an adapter card, and supported operations include creating, extending, deleting, masking, and unmasking LUNs.

When an application initiates a connection to the VDS API and the VDS service isn't started, the Svchost process hosting the RPC service starts the VDS loader process (%SystemRoot%\System32\Vdsldr.exe), which starts the VDS service process and then exits. When the last connection to the VDS API closes, the VDS service process exits.

Virtual Hard Disk Support

Windows includes extensive built-in support for VHD (Virtual Hard Disk, the Microsoft virtual machine disk format) files. Using disk-management utilities, you can create, delete, and merge VHDs, as well as attach them to the system as though they were physical disks. Windows also includes support for booting Windows installations stored in NTFS volumes within VHDs.

There are three types of VHDs, all of which are supported by the VHD functionality in Windows:

- **Dynamic**   The VHD does not necessarily contain all the blocks it is advertising (thinly provisioned) and will be grown as necessary, up to its maximum size. In other words, the amount of space being consumed by the VHD is equal to the amount of data that is being stored in it (plus a small amount of overhead for the VHD container).

- **Fixed**   The VHD is of fixed size, cannot grow, and contains all the disk blocks it is advertising (fully provisioned).

- **Differencing**   Similar to a dynamic VHD, but contains only the sectors that would have been modified when compared with a parent VHD (which is read-only). The parent VHD may be of any of the three VHD types (including another differencing VHD). Differencing VHDs are generally used for taking a snapshot of the state of a parent VHD. That state can then be recovered by simply deleting the differencing VHD. This is often used in checkpointing virtual machines (VMs) to enable the user to return the VM to a particular state. Note that the differencing VHD must be kept in the same directory as the parent VHD.

When presented to the system, the standard partition manager and volume manager mounting volume recognition and mounting processes take place, making file systems stored in the VHD accessible using Windows file system APIs and utilities.

VHDs can be contained within a VHD, so Windows limits the number of nesting levels of VHDs that it will present to the system as a disk to two, with the maximum number of nesting levels specified by the registry value HKLM\System\CurrentControlSet\Services\FsDepends\Parameters\VirtualDiskMaxTreeDepth. Mounting VHDs can be prevented by setting the registry value HKLM\System\CurrentControlSet\Services\FsDepends\Parameters\VirtualDiskNoLocalMount to 1.

Windows can also boot from a VHD. A bootable VHD may be created from scratch during installation (when booting the Windows installation disk) or from a running system using various tools, including ImageX or Sysinternals's Disk2VHD. That "system in a VHD" can be run under Virtual PC or Hyper-V (on Windows Server), and Windows Ultimate and Enterprise editions can directly boot from a VHD.

Windows also extends its support of VHDs to all its built-in disk-management utilities. Creating, mounting, and dismounting a VHD can be done while Windows is running using the Disk Management MMC snap-in (%SystemRoot%\System32\Diskmgmt.msc) or the DiskPart (%SystemRoot%\System32\Diskpart.exe) command-line tool. These tools are implemented using Virtual Disk Service (VDS) APIs, which can also be used by third-party utilities for managing and manipulating VHDs.

Attaching VHDs

The root-enumerated bus driver Vdrvroot (%SystemRoot%\System32\Drivers\Vdrvroot.sys) creates a physical device object (PDO) for each nested file system to be mounted. The PnP manager loads the Vhdmp (%SystemRoot%\System32\Drivers\Vhdmp.sys) Storport miniport driver as the function driver on the PDO, exposing what to the rest of the system looks like a physical disk. The I/O manager then layers the rest of the storage stack (disk class driver, partition manager, volume manager, and file system driver) on top of the device stack (DevStack) containing Vhdmp. When Vhdmp receives sector read and write requests, it translates those requests into offsets within the VHD file and then forwards the requests to the storage stack where the VHD file is located.

Nested File Systems

To support nested file systems, a dependency tree is created to track which file systems have dependencies on other file systems. This is important for several systemwide operations to function properly, such as dismounting a volume (dependent file systems would have to be dismounted first), system shutdown (similar to volume dismounting), and volume snapshots (dependent volumes need to be flushed before the parent during a FlushAndHold operation). Dependencies are tracked by a file system minifilter driver (%SystemRoot%\System32\Drivers\Fsdepends.sys), which sits above the file system driver. Dependencies are tracked by Fsdepends using PnP removal relations, instead of parent-child relationships, because removal relations are more dynamic and are queried at run time rather than set up statically. (This is important because nested drivers can set up additional dependency relationships after a VHD is mounted.)

As far as most Windows components are concerned, a mounted VHD volume is identical to a volume residing on a physical disk, with the limitations that neither paging files, the hibernation file, or the crash dump file can be located on a mounted VHD and VHDs cannot be larger than 2 TB.

BitLocker Drive Encryption

An operating system can enforce its security policies only while it's active, so you have to take additional measures to protect data when the physical security of a system can be compromised and the data accessed from outside the operating system. Hardware-based mechanisms such as BIOS passwords and encryption are two technologies commonly used to prevent unauthorized access, especially on laptops, which are the computers most likely to be lost or stolen.

While Windows supports the Encrypting File System (EFS), you can't use EFS to protect access to sensitive areas of the system, such as the registry hive files. For example, if Group Policy allows you to log on to your laptop even when you're not connected to a domain, then your domain credential verifiers are cached in the registry, so an attacker could use tools to obtain your domain account password hash and use that to try to obtain your password with a password cracker. The password would provide access to your account and EFS files (assuming you didn't store the EFS key on a smartcard). To make it easy to encrypt the entire boot volume, including all its system files and data, Windows includes a full-volume encryption feature called Windows BitLocker Drive Encryption.

BitLocker operates in two modes:

- **Standard**   Protects the fixed disks in a system.

- **BitLocker To Go**   Protects removable disks formatted using the FAT file system, including USB flash disks.

In standard mode, BitLocker helps prevent unauthorized access to data on lost or stolen computers by combining two major data-protection procedures:

- Encrypting the entire Windows operating system volume on the hard disk.

- Verifying the integrity of early boot components and boot configuration data.

The most secure implementation of BitLocker leverages the enhanced security capabilities of a Trusted Platform Module (TPM) version 1.2. The TPM is a cryptographic coprocessor installed in many newer computers by computer manufacturers. The TPM implements a variety of functions, including public key cryptography. Information on the operation of the TPM can be found at *http://www.TrustedComputingGroup.org/.* The TPM works with BitLocker to help protect user data and to ensure that a computer running Windows has not been tampered with while the system was offline. On computers that do not have a TPM version 1.2, BitLocker can still encrypt the Windows operating system volume. However, this implementation requires the user to insert a USB startup flash disk to start the computer or resume from hibernation, and it does not provide the full offline and preboot protection that a TPM-enabled system does.

BitLocker's architecture provides functionality and management mechanisms in both kernel mode and user mode. At a high level, the main components of BitLocker are:

- The Trusted Platform Module driver (%SystemRoot%\System32\Drivers\Tpm.sys), a kernel-mode driver that accesses the TPM chip.

- The TPM Base Services, which include a user-mode service that provides user-mode access to the TPM (%SystemRoot%\System32\Tbssvc.dll), a WMI provider, and an MMC snap-in for configuration (%SystemRoot%\System32\Tpm.msc).

- The BitLocker-related code in the Boot Manager (\Bootmgr, on the system volume) that authenticates access to the disk, handles boot-related unlocking, and allows recovery.

- The BitLocker filter driver (%SystemRoot%\System32\Drivers\Fvevol.sys), a kernel-mode filter driver that performs on-the-fly encryption and decryption of the volume.

- The BitLocker WMI provider and management script, which allow configuration and scripting of the BitLocker interface.

In the next sections, we'll take a look at these various components and the services they provide. Figure 9-19 provides an overview of the BitLocker architecture.

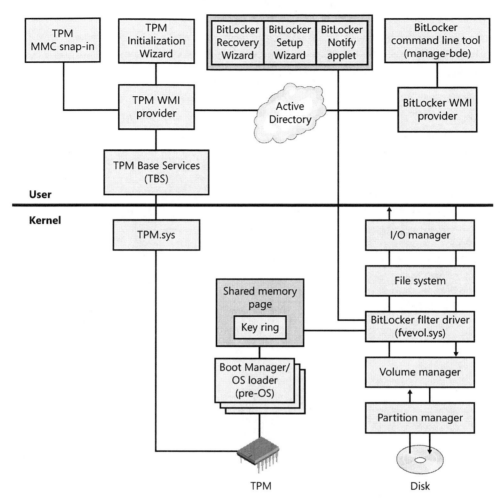

FIGURE 9-19 BitLocker architecture

Encryption Keys

BitLocker encrypts the contents of the volume using a full-volume encryption key (FVEK) and cryptography that uses the AES128-CBC (by default) or AES256-CBC algorithm, with a Microsoft-specific extension called a diffuser. In turn, the FVEK is encrypted with a volume master key (VMK) and stored in a special metadata region of the volume. Securing the volume master key is an indirect way of protecting data on the volume: the addition of the volume master key allows the system to be rekeyed easily when keys upstream in the trust chain are lost or compromised. This ability to rekey the system saves the time and expense of decrypting and re-encrypting the entire volume again.

When you configure BitLocker, you have a number of options for how the VMK will be protected, depending on the system's hardware capabilities. If the system has a TPM, you can encrypt the VMK with the TPM, have the system encrypt the VMK using a key stored in the TPM and one stored on a USB flash device, encrypt the VMK using a TPM-stored key and a PIN you enter when the system boots, or encrypt the VMK with a combination of both a PIN and a USB flash device. For systems that don't have a compatible TPM, BitLocker offers the option of encrypting the VMK using a key stored on an external USB flash device.

In any case you'll need an unencrypted 100-MB NTFS system volume, the volume where the Boot Manager and BCD are stored, because the MBR and boot-sector code are legacy code, run in 16-bit real mode (as discussed in Chapter 13), and do not have the ability to perform any on-the-fly decryption of the same volume they're running on. This means that these components must remain on an unencrypted volume so that the BIOS can access them and they can run and locate Bootmgr.

As covered earlier in this chapter, the system volume is created automatically when Windows is installed on a system, regardless of whether or not you are using BitLocker. This places the system volume at the beginning of the disk (the first partition), which keeps the rest of the disk contiguous.

Figure 9-20 and Table 9-1 summarize the various ways in which the VMK can be generated.

TABLE 9-1 VMK Sources

Source	Identifies	Security	User Impact
TPM only	What it is	Protects against software attacks, but vulnerable to hardware attacks.	None
TPM + PIN	What it is + What you know	Adds protection against most hardware attacks as well.	User must enter PIN each boot
TPM + USB key	What it is + What you have	Fully protects against hardware attacks, but vulnerable to stolen USB key.	User must insert USB key each boot
TPM + USB key + PIN	What it is + What you have + What you know	Maximum level of protection.	User must enter PIN and insert USB key each boot
USB key only	What you have	Minimum level of protection for systems without TPM, but vulnerable to stolen key.	User must insert USB key each boot

Finally, BitLocker also provides a simple encryption-based authentication scheme to ensure the integrity of the drive contents. Although AES encryption is currently considered uncrackable through brute-force attacks and is one of the most widely used algorithms in the industry today, it doesn't provide a way to ensure that modified encrypted data can't in some way be modified such that it is translated back to plaintext data that an attacker could make use of. For example, by precise manipulation of the encrypted data, a hacker might be able to cause a certain logon function to behave differently and allow all logons.

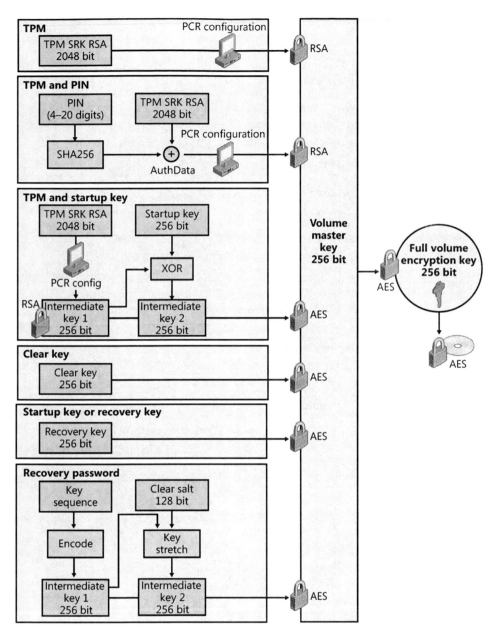

FIGURE 9-20 BitLocker key generation

To protect the system against this type of attack, BitLocker includes a *diffuser* algorithm called Elephant. The job of the diffuser is to make sure that even a single bit change in the ciphertext (encrypted data) will result in a totally random plaintext data output, ensuring that the modified executable code will most likely arbitrarily crash instead of performing a specific malicious function. Additionally, when combined with code integrity (see Chapter 3 in Part 1 for more information on code integrity), the diffuser will also cause core system files to fail their signature checks, rendering the system unbootable.

Trusted Platform Module (TPM)

A TPM is a tamper-resistant processor mounted on a motherboard that provides various cryptographic services such as key and random number generation and sealed storage. Support for TPM in Windows reaches beyond supporting BitLocker, however. Through the TPM Base Services (TBS), other applications on the system can also take advantage of compatible hardware TPM chips and use WMI to administer and script access to the TPM. For example, Windows uses a TPM as an additional seed into random number generation, which enhances the overall security of all applications on the system that depend on strong security or hashing algorithms (including mechanisms such as logons).

Although your computer may have a TPM, that does not necessarily mean that Windows will be able to support it. There are two requirements for Windows TPM support:

- The computer must have a TPM version 1.2 or higher.

- The computer must have a Trusted Computing Group (TCG)–compliant BIOS. The BIOS establishes a chain of trust for the preboot environment and must include support for TCG-specific Static Root of Trust Measurement (SRTM).

The easiest way to determine whether your machine contains a compatible TPM is to run the TPM MMC snap-in (%SystemRoot%\System32\Tpm.msc). If Windows detects a compatible TPM, you should see a window similar to the one shown in Figure 9-21. Otherwise, an error message will appear.

As stated earlier, BitLocker can be configured to use the TPM to perform system integrity checks on critical early boot components. At a high level, the TPM collects and stores measurements from multiple early boot components and boot configuration data to create a system identifier (much like a fingerprint) for that computer. It stores each part of this fingerprint as a hash in a 160-bit *platform configuration register* (PCR). BitLocker uses the hash of these functions to *seal* the VMK, which is the key that BitLocker uses to protect other keys, including the FVEKs used to encrypt volumes.

If the early boot components are changed or tampered with, such as by changing the BIOS or MBR, changing an operating system file, or moving the hard disk to a different computer, the TPM prevents BitLocker from unsealing the VMK, and Windows enters a key recovery mode (described later in the chapter). If the PCR values match those used to seal the key, the system is deemed to be tamper free, and it unseals the key, and BitLocker can decrypt the keys used to encrypt the volumes. Once the keys are unsealed, Windows starts and system protection becomes the responsibility of the user and the operating system.

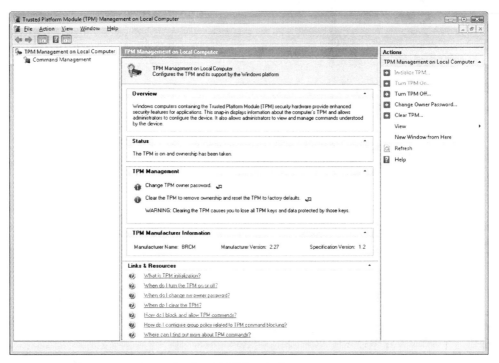

FIGURE 9-21 The TPM MMC snap-in after initializing the TPM.

A platform validation profile supported by TPMs consists of at least 16, and as many as 24, PCRs that contain additional information and only reset after a TPM reset (implying a machine reboot). Each PCR is associated with components that run when an operating system starts, as shown in Table 9-2.

TABLE 9-2 Platform Configuration Registers

Index	Meaning
0	Core Root of Trust of Measurement (CRTM), BIOS, and platform extensions
1	Platform and motherboard configuration and data (BIOS data and CPU microcode)
2	Option ROM code
3	Option ROM configuration and data
4	Master Boot Record (MBR) code
5	Master Boot Record (MBR) partition table
6	Power-state transition and wake events
7	Computer manufacturer-specific
8	First NTFS boot sector (volume boot record)
9	Remaining NTFS boot sectors (volume boot record)
10	Boot Manager

Index	Meaning
11	BitLocker Access Control
12	Defined for use by the static operating system
13	Defined for use by the static operating system
14	Defined for use by the static operating system
15	Defined for use by the static operating system
16	Used for debugging
17	Dynamic CRTM
18	Platform defined
19	Used by a trusted operating system
20	Used by a trusted operating system
21	Used by a trusted operating system
22	Used by a trusted operating system
23	Application support

By default, BitLocker uses registers 0, 2, 4, 5, 8, 9, 10, and 11 to seal the VMK. The set of PCRs used by BitLocker is known as the Platform Validation Profile, which can be configured via Group Policy (Computer Configuration\Administrative Templates\Windows Components\BitLocker Drive Encryption\Operating System Drives\Configure TPM platform validation profile) and depends on the security requirements of your organization, as shown in Table 9-2. PCR 11 must be selected to enable BitLocker protection.

> **Note** If you change anything protected by the PCRs specified in your Platform Validation Profile, your system will not boot without either the recovery key or recovery password. For example, if you need to update the BIOS on your system, suspend BitLocker (using the BitLocker Drive Encryption Control Panel applet) before performing the update.

BitLocker Boot Process

The actual measurements stored in the TPM PCRs are generated by the TPM itself, the TPM BIOS, and Windows. When the system boots, the TPM does a self-test, following which the CRTM in the BIOS measures its own hashing and PCR loading code and writes the hash to the first PCR of the TPM. It then hashes the BIOS and stores that measurement in the first PCR as well. The BIOS in turn hashes the next component in the boot sequence, the MBR of the boot drive, and this process continues until the operating system loader is measured. Each subsequent piece of code that runs is responsible for measuring the code that it loads and for storing the measurement in the appropriate PCR in the TPM.

Finally, when the user selects which operating system to boot, the Boot Manager (Bootmgr) reads the encrypted VMK from the volume and asks the TPM to unseal it. As described previously, only if all the measurements are the same as when the VMK was sealed, including the optional PIN (password), will the TPM successfully decrypt the VMK. This process not only guarantees that the machine and system files are identical to the applications or operating systems that are allowed to read the drive, but also verifies the uniqueness of the operating system installation. For example, even another identical Windows operating system installed on the same machine will not get access to the drive because Bootmgr takes an active role in protecting the VMK from being passed to an operating system to which it doesn't belong (by generating a MAC hash of several system configuration options).

You can think of this scheme as a verification chain, where each component in the boot sequence describes the next component to the TPM. In effect, the TPM acts like a safe with 12 combination dials, with each dial containing 2,160 numbers. Only if all the PCRs match the original ones given to it when BitLocker was enabled will the TPM divulge its secret. BitLocker therefore protects the encrypted data even when the disk is removed and placed in another system, the system is booted using a different operating system, or the unencrypted files on the boot volume are compromised. Figure 9-22 shows the various steps of the preboot process up until Winload begins loading the operating system.

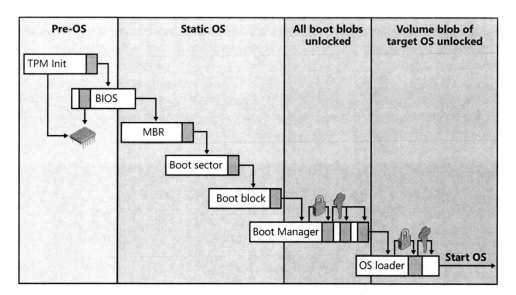

FIGURE 9-22 BitLocker preboot process

The administrator may need to temporarily suspend BitLocker protection because a component specified in the Platform Validation Profile needs to be changed (for example, updating BIOS, changing a drive's partition table, installing another operating system on the same disk, and so on). The BitLocker Drive Encryption Control Panel applet provides a simple mechanism for suspending BitLocker (click Suspend Protection for the volume). When BitLocker is suspended, the contents of the volume are still encrypted, but the volume master key is encrypted with a symmetric *clear key*, which is written to the volume's BitLocker metadata. When a volume is mounted, BitLocker automatically looks for a clear key and will be able to decrypt the contents of the volume. When BitLocker protection on a volume is resumed, the clear key is removed from the metadata.

Note Exposing the volume master key even for a brief period of time is a security risk because an attacker could access the volume master key and FVEK when these keys were exposed by the clear key, so do not leave a volume suspended for any longer than absolutely necessary.

BitLocker Key Recovery

For recovery purposes, BitLocker uses a recovery key (stored on a USB device) or a recovery password (numerical password), as shown earlier in Figure 9-20. BitLocker creates the recovery key and recovery password during initialization. A copy of the VMK is encrypted with a 256-bit AES-CCM key that can be computed with the recovery password and a salt stored in the metadata block. The password is a 48-digit number, eight groups of 6 digits, with three properties for checksumming:

- Each group of 6 digits must be divisible by 11. This check can be used to identify groups mistyped by the user.

- Each group of 6 digits must be less than 216 * 11. Each group contains 16 bits of key information. The eight groups, therefore, hold 128 bits of key.

- The sixth digit in each group is a checksum digit.

Inserting the recovery key or typing the recovery password enables an authorized user to regain access to the encrypted volume in the event of an attempted security breach or system failure. Figure 9-23 displays the prompt requesting the user to type the recovery password.

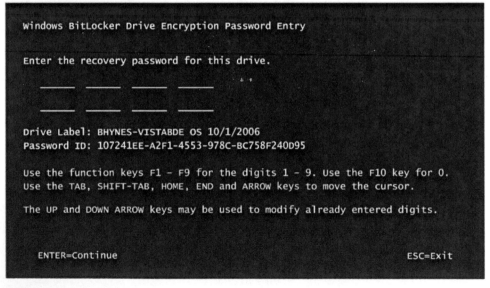

```
Windows BitLocker Drive Encryption Password Entry

Enter the recovery password for this drive.

_____  _____  _____  _____

_____  _____  _____  _____

Drive Label: BHYNES-VISTABDE OS 10/1/2006
Password ID: 107241EE-A2F1-4553-978C-BC758F240D95

Use the function keys F1 - F9 for the digits 1 - 9. Use the F10 key for 0.
Use the TAB, SHIFT-TAB, HOME, END and ARROW keys to move the cursor.

The UP and DOWN ARROW keys may be used to modify already entered digits.

    ENTER=Continue                                    ESC=Exit
```

FIGURE 9-23 BitLocker recovery screen

The recovery key or password is also used in cases when parts of the system have changed, resulting in different measurements. One common example of this is when a user has modified the BCD, such as by adding the *debug* option. Upon reboot, Bootmgr will detect the change and ask the user to validate it by inputting the recovery key. For this reason, it is extremely important not to lose this key, because it isn't only used for recovery but for validating system changes. Another application of the recovery key is for *foreign volumes*. Foreign volumes are operating system volumes that were BitLocker-enabled on another computer and have been transferred to a different Windows computer. An administrator can unlock these volumes by entering the recovery password.

Full-Volume Encryption Driver

Unlike EFS, which is implemented by the NTFS file system driver and operates at the file level, BitLocker encrypts at the volume level using the full-volume encryption (FVE) driver (%SystemRoot%\System32\Drivers\Fvevol.sys), as shown in Figure 9-24.

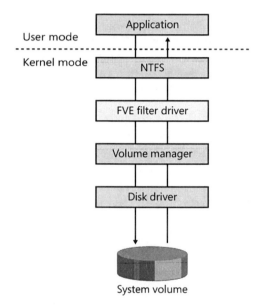

FIGURE 9-24 BitLocker filter driver implementation

FVE is a filter driver, so it automatically sees all the I/O requests sent to the volume, encrypting blocks as they're written and decrypting them as they're read using the FVEK assigned to the volume when it's initially configured to use BitLocker. Because the encryption and decryption happen beneath NTFS in the I/O system, the volume appears to NTFS as if it's unencrypted, and NTFS is not aware that BitLocker is enabled. If you attempt to read data from the volume from outside Windows, however, it appears to be random data.

BitLocker also uses an extra measure to make plaintext attacks in which an attacker knows the contents of a sector and uses that information to try and derive the key used to encrypt it more difficult. By combining the FVEK with the sector number to create the key used to encrypt a particular sector, and passing the encrypted data through the Elephant diffuser, BitLocker ensures that every sector is encrypted with a slightly different key, resulting in different encrypted data for different sectors even if their contents are identical.

BitLocker encrypts every sector (including unallocated sectors) on a volume with the exception of the first sector and three unencrypted metadata blocks containing the encrypted VMK and other data used by BitLocker. The metadata is surfaced in the volume's System Volume Information directory.

BitLocker Management

BitLocker provides a variety of administrative interfaces, each suited to a particular role or task. It provides a WMI interface (and works with the TBS—TPM Base Services—WMI interface) for programmatic access to the BitLocker functionality, a set of group policies that allow administrators to define the behavior across the network or a series of machines, integration with Active Directory, and a command-line management program (%SystemRoot%\System32\Manage-bde.exe).

Developers and system administrators with scripting familiarity can access the *Win32_Tpm* and *Win32_EncryptableVolume* interfaces to protect keys, define authentication methods, define which PCR registers are used as part of the BitLocker Platform Validation Profile, and manually initiate encryption or decryption of an entire volume. The *Manage-bde.exe* program, located in %SystemRoot%\System32, uses these interfaces to allow command-line management of the BitLocker service.

On systems that are joined to a domain, the key for each machine can automatically be backed up as part of a key escrow service, allowing IT administrators to easily recover and gain access to machines that are part of the corporate network. Additionally, various group policies related to BitLocker can be configured. You can access these by using the Local Group Policy Editor, under the Computer Configuration, Administrative Templates, Windows Components, BitLocker Drive Encryption entry. For example, Figure 9-25 displays the option for enabling the Active Directory key backup functionality.

If a TPM chip is present on the system, additional options (such as TPM Key Backup) can be accessed from the Trusted Platform Module Services entry under Windows Components.

To ensure easy access to corporate data, the Data Recovery Agent (DRA) feature has been added to BitLocker. The DRA is most commonly configured via Group Policy and allows a certificate to be specified as a key protector. This allows anyone holding that certificate (or a smartcard containing the certificate) to access (or unlock) a BitLocker-protected volume. See *http://technet.microsoft.com/en-us/library/dd875560(WS.10).aspx* for more information on configuring DRA.

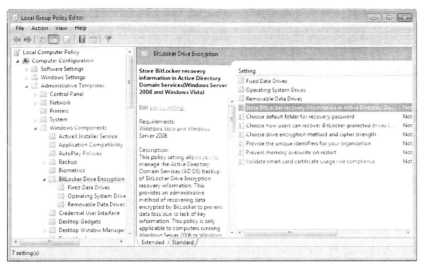

FIGURE 9-25 BitLocker Group Policy settings

BitLocker To Go

USB flash disks have become a popular method for transporting data because of their small size, low cost, and large capacity. However, it is precisely these qualities that make USB flash disks a security threat. Gigabytes of confidential information can be stored on a device the size of an AA battery that is easily lost or stolen. Standard BitLocker only encrypts NTFS volumes, and all USB flash disks use the FAT file system by default. BitLocker To Go (BTG) now brings the security of BitLocker full-volume encryption to disk devices using the FAT file system. BTG-encrypted flash disks can be created only on the Enterprise, Ultimate, or Server editions of Windows. They can be read on any edition—even on older operating systems such as Windows XP and Windows Vista—but can be written only on Windows 7 or Windows Server 2008/R2. To ensure that BTG is used, Group Policy can be used to restrict writing to removable media unless it is protected with BTG.

Like standard BitLocker, BTG encrypts the volume using AES, the decryption key is encrypted with multiple key protectors, and a recovery key can be saved to a file or escrowed through Active Directory. Unlike standard BitLocker, BTG does not make use of the TPM or public key cryptography. One of the key protectors may be either a user-supplied password or a smartcard.

BTG can be enabled in Explorer (right-click on the flash disk, and select Turn On BitLocker) or from the BitLocker Control Panel applet. Once it's enabled, BTG will create a FAT32 *discovery* volume containing the files shown in Figure 9-26. The purpose of the discovery volume is to provide the standalone BitLockerToGo application and its MUI files (user interface strings in various languages) and metadata to the host operating system.

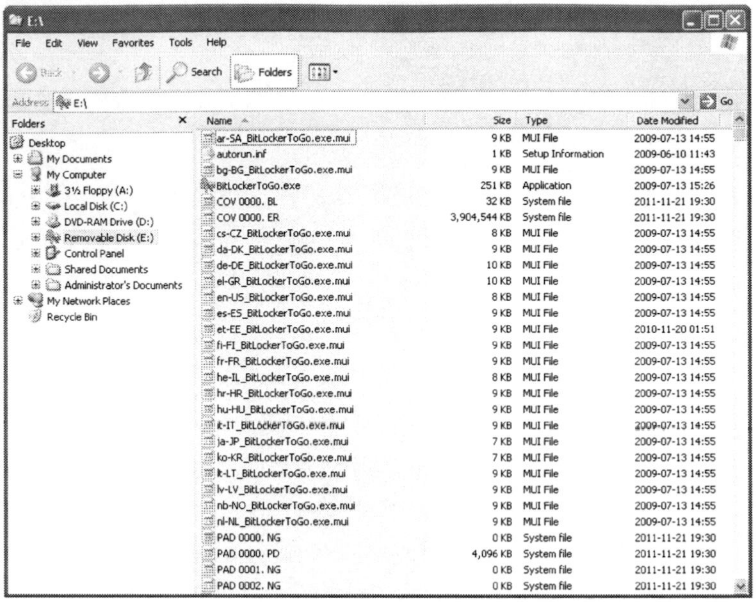

FIGURE 9-26 BitLocker To Go files

The encrypted volume is implemented as one or more *cover files*, named COV 0000. ER to COV 9999. ER, each of which can have a maximum size of 4 GB, as shown in Figures 9-26 and 9-27. Any extra space left on the volume will be filled with padding files to prevent any additional files from being added to the discovery volume.

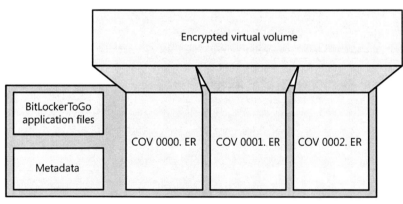

Discovery volume

FIGURE 9-27 BitLocker To Go layout

When the BitLockerToGo application mounts the encrypted virtual volume, the discovery volume will be hidden and is not accessible. The virtual volume may then be accessed like any other disk.

Volume Shadow Copy Service

The Volume Shadow Copy Service (VSS) is a built-in Windows mechanism that enables the creation of consistent, point-in-time copies of data, known as *shadow copies* or *snapshots*. VSS coordinates with applications, file-system services, backup applications, fast-recovery solutions, and storage hardware to produce consistent shadow copies.

Shadow Copies

Shadow copies are created through one of two mechanisms—*clone* and *copy-on-write*. The VSS provider (described in more detail later) determines the method to use. (Providers can implement the snapshot as they see fit. For example, certain hardware providers will take a hybrid approach: clone first, and then copy-on-write.)

Clone Shadow Copies

A clone shadow copy, also called a *split mirror*, is a full duplicate of the original data on a volume, created either by software or hardware mirroring. Software or hardware keeps a clone synchronized with the master copy until the mirror connection is broken in order to create a shadow copy. At that moment, the live volume (also called the *original volume*) and the shadow volume become independent. The live volume is writable and still accepts changes, but the shadow volume is read-only and stores contents of the live volume at the time it was created.

Copy-on-Write Shadow Copies

A copy-on-write shadow copy, also called a *differential copy*, is a differential, rather than a full, duplicate of the original data. Similar to a clone copy, differential copies can be created by software or hardware mechanisms. Whenever a change is made to the live data, the block of data being modified is copied to a "differences area" associated with the shadow copy before the change is written to the live data block. Overlaying the modified data on the live data creates a view of the live data at the point in time when the shadow copy was created.

> **Note** The in-box VSS provider that ships with Windows supports only copy-on-write shadow copies.

VSS Architecture

VSS (%SystemRoot%\System32\Vssvc.exe) coordinates VSS writers, VSS providers, and VSS requestors. A VSS writer is a software component that enables shadow-copy-aware applications, such as Microsoft SQL Server, Microsoft Exchange Server, and Active Directory, to receive freeze and thaw notifications to ensure that backup copies of their data files are internally consistent. Implementing a VSS provider allows an ISV or IHV with unique storage schemes to integrate with the shadow copy service. For instance, an IHV with mirrored storage devices might define a shadow copy as the frozen half of a split mirrored volume. VSS requestors are the applications that request the creation of volume shadow copies and include backup utilities and the Windows System Restore feature. Figure 9-28 shows the relationship between the VSS shadow copy service, writers, providers, and requestors.

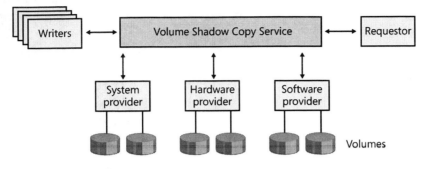

FIGURE 9-28 VSS architecture

VSS Operation

Regardless of the specific purpose for the copy and the application making use of VSS, shadow copy creation follows the same steps, shown in Figure 9-29. First, a requestor sends a command to VSS to enumerate writers, gather metadata, and prepare for the copy (1). VSS asks each writer to return information on its restore capabilities and an XML description of its backup components (2). Next, each writer prepares for the copy in its own appropriate way, which might include completing outstanding transactions and flushing caches. A prepare command is sent to all involved providers as well (3).

At this point, VSS initiates the *commit* phase of the copy (4). VSS instructs each writer to quiesce its data and temporarily freeze all write I/O requests (read requests are still passed through). VSS then flushes volume file system buffers and requests that the volume file system drivers freeze their I/O by sending them the IOCTL_VOLSNAP_FLUSH_AND_HOLD_WRITES device I/O control command, ensuring that all the file system metadata is written out to disk consistently (5). Once the system is in this state, VSS sends a command telling the provider to perform the actual copy creation (6). VSS allows up to 10 seconds for the creation, after which it aborts the operation if it is not already completed in this interval. After the provider has created the shadow copy, VSS asks the file systems to *thaw*, or resume write I/O operations, by sending them the IOCTL_VOLSNAP_RELEASE_WRITES command, and it releases the writers from their temporary freeze. All queued write I/O operations then proceed (7).

VSS next queries the writers to confirm that I/O operations were successfully held during the creation to ensure that the created shadow copy is consistent. If the shadow copy is inconsistent as the result of file system damage, the shadow copy is deleted by VSS. In other cases of writer failure, VSS simply notifies the requestor. At this point, the requestor can retry the procedure from (1) or wait for user action. If the copy was created consistently, VSS tells the requestor the location of the copy.

An optional final step is to make the snapshot device(s) writable, such that interested writers such as TxF (transactional NTFS) can perform additional recovery actions on the snapshot device itself. After this recovery step, the snapshot is sealed read-only and handed out to the requestor.

> **Note** VSS also allows the surfacing of shadow copy devices on a different server—called *transportable* shadow copies.

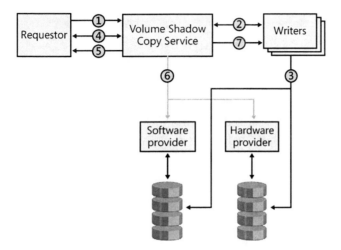

FIGURE 9-29 VSS shadow copy creation

Shadow Copy Provider

The Shadow Copy Provider (%SystemRoot%\System32\Drivers\Swprov.dll) implements software-based differential copies with the aid of the Volume Shadow Copy Driver (Volsnap—%SystemRoot%\System32\Drivers\Volsnap.sys). Volsnap is a storage filter driver that resides between file system drivers and volume manager drivers (the drivers that present views of the sectors that represent a volume) so that the I/O system forwards it I/O operations directed at a volume.

When asked by VSS to create a shadow copy, Volsnap queues I/O operations directed at the target volume and creates a differential file in the volume's System Volume Information directory to store volume data that subsequently changes. Volsnap also creates a virtual volume through which applications can access the shadow copy. For example, if a volume's name in the object manager namespace is \Device\HarddiskVolume1, the shadow volume would have a name like \Device\HarddiskVolume-ShadowCopy*N*, where *N* is a unique ID.

Whenever Volsnap sees a write operation directed at a live volume, it reads a copy of the sectors that will be overwritten into a paging file—a backed memory section that's associated with the corresponding shadow copy. It services read operations directed at the shadow copy of modified sectors from this memory section, and it services reads to unmodified areas by reading from the live volume. Because the backup utility won't save the paging file or the contents of the system-managed System Volume Information directory located on every volume (which includes shadow copy differential files), Volsnap uses the defragmentation API to determine the location of these files and directories and does not record changes to them.

Figure 9-30 demonstrates the behavior of applications accessing a volume and a backup application accessing the volume's shadow volume copy. When an application writes to a sector after the snapshot time, the Volsnap driver makes a backup copy, like it has for sectors a, b, and c of volume C: in the figure. Subsequently, when an application reads from sector c, Volsnap directs the read to volume C:, but when a backup application reads from sector c, Volsnap reads the sector from the snapshot. When a read occurs for any unmodified sector, such as d, Volsnap routes the read to volume C:.

Note Volsnap avoids copy-on-write operations for the paging file, hibernation file, and the difference data stored in the System Volume Information folder. All other files will get copy-on-write protection.

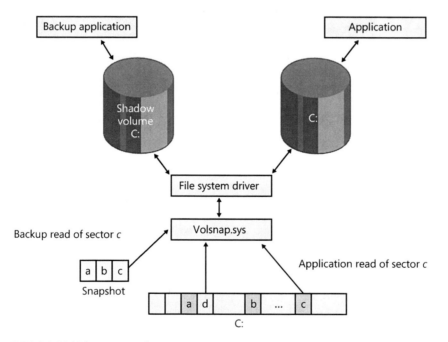

FIGURE 9-30 Volsnap operation

Uses in Windows

Several features in Windows make use of VSS, including Backup, System Restore, Previous Versions, and Shadow Copies for Shared Folders. We'll look at some of these uses and describe why VSS is needed and which VSS functionality is applicable to the applications.

Backup

A limitation of many backup utilities relates to open files. If an application has a file open for exclusive access, a backup utility can't gain access to the file's contents. Even if the backup utility can access an open file, the utility runs the risk of creating an inconsistent backup. Consider an application that updates a file at its beginning and then at its end. A backup utility saving the file during this operation might record an image of the file that reflects the start of the file before the application's modification and the end after the modification. If the file is later restored the application might deem the entire file corrupt because it might be prepared to handle the case where the beginning has been modified and not the end, but not vice versa. These two problems illustrate why most backup utilities skip open files altogether.

EXPERIMENT: Viewing Shadow Volume Device Objects

You can see the existence of shadow volume device objects in the object manager namespace by starting the Windows backup application (under System Tools in the Accessories folder of the Start menu), and then running WinObj to see the objects in the \Device subdirectory, as shown here.

Name	Type	SymLink
HarddiskVolume15	Device	
HarddiskVolume2	Device	
HarddiskVolume3	Device	
HarddiskVolume4	Device	
HarddiskVolume5	Device	
HarddiskVolume6	Device	
HarddiskVolume7	Device	
HarddiskVolume8	Device	
HarddiskVolume9	Device	
HarddiskVolumeShadowCopy100	Device	
HarddiskVolumeShadowCopy101	Device	
HarddiskVolumeShadowCopy102	Device	
HarddiskVolumeShadowCopy103	Device	
HarddiskVolumeShadowCopy104	Device	
HarddiskVolumeShadowCopy105	Device	
HarddiskVolumeShadowCopy106	Device	
HarddiskVolumeShadowCopy107	Device	
HarddiskVolumeShadowCopy108	Device	
HarddiskVolumeShadowCopy109	Device	
HarddiskVolumeShadowCopy110	Device	
HarddiskVolumeShadowCopy111	Device	
HarddiskVolumeShadowCopy112	Device	
HarddiskVolumeShadowCopy113	Device	
HarddiskVolumeShadowCopy114	Device	
HarddiskVolumeShadowCopy115	Device	

\Device\HarddiskVolumeShadowCopy101

Instead of opening files to back up on the live volume, the backup utility opens them on the shadow volume. A shadow volume represents a point-in-time view of a volume, so by relying on the shadow copy facility, the backup utility overcomes both the backup problems related to open files.

Previous Versions and System Restore

The Windows Previous Versions feature also integrates support for automatically creating volume snapshots, typically one per day, that you can access through Explorer (by opening a Properties dialog box) using the same interface used by Shadow Copies for Shared Folders. This enables you to view, restore, or copy old versions of files and directories that you might have accidentally modified or deleted.

Windows also takes advantage of volume snapshots to unify user and system data-protection mechanisms and avoid saving redundant backup data. When an application installation or configuration change causes incorrect or undesirable behaviors, you can use System Restore to restore system files and data to their state as it existed when a restore point was created. When you use the System Restore user interface in Windows 7 to go back to a restore point, you're actually copying earlier versions of modified system files from the snapshot associated with the restore point to the live volume.

EXPERIMENT: Navigating Through Previous Versions

As you saw earlier, each time Windows creates a new system restore point, this results in a shadow copy being taken for that volume. You can use Windows Explorer to navigate through time and see older copies of each drive being shadowed. To see a list of all previous versions of an entire volume, right-click on a partition, such as C:, and select Restore Previous Versions. You will see a dialog box similar to the one shown here.

Pick any of the versions shown, and then click the Open button. This opens a new Explorer window displaying that volume at the point in time when the snapshot was taken. The path shown will include localhost\C$\<volume label> (<drive>:) (<date>, <time>), which is how Explorer virtualizes the different shadow copies taken. (C$ is the local hidden default share that Windows networking uses; for more information, see Chapter 7, "Networking," in Part 1.) Note that Explorer will normally display a path as a friendly name in its address bar. To see the actual path, click once within the address bar.

Note If your disk is drastically low on free space, the space consumed by the shadow copy will be reclaimed, in which case you might not have any previous versions.

Internally, each volume shadow copy shown isn't a complete copy of the drive, so it doesn't duplicate the entire contents twice, which would double disk space requirements for every single copy. Previous Versions uses the copy-on-write mechanism described earlier to create shadow copies. For example, if the only file that changed between time A and time B, when a volume shadow copy was taken, is New.txt, the shadow copy will contain only New.txt. This allows VSS to be used in client scenarios with minimal visible impact on the user, since entire drive contents are not duplicated and size constraints remain small.

Although shadow copies for previous versions are taken daily (or whenever a Windows Update or software installation is performed, for example), you can manually request a copy to be taken. This can be useful if, for example, you're about to make major changes to the system or have just copied a set of files you want to save immediately for the purpose of creating a previous version. You can access these settings by right-clicking Computer on the Start Menu or desktop, selecting Properties, and then clicking System Protection. You can also open Control Panel, click System And Maintenance, and then click System. The dialog box shown in Figure 9-31 allows you to select the volumes on which to enable System Restore (which also affects previous versions) and to create an immediate restore point and name it.

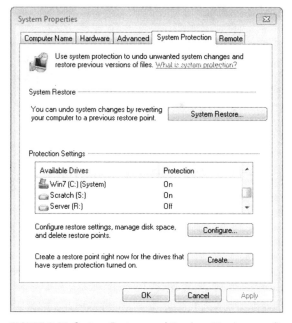

FIGURE 9-31 System Restore and Previous Versions configuration

EXPERIMENT: Mapping Volume Shadow Device Objects

Although you can browse previous versions by using Explorer, this doesn't give you a permanent interface through which you can access that view of the drive in an application-independent, persistent way. You can use the Vssadmin utility (%SystemRoot%\System32\Vssadmin.exe) included with Windows to view all the shadow copies taken, and you can then take advantage of symbolic links to map a copy. This experiment will show you how.

1. List all shadow copies available on the system by using the *list shadows* command:

   vssadmin list shadows

   You'll see output that resembles the following. Each entry is either a previous version copy or a shared folder with shadow copies enabled.

   ```
   vssadmin 1.1 - Volume Shadow Copy Service administrative command-line tool
   (C) Copyright 2001-2005 Microsoft Corp.

   Contents of shadow copy set ID: {dfe617b7-ef2b-4280-9f4e-ddf94c2ccfac}
      Contained 1 shadow copies at creation time: 8/27/2008 1:59:58 PM
         Shadow Copy ID: {f455a794-6b0c-49e4-9ae5-e54647fd1f31}
            Original Volume: (C:)\\?\Volume{f5f9d9c3-7466-11dd-9ba5-806e6f6e6963}\
            Shadow Copy Volume: \\?\GLOBALROOT\Device\HarddiskVolumeShadowCopy1
            Originating Machine: WIN-SL5V78KD01W
            Service Machine: WIN-SL5V78KD01W
            Provider: 'Microsoft Software Shadow Copy provider 1.0'
            Type: ClientAccessibleWriters
            Attributes: Persistent, Client-accessible, No auto release,
               Differential, Auto recovered

   Contents of shadow copy set ID: {02dad996-e7b0-4d2d-9fb9-7e692be8fe3c}
      Contained 1 shadow copies at creation time: 8/29/2008 1:51:14 AM
         Shadow Copy ID: {79c9ee14-ca1f-4e46-b3f0-0dc98f8eb0d4}
            Original Volume: (C:)\\?\Volume{f5f9d9c3-7466-11dd-9ba5-806e6f6e6963}\
            Shadow Copy Volume: \\?\GLOBALROOT\Device\HarddiskVolumeShadowCopy2.
   ...
   ```

   Note that each *shadow copy set ID* displayed in this output matches the C$ entries shown by Explorer in the previous experiment (although the date and time may be formatted differently), and the tool also displays the *shadow copy volume*, which corresponds to the shadow copy device objects that you can see with WinObj.

2. You can now use the Mklink.exe utility to create a directory symbolic link (for more information on symbolic links, see Chapter 12), which will let you map a shadow copy into an actual location. Use the */d* flag to create a directory link, and specify a folder on your drive to map to the given volume device object. Make sure to append the path with a backslash (\) as shown here:

   mklink /d c:\old \\?\GLOBALROOT\Device\HarddiskVolumeShadowCopy2

3. Finally, with the Subst.exe utility, you can map the c:\old directory to a real volume using the command shown here:

subst g: c:\old

You can now access the old contents of your drive from any application by using the c:\old path, or from any command-prompt utility by using the g:\ path—for example, try **dir g:** to list the contents of your drive.

Conclusion

In this chapter, we've reviewed the on-disk organization, components, and operation of Windows disk storage management. In Chapter 11, we'll delve into the cache manager, an executive component integral to the operation of file system drivers that mount the volume types presented in this chapter. However, next, we'll take a close look at an integral component of the Windows kernel: the memory manager.

CHAPTER 10

Memory Management

I n this chapter, you'll learn how Windows implements virtual memory and how it manages the subset of virtual memory kept in physical memory. We'll also describe the internal structure and components that make up the memory manager, including key data structures and algorithms. Before examining these mechanisms, we'll review the basic services provided by the memory manager and key concepts such as reserved memory versus committed memory and shared memory.

Introduction to the Memory Manager

By default, the virtual size of a process on 32-bit Windows is 2 GB. If the image is marked specifically as large address space aware, and the system is booted with a special option (described later in this chapter), a 32-bit process can grow to be 3 GB on 32-bit Windows and to 4 GB on 64-bit Windows. The process virtual address space size on 64-bit Windows is 7,152 GB on IA64 systems and 8,192 GB on x64 systems. (This value could be increased in future releases.)

As you saw in Chapter 2, "System Architecture," in Part 1 (specifically in Table 2-2), the maximum amount of physical memory currently supported by Windows ranges from 2 GB to 2,048 GB, depending on which version and edition of Windows you are running. Because the virtual address space might be larger or smaller than the physical memory on the machine, the memory manager has two primary tasks:

- Translating, or mapping, a process's virtual address space into physical memory so that when a thread running in the context of that process reads or writes to the virtual address space, the correct physical address is referenced. (The subset of a process's virtual address space that is physically resident is called the *working set*. Working sets are described in more detail later in this chapter.)

- Paging some of the contents of memory to disk when it becomes overcommitted—that is, when running threads or system code try to use more physical memory than is currently available—and bringing the contents back into physical memory when needed.

In addition to providing virtual memory management, the memory manager provides a core set of services on which the various Windows environment subsystems are built. These services include memory mapped files (internally called *section objects*), copy-on-write memory, and support for applications using large, sparse address spaces. In addition, the memory manager provides a way for a process to allocate and use larger amounts of physical memory than can be mapped into the process virtual address space at one time (for example, on 32-bit systems with more than 3 GB of physical memory). This is explained in the section "Address Windowing Extensions" later in this chapter.

> **Note** There is a Control Panel applet that provides control over the size, number, and locations of the paging files, and its nomenclature suggests that "virtual memory" is the same thing as the paging file. This is not the case. The paging file is only one aspect of virtual memory. In fact, even if you run with no page file at all, Windows will still be using virtual memory. This distinction is explained in more detail later in this chapter.

Memory Manager Components

The memory manager is part of the Windows executive and therefore exists in the file Ntoskrnl.exe. No parts of the memory manager exist in the HAL. The memory manager consists of the following components:

- A set of executive system services for allocating, deallocating, and managing virtual memory, most of which are exposed through the Windows API or kernel-mode device driver interfaces

- A translation-not-valid and access fault trap handler for resolving hardware-detected memory management exceptions and making virtual pages resident on behalf of a process

- Six key top-level routines, each running in one of six different kernel-mode threads in the System process (see the experiment "Mapping a System Thread to a Device Driver," which shows how to identify system threads, in Chapter 2 in Part 1):

  - The *balance set manager* (*KeBalanceSetManager*, priority 16). It calls an inner routine, the *working set manager (MmWorkingSetManager)*, once per second as well as when free memory falls below a certain threshold. The working set manager drives the overall memory management policies, such as working set trimming, aging, and modified page writing.

  - The *process/stack swapper* (*KeSwapProcessOrStack*, priority 23) performs both process and kernel thread stack inswapping and outswapping. The balance set manager and the thread-scheduling code in the kernel awaken this thread when an inswap or outswap operation needs to take place.

  - The *modified page writer* (*MiModifiedPageWriter*, priority 17) writes dirty pages on the modified list back to the appropriate paging files. This thread is awakened when the size of the modified list needs to be reduced.

  - The *mapped page writer* (*MiMappedPageWriter*, priority 17) writes dirty pages in mapped files to disk (or remote storage). It is awakened when the size of the modified list needs to be reduced or if pages for mapped files have been on the modified list for more than 5 minutes. This second modified page writer thread is necessary because it can generate page faults that result in requests for free pages. If there were no free pages and there was only one modified page writer thread, the system could deadlock waiting for free pages.

- The *segment dereference thread* (*MiDereferenceSegmentThread*, priority 18) is responsible for cache reduction as well as for page file growth and shrinkage. (For example, if there is no virtual address space for paged pool growth, this thread trims the page cache so that the paged pool used to anchor it can be freed for reuse.)

- The *zero page thread* (*MmZeroPageThread*, base priority 0) zeroes out pages on the free list so that a cache of zero pages is available to satisfy future demand-zero page faults. Unlike the other routines described here, this routine is not a top-level thread function but is called by the top-level thread routine *Phase1Initialization*. *MmZeroPageThread* never returns to its caller, so in effect the Phase 1 Initialization thread becomes the zero page thread by calling this routine. Memory zeroing in some cases is done by a faster function called *MiZeroInParallel*. See the note in the section "Page List Dynamics" later in this chapter.

Each of these components is covered in more detail later in the chapter.

Internal Synchronization

Like all other components of the Windows executive, the memory manager is fully reentrant and supports simultaneous execution on multiprocessor systems—that is, it allows two threads to acquire resources in such a way that they don't corrupt each other's data. To accomplish the goal of being fully reentrant, the memory manager uses several different internal synchronization mechanisms, such as spinlocks, to control access to its own internal data structures. (Synchronization objects are discussed in Chapter 3, "System Mechanisms," in Part 1.)

Some of the systemwide resources to which the memory manager must synchronize access include:

- Dynamically allocated portions of the system virtual address space

- System working sets

- Kernel memory pools

- The list of loaded drivers

- The list of paging files

- Physical memory lists

- Image base randomization (ASLR) structures

- Each individual entry in the page frame number (PFN) database

Per-process memory management data structures that require synchronization include the working set lock (held while changes are being made to the working set list) and the address space lock (held whenever the address space is being changed). Both these locks are implemented using pushlocks.

Examining Memory Usage

The Memory and Process performance counter objects provide access to most of the details about system and process memory utilization. Throughout the chapter, we'll include references to specific performance counters that contain information related to the component being described. We've included relevant examples and experiments throughout the chapter. One word of caution, however: different utilities use varying and sometimes inconsistent or confusing names when displaying memory information. The following experiment illustrates this point. (We'll explain the terms used in this example in subsequent sections.)

EXPERIMENT: Viewing System Memory Information

The Performance tab in the Windows Task Manager, shown in the following screen shot, displays basic system memory information. This information is a subset of the detailed memory information available through the performance counters. It includes data on both physical and virtual memory usage.

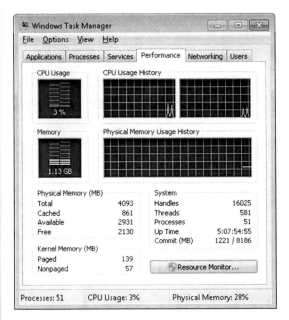

The following table shows the meaning of the memory-related values.

Task Manager Value	Definition
Memory bar histogram	Bar/chart line height shows physical memory in use by Windows (not available as a performance counter). The remaining height of the graph is equal to the Available counter in the Physical Memory section, described later in the table. The total height of the graph is equal to the Total counter in that section. This represents the total RAM usable by the operating system, and does not include BIOS shadow pages, device memory, and so on.

Task Manager Value	Definition
Physical Memory (MB): Total	Physical memory usable by Windows
Physical Memory (MB): Cached	Sum of the following performance counters in the Memory object: Cache Bytes, Modified Page List Bytes, Standby Cache Core Bytes, Standby Cache Normal Priority Bytes, and Standby Cache Reserve Bytes (all in Memory object)
Physical Memory (MB): Available	Amount of memory that is immediately available for use by the operating system, processes, and drivers. Equal to the combined size of the standby, free, and zero page lists.
Physical Memory (MB): Free	Free and zero page list bytes
Kernel Memory (MB): Paged	Pool paged bytes. This is the total size of the pool, including both free and allocated regions
Kernel Memory (MB): Nonpaged	Pool nonpaged bytes. This is the total size of the pool, including both free and allocated regions
System: Commit (two numbers shown)	Equal to performance counters Committed Bytes and Commit Limit, respectively

To see the specific usage of paged and nonpaged pool, use the Poolmon utility, described in the "Monitoring Pool Usage" section.

The Process Explorer tool from Windows Sysinternals (*http://www.microsoft.com/technet/sysinternals*) can show considerably more data about physical and virtual memory. On its main screen, click View and then System Information, and then choose the Memory tab. Here is an example display from a 32-bit Windows system:

We will explain most of these additional counters in the relevant sections later in this chapter.

Two other Sysinternals tools show extended memory information:

- VMMap shows the usage of virtual memory within a process to an extremely fine level of detail.

- RAMMap shows detailed physical memory usage.

These tools will be featured in experiments found later in this chapter.

Finally, the *!vm* command in the kernel debugger shows the basic memory management information available through the memory-related performance counters. This command can be useful if you're looking at a crash dump or hung system. Here's an example of its output from a 4-GB Windows client system:

```
1: kd> !vm

*** Virtual Memory Usage ***
        Physical Memory:       851757  (   3407028 Kb)
        Page File: \??\C:\pagefile.sys
          Current:    3407028 Kb  Free Space:    3407024 Kb
          Minimum:    3407028 Kb  Maximum:       4193280 Kb
        Available Pages:       699186  (   2796744 Kb)
        ResAvail Pages:        757454  (   3029816 Kb)
        Locked IO Pages:            0  (         0 Kb)
        Free System PTEs:      370673  (   1482692 Kb)
        Modified Pages:          9799  (     39196 Kb)
        Modified PF Pages:       9798  (     39192 Kb)
        NonPagedPool Usage:         0  (         0 Kb)
        NonPagedPoolNx Usage:    8735  (     34940 Kb)
        NonPagedPool Max:      522368  (   2089472 Kb)
        PagedPool 0 Usage:      17573  (     70292 Kb)
        PagedPool 1 Usage:       2417  (      9668 Kb)
        PagedPool 2 Usage:          0  (         0 Kb)
        PagedPool 3 Usage:          0  (         0 Kb)
        PagedPool 4 Usage:         28  (       112 Kb)
        PagedPool Usage:        20018  (     80072 Kb)
        PagedPool Maximum:     523264  (   2093056 Kb)
        Session Commit:          6218  (     24872 Kb)
        Shared Commit:          18591  (     74364 Kb)
        Special Pool:               0  (         0 Kb)
        Shared Process:          2151  (      8604 Kb)
        PagedPool Commit:       20031  (     80124 Kb)
        Driver Commit:           4531  (     18124 Kb)
        Committed pages:       179178  (    716712 Kb)
        Commit limit:         1702548  (   6810192 Kb)

        Total Private:          66073  (    264292 Kb)
         0a30 CCC.exe           11078  (     44312 Kb)
         0548 dwm.exe            6548  (     26192 Kb)
         091c MOM.exe            6103  (     24412 Kb)
    ...
```

We will describe many of the details of the output of this command later in this chapter.

Services Provided by the Memory Manager

The memory manager provides a set of system services to allocate and free virtual memory, share memory between processes, map files into memory, flush virtual pages to disk, retrieve information about a range of virtual pages, change the protection of virtual pages, and lock the virtual pages into memory.

Like other Windows executive services, the memory management services allow their caller to supply a process handle indicating the particular process whose virtual memory is to be manipulated. The caller can thus manipulate either its own memory or (with the proper permissions) the memory of another process. For example, if a process creates a child process, by default it has the right to manipulate the child process's virtual memory. Thereafter, the parent process can allocate, deallocate, read, and write memory on behalf of the child process by calling virtual memory services and passing a handle to the child process as an argument. This feature is used by subsystems to manage the memory of their client processes. It is also essential for implementing debuggers because debuggers must be able to read and write to the memory of the process being debugged.

Most of these services are exposed through the Windows API. The Windows API has three groups of functions for managing memory in applications: heap functions (*Heapxxx* and the older interfaces *Localxxx* and *Globalxxx*, which internally make use of the *Heapxxx* APIs), which may be used for allocations smaller than a page; virtual memory functions, which operate with page granularity (*Virtualxxx*); and memory mapped file functions (*CreateFileMapping*, *CreateFileMappingNuma*, *MapViewOfFile*, *MapViewOfFileEx*, and *MapViewOfFileExNuma*). (We'll describe the heap manager later in this chapter.)

The memory manager also provides a number of services (such as allocating and deallocating physical memory and locking pages in physical memory for direct memory access [DMA] transfers) to other kernel-mode components inside the executive as well as to device drivers. These functions begin with the prefix *Mm*. In addition, though not strictly part of the memory manager, some executive support routines that begin with *Ex* are used to allocate and deallocate from the system heaps (paged and nonpaged pool) as well as to manipulate look-aside lists. We'll touch on these topics later in this chapter in the section "Kernel-Mode Heaps (System Memory Pools)."

Large and Small Pages

The virtual address space is divided into units called pages. That is because the hardware memory management unit translates virtual to physical addresses at the granularity of a page. Hence, a page is the smallest unit of protection at the hardware level. (The various page protection options are described in the section "Protecting Memory" later in the chapter.) The processors on which Windows runs support two page sizes, called small and large. The actual sizes vary based on the processor architecture, and they are listed in Table 10-1.

TABLE 10-1 Page Sizes

Architecture	Small Page Size	Large Page Size	Small Pages per Large Page
x86	4 KB	4 MB (2 MB if Physical Address Extension (PAE) enabled (PAE is described later in the chapter)	1,024 (512 with PAE)
x64	4 KB	2 MB	512
IA64	8 KB	16 MB	2,048

Note IA64 processors support a variety of dynamically configurable page sizes, from 4 KB up to 256 MB. Windows on Itanium uses 8 KB and 16 MB for small and large pages, respectively, as a result of performance tests that confirmed these values as optimal. Additionally, recent x64 processors support a size of 1 GB for large pages, but Windows does not use this feature.

The primary advantage of large pages is speed of address translation for references to other data within the large page. This advantage exists because the first reference to any byte within a large page will cause the hardware's translation look-aside buffer (TLB, described in a later section) to have in its cache the information necessary to translate references to any other byte within the large page. If small pages are used, more TLB entries are needed for the same range of virtual addresses, thus increasing recycling of entries as new virtual addresses require translation. This, in turn, means having to go back to the page table structures when references are made to virtual addresses outside the scope of a small page whose translation has been cached. The TLB is a very small cache, and thus large pages make better use of this limited resource.

To take advantage of large pages on systems with more than 2 GB of RAM, Windows maps with large pages the core operating system images (Ntoskrnl.exe and Hal.dll) as well as core operating system data (such as the initial part of nonpaged pool and the data structures that describe the state of each physical memory page). Windows also automatically maps I/O space requests (calls by device drivers to *MmMapIoSpace*) with large pages if the request is of satisfactory large page length and alignment. In addition, Windows allows applications to map their images, private memory, and page-file-backed sections with large pages. (See the MEM_LARGE_PAGE flag on the *VirtualAlloc*, *VirtualAllocEx*, and *VirtualAllocExNuma* functions.) You can also specify other device drivers to be mapped with large pages by adding a multistring registry value to HKLM\SYSTEM\CurrentControlSet\Control\Session Manager\Memory Management\LargePageDrivers and specifying the names of the drivers as separately null-terminated strings.

Attempts to allocate large pages may fail after the operating system has been running for an extended period, because the physical memory for each large page must occupy a significant number (see Table 10-1) of physically contiguous small pages, and this extent of physical pages must furthermore begin on a large page boundary. (For example, physical pages 0 through 511 could be used as a large page on an x64 system, as could physical pages 512 through 1,023, but pages 10 through 521 could not.) Free physical memory does become fragmented as the system runs. This is not a problem for allocations using small pages but can cause large page allocations to fail.

It is not possible to specify anything but read/write access to large pages. The memory is also always nonpageable, because the page file system does not support large pages. And, because the memory is nonpageable, it is not considered part of the process working set (described later). Nor are large page allocations subject to job-wide limits on virtual memory usage.

There is an unfortunate side effect of large pages. Each page (whether large or small) must be mapped with a single protection that applies to the entire page (because hardware memory protection is on a per-page basis). If a large page contains, for example, both read-only code and read/write data, the page must be marked as read/write, which means that the code will be writable. This means that device drivers or other kernel-mode code could, as a result of a bug, modify what is supposed to be read-only operating system or driver code without causing a memory access violation. If small pages are used to map the operating system's kernel-mode code, the read-only portions of Ntoskrnl.exe and Hal.dll can be mapped as read-only pages. Using small pages does reduce efficiency of address translation, but if a device driver (or other kernel-mode code) attempts to modify a read-only part of the operating system, the system will crash immediately with the exception information pointing at the offending instruction in the driver. If the write was allowed to occur, the system would likely crash later (in a harder-to-diagnose way) when some other component tried to use the corrupted data.

If you suspect you are experiencing kernel code corruptions, enable Driver Verifier (described later in this chapter), which will disable the use of large pages.

Reserving and Committing Pages

Pages in a process virtual address space are *free*, *reserved*, *committed*, or *shareable*. Committed and shareable pages are pages that, when accessed, ultimately translate to valid pages in physical memory.

Committed pages are also referred to as *private* pages. This reflects the fact that committed pages cannot be shared with other processes, whereas shareable pages can be (but, of course, might be in use by only one process).

Private pages are allocated through the Windows *VirtualAlloc*, *VirtualAllocEx*, and *VirtualAllocExNuma* functions. These functions allow a thread to reserve address space and then commit portions of the reserved space. The intermediate "reserved" state allows the thread to set aside a range of contiguous virtual addresses for possible future use (such as an array), while consuming negligible system resources, and then commit portions of the reserved space as needed as the application runs. Or, if the size requirements are known in advance, a thread can reserve and commit in the same function call. In either case, the resulting committed pages can then be accessed by the thread. Attempting to access free or reserved memory results in an exception because the page isn't mapped to any storage that can resolve the reference.

If committed (private) pages have never been accessed before, they are created at the time of first access as zero-initialized pages (or *demand zero*). Private committed pages may later be automatically written to the paging file by the operating system if required by demand for physical memory. "Private" refers to the fact that these pages are normally inaccessible to any other process.

> **Note** There are functions, such as *ReadProcessMemory* and *WriteProcessMemory*, that apparently permit cross-process memory access, but these are implemented by running kernel-mode code in the context of the target process (this is referred to as *attaching to the process*). They also require that either the security descriptor of the target process grant the accessor the PROCESS_VM_READ or PROCESS_VM_WRITE right, respectively, or that the accessor holds SeDebugPrivilege, which is by default granted only to members of the Administrators group.

Shared pages are usually mapped to a view of a *section*, which in turn is part or all of a file, but may instead represent a portion of page file space. All shared pages can potentially be shared with other processes. Sections are exposed in the Windows API as file mapping objects.

When a shared page is first accessed by any process, it will be read in from the associated mapped file (unless the section is associated with the paging file, in which case it is created as a zero-initialized page). Later, if it is still *resident* in physical memory, the second and subsequent processes accessing it can simply use the same page contents that are already in memory. Shared pages might also have been *prefetched* by the system.

Two upcoming sections of this chapter, "Shared Memory and Mapped Files" and "Section Objects," go into much more detail about shared pages. Pages are written to disk through a mechanism called *modified page writing*. This occurs as pages are moved from a process's *working set* to a systemwide list called the *modified page list;* from there, they are written to disk (or remote storage). (Working sets and the modified list are explained later in this chapter.) Mapped file pages can also be written back to their original files on disk as a result of an explicit call to *FlushViewOfFile* or by the mapped page writer as memory demands dictate.

You can decommit private pages and/or release address space with the *VirtualFree* or *VirtualFreeEx* function. The difference between decommittal and release is similar to the difference between reservation and committal—decommitted memory is still reserved, but released memory has been freed; it is neither committed nor reserved.

Using the two-step process of reserving and then committing virtual memory defers committing pages—and, thereby, defers adding to the system "commit charge" described in the next section—until needed, but keeps the convenience of virtual contiguity. Reserving memory is a relatively inexpensive operation because it consumes very little actual memory. All that needs to be updated or constructed is the relatively small internal data structures that represent the state of the process address space. (We'll explain these data structures, called *page tables* and *virtual address descriptors*, or VADs, later in the chapter.)

One extremely common use for reserving a large space and committing portions of it as needed is the user-mode stack for each thread. When a thread is created, a stack is created by reserving a contiguous portion of the process address space. (1 MB is the default; you can override this size with the

CreateThread and *CreateRemoteThread* function calls or change it on an imagewide basis by using the /STACK linker flag.) By default, the initial page in the stack is committed and the next page is marked as a guard page (which isn't committed) that traps references beyond the end of the committed portion of the stack and expands it.

EXPERIMENT: Reserved vs. Committed Pages

The TestLimit utility (which you can download from the *Windows Internals* book webpage) can be used to allocate large amounts of either reserved or private committed virtual memory, and the difference can be observed via Process Explorer. First, open two Command Prompt windows. Invoke TestLimit in one of them to create a large amount of reserved memory:

```
C:\temp>testlimit -r 1 -c 800

Testlimit v5.2 - test Windows limits
Copyright (C) 2012 Mark Russinovich
Sysinternals - www.sysinternals.com

Process ID: 1544

Reserving private bytes 1 MB at a time ...
Leaked 800 MB of reserved memory (800 MB total leaked). Lasterror: 0
The operation completed successfully.
```

In the other window, create a similar amount of committed memory:

```
C:\temp>testlimit -m 1 -c 800

Testlimit v5.2 - test Windows limits
Copyright (C) 2012 Mark Russinovich
Sysinternals - www.sysinternals.com

Process ID: 2828

Leaking private bytes 1 KB at a time ...
Leaked 800 MB of private memory (800 MB total leaked). Lasterror: 0
The operation completed successfully.
```

Now run Task Manager, go to the Processes tab, and use the Select Columns command on the View menu to include Memory—Commit Size in the display. Find the two instances of Test-Limit in the list. They should appear something like the following figure.

Task Manager shows the committed size, but it has no counters that will reveal the reserved memory in the other TestLimit process.

Finally, invoke Process Explorer. Choose View, Select Columns, select the Process Memory tab, and enable the Private Bytes and Virtual Size counters. Find the two TestLimit processes in the main display:

Notice that the virtual sizes of the two processes are identical, but only one shows a value for Private Bytes comparable to that for Virtual Size. The large difference in the other TestLimit process (process ID 1544) is due to the reserved memory. The same comparison could be made in Performance Monitor by looking at the Process | Virtual Bytes and Process | Private Bytes counters.

Commit Limit

On Task Manager's Performance tab, there are two numbers following the legend Commit. The memory manager keeps track of private committed memory usage on a global basis, termed *commitment* or *commit charge*; this is the first of the two numbers, which represents the total of all committed virtual memory in the system.

There is a systemwide limit, called the *system commit limit* or simply the *commit limit*, on the amount of committed virtual memory that can exist at any one time. This limit corresponds to the current total size of all paging files, plus the amount of RAM that is usable by the operating system. This is the second of the two numbers displayed as Commit on Task Manager's Performance tab. The memory manager can increase the commit limit automatically by expanding one or more of the paging files, if they are not already at their configured maximum size.

Commit charge and the system commit limit will be explained in more detail in a later section.

Locking Memory

In general, it's better to let the memory manager decide which pages remain in physical memory. However, there might be special circumstances where it might be necessary for an application or device driver to lock pages in physical memory. Pages can be locked in memory in two ways:

- Windows applications can call the *VirtualLock* function to lock pages in their process working set. Pages locked using this mechanism remain in memory until explicitly unlocked or until the process that locked them terminates. The number of pages a process can lock can't exceed its minimum working set size minus eight pages. Therefore, if a process needs to lock more pages, it can increase its working set minimum with the *SetProcessWorkingSetSizeEx* function (referred to in the section "Working Set Management").

- Device drivers can call the kernel-mode functions *MmProbeAndLockPages*, *MmLockPagableCodeSection*, *MmLockPagableDataSection*, or *MmLockPagableSectionByHandle*. Pages locked using this mechanism remain in memory until explicitly unlocked. The last three of these APIs enforce no quota on the number of pages that can be locked in memory because the resident available page charge is obtained when the driver first loads; this ensures that it can never cause a system crash due to overlocking. For the first API, quota charges must be obtained or the API will return a failure status.

Allocation Granularity

Windows aligns each region of reserved process address space to begin on an integral boundary defined by the value of the system *allocation granularity*, which can be retrieved from the Windows *GetSystemInfo* or *GetNativeSystemInfo* function. This value is 64 KB, a granularity that is used by the memory manager to efficiently allocate metadata (for example, VADs, bitmaps, and so on) to support various process operations. In addition, if support were added for future processors with larger page sizes (for example, up to 64 KB) or virtually indexed caches that require systemwide physical-to-virtual page alignment, the risk of requiring changes to applications that made assumptions about allocation alignment would be reduced.

> **Note** Windows kernel-mode code isn't subject to the same restrictions; it can reserve memory on a single-page granularity (although this is not exposed to device drivers for the reasons detailed earlier). This level of granularity is primarily used to pack TEB allocations more densely, and because this mechanism is internal only, this code can easily be changed if a future platform requires different values. Also, for the purposes of supporting 16-bit and MS-DOS applications on x86 systems only, the memory manager provides the MEM_DOS_LIM flag to the *MapViewOfFileEx* API, which is used to force the use of single-page granularity.

Finally, when a region of address space is reserved, Windows ensures that the size and base of the region is a multiple of the system page size, whatever that might be. For example, because x86 systems use 4-KB pages, if you tried to reserve a region of memory 18 KB in size, the actual amount reserved on an x86 system would be 20 KB. If you specified a base address of 3 KB for an 18-KB region, the actual amount reserved would be 24 KB. Note that the VAD for the allocation would then also be rounded to 64-KB alignment/length, thus making the remainder of it inaccessible. (VADs will be described later in this chapter.)

Shared Memory and Mapped Files

As is true with most modern operating systems, Windows provides a mechanism to share memory among processes and the operating system. *Shared memory* can be defined as memory that is visible to more than one process or that is present in more than one process virtual address space. For example, if two processes use the same DLL, it would make sense to load the referenced code pages for that DLL into physical memory only once and share those pages between all processes that map the DLL, as illustrated in Figure 10-1.

Each process would still maintain its private memory areas in which to store private data, but the DLL code and unmodified data pages could be shared without harm. As we'll explain later, this kind of sharing happens automatically because the code pages in executable images (.exe and .dll files, and several other types like screen savers (.scr), which are essentially DLLs under other names) are mapped as execute-only and writable pages are mapped as copy-on-write. (See the section "Copy-on-Write" for more information.)

The underlying primitives in the memory manager used to implement shared memory are called *section objects*, which are exposed as *file mapping objects* in the Windows API. The internal structure and implementation of section objects are described in the section "Section Objects" later in this chapter.

This fundamental primitive in the memory manager is used to map virtual addresses, whether in main memory, in the page file, or in some other file that an application wants to access as if it were in memory. A section can be opened by one process or by many; in other words, section objects don't necessarily equate to shared memory.

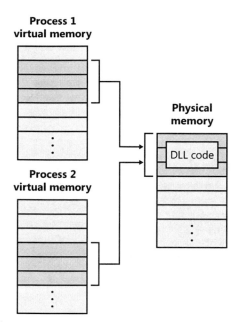

Process 1 virtual memory

Physical memory

DLL code

Process 2 virtual memory

FIGURE 10-1 Sharing memory between processes

A section object can be connected to an open file on disk (called a mapped file) or to committed memory (to provide shared memory). Sections mapped to committed memory are called *page-file-backed sections* because the pages are written to the paging file (as opposed to a mapped file) if demands on physical memory require it. (Because Windows can run with no paging file, page-file-backed sections might in fact be "backed" only by physical memory.) As with any other empty page that is made visible to user mode (such as private committed pages), shared committed pages are always zero-filled when they are first accessed to ensure that no sensitive data is ever leaked.

To create a section object, call the Windows *CreateFileMapping* or *CreateFileMappingNuma* function, specifying the file handle to map it to (or INVALID_HANDLE_VALUE for a page-file-backed section) and optionally a name and security descriptor. If the section has a name, other processes can open it with *OpenFileMapping*. Or you can grant access to section objects through either handle inheritance (by specifying that the handle be inheritable when opening or creating the handle) or handle duplication (by using *DuplicateHandle*). Device drivers can also manipulate section objects with the *ZwOpenSection*, *ZwMapViewOfSection*, and *ZwUnmapViewOfSection* functions.

A section object can refer to files that are much larger than can fit in the address space of a process. (If the paging file backs a section object, sufficient space must exist in the paging file and/or RAM to contain it.) To access a very large section object, a process can map only the portion of the section object that it requires (called a *view* of the section) by calling the *MapViewOfFile, MapViewOfFileEx, or MapViewOfFileExNuma* function and then specifying the range to map. Mapping views permits processes to conserve address space because only the views of the section object needed at the time must be mapped into memory.

Windows applications can use mapped files to conveniently perform I/O to files by simply making them appear in their address space. User applications aren't the only consumers of section objects: the image loader uses section objects to map executable images, DLLs, and device drivers into memory, and the cache manager uses them to access data in cached files. (For information on how the cache manager integrates with the memory manager, see Chapter 11, "Cache Manager.") The implementation of shared memory sections, both in terms of address translation and the internal data structures, is explained later in this chapter.

EXPERIMENT: Viewing Memory Mapped Files

You can list the memory mapped files in a process by using Process Explorer from Sysinternals. To view the memory mapped files by using Process Explorer, configure the lower pane to show the DLL view. (Click on View, Lower Pane View, DLLs.) Note that this is more than just a list of DLLs—it represents all memory mapped files in the process address space. Some of these are DLLs, one is the image file (EXE) being run, and additional entries might represent memory mapped data files.

For example, the following display from Process Explorer shows a WinDbg process using several different memory mappings to access the memory dump file being examined. Like most Windows programs, it (or one of the Windows DLLs it is using) is also using memory mapping to access a Windows data file called Locale.nls, which is part of the internationalization support in Windows.

Name	Description	Version	Base	ASLR	Mapping
kernel32.dll	Windows NT BASE API Client DLL	6.1.7601.17651	0x77650000	ASLR	Image
KernelBase.dll	Windows NT BASE API Client DLL	6.1.7601.17651	0x75EC0000	ASLR	Image
kext.dll	Debugger Extensions	6.12.2.633	0x737E0000	ASLR	Image
linkinfo.dll	Windows Volume Tracking	6.1.7600.16385	0x701A0000	ASLR	Image
locale.nls			0x110000	n/a	Data
lpk.dll	Language Pack	6.1.7600.16385	0x77CF0000	ASLR	Image
MEMORY.DMP			0x1410000	n/a	Data
MEMORY.DMP			0x1420000	n/a	Data
MEMORY.DMP			0x1550000	n/a	Data

CPU Usage: 3.04% Commit Charge: 35.03% Processes: 50 Physical Usage: 44.15%

You can also search for memory mapped files by clicking Find, DLL. This can be useful when trying to determine which process(es) are using a DLL or a memory mapped file that you are trying to replace.

Protecting Memory

As explained in Chapter 1, "Concepts and Tools," in Part 1, Windows provides memory protection so that no user process can inadvertently or deliberately corrupt the address space of another process or of the operating system. Windows provides this protection in four primary ways.

First, all systemwide data structures and memory pools used by kernel-mode system components can be accessed only while in kernel mode—user-mode threads can't access these pages. If they attempt to do so, the hardware generates a fault, which in turn the memory manager reports to the thread as an access violation.

Second, each process has a separate, private address space, protected from being accessed by any thread belonging to another process. Even shared memory is not really an exception to this because each process accesses the shared regions using addresses that are part of its own virtual address space. The only exception is if another process has virtual memory read or write access to the process object (or holds SeDebugPrivilege) and thus can use the *ReadProcessMemory* or *WriteProcessMemory* function. Each time a thread references an address, the virtual memory hardware, in concert with the memory manager, intervenes and translates the virtual address into a physical one. By controlling how virtual addresses are translated, Windows can ensure that threads running in one process don't inappropriately access a page belonging to another process.

Third, in addition to the implicit protection virtual-to-physical address translation offers, all processors supported by Windows provide some form of hardware-controlled memory protection (such as read/write, read-only, and so on); the exact details of such protection vary according to the processor. For example, code pages in the address space of a process are marked read-only and are thus protected from modification by user threads.

Table 10-2 lists the memory protection options defined in the Windows API. (See the *Virtual-Protect*, *VirtualProtectEx*, *VirtualQuery*, and *VirtualQueryEx* functions.)

TABLE 10-2 Memory Protection Options Defined in the Windows API

Attribute	Description
PAGE_NOACCESS	Any attempt to read from, write to, or execute code in this region causes an access violation.
PAGE_READONLY	Any attempt to write to (and on processors with no execute support, execute code in) memory causes an access violation, but reads are permitted.
PAGE_READWRITE	The page is readable and writable but not executable.
PAGE_EXECUTE	Any attempt to write to code in memory in this region causes an access violation, but execution (and read operations on all existing processors) is permitted.
PAGE_EXECUTE_READ*	Any attempt to write to memory in this region causes an access violation, but executes and reads are permitted.
PAGE_EXECUTE_READWRITE*	The page is readable, writable, and executable—any attempted access will succeed.
PAGE_WRITECOPY	Any attempt to write to memory in this region causes the system to give the process a private copy of the page. On processors with no-execute support, attempts to execute code in memory in this region cause an access violation.

Attribute	Description
PAGE_EXECUTE_WRITECOPY	Any attempt to write to memory in this region causes the system to give the process a private copy of the page. Reading and executing code in this region is permitted. (No copy is made in this case.)
PAGE_GUARD	Any attempt to read from or write to a guard page raises an EXCEPTION_GUARD_PAGE exception and turns off the guard page status. Guard pages thus act as a one-shot alarm. Note that this flag can be specified with any of the page protections listed in this table except PAGE_NOACCESS.
PAGE_NOCACHE	Uses physical memory that is not cached. This is not recommended for general usage. It is useful for device drivers—for example, mapping a video frame buffer with no caching.
PAGE_WRITECOMBINE	Enables write-combined memory accesses. When enabled, the processor does not cache memory writes (possibly causing significantly more memory traffic than if memory writes were cached), but it does try to aggregate write requests to optimize performance. For example, if multiple writes are made to the same address, only the most recent write might occur. Separate writes to adjacent addresses may be similarly collapsed into a single large write. This is not typically used for general applications, but it is useful for device drivers—for example, mapping a video frame buffer as write combined.

* No execute protection is supported on processors that have the necessary hardware support (for example, all x64 and IA64 processors) but not in older x86 processors.

And finally, shared memory section objects have standard Windows access control lists (ACLs) that are checked when processes attempt to open them, thus limiting access of shared memory to those processes with the proper rights. Access control also comes into play when a thread creates a section to contain a mapped file. To create the section, the thread must have at least read access to the underlying file object or the operation will fail.

Once a thread has successfully opened a handle to a section, its actions are still subject to the memory manager and the hardware-based page protections described earlier. A thread can change the page-level protection on virtual pages in a section if the change doesn't violate the permissions in the ACL for that section object. For example, the memory manager allows a thread to change the pages of a read-only section to have copy-on-write access but not to have read/write access. The copy-on-write access is permitted because it has no effect on other processes sharing the data.

No Execute Page Protection

No execute page protection (also referred to as data execution prevention, or DEP) causes an attempt to transfer control to an instruction in a page marked as "no execute" to generate an access fault. This can prevent certain types of malware from exploiting bugs in the system through the execution of code placed in a data page such as the stack. DEP can also catch poorly written programs that don't correctly set permissions on pages from which they intend to execute code. If an attempt is made in kernel mode to execute code in a page marked as no execute, the system will crash with the ATTEMPTED_EXECUTE_OF_NOEXECUTE_MEMORY bugcheck code. (See Chapter 14, "Crash Dump Analysis," for an explanation of these codes.) If this occurs in user mode, a STATUS_ACCESS_VIOLATION (0xc0000005) exception is delivered to the thread attempting the illegal reference. If a process allocates memory that needs to be executable, it must explicitly mark such pages by specifying the PAGE_EXECUTE, PAGE_EXECUTE_READ, PAGE_EXECUTE_READWRITE, or PAGE_EXECUTE_WRITECOPY flags on the page granularity memory allocation functions.

On 32-bit x86 systems that support DEP, bit 63 in the page table entry (PTE) is used to mark a page as nonexecutable. Therefore, the DEP feature is available only when the processor is running in Physical Address Extension (PAE) mode, without which page table entries are only 32 bits wide. (See the section "Physical Address Extension (PAE)" later in this chapter.) Thus, support for hardware DEP on 32-bit systems requires loading the PAE kernel (%SystemRoot%\System32\Ntkrnlpa.exe), even if that system does not require extended physical addressing (for example, physical addresses greater than 4 GB). The operating system loader automatically loads the PAE kernel on 32-bit systems that support hardware DEP. To force the non-PAE kernel to load on a system that supports hardware DEP, the BCD option *nx* must be set to *AlwaysOff*, and the *pae* option must be set to *ForceDisable*.

On 64-bit versions of Windows, execution protection is always applied to all 64-bit processes and device drivers and can be disabled only by setting the *nx* BCD option to *AlwaysOff*. Execution protection for 32-bit programs depends on system configuration settings, described shortly. On 64-bit Windows, execution protection is applied to thread stacks (both user and kernel mode), user-mode pages not specifically marked as executable, kernel paged pool, and kernel session pool (for a description of kernel memory pools, see the section "Kernel-Mode Heaps (System Memory Pools)." However, on 32-bit Windows, execution protection is applied only to thread stacks and user-mode pages, not to paged pool and session pool.

The application of execution protection for 32-bit processes depends on the value of the BCD *nx* option. The settings can be changed by going to the Data Execution Prevention tab under Computer, Properties, Advanced System Settings, Performance Settings. (See Figure 10-2.) When you configure no execute protection in the Performance Options dialog box, the BCD *nx* option is set to the appropriate value. Table 10-3 lists the variations of the values and how they correspond to the DEP settings tab. The registry lists 32-bit applications that are excluded from execution protection under the key HKLM\SOFTWARE\Microsoft\Windows NT\CurrentVersion\AppCompatFlags\Layers, with the value name being the full path of the executable and the data set to "DisableNXShowUI".

On Windows client versions (both 64-bit and 32-bit) execution protection for 32-bit processes is configured by default to apply only to core Windows operating system executables (the *nx* BCD option is set to *OptIn*) so as not to break 32-bit applications that might rely on being able to execute code in pages not specifically marked as executable, such as self-extracting or packed applications. On Windows server systems, execution protection for 32-bit applications is configured by default to apply to all 32-bit programs (the *nx* BCD option is set to *OptOut*).

> **Note** To obtain a complete list of which programs are protected, install the Windows Application Compatibility Toolkit (downloadable from *www.microsoft.com*) and run the Compatibility Administrator Tool. Click System Database, Applications, and then Windows Components. The pane at the right shows the list of protected executables.

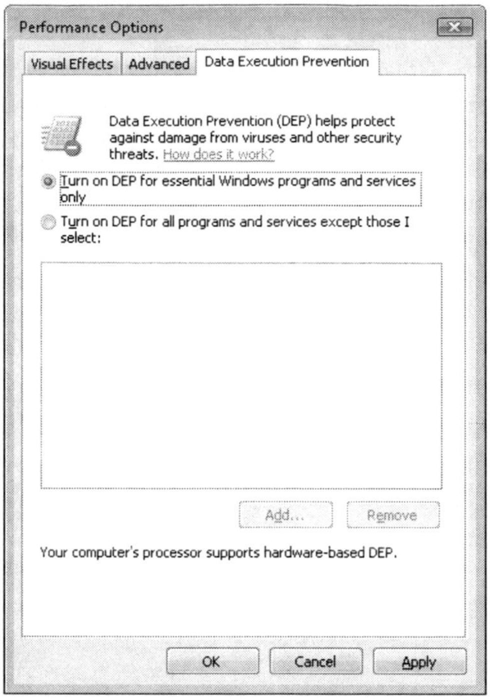

FIGURE 10-2 Data Execution Prevention tab settings

TABLE 10-3 BCD *nx* Values

BCD *nx* Value	Option on DEP Settings Tab	Meaning
OptIn	Turn on DEP for essential Windows programs and services only	Enables DEP for core Windows system images. Enables 32-bit processes to dynamically configure DEP for their lifetime.
OptOut	Turn on DEP for all programs and services except those I select	Enables DEP for all executables except those specified. Enables 32-bit processes to dynamically configure DEP for their lifetime. Enables system compatibility fixes for DEP.
AlwaysOn	No dialog box option for this setting	Enables DEP for all components with no ability to exclude certain applications. Disables dynamic configuration for 32-bit processes, and disables system compatibility fixes.
AlwaysOff	No dialog box option for this setting	Disables DEP (not recommended). Disables dynamic configuration for 32-bit processes.

Even if you force DEP to be enabled, there are still other methods through which applications can disable DEP for their own images. For example, regardless of the execution protection options that are enabled, the image loader (see Chapter 3 in Part 1 for more information about the image loader) will verify the signature of the executable against known copy-protection mechanisms (such as SafeDisc and SecuROM) and disable execution protection to provide compatibility with older copy-protected software such as computer games.

EXPERIMENT: Looking at DEP Protection on Processes

Process Explorer can show you the current DEP status for all the processes on your system, including whether the process is opted in or benefiting from permanent protection. To look at the DEP status for processes, right-click any column in the process tree, choose Select Columns, and then select DEP Status on the Process Image tab. Three values are possible:

- **DEP (permanent)** This means that the process has DEP enabled because it is a "necessary Windows program or service."

- **DEP** This means that the process opted in to DEP. This may be due to a systemwide policy to opt in all 32-bit processes, an API call such as *SetProcessDEPPolicy*, or setting the linker flag /NXCOMPAT when the image was built.

- **Nothing** If the column displays no information for this process, DEP is disabled, either because of a systemwide policy or an explicit API call or shim.

The following Process Explorer window shows an example of a system on which DEP is set to OptOut, Turn On DEP For All Programs And Services Except Those That I Select. Note that two processes running in the user's login, a third-party sound-card manager and a USB port monitor, show simply DEP, meaning that DEP can be turned off for them via the dialog box shown in Figure 10-2. The other processes shown are running Windows in-box programs and show DEP (Permanent), indicating that DEP cannot be disabled for them.

Process	PID	CPU	Description	Company Name	DEP
sppsvc.exe	3756		Microsoft Software Protection Platf...	Microsoft Corporation	DEP (permanent)
svchost.exe	3792		Host Process for Windows Services	Microsoft Corporation	DEP (permanent)
lsass.exe	576	< 0.01	Local Security Authority Process	Microsoft Corporation	DEP (permanent)
lsm.exe	584		Local Session Manager Service	Microsoft Corporation	DEP (permanent)
csrss.exe	512	0.06	Client Server Runtime Process	Microsoft Corporation	DEP (permanent)
conhost.exe	2516	< 0.01	Console Window Host	Microsoft Corporation	DEP (permanent)
conhost.exe	2032	< 0.01	Console Window Host	Microsoft Corporation	DEP (permanent)
conhost.exe	2884	< 0.01	Console Window Host	Microsoft Corporation	DEP (permanent)
conhost.exe	3228	< 0.01	Console Window Host	Microsoft Corporation	DEP (permanent)
winlogon.exe	680		Windows Logon Application	Microsoft Corporation	DEP (permanent)
explorer.exe	1420	0.07	Windows Explorer	Microsoft Corporation	DEP (permanent)
RtHDVCpl.exe	2232		Realtek HD Audio Manager	Realtek Semiconductor	DEP
nusb3mon.exe	2248		USB 3.0 Monitor	Renesas Electronics C...	DEP
cmd.exe	2520		Windows Command Processor	Microsoft Corporation	DEP (permanent)
procexp.exe	2620	0.97	Sysinternals Process Explorer	Sysinternals - www.sys...	DEP (permanent)
RAMMap.exe	1148	< 0.01	RamMap - physical memory analyzer	Sysinternals - www.sys...	DEP (permanent)

CPU Usage: 1.81%   Commit Charge: 35.38%   Processes: 49   Physical Usage: 44.75%

Additionally, to provide compatibility with older versions of the Active Template Library (ATL) framework (version 7.1 or earlier), the Windows kernel provides an ATL thunk emulation environment. This environment detects ATL thunk code sequences that have caused the DEP exception and emulates the expected operation. Application developers can request that ATL thunk emulation not be applied by using the latest Microsoft C++ compiler and specifying the /NXCOMPAT flag (which sets the IMAGE_DLLCHARACTERISTICS_NX_COMPAT flag in the PE header), which tells the system that the executable fully supports DEP. Note that ATL thunk emulation is permanently disabled if the *AlwaysOn* value is set.

Finally, if the system is in *OptIn* or *OptOut* mode and executing a 32-bit process, the *SetProcess-DEPPolicy* function allows a process to dynamically disable DEP or to permanently enable it. (Once enabled through this API, DEP cannot be disabled programmatically for the lifetime of the process.) This function can also be used to dynamically disable ATL thunk emulation in case the image wasn't compiled with the /NXCOMPAT flag. On 64-bit processes or systems booted with *AlwaysOff* or *AlwaysOn*, the function always returns a failure. The *GetProcessDEPPolicy* function returns the 32-bit per-process DEP policy (it fails on 64-bit systems, where the policy is always the same—enabled), while *GetSystemDEPPolicy* can be used to return a value corresponding to the policies in Table 10-3.

Software Data Execution Prevention

For older processors that do not support hardware no execute protection, Windows supports limited *software data execution prevention* (DEP). One aspect of software DEP reduces exploits of the exception handling mechanism in Windows. (See Chapter 3 in Part 1 for a description of structured exception handling.) If the program's image files are built with safe structured exception handling (a feature in the Microsoft Visual C++ compiler that is enabled with the /SAFESEH flag), before an exception is dispatched, the system verifies that the exception handler is registered in the function table (built by the compiler) located within the image file.

The previous mechanism depends on the program's image files being built with safe structured exception handling. If they are not, software DEP guards against overwrites of the structured exception handling chain on the stack in x86 processes via a mechanism known as Structured Exception Handler Overwrite Protection (SEHOP). A new *symbolic exception registration record* is added on the stack when a thread first begins user-mode execution. The normal exception registration chain will lead to this record. When an exception occurs, the exception dispatcher will first walk the list of exception handler registration records to ensure that the chain leads to this symbolic record. If it does not, the exception chain must have been corrupted (either accidentally or deliberately), and the exception dispatcher will simply terminate the process without calling any of the exception handlers described on the stack. Address Space Layout Randomization (ASLR) contributes to the robustness of this method by making it more difficult for attacking code to know the location of the function pointed to by the symbolic exception registration record, and so to construct a fake symbolic record of its own.

To further validate the SEH handler when /SAFESEH is not present, a mechanism called *Image Dispatch Mitigation* ensures that the SEH handler is located within the same image section as the function that raised an exception, which is normally the case for most programs (although not necessarily, since some DLLs might have exception handlers that were set up by the main executable, which is why this mitigation is off by default). Finally, *Executable Dispatch Mitigation* further makes sure that the SEH handler is located within an executable page—a less strong requirement than Image Dispatch Mitigation, but one with fewer compatibility issues.

Two other methods for software DEP that the system implements are *stack cookies* and *pointer encoding*. The first relies on the compiler to insert special code at the beginning and end of each potentially exploitable function. The code saves a special numerical value (the *cookie*) on the stack on entry and validates the cookie's value before returning to the caller saved on the stack (which would have now been corrupted to point to a piece of malicious code). If the cookie value is mismatched, the application is terminated and not allowed to continue executing. The cookie value is computed for each boot when executing the first user-mode thread, and it is saved in the KUSER_SHARED_DATA structure. The image loader reads this value and initializes it when a process starts executing in user mode. (See Chapter 3 in Part 1 for more information on the shared data section and the image loader.)

The cookie value that is calculated is also saved for use with the *EncodeSystemPointer* and *DecodeSystemPointer* APIs, which implement pointer encoding. When an application or a DLL has static pointers that are dynamically called, it runs the risk of having malicious code overwrite the pointer values with code that the malware controls. By encoding all pointers with the cookie value and then decoding them, when malicious code sets a nonencoded pointer, the application will still attempt to decode the pointer, resulting in a corrupted value and causing the program to crash. The *EncodePointer* and *DecodePointer* APIs provide similar protection but with a per-process cookie (created on demand) instead of a per-system cookie.

> **Note** The system cookie is a combination of the system time at generation, the stack value of the saved system time, the number of page faults, and the current interrupt time.

Copy-on-Write

Copy-on-write page protection is an optimization the memory manager uses to conserve physical memory. When a process maps a copy-on-write view of a section object that contains read/write pages, instead of making a process private copy at the time the view is mapped, the memory manager defers making a copy of the pages until the page is written to. For example, as shown in Figure 10-3, two processes are sharing three pages, each marked copy-on-write, but neither of the two processes has attempted to modify any data on the pages.

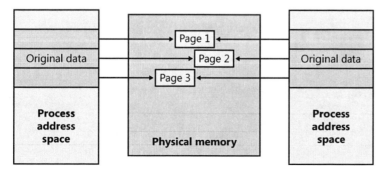

FIGURE 10-3 The "before" of copy-on-write

If a thread in either process writes to a page, a memory management fault is generated. The memory manager sees that the write is to a copy-on-write page, so instead of reporting the fault as an access violation, it allocates a new read/write page in physical memory, copies the contents of the original page to the new page, updates the corresponding page-mapping information (explained later in this chapter) in this process to point to the new location, and dismisses the exception, thus causing the instruction that generated the fault to be reexecuted. This time, the write operation succeeds, but as shown in Figure 10-4, the newly copied page is now private to the process that did the writing and isn't visible to the other process still sharing the copy-on-write page. Each new process that writes to that same shared page will also get its own private copy.

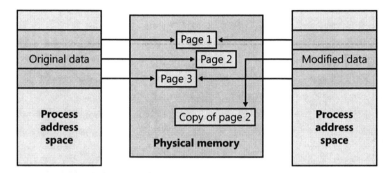

FIGURE 10-4 The "after" of copy-on-write

One application of copy-on-write is to implement breakpoint support in debuggers. For example, by default, code pages start out as execute-only. If a programmer sets a breakpoint while debugging a program, however, the debugger must add a breakpoint instruction to the code. It does this by first changing the protection on the page to PAGE_EXECUTE_READWRITE and then changing the instruction stream. Because the code page is part of a mapped section, the memory manager creates a private copy for the process with the breakpoint set, while other processes continue using the unmodified code page.

Copy-on-write is one example of an evaluation technique known as *lazy evaluation* that the memory manager uses as often as possible. Lazy-evaluation algorithms avoid performing an expensive operation until absolutely required—if the operation is never required, no time is wasted on it.

To examine the rate of copy-on-write faults, see the performance counter Memory: Write Copies/sec.

Address Windowing Extensions

Although the 32-bit version of Windows can support up to 64 GB of physical memory (as shown in Table 2-2 in Part 1), each 32-bit user process has by default only a 2-GB virtual address space. (This can be configured up to 3 GB when using the *increaseuserva* BCD option, described in the upcoming section "User Address Space Layout.") An application that needs to make more than 2 GB (or 3 GB) of data easily available in a single process could do so via file mapping, remapping a part of its address space into various portions of a large file. However, significant paging would be involved upon each remap.

For higher performance (and also more fine-grained control), Windows provides a set of functions called *Address Windowing Extensions* (AWE). These functions allow a process to allocate more physical memory than can be represented in its virtual address space. It then can access the physical memory by mapping a portion of its virtual address space into selected portions of the physical memory at various times.

Allocating and using memory via the AWE functions is done in three steps:

1. Allocating the physical memory to be used. The application uses the Windows functions *AllocateUserPhysicalPages* or *AllocateUserPhysicalPagesNuma*. (These require the Lock Pages In Memory user right.)

2. Creating one or more regions of virtual address space to act as windows to map views of the physical memory. The application uses the Win32 *VirtualAlloc*, *VirtualAllocEx*, or *VirtualAllocExNuma* function with the MEM_PHYSICAL flag.

3. The preceding steps are, generally speaking, initialization steps. To actually use the memory, the application uses *MapUserPhysicalPages* or *MapUserPhysicalPagesScatter* to map a portion of the physical region allocated in step 1 into one of the virtual regions, or windows, allocated in step 2.

Figure 10-5 shows an example. The application has created a 256-MB window in its address space and has allocated 4 GB of physical memory (on a system with more than 4 GB of physical memory). It can then use *MapUserPhysicalPages* or *MapUserPhysicalPagesScatter* to access any portion of the physical memory by mapping the desired portion of memory into the 256-MB window. The size of the application's virtual address space window determines the amount of physical memory that the application can access with any given mapping. To access another portion of the allocated RAM, the application can simply remap the area.

The AWE functions exist on all editions of Windows and are usable regardless of how much physical memory a system has. However, AWE is most useful on 32-bit systems with more than 2 GB of physical memory because it provides a way for a 32-bit process to access more RAM than its virtual address space would otherwise allow. Another use is for security purposes: because AWE memory is never paged out, the data in AWE memory can never have a copy in the paging file that someone could examine by rebooting into an alternate operating system. (*VirtualLock* provides the same guarantee for pages in general.)

Finally, there are some restrictions on memory allocated and mapped by the AWE functions:

- Pages can't be shared between processes.

- The same physical page can't be mapped to more than one virtual address in the same process.

- Page protection is limited to read/write, read-only, and no access.

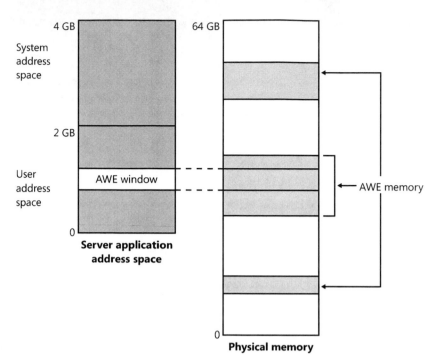

FIGURE 10-5 Using AWE to map physical memory

AWE is less useful on x64 or IA64 Windows systems because these systems support 8 TB or 7 TB (respectively) of virtual address space per process, while allowing a maximum of only 2 TB of RAM. Therefore, AWE is not necessary to allow an application to use more RAM than it has virtual address space; the amount of RAM on the system will always be smaller than the process virtual address space. AWE remains useful, however, for setting up nonpageable regions of a process address space. It provides finer granularity than the file mapping APIs (the system page size, 4 KB or 8 KB, versus 64 KB).

For a description of the page table data structures used to map memory on systems with more than 4 GB of physical memory, see the section "Physical Address Extension (PAE)."

Kernel-Mode Heaps (System Memory Pools)

At system initialization, the memory manager creates two dynamically sized memory pools, or heaps, that most kernel-mode components use to allocate system memory:

- **Nonpaged pool** Consists of ranges of system virtual addresses that are guaranteed to reside in physical memory at all times and thus can be accessed at any time without incurring a page fault; therefore, they can be accessed from any IRQL. One of the reasons nonpaged pool is required is because of the rule described in Chapter 2 in Part 1: page faults can't be satisfied at

DPC/dispatch level or above. Therefore, any code and data that might execute or be accessed at or above DPC/dispatch level must be in nonpageable memory.

- **Paged pool**   A region of virtual memory in system space that can be paged into and out of the system. Device drivers that don't need to access the memory from DPC/dispatch level or above can use paged pool. It is accessible from any process context.

Both memory pools are located in the system part of the address space and are mapped in the virtual address space of every process. The executive provides routines to allocate and deallocate from these pools; for information on these routines, see the functions that start with *ExAllocatePool* and *ExFreePool* in the WDK documentation.

Systems start with four paged pools (combined to make the overall system paged pool) and one nonpaged pool; more are created, up to a maximum of 64, depending on the number of NUMA nodes on the system. Having more than one paged pool reduces the frequency of system code blocking on simultaneous calls to pool routines. Additionally, the different pools created are mapped across different virtual address ranges that correspond to different NUMA nodes on the system. (The different data structures, such as the large page look-aside lists, to describe pool allocations are also mapped across different NUMA nodes. More information on NUMA optimizations will follow later.)

In addition to the paged and nonpaged pools, there are a few other pools with special attributes or uses. For example, there is a pool region in session space, which is used for data that is common to all processes in the session. (Sessions are described in Chapter 1 in Part 1.) There is a pool called, quite literally, *special pool*. Allocations from special pool are surrounded by pages marked as no-access to help isolate problems in code that accesses memory before or after the region of pool it allocated. Special pool is described in Chapter 14.

Pool Sizes

Nonpaged pool starts at an initial size based on the amount of physical memory on the system and then grows as needed. For nonpaged pool, the initial size is 3 percent of system RAM. If this is less than 40 MB, the system will instead use 40 MB as long as 10 percent of RAM results in more than 40 MB; otherwise 10 percent of RAM is chosen as a minimum.

Windows dynamically chooses the maximum size of the pools and allows a given pool to grow from its initial size to the maximums shown in Table 10-4.

TABLE 10-4 Maximum Pool Sizes

Pool Type	Maximum on 32-Bit Systems	Maximum on 64-Bit Systems
Nonpaged	75% of physical memory or 2 GB, whichever is smaller	75% of physical memory or 128 GB, whichever is smaller
Paged	2 GB	128 GB

Four of these computed sizes are stored in kernel variables, three of which are exposed as performance counters, and one is computed only as a performance counter value. These variables and counters are listed in Table 10-5.

TABLE 10-5 System Pool Size Variables and Performance Counters

Kernel Variable	Performance Counter	Description
MmSizeOfNonPagedPoolInBytes	Memory: Pool Nonpaged Bytes	Size of the initial nonpaged pool. This can be reduced or enlarged automatically by the system if memory demands dictate. The kernel variable will not show these changes, but the performance counter will.
MmMaximumNonPagedPoolInBytes	Not available	Maximum size of nonpaged pool
Not available	Memory: Pool Paged Bytes	Current total virtual size of paged pool
WorkingSetSize (number of pages) in the *MmPagedPoolWs* struct (type _MMSUPPORT)	Memory: Pool Paged Resident Bytes	Current physical (resident) size of paged pool
MmSizeOfPagedPoolInBytes	Not available	Maximum (virtual) size of paged pool

EXPERIMENT: Determining the Maximum Pool Sizes

You can obtain the pool maximums by using either Process Explorer or live kernel debugging (explained in Chapter 1 in Part 1). To view pool maximums with Process Explorer, click on View, System Information, and then click the Memory tab. The pool limits are displayed in the Kernel Memory middle section, as shown here:

Note that for Process Explorer to retrieve this information, it must have access to the symbols for the kernel running on your system. (For a description of how to configure Process Explorer to use symbols, see the experiment "Viewing Process Details with Process Explorer" in Chapter 1 in Part 1.)

To view the same information by using the kernel debugger, you can use the *!vm* command as shown here:

```
kd> !vm

1: kd> !vm

*** Virtual Memory Usage ***
        Physical Memory:       851757 (    3407028 Kb)
        Page File: \??\C:\pagefile.sys
          Current:    3407028 Kb  Free Space:     3407024 Kb
          Minimum:    3407028 Kb  Maximum:        4193280 Kb
        Available Pages:       699186 (   2796744 Kb)
        ResAvail Pages:        757454 (   3029816 Kb)
        Locked IO Pages:            0 (         0 Kb)
        Free System PTEs:      370673 (   1482692 Kb)
        Modified Pages:          9799 (     39196 Kb)
        Modified PF Pages:       9798 (     39192 Kb)
        NonPagedPool Usage:         0 (         0 Kb)
        NonPagedPoolNx Usage:    8735 (     34940 Kb)
        NonPagedPool Max:      522368 (   2089472 Kb)
        PagedPool 0 Usage:      17573 (     70292 Kb)
        PagedPool 1 Usage:       2417 (      9668 Kb)
        PagedPool 2 Usage:          0 (         0 Kb)
        PagedPool 3 Usage:          0 (         0 Kb)
        PagedPool 4 Usage:         28 (       112 Kb)
        PagedPool Usage:        20018 (     80072 Kb)
        PagedPool Maximum:     523264 (   2093056 Kb)
        . . .
```

On this 4-GB, 32-bit system, nonpaged and paged pool were far from their maximums.

You can also examine the values of the kernel variables listed in Table 10-5. The following were taken from a 32-bit system:

```
lkd> ? poi(MmMaximumNonPagedPoolInBytes)
Evaluate expression: 2139619328 = 7f880000

lkd> ? poi(MmSizeOfPagedPoolInBytes)
Evaluate expression: 2143289344 = 7fc00000
```

From this example, you can see that the maximum size of both nonpaged and paged pool is approximately 2 GB, typical values on 32-bit systems with large amounts of RAM. On the system used for this example, current nonpaged pool usage was 35 MB and paged pool usage was 80 MB, so both pools were far from full.

Monitoring Pool Usage

The Memory performance counter object has separate counters for the size of nonpaged pool and paged pool (both virtual and physical). In addition, the Poolmon utility (in the WDK) allows you to monitor the detailed usage of nonpaged and paged pool. When you run Poolmon, you should see a display like the one shown in Figure 10-6.

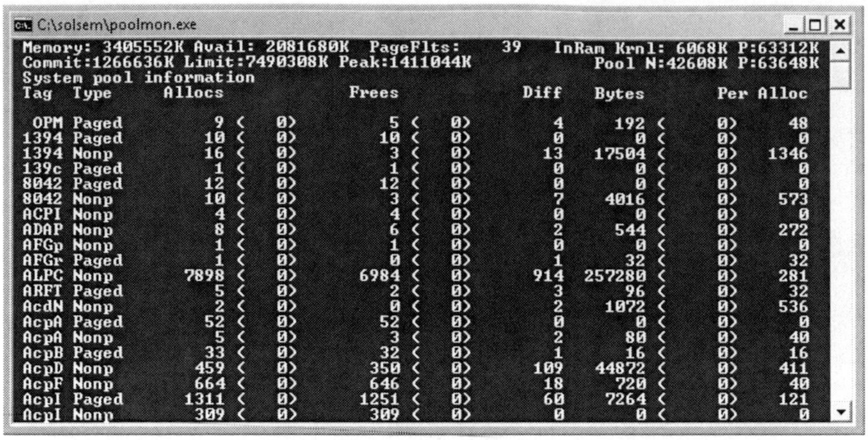

FIGURE 10-6 Poolmon output

The highlighted lines you might see represent changes to the display. (You can disable the highlighting feature by typing a slash (/) while running Poolmon. Type / again to reenable highlighting.) Type ? while Poolmon is running to bring up its help screen. You can configure which pools you want to monitor (paged, nonpaged, or both) and the sort order. For example, by pressing the P key until only nonpaged allocations are shown, and then the D key to sort by the Diff (differences) column, you can find out what kind of structures are most numerous in nonpaged pool. Also, the command-line options are shown, which allow you to monitor specific tags (or every tag but one tag). For example, the command *poolmon –iCM* will monitor only CM tags (allocations from the configuration manager, which manages the registry). The columns have the meanings shown in Table 10-6.

TABLE 10-6 Poolmon Columns

Column	Explanation
Tag	Four-byte tag given to the pool allocation
Type	Pool type (paged or nonpaged pool)
Allocs	Count of all allocations (The number in parentheses shows the difference in the Allocs column since the last update.)
Frees	Count of all Frees (The number in parentheses shows the difference in the Frees column since the last update.)
Diff	Count of Allocs minus Frees
Bytes	Total bytes consumed by this tag (The number in parentheses shows the difference in the Bytes column since the last update.)
Per Alloc	Size in bytes of a single instance of this tag

For a description of the meaning of the pool tags used by Windows, see the file \Program Files\ Debugging Tools for Windows\Triage\Pooltag.txt. (This file is installed as part of the Debugging Tools for Windows, described in Chapter 1 in Part 1.) Because third-party device driver pool tags are not listed in this file, you can use the *–c* switch on the 32-bit version of Poolmon that comes with the WDK to generate a local pool tag file (Localtag.txt). This file will contain pool tags used by drivers found on your system, including third-party drivers. (Note that if a device driver binary has been deleted after it was loaded, its pool tags will not be recognized.)

Alternatively, you can search the device drivers on your system for a pool tag by using the Strings.exe tool from Sysinternals. For example, the command

```
strings %SYSTEMROOT%\system32\drivers\*.sys | findstr /i "abcd"
```

will display drivers that contain the string "abcd". Note that device drivers do not necessarily have to be located in %SystemRoot%\System32\Drivers—they can be in any folder. To list the full path of all loaded drivers, open the Run dialog box from the Start menu, and then type **Msinfo32**. Click Software Environment, and then click System Drivers. As already noted, if a device driver has been loaded and then deleted from the system, it will not be listed here.

An alternative to view pool usage by device driver is to enable the pool tracking feature of Driver Verifier, explained later in this chapter. While this makes the mapping from pool tag to device driver unnecessary, it does require a reboot (to enable Driver Verifier on the desired drivers). After rebooting with pool tracking enabled, you can either run the graphical Driver Verifier Manager (%SystemRoot%\System32\Verifier.exe) or use the Verifier /Log command to send the pool usage information to a file.

Finally, you can view pool usage with the kernel debugger *!poolused* command. The command *!poolused 2* shows nonpaged pool usage sorted by pool tag using the most amount of pool. The command *!poolused 4* lists paged pool usage, again sorted by pool tag using the most amount of pool. The following example shows the partial output from these two commands:

```
lkd> !poolused 2
   Sorting by  NonPaged Pool Consumed
   Pool Used:
            NonPaged          Paged
   Tag   Allocs      Used   Allocs     Used
   Cont   1669  15801344        0        0   Contiguous physical memory allocations for
                                             device drivers
   Int2    414   5760072        0        0   UNKNOWN pooltag 'Int2', please update
                                             pooltag.txt
   LSwi      1   2623568        0        0   initial work context
   EtwB    117   2327832       10   409600   Etw Buffer , Binary: nt!etw
   Pool      5   1171880        0        0   Pool tables, etc.

lkd> !poolused 4
   Sorting by  Paged Pool Consumed
   Pool Used:
            NonPaged          Paged
   Tag   Allocs      Used   Allocs       Used
   CM25      0         0     3921   16777216   Internal Configuration manager allocations ,
                                               Binary: nt!cm
   MmRe      0         0      720   13508136   UNKNOWN pooltag 'MmRe', please update
                                               pooltag.txt
   MmSt      0         0     5369   10827440   Mm section object prototype ptes ,
                                               Binary: nt!mm
   Ntff      9      2232     4210    3738480   FCB_DATA , Binary: ntfs.sys
   AlMs      0         0      212    2450448   ALPC message , Binary: nt!alpc
   ViMm    469    440584      608    1468888   Video memory manager , Binary: dxgkrnl.sys
```

EXPERIMENT: Troubleshooting a Pool Leak

In this experiment, you will fix a real paged pool leak on your system so that you can put to use the techniques described in the previous section to track down the leak. The leak will be generated by the Notmyfault tool from Sysinternals. When you run Notmyfault.exe, it loads the device driver Myfault.sys and presents the following dialog box:

![Not My Fault dialog box showing the Leak tab with Options and Status sections, a Leak/second field set to 1000 KB, and Leak Paged / Leak Nonpaged buttons]

1. Click the Leak tab, ensure that Leak/Second is set to 1000 KB, and click the Leak Paged button. This causes Notmyfault to begin sending requests to the Myfault device driver to allocate paged pool. Notmyfault will continue sending requests until you click the Stop Paged button. Note that paged pool is not normally released even when you close a program that has caused it to occur (by interacting with a buggy device driver); the pool is permanently leaked until you reboot the system. However, to make testing easier, the Myfault device driver detects that the process was closed and frees its allocations.

2. While the pool is leaking, first open Task Manager and click on the Performance tab. You should notice Kernel Memory (MB): Paged climbing. You can also check this with Process Explorer's System Information display. (Click View, System Information, and then the Memory tab.)

3. To determine the pool tag that is leaking, run Poolmon and press the B key to sort by the number of bytes. Press P twice so that Poolmon is showing only paged pool. You should notice the pool tag "Leak" climbing to the top of the list. (Poolmon shows changes to pool allocations by highlighting the lines that change.)

4. Now press the Stop Paged button so that you don't exhaust paged pool on your system.

5. Using the technique described in the previous section, run Strings (from Sysinternals) to look for driver binaries that contain the pool tag "Leak":

```
Strings %SystemRoot%\system32\drivers\*.sys | findstr Leak
```

This should display a match on the file Myfault.sys, thus confirming it as the driver using the "Leak" pool tag.

Look-Aside Lists

Windows also provides a fast memory allocation mechanism called *look-aside lists*. The basic difference between pools and look-aside lists is that while general pool allocations can vary in size, a look-aside list contains only fixed-sized blocks. Although the general pools are more flexible in terms of what they can supply, look-aside lists are faster because they don't use any spinlocks.

Executive components and device drivers can create look-aside lists that match the size of frequently allocated data structures by using the *ExInitializeNPagedLookasideList* and *ExInitialize-PagedLookasideList* functions (documented in the WDK). To minimize the overhead of multiprocessor synchronization, several executive subsystems (such as the I/O manager, cache manager, and object manager) create separate look-aside lists for each processor for their frequently accessed data structures. The executive also creates a general per-processor paged and nonpaged look-aside list for small allocations (256 bytes or less).

If a look-aside list is empty (as it is when it's first created), the system must allocate from paged or nonpaged pool. But if it contains a freed block, the allocation can be satisfied very quickly. (The list grows as blocks are returned to it.) The pool allocation routines automatically tune the number of freed buffers that look-aside lists store according to how often a device driver or executive subsystem allocates from the list—the more frequent the allocations, the more blocks are stored on a list. Look-aside lists are automatically reduced in size if they aren't being allocated from. (This check happens once per second when the balance set manager system thread wakes up and calls the function *ExAdjustLookasideDepth*.)

Heap Manager

Most applications allocate smaller blocks than the 64-KB minimum allocation granularity possible using page granularity functions such as *VirtualAlloc* and *VirtualAllocExNuma*. Allocating such a large area for relatively small allocations is not optimal from a memory usage and performance standpoint. To address this need, Windows provides a component called the *heap manager*, which manages allocations inside larger memory areas reserved using the page granularity memory allocation functions. The allocation granularity in the heap manager is relatively small: 8 bytes on 32-bit systems, and 16 bytes on 64-bit systems. The heap manager has been designed to optimize memory usage and performance in the case of these smaller allocations.

The heap manager exists in two places: Ntdll.dll and Ntoskrnl.exe. The subsystem APIs (such as the Windows heap APIs) call the functions in Ntdll, and various executive components and device drivers call the functions in Ntoskrnl. Its native interfaces (prefixed with *Rtl*) are available only for use in internal Windows components or kernel-mode device drivers. The documented Windows API interfaces to the heap (prefixed with *Heap*) are forwarders to the native functions in Ntdll.dll. In addition, legacy APIs (prefixed with either *Local* or *Global*) are provided to support older Windows applications, which also internally call the heap manager, using some of its specialized interfaces to support legacy behavior. The C runtime (CRT) also uses the heap manager when using functions such as *malloc*, *free*, and the C++ *new* operator. The most common Windows heap functions are:

- *HeapCreate* or *HeapDestroy*   Creates or deletes, respectively, a heap. The initial reserved and committed size can be specified at creation.

- *HeapAlloc*   Allocates a heap block.

- *HeapFree*   Frees a block previously allocated with *HeapAlloc*.

- *HeapReAlloc*   Changes the size of an existing allocation (grows or shrinks an existing block).

- *HeapLock* or *HeapUnlock*   Controls mutual exclusion to the heap operations.

- *HeapWalk*   Enumerates the entries and regions in a heap.

Types of Heaps

Each process has at least one heap: the default process heap. The default heap is created at process startup and is never deleted during the process's lifetime. It defaults to 1 MB in size, but it can be made bigger by specifying a starting size in the image file by using the /HEAP linker flag. This size is just the initial reserve, however—it will expand automatically as needed. (You can also specify the initial committed size in the image file.)

The default heap can be explicitly used by a program or implicitly used by some Windows internal functions. An application can query the default process heap by making a call to the Windows function *GetProcessHeap*. Processes can also create additional private heaps with the *HeapCreate* function. When a process no longer needs a private heap, it can recover the virtual address space by calling *HeapDestroy*. An array with all heaps is maintained in each process, and a thread can query them with the Windows function *GetProcessHeaps*.

A heap can manage allocations either in large memory regions reserved from the memory manager via *VirtualAlloc* or from memory mapped file objects mapped in the process address space. The latter approach is rarely used in practice, but it's suitable for scenarios where the content of the blocks needs to be shared between two processes or between a kernel-mode and a user-mode component. The Win32 GUI subsystem driver (Win32k.sys) uses such a heap for sharing GDI and User objects with user mode. If a heap is built on top of a memory mapped file region, certain constraints apply with respect to the component that can call heap functions. First, the internal heap structures use pointers, and therefore do not allow remapping to different addresses in other processes. Second, the synchronization across multiple processes or between a kernel component and a user process is not supported by the heap functions. Also, in the case of a shared heap between user mode and kernel mode, the user-mode mapping should be read-only to prevent user-mode code from corrupting the heap's internal structures, which would result in a system crash. The kernel-mode driver is also responsible for not putting any sensitive data in a shared heap to avoid leaking it to user mode.

Heap Manager Structure

As shown in Figure 10-7, the heap manager is structured in two layers: an optional front-end layer and the core heap. The core heap handles the basic functionality and is mostly common across the user-mode and kernel-mode heap implementations. The core functionality includes the management of blocks inside segments, the management of the segments, policies for extending the heap, committing and decommitting memory, and management of the large blocks.

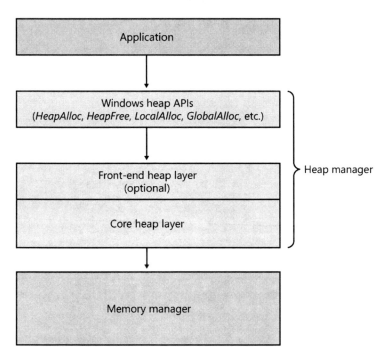

FIGURE 10-7 Heap manager layers

For user-mode heaps only, an optional front-end heap layer can exist on top of the existing core functionality. The only front-end supported on Windows is the Low Fragmentation Heap (LFH). Only one front-end layer can be used for one heap at one time.

Heap Synchronization

The heap manager supports concurrent access from multiple threads by default. However, if a process is single threaded or uses an external mechanism for synchronization, it can tell the heap manager to avoid the overhead of synchronization by specifying HEAP_NO_SERIALIZE either at heap creation or on a per-allocation basis.

A process can also lock the entire heap and prevent other threads from performing heap operations for operations that would require consistent states across multiple heap calls. For instance, enumerating the heap blocks in a heap with the Windows function *HeapWalk* requires locking the heap if multiple threads can perform heap operations simultaneously.

If heap synchronization is enabled, there is one lock per heap that protects all internal heap structures. In heavily multithreaded applications (especially when running on multiprocessor systems), the heap lock might become a significant contention point. In that case, performance might be improved by enabling the front-end heap, described in an upcoming section.

The Low Fragmentation Heap

Many applications running in Windows have relatively small heap memory usage (usually less than 1 MB). For this class of applications, the heap manager's best-fit policy helps keep a low memory footprint for each process. However, this strategy does not scale for large processes and multiprocessor machines. In these cases, memory available for heap usage might be reduced as a result of heap fragmentation. Performance can suffer in scenarios where only certain sizes are often used concurrently from different threads scheduled to run on different processors. This happens because several processors need to modify the same memory location (for example, the head of the look-aside list for that particular size) at the same time, thus causing significant contention for the corresponding cache line.

The LFH avoids fragmentation by managing allocated blocks in predetermined different block-size ranges called buckets. When a process allocates memory from the heap, the LFH chooses the bucket that maps to the smallest block large enough to hold the required size. (The smallest block is 8 bytes.) The first bucket is used for allocations between 1 and 8 bytes, the second for allocations between 9 and 16 bytes, and so on, until the thirty-second bucket, which is used for allocations between 249 and 256 bytes, followed by the thirty-third bucket, which is used for allocations between 257 and 272 bytes, and so on. Finally, the one hundred twenty-eighth bucket, which is the last, is used for allocations between 15,873 and 16,384 bytes. (This is known as a *binary buddy* system.) Table 10-7 summarizes the different buckets, their granularity, and the range of sizes they map to.

TABLE 10-7 Buckets

Buckets	Granularity	Range
1–32	8	1–256
33–48	16	257–512
49–64	32	513–1,024
65–80	64	1,025–2,048
81–96	128	2,049–4,096
97–112	256	4,097–8,194
113–128	512	8,195–16,384

The LFH addresses these issues by using the core heap manager and look-aside lists. The Windows heap manager implements an automatic tuning algorithm that can enable the LFH by default under certain conditions, such as lock contention or the presence of popular size allocations that have shown better performance with the LFH enabled. For large heaps, a significant percentage of allocations is frequently grouped in a relatively small number of buckets of certain sizes. The allocation strategy used by LFH is to optimize the usage for these patterns by efficiently handling same-size blocks.

To address scalability, the LFH expands the frequently accessed internal structures to a number of slots that is two times larger than the current number of processors on the machine. The assignment of threads to these slots is done by an LFH component called the *affinity manager*. Initially, the LFH starts using the first slot for heap allocations; however, if a contention is detected when accessing some internal data, the LFH switches the current thread to use a different slot. Further contentions will spread threads on more slots. These slots are controlled for each size bucket to improve locality and minimize the overall memory consumption.

Even if the LFH is enabled as a front-end heap, the less frequent allocation sizes may still continue to use the core heap functions to allocate memory, while the most popular allocation classes will be performed from the LFH. The LFH can also be disabled by using the *HeapSetInformation* API with the *HeapCompatibilityInformation* class.

Heap Security Features

As the heap manager has evolved, it has taken an increased role in early detection of heap usage errors and in mitigating effects of potential heap-based exploits. These measures exist to lessen the security effect of potential vulnerabilities in applications. The metadata used by the heap for internal management is packed with a high degree of randomization to make it difficult for an attempted exploit to patch the internal structures to prevent crashes or conceal the attack attempt. These blocks are also subject to an integrity check mechanism on the header to detect simple corruptions such as buffer overruns. Finally, the heap also uses a small degree of randomization of the base address (or handle). By using the *HeapSetInformation* API with the *HeapEnableTerminationOnCorruption* class, processes can opt in for an automatic termination in case of detected inconsistencies to avoid executing unknown code.

As an effect of block metadata randomization, using the debugger to simply dump a block header as an area of memory is not that useful. For example, the size of the block and whether it is busy or not are not easy to spot from a regular dump. The same applies to LFH blocks; they have a different type of metadata stored in the header, partially randomized as well. To dump these details, the *!heap −i* command in the debugger does all the work to retrieve the metadata fields from a block, flagging checksum or free list inconsistencies as well if they exist. The command works for both the LFH and regular heap blocks. The total size of the blocks, the user requested size, the segment owning the block, as well as the header partial checksum are available in the output, as shown in the following sample. Because the randomization algorithm uses the heap granularity, the *!heap −i* command should be used only in the proper context of the heap containing the block. In the example, the heap handle is 0x001a0000. If the current heap context was different, the decoding of the header would be incorrect. To set the proper context, the same *!heap −i* command with the heap handle as an argument needs to be executed first.

```
0:000> !heap -i 001a0000
Heap context set to the heap 0x001a0000
0:000> !heap -i 1e2570
Detailed information for block entry 001e2570
Assumed heap        : 0x001a0000 (Use !heap -i NewHeapHandle to change)
Header content      : 0x1570F4EC 0x0C0015BE (decoded : 0x07010006 0x0C00000D)
Owning segment      : 0x001a0000 (offset 0)
Block flags         : 0x1 (busy )
Total block size    : 0x6 units (0x30 bytes)
Requested size      : 0x24 bytes (unused 0xc bytes)
Previous block size: 0xd units (0x68 bytes)
Block CRC           : OK - 0x7
Previous block      : 0x001e2508
Next block          : 0x001e25a0
```

Heap Debugging Features

The heap manager leverages the 8 bytes used to store internal metadata as a consistency checkpoint, which makes potential heap usage errors more obvious, and also includes several features to help detect bugs by using the following heap functions:

- **Enable tail checking** The end of each block carries a signature that is checked when the block is released. If a buffer overrun destroyed the signature entirely or partially, the heap will report this error.

- **Enable free checking** A free block is filled with a pattern that is checked at various points when the heap manager needs to access the block (such as at removal from the free list to satisfy an allocate request). If the process continued to write to the block after freeing it, the heap manager will detect changes in the pattern and the error will be reported.

- **Parameter checking** This function consists of extensive checking of the parameters passed to the heap functions.

- **Heap validation**   The entire heap is validated at each heap call.

- **Heap tagging and stack traces support**   This function supports specifying tags for allocation and/or captures user-mode stack traces for the heap calls to help narrow the possible causes of a heap error.

The first three options are enabled by default if the loader detects that a process is started under the control of a debugger. (A debugger can override this behavior and turn off these features.) The heap debugging features can be specified for an executable image by setting various debugging flags in the image header using the Gflags tool. (See the section "Windows Global Flags" in Chapter 3 in Part 1.) Or, heap debugging options can be enabled using the *!heap* command in the standard Windows debuggers. (See the debugger help for more information.)

Enabling heap debugging options affects all heaps in the process. Also, if any of the heap debugging options are enabled, the LFH will be disabled automatically and the core heap will be used (with the required debugging options enabled). The LFH is also not used for heaps that are not expandable (because of the extra overhead added to the existing heap structures) or for heaps that do not allow serialization.

Pageheap

Because the tail and free checking options described in the preceding sections might be discovering corruptions that occurred well before the problem was detected, an additional heap debugging capability, called *pageheap*, is provided that directs all or part of the heap calls to a different heap manager. Pageheap is enabled using the Gflags tool (which is part of the Debugging Tools for Windows). When enabled, the heap manager places allocations at the end of pages and reserves the immediately following page. Since reserved pages are not accessible, if a buffer overrun occurs it will cause an access violation, making it easier to detect the offending code. Optionally, pageheap allows placing the blocks at the beginning of the pages, with the preceding page reserved, to detect buffer underrun problems. (This is a rare occurrence.) The pageheap also can protect freed pages against any access to detect references to heap blocks after they have been freed.

Note that using the pageheap can result in running out of address space because of the significant overhead added for small allocations. Also, performance can suffer as a result of the increase of references to demand zero pages, loss of locality, and additional overhead caused by frequent calls to validate heap structures. A process can reduce the impact by specifying that the pageheap be used only for blocks of certain sizes, address ranges, and/or originating DLLs.

For more information on pageheap, see the Debugging Tools for Windows Help file.

Fault Tolerant Heap

Corruption of heap metadata has been identified by Microsoft as one of the most common causes of application failures. Windows includes a feature called the *fault tolerant heap*, or FTH, in an attempt to mitigate these problems and to provide better problem-solving resources to application developers. The fault tolerant heap is implemented in two primary components: the *detection* component, or FTH server, and the *mitigation* component, or FTH client.

The detection component is a DLL, Fthsvc.dll, that is loaded by the Windows Security Center service (Wscsvc.dll, which in turn runs in one of the shared service processes under the local service account). It is notified of application crashes by the Windows Error Reporting service.

When an application crashes in Ntdll.dll, with an error status indicating either an access violation or a heap corruption exception, if it is not already on the FTH service's list of "watched" applications, the service creates a "ticket" for the application to hold the FTH data. If the application subsequently crashes more than four times in an hour, the FTH service configures the application to use the FTH client in the future.

The FTH client is an application compatibility shim. This mechanism has been used since Windows XP to allow applications that depend on particular behavior of older Windows systems to run on later systems. In this case, the shim mechanism intercepts the calls to the heap routines and redirects them to its own code. The FTH code implements a number of "mitigations" that attempt to allow the application to survive despite various heap-related errors.

For example, to protect against small buffer overrun errors, the FTH adds 8 bytes of padding and an FTH reserved area to each allocation. To address a common scenario in which a block of heap is accessed after it is freed, *HeapFree* calls are implemented only after a delay: "freed" blocks are put on a list, and only freed when the total size of the blocks on the list exceeds 4 MB. Attempts to free regions that are not actually part of the heap, or not part of the heap identified by the heap handle argument to *HeapFree*, are simply ignored. In addition, no blocks are actually freed once *exit* or *RtlExitUserProcess* has been called.

The FTH server continues to monitor the failure rate of the application after the mitigations have been installed. If the failure rate does not improve, the mitigations are removed.

The activity of the fault tolerant heap can be observed in the Event Viewer. Type **eventvwr.msc** at a Run prompt, and then navigate in the left pane to Event Viewer, Applications And Services Logs, Microsoft, Windows, Fault-Tolerant-Heap. Click on the Operational log. It may be disabled completely in the registry: in the key HKLM\Software\Microsoft\FTH, set the value Enabled to 0.

The FTH does not normally operate on services, only applications, and it is disabled on Windows server systems for performance reasons. A system administrator can manually apply the shim to an application or service executable by using the Application Compatibility Toolkit.

Virtual Address Space Layouts

This section describes the components in the user and system address space, followed by the specific layouts on 32-bit and 64-bit systems. This information helps you to understand the limits on process and system virtual memory on both platforms.

Three main types of data are mapped into the virtual address space in Windows: per-process private code and data, sessionwide code and data, and systemwide code and data.

As explained in Chapter 1 in Part 1, each process has a private address space that cannot be accessed by other processes. That is, a virtual address is always evaluated in the context of the current process and cannot refer to an address defined by any other process. Threads within the process can therefore never access virtual addresses outside this private address space. Even shared memory is not an exception to this rule, because shared memory regions are mapped into each participating process, and so are accessed by each process using per-process addresses. Similarly, the cross-process memory functions (*ReadProcessMemory* and *WriteProcessMemory*) operate by running kernel-mode code in the context of the target process.

The information that describes the process virtual address space, called *page tables*, is described in the section on address translation. Each process has its own set of page tables. They are stored in kernel-mode-only accessible pages so that user-mode threads in a process cannot modify their own address space layout.

Session space contains information that is common to each session. (For a description of sessions, see Chapter 2 in Part 1.) A *session* consists of the processes and other system objects (such as the window station, desktops, and windows) that represent a single user's logon session. Each session has a session-specific paged pool area used by the kernel-mode portion of the Windows subsystem (Win32k.sys) to allocate session-private GUI data structures. In addition, each session has its own copy of the Windows subsystem process (Csrss.exe) and logon process (Winlogon.exe). The session manager process (Smss.exe) is responsible for creating new sessions, which includes loading a session-private copy of Win32k.sys, creating the session-private object manager namespace, and creating the session-specific instances of the Csrss and Winlogon processes. To virtualize sessions, all sessionwide data structures are mapped into a region of system space called *session space*. When a process is created, this range of addresses is mapped to the pages associated with the session that the process belongs to.

Finally, *system space* contains global operating system code and data structures visible by kernel-mode code regardless of which process is currently executing. System space consists of the following components:

- **System code**   Contains the operating system image, HAL, and device drivers used to boot the system.

- **Nonpaged pool**   Nonpageable system memory heap.

- **Paged pool**   Pageable system memory heap.

- **System cache**   Virtual address space used to map files open in the system cache. (See Chapter 11 for detailed information.)

- **System page table entries (PTEs)**   Pool of system PTEs used to map system pages such as I/O space, kernel stacks, and memory descriptor lists. You can see how many system PTEs are available by examining the value of the Memory: Free System Page Table Entries counter in Performance Monitor.

- **System working set lists**   The working set list data structures that describe the three system working sets (the system cache working set, the paged pool working set, and the system PTEs working set).

- **System mapped views**   Used to map Win32k.sys, the loadable kernel-mode part of the Windows subsystem, as well as kernel-mode graphics drivers it uses. (See Chapter 2 in Part 1 for more information on Win32k.sys.)

- **Hyperspace**   A special region used to map the process working set list and other per-process data that doesn't need to be accessible in arbitrary process context. Hyperspace is also used to temporarily map physical pages into the system space. One example of this is invalidating page table entries in page tables of processes other than the current one (such as when a page is removed from the standby list).

- **Crash dump information**   Reserved to record information about the state of a system crash.

- **HAL usage**   System memory reserved for HAL-specific structures.

Now that we've described the basic components of the virtual address space in Windows, let's examine the specific layout on the x86, IA64, and x64 platforms.

x86 Address Space Layouts

By default, each user process on 32-bit versions of Windows has a 2-GB private address space; the operating system takes the remaining 2 GB. However, the system can be configured with the *increase-userva* BCD boot option to permit user address spaces up to 3 GB. Two possible address space layouts are shown in Figure 10-8.

The ability for a 32-bit process to grow beyond 2 GB was added to accommodate the need for 32-bit applications to keep more data in memory than could be done with a 2-GB address space. Of course, 64-bit systems provide a much larger address space.

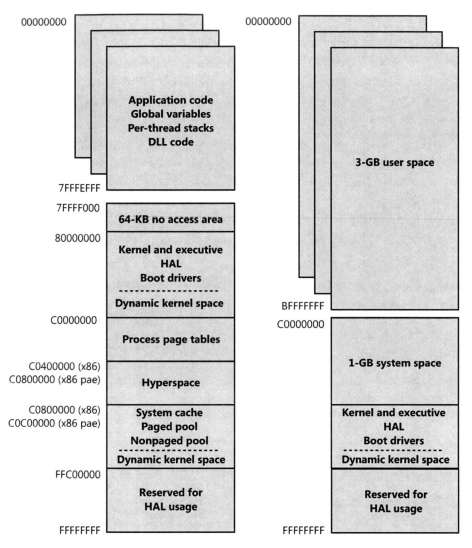

FIGURE 10-8 x86 virtual address space layouts

For a process to grow beyond 2 GB of address space, the image file must have the IMAGE_FILE_ LARGE_ADDRESS_AWARE flag set in the image header. Otherwise, Windows reserves the additional address space for that process so that the application won't see virtual addresses greater than 0x7FFFFFFF. Access to the additional virtual memory is opt-in because some applications have assumed that they'd be given at most 2 GB of the address space. Since the high bit of a pointer referencing an address below 2 GB is always zero, these applications would use the high bit in their pointers as a flag for their own data, clearing it, of course, before referencing the data. If they ran with a 3-GB address space, they would inadvertently truncate pointers that have values greater than 2 GB, causing program errors, including possible data corruption. You set this flag by specifying the linker flag /LARGEADDRESSAWARE when building the executable. This flag has no effect when running the application on a system with a 2-GB user address space.

Several system images are marked as large address space aware so that they can take advantage of systems running with large process address spaces. These include:

- **Lsass.exe**   The Local Security Authority Subsystem

- **Inetinfo.exe**   Internet Information Server

- **Chkdsk.exe**   The Check Disk utility

- **Smss.exe**   The Session Manager

- **Dllhst3g.exe**   A special version of Dllhost.exe (for COM+ applications)

- **Dispdiag.exe**   The display diagnostic dump utility

- **Esentutl.exe**   The Active Directory Database Utility tool

EXPERIMENT: Checking If an Application Is Large Address Aware

You can use the Dumpbin utility from the Windows SDK to check other executables to see if they support large address spaces. Use the /HEADERS flag to display the results. Here's a sample output of Dumpbin on the Session Manager:

```
C:\Program Files\Microsoft SDKs\Windows\v7.1>dumpbin /headers c:\windows\system32\smss.exe
Microsoft (R) COFF/PE Dumper Version 10.00.40219.01
Copyright (C) Microsoft Corporation.  All rights reserved.


Dump of file c:\windows\system32\smss.exe

PE signature found

File Type: EXECUTABLE IMAGE

FILE HEADER VALUES
            8664 machine (x64)
               5 number of sections
        4A5BC116 time date stamp Mon Jul 13 16:19:50 2009
               0 file pointer to symbol table
               0 number of symbols
              F0 size of optional header
              22 characteristics
                   Executable
                   Application can handle large (>2GB) addresses
```

Finally, because memory allocations using *VirtualAlloc*, *VirtualAllocEx*, and *VirtualAllocExNuma* start with low virtual addresses and grow higher by default, unless a process allocates a lot of virtual memory or it has a very fragmented virtual address space, it will never get back very high virtual addresses. Therefore, for testing purposes, you can force memory allocations to start from high addresses by using the MEM_TOP_DOWN flag or by adding a DWORD registry value, HKLM\SYSTEM\CurrentControlSet\Control\Session Manager\Memory Management\AllocationPreference, and setting it to 0x100000.

Figure 10-9 shows two screen shots of the TestLimit utility (shown in previous experiments) leaking memory on a 32-bit Windows machine booted with and without the *increaseuserva* option set to 3 GB.

Note that in the second screen shot, TestLimit was able to leak almost 3 GB, as expected. This is only possible because TestLimit was linked with /LARGEADDRESSAWARE. Had it not been, the results would have been essentially the same as on the system booted without *increaseuserva*.

```
C:\temp>testlimit -r

Testlimit v5.1 - test Windows limits
Copyright (C) 2012 Mark Russinovich
Sysinternals - www.sysinternals.com

Reserving private bytes (MB)...
Leaked 2016 MB of reserved memory (2016 MB total leaked). Lasterror: 8
Not enough storage is available to process this command.
```

```
C:\temp>testlimit -r

Testlimit v5.1 - test Windows limits
Copyright (C) 2012 Mark Russinovich
Sysinternals - www.sysinternals.com

Reserving private bytes (MB)...
Leaked 3038 MB of reserved memory (3038 MB total leaked). Lasterror: 8
Not enough storage is available to process this command.
```

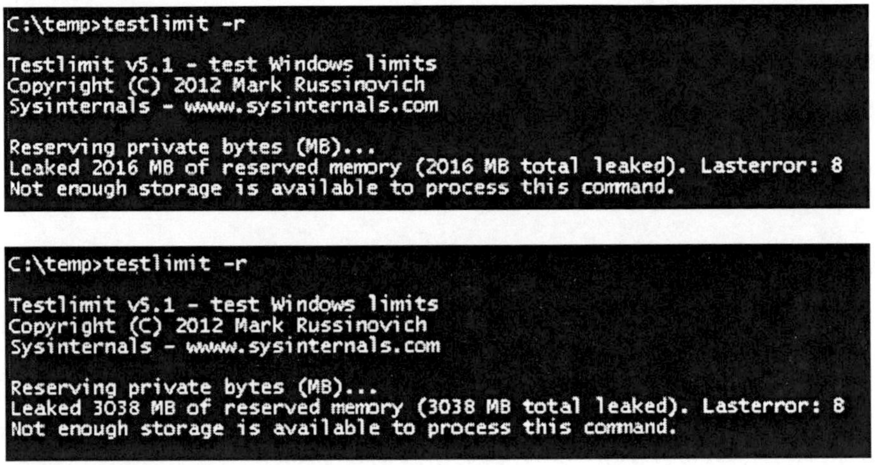

FIGURE 10-9 TestLimit leaking memory on a 32-bit Windows computer, with and without *increaseuserva* set to 3 GB

x86 System Address Space Layout

The 32-bit versions of Windows implement a dynamic system address space layout by using a virtual address allocator (we'll describe this functionality later in this section). There are still a few specifically reserved areas, as shown in Figure 10-8. However, many kernel-mode structures use dynamic address space allocation. These structures are therefore not necessarily virtually contiguous with themselves. Each can easily exist in several disjointed pieces in various areas of system address space. The uses of system address space that are allocated in this way include:

- Nonpaged pool
- Special pool
- Paged pool
- System page table entries (PTEs)
- System mapped views
- File system cache

- File system structures (metadata)

- Session space

x86 Session Space

For systems with multiple sessions, the code and data unique to each session are mapped into system address space but shared by the processes in that session. Figure 10-10 shows the general layout of session space.

Win32k.sys & video drivers
MM_SESSION_SPACE & session WSLs
Mapped views for this session
Paged pool for this session

FIGURE 10-10 x86 session space layout (not proportional)

The sizes of the components of session space, just like the rest of kernel system address space, are dynamically configured and resized by the memory manager on demand.

EXPERIMENT: Viewing Sessions

You can display which processes are members of which sessions by examining the session ID. This can be viewed with Task Manager, Process Explorer, or the kernel debugger. Using the kernel debugger, you can list the active sessions with the *!session* command as follows:

```
lkd> !session
Sessions on machine: 3
Valid Sessions: 0 1 3
Current Session 1
```

Then you can set the active session using the *!session –s* command and display the address of the session data structures and the processes in that session with the *!sprocess* command:

```
lkd> !session -s 3
Sessions on machine: 3
Implicit process is now 84173500
```

```
Using session 3

lkd> !sprocess
Dumping Session 3

_MM_SESSION_SPACE 9a83c000
_MMSESSION        9a83cd00
PROCESS 84173500  SessionId: 3  Cid: 0d78    Peb: 7ffde000  ParentCid: 0e80
    DirBase: 3ef53500  ObjectTable: 8588d820  HandleCount:  76.
    Image: csrss.exe

PROCESS 841a6030  SessionId: 3  Cid: 0c6c    Peb: 7ffdc000  ParentCid: 0e80
    DirBase: 3ef53520  ObjectTable: 85897208  HandleCount:  94.
    Image: winlogon.exe

PROCESS 841d9cf0  SessionId: 3  Cid: 0d38    Peb: 7ffd6000  ParentCid: 0c6c
    DirBase: 3ef53540  ObjectTable: 8589d248  HandleCount: 165.
    Image: LogonUI.exe

...
```

To view the details of the session, dump the MM_SESSION_SPACE structure using the *dt*
command, as follows:

```
lkd> dt nt!_MM_SESSION_SPACE 9a83c000
   +0x000 ReferenceCount    : 0n3
   +0x004 u                 : <unnamed-tag>
   +0x008 SessionId         : 3
   +0x00c ProcessReferenceToSession : 0n4
   +0x010 ProcessList       : _LIST_ENTRY [ 0x841735e4 - 0x841d9dd4 ]
   +0x018 LastProcessSwappedOutTime : _LARGE_INTEGER 0x0
   +0x020 SessionPageDirectoryIndex : 0x31fa3
   +0x024 NonPagablePages   : 0x19
   +0x028 CommittedPages    : 0x867
   +0x02c PagedPoolStart    : 0x80000000 Void
   +0x030 PagedPoolEnd      : 0xffbfffff Void
   +0x034 SessionObject     : 0x854e2040 Void
   +0x038 SessionObjectHandle : 0x8000020c Void
   +0x03c ResidentProcessCount : 0n3
   +0x040 SessionPoolAllocationFailures : [4] 0
   +0x050 ImageList         : _LIST_ENTRY [ 0x8519bef8 - 0x85296370 ]
   +0x058 LocaleId          : 0x409
   +0x05c AttachCount       : 0
   +0x060 AttachGate        : _KGATE
   +0x070 WsListEntry       : _LIST_ENTRY [ 0x82772408 - 0x97044070 ]
   +0x080 Lookaside         : [25] _GENERAL_LOOKASIDE
...
```

EXPERIMENT: Viewing Session Space Utilization

You can view session space memory utilization with the *!vm 4* command in the kernel debugger. For example, the following output was taken from a 32-bit Windows client system with the default two sessions created at system startup:

```
lkd> !vm 4
.

.

    Terminal Server Memory Usage By Session:


    Session ID 0 @ 9a8c7000:
    Paged Pool Usage:          2372K
    Commit Usage:              4832K

    Session ID 1 @ 9a881000:
    Paged Pool Usage:         14120K
    Commit Usage:             16704K
```

System Page Table Entries

System page table entries (PTEs) are used to dynamically map system pages such as I/O space, kernel stacks, and the mapping for memory descriptor lists. System PTEs aren't an infinite resource. On 32-bit Windows, the number of available system PTEs is such that the system can theoretically describe 2 GB of contiguous system virtual address space. On 64-bit Windows, system PTEs can describe up to 128 GB of contiguous virtual address space.

EXPERIMENT: Viewing System PTE Information

You can see how many system PTEs are available by examining the value of the Memory: Free System Page Table Entries counter in Performance Monitor or by using the *!sysptes* or *!vm* command in the debugger. You can also dump the _MI_SYSTEM_PTE_TYPE structure associated with the *MiSystemPteInfo* global variable. This will also show you how many PTE allocation failures occurred on the system—a high count indicates a problem and possibly a system PTE leak.

```
0: kd> !sysptes

System PTE Information
  Total System Ptes 307168

    starting PTE: c0200000

  free blocks: 32    total free: 3856    largest free block: 542
```

```
Kernel Stack PTE Information
Unable to get syspte index array - skipping bins

    starting PTE: c0200000

  free blocks: 165    total free: 1503    largest free block: 75

0: kd> ? nt!MiSystemPteInfo
Evaluate expression: -2100014016 = 82d45440

0: kd> dt _MI_SYSTEM_PTE_TYPE 82d45440
nt!_MI_SYSTEM_PTE_TYPE
    +0x000 Bitmap             : _RTL_BITMAP
    +0x008 Flags              : 3
    +0x00c Hint               : 0x2271f
    +0x010 BasePte            : 0xc0200000 _MMPTE
    +0x014 FailureCount       : 0x82d45468  -> 0
    +0x018 Vm                 : 0x82d67300 _MMSUPPORT
    +0x01c TotalSystemPtes    : 0n7136
    +0x020 TotalFreeSystemPtes : 0n4113
    +0x024 CachedPteCount     : 0n0
    +0x028 PteFailures        : 0
    +0x02c SpinLock           : 0
    +0x02c GlobalMutex        : (null)
```

If you are seeing lots of system PTE failures, you can enable system PTE tracking by creating a new DWORD value in the HKLM\SYSTEM\CurrentControlSet\Control\Session Manager\Memory Management key called TrackPtes and setting its value to 1. You can then use *!sysptes 4* to show a list of allocators, as shown here:

```
lkd>!sysptes 4
0x1ca2 System PTEs allocated to mapping locked pages

VA        MDL       PageCount  Caller/CallersCaller
ecbfdee8  f0ed0958         2  netbt!DispatchIoctls+0x56a/netbt!NbtDispatchDevCtrl+0xcd
f0a8d050  f0ed0510         1  netbt!DispatchIoctls+0x64e/netbt!NbtDispatchDevCtrl+0xcd
ecef5000         1        20  nt!MiFindContiguousMemory+0x63
ed447000         0         2  Ntfs!NtfsInitializeVcb+0x30e/Ntfs!NtfsInitializeDevice+0x95
ee1ce000         0         2  Ntfs!NtfsInitializeVcb+0x30e/Ntfs!NtfsInitializeDevice+0x95
ed9c4000         1        ca  nt!MiFindContiguousMemory+0x63
eda8e000         1        ca  nt!MiFindContiguousMemory+0x63
efb23d68  f8067888         2  mrxsmb!BowserMapUsersBuffer+0x28
efac5af4  f8b15b98         2  ndisuio!NdisuioRead+0x54/nt!NtReadFile+0x566
f0ac688c  f848ff88         1  ndisuio!NdisuioRead+0x54/nt!NtReadFile+0x566
efac7b7c  f82fc2a8         2  ndisuio!NdisuioRead+0x54/nt!NtReadFile+0x566
ee4d1000         1        38  nt!MiFindContiguousMemory+0x63
efa4f000         0         2  Ntfs!NtfsInitializeVcb+0x30e/Ntfs!NtfsInitializeDevice+0x95
efa53000         0         2  Ntfs!NtfsInitializeVcb+0x30e/Ntfs!NtfsInitializeDevice+0x95
eea89000         0         1  TDI!DllInitialize+0x4f/nt!MiResolveImageReferences+0x4bc
ee798000         1        20  VIDEOPRT!pVideoPortGetDeviceBase+0x1f1
f0676000         1        10  hal!HalpGrowMapBuffers+0x134/hal!HalpAllocateAdapterEx+0x1ff
f0b75000         1         1  cpqasm2+0x2af67/cpqasm2+0x7847
f0afa000         1         1  cpqasm2+0x2af67/cpqasm2+0x6d82
```

64-Bit Address Space Layouts

The theoretical 64-bit virtual address space is 16 exabytes (18,446,744,073,709,551,616 bytes, or approximately 18.44 billion billion bytes). Unlike on x86 systems, where the default address space is divided in two parts (half for a process and half for the system), the 64-bit address is divided into a number of different size regions whose components match conceptually the portions of user, system, and session space. The various sizes of these regions, listed in Table 10-8, represent current implementation limits that could easily be extended in future releases. Clearly, 64 bits provides a tremendous leap in terms of address space sizes.

TABLE 10-8 64-Bit Address Space Sizes

Region	IA64	x64
Process Address Space	7,152 GB	8,192 GB
System PTE Space	128 GB	128 GB
System Cache	1 TB	1 TB
Paged Pool	128 GB	128 GB
Nonpaged Pool	75% of physical memory	75% of physical memory

Also, on 64-bit Windows, another useful feature of having an image that is large address space aware is that while running on 64-bit Windows (under Wow64), such an image will actually receive all 4 GB of user address space available—after all, if the image can support 3-GB pointers, 4-GB pointers should not be any different, because unlike the switch from 2 GB to 3 GB, there are no additional bits involved. Figure 10-11 shows TestLimit, running as a 32-bit application, reserving address space on a 64-bit Windows machine, followed by the 64-bit version of TestLimit leaking memory on the same machine.

```
C:\temp>testlimit -r

Testlimit v5.1 - test Windows limits
Copyright (C) 2012 Mark Russinovich
Sysinternals - www.sysinternals.com

Reserving private bytes (MB)...
Leaked 4031 MB of reserved memory (4031 MB total leaked). Lasterror: 8
Not enough storage is available to process this command.
```

```
C:\temp>testlimit64 -r

Testlimit v5.1 - test Windows limits
Copyright (C) 2012 Mark Russinovich
Sysinternals - www.sysinternals.com

Reserving private bytes (MB)...
Leaked 8388548 MB of reserved memory (8388548 MB total leaked). Lasterror: 8
Not enough storage is available to process this command.
```

FIGURE 10-11 32-bit and 64-bit TestLimit reserving address space on a 64-bit Windows computer

Note that these results depend on the two versions of TestLimit having been linked with the /LARGEADDRESSAWARE option. Had they not been, the results would have been about 2 GB for each. 64-bit applications linked without /LARGEADDRESSAWARE are constrained to the first 2 GB of the process virtual address space, just like 32-bit applications.

The detailed IA64 and x64 address space layouts vary slightly. The IA64 address space layout is shown in Figure 10-12, and the x64 address space layout is shown in Figure 10-13.

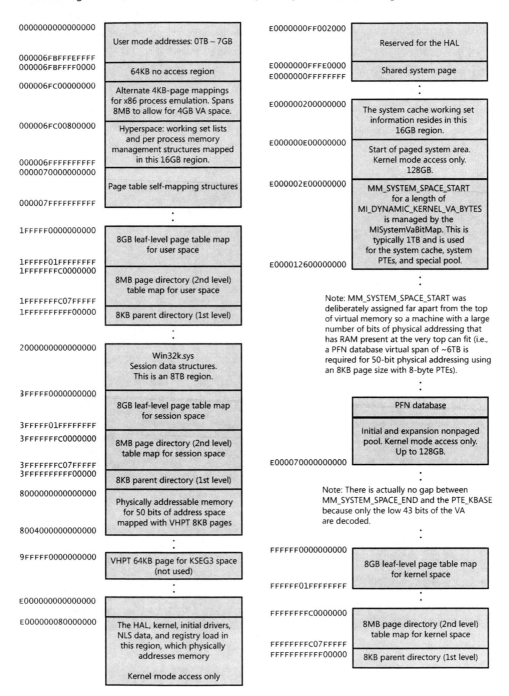

FIGURE 10-12 IA64 address space layout

0000000000000000 000007FFFFFEFFFF	User mode addresses: 8TB minus 64KB
000007FFFFFF0000 000007FFFFFFFFFF	64KB no access region

.
.

FFFF080000000000	Start of system space
FFFFF68000000000	512GB four-level page table map
FFFFF70000000000	Hyperspace: working set lists and per process memory management struc-tures mapped in this 512GB region
FFFFF78000000000	Shared system page
FFFFF78000001000	The system cache working set information resides in this 512GB – 4K region

.
.

Note: The ranges below are sign-extended for >43 bits and therefore can be used with interlocked slists. The system address space above is NOT.

.
.

FFFFF80000000000	Mappings initialized by the loader. This is a 512GB region.
FFFFF88000000000	Start of system PTEs area. Kernel mode access only. 128GB.
FFFFF8A000000000	Start of paged system area. Kernel mode access only. 128GB.
FFFFF90000000000	Win32k.sys. Session data structures. This is a 512GB region.
FFFFF98000000000	MM_SYSTEM_SPACE_START for a length of MI_DYNAMIC_KERNEL_VA_BYTES is managed by the MiSystemVaBitMap. This is typically 1TB and is used for the system cache, system PTEs, and special pool.
FFFFFA8000000000	

.
.

Note: A large VA range is deliberately reserved here to support machines with a large number of bits of physical addressing with RAM present at the very top (i.e., a PFN database virtual span of ~6TB is required for 49-bit physical addressing using a 4KB page size with 8 byte PTEs).

.
.

	PFN database
	Initial and expansion nonpaged pool. Kernel mode access only. Up to 128GB.

.
.

FFFFFFFF00C00000	Minimum 4MB reserved for the HAL. Loader/HAL can consume additional virtual accesss memory by leaving it mapped at kernel bootup.
FFFFFFFFFFFFFFFF	

FIGURE 10-13 x64 address space layout

x64 Virtual Addressing Limitations

As discussed previously, 64 bits of virtual address space allow for a possible maximum of 16 exabytes (EB) of virtual memory, a notable improvement over the 4 GB offered by 32-bit addressing. With such a copious amount of memory, it is obvious that today's computers, as well as tomorrow's foreseeable machines, are not even close to requiring support for that much memory.

Accordingly, to simplify chip architecture and avoid unnecessary overhead, particularly in address translation (to be described later), AMD's and Intel's current x64 processors implement only 256 TB of virtual address space. That is, only the low-order 48 bits of a 64-bit virtual address are implemented. However, virtual addresses are still 64 bits wide, occupying 8 bytes in registers or when stored in memory. The high-order 16 bits (bits 48 through 63) must be set to the same value as the highest order implemented bit (bit 47), in a manner similar to sign extension in two's complement arithmetic. An address that conforms to this rule is said to be a "canonical" address.

Under these rules, the bottom half of the address space thus starts at 0x0000000000000000, as expected, but it ends at 0x00007FFFFFFFFFFF. The top half of the address space starts at 0xFFFF800000000000 and ends at 0xFFFFFFFFFFFFFFFF. Each "canonical" portion is 128 TB. As newer processors implement more of the address bits, the lower half of memory will expand upward, toward 0x7FFFFFFFFFFFFFFF, while the upper half of memory will expand downward, toward 0x8000000000000000 (a similar split to today's memory space but with 32 more bits).

Windows x64 16-TB Limitation

Windows on x64 has a further limitation: of the 256 TB of virtual address space available on x64 processors, Windows at present allows only the use of a little more than 16 TB. This is split into two 8-TB regions, the user mode, per-process region starting at 0 and working toward higher addresses (ending at 0x000007FFFFFFFFFF), and a kernel-mode, systemwide region starting at "all Fs" and working toward lower addresses, ending at 0xFFFFF80000000000 for most purposes. This section describes the origin of this 16-TB limit.

A number of Windows mechanisms have made, and continue to make, assumptions about usable bits in addresses. Pushlocks, fast references, Patchguard DPC contexts, and singly linked lists are common examples of data structures that use bits within a pointer for nonaddressing purposes. Singly linked lists, combined with the lack of a CPU instruction in the original x64 CPUs required to "port" the data structure to 64-bit Windows, are responsible for this memory addressing limit on Windows for x64.

Here is the SLIST_HEADER, the data structure Windows uses to represent an entry inside a list:

```
typedef union _SLIST_HEADER {
    ULONGLONG Alignment;
    struct {
        SLIST_ENTRY Next;
        USHORT Depth;
        USHORT Sequence;
    } DUMMYSTRUCTNAME;
} SLIST_HEADER, *PSLIST_HEADER;
```

Note that this is an 8-byte structure, guaranteed to be aligned as such, composed of three elements: the pointer to the next entry (32 bits, or 4 bytes) and depth and sequence numbers, each 16 bits (or 2 bytes). To create lock-free push and pop operations, the implementation makes use of an instruction present on Pentium processors or higher—CMPXCHG8B (Compare and Exchange 8 bytes), which allows the atomic modification of 8 bytes of data. By using this native CPU instruction, which also supports the LOCK prefix (guaranteeing atomicity on a multiprocessor system), the need for a spinlock to combine two 32-bit accesses is eliminated, and all operations on the list become lock free (increasing speed and scalability).

On 64-bit computers, addresses are 64 bits, so the pointer to the next entry should logically be 64 bits. If the depth and sequence numbers remain within the same parameters, the system must provide a way to modify at minimum 64+32 bits of data—or better yet, 128 bits, in order to increase the entropy of the depth and sequence numbers. However, the first x64 processors did not implement the essential CMPXCHG16B instruction to allow this. The implementation, therefore, was written to pack as much information as possible into only 64 bits, which was the most that could be modified atomically at once. The 64-bit SLIST_HEADER thus looks like this:

```
struct {  // 8-byte header
        ULONGLONG Depth:16;
        ULONGLONG Sequence:9;
        ULONGLONG NextEntry:39;
} Header8;
```

The first change is the reduction of the space for the sequence number to 9 bits instead of 16 bits, reducing the maximum sequence number the list can achieve. This leaves only 39 bits for the pointer, still far from 64 bits. However, by forcing the structure to be 16-byte aligned when allocated, 4 more bits can be used because the bottom bits can now always be assumed to be 0. This gives 43 bits for addresses, but there is one more assumption that can be made. Because the implementation of linked lists is used either in kernel mode or user mode but cannot be used across address spaces, the top bit can be ignored, just as on 32-bit machines. The code will assume the address to be kernel mode if called in kernel mode and vice versa. This allows us to address up to 44 bits of memory in the *NextEntry* pointer and is the defining constraint of the addressing limit in Windows.

Forty-four bits is a much better number than 32. It allows 16 TB of virtual memory to be described and thus splits Windows into two even chunks of 8 TB for user-mode and kernel-mode memory. Nevertheless, this is still 16 times smaller than the CPU's own limit (48 bits is 256 TB), and even farther still from the maximum that 64 bits can describe. So, with scalability in mind, some other bits do exist in the SLIST_HEADER that define the type of header being dealt with. This means that when the day comes when all x64 CPUs support 128-bit Compare and Exchange, Windows can easily take advantage of it (and to do so before then would mean distributing two different kernel images). Here's a look at the full 8-byte header:

```
struct {  // 8-byte header
     ULONGLONG Depth:16;
     ULONGLONG Sequence:9;
     ULONGLONG NextEntry:39;
     ULONGLONG HeaderType:1; // 0: 8-byte; 1: 16-byte
     ULONGLONG Init:1;       // 0: uninitialized; 1: initialized
     ULONGLONG Reserved:59;
     ULONGLONG Region:3;
} Header8;
```

Note how the *HeaderType* bit is overlaid with the *Depth* bits and allows the implementation to deal with 16-byte headers whenever support becomes available. For the sake of completeness, here is the definition of the 16-byte header:

```
struct {  // 16-byte header
     ULONGLONG Depth:16;
     ULONGLONG Sequence:48;
     ULONGLONG HeaderType:1; // 0: 8-byte; 1: 16-byte
     ULONGLONG Init:1;       // 0: uninitialized; 1: initialized
     ULONGLONG Reserved:2;
     ULONGLONG NextEntry:60; // last 4 bits are always 0's
} Header16;
```

Notice how the *NextEntry* pointer has now become 60 bits, and because the structure is still 16-byte aligned, with the 4 free bits, leads to the full 64 bits being addressable.

Conversely, kernel-mode data structures that do not involve SLISTs are not limited to the 8-TB address space range. System page table entries, hyperspace, and the cache working set all occupy virtual addresses below 0xFFFFF80000000000 because these structures do not use SLISTs.

Dynamic System Virtual Address Space Management

Thirty-two-bit versions of Windows manage the system address space through an internal kernel virtual allocator mechanism that we'll describe in this section. Currently, 64-bit versions of Windows have no need to use the allocator for virtual address space management (and thus bypass the cost), because each region is statically defined as shown in Table 10-8 earlier.

When the system initializes, the *MiInitializeDynamicVa* function sets up the basic dynamic ranges (the ranges currently supported are described in Table 10-9) and sets the available virtual address to all available kernel space. It then initializes the address space ranges for boot loader images, process space (hyperspace), and the HAL through the *MiIntializeSystemVaRange* function, which is used to set hard-coded address ranges. Later, when nonpaged pool is initialized, this function is used again to reserve the virtual address ranges for it. Finally, whenever a driver loads, the address range is relabeled to a driver image range (instead of a boot loaded range).

After this point, the rest of the system virtual address space can be dynamically requested and released through *MiObtainSystemVa* (and its analogous *MiObtainSessionVa*) and *MiReturnSystemVa*.

Operations such as expanding the system cache, the system PTEs, nonpaged pool, paged pool, and/or special pool; mapping memory with large pages; creating the PFN database; and creating a new session all result in dynamic virtual address allocations for a specific range. Each time the kernel virtual address space allocator obtains virtual memory ranges for use by a certain type of virtual address, it updates the *MiSystemVaType* array, which contains the virtual address type for the newly allocated range. The values that can appear in *MiSystemVaType* are shown in Table 10-9.

TABLE 10-9 System Virtual Address Types

Region	Description	Limitable
MiVaSessionSpace (0x1)	Addresses for session space	Yes
MiVaProcessSpace (0x2)	Addresses for process address space	No
MiVaBootLoaded (0x3)	Addresses for images loaded by the boot loader	No
MiVaPfnDatabase (0x4)	Addresses for the PFN database	No
MiVaNonPagedPool (0x5)	Addresses for the nonpaged pool	Yes
MiVaPagedPool (0x6)	Addresses for the paged pool	Yes
MiVaSpecialPool (0x7)	Addresses for the special pool	No
MiVaSystemCache (0x8)	Addresses for the system cache	Yes
MiVaSystemPtes (0x9)	Addresses for system PTEs	Yes
MiVaHal (0xA)	Addresses for the HAL	No
MiVaSessionGlobalSpace (0xB)	Addresses for session global space	No
MiVaDriverImages (0xC)	Addresses for loaded driver images	No

Although the ability to dynamically reserve virtual address space on demand allows better management of virtual memory, it would be useless without the ability to free this memory. As such, when paged pool or the system cache can be shrunk, or when special pool and large page mappings are freed, the associated virtual address is freed. (Another case is when the boot registry is released.) This allows dynamic management of memory depending on each component's use. Additionally, components can reclaim memory through *MiReclaimSystemVa*, which requests virtual addresses associated with the system cache to be flushed out (through the dereference segment thread) if available virtual address space has dropped below 128 MB. (Reclaiming can also be satisfied if initial nonpaged pool has been freed.)

In addition to better proportioning and better management of virtual addresses dedicated to different kernel memory consumers, the dynamic virtual address allocator also has advantages when it comes to memory footprint reduction. Instead of having to manually preallocate static page table entries and page tables, paging-related structures are allocated on demand. On both 32-bit and 64-bit systems, this reduces boot-time memory usage because unused addresses won't have their page tables allocated. It also means that on 64-bit systems, the large address space regions that are reserved don't need to have their page tables mapped in memory, which allows them to have arbitrarily large limits, especially on systems that have little physical RAM to back the resulting paging structures.

EXPERIMENT: Querying System Virtual Address Usage

You can look at the current usage and peak usage of each system virtual address type by using the kernel debugger. For each system virtual address type described in Table 10-9, the *MiSystemVaTypeCount, MiSystemVaTypeCountFailures,* and *MiSystemVaTypeCountPeak* arrays in the kernel contain the sizes, count failures, and peak sizes for each type. Here's how you can dump the usage for the system, followed by the peak usage (you can use a similar technique for the failure counts):

```
lkd> dd /c 1 MiSystemVaTypeCount 1 c
81f4f880  00000000
81f4f884  00000028
81f4f888  00000008
81f4f88c  0000000c
81f4f890  0000000b
81f4f894  0000001a
81f4f898  0000002f
81f4f89c  00000000
81f4f8a0  000001b6
81f4f8a4  00000030
81f4f8a8  00000002
81f4f8ac  00000006
lkd> dd /c 1 MiSystemVaTypeCountPeak  1 c
81f4f840  00000000
81f4f844  00000038
81f4f848  00000000
81f4f84c  00000000
81f4f850  0000003d
81f4f854  0000001e
81f4f858  00000032
81f4f85c  00000000
81f4f860  00000238
81f4f864  00000031
81f4f868  00000000
81f4f86c  00000006
```

Theoretically, the different virtual address ranges assigned to components can grow arbitrarily in size as long as enough system virtual address space is available. In practice, on 32-bit systems, the kernel allocator implements the ability to set limits on each virtual address type for the purposes of both reliability and stability. (On 64-bit systems, kernel address space exhaustion is currently not a concern.) Although no limits are imposed by default, system administrators can use the registry to modify these limits for the virtual address types that are currently marked as limitable (see Table 10-9).

If the current request during the *MiObtainSystemVa* call exceeds the available limit, a failure is marked (see the previous experiment) and a reclaim operation is requested regardless of available memory. This should help alleviate memory load and might allow the virtual address allocation to work during the next attempt. (Recall, however, that reclaiming affects only system cache and non-paged pool).

System Virtual Address Space Quotas

The system virtual address space limits described in the previous section allow for limiting systemwide virtual address space usage of certain kernel components, but they work only on 32-bit systems when applied to the system as a whole. To address more specific quota requirements that system administrators might have, the memory manager also collaborates with the process manager to enforce either systemwide or user-specific quotas for each process.

The PagedPoolQuota, NonPagedPoolQuota, PagingFileQuota, and WorkingSetPagesQuota values in the HKLM\SYSTEM\CurrentControlSet\Control\Session Manager\Memory Management key can be configured to specify how much memory of each type a given process can use. This information is read at initialization, and the default system quota block is generated and then assigned to all system processes (user processes will get a copy of the default system quota block unless per-user quotas have been configured as explained next).

To enable per-user quotas, subkeys under the registry key HKLM\SYSTEM\CurrentControlSet\ Session Manager\Quota System can be created, each one representing a given user SID. The values mentioned previously can then be created under this specific SID subkey, enforcing the limits only for the processes created by that user. Table 10-10 shows how to configure these values, which can be configured at run time or not, and which privileges are required.

TABLE 10-10 Process Quota Types

Value Name	Description	Value Type	Dynamic	Privilege
PagedPoolQuota	Maximum size of paged pool that can be allocated by this process	Size in MB	Only for processes running with the system token	SeIncreaseQuotaPrivilege
NonPagedPoolQuota	Maximum size of nonpaged pool that can be allocated by this process	Size in MB	Only for processes running with the system token	SeIncreaseQuotaPrivilege
PagingFileQuota	Maximum number of pages that a process can have backed by the page file	Pages	Only for processes running with the system token	SeIncreaseQuotaPrivilege
WorkingSetPagesQuota	Maximum number of pages that a process can have in its working set (in physical memory)	Pages	Yes	SeIncreaseBasePriorityPrivilege unless operation is a purge request

User Address Space Layout

Just as address space in the kernel is dynamic, the user address space is also built dynamically—the addresses of the thread stacks, process heaps, and loaded images (such as DLLs and an application's executable) are dynamically computed (if the application and its images support it) through a mechanism known as Address Space Layout Randomization, or ASLR.

At the operating system level, user address space is divided into a few well-defined regions of memory, shown in Figure 10-14. The executable and DLLs themselves are present as memory mapped image files, followed by the heap(s) of the process and the stack(s) of its thread(s). Apart from these regions (and some reserved system structures such as the TEBs and PEB), all other memory allocations are run-time dependent and generated. ASLR is involved with the location of all these run-time-dependent regions and, combined with DEP, provides a mechanism for making remote exploitation of a system through memory manipulation harder to achieve. Since Windows code and data are placed at dynamic locations, an attacker cannot typically hardcode a meaningful offset into either a program or a system-supplied DLL.

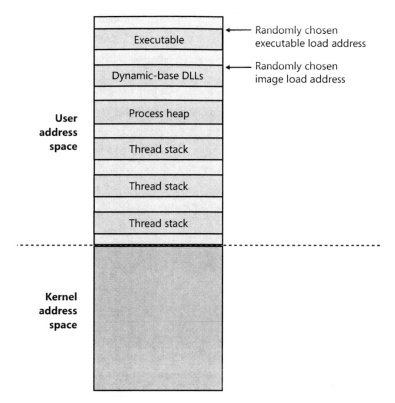

User
address
space

Executable ← Randomly chosen executable load address

Dynamic-base DLLs ← Randomly chosen image load address

Process heap

Thread stack

Thread stack

Thread stack

Kernel
address
space

FIGURE 10-14 User address space layout with ASLR enabled

EXPERIMENT: Analyzing User Virtual Address Space

The VMMap utility from Sysinternals can show you a detailed view of the virtual memory being utilized by any process on your machine, divided into categories for each type of allocation, summarized as follows:

- **Image**   Displays memory allocations used to map the executable and its dependencies (such as dynamic libraries) and any other memory mapped image (portable executable format) files

- **Private**   Displays memory allocations marked as private, such as internal data structures, other than the stack and heap

- **Shareable**   Displays memory allocations marked as shareable, typically including shared memory (but not memory mapped files, which are either Image or Mapped File)

- **Mapped File**   Displays memory allocations for memory mapped data files

- **Heap**   Displays memory allocated for the heap(s) that this process owns

- **Stack** Displays memory allocated for the stack of each thread in this process

- **System** Displays kernel memory allocated for the process (such as the process object)

The following screen shot shows a typical view of Explorer as seen through VMMap.

Depending on the type of memory allocation, VMMap can show additional information, such as file names (for mapped files), heap IDs (for heap allocations), and thread IDs (for stack allocations). Furthermore, each allocation's cost is shown both in committed memory and working set memory. The size and protection of each allocation is also displayed.

ASLR begins at the image level, with the executable for the process and its dependent DLLs. Any image file that has specified ASLR support in its PE header (IMAGE_DLL_CHARACTERISTICS_DYNAMIC_BASE), typically specified by using the /DYNAMICBASE linker flag in Microsoft Visual Studio, and contains a relocation section will be processed by ASLR. When such an image is found, the system selects an image offset valid globally for the current boot. This offset is selected from a bucket of 256 values, all of which are 64-KB aligned.

Image Randomization

For executables, the load offset is calculated by computing a delta value each time an executable is loaded. This value is a pseudo-random 8-bit number from 0x10000 to 0xFE0000, calculated by taking the current processor's time stamp counter (TSC), shifting it by four places, and then performing a division modulo 254 and adding 1. This number is then multiplied by the allocation granularity of

64 KB discussed earlier. By adding 1, the memory manager ensures that the value can never be 0, so executables will never load at the address in the PE header if ASLR is being used. This delta is then added to the executable's preferred load address, creating one of 256 possible locations within 16 MB of the image address in the PE header.

For DLLs, computing the load offset begins with a per-boot, systemwide value called the *image bias*, which is computed by *MiInitializeRelocations* and stored in *MiImageBias*. This value corresponds to the time stamp counter (TSC) of the current CPU when this function was called during the boot cycle, shifted and masked into an 8-bit value, which provides 256 possible values. Unlike executables, this value is computed only once per boot and shared across the system to allow DLLs to remain shared in physical memory and relocated only once. If DLLs were remapped at different locations inside different processes, the code could not be shared. The loader would have to fix up address references differently for each process, thus turning what had been shareable read-only code into process-private data. Each process using a given DLL would have to have its own private copy of the DLL in physical memory.

Once the offset is computed, the memory manager initializes a bitmap called the *MiImageBitMap*. This bitmap is used to represent ranges from 0x50000000 to 0x78000000 (stored in *MiImage-BitMapHighVa*), and each bit represents one unit of allocation (64 KB, as mentioned earlier). Whenever the memory manager loads a DLL, the appropriate bit is set to mark its location in the system; when the same DLL is loaded again, the memory manager shares its section object with the already relocated information.

As each DLL is loaded, the system scans the bitmap from top to bottom for free bits. The *MiImage-Bias* value computed earlier is used as a start index from the top to randomize the load across different boots as suggested. Because the bitmap will be entirely empty when the first DLL (which is always Ntdll.dll) is loaded, its load address can easily be calculated: 0x78000000 – *MiImageBias* * 0x10000. Each subsequent DLL will then load in a 64-KB chunk below. Because of this, if the address of Ntdll.dll is known, the addresses of other DLLs could easily be computed. To mitigate this possibility, the order in which known DLLs are mapped by the Session Manager during initialization is also randomized when Smss loads.

Finally, if no free space is available in the bitmap (which would mean that most of the region defined for ASLR is in use, the DLL relocation code defaults back to the executable case, loading the DLL at a 64-KB chunk within 16 MB of its preferred base address.

Stack Randomization

The next step in ASLR is to randomize the location of the initial thread's stack (and, subsequently, of each new thread). This randomization is enabled unless the flag *StackRandomizationDisabled* was enabled for the process and consists of first selecting one of 32 possible stack locations separated by either 64 KB or 256 KB. This base address is selected by finding the first appropriate free memory region and then choosing the *x*th available region, where *x* is once again generated based on the current processor's TSC shifted and masked into a 5-bit value (which allows for 32 possible locations).

Once this base address has been selected, a new TSC-derived value is calculated, this one 9 bits long. The value is then multiplied by 4 to maintain alignment, which means it can be as large as 2,048 bytes (half a page). It is added to the base address to obtain the final stack base.

Heap Randomization

Finally, ASLR randomizes the location of the initial process heap (and subsequent heaps) when created in user mode. The *RtlCreateHeap* function uses another pseudo-random, TSC-derived value to determine the base address of the heap. This value, 5 bits this time, is multiplied by 64 KB to generate the final base address, starting at 0, giving a possible range of 0x00000000 to 0x001F0000 for the initial heap. Additionally, the range before the heap base address is manually deallocated in an attempt to force an access violation if an attack is doing a brute-force sweep of the entire possible heap address range.

ASLR in Kernel Address Space

ASLR is also active in kernel address space. There are 64 possible load addresses for 32-bit drivers and 256 for 64-bit drivers. Relocating user-space images requires a significant amount of work area in kernel space, but if kernel space is tight, ASLR can use the user-mode address space of the System process for this work area.

Controlling Security Mitigations

As we've seen, ASLR and many of the other security mitigations in Windows are optional because of their potential compatibility effects: ASLR applies only to images with the IMAGE_DLL_CHARACTER-ISTICS_DYNAMIC_BASE bit in their image headers, hardware no-execute (data execution protection) can be controlled by a combination of boot options and linker options, and so on. To allow both enterprise customers and individual users more visibility and control of these features, Microsoft publishes the Enhanced Mitigation Experience Toolkit (EMET). EMET offers centralized control of the mitigations built into Windows and also adds several more mitigations not yet part of the Windows product. Additionally, EMET provides notification capabilities through the Event Log to let administrators know when certain software has experienced access faults because mitigations have been applied. Finally, EMET also enables manual opt-out for certain applications that might exhibit compatibility issues in certain environments, even though they were opted in by the developer.

EXPERIMENT: Looking at ASLR Protection on Processes

You can use Process Explorer from Sysinternals to look over your processes (and, just as important, the DLLs they load) to see if they support ASLR. Note that even if just one DLL loaded by a process does not support ASLR, it can make the process much more vulnerable to attacks.

To look at the ASLR status for processes, right-click on any column in the process tree, choose Select Columns, and then check ASLR Enabled on the Process Image tab. Notice that not all in-box Windows programs and services are running with ASLR enabled, and there is one visible example of a third-party application that does not have ASLR enabled either.

In the example, we have highlighted the Notepad.exe process. In this case, its load address is 0xFE0000. If you were to close all instances of Notepad and then start another, you would find it at a different load address. If you shut down and reboot the system and then try the experiment again, you would find that the ASLR-enabled DLLs are at different load addresses after each boot.

Process	PID	CPU	Description	Company Name	ASLR
notepad.exe	2956	< 0.01	Notepad	Microsoft Corporation	ASLR
taskmgr.exe	3048	0.21	Windows Task Manager	Microsoft Corporation	ASLR

Name	Description	Version	Base	ASLR	Mapping
kernel32.dll	Windows NT BASE API Client DLL	6.1.7601.17651	0x77650000	ASLR	Image
KernelBase.dll	Windows NT BASE API Client DLL	6.1.7601.17651	0x75EC0000	ASLR	Image
locale.nls			0x1E0000	n/a	Data
lpk.dll	Language Pack	6.1.7600.16385	0x77CF0000	ASLR	Image
msctf.dll	MSCTF Server DLL	6.1.7600.16385	0x762E0000	ASLR	Image
msvcrt.dll	Windows NT CRT DLL	7.0.7601.17744	0x771E0000	ASLR	Image
notepad.exe	Notepad	6.1.7600.16385	0xFE0000	ASLR	Image
notepad.exe.mui	Notepad	6.1.7600.16385	0x70000	n/a	Data
ntdll.dll	NT Layer DLL	6.1.7601.17725	0x77AD0000	ASLR	Image

CPU Usage: 1.57%   Commit Charge: 34.48%   Processes: 49   Physical Usage: 44.13%

Address Translation

Now that you've seen how Windows structures the virtual address space, let's look at how it maps these address spaces to real physical pages. User applications and system code reference virtual addresses. This section starts with a detailed description of 32-bit x86 address translation (in both non-PAE and PAE modes) and continues with a brief description of the differences on the 64-bit IA64 and x64 platforms. In the next section, we'll describe what happens when such a translation doesn't resolve to a physical memory address (paging) and explain how Windows manages physical memory via working sets and the page frame database.

x86 Virtual Address Translation

Using data structures the memory manager creates and maintains called *page tables*, the CPU translates virtual addresses into physical addresses. Each page of virtual address space is associated with a system-space structure called a *page table entry* (PTE), which contains the physical address to which the virtual one is mapped. For example, Figure 10-15 shows how three consecutive virtual pages might be mapped to three physically discontiguous pages on an x86 system. There may not even be any PTEs for regions that have been marked as reserved or committed but never accessed, because the page table itself might be allocated only when the first page fault occurs.

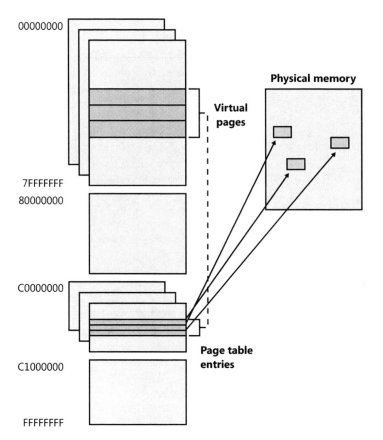

FIGURE 10-15 Mapping virtual addresses to physical memory (x86)

The dashed line connecting the virtual pages to the PTEs in Figure 10-15 represents the indirect relationship between virtual pages and physical memory.

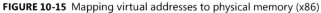

Note Even kernel-mode code (such as device drivers) cannot reference physical memory addresses directly, but it may do so indirectly by first creating virtual addresses mapped to them. For more information, see the memory descriptor list (MDL) support routines described in the WDK documentation.

As mentioned previously, Windows on x86 can use either of two schemes for address translation: non-PAE and PAE. We'll discuss the non-PAE mode first and cover PAE in the next section. The PAE material does depend on the non-PAE material, so even if you are primarily interested in PAE, you should study this section first. The description of x64 address translation similarly builds on the PAE information.

Non-PAE x86 systems use a two-level page table structure to translate virtual to physical addresses. A 32-bit virtual address mapped by a normal 4-KB page is interpreted as two fields: the *virtual page number* and the byte within the page, called the *byte offset*. The virtual page number is further divided into two subfields, called the *page directory index* and the *page table index*, as illustrated in Figure 10-16. These two fields are used to locate entries in the page directory and in a page table.

The sizes of these bit fields are dictated by the structures they reference. For example, the byte offset is 12 bits because it denotes a byte within a page, and pages are 4,096 bytes (2^{12} = 4,096). The other indexes are 10 bits because the structures they index have 1,024 entries (2^{10} = 1,024).

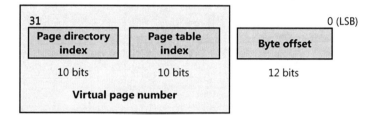

FIGURE 10-16 Components of a 32-bit virtual address on x86 systems

The job of virtual address translation is to convert these virtual addresses into physical addresses—that is, addresses of locations in RAM. The format of a physical address on an x86 non-PAE system is shown in Figure 10-17.

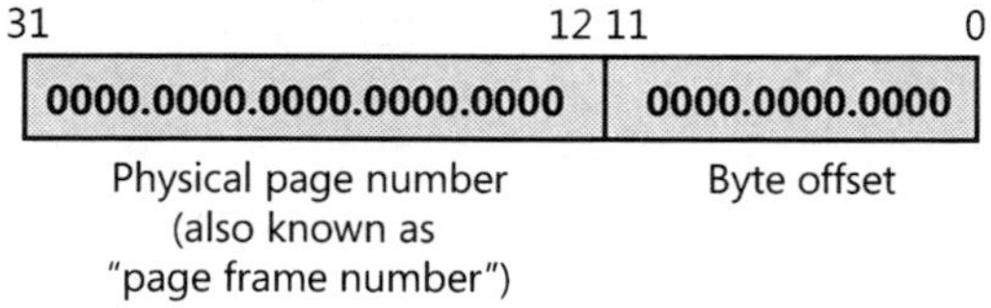

```
31                        12 11              0
┌─────────────────────────┬─────────────────┐
│ 0000.0000.0000.0000.0000 │ 0000.0000.0000  │
└─────────────────────────┴─────────────────┘
   Physical page number        Byte offset
     (also known as
   "page frame number")
```

FIGURE 10-17 Components of a physical address on x86 non-PAE systems

As you can see, the format is very similar to that of a virtual address. Furthermore, the byte offset value from a virtual address will be the same in the resulting physical address. We can say, then, that address translation involves converting virtual page numbers to physical page numbers (also referred to as *page frame numbers*, or PFNs). The byte offset does not participate in, and does not change as a result of, address translation. It is simply copied from the virtual address to the physical address,

Figure 10-18 shows the relationship of these three values and how they are used to perform address translation.

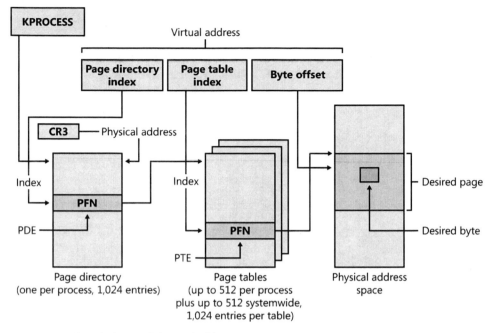

FIGURE 10-18 Translating a valid virtual address (x86 non-PAE)

The following basic steps are involved in translating a virtual address:

1. The memory management unit (MMU) uses a privileged CPU register, CR3, to obtain the physical address of the page directory.

2. The page directory index portion of the virtual address is used as an index into the page directory. This locates the page directory entry (PDE) that contains the location of the page table needed to map the virtual address. The PDE in turn contains the physical page number, also called the *page frame number*, or PFN, of the desired page table, provided the page table is resident—page tables can be paged out or not yet created, and in those cases, the page table is first made resident before proceeding. If a flag in the PDE indicates that it describes a large page, then it simply contains the PFN of the target large page, and the rest of the virtual address is treated as the byte offset within the large page.

3. The page table index is used as an index into the page table to locate the PTE that describes the virtual page in question.

4. If the PTE's valid bit is clear, this triggers a page fault (memory management fault). The operating system's memory management fault handler (pager) locates the page and tries to make it valid; after doing so, this sequence continues at step 5. (See the section "Page Fault Handling.") If the page cannot or should not be made valid (for example, because of a protection fault), the fault handler generates an access violation or a bug check.

5. When the PTE describes a valid page (whether immediately or after page fault resolution), the desired physical address is constructed from the PFN field of the PTE, followed by the byte offset field from the original virtual address.

Now that you have the overall picture, let's look at the detailed structure of page directories, page tables, and PTEs.

Page Directories

On non-PAE x86 systems, each process has a single *page directory*, a page the memory manager creates to map the location of all page tables for that process. The physical address of the process page directory is stored in the kernel process (KPROCESS) block, but it is also mapped virtually at address 0xC0300000 on x86 non-PAE systems. (For more detailed information about the KPROCESS and other process data structures, refer to Chapter 5, "Processes, Threads, and Jobs" in Part 1.)

The CPU obtains the location of the page directory from a privileged CPU register called CR3. It contains the page frame number of the page directory. (Since the page directory is itself always page-aligned, the low-order 12 bits of its address are always zero, so there is no need for CR3 to supply these.) Each time a context switch occurs to a thread that is in a different process than that of the currently executing thread, the context switch routine in the kernel loads this register from a field in the KPROCESS block of the new process. Context switches between threads in the same process don't result in reloading the physical address of the page directory because all threads within the same process share the same process address space and thus use the same page directory and page tables.

The page directory is composed of *page directory entries* (PDEs), each of which is 4 bytes long. The PDEs in the page directory describe the state and location of all the possible page tables for the process. As described later in the chapter, page tables are created on demand, so the page directory for most processes points only to a small set of page tables. (If a page table does not yet exist, the VAD tree is consulted to determine whether an access should materialize it.) The format of a PDE isn't repeated here because it's mostly the same as a hardware PTE, which is described shortly.

To describe the full 4-GB virtual address space, 1,024 page tables are required. The process page directory that maps these page tables contains 1,024 PDEs. Therefore, the page directory index needs to be 10 bits wide (2^{10} = 1,024).

Because Windows provides a private address space for each process, each process has its own page directory and page tables to map that process's private address space. However, the page tables that describe system space are shared among all processes (and session space is shared only among processes in a session). To avoid having multiple page tables describing the same virtual memory, when a process is created, the page directory entries that describe system space are initialized to point to the existing system page tables. If the process is part of a session, session space page tables are also shared by pointing the session space page directory entries to the existing session page tables.

Page Tables and Page Table Entries

Each page directory entry points to a page table. A page table is a simple array of PTEs. The virtual address's page table index field (as shown in Figure 10-18) indicates which PTE within the page table corresponds to and describes the data page in question. The page table index is 10 bits wide, allowing you to reference up to 1,024 4-byte PTEs. Of course, because x86 provides a 4-GB virtual address space, more than one page table is needed to map the entire address space. To calculate the number of page tables required to map the entire 4-GB virtual address space, divide 4 GB by the virtual memory mapped by a single page table. Recall that each page table on an x86 system maps 4 MB of data pages. Thus, 1,024 page tables (4 GB / 4 MB) are required to map the full 4-GB address space. This corresponds with the 1,024 entries in the page directory.

You can use the *!pte* command in the kernel debugger to examine PTEs. (See the experiment "Translating Addresses.") We'll discuss valid PTEs here and invalid PTEs in a later section. Valid PTEs have two main fields: the page frame number (PFN) of the physical page containing the data or of the physical address of a page in memory, and some flags that describe the state and protection of the page, as shown in Figure 10-19.

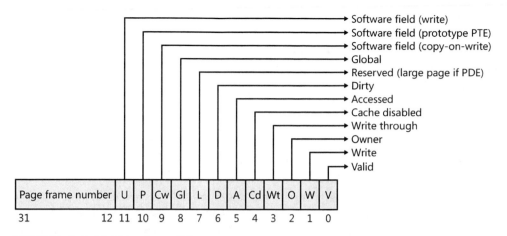

FIGURE 10-19 Valid x86 hardware PTEs

As you'll see later, the bits labeled "Software field" and "Reserved" in Figure 10-19 are ignored by the MMU, whether or not the PTE is valid. These bits are stored and interpreted by the memory manager. Table 10-11 briefly describes the hardware-defined bits in a valid PTE.

TABLE 10-11 PTE Status and Protection Bits

Name of Bit	Meaning
Accessed	Page has been accessed.
Cache disabled	Disables CPU caching for that page.
Copy-on-write	Page is using copy-on-write (described earlier).
Dirty	Page has been written to.
Global	Translation applies to all processes. (For example, a translation buffer flush won't affect this PTE.)
Large page	Indicates that the PDE maps a 4-MB page (or 2 MB on PAE systems). See the section "Large and Small Pages" earlier in the chapter.
Owner	Indicates whether user-mode code can access the page or whether the page is limited to kernel-mode access.
Prototype	The PTE is a prototype PTE, which is used as a template to describe shared memory associated with section objects.
Valid	Indicates whether the translation maps to a page in physical memory.
Write through	Marks the page as write-through or (if the processor supports the page attribute table) write-combined. This is typically used to map video frame buffer memory.
Write	Indicates to the MMU whether the page is writable.

On x86 systems, a hardware PTE contains two bits that can be changed by the MMU, the Dirty bit and the Accessed bit. The MMU sets the Accessed bit whenever the page is read or written (provided it is not already set). The MMU sets the Dirty bit whenever a write operation occurs to the page. The operating system is responsible for clearing these bits at the appropriate times; they are never cleared by the MMU.

The x86 MMU uses a Write bit to provide page protection. When this bit is clear, the page is read-only; when it is set, the page is read/write. If a thread attempts to write to a page with the Write bit clear, a memory management exception occurs, and the memory manager's access fault handler (described later in the chapter) must determine whether the thread can be allowed to write to the page (for example, if the page was really marked copy-on-write) or whether an access violation should be generated.

Hardware vs. Software Write Bits in Page Table Entries

The additional Write bit implemented in software (as mentioned in Table 10-11) is used to force updating of the Dirty bit to be synchronized with updates to Windows memory management data. In a simple implementation, the memory manager would set the hardware Write bit (bit 1) for any writable page, and a write to any such page will cause the MMU to set the Dirty bit in the page table entry. Later, the Dirty bit will tell the memory manager that the contents of that physical page must be written to backing store before the physical page can be used for something else.

In practice, on multiprocessor systems, this can lead to race conditions that are expensive to resolve. The MMUs of the various processors can, at any time, set the Dirty bit of any PTE that has its hardware Write bit set. The memory manager must, at various times, update the process working set list to reflect the state of the Dirty bit in a PTE. The memory manager uses a pushlock to synchronize access to the working set list. But on a multiprocessor system, even while one processor is holding the lock, the Dirty bit might be changed by MMUs of other CPUs. This raises the possibility of missing an update to a Dirty bit.

To avoid this, the Windows memory manager initializes both read-only and writable pages with the hardware Write bit (bit 1) of their PTEs set to 0 and records the true writable state of the page in the software Write bit (bit 11). On the first write access to such a page, the processor will raise a memory management exception because the hardware Write bit is clear, just as it would be for a true read-only page. In this case, though, the memory manager learns that the page actually is writable (via the software Write bit), acquires the working set pushlock, sets the Dirty bit and the hardware Write bit in the PTE, updates the working set list to note that the page has been changed, releases the working set pushlock, and dismisses the exception. The hardware write operation then proceeds as usual, but the setting of the Dirty bit is made to happen with the working set list pushlock held.

On subsequent writes to the page, no exceptions occur because the hardware Write bit is set. The MMU will redundantly set the Dirty bit, but this is benign because the "written-to" state of the page is already recorded in the working set list. Forcing the first write to a page to go through this exception handling may seem to be excessive overhead. However, it happens only once per writable page as long as the page remains valid. Furthermore, the first access to almost any page already goes through memory management exception handling because pages are usually initialized in the invalid state (PTE bit 0 is clear). If the first access to a page is also the first write access to the page, the Dirty bit handling just described will occur within the handling of the first-access page fault, so the additional overhead is small. Finally, on both uniprocessor and multiprocessor systems, this implementation allows flushing of the *translation look-aside buffer* (described later) without holding a lock for each page being flushed.

Byte Within Page

Once the memory manager has determined the physical page number, it must locate the requested data within that page. This is the purpose of the byte offset field. The byte offset from the original virtual address is simply copied to the corresponding field in the physical address. On x86 systems, the byte offset is 12 bits wide, allowing you to reference up to 4,096 bytes of data (the size of a page). Another way to interpret this is that the byte offset from the virtual address is concatenated to the physical page number retrieved from the PTE. This completes the translation of a virtual address to a physical address.

Translation Look-Aside Buffer

As you've learned so far, each hardware address translation requires two lookups: one to find the right entry in the page directory (which provides the location of the page table) and one to find the right entry *in* the page table. Because doing two additional memory lookups for every reference to a virtual address would triple the required bandwidth to memory, resulting in poor performance, all CPUs cache address translations so that repeated accesses to the same addresses don't have to be repeatedly translated. This cache is an array of associative memory called the *translation look-aside buffer*, or TLB. Associative memory is a vector whose cells can be read simultaneously and compared to a target value. In the case of the TLB, the vector contains the virtual-to-physical page mappings of the most recently used pages, as shown in Figure 10-20, and the type of page protection, size, attributes, and so on applied to each page. Each entry in the TLB is like a cache entry whose tag holds portions of the virtual address and whose data portion holds a physical page number, protection field, valid bit, and usually a dirty bit indicating the condition of the page to which the cached PTE corresponds. If a PTE's global bit is set (as is done by Windows for system space pages that are visible to all processes), the TLB entry isn't invalidated on process context switches.

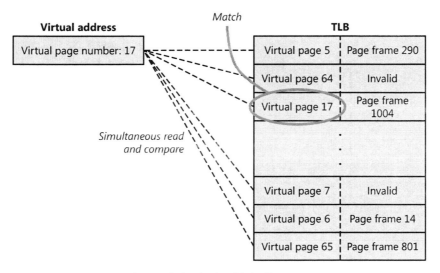

FIGURE 10-20 Accessing the translation look-aside buffer

Virtual addresses that are used frequently are likely to have entries in the TLB, which provides extremely fast virtual-to-physical address translation and, therefore, fast memory access. If a virtual address isn't in the TLB, it might still be in memory, but multiple memory accesses are needed to find it, which makes the access time slightly slower. If a virtual page has been paged out of memory or if the memory manager changes the PTE, the memory manager is required to explicitly invalidate the TLB entry. If a process accesses it again, a page fault occurs, and the memory manager brings the page back into memory (if needed) and re-creates its PTE entry (which then results in an entry for it in the TLB).

Physical Address Extension (PAE)

The Intel x86 Pentium Pro processor introduced a memory-mapping mode called *Physical Address Extension* (PAE). With the proper chipset, the PAE mode allows 32-bit operating systems access to up to 64 GB of physical memory on current Intel x86 processors (up from 4 GB without PAE) and up to 1,024 GB of physical memory when running on x64 processors in legacy mode (although Windows currently limits this to 64 GB due to the size of the PFN database required to describe so much memory). When the processor is running in PAE mode, the memory management unit (MMU) divides virtual addresses mapped by normal pages into four fields, as shown in Figure 10-21. The MMU still implements page directories and page tables, but under PAE a third level, the page directory pointer table, exists above them.

One way in which 32-bit applications can take advantage of such large memory configurations is described in the earlier section "Address Windowing Extensions." However, even if applications are not using such functions, the memory manager will use all available physical memory for multiple processes' working sets, file cache, and trimmed private data through the use of the system cache, standby, and modified lists (described in the section "Page Frame Number Database").

PAE mode is selected at boot time and cannot be changed without rebooting. As explained in Chapter 2 in Part 1, there is a special version of the 32-bit Windows kernel with support for PAE called Ntkrnlpa.exe. Thirty-two-bit systems that have hardware support for nonexecutable memory (described earlier, in the section "No Execute Page Protection") are booted by default using this PAE kernel, because PAE mode is required to implement the no-execute feature. To force the loading of the PAE-enabled kernel, you can set the *pae* BCD option to *ForceEnable*.

Note that the PAE kernel is installed on the disk on all 32-bit Windows systems, even systems with small memory and without hardware no-execute support. This is to allow testing of PAE-related code, even on small memory systems, and to avoid the need for reinstalling Windows should more RAM be added later. Another BCD option relevant to PAE is *nolowmem*, which discards memory below 4 GB (assuming you have at least 5 GB of physical memory) and relocates device drivers above this range. This guarantees that drivers will be presented with physical addresses greater than 32 bits, which makes any possible driver sign extension bugs easier to find.

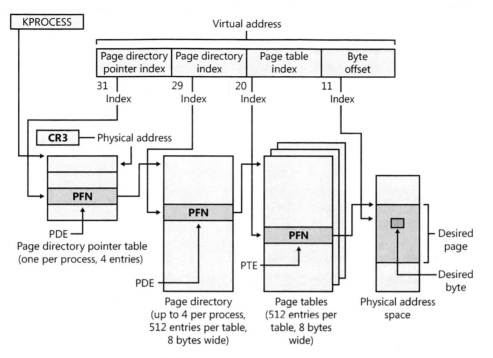

FIGURE 10-21 Page mappings with PAE

To understand PAE, it is useful to understand the derivation of the sizes of the various structures and bit fields. Recall that the goal of PAE is to allow addressing of more than 4 GB of RAM. The 4-GB limit for RAM addresses without PAE comes from the 12-bit byte offset and the 20-bit page frame number fields of physical addresses: 12 + 20 = 32 bits of physical address, and 2^{32} bytes = 4 GB. (Note that this is due to a limit of the physical address format and the number of bits allocated for the PFN within a page table entry. The fact that virtual addresses are 32 bits wide on x86, with or without PAE, does not limit the physical address space.)

Under PAE, the PFN is expanded to 24 bits. Combined with the 12-bit byte offset, this allows addressing of 224 + 12 bytes, or 64 GB, of memory.

To provide the 24-bit PFN, PAE expands the PFN fields of page table and page directory entries from 20 to 24 bits. To allow room for this expansion, the page table and page directory entries are 8 bytes wide instead of 4. (This would seem to expand the PFN field of the PTE and PDE by 32 bits rather than just 4, but in x86 processors, PFNs are limited to 24 bits. This does leave a large number of bits in the PDE unused—or, rather, available for future expansion.)

Since both page tables and page directories have to fit in one page, these tables can then have only 512 entries instead of 1,024. So the corresponding index fields of the virtual address are accordingly reduced from 10 to 9 bits.

This then leaves the two high-order bits of the virtual address unaccounted for. So PAE expands the number of page directories from one to four and adds a third-level address translation table, called the *page directory pointer table,* or PDPT. This table contains only four entries, 8 bytes each, which provide the PFNs of the four page directories. The two high-order bits of the virtual address are used to index into the PDPT and are called the *page directory pointer index.*

As before, CR3 provides the location of the top-level table, but that is now the PDPT rather than the page directory. The PDPT must be aligned on a 32-byte boundary and must furthermore reside in the first 4 GB of RAM (because CR3 on x86 is only a 32-bit register, even with PAE enabled).

Note that PAE mode can address more memory than the standard translation mode not directly because of the extra level of translation, but because the physical address format has been expanded. The extra level of translation is required to allow processing of all 32 bits of a virtual address.

EXPERIMENT: Translating Addresses

To clarify how address translation works, this experiment shows a real example of translating a virtual address on an x86 PAE system, using the available tools in the kernel debugger to examine the PDPT, page directories, page tables, and PTEs. (It is common for Windows on today's x86 processors, even with less than 4 GB of RAM, to run in PAE mode because PAE mode is required to enable no-execute memory access protection.) In this example, we'll work with a process that has virtual address 0x30004, currently mapped to a valid physical address. In later examples, you'll see how to follow address translation for invalid addresses with the kernel debugger.

First let's convert 0x30004 to binary and break it into the three fields that are used to translate an address. In binary, 0x30004 is 11.0000.0000.0000.0100. Breaking it into the component fields yields the following:

31 30 29		21 20	12 11	0
00	00.0000.000	0.0011.0000	0000.0000.0100	
Page directory pointer index (0)	Page directory index (0)	Page table index (0x30 or 48 decimal)	Byte offset (4)	

To start the translation process, the CPU needs the physical address of the process's page directory pointer table, found in the CR3 register while a thread in that process is running. You can display this address by looking at the *DirBase* field in the output of the *!process* command, as shown here:

```
lkd> !process -1 0
PROCESS 852d1030  SessionId: 1  Cid: 0dec    Peb: 7ffdf000  ParentCid: 05e8
    DirBase: ced25440  ObjectTable: a2014a08  HandleCount: 221.
    Image: windbg.exe
```

The *DirBase* field shows that the page directory pointer table is at physical address 0xced25440. As shown in the preceding illustration, the page directory pointer table index field in our example virtual address is 0. Therefore, the PDPT entry that contains the physical address of the relevant page directory is the first entry in the PDPT, at physical address 0xced25440.

As under x86 non-PAE systems, the kernel debugger *!pte* command displays the PDE and PTE that describe a virtual address, as shown here:

```
1kd> !pte 30004
                    VA 00030004
PDE at C0600000        PTE at C0000180
contains 000000002EBF3867  contains 800000005AF4D025
pfn 2ebf3    ---DA--UWEV  pfn 5af4d    ----A--UR-V
```

The debugger does not show the page directory pointer table, but it is easy to display given its physical address:

```
1kd> !dq ced25440 L 4
#ced25440 00000000`2e8ff801 00000000`2c9d8801
#ced25450 00000000`2e6b1801 00000000`2e73a801
```

Here we have used the debugger extension command *!dq*. This is similar to the *dq* command (display as quadwords—"quadwords" being a name for a 64-bit field; this came from the day when "words" were often 16 bits), but it lets us examine memory by physical rather than virtual address. Since we know that the PDPT is only four entries long, we added the *L 4* length argument to keep the output uncluttered.

As illustrated previously, the PDPT index (the two most significant bits) from our example virtual address equal 0, so the PDPT entry we want is the first displayed quadword. PDPT entries have a format similar to PD entries and PT entries, so we can see by inspection that this one contains a PFN of 0x2e8ff, for a physical address of 2e8ff000. That's the physical address of the page directory.

The *!pte* output shows the PDE address as a virtual address, not physical. On x86 systems with PAE, the first process page directory starts at virtual address 0xC0600000. The page directory index field of our example virtual address is 0, so we're looking at the first PDE in the page directory. Therefore, in this case, the PDE address is the same as the page directory address.

As with non-PAE, the page directory entry provides the PFN of the needed page table; in this example, the PFN is 0x2ebf3. So the page table starts at physical address 0x2ebf3000. To this the MMU will add the page table index field (0x30) from the virtual address, multiplied by 8 (the size of a PTE in bytes; this would be 4 on a non-PAE system). The resulting physical address of the PTE is then 0x2ebf3180.

The debugger shows that this PTE is at *virtual* address 0xC0000180. Notice that the byte offset portion (0x180) is the same as that from the physical address, as is always the case in address translation. Because the memory manager maps page tables starting at 0xC0000000, adding 0x180 to 0xC0000000 yields the virtual address shown in the kernel debugger output: 0xC0000180. The debugger shows that the PFN field of the PTE is 0x5af4d.

Finally, we can consider the byte offset from the original address. As described previously, the MMU will concatenate the byte offset to the PFN from the PTE, giving a physical address of 0x5af4d004. This is the physical address that corresponds to the original virtual address of 0x30004—at the moment.

The flags bits from the PTE are interpreted to the right of the PFN number. For example, the PTE that describes the page being referenced has flags of --A--UR-V. Here, *A* stands for accessed (the page has been read), *U* for user-mode accessible (as opposed to kernel-mode accessible only), *R* for read-only page (rather than writable), and *V* for valid (the PTE represents a valid page in physical memory).

To confirm our calculation of the physical address, we can look at the memory in question via both its virtual and its physical addresses. First, using the debugger's *dd* command (display dwords) on the virtual address, we see the following:

```
1kd> dd 30004
00030004  00000020 00000001 00003020 000000dc
00030014  00000000 00000020 00000000 00000014
00030024  00000001 00000007 00000034 0000017c
00030034  00000001 00000000 00000000 00000000
00030044  00000000 00000000 00000002 1a26ef4e
00030054  00000298 00000044 000002e0 00000260
00030064  00000000 f33271ba 00000540 0000004a
00030074  0000058c 0000031e 00000000 2d59495b
```

And with the *!dd* command on the physical address just computed, we see the same contents:

```
1kd> !dd 5af4d004
#5af4d004  00000020 00000001 00003020 000000dc
#5af4d014  00000000 00000020 00000000 00000014
#5af4d024  00000001 00000007 00000034 0000017c
#5af4d034  00000001 00000000 00000000 00000000
#5af4d044  00000000 00000000 00000002 1a26ef4e
#5af4d054  00000298 00000044 000002e0 00000260
#5af4d064  00000000 f33271ba 00000540 0000004a
#5af4d074  0000058c 0000031e 00000000 2d59495b
```

We could similarly compare the displays from the virtual and physical addresses of the PTE and PDE.

x64 Virtual Address Translation

Address translation on x64 is similar to x86 PAE, but with a fourth level added. Each process has a top-level extended page directory (called the *page map level 4* table) that contains the physical locations of 512 third-level structures, called *page parent directories*. The page parent directory is analogous to the x86 PAE page directory pointer table, but there are 512 of them instead of just 1, and each page parent directory is an entire page, containing 512 entries instead of just 4. Like the PDPT, the page parent directory's entries contain the physical locations of second-level page directories, each of which in turn contains 512 entries providing the locations of the individual page tables. Finally, the page tables (each of which contain 512 page table entries) contain the physical locations of the pages in memory. (All of the "physical locations" in the preceding description are stored in these structures as page frame numbers, or PFNs.)

Current implementations of the x64 architecture limit virtual addresses to 48 bits. The components that make up this 48-bit virtual address are shown in Figure 10-22. The connections between these structures are shown in Figure 10-23. Finally, the format of an x64 hardware page table entry is shown in Figure 10-24.

x64 64-bit (48-bit in today's processors)

47 39	38 30	29 21	20 12	11 0
Page map level 4 selector	Page directory pointer selector	Page table selector	Page table entry selector	Byte within page
9 bits	9 bits	9 bits	9 bits	12 bits

FIGURE 10-22 x64 virtual address

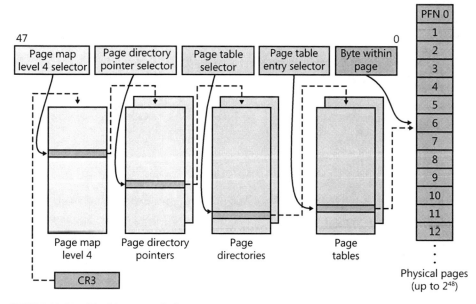

FIGURE 10-23 x64 address translation structures

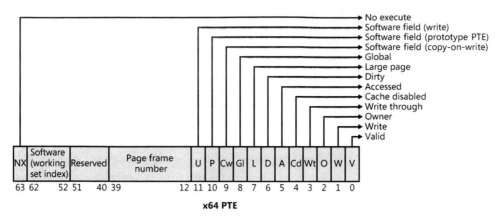

FIGURE 10-24 x64 hardware page table entry

IA64 Virtual Address Translation

The virtual address space for IA64 is divided into eight regions by the hardware. Each region can have its own set of page tables. Windows uses five of the regions, three of which have page tables. Table 10-12 lists the regions and how they are used.

TABLE 10-12 The IA64 Regions

Region	Use
0	User code and data
1	Session space code and data
2	Unused
3	Unused
4	Kseg3, which is a cached, 1-to-1 mapping of physical memory. No page tables are needed for this region because the necessary TLB inserts are done directly by the memory manager.
5	Kseg4, which is a noncached, 1-to-1 mapping for physical memory. This is used only in a few places for accessing I/O locations such as the I/O port range. There are no page tables needed for this region.
6	Unused
7	Kernel code and data

Address translation by 64-bit Windows on the IA64 platform uses a three-level page table scheme. Each process has a page directory pointer structure that contains 1,024 pointers to page directories. Each page directory contains 1,024 pointers to page tables, which in turn point to physical pages. Figure 10-25 shows the format of an IA64 hardware PTE.

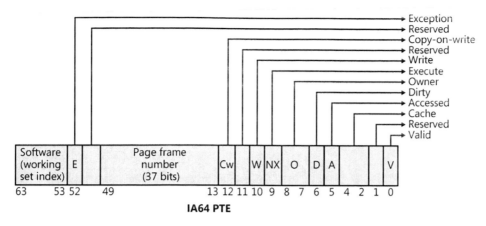

FIGURE 10-25 IA64 page table entry

Page Fault Handling

Earlier, you saw how address translations are resolved when the PTE is valid. When the PTE valid bit is clear, this indicates that the desired page is for some reason not currently accessible to the process. This section describes the types of invalid PTEs and how references to them are resolved.

Note Only the 32-bit x86 PTE formats are detailed in this section. PTEs for 64-bit systems contain similar information, but their detailed layout is not presented.

A reference to an invalid page is called a *page fault*. The kernel trap handler (introduced in the section "Trap Dispatching" in Chapter 3 in Part 1) dispatches this kind of fault to the memory manager fault handler (*MmAccessFault*) to resolve. This routine runs in the context of the thread that incurred the fault and is responsible for attempting to resolve the fault (if possible) or raise an appropriate exception. These faults can be caused by a variety of conditions, as listed in Table 10-13.

TABLE 10-13 Reasons for Access Faults

Reason for Fault	Result
Accessing a page that isn't resident in memory but is on disk in a page file or a mapped file	Allocate a physical page, and read the desired page from disk and into the relevant working set
Accessing a page that is on the standby or modified list	Transition the page to the relevant process, session, or system working set
Accessing a page that isn't committed (for example, reserved address space or address space that isn't allocated)	Access violation
Accessing a page from user mode that can be accessed only in kernel mode	Access violation
Writing to a page that is read-only	Access violation

Reason for Fault	Result
Accessing a demand-zero page	Add a zero-filled page to the relevant working set
Writing to a guard page	Guard-page violation (if a reference to a user-mode stack, perform automatic stack expansion)
Writing to a copy-on-write page	Make process-private (or session-private) copy of page, and replace original in process, session, or system working set
Writing to a page that is valid but hasn't been written to the current backing store copy	Set Dirty bit in PTE
Executing code in a page that is marked as no execute	Access violation (supported only on hardware platforms that support no execute protection)

The following section describes the four basic kinds of invalid PTEs that are processed by the access fault handler. Following that is an explanation of a special case of invalid PTEs, prototype PTEs, which are used to implement shareable pages.

Invalid PTEs

If the valid bit of a PTE encountered during address translation is zero, the PTE represents an invalid page—one that will raise a memory management exception, or page fault, upon reference. The MMU ignores the remaining bits of the PTE, so the operating system can use these bits to store information about the page that will assist in resolving the page fault.

The following list details the four kinds of invalid PTEs and their structure. These are often referred to as *software PTEs* because they are interpreted by the memory manager rather than the MMU. Some of the flags are the same as those for a hardware PTE as described in Table 10-11, and some of the bit fields have either the same or similar meanings to corresponding fields in the hardware PTE.

■ **Page file** The desired page resides within a paging file. As illustrated in Figure 10-26, 4 bits in the PTE indicate in which of 16 possible page files the page resides, and 20 bits (in x86 non-PAE; more in other modes) provide the page number within the file. The pager initiates an in-page operation to bring the page into memory and make it valid. The page file offset is always non-zero and never all 1s (that is, the very first and last pages in the page file are not used for paging) in order to allow for other formats, described next.

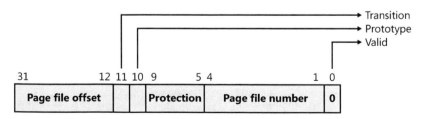

FIGURE 10-26 A page table entry representing a page in a page file

- **Demand zero**   This PTE format is the same as the page file PTE shown in the previous entry, but the page file offset is zero. The desired page must be satisfied with a page of zeros. The pager looks at the zero page list. If the list is empty, the pager takes a page from the free list and zeroes it. If the free list is also empty, it takes a page from one of the standby lists and zeroes it.

- **Virtual address descriptor**   This PTE format is the same as the page file PTE shown previously, but in this case the page file offset field is all 1s. This indicates a page whose definition and backing store, if any, can be found in the process's virtual address descriptor (VAD) tree. This format is used for pages that are backed by sections in mapped files. The pager finds the VAD that defines the virtual address range encompassing the virtual page and initiates an in-page operation from the mapped file referenced by the VAD. (VADs are described in more detail in a later section.)

- **Transition**   The desired page is in memory on either the standby, modified, or modified-no-write list or not on any list. As shown in Figure 10-27, the PTE contains the page frame number of the page. The pager will remove the page from the list (if it is on one) and add it to the process working set.

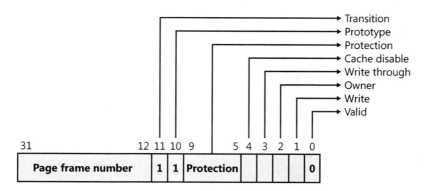

FIGURE 10-27 A page table entry representing a page in transition

- **Unknown**   The PTE is zero, or the page table doesn't yet exist (the page directory entry that would provide the physical address of the page table contains zero). In both cases, the memory manager pager must examine the virtual address descriptors (VADs) to determine whether this virtual address has been committed. If so, page tables are built to represent the newly committed address space. (See the discussion of VADs later in the chapter.) If not (if the page is reserved or hasn't been defined at all), the page fault is reported as an access violation exception.

Prototype PTEs

If a page can be shared between two processes, the memory manager uses a software structure called *prototype page table entries* (prototype PTEs) to map these potentially shared pages. For page-file-backed sections, an array of prototype PTEs is created when a section object is first created;

for mapped files, portions of the array are created on demand as each view is mapped. These proto-type PTEs are part of the *segment* structure, described at the end of this chapter.

When a process first references a page mapped to a view of a section object (recall that the VADs are created only when the view is mapped), the memory manager uses the information in the proto-type PTE to fill in the real PTE used for address translation in the process page table. When a shared page is made valid, both the process PTE and the prototype PTE point to the physical page containing the data. To track the number of process PTEs that reference a valid shared page, a counter in its PFN database entry is incremented. Thus, the memory manager can determine when a shared page is no longer referenced by any page table and thus can be made invalid and moved to a transition list or written out to disk.

When a shareable page is invalidated, the PTE in the process page table is filled in with a special PTE that points to the prototype PTE entry that describes the page, as shown in Figure 10-28.

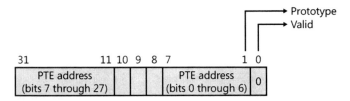

FIGURE 10-28 Structure of an invalid PTE that points to the prototype PTE

Thus, when the page is later accessed, the memory manager can locate the prototype PTE using the information encoded in this PTE, which in turn describes the page being referenced. A shared page can be in one of six different states as described by the prototype PTE entry:

- **Active/valid**   The page is in physical memory as a result of another process that accessed it.

- **Transition**   The desired page is in memory on the standby or modified list (or not on any list).

- **Modified-no-write**   The desired page is in memory and on the modified-no-write list. (See Table 10-19.)

- **Demand zero**   The desired page should be satisfied with a page of zeros.

- **Page file**   The desired page resides within a page file.

- **Mapped file**   The desired page resides within a mapped file.

Although the format of these prototype PTE entries is the same as that of the real PTE entries de-scribed earlier, these prototype PTEs aren't used for address translation—they are a layer between the page table and the page frame number database and never appear directly in page tables.

By having all the accessors of a potentially shared page point to a prototype PTE to resolve faults, the memory manager can manage shared pages without needing to update the page tables of each process sharing the page. For example, a shared code or data page might be paged out to disk at some point. When the memory manager retrieves the page from disk, it needs only to update the prototype PTE to point to the page's new physical location—the PTEs in each of the processes sharing the page remain the same (with the valid bit clear and still pointing to the prototype PTE). Later, as processes reference the page, the real PTE will get updated.

Figure 10-29 illustrates two virtual pages in a mapped view. One is valid, and the other is invalid. As shown, the first page is valid and is pointed to by the process PTE and the prototype PTE. The second page is in the paging file—the prototype PTE contains its exact location. The process PTE (and any other processes with that page mapped) points to this prototype PTE.

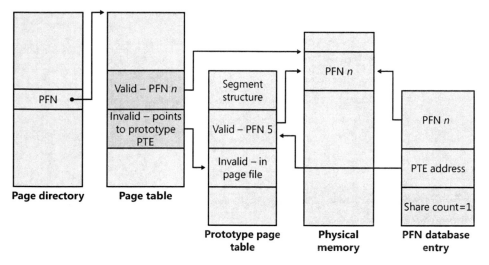

FIGURE 10-29 Prototype page table entries

In-Paging I/O

In-paging I/O occurs when a read operation must be issued to a file (paging or mapped) to satisfy a page fault. Also, because page tables are pageable, the processing of a page fault can incur additional I/O if necessary when the system is loading the page table page that contains the PTE or the prototype PTE that describes the original page being referenced.

The in-page I/O operation is synchronous—that is, the thread waits on an event until the I/O completes—and isn't interruptible by asynchronous procedure call (APC) delivery. The pager uses a special modifier in the I/O request function to indicate paging I/O. Upon completion of paging I/O, the I/O system triggers an event, which wakes up the pager and allows it to continue in-page processing.

While the paging I/O operation is in progress, the faulting thread doesn't own any critical memory management synchronization objects. Other threads within the process are allowed to issue virtual memory functions and handle page faults while the paging I/O takes place. But a number of interesting conditions that the pager must recognize when the I/O completes are exposed:

■ Another thread in the same process or a different process could have faulted the same page (called a *collided page fault* and described in the next section).

■ The page could have been deleted (and remapped) from the virtual address space.

- The protection on the page could have changed.

- The fault could have been for a prototype PTE, and the page that maps the prototype PTE could be out of the working set.

The pager handles these conditions by saving enough state on the thread's kernel stack before the paging I/O request such that when the request is complete, it can detect these conditions and, if necessary, dismiss the page fault without making the page valid. When and if the faulting instruction is reissued, the pager is again invoked and the PTE is reevaluated in its new state.

Collided Page Faults

The case when another thread in the same process or a different process faults a page that is currently being in-paged is known as a *collided page fault*. The pager detects and handles collided page faults optimally because they are common occurrences in multithreaded systems. If another thread or process faults the same page, the pager detects the collided page fault, noticing that the page is in transition and that a read is in progress. (This information is in the PFN database entry.) In this case, the pager may issue a wait operation on the event specified in the PFN database entry, or it can choose to issue a parallel I/O to protect the file systems from deadlocks (the first I/O to complete "wins," and the others are discarded). This event was initialized by the thread that first issued the I/O needed to resolve the fault.

When the I/O operation completes, all threads waiting on the event have their wait satisfied. The first thread to acquire the PFN database lock is responsible for performing the in-page completion operations. These operations consist of checking I/O status to ensure that the I/O operation completed successfully, clearing the read-in-progress bit in the PFN database, and updating the PTE.

When subsequent threads acquire the PFN database lock to complete the collided page fault, the pager recognizes that the initial updating has been performed because the read-in-progress bit is clear and checks the in-page error flag in the PFN database element to ensure that the in-page I/O completed successfully. If the in-page error flag is set, the PTE isn't updated and an in-page error exception is raised in the faulting thread.

Clustered Page Faults

The memory manager prefetches large clusters of pages to satisfy page faults and populate the system cache. The prefetch operations read data directly into the system's page cache instead of into a working set in virtual memory, so the prefetched data does not consume virtual address space, and the size of the fetch operation is not limited to the amount of virtual address space that is available. (Also, no expensive TLB-flushing Inter-Processor Interrupt is needed if the page will be repurposed.) The prefetched pages are put on the standby list and marked as in transition in the PTE. If a prefetched page is subsequently referenced, the memory manager adds it to the working set. However, if it is never referenced, no system resources are required to release it. If any pages in the prefetched cluster are already in memory, the memory manager does not read them again. Instead, it uses a dummy page to represent them so that an efficient single large I/O can still be issued, as Figure 10-30 shows.

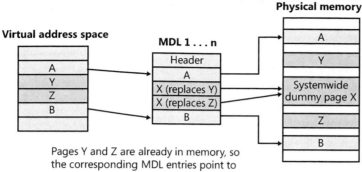

Physical memory

Pages Y and Z are already in memory, so the corresponding MDL entries point to the systemwide dummy page.

FIGURE 10-30 Usage of dummy page during virtual address to physical address mapping in an MDL

In the figure, the file offsets and virtual addresses that correspond to pages A, Y, Z, and B are logically contiguous, although the physical pages themselves are not necessarily contiguous. Pages A and B are nonresident, so the memory manager must read them. Pages Y and Z are already resident in memory, so it is not necessary to read them. (In fact, they might already have been modified since they were last read in from their backing store, in which case it would be a serious error to overwrite their contents.) However, reading pages A and B in a single operation is more efficient than performing one read for page A and a second read for page B. Therefore, the memory manager issues a single read request that comprises all four pages (A, Y, Z, and B) from the backing store. Such a read request includes as many pages as make sense to read, based on the amount of available memory, the current system usage, and so on.

When the memory manager builds the memory descriptor list (MDL) that describes the request, it supplies valid pointers to pages A and B. However, the entries for pages Y and Z point to a single systemwide dummy page X. The memory manager can fill the dummy page X with the potentially stale data from the backing store because it does not make X visible. However, if a component accesses the Y and Z offsets in the MDL, it sees the dummy page X instead of Y and Z.

The memory manager can represent any number of discarded pages as a single dummy page, and that page can be embedded multiple times in the same MDL or even in multiple concurrent MDLs that are being used for different drivers. Consequently, the contents of the locations that represent the discarded pages can change at any time.

Page Files

Page files are used to store modified pages that are still in use by some process but have had to be written to disk (because they were unmapped or memory pressure resulted in a trim). Page file space is reserved when the pages are initially committed, but the actual optimally clustered page file locations cannot be chosen until pages are written out to disk.

When the system boots, the Session Manager process (described in Chapter 13, "Startup and Shutdown") reads the list of page files to open by examining the registry value HKLM\SYSTEM\CurrentControlSet\Control\Session Manager\Memory Management\PagingFiles. This multistring registry value contains the name, minimum size, and maximum size of each paging file. Windows supports up to 16 paging files. On x86 systems running the normal kernel, each page file can be a maximum of 4,095 MB. On x86 systems running the PAE kernel and x64 systems, each page file can be 16 terabytes (TB) while the maximum is 32 TB on IA64 systems. Once open, the page files can't be deleted while the system is running because the System process (described in Chapter 2 in Part 1) maintains an open handle to each page file. The fact that the paging files are open explains why the built-in defragmentation tool cannot defragment the paging file while the system is up. To defragment your paging file, use the freeware Pagedefrag tool from Sysinternals. It uses the same approach as other third-party defragmentation tools—it runs its defragmentation process early in the boot process before the page files are opened by the Session Manager.

Because the page file contains parts of process and kernel virtual memory, for security reasons the system can be configured to clear the page file at system shutdown. To enable this, set the registry value HKLM\SYSTEM\CurrentControlSet\Control\Session Manager\Memory Management\ClearPage-FileAtShutdown to 1. Otherwise, after shutdown, the page file will contain whatever data happened to have been paged out while the system was up. This data could then be accessed by someone who gained physical access to the machine.

If the minimum and maximum paging file sizes are both zero, this indicates a system-managed paging file, which causes the system to choose the page file size as follows:

- Minimum size: set to the amount of RAM or 1 GB, whichever is larger.

- Maximum size: set to 3 * RAM or 4 GB, whichever is larger.

As you can see, by default the initial page file size is proportional to the amount of RAM. This policy is based on the assumption that machines with more RAM are more likely to be running workloads that commit large amounts of virtual memory.

EXPERIMENT: Viewing Page Files

To view the list of page files, look in the registry at HKLM\SYSTEM\CurrentControlSet\Control\ Session Manager\Memory Management\PagingFiles. This entry contains the paging file configuration settings modified through the Advanced System Settings dialog box. Open Control Panel, click System And Security, and then System. This is the System Properties dialog box, also reachable by right-clicking on Computer in Explorer and selecting Properties. From there, click Advanced System Settings, then Settings in the Performance area. In the Performance Options dialog box, click the Advanced tab, and then click Change in the Virtual Memory area.

To add a new page file, Control Panel uses the (internal only) *NtCreatePagingFile* system service defined in Ntdll.dll. Page files are always created as noncompressed files, even if the directory they are in is compressed. To keep new page files from being deleted, a handle is duplicated into the System process so that even after the creating process closes the handle to the new page file, a handle is nevertheless always open to it.

Commit Charge and the System Commit Limit

We are now in a position to more thoroughly discuss the concepts of commit charge and the system commit limit.

Whenever virtual address space is created, for example by a *VirtualAlloc* (for committed memory) or *MapViewOfFile* call, the system must ensure that there is room to store it, either in RAM or in backing store, before successfully completing the create request. For mapped memory (other than sections mapped to the page file), the file associated with the mapping object referenced by the *MapViewOfFile* call provides the required backing store.

All other virtual allocations rely for storage on system-managed shared resources: RAM and the paging file(s). The purpose of the system commit limit and commit charge is to track all uses of these resources to ensure that they are never overcommitted—that is, that there is never more virtual address space defined than there is space to store its contents, either in RAM or in backing store (on disk).

> **Note** This section makes frequent references to paging files. It is possible, though not generally recommended, to run Windows without any paging files. Every reference to paging files here may be considered to be qualified by "if one or more paging files exist."

Conceptually, the system commit limit represents the total virtual address space that can be created in addition to virtual allocations that are associated with their own backing store—that is, in addition to sections mapped to files. Its numeric value is simply the amount of RAM available to Windows plus the current sizes of any page files. If a page file is expanded, or new page files are created, the commit limit increases accordingly. If no page files exist, the system commit limit is simply the total amount of RAM available to Windows.

Commit charge is the systemwide total of all "committed" memory allocations that must be kept in either RAM or in a paging file. From the name, it should be apparent that one contributor to commit charge is process-private committed virtual address space. However, there are many other contributors, some of them not so obvious.

Windows also maintains a per-process counter called the *process page file quota*. Many of the allocations that contribute to commit charge contribute to the process page file quota as well. This represents each process's private contribution to the system commit charge. Note, however, that this does not represent current page file usage. It represents the potential or maximum page file usage, should all of these allocations have to be stored there.

The following types of memory allocations contribute to the system commit charge and, in many cases, to the process page file quota. (Some of these will be described in detail in later sections of this chapter.)

- Private committed memory is memory allocated with the *VirtualAlloc* call with the COMMIT option. This is the most common type of contributor to the commit charge. These allocations are also charged to the process page file quota.

- Page-file-backed mapped memory is memory allocated with a *MapViewOfFile* call that references a section object, which in turn is not associated with a file. The system uses a portion of the page file as the backing store instead. These allocations are not charged to the process page file quota.

- Copy-on-write regions of mapped memory, even if it is associated with ordinary mapped files. The mapped file provides backing store for its own unmodified content, but should a page in the copy-on-write region be modified, it can no longer use the original mapped file for backing store. It must be kept in RAM or in a paging file. These allocations are not charged to the process page file quota.

- Nonpaged and paged pool and other allocations in system space that are not backed by explicitly associated files. Note that even the currently free regions of the system memory pools contribute to commit charge. The nonpageable regions are counted in the commit charge, even though they will never be written to the page file because they permanently reduce the amount of RAM available for private pageable data. These allocations are not charged to the process page file quota.

- Kernel stacks.

- Page tables, most of which are themselves pageable, and they are not backed by mapped files. Even if not pageable, they occupy RAM. Therefore, the space required for them contributes to commit charge.

- Space for page tables that are not yet actually allocated. As we'll see later, where large areas of virtual space have been defined but not yet referenced (for example, private committed virtual space), the system need not actually create page tables to describe it. But the space for these as-yet-nonexistent page tables is charged to commit charge to ensure that the page tables can be created when they are needed.

- Allocations of physical memory made via the Address Windowing Extension (AWE) APIs.

For many of these items, the commit charge may represent the potential use of storage rather than the actual. For example, a page of private committed memory does not actually occupy either a physical page of RAM or the equivalent page file space until it's been referenced at least once. Until then, it is a *demand-zero page* (described later). But commit charge accounts for such pages when the virtual space is first created. This ensures that when the page is later referenced, actual physical storage space will be available for it.

A region of a file mapped as copy-on-write has a similar requirement. Until the process writes to the region, all pages in it are backed by the mapped file. But the process may write to any of the pages in the region at any time, and when that happens, those pages are thereafter treated as private to the process. Their backing store is, thereafter, the page file. Charging the system commit for them when the region is first created ensures that there will be private storage for them later, if and when the write accesses occur.

A particularly interesting case occurs when reserving private memory and later committing it. When the reserved region is created with *VirtualAlloc*, system commit charge is not charged for the actual virtual region. It is, however, charged for any new page table pages that will be required to describe the region, even though these might not yet exist. If the region or a part of it is later committed, system commit is charged to account for the size of the region (as is the process page file quota).

To put it another way, when the system successfully completes (for example) a *VirtualAlloc* or *MapViewOfFile* call, it makes a "commitment" that the needed storage will be available when needed, even if it wasn't needed at that moment. Thus, a later memory reference to the allocated region can never fail for lack of storage space. (It could fail for other reasons, such as page protection, the region being deallocated, and so on.) The commit charge mechanism allows the system to keep this commitment.

The commit charge appears in the Performance Monitor counters as Memory: Committed Bytes. It is also the first of the two numbers displayed on Task Manager's Performance tab with the legend Commit (the second being the commit limit), and it is displayed by Process Explorer's System Information Memory tab as Commit Charge—Current.

The process page file quota appears in the performance counters as Process: Page File Bytes. The same data appears in the Process: Private Bytes performance counter. (Neither term exactly describes the true meaning of the counter.)

If the commit charge ever reaches the commit limit, the memory manager will attempt to increase the commit limit by expanding one or more page files. If that is not possible, subsequent attempts to allocate virtual memory that uses commit charge will fail until some existing committed memory is freed. The performance counters listed in Table 10-14 allow you to examine private committed memory usage on a systemwide, per-process, or per-page-file, basis.

TABLE 10-14 Committed Memory and Page File Performance Counters

Performance Counter	Description
Memory: Committed Bytes	Number of bytes of virtual (not reserved) memory that has been committed. This number doesn't necessarily represent page file usage because it includes private committed pages in physical memory that have never been paged out. Rather, it represents the charged amount that must be backed by page file space and/or RAM.
Memory: Commit Limit	Number of bytes of virtual memory that can be committed without having to extend the paging files; if the paging files can be extended, this limit is soft.
Process: Page File Quota	The process's contribution to Memory: Committed Bytes.
Process: Private Bytes	Same as Process: Page File Quota
Process: Working Set—Private	The subset of Process: Page File Quota that is currently in RAM and can be referenced without a page fault. Also a subset of Process: Working Set.
Process: Working Set	The subset of Process: Virtual Bytes that is currently in RAM and can be referenced without a page fault.
Process: Virtual Bytes	The total virtual memory allocation of the process, including mapped regions, private committed regions, and private reserved regions.
Paging File: % Usage	Percentage of the page file space that is currently in use.
Paging File: % Usage Peak	The highest observed value of Paging File: % Usage

Commit Charge and Page File Size

The counters in Table 10-14 can assist you in choosing a custom page file size. The default policy based on the amount of RAM works acceptably for most machines, but depending on the workload it can result in a page file that's unnecessarily large, or not large enough.

To determine how much page file space your system really needs based on the mix of applications that have run since the system booted, examine the peak commit charge in the Memory tab of Process Explorer's System Information display. This number represents the peak amount of page file space since the system booted that would have been needed if the system had to page out the majority of private committed virtual memory (which rarely happens).

If the page file on your system is too big, the system will not use it any more or less—in other words, increasing the size of the page file does not change system performance, it simply means the system can have more committed virtual memory. If the page file is too small for the mix of applications you are running, you might get the "system running low on virtual memory" error message. In this case, first check to see whether a process has a memory leak by examining the process private bytes count. If no process appears to have a leak, check the system paged pool size—if a device driver is leaking paged pool, this might also explain the error. (See the "Troubleshooting a Pool Leak" experiment in the "Kernel-Mode Heaps (System Memory Pools)" section for how to troubleshoot a pool leak.)

EXPERIMENT: Viewing Page File Usage with Task Manager

You can also view committed memory usage with Task Manager by clicking its Performance tab. You'll see the following counters related to page files:

![Windows Task Manager screenshot showing the Performance tab. CPU Usage at 3%, Memory at 1.13 GB. Physical Memory (MB): Total 4093, Cached 861, Available 2931, Free 2130. Kernel Memory (MB): Paged 139, Nonpaged 57. System: Handles 16025, Threads 581, Processes 51, Up Time 5:07:54:55, Commit (MB) 1221 / 8186. Status bar: Processes: 51, CPU Usage: 3%, Physical Memory: 28%.]

The system commit total is displayed in the lower-right System area as two numbers. The first number represents *potential* page file usage, not actual page file usage. It is how much page file space would be used if all of the private committed virtual memory in the system had to be paged out all at once. The second number displayed is the *commit limit*, which displays the maximum virtual memory usage that the system can support before running out of virtual memory (it includes virtual memory backed in physical memory as well as by the paging files). The commit limit is essentially the size of RAM plus the current size of the paging files. It therefore does not account for possible page file expansion.

Process Explorer's System Information display shows an additional item of information about system commit usage, namely the percentage of the peak as compared to the limit and the current usage as compared to the limit:

Stacks

Whenever a thread runs, it must have access to a temporary storage location in which to store function parameters, local variables, and the return address after a function call. This part of memory is called a *stack*. On Windows, the memory manager provides two stacks for each thread, the *user stack* and the *kernel stack*, as well as per-processor stacks called *DPC stacks*. We have already described how the stack can be used to generate stack traces and how exceptions and interrupts store structures on the stack, and we have also talked about how system calls, traps, and interrupts cause the thread to switch from a user stack to its kernel stack. Now, we'll look at some extra services the memory manager provides to efficiently use stack space.

User Stacks

When a thread is created, the memory manager automatically reserves a predetermined amount of virtual memory, which by default is 1 MB. This amount can be configured in the call to the *CreateThread* or *CreateRemoteThread* function or when compiling the application, by using the /STACK:reserve switch in the Microsoft C/C++ compiler, which will store the information in the image header. Although 1 MB is reserved, only the first page of the stack will be committed (unless the PE header of the image specifies otherwise), along with a guard page. When a thread's stack grows large enough to touch the guard page, an exception will occur, causing an attempt to allocate another guard. Through this mechanism, a user stack doesn't immediately consume all 1 MB of committed memory but instead grows with demand. (However, it will never shrink back.)

EXPERIMENT: Creating the Maximum Number of Threads

With only 2 GB of user address space available to each 32-bit process, the relatively large memory that is reserved for each thread's stack allows for an easy calculation of the maximum number of threads that a process can support: a little less than 2,048, for a total of nearly 2 GB of memory (unless the *increaseuserva* BCD option is used and the image is large address space aware). By forcing each new thread to use the smallest possible stack reservation size, 64 KB, the limit can grow to about 30,400 threads, which you can test for yourself by using the TestLimit utility from Sysinternals. Here is some sample output:

```
C:\>testlimit -t
Testlimit - tests Windows limits
By Mark Russinovich

Creating threads ...
Created 30399 threads. Lasterror: 8
```

If you attempt this experiment on a 64-bit Windows installation (with 8 TB of user address space available), you would expect to see potentially hundreds of thousands of threads created (as long as sufficient memory were available). Interestingly, however, TestLimit will actually create fewer threads than on a 32-bit machine, which has to do with the fact that Testlimit.exe is a 32-bit application and thus runs under the Wow64 environment. (See Chapter 3 in Part 1 for more information on Wow64.) Each thread will therefore have not only its 32-bit Wow64 stack but also its 64-bit stack, thus consuming more than twice the memory, while still keeping only 2 GB of address space. To properly test the thread-creation limit on 64-bit Windows, use the Testlimit64.exe binary instead.

Note that you will need to terminate TestLimit with Process Explorer or Task Manager—using Ctrl+C to break the application will not function because this operation itself creates a new thread, which will not be possible once memory is exhausted.

Kernel Stacks

Although user stack sizes are typically 1 MB, the amount of memory dedicated to the kernel stack is significantly smaller: 12 KB on x86 and 16 KB on x64, followed by another guard PTE (for a total of 16 or 20 KB of virtual address space). Code running in the kernel is expected to have less recursion than user code, as well as contain more efficient variable use and keep stack buffer sizes low. Because kernel stacks live in system address space (which is shared by all processes), their memory usage has a bigger impact of the system.

Although kernel code is usually not recursive, interactions between graphics system calls handled by Win32k.sys and its subsequent callbacks into user mode can cause recursive re-entries in the kernel on the same kernel stack. As such, Windows provides a mechanism for dynamically expanding and shrinking the kernel stack from its initial size of 16 KB. As each additional graphics call is performed from the same thread, another 16-KB kernel stack is allocated (anywhere in system address space; the memory manager provides the ability to jump stacks when nearing the guard page). Whenever each call returns to the caller (unwinding), the memory manager frees the additional kernel stack that had been allocated, as shown in Figure 10-31.

This mechanism allows reliable support for recursive system calls, as well as efficient use of system address space, and is also provided for use by driver developers when performing recursive callouts through the *KeExpandKernelStackAndCallout* API, as necessary.

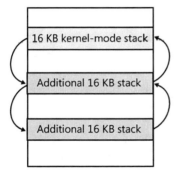

Unwind when nested callback is complete

FIGURE 10-31 Kernel stack jumping

DPC Stack

Finally, Windows keeps a per-processor DPC stack available for use by the system whenever DPCs are executing, an approach that isolates the DPC code from the current thread's kernel stack (which is unrelated to the DPC's actual operation because DPCs run in arbitrary thread context). The DPC stack is also configured as the initial stack for handling the SYSENTER or SYSCALL instruction during a system call. The CPU is responsible for switching the stack when SYSENTER or SYSCALL is executed, based on one of the model-specific registers (MSRs), but Windows does not want to reprogram the MSR for every context switch, because that is an expensive operation. Windows therefore configures the per-processor DPC stack pointer in the MSR.

Virtual Address Descriptors

The memory manager uses a demand-paging algorithm to know when to load pages into memory, waiting until a thread references an address and incurs a page fault before retrieving the page from disk. Like copy-on-write, demand paging is a form of *lazy evaluation*—waiting to perform a task until it is required.

The memory manager uses lazy evaluation not only to bring pages into memory but also to construct the page tables required to describe new pages. For example, when a thread commits a large region of virtual memory with *VirtualAlloc* or *VirtualAllocExNuma*, the memory manager could immediately construct the page tables required to access the entire range of allocated memory. But what if some of that range is never accessed? Creating page tables for the entire range would be a wasted effort. Instead, the memory manager waits to create a page table until a thread incurs a page fault, and then it creates a page table for that page. This method significantly improves performance for processes that reserve and/or commit a lot of memory but access it sparsely.

The virtual address space that would be occupied by such as-yet-nonexistent page tables is charged to the process page file quota and to the system commit charge. This ensures that space will be available for them should they be actually created. With the lazy-evaluation algorithm, allocating even large blocks of memory is a fast operation. When a thread allocates memory, the memory manager must respond with a range of addresses for the thread to use. To do this, the memory manager maintains another set of data structures to keep track of which virtual addresses have been reserved in the process's address space and which have not. These data structures are known as *virtual address descriptors* (VADs). VADs are allocated in nonpaged pool.

Process VADs

For each process, the memory manager maintains a set of VADs that describes the status of the process's address space. VADs are organized into a self-balancing AVL tree (named after its inventors, Adelson-Velskii and Landis) that optimally balances the tree. This results in, on average, the fewest number of comparisons when searching for a VAD corresponding with a virtual address. There is one virtual address descriptor for each virtually contiguous range of not-free virtual addresses that all have the same characteristics (reserved versus committed versus mapped, memory access protection, and so on). A diagram of a VAD tree is shown in Figure 10-32.

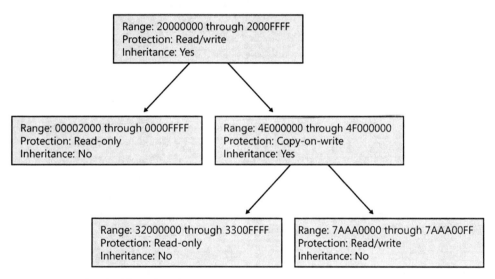

FIGURE 10-32 Virtual address descriptors

When a process reserves address space or maps a view of a section, the memory manager creates a VAD to store any information supplied by the allocation request, such as the range of addresses being reserved, whether the range will be shared or private, whether a child process can inherit the contents of the range, and the page protection applied to pages in the range.

When a thread first accesses an address, the memory manager must create a PTE for the page containing the address. To do so, it finds the VAD whose address range contains the accessed address and uses the information it finds to fill in the PTE. If the address falls outside the range covered by the VAD or in a range of addresses that are reserved but not committed, the memory manager knows that the thread didn't allocate the memory before attempting to use it and therefore generates an access violation.

EXPERIMENT: Viewing Virtual Address Descriptors

You can use the kernel debugger's *!vad* command to view the VADs for a given process. First find the address of the root of the VAD tree with the *!process* command. Then specify that address to the *!vad* command, as shown in the following example of the VAD tree for a process running Notepad.exe:

```
lkd> !process 0 1 notepad.exe
PROCESS 8718ed90  SessionId: 1  Cid: 1ea68     Peb: 7ffdf000  ParentCid: 0680
    DirBase: ce2aa880  ObjectTable: ee6e01b0  HandleCount:  48.
    Image: notepad.exe
    VadRoot 865f10e0 Vads 51 Clone 0 Private 210. Modified 0. Locked 0.

lkd> !vad 865f10e0
VAD      level      start     end     commit
8a05bf88 ( 6)          10      1f        0 Mapped      READWRITE
88390ad8 ( 5)          20      20        1 Private     READWRITE
87333740 ( 6)          30      33        0 Mapped      READONLY
86d09d10 ( 4)          40      41        0 Mapped      READONLY
882b49a0 ( 6)          50      50        1 Private     READWRITE
...
Total VADs:     51  average level:     5  maximum depth: 6
```

Rotate VADs

A video card driver must typically copy data from the user-mode graphics application to various other system memory, including the video card memory and the AGP port's memory, both of which have different caching attributes as well as addresses. In order to quickly allow these different views of memory to be mapped into a process, and to support the different cache attributes, the memory manager implements *rotate VADs*, which allow video drivers to transfer data directly by using the GPU and to rotate unneeded memory in and out of the process view pages on demand. Figure 10-33 shows an example of how the same virtual address can rotate between video RAM and virtual memory.

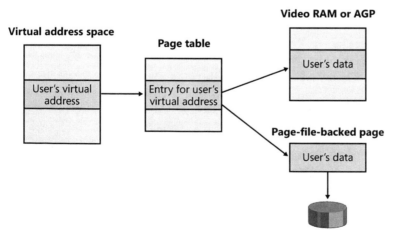

FIGURE 10-33 Rotate virtual address descriptors

NUMA

Each new release of Windows provides new enhancements to the memory manager to better make use of Non Uniform Memory Architecture (NUMA) machines, such as large server systems (but also Intel i7 and AMD Opteron SMP workstations). The NUMA support in the memory manager adds intelligent knowledge of node information such as location, topology, and access costs to allow applications and drivers to take advantage of NUMA capabilities, while abstracting the underlying hardware details.

When the memory manager is initializing, it calls the *MiComputeNumaCosts* function to perform various page and cache operations on different nodes and then computes the time it took for those operations to complete. Based on this information, it builds a node graph of access costs (the distance between a node and any other node on the system). When the system requires pages for a given operation, it consults the graph to choose the most optimal node (that is, the closest). If no memory is available on that node, it chooses the next closest node, and so on.

Although the memory manager ensures that, whenever possible, memory allocations come from the ideal processor's node (the *ideal node*) of the thread making the allocation, it also provides functions that allow applications to choose their own node, such as the *VirtualAllocExNuma*, *CreateFileMappingNuma*, *MapViewOfFileExNuma*, and *AllocateUserPhysicalPagesNuma* APIs.

The ideal node isn't used only when applications allocate memory but also during kernel operation and page faults. For example, when a thread is running on a nonideal processor and takes a page fault, the memory manager won't use the current node but will instead allocate memory from the thread's ideal node. Although this might result in slower access time while the thread is still running on this CPU, overall memory access will be optimized as the thread migrates back to its ideal node. In any case, if the ideal node is out of resources, the closest node to the ideal node is chosen and not a random other node. Just like user-mode applications, however, drivers can specify their own node when using APIs such as *MmAllocatePagesforMdlEx* or *MmAllocateContiguousMemorySpecifyCacheNode*.

Various memory manager pools and data structures are also optimized to take advantage of NUMA nodes. The memory manager tries to evenly use physical memory from all the nodes on the system to hold the nonpaged pool. When a nonpaged pool allocation is made, the memory manager looks at the ideal node and uses it as an index to choose a virtual memory address range inside nonpaged pool that corresponds to physical memory belonging to this node. In addition, per-NUMA node pool freelists are created to efficiently leverage these types of memory configurations. Apart from nonpaged pool, the system cache and system PTEs are also similarly allocated across all nodes, as well as the memory manager's look-aside lists.

Finally, when the system needs to zero pages, it does so in parallel across different NUMA nodes by creating threads with NUMA affinities that correspond to the nodes in which the physical memory is located. The logical prefetcher and Superfetch (described later) also use the ideal node of the target process when prefetching, while soft page faults cause pages to migrate to the ideal node of the faulting thread.

Section Objects

As you'll remember from the section on shared memory earlier in the chapter, the *section object*, which the Windows subsystem calls a *file mapping object*, represents a block of memory that two or more processes can share. A section object can be mapped to the paging file or to another file on disk.

The executive uses sections to load executable images into memory, and the cache manager uses them to access data in a cached file. (See Chapter 11 for more information on how the cache manager uses section objects.) You can also use section objects to map a file into a process address space. The file can then be accessed as a large array by mapping different views of the section object and reading or writing to memory rather than to the file (an activity called *mapped file I/O*). When the program accesses an invalid page (one not in physical memory), a page fault occurs and the memory manager automatically brings the page into memory from the mapped file (or page file). If the application modifies the page, the memory manager writes the changes back to the file during its normal paging operations (or the application can flush a view by using the Windows *FlushViewOfFile* function).

Section objects, like other objects, are allocated and deallocated by the object manager. The object manager creates and initializes an object header, which it uses to manage the objects; the memory manager defines the body of the section object. The memory manager also implements services that user-mode threads can call to retrieve and change the attributes stored in the body of section objects. The structure of a section object is shown in Figure 10-34.

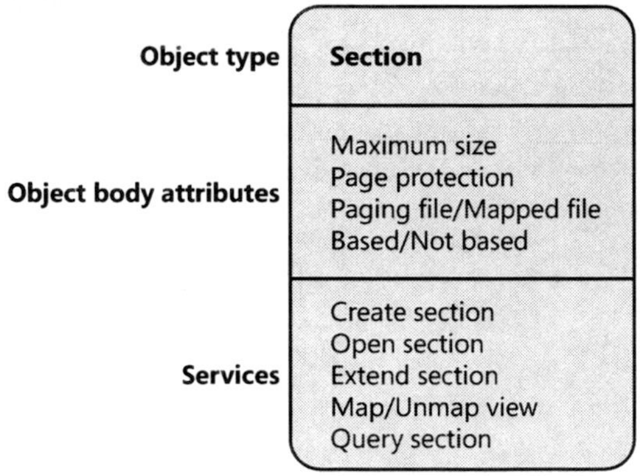

Object type	Section
Object body attributes	Maximum size Page protection Paging file/Mapped file Based/Not based
Services	Create section Open section Extend section Map/Unmap view Query section

FIGURE 10-34 A section object

Table 10-15 summarizes the unique attributes stored in section objects.

TABLE 10-15 Section Object Body Attributes

Attribute	Purpose
Maximum size	The largest size to which the section can grow in bytes; if mapping a file, the maximum size is the size of the file.
Page protection	Page-based memory protection assigned to all pages in the section when it is created.
Paging file/Mapped file	Indicates whether the section is created empty (backed by the paging file—as explained earlier, page-file-backed sections use page-file resources only when the pages need to be written out to disk) or loaded with a file (backed by the mapped file).
Based/Not based	Indicates whether a section is a based section, which must appear at the same virtual address for all processes sharing it, or a nonbased section, which can appear at different virtual addresses for different processes.

EXPERIMENT: Viewing Section Objects

With the Object Viewer (Winobj.exe from Sysinternals), you can see the list of sections that have names. You can list the open handles to section objects with any of the tools described in the "Object Manager" section in Chapter 3 in Part 1 that list the open handle table. (As explained in Chapter 3, these names are stored in the object manager directory \Sessions\x\BaseNamed-Objects, where x is the appropriate Session directory. Unnamed section objects are not visible.

As mentioned earlier, you can use Process Explorer from Sysinternals to see files mapped by a process. Select DLLs from the Lower Pane View entry of the View menu, and enable the Mapping Type column in the DLL section of View | Select Columns. Files marked as "Data" in the Mapping column are mapped files (rather than DLLs and other files the image loader loads as modules). We saw this example earlier:

Name	Description	Version	Base	ASLR	Mapping
kernel32.dll	Windows NT BASE API Client DLL	6.1.7601.17651	0x77650000	ASLR	Image
KernelBase.dll	Windows NT BASE API Client DLL	6.1.7601.17651	0x75EC0000	ASLR	Image
kext.dll	Debugger Extensions	6.12.2.633	0x737E0000	ASLR	Image
linkinfo.dll	Windows Volume Tracking	6.1.7600.16385	0x701A0000	ASLR	Image
locale.nls			0x110000	n/a	Data
lpk.dll	Language Pack	6.1.7600.16385	0x77CF0000	ASLR	Image
MEMORY.DMP			0x1410000	n/a	Data
MEMORY.DMP			0x1420000	n/a	Data
MEMORY.DMP			0x1550000	n/a	Data

CPU Usage: 3.04%   Commit Charge: 35.03%   Processes: 50   Physical Usage: 44.15%

The data structures maintained by the memory manager that describe mapped sections are shown in Figure 10-35. These structures ensure that data read from mapped files is consistent, regardless of the type of access (open file, mapped file, and so on).

For each open file (represented by a file object), there is a single *section object pointers* structure. This structure is the key to maintaining data consistency for all types of file access as well as to providing caching for files. The section object pointers structure points to one or two *control areas*. One control area is used to map the file when it is accessed as a data file, and one is used to map the file when it is run as an executable image.

A control area in turn points to *subsection* structures that describe the mapping information for each section of the file (read-only, read/write, copy-on-write, and so on). The control area also points to a *segment* structure allocated in paged pool, which in turn points to the prototype PTEs used to map to the actual pages mapped by the section object. As described earlier in the chapter, process page tables point to these prototype PTEs, which in turn map the pages being referenced.

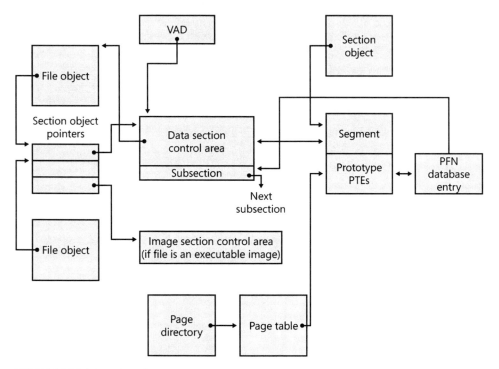

FIGURE 10-35 Internal section structures

Although Windows ensures that any process that accesses (reads or writes) a file will always see the same, consistent data, there is one case in which two copies of pages of a file can reside in physical memory (but even in this case, all accessors get the latest copy and data consistency is maintained). This duplication can happen when an image file has been accessed as a data file (having been read or written) and then run as an executable image (for example, when an image is linked and then run—the linker had the file open for data access, and then when the image was run, the image loader mapped it as an executable). Internally, the following actions occur:

1. If the executable file was created using the file mapping APIs (or the cache manager), a data control area is created to represent the data pages in the image file being read or written.

2. When the image is run and the section object is created to map the image as an executable, the memory manager finds that the section object pointers for the image file point to a data control area and flushes the section. This step is necessary to ensure that any modified pages have been written to disk before accessing the image through the image control area.

3. The memory manager then creates a control area for the image file.

4. As the image begins execution, its (read-only) pages are faulted in from the image file (or copied directly over from the data file if the corresponding data page is resident).

Because the pages mapped by the data control area might still be resident (on the standby list), this is the one case in which two copies of the same data are in two different pages in memory. However, this duplication doesn't result in a data consistency issue because, as mentioned, the data control area has already been flushed to disk, so the pages read from the image are up to date (and these pages are never written back to disk).

EXPERIMENT: Viewing Control Areas

To find the address of the control area structures for a file, you must first get the address of the file object in question. You can obtain this address through the kernel debugger by dumping the process handle table with the *!handle* command and noting the object address of a file object. Although the kernel debugger *!file* command displays the basic information in a file object, it doesn't display the pointer to the section object pointers structure. Then, using the *dt* command, format the file object to get the address of the section object pointers structure. This structure consists of three pointers: a pointer to the data control area, a pointer to the shared cache map (explained in Chapter 11), and a pointer to the image control area. From the section object pointers structure, you can obtain the address of a control area for the file (if one exists) and feed that address into the *!ca* command.

For example, if you open a PowerPoint file and display the handle table for that process using *!handle*, you will find an open handle to the PowerPoint file as shown here. (For information on using *!handle*, see the "Object Manager" section in Chapter 3 in Part 1.)

```
lkd> !handle 1 f 86f57d90 File
   .
   .
   .
0324: Object: 865d2768  GrantedAccess: 00120089 Entry: c848e648
Object: 865d2768  Type: (8475a2c0) File
    ObjectHeader: 865d2750 (old version)
        HandleCount: 1  PointerCount: 1
        Directory Object: 00000000  Name: \Users\Administrator\Documents\Downloads\
SVR-T331_WH07 (1).pptx {HarddiskVolume3}
```

Taking the file object address (865d2768) and formatting it with *dt* results in this:

```
lkd> dt nt!_FILE_OBJECT 865d2768
   +0x000 Type             : 5
   +0x002 Size             : 128
   +0x004 DeviceObject     : 0x84a62320 _DEVICE_OBJECT
   +0x008 Vpb              : 0x84a60590 _VPB
   +0x00c FsContext        : 0x8cee4390
   +0x010 FsContext2       : 0xbf910c80
   +0x014 SectionObjectPointer : 0x86c45584 _SECTION_OBJECT_POINTERS
```

Then taking the address of the section object pointers structure (0x86c45584) and formatting it with *dt* results in this:

```
lkd> dt 0x86c45584 nt!_SECTION_OBJECT_POINTERS
   +0x000 DataSectionObject : 0x863d3b00
   +0x004 SharedCacheMap    : 0x86f10ec0
   +0x008 ImageSectionObject : (null)
```

Finally, use *!ca* to display the control area using the address:

```
lkd> !ca 0x863d3b00

ControlArea  @ 863d3b00
   Segment      b1de9d48  Flink      00000000  Blink        8731f80c
   Section Ref        1  Pfn Ref          48  Mapped Views        2
   User Ref           0  WaitForDel        0  Flush Count         0
   File Object  86cf6188  ModWriteCount     0  System Views        2
   WritableRefs       0
   Flags (c080) File WasPurged Accessed

      No name for file


Segment @ b1de9d48
   ControlArea      863d3b00  ExtendInfo      00000000
   Total Ptes           100
   Segment Size      100000  Committed            0
   Flags (c0000) ProtectionMask


Subsection 1 @ 863d3b48
   ControlArea  863d3b00  Starting Sector      0  Number Of Sectors  100
   Base Pte     bf85e008  Ptes In Subsect    100  Unused Ptes          0
   Flags             d  Sector Offset        0  Protection           6
   Accessed
   Flink        00000000  Blink           8731f87c  MappedViews          2
```

Another technique is to display the list of all control areas with the *!memusage* command. The following excerpt is from the output of this command:

```
lkd> !memusage
 loading PFN database
loading (100% complete)
Compiling memory usage data (99% Complete).
             Zeroed:   2654 ( 10616 kb)
               Free:    584 (  2336 kb)
            Standby: 402938 (1611752 kb)
           Modified:  12732 ( 50928 kb)
    ModifiedNoWrite:      3 (    12 kb)
       Active/Valid: 431478 (1725912 kb)
         Transition:   1186 (  4744 kb)
                Bad:      0 (     0 kb)
            Unknown:      0 (     0 kb)
              TOTAL: 851575 (3406300 kb)
  Building kernel map
  Finished building kernel map
Scanning PFN database - (100% complete)

  Usage Summary (in Kb):
Control Valid Standby Dirty Shared Locked PageTables  name
86d75f18    0    64     0     0     0     0  mapped_file( netcfgx.dll )
8a124ef8    0     4     0     0     0     0   No Name for File
8747af80    0    52     0     0     0     0  mapped_file( iebrshim.dll )
883a2e58   24     8     0     0     0     0  mapped_file( WINWORD.EXE )
86d6eae0    0    16     0     0     0     0  mapped_file( oem13.CAT )
84b19af8    8     0     0     0     0     0   No Name for File
b1672ab0    4     0     0     0     0     0   No Name for File
88319da8    0    20     0     0     0     0  mapped_file( Microsoft-Windows-MediaPlayer-
Package~31bf3856ad364e35~x86~en-US~6.0.6001.18000.cat )
8a04db00    0    48     0     0     0     0  mapped_file( eapahost.dll )
```

The Control column points to the control area structure that describes the mapped file. You can display control areas, segments, and subsections with the kernel debugger *!ca* command. For example, to dump the control area for the mapped file Winword.exe in this example, type the *!ca* command followed by the Control number, as shown here:

```
lkd> !ca 883a2e58

ControlArea @ 883a2e58
  Segment      ee613998  Flink      00000000  Blink         88a985a4
  Section Ref         1  Pfn Ref           8  Mapped Views         1
  User Ref            2  WaitForDel        0  Flush Count          0
  File Object  88b45180  ModWriteCount     0  System Views      ffff
  WritableRefs 80000006
  Flags (40a0) Image File Accessed

    File: \PROGRA~1\MICROS~1\Office12\WINWORD.EXE
```

```
Segment @ ee613998
    ControlArea      883a2e58   BasedAddress    2f510000
    Total Ptes            57
    Segment Size      57000   Committed             0
    Image Commit          1   Image Info      ee613c80
    ProtoPtes       ee6139c8
    Flags (20000) ProtectionMask


Subsection 1 @ 883a2ea0
    ControlArea  883a2e58   Starting Sector     0   Number Of Sectors    2
    Base Pte     ee6139c8   Ptes In Subsect     1   Unused Ptes          0
    Flags               2   Sector Offset       0   Protection           1

Subsection 2 @ 883a2ec0
    ControlArea  883a2e58   Starting Sector     2   Number Of Sectors    a
    Base Pte     ee6139d0   Ptes In Subsect     2   Unused Ptes          0
    Flags               6   Sector Offset       0   Protection           3

Subsection 3 @ 883a2ee0
    ControlArea  883a2e58   Starting Sector     c   Number Of Sectors    1
    Base Pte     ee6139e0   Ptes In Subsect     1   Unused Ptes          0
    Flags               a   Sector Offset       0   Protection           5

Subsection 4 @ 883a2f00
    ControlArea  883a2e58   Starting Sector     d   Number Of Sectors  28b
    Base Pte     ee6139e8   Ptes In Subsect    52   Unused Ptes          0
    Flags               2   Sector Offset       0   Protection           1

Subsection 5 @ 883a2f20
    ControlArea  883a2e58   Starting Sector   298   Number Of Sectors    1
    Base Pte     ee613c78   Ptes In Subsect     1   Unused Ptes          0
    Flags               2   Sector Offset       0   Protection           1
```

Driver Verifier

As introduced in Chapter 8, "I/O System," Driver Verifier is a mechanism that can be used to help find and isolate commonly found bugs in device driver or other kernel-mode system code. This section describes the memory management–related verification options Driver Verifier provides (the options related to device drivers are described in Chapter 8).

The verification settings are stored in the registry under HKLM\SYSTEM\CurrentControlSet\ Control\Session Manager\Memory Management. The value VerifyDriverLevel contains a bitmask that represents the verification types enabled. The VerifyDrivers value contains the names of the drivers to validate. (These values won't exist in the registry until you select drivers to verify in the Driver Verifier Manager.) If you choose to verify all drivers, VerifyDrivers is set to an asterisk (*) character. Depending on the settings you have made, you might need to reboot the system for the selected verification to occur.

Early in the boot process, the memory manager reads the Driver Verifier registry values to determine which drivers to verify and which Driver Verifier options you enabled. (Note that if you boot in safe mode, any Driver Verifier settings are ignored.) Subsequently, if you've selected at least one driver for verification, the kernel checks the name of every device driver it loads into memory against the list of drivers you've selected for verification. For every device driver that appears in both places, the kernel invokes the *VfLoadDriver* function, which calls other internal *Vf** functions to replace the driver's references to a number of kernel functions with references to Driver Verifier–equivalent versions of those functions. For example, *ExAllocatePool* is replaced with a call to *VerifierAllocatePool*. The windowing system driver (Win32k.sys) also makes similar changes to use Driver Verifier–equivalent functions.

Now that we've reviewed how Driver Verifier is set up, we'll examine the six memory-related verification options that can be applied to device drivers: Special Pool, Pool Tracking, Force IRQL Checking, Low Resources Simulation, Miscellaneous Checks, and Automatic Checks

Special Pool   The Special Pool option causes the pool allocation routines to bracket pool allocations with an invalid page so that references before or after the allocation will result in a kernel-mode access violation, thus crashing the system with the finger pointed at the buggy driver. Special pool also causes some additional validation checks to be performed when a driver allocates or frees memory.

When special pool is enabled, the pool allocation routines allocate a region of kernel memory for Driver Verifier to use. Driver Verifier redirects memory allocation requests that drivers under verification make to the special pool area rather than to the standard kernel-mode memory pools. When a device driver allocates memory from special pool, Driver Verifier rounds up the allocation to an even-page boundary. Because Driver Verifier brackets the allocated page with invalid pages, if a device driver attempts to read or write past the end of the buffer, the driver will access an invalid page, and the memory manager will raise a kernel-mode access violation.

Figure 10-36 shows an example of the special pool buffer that Driver Verifier allocates to a device driver when Driver Verifier checks for overrun errors.

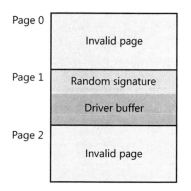

FIGURE 10-36 Layout of special pool allocations

By default, Driver Verifier performs *overrun* detection. It does this by placing the buffer that the device driver uses at the end of the allocated page and fills the beginning of the page with a random pattern. Although the Driver Verifier Manager doesn't let you specify underrun detection, you can set this type of detection manually by adding the DWORD registry value HKLM\SYSTEM\Current-ControlSet\Control\Session Manager\Memory Management\PoolTagOverruns and setting it to 0 (or by running the Gflags utility and selecting the Verify Start option instead of the default option, Verify End). When Windows enforces underrun detection, Driver Verifier allocates the driver's buffer at the beginning of the page rather than at the end.

The overrun-detection configuration includes some measure of underrun detection as well. When the driver frees its buffer to return the memory to Driver Verifier, Driver Verifier ensures that the pattern preceding the buffer hasn't changed. If the pattern is modified, the device driver has underrun the buffer and written to memory outside the buffer.

Special pool allocations also check to ensure that the processor IRQL at the time of an allocation and deallocation is legal. This check catches an error that some device drivers make: allocating pageable memory from an IRQL at DPC/dispatch level or above.

You can also configure special pool manually by adding the DWORD registry value HKLM\SYSTEM\CurrentControlSet\Control\Session Manager\Memory Management\PoolTag, which represents the allocation tags the system uses for special pool. Thus, even if Driver Verifier isn't configured to verify a particular device driver, if the tag the driver associates with the memory it allocates matches what is specified in the PoolTag registry value, the pool allocation routines will allocate the memory from special pool. If you set the value of PoolTag to 0x0000002a or to the wildcard (*), all memory that drivers allocate is from special pool, provided there's enough virtual and physical memory. (The drivers will revert to allocating from regular pool if there aren't enough free pages—bounding exists, but each allocation uses two pages.)

Pool Tracking   If pool tracking is enabled, the memory manager checks at driver unload time whether the driver freed all the memory allocations it made. If it didn't, it crashes the system, indicating the buggy driver. Driver Verifier also shows general pool statistics on the Driver Verifier Manager's Pool Tracking tab. You can also use the *!verifier* kernel debugger command. This command shows more information than Driver Verifier and is useful to driver writers.

Pool tracking and special pool cover not only explicit allocation calls, such as *ExAllocatePoolWith-Tag*, but also calls to other kernel APIs that implicitly allocate pool: *IoAllocateMdl*, *IoAllocateIrp*, and other IRP allocation calls; various *Rtl* string APIs; and *IoSetCompletionRoutineEx*.

Another driver verified function enabled by the Pool Tracking option has to do with pool quota charges. The call *ExAllocatePoolWithQuotaTag* charges the current process's pool quota for the number of bytes allocated. If such a call is made from a deferred procedure call (DPC) routine, the process that is charged is unpredictable because DPC routines may execute in the context of any process. The Pool Tracking option checks for calls to this routine from DPC routine context.

Driver Verifier can also perform locked memory page tracking, which additionally checks for pages that have been left locked after an I/O operation and generates the DRIVER_LEFT_LOCKED_PAGES_IN_PROCESS instead of the PROCESS_HAS_LOCKED_PAGES crash code—the former indicates the driver responsible for the error as well as the function responsible for the locking of the pages.

Force IRQL Checking   One of the most common device driver bugs occurs when a driver accesses pageable data or code when the processor on which the device driver is executing is at an elevated IRQL. As explained in Chapter 3 in Part 1, the memory manager can't service a page fault when the IRQL is DPC/dispatch level or above. The system often doesn't detect instances of a device driver accessing pageable data when the processor is executing at a high IRQL level because the pageable data being accessed happens to be physically resident at the time. At other times, however, the data might be paged out, which results in a system crash with the stop code IRQL_NOT_LESS_OR_EQUAL (that is, the IRQL wasn't less than or equal to the level required for the operation attempted—in this case, accessing pageable memory).

Although testing device drivers for this kind of bug is usually difficult, Driver Verifier makes it easy. If you select the Force IRQL Checking option, Driver Verifier forces all kernel-mode pageable code and data out of the system working set whenever a device driver under verification raises the IRQL. The internal function that does this is *MiTrimAllSystemPagableMemory*. With this setting enabled, whenever a device driver under verification accesses pageable memory when the IRQL is elevated, the system instantly detects the violation, and the resulting system crash identifies the faulty driver.

Another common driver crash that results from incorrect IRQL usage occurs when synchronization objects are part of data structures that are paged and then waited on. Synchronization objects should never be paged because the dispatcher needs to access them at an elevated IRQL, which would cause a crash. Driver Verifier checks whether any of the following structures are present in pageable memory: KTIMER, KMUTEX, KSPIN_LOCK, KEVENT, KSEMAPHORE, ERESOURCE, FAST_MUTEX.

Low Resources Simulation   Enabling Low Resources Simulation causes Driver Verifier to randomly fail memory allocations that verified device drivers perform. In the past, developers wrote many device drivers under the assumption that kernel memory would always be available and that if memory ran out, the device driver didn't have to worry about it because the system would crash anyway. However, because low-memory conditions can occur temporarily, it's important that device drivers properly handle allocation failures that indicate kernel memory is exhausted.

The driver calls that will be injected with random failures include the *ExAllocatePool**, *MmProbe-AndLockPages*, *MmMapLockedPagesSpecifyCache*, *MmMapIoSpace*, *MmAllocateContiguousMemory*, *MmAllocatePagesForMdl*, *IoAllocateIrp*, *IoAllocateMdl*, *IoAllocateWorkItem*, *IoAllocateErrorLogEntry*, *IOSetCompletionRoutineEx*, and various *Rtl* string APIs that allocate pool. Additionally, you can specify the probability that allocation will fail (6 percent by default), which applications should be subject to the simulation (all are by default), which pool tags should be affected (all are by default), and what delay should be used before fault injection starts (the default is 7 minutes after the system boots, which is enough time to get past the critical initialization period in which a low-memory condition might prevent a device driver from loading).

After the delay period, Driver Verifier starts randomly failing allocation calls for device drivers it is verifying. If a driver doesn't correctly handle allocation failures, this will likely show up as a system crash.

Miscellaneous Checks   Some of the checks that Driver Verifier calls "miscellaneous" allow Driver Verifier to detect the freeing of certain system structures in the pool that are still active. For example, Driver Verifier will check for:

- Active work items in freed memory (a driver calls *ExFreePool* to free a pool block in which one or more work items queued with *IoQueueWorkItem* are present).

- Active resources in freed memory (a driver calls *ExFreePool* before calling *ExDeleteResource* to destroy an ERESOURCE object).

- Active look-aside lists in freed memory (a driver calls *ExFreePool* before calling *ExDeleteNPagedLookasideList* or *ExDeletePagedLookasideList* to delete the look-aside list).

Finally, when verification is enabled, Driver Verifier also performs certain automatic checks that cannot be individually enabled or disabled. These include:

- Calling *MmProbeAndLockPages* or *MmProbeAndLockProcessPages* on a memory descriptor list (MDL) having incorrect flags. For example, it is incorrect to call *MmProbeAndLockPages* for an MDL setup by calling *MmBuildMdlForNonPagedPool*.

- Calling *MmMapLockedPages* on an MDL having incorrect flags. For example, it is incorrect to call *MmMapLockedPages* for an MDL that is already mapped to a system address. Another example of incorrect driver behavior is calling *MmMapLockedPages* for an MDL that was not locked.

- Calling *MmUnlockPages* or *MmUnmapLockedPages* on a partial MDL (created by using *IoBuildPartialMdl*).

- Calling *MmUnmapLockedPages* on an MDL that is not mapped to a system address.

- Allocating synchronization objects such as events or mutexes from NonPagedPoolSession memory.

Driver Verifier is a valuable addition to the arsenal of verification and debugging tools available to device driver writers. Many device drivers that first ran with Driver Verifier had bugs that Driver Verifier was able to expose. Thus, Driver Verifier has resulted in an overall improvement in the quality of all kernel-mode code running in Windows.

Page Frame Number Database

In several previous sections, we've concentrated on the virtual view of a Windows process—page tables, PTEs, and VADs. In the remainder of this chapter, we'll explain how Windows manages physical memory, starting with how Windows keeps track of physical memory. Whereas working sets describe the resident pages owned by a process or the system, the *page frame number (PFN) database* describes the state of each page in physical memory. The page states are listed in Table 10-16.

TABLE 10-16 Page States

Status	Description
Active (also called Valid)	The page is part of a working set (either a process working set, a session working set, or a system working set), or it's not in any working set (for example, nonpaged kernel page) and a valid PTE usually points to it.
Transition	A temporary state for a page that isn't owned by a working set and isn't on any paging list. A page is in this state when an I/O to the page is in progress. The PTE is encoded so that collided page faults can be recognized and handled properly. (Note that this use of the term "transition" differs from the use of the word in the section on invalid PTEs; an invalid transition PTE refers to a page on the standby or modified list.)
Standby	The page previously belonged to a working set but was removed (or was prefetched/clustered directly into the standby list). The page wasn't modified since it was last written to disk. The PTE still refers to the physical page but is marked invalid and in transition.
Modified	The page previously belonged to a working set but was removed. However, the page was modified while it was in use and its current contents haven't yet been written to disk or remote storage. The PTE still refers to the physical page but is marked invalid and in transition. It must be written to the backing store before the physical page can be reused.
Modified no-write	Same as a modified page, except that the page has been marked so that the memory manager's modified page writer won't write it to disk. The cache manager marks pages as modified no-write at the request of file system drivers. For example, NTFS uses this state for pages containing file system metadata so that it can first ensure that transaction log entries are flushed to disk before the pages they are protecting are written to disk. (NTFS transaction logging is explained in Chapter 12, "File Systems.")
Free	The page is free but has unspecified dirty data in it. (These pages can't be given as a user page to a user process without being initialized with zeros, for security reasons.)
Zeroed	The page is free and has been initialized with zeros by the zero page thread (or was determined to already contain zeros).
Rom	The page represents read-only memory
Bad	The page has generated parity or other hardware errors and can't be used.

The PFN database consists of an array of structures that represent each physical page of memory on the system. The PFN database and its relationship to page tables are shown in Figure 10-37. As this figure shows, valid PTEs usually point to entries in the PFN database, and the PFN database entries (for nonprototype PFNs) point back to the page table that is using them (if it is being used by a page table). For prototype PFNs, they point back to the prototype PTE.

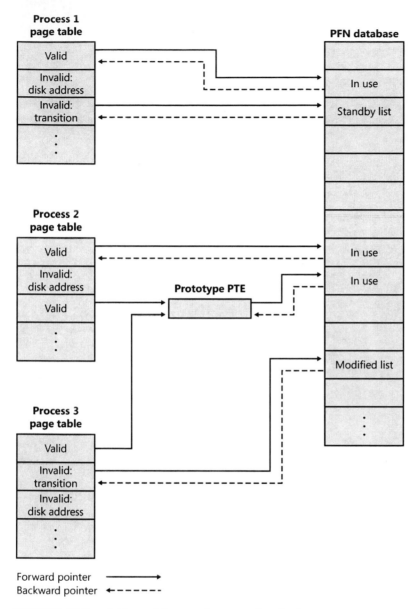

FIGURE 10-37 Page tables and the page frame number database

Of the page states listed in Table 10-16, six are organized into linked lists so that the memory manager can quickly locate pages of a specific type. (Active/valid pages, transition pages, and overloaded "bad" pages aren't in any systemwide page list.) Additionally, the standby state is actually associated with eight different lists ordered by priority (we'll talk about page priority later in this section). Figure 10-38 shows an example of how these entries are linked together.

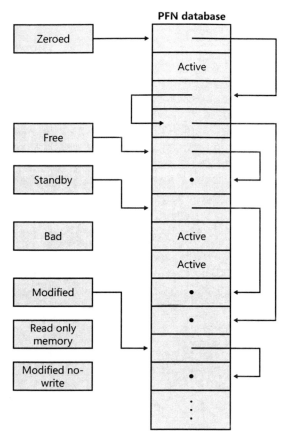

FIGURE 10-38 Page lists in the PFN database

In the next section, you'll find out how these linked lists are used to satisfy page faults and how pages move to and from the various lists.

> **EXPERIMENT: Viewing the PFN Database**
>
> You can use the MemInfo tool from Winsider Seminars & Solutions to dump the size of the various paging lists by using the *–s* flag. The following is the output from this command:
>
> ```
> C:\>MemInfo.exe -s
>
> MemInfo v2.10 - Show PFN database information
> Copyright (C) 2007-2009 Alex Ionescu
> www.alex-ionescu.com
>
> Initializing PFN Database... Done
>
> PFN Database List Statistics
>             Zeroed:    487 (    1948 kb)
>               Free:      0 (       0 kb)
>            Standby: 379745 (1518980 kb)
>           Modified:   1052 (    4208 kb)
>    ModifiedNoWrite:      0 (       0 kb)
>       Active/Valid: 142703 ( 570812 kb)
>         Transition:    184 (     736 kb)
>                Bad:      0 (       0 kb)
>            Unknown:      2 (       8 kb)
>              TOTAL: 524173 (2096692 kb)
> ```
>
> Using the kernel debugger *!memusage* command, you can obtain similar information, although this will take considerably longer and will require booting into debugging mode.

Page List Dynamics

Figure 10-39 shows a state diagram for page frame transitions. For simplicity, the modified-no-write list isn't shown.

Page frames move between the paging lists in the following ways:

- When the memory manager needs a zero-initialized page to service a demand-zero page fault (a reference to a page that is defined to be all zeros or to a user-mode committed private page that has never been accessed), it first attempts to get one from the zero page list. If the list is empty, it gets one from the free page list and zeroes the page. If the free list is empty, it goes to the standby list and zeroes that page.

  One reason zero-initialized pages are required is to meet various security requirements, such as the Common Criteria. Most Common Criteria profiles specify that user-mode processes must be given initialized page frames to prevent them from reading a previous process's memory contents. Therefore, the memory manager gives user-mode processes zeroed page frames unless the page is being read in from a backing store. If that's the case, the memory manager prefers to use nonzeroed page frames, initializing them with the data off the disk or remote storage.

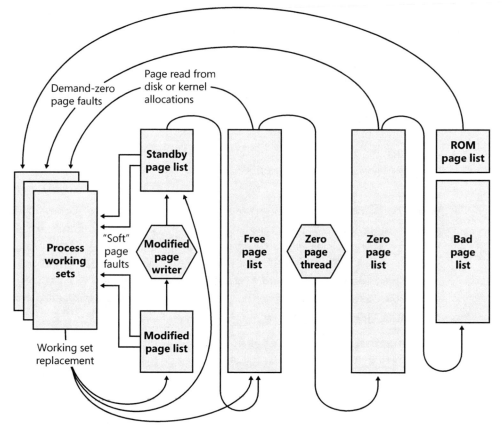

FIGURE 10-39 State diagram for page frames

The zero page list is populated from the free list by a system thread called the *zero page thread* (thread 0 in the System process). The zero page thread waits on a gate object to signal it to go to work. When the free list has eight or more pages, this gate is signaled. However, the zero page thread will run only if at least one processor has no other threads running, because the zero page thread runs at priority 0 and the lowest priority that a user thread can be set to is 1.

> **Note** Because the zero page thread actually waits on an event dispatcher object, it receives a priority boost (see the section "Priority Boosts" in Chapter 5 in Part 1), which results in it executing at priority 1 for at least part of the time. This is a bug in the current implementation.

Note When memory needs to be zeroed as a result of a physical page allocation by a driver that calls *MmAllocatePagesForMdl* or *MmAllocatePagesForMdlEx*, by a Windows application that calls *AllocateUserPhysicalPages* or *AllocateUserPhysicalPagesNuma*, or when an application allocates large pages, the memory manager zeroes the memory by using a higher performing function called *MiZeroInParallel* that maps larger regions than the zero page thread, which only zeroes a page at a time. In addition, on multiprocessor systems, the memory manager creates additional system threads to perform the zeroing in parallel (and in a NUMA-optimized fashion on NUMA platforms).

- When the memory manager doesn't require a zero-initialized page, it goes first to the free list. If that's empty, it goes to the zeroed list. If the zeroed list is empty, it goes to the standby lists. Before the memory manager can use a page frame from the standby lists, it must first backtrack and remove the reference from the invalid PTE (or prototype PTE) that still points to the page frame. Because entries in the PFN database contain pointers back to the previous user's page table page (or to a page of prototype PTE pool for shared pages), the memory manager can quickly find the PTE and make the appropriate change.

- When a process has to give up a page out of its working set (either because it referenced a new page and its working set was full or the memory manager trimmed its working set), the page goes to the standby lists if the page was clean (not modified) or to the modified list if the page was modified while it was resident.

- When a process exits, all the private pages go to the free list. Also, when the last reference to a page-file-backed section is closed, and the section has no remaining mapped views, these pages also go to the free list.

EXPERIMENT: The Free and Zero Page Lists

You can observe the release of private pages at process exit with Process Explorer's System Information display. Begin by creating a process with a large number of private pages in its working set. We did this in an earlier experiment with the TestLimit utility:

```
C:\temp>testlimit -d 1 -c 800

Testlimit v5.1 - test Windows limits
Copyright (C) 2012 Mark Russinovich
Sysinternals - www.sysinternals.com

Leaking private bytes 1 MB at a time ...
Leaked 800 MB of private memory (800 MB total leaked). Lasterror: 0
The operation completed successfully.
```

The *–d* option causes TestLimit to not only allocate the memory as private committed, but to "touch" it—that is, to access it. This causes physical memory to be allocated and assigned to the process to realize the area of private committed virtual memory. If there is sufficient available RAM on the system, the entire 800 MB should be in RAM for the process.

This process will now wait until you cause it to exit or terminate (perhaps by using Ctrl+C in its command window). Open Process Explorer and select View, System Information. Observe the Free and Zeroed list sizes.

Now terminate or exit the TestLimit process. You *may* see the free page list briefly increase in size:

```
System Information                                                    _ □ ✕

 Summary   CPU   Memory   I/O   GPU

  System Commit

  ┌──┐  ┌──────────────────────────────────────────────────────┐
  │  │  │                                                        │
  └──┘  └──────────────────────────────────────────────────────┘
  2.3 GB

  Physical Memory

  ┌──┐  ┌──────────────────────────────────────────────────────┐
  │  │  │                                                        │
  └──┘  └──────────────────────────────────────────────────────┘
  1.4 GB

  Commit Charge (K)          Kernel Memory (K)              Paging Lists (K)
  Current     2,421,636      Paged WS          102,984      Zeroed          1,119,800
  Limit       6,812,300      Paged Virtual     130,028      Free              137,644
  Peak        7,807,568      Paged Limit     no symbols     Modified           25,876
                                                            ModifiedNoWrite        28
  Peak/Limit    114.61%      Nonpaged           29,464      Standby           838,168
  Current/Limit  35.55%      Nonpaged Limit  no symbols       Priority 0        5,180
                                                               Priority 1      135,320
  Physical Memory (K)        Paging                           Priority 2      466,056
  Total       3,407,028      Page Fault Delta        271      Priority 3       86,284
  Available   2,095,612      Page Read Delta           0      Priority 4       35,660
  Cache WS       29,788      Paging File Write Delta    0      Priority 5       78,044
  Kernel WS       1,568      Mapped File Write Delta    0      Priority 6       10,348
  Driver WS       4,224                                        Priority 7       21,276

                                                                    [  OK  ]
```

We say "may" because the zero page thread is awakened as soon as there are only eight pages on the zero list, and it acts very quickly. Notice that in this example, we freed 800 MB of private memory but only about 138 MB appear here on the free list. Process Explorer updates this display only once per second, and it is likely that the rest of the pages were already zeroed and moved to the zeroed page list before it happened to "catch" this state.

If you are able to see the temporary increase in the free list, you will then see it drop to zero, and a corresponding increase will occur in the zeroed page list. If not, you will simply see the increase in the zeroed list.

EXPERIMENT: The Modified and Standby Page Lists

The movement of pages from process working set to the modified page list and then to the standby page list can also be observed with the Sysinternals tools VMMap and RAMMap and the live kernel debugger.

The first step is to open RAMMap and observe the state of the quiet system:

Usage	Total	Active	Standby	Modified	...	...	Zeroed	Free	
Process Private	232,416 K	141,908 K	88,700 K	1,808 K					
Mapped File	937,972 K	32,408 K	905,556 K	8 K					
Shareable	35,156 K	8,812 K	20,552 K	5,792 K					
Page Table	8,044 K	7,660 K	140 K	244 K					
Paged Pool	185,456 K	89,764 K	95,684 K	8 K					
Nonpaged Pool	136,584 K	136,576 K				8 K			
System PTE	29,024 K	23,024 K	6,000 K						
Session Private	15,328 K	9,244 K	6,076 K	8 K					
Metafile	580,528 K	2,648 K	577,436 K		444 K				
AWE									
Driver Locked	1,080 K	1,080 K							
Kernel Stack	6,052 K	5,384 K	496 K	172 K					
Unused	1,239,388 K						1,238,836 K	552 K	
Total	3,407,028 K	458,508 K	1,700,640 K	8,040 K	444 K	8 K	1,238,836 K	552 K	

This is an x86 system with about 3.4 GB of RAM usable by Windows. The columns in this display represent the various page states shown in Figure 10-39. (A few of the columns not important to this discussion have been narrowed for ease of reference.)

The system has about 1.2 GB of RAM free (sum of the free and zeroed page lists). About 1,700 MB is on the standby list (hence part of "available," but likely containing data recently lost from processes or being used by Superfetch). About 448 MB is "active," being mapped directly to virtual addresses via valid page table entries.

Each row further breaks down into page state by usage or origin (process private, mapped file, and so on). For example, at the moment, of the active 448 MB, about 138 MB is due to process private allocations.

Now, as in the previous experiment, use the TestLimit utility to create a process with a large number of pages in its working set. Again we will use the −d option to cause TestLimit to write to each page, but this time we will use it without a limit, so as to create as many private modified pages as possible:

```
C:\Users\user1>testlimit -d

Testlimit v5.21 - test Windows limits
Copyright (C) 2012 Mark Russinovich
Sysinternals - www.sysinternals.com

Process ID: 1000

Leaking private bytes with touch (MB) ...
Leaked 2017 MB of private memory (2017 MB total leaked). Lasterror: 8
Not enough storage is available to process this command.
```

TestLimit has now created 2,017 allocations of 1 MB each.

In RAMMap, use the File, Refresh command to update the display (because of the cost of gathering its information, RAMMap does not update continuously).

You will see that over 2 GB are now active and in the Process Private row. This is due to the memory allocated and accessed by the TestLimit process. Note also that the standby, zeroed, and free lists are now much smaller. Most of the RAM allocated to TestLimit came from these lists.

Next, in RAMMap, check the process's physical page allocations. Change to the Physical Pages tab, and set the filter at the bottom to the column Process and the value Testlimit.exe. This display shows all the physical pages that are part of the process working set.

RamMap - Sysinternals: www.sysinternals.com

File   Empty   Help

Use Counts | Processes | Priority Summary | **Physical Pages** | Physical Ranges | File Summary | File Details

Physical Addr...	List	Use	Priority	Process	Virtual Address	Image	Offset	File Name
0x11C000	Active	Process Pri...	5	Testlimit.exe (1184)	0x4C9C9000			
0x11D000	Active	Process Pri...	5	Testlimit.exe (1184)	0x4C8CA000			
0x11E000	Active	Process Pri...	5	Testlimit.exe (1184)	0x4CA42000			
0x11F000	Active	Process Pri...	5	Testlimit.exe (1184)	0x4C6B6000			
0x160000	Active	Process Pri...	5	Testlimit.exe (1184)	0x4A382000			
0x161000	Active	Process Pri...	5	Testlimit.exe (1184)	0x4C728000			
0x162000	Active	Process Pri...	5	Testlimit.exe (1184)	0x4C5B2000			
0x163000	Active	Process Pri...	5	Testlimit.exe (1184)	0x4C78A000			
0x164000	Active	Process Pri...	5	Testlimit.exe (1184)	0x4C9C1000			
0x165000	Active	Process Pri...	5	Testlimit.exe (1184)	0x4C8C2000			
0x166000	Active	Process Pri...	5	Testlimit.exe (1184)	0x4CA3A000			
0x167000	Active	Process Pri...	5	Testlimit.exe (1184)	0x4C6AE000			
0x168000	Active	Process Pri...	5	Testlimit.exe (1184)	0x4A37A000			
0x169000	Active	Process Pri...	5	Testlimit.exe (1184)	0x4C720000			
0x16A000	Active	Process Pri...	5	Testlimit.exe (1184)	0x4C5AA000			
0x16B000	Active	Process Pri...	5	Testlimit.exe (1184)	0x4C782000			
0x16C000	Active	Process Pri...	5	Testlimit.exe (1184)	0x4C9B9000			
0x16D000	Active	Process Pri...	5	Testlimit.exe (1184)	0x4C8BA000			
0x16E000	Active	Process Pri	5	Testlimit.exe (1184)	0x4CA32000			

Filter: Process   ▼   is   Testlimit.exe (1184)

We would like to identify a physical page involved in the allocation of virtual address space done by TestLimit's *–d* option. RAMMap does not give an indication about which virtual allocations are associated with RAMMap's *VirtualAlloc* calls. However, we can get a good hint of this through the VMMap tool. Using VMMap on the same process, we find the following:

VMMap - Sysinternals: www.sysinternals.com

File   Edit   View   Options   Help

Process: Testlimit.exe
PID: 1000

Committed: 2,085,880 K

Private Bytes: 2,074,792 K

Working Set: 2,076,208 K

Type	Size	Committed	Private	Total WS	Private WS	Shareable WS	Shared WS	Locked WS	Blocks	Largest
Total	2,100,804 K	2,085,880 K	2,074,792 K	2,076,208 K	2,074,724 K	1,484 K	1,340 K		2121	
Image	7,360 K	7,360 K	208 K	1,184 K	148 K	1,036 K	956 K		70	1,264 K
Mapped File	1,190 K	1,180 K		224 K		224 K	168 K		2	768 K
Shareable	15,464 K	1,820 K		220 K		220 K	212 K		16	12,288 K
Heap										
Managed Heap										
Stack	256 K	16 K	16 K	12 K	12 K				3	256 K
Private Data	2,066,644 K	2,065,604 K	2,065,604 K	2,065,604 K	2,065,600 K	4 K	4 K		2030	1,024 K
Page Table	8,964 K	8,964 K	8,964 K	8,964 K	8,964 K					
Unusable	936 K	936 K								60 K
Free	5,248 K								15	768 K

Address	Type	Size	Committed	Private	Total WS	Private WS	Shareable WS	Shared WS	Locked WS	Blocks	Prot
002A0000	Mapped File	768 K	768 K	768 K	64 K		64 K	8 K		1	Copy
00370000	Private Data	1,024 K	140 K	140 K	140 K	140 K				2	Rea
00470000	Shareable	1,028 K	1,028 K		44 K		44 K	44 K		1	Rea
00580000	Private D #a	1,024 K	1,024 K	1,024 K	1,024 K	1,024 K				1	Rea
006E0000	Private Data	64 K	20 K	20 K	20 K	20 K				2	Rea
006F0000	Private Data	1,024 K	1,024 K	1,024 K	1,024 K	1,024 K				1	Rea
007F0000	Private Data	1,024 K	1,024 K	1,024 K	1,024 K	1,024 K				1	Rea
008F0000											

Timeline...   Heap Allocations...   Call Tree...   Trace...

In the lower part of the display, we find hundreds of allocations of process private data, each 1 MB in size and with 1 MB committed. These match the size of the allocations done by TestLimit. The first of these is highlighted in the preceding screen shot. Note the starting virtual address, 0x580000.

Now go back to RAMMap's physical memory display. Arrange the columns to make the Virtual Address column easily visible, click on it to sort by that value, and you can find that virtual address:

This shows that the virtual page starting at 0x01340000 is currently mapped to physical address 0x97D78000.

TestLimit's –d option writes the program's own name to the first bytes of each allocation. We can demonstrate this with the !dc (display characters using physical address) command in the local kernel debugger:

```
1kd> !dc 0x97d78000
#97d78000 74736554 696d694c 00000074 00000000 TestLimit.......
#97d78010 00000000 00000000 00000000 00000000 ................
#97d78020 00000000 00000000 00000000 00000000 ................
...
```

For the final leg of the experiment, we will demonstrate that this data remains intact (for a while, anyway) after the process working set is reduced and this page is moved to the modified and then the standby page list.

In VMMap, having selected the TestLimit process, use the View, Empty Working Set command to reduce the process's working set to the bare minimum. VMMap's display should now look like this:

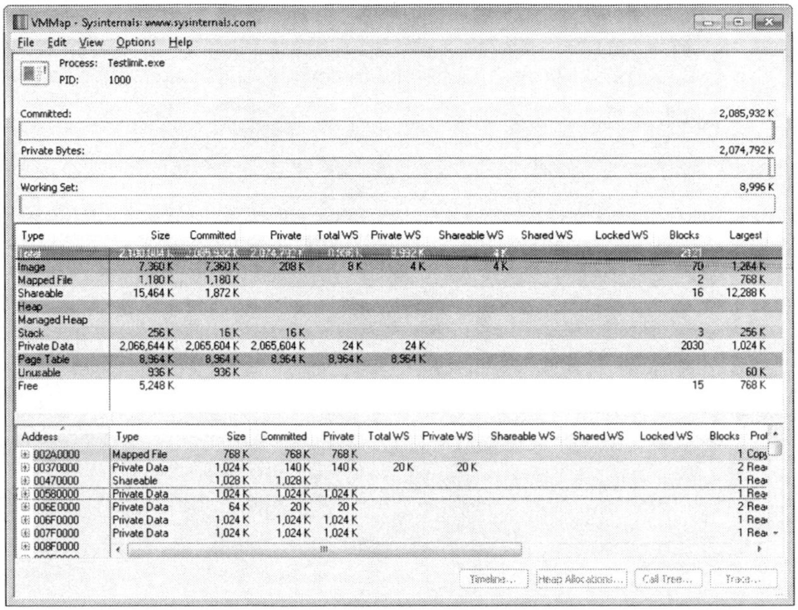

Notice that the Working Set bar graph is practically empty. In the middle section, the process shows a total working set of only 9 MB, and almost all of it is in page tables, with a tiny 32 KB total paged in of image files and private data. Now return to RAMMap. On the Use Counts tab, you will find that active pages have been reduced tremendously, with a large number of pages on the modified list and a significant number on the standby list:

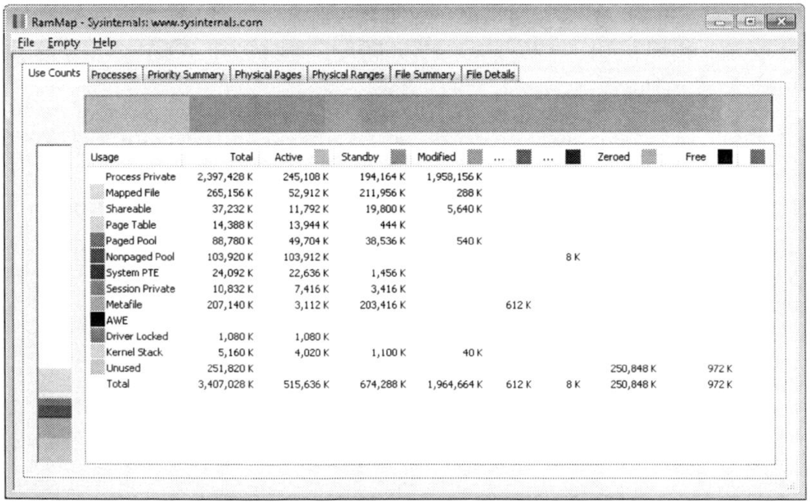

RAMMap's Processes tab confirms that the TestLimit process contributed most of those pages to those lists:

Still in RAMMap, show the Physical Pages tab. Sort by Physical Address, and find the page previously examined (in this case, physical address 0xc09fa000). RAMMap will almost certainly show that it is on the standby or modified list.

Note that the page is still associated with the TestLimit process and with its virtual address.

Finally, we can again use the kernel debugger to verify the page has not been overwritten:

```
lkd> !dc 0x97d78000
#97d78000 74736554 696d694c 00000074 00000000 TestLimit.......
#97d78010 00000000 00000000 00000000 00000000 ...............
#97d78020 00000000 00000000 00000000 00000000 ...............
...
```

We can also use the local kernel debugger to show the page frame number, or PFN, entry for the page. (The PFN database is described earlier in the chapter.)

```
lkd> !pfn 97d78
    PFN 00097D78 at address 84E9B920
    flink        000A0604  blink / share count 000A05C1  pteaddress C0002C00
    reference count 0000   Cached        color 0   Priority 5
    restore pte 00000080   containing page        097D60  Modified   M
    Modified
```

Note that the page is still associated with the TestLimit process and with its virtual address.

Page Priority

Every physical page in the system has a *page priority* value assigned to it by the memory manager. The page priority is a number in the range 0 to 7. Its main purpose is to determine the order in which pages are consumed from the standby list. The memory manager divides the standby list into eight sublists that each store pages of a particular priority. When the memory manager wants to take a page from the standby list, it takes pages from low-priority lists first, as shown in Figure 10-40.

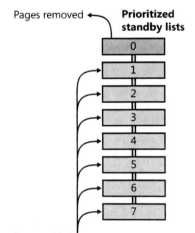

FIGURE 10-40 Prioritized standby lists

Each thread and process in the system is also assigned a page priority. A page's priority usually reflects the page priority of the thread that first causes its allocation. (If the page is shared, it reflects the highest page priority among the sharing threads.) A thread inherits its page-priority value from the process to which it belongs. The memory manager uses low priorities for pages it reads from disk speculatively when anticipating a process's memory accesses.

By default, processes have a page-priority value of 5, but functions allow applications and the system to change process and thread page-priority values. You can look at the memory priority of a thread with Process Explorer (per-page priority can be displayed by looking at the PFN entries, as you'll see in an experiment later in the chapter). Figure 10-41 shows Process Explorer's Threads tab displaying information about Winlogon's main thread. Although the thread priority itself is high, the memory priority is still the standard 5.

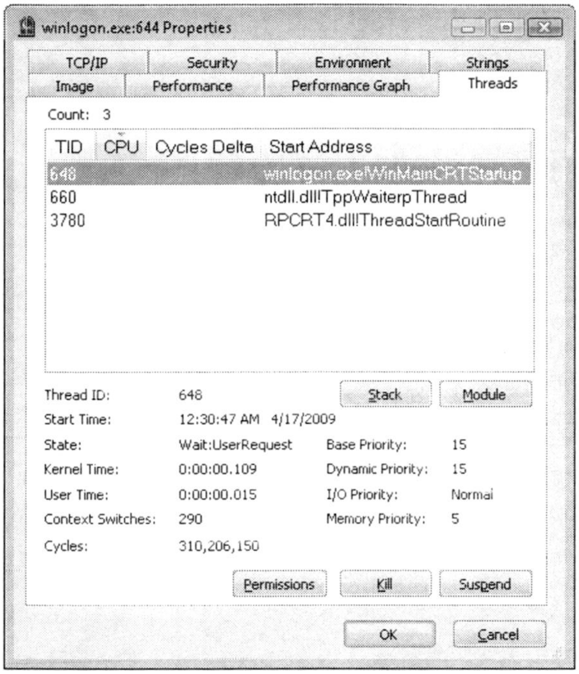

FIGURE 10-41 Process Explorer's Threads tab.

The real power of memory priorities is realized only when the relative priorities of pages are understood at a high level, which is the role of Superfetch, covered at the end of this chapter.

EXPERIMENT: Viewing the Prioritized Standby Lists

You can use the MemInfo tool from Winsider Seminars & Solutions to dump the size of each standby paging list by using the –c flag. MemInfo will also display the number of repurposed pages for each standby list—this corresponds to the number of pages in each list that had to be reused to satisfy a memory allocation, and thus thrown out of the standby page lists. The following is the relevant output from the following command.

```
C:\Windows\system32>meminfo -c
MemInfo v2.10 - Show PFN database information
Copyright (C) 2007-2009 Alex Ionescu
www.alex-ionescu.com

Initializing PFN Database... Done


Priority              Standby              Repurposed
0 - Idle           0 (      0 KB)        0 (      0 KB)
1 - Very Low    41352 ( 165408 KB)       0 (      0 KB)
2 - Low          7201 (  28804 KB)       0 (      0 KB)
3 - Background    2043 (   8172 KB)       0 (      0 KB)
4 - Background   24715 (  98860 KB)       0 (      0 KB)
5 - Normal        7895 (  31580 KB)       0 (      0 KB)
6 - Superfetch   23877 (  95508 KB)       0 (      0 KB)
7 - Superfetch    8435 (  33740 KB)       0 (      0 KB)
TOTAL           115518 ( 462072 KB)       0 (      0 KB)
```

You can add the *–i* flag to MemInfo to continuously display the state of the standby page lists and repurpose counts, which is useful for tracking memory usage as well as the following experiment. Additionally, the System Information panel in Process Explorer (choose View, System Information) can also be used to display the live state of the prioritized standby lists, as shown in this screen shot:

On the recently started x64 system used in this experiment (see the previous MemInfo output), there is no data cached at priority 0, about 165 MB at priority 1, and about 29 MB at priority 2. Your system probably has some data in those priorities as well.

The following shows what happens when we use the TestLimit tool from Sysinternals to commit and touch 1 GB of memory. Here is the command you use (to leak and touch memory in 20 chunks of 50 MB):

```
testlimit -d 50 -c 20
```

Here is the output of MemInfo just before the run:

```
Priority                Standby              Repurposed
0 - Idle             0 (       0 KB)    2554 (  10216 KB)
1 - Very Low     92915 ( 371660 KB)  141352 ( 565408 KB)
2 - Low          35783 ( 143132 KB)       0 (      0 KB)
3 - Background   50666 ( 202664 KB)       0 (      0 KB)
4 - Background   15236 (  60944 KB)       0 (      0 KB)
5 - Normal       34197 ( 136788 KB)       0 (      0 KB)
6 - Superfetch    2912 (  11648 KB)       0 (      0 KB)
7 - Superfetch    5876 (  23504 KB)       0 (      0 KB)
TOTAL           237585 ( 950340 KB)  143906 ( 575624 KB)
```

And here is the output after the allocations are done but the TestLimit process still exists:

```
Priority                Standby              Repurposed
0 - Idle             0 (       0 KB)    2554 (  10216 KB)
1 - Very Low         5 (      20 KB)  234351 ( 937404 KB)
2 - Low              0 (       0 KB)   35830 ( 143320 KB)
3 - Background    9586 (  38344 KB)   41654 ( 166616 KB)
4 - Background   15371 (  61484 KB)       0 (      0 KB)
5 - Normal       34208 ( 136832 KB)       0 (      0 KB)
6 - Superfetch    2914 (  11656 KB)       0 (      0 KB)
7 - Superfetch    5881 (  23524 KB)       0 (      0 KB)
TOTAL            67965 ( 271860 KB)  314389 (1257556 KB)
```

Note how the lower-priority standby page lists were used first (shown by the repurposed count) and are now depleted, while the higher lists still contain valuable cached data.

Modified Page Writer

The memory manager employs two system threads to write pages back to disk and move those pages back to the standby lists (based on their priority). One system thread writes out modified pages (*MiModifiedPageWriter*) to the paging file, and a second one writes modified pages to mapped files (*MiMappedPageWriter*). Two threads are required to avoid creating a deadlock, which would occur if the writing of mapped file pages caused a page fault that in turn required a free page when no free pages were available (thus requiring the modified page writer to create more free pages). By having the modified page writer perform mapped file paging I/Os from a second system thread, that thread can wait without blocking regular page file I/O.

Both threads run at priority 17, and after initialization they wait for separate objects to trigger their operation. The mapped page writer waits on an event, *MmMappedPageWriterEvent*. It can be signaled in the following cases:

- During a page list operation (*MiInsertPageInLockedList* or *MiInsertPageInList*). These routines signal this event if the number of file-system-destined pages on the modified page list has reached more than 800 and the number of available pages has fallen below 1,024, or if the number of available pages is less than 256.

- In an attempt to obtain free pages (*MiObtainFreePages*).

- By the memory manager's working set manager (*MmWorkingSetManager*), which runs as part of the kernel's balance set manager (once every second). The working set manager signals this event if the number of file-system-destined pages on the modified page list has reached more than 800.

- Upon a request to flush all modified pages (*MmFlushAllPages*).

- Upon a request to flush all file-system-destined modified pages (*MmFlushAllFilesystemPages*). Note that in most cases, writing modified mapped pages to their backing store files does not occur if the number of mapped pages on the modified page list is less than the maximum "write cluster" size, which is 16 pages. This check is not made in *MmFlushAllFilesystemPages* or *MmFlushAllPages*.

The mapped page writer also waits on an array of *MiMappedPageListHeadEvent* events associated with the 16 mapped page lists. Each time a mapped page is dirtied, it is inserted into one of these 16 mapped page lists based on a bucket number (*MiCurrentMappedPageBucket*). This bucket number is updated by the working set manager whenever the system considers that mapped pages have gotten old enough, which is currently 100 seconds (the *MiWriteGapCounter* variable controls this and is incremented whenever the working set manager runs). The reason for these additional events is to reduce data loss in the case of a system crash or power failure by eventually writing out modified mapped pages even if the modified list hasn't reached its threshold of 800 pages.

The modified page writer waits on a single gate object (*MmModifiedPageWriterGate*), which can be signaled in the following scenarios:

- A request to flush all pages has been received.

- The number of available pages (*MmAvailablePages*) drops below 128 pages.

- The total size of the zeroed and free page lists has dropped below 20,000 pages, and the number of modified pages destined for the paging file is greater than the smaller of one-sixteenth of the available pages or 64 MB (16,384 pages).

- When a working set is being trimmed to accommodate additional pages, if the number of pages available is less than 15,000.

- During a page list operation (*MiInsertPageInLockedList* or *MiInsertPageInList*). These routines signal this gate if the number of page-file-destined pages on the modified page list has reached more than 800 and the number of available pages has fallen below 1,024, or if the number of available pages is less than 256.

Additionally, the modified page writer waits on an event (*MiRescanPageFilesEvent*) and an internal event in the paging file header (*MmPagingFileHeader*), which allows the system to manually request flushing out data to the paging file when needed.

When invoked, the mapped page writer attempts to write as many pages as possible to disk with a single I/O request. It accomplishes this by examining the original PTE field of the PFN database elements for pages on the modified page list to locate pages in contiguous locations on the disk. Once a list is created, the pages are removed from the modified list, an I/O request is issued, and, at successful completion of the I/O request, the pages are placed at the tail of the standby list corresponding to their priority.

Pages that are in the process of being written can be referenced by another thread. When this happens, the reference count and the share count in the PFN entry that represents the physical page are incremented to indicate that another process is using the page. When the I/O operation completes, the modified page writer notices that the reference count is no longer 0 and doesn't place the page on any standby list.

PFN Data Structures

Although PFN database entries are of fixed length, they can be in several different states, depending on the state of the page. Thus, individual fields have different meanings depending on the state. Figure 10-42 shows the formats of PFN entries for different states.

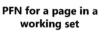

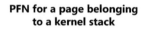

PFN for a page in a working set

Working set index		
PTE address | Lock		
Share count		
Flags	Type	Priority
Caching attributes		Reference count
Original PTE contents		
PFN of PTE	Flags	Page color

PFN for a page on the standby or the modified list

Forward link		
PTE address | Lock		
Backward link		
Flags	Type	Priority
Caching attributes		Reference count
Original PTE contents		
PFN of PTE	Flags	Page color

PFN for a page belonging to a kernel stack

Kernel stack owner	Link to next stack PFN	
PTE address | Lock		
Share count		
Flags	Type	Priority
Caching attributes		Reference count
Original PTE contents		
PFN of PTE	Flags	Page color

PFN for a page with an I/O in progress

Event address		
PTE address | Lock		
Share count		
Flags	Type	Priority
Caching attributes		Reference count
Original PTE contents		
PFN of PTE	Flags	Page color

FIGURE 10-42 States of PFN database entries. (Specific layouts are conceptual)

Several fields are the same for several PFN types, but others are specific to a given type of PFN. The following fields appear in more than one PFN type:

- **PTE address** Virtual address of the PTE that points to this page. Also, since PTE addresses will always be aligned on a 4-byte boundary (8 bytes on 64-bit systems), the two low-order bits are used as a locking mechanism to serialize access to the PFN entry.

- **Reference count** The number of references to this page. The reference count is incremented when a page is first added to a working set and/or when the page is locked in memory for I/O (for example, by a device driver). The reference count is decremented when the share count becomes 0 or when pages are unlocked from memory. When the share count becomes 0, the page is no longer owned by a working set. Then, if the reference count is also zero, the PFN database entry that describes the page is updated to add the page to the free, standby, or modified list.

- **Type** The type of page represented by this PFN. (Types include active/valid, standby, modified, modified-no-write, free, zeroed, bad, and transition.)

- **Flags** The information contained in the flags field is shown in Table 10-17.

- **Priority** The priority associated with this PFN, which will determine on which standby list it will be placed.

- **Original PTE contents** All PFN database entries contain the original contents of the PTE that pointed to the page (which could be a prototype PTE). Saving the contents of the PTE allows it to be restored when the physical page is no longer resident. PFN entries for AWE allocations are exceptions; they store the AWE reference count in this field instead.

- **PFN of PTE** Physical page number of the page table page containing the PTE that points to this page.

- **Color** Besides being linked together on a list, PFN database entries use an additional field to link physical pages by "color," which is the page's NUMA node number.

- **Flags** A second flags field is used to encode additional information on the PTE. These flags are described in Table 10-18.

TABLE 10-17 Flags Within PFN Database Entries

Flag	Meaning
Write in progress	Indicates that a page write operation is in progress. The first DWORD contains the address of the event object that will be signaled when the I/O is complete.
Modified state	Indicates whether the page was modified. (If the page was modified, its contents must be saved to disk before removing it from memory.)
Read in progress	Indicates that an in-page operation is in progress for the page. The first DWORD contains the address of the event object that will be signaled when the I/O is complete.
Rom	Indicates that this page comes from the computer's firmware or another piece of read-only memory such as a device register.
In-page error	Indicates that an I/O error occurred during the in-page operation on this page. (In this case, the first field in the PFN contains the error code.)
Kernel stack	Indicates that this page is being used to contain a kernel stack. In this case, the PFN entry contains the owner of the stack and the next stack PFN for this thread.
Removal requested	Indicates that the page is the target of a remove (due to ECC/scrubbing or hot memory removal).
Parity error	Indicates that the physical page contains parity or error correction control errors.

TABLE 10-18 Secondary Flags Within PFN Database Entries

Flag	Meaning
PFN image verified	The code signature for this PFN (contained in the cryptographic signature catalog for the image being backed by this PFN) has been verified.
AWE allocation	This PFN backs an AWE allocation.
Prototype PTE	Indicates that the PTE referenced by the PFN entry is a prototype PTE. (For example, this page is shareable.)

The remaining fields are specific to the type of PFN. For example, the first PFN in Figure 10-42 represents a page that is active and part of a working set. The share count field represents the number of PTEs that refer to this page. (Pages marked read-only, copy-on-write, or shared read/write can be shared by multiple processes.) For page table pages, this field is the number of valid and transition PTEs in the page table. As long as the share count is greater than 0, the page isn't eligible for removal from memory.

The working set index field is an index into the process working set list (or the system or session working set list, or zero if not in any working set) where the virtual address that maps this physical page resides. If the page is a private page, the working set index field refers directly to the entry in the working set list because the page is mapped only at a single virtual address. In the case of a shared page, the working set index is a hint that is guaranteed to be correct only for the first process that made the page valid. (Other processes will try to use the same index where possible.) The process that initially sets this field is guaranteed to refer to the proper index and doesn't need to add a working set list hash entry referenced by the virtual address into its working set hash tree. This guarantee reduces the size of the working set hash tree and makes searches faster for these particular direct entries.

The second PFN in Figure 10-42 is for a page on either the standby or the modified list. In this case, the forward and backward link fields link the elements of the list together within the list. This linking allows pages to be easily manipulated to satisfy page faults. When a page is on one of the lists, the share count is by definition 0 (because no working set is using the page) and therefore can be overlaid with the backward link. The reference count is also 0 if the page is on one of the lists. If it is nonzero (because an I/O could be in progress for this page—for example, when the page is being written to disk), it is first removed from the list.

The third PFN in Figure 10-42 is for a page that belongs to a kernel stack. As mentioned earlier, kernel stacks in Windows are dynamically allocated, expanded, and freed whenever a callback to user mode is performed and/or returns, or when a driver performs a callback and requests stack expansion. For these PFNs, the memory manager must keep track of the thread actually associated with the kernel stack, or if it is free it keeps a link to the next free look-aside stack.

The fourth PFN in Figure 10-42 is for a page that has an I/O in progress (for example, a page read). While the I/O is in progress, the first field points to an event object that will be signaled when the I/O completes. If an in-page error occurs, this field contains the Windows error status code representing the I/O error. This PFN type is used to resolve collided page faults.

In addition to the PFN database, the system variables in Table 10-19 describe the overall state of physical memory.

TABLE 10-19 System Variables That Describe Physical Memory

Variable	Description
MmNumberOfPhysicalPages	Total number of physical pages available on the system
MmAvailablePages	Total number of available pages on the system—the sum of the pages on the zeroed, free, and standby lists
MmResidentAvailablePages	Total number of physical pages that would be available if every process was trimmed to its minimum working set size and all modified pages were flushed to disk

EXPERIMENT: Viewing PFN Entries

You can examine individual PFN entries with the kernel debugger *!pfn* command. You need to supply the PFN as an argument. (For example, *!pfn 1* shows the first entry, *!pfn 2* shows the second, and so on.) In the following example, the PTE for virtual address 0x50000 is displayed, followed by the PFN that contains the page directory, and then the actual page:

```
lkd> !pte 50000
              VA 00050000
PDE at 00000000C0600000      PTE at 00000000C0000280
contains 000000002C9F7867   contains 800000002D6C1867
pfn 2c9f7      ---DA--UWEV    pfn 2d6c1      ---DA--UW-V

lkd> !pfn 2c9f7
    PFN 0002C9F7 at address 834E1704
    flink        00000026  blink / share count 00000091  pteaddress C0600000
    reference count 0001   Cached      color 0   Priority 5
    restore pte 00000080  containing page        02BAA5  Active    M
    Modified

lkd> !pfn 2d6c1
    PFN 0002D6C1 at address 834F7D1C
    flink        00000791  blink / share count 00000001  pteaddress C0000280
    reference count 0001   Cached      color 0   Priority 5
    restore pte 00000080  containing page        02C9F7  Active    M
    Modified
```

You can also use the MemInfo tool to obtain information about a PFN. MemInfo can sometimes give you more information than the debugger's output, and it does not require being booted into debugging mode. Here's MemInfo's output for those same two PFNs:

```
C:\>meminfo -p 2c9f7

PFN: 2c9f7
PFN List: Active and Valid
PFN Type: Page Table
PFN Priority: 5
Page Directory: 0x866168C8
Physical Address: 0x2C9F7000

C:\>meminfo -p 2d6c1

PFN: 2d6c1
PFN List: Active and Valid
PFN Type: Process Private
PFN Priority: 5
EPROCESS: 0x866168C8 [windbg.exe]
Physical Address: 0x2D6C1000
```

MemInfo correctly recognized that the first PFN was a page table and that the second PFN belongs to WinDbg, which was the active process when the *!pte 50000* command was used in the debugger.

Physical Memory Limits

Now that you've learned how Windows keeps track of physical memory, we'll describe how much of it Windows can actually support. Because most systems access more code and data than can fit in physical memory as they run, physical memory is in essence a window into the code and data used over time. The amount of memory can therefore affect performance, because when data or code that a process or the operating system needs is not present, the memory manager must bring it in from disk or remote storage.

Besides affecting performance, the amount of physical memory impacts other resource limits. For example, the amount of nonpaged pool, operating system buffers backed by physical memory, is obviously constrained by physical memory. Physical memory also contributes to the system virtual memory limit, which is the sum of roughly the size of physical memory plus the current configured size of any paging files. Physical memory also can indirectly limit the maximum number of processes.

Windows support for physical memory is dictated by hardware limitations, licensing, operating system data structures, and driver compatibility. Table 10-20 lists the currently supported amounts of physical memory across the various editions of Windows along with the limiting factors.

TABLE 10-20 Physical Memory Support

Version	32-Bit Limit	64-Bit Limit	Limiting Factors
Ultimate, Enterprise, and Professional	4 GB	192 GB	Licensing on 64-bit; licensing, hardware support, and driver compatibility on 32-bit
Home Premium	4 GB	16 GB	Licensing on 64-bit; licensing, hardware support, and driver compatibility on 32-bit
Home Basic	4 GB	8 GB	Licensing on 64-bit; licensing, hardware support, and driver compatibility on 32-bit
Starter	2 GB	2 GB	Licensing
Server Datacenter, Enterprise, and Server for Itanium	N/A	2 TB	Testing and available systems
Server Foundation	N/A	8 GB	Licensing
Server Standard and Web Server	N/A	32 GB	Licensing
Server HPC Edition	N/A	128 GB	Licensing

The maximum 2-TB physical memory limit doesn't come from any implementation or hardware limitation, but because Microsoft will support only configurations it can test. As of this writing, the largest tested and supported memory configuration was 2 TB.

Windows Client Memory Limits

64-bit Windows client editions support different amounts of memory as a differentiating feature, with the low end being 2 GB for Starter Edition, increasing to 192 GB for the Ultimate, Enterprise, and Professional editions. All 32-bit Windows client editions, however, support a maximum of 4 GB of physical memory, which is the highest physical address accessible with the standard x86 memory management mode.

Although client SKUs support PAE addressing modes on x86 systems in order to provide hardware no-execute protection (which would also enable access to more than 4 GB of physical memory), testing revealed that systems would crash, hang, or become unbootable because some device drivers, commonly those for video and audio devices found typically on clients but not servers, were not programmed to expect physical addresses larger than 4 GB. As a result, the drivers truncated such addresses, resulting in memory corruptions and corruption side effects. Server systems commonly have more generic devices, with simpler and more stable drivers, and therefore had not generally revealed these problems. The problematic client driver ecosystem led to the decision for client editions to ignore physical memory that resides above 4 GB, even though they can theoretically address it. Driver developers are encouraged to test their systems with the *nolowmem* BCD option, which will force the kernel to use physical addresses above 4 GB only if sufficient memory exists on the system to allow it. This will immediately lead to the detection of such issues in faulty drivers.

32-Bit Client Effective Memory Limits

While 4 GB is the licensed limit for 32-bit client editions, the effective limit is actually lower and dependent on the system's chipset and connected devices. The reason is that the physical address map includes not only RAM but device memory, and x86 and x64 systems typically map all device memory below the 4 GB address boundary to remain compatible with 32-bit operating systems that don't know how to handle addresses larger than 4 GB. Newer chipsets do support PAE-based device remapping, but client editions of Windows do not support this feature for the driver compatibility problems explained earlier (otherwise, drivers would receive 64-bit pointers to their device memory).

If a system has 4 GB of RAM and devices such as video, audio, and network adapters that implement windows into their device memory that sum to 500 MB, 500 MB of the 4 GB of RAM will reside above the 4 GB address boundary, as seen in Figure 10-43.

The result is that if you have a system with 3 GB or more of memory and you are running a 32-bit Windows client, you may not be getting the benefit of all of the RAM. You can see how much RAM Windows has detected as being installed in the System Properties dialog box, but to see how much memory is actually available to Windows, you need to look at Task Manager's Performance page or the Msinfo32 and Winver utilities. On one particular 4-GB laptop, when booted with 32-bit Windows, the amount of physical memory available is 3.5 GB, as seen in the Msinfo32 utility:

Installed Physical Memory (RAM)   4.00 GB
Total Physical Memory   3.50 GB

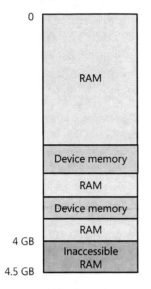

FIGURE 10-43 Physical memory layout on a 4-GB system

You can see the physical memory layout with the MemInfo tool from Winsider Seminars & Solutions. Figure 10-44 shows the output of MemInfo when run on a 32-bit system, using the −r switch to dump physical memory ranges:

```
C:\>MemInfo.exe -r

MemInfo v1.11 - Show PFN database information
Copyright (C) 2007-2008 Alex Ionescu
www.alex-ionescu.com

Physical Memory Range: 00001000 to 0009F000 (158 pages, 632 KB)
Physical Memory Range: 00100000 to DFE6D000 (916845 pages, 3667380 KB)
MmHighestPhysicalPage: 917101
```

FIGURE 10-44 Memory ranges on a 32-bit Windows system

Note the gap in the memory address range from page 9F0000 to page 100000, and another gap from DFE6D000 to FFFFFFFF (4 GB). When the system is booted with 64-bit Windows, on the other hand, all 4 GB show up as available (see Figure 10-45), and you can see how Windows uses the remaining 500 MB of RAM that are above the 4-GB boundary.

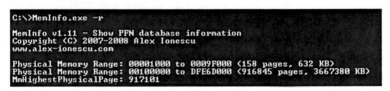

```
MemInfo v1.11 - Show PFN database information
Copyright (C) 2007-2008 Alex Ionescu
www.alex-ionescu.com

Physical Memory Range: 0000000000001000 to 000000000009F000 (158 pages, 632 KB)
Physical Memory Range: 0000000000100000 to 00000000DFE6D000 (916845 pages, 3667380 KB)
Physical Memory Range: 0000000100002000 to 0000000120000000 (131070 pages, 524280 KB)
MmHighestPhysicalPage: 1179648
```

FIGURE 10-45 Memory ranges on an x64 Windows system

You can use Device Manager on your machine to see what is occupying the various reserved memory regions that can't be used by Windows (and that will show up as holes in MemInfo's output). To check Device Manager, run Devmgmt.msc, select Resources By Connection on the View menu, and then expand the Memory node. On the laptop computer used for the output shown in Figure 10-46, the primary consumer of mapped device memory is, unsurprisingly, the video card, which consumes 256 MB in the range E0000000-EFFFFFFF.

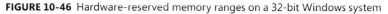

FIGURE 10-46 Hardware-reserved memory ranges on a 32-bit Windows system

Other miscellaneous devices account for most of the rest, and the PCI bus reserves additional ranges for devices as part of the conservative estimation the firmware uses during boot.

The consumption of memory addresses below 4 GB can be drastic on high-end gaming systems with large video cards. For example, on a test machine with 8 GB of RAM and two 1-GB video cards, only 2.2 GB of the memory was accessible by 32-bit Windows. A large memory hole from 8FEF0000 to FFFFFFFF is visible in the MemInfo output from the system on which 64-bit Windows is installed, shown in Figure 10-47.

```
C:\>meminfo64.exe -r

MemInfo v1.11 - Show PFN database information
Copyright (C) 2007-2008 Alex Ionescu
www.alex-ionescu.com

Physical Memory Range: 0000000000001000 to 000000000009B000 (154 pages, 616 KB)
Physical Memory Range: 0000000000100000 to 000000008FEF0000 (589296 pages, 2357184 KB)
Physical Memory Range: 0000000100000000 to 0000000270000000 (1507328 pages, 6029312 KB)
MmHighestPhysicalPage: 2555904
```

FIGURE 10-47 Memory ranges on a 64-bit Windows system

Device Manager revealed that 512 MB of the more than 2-GB gap is for the video cards (256 MB each) and that the PCI bus driver had reserved more either for dynamic mappings or alignment requirements, or perhaps because the devices claimed larger areas than they actually needed. Finally, even systems with as little as 2 GB can be prevented from having all their memory usable under 32-bit Windows because of chipsets that aggressively reserve memory regions for devices.

Working Sets

Now that we've looked at how Windows keeps track of physical memory, and how much memory it can support, we'll explain how Windows keeps a subset of virtual addresses in physical memory.

As you'll recall, the term used to describe a subset of virtual pages resident in physical memory is called a *working set*. There are three kinds of working sets:

- Process working sets contain the pages referenced by threads within a single process.

- System working sets contains the resident subset of the pageable system code (for example, Ntoskrnl.exe and drivers), paged pool, and the system cache.

- Each session has a working set that contains the resident subset of the kernel-mode session-specific data structures allocated by the kernel-mode part of the Windows subsystem (Win32k.sys), session paged pool, session mapped views, and other session-space device drivers.

Before examining the details of each type of working set, let's look at the overall policy for deciding which pages are brought into physical memory and how long they remain. After that, we'll explore the various types of working sets.

Demand Paging

The Windows memory manager uses a demand-paging algorithm with clustering to load pages into memory. When a thread receives a page fault, the memory manager loads into memory the faulted page plus a small number of pages preceding and/or following it. This strategy attempts to minimize the number of paging I/Os a thread will incur. Because programs, especially large ones, tend to execute in small regions of their address space at any given time, loading clusters of virtual pages reduces the number of disk reads. For page faults that reference data pages in images, the cluster size is three pages. For all other page faults, the cluster size is seven pages.

However, a demand-paging policy can result in a process incurring many page faults when its threads first begin executing or when they resume execution at a later point. To optimize the startup of a process (and the system), Windows has an intelligent prefetch engine called the *logical prefetcher*, described in the next section. Further optimization and prefetching is performed by another component, called Superfetch, that we'll describe later in the chapter.

Logical Prefetcher

During a typical system boot or application startup, the order of faults is such that some pages are brought in from one part of a file, then perhaps from a distant part of the same file, then from a different file, perhaps from a directory, and then again from the first file. This jumping around slows down each access considerably and, thus, analysis shows that disk seek times are a dominant factor in slowing boot and application startup times. By prefetching batches of pages all at once, a more sensible ordering of access, without excessive backtracking, can be achieved, thus improving the overall time for system and application startup. The pages that are needed can be known in advance because of the high correlation in accesses across boots or application starts.

The prefetcher tries to speed the boot process and application startup by monitoring the data and code accessed by boot and application startups and using that information at the beginning of a subsequent boot or application startup to read in the code and data. When the prefetcher is active, the memory manager notifies the prefetcher code in the kernel of page faults, both those that require that data be read from disk (hard faults) and those that simply require data already in memory be added to a process's working set (soft faults). The prefetcher monitors the first 10 seconds of application startup. For boot, the prefetcher by default traces from system start through the 30 seconds following the start of the user's shell (typically Explorer) or, failing that, up through 60 seconds following Windows service initialization or through 120 seconds, whichever comes first.

The trace assembled in the kernel notes faults taken on the NTFS master file table (MFT) metadata file (if the application accesses files or directories on NTFS volumes), on referenced files, and on referenced directories. With the trace assembled, the kernel prefetcher code waits for requests from the prefetcher component of the Superfetch service (%SystemRoot%\System32\Sysmain.dll), running in a copy of Svchost. The Superfetch service is responsible for both the logical prefetching component in the kernel and for the Superfetch component that we'll talk about later. The prefetcher signals the event \KernelObjects\PrefetchTracesReady to inform the Superfetch service that it can now query trace data.

> **Note** You can enable or disable prefetching of the boot or application startups by editing the DWORD registry value HKLM\SYSTEM\CurrentControlSet\Control\Session Manager\ Memory Management\PrefetchParameters\EnablePrefetcher. Set it to 0 to disable prefetching altogether, 1 to enable prefetching of only applications, 2 for prefetching of boot only, and 3 for both boot and applications.

The Superfetch service (which hosts the logical prefetcher, although it is a completely separate component from the actual Superfetch functionality) performs a call to the internal *NtQuerySystem-Information* system call requesting the trace data. The logical prefetcher post-processes the trace data, combining it with previously collected data, and writes it to a file in the %SystemRoot%\Prefetch folder, which is shown in Figure 10-48. The file's name is the name of the application to which the trace applies followed by a dash and the hexadecimal representation of a hash of the file's path. The file has a .pf extension; an example would be NOTEPAD.EXE-AF43252301.PF.

There are two exceptions to the file name rule. The first is for images that host other components, including the Microsoft Management Console (%SystemRoot%\System32\Mmc.exe), the Service Hosting Process (%SystemRoot%\System32\Svchost.exe), the Run DLL Component (%SystemRoot%\ System32\Rundll32.exe), and Dllhost (%SystemRoot%\System32\Dllhost.exe). Because add-on components are specified on the command line for these applications, the prefetcher includes the command line in the generated hash. Thus, invocations of these applications with different components on the command line will result in different traces.

The other exception to the file name rule is the file that stores the boot's trace, which is always named NTOSBOOT-B00DFAAD.PF. (If read as a word, "boodfaad" sounds similar to the English words *boot fast*.) Only after the prefetcher has finished the boot trace (the time of which was defined earlier) does it collect page fault information for specific applications.

Name	Date modified	Type	Size
ReadyBoot	4/17/2009 12:47 AM	File Folder	
AgAppLaunch.db	8/27/2008 2:37 PM	Data Base File	325 KB
AgCx_SC1.db	4/15/2009 12:22 PM	Data Base File	456 KB
AgCx_SC1.db.trx	4/15/2009 12:20 PM	TRX File	51 KB
AgGlFaultHistory.db	4/17/2009 12:44 AM	Data Base File	740 KB
AgGlFgAppHistory.db	4/17/2009 12:44 AM	Data Base File	426 KB
AgGlGlobalHistory.db	4/17/2009 12:44 AM	Data Base File	782 KB
AgGIUAD_P_S-1-5-21-3341607578-99054...	4/15/2009 7:58 PM	Data Base File	972 KB
AgGIUAD_S-1-5-21-3341607578-9905412...	4/15/2009 7:58 PM	Data Base File	872 KB
AgRobust.db	4/17/2009 12:44 AM	Data Base File	186 KB
BCDEDIT.EXE-23D6A12E.pf	3/30/2009 6:49 PM	PF File	7 KB
CMD.EXE-89305D47.pf	4/9/2009 4:29 PM	PF File	8 KB
CONSENT.EXE-65F6206D.pf	4/17/2009 12:55 AM	PF File	112 KB
CONSS.EXE-80CDC9F0.pf	10/27/2008 11:31 ...	PF File	5 KB
CONTROL.EXE-9459D5A0.pf	4/9/2009 4:32 PM	PF File	31 KB
CSRSS.EXE-8C04D631.pf	4/17/2009 12:39 AM	PF File	116 KB

126 items

FIGURE 10-48 Prefetch folder

EXPERIMENT: Looking Inside a Prefetch File

A prefetch file's contents serve as a record of files and directories accessed during the boot or an application startup, and you can use the Strings utility from Sysinternals to see the record. The following command lists all the files and directories referenced during the last boot:

```
C:\Windows\Prefetch>Strings -n 5 ntosboot-b00dfaad.pf

Strings v2.4
Copyright (C) 1999-2007 Mark Russinovich
Sysinternals - www.sysinternals.com

4NTOSBOOT
\DEVICE\HARDDISKVOLUME1\$MFT
\DEVICE\HARDDISKVOLUME1\WINDOWS\SYSTEM32\DRIVERS\TUNNEL.SYS
\DEVICE\HARDDISKVOLUME1\WINDOWS\SYSTEM32\DRIVERS\TUNMP.SYS
\DEVICE\HARDDISKVOLUME1\WINDOWS\SYSTEM32\DRIVERS\I8042PRT.SYS
\DEVICE\HARDDISKVOLUME1\WINDOWS\SYSTEM32\DRIVERS\KBDCLASS.SYS
\DEVICE\HARDDISKVOLUME1\WINDOWS\SYSTEM32\DRIVERS\VMMOUSE.SYS
\DEVICE\HARDDISKVOLUME1\WINDOWS\SYSTEM32\DRIVERS\MOUCLASS.SYS
\DEVICE\HARDDISKVOLUME1\WINDOWS\SYSTEM32\DRIVERS\PARPORT.SYS
...
```

When the system boots or an application starts, the prefetcher is called to give it an opportunity to perform prefetching. The prefetcher looks in the prefetch directory to see if a trace file exists for the prefetch scenario in question. If it does, the prefetcher calls NTFS to prefetch any MFT metadata file references, reads in the contents of each of the directories referenced, and finally opens each file referenced. It then calls the memory manager function *MmPrefetchPages* to read in any data and code specified in the trace that's not already in memory. The memory manager initiates all the reads asynchronously and then waits for them to complete before letting an application's startup continue.

EXPERIMENT: Watching Prefetch File Reads and Writes

If you capture a trace of application startup with Process Monitor from Sysinternals on a client edition of Windows (Windows Server editions disable prefetching by default), you can see the prefetcher check for and read the application's prefetch file (if it exists), and roughly 10 seconds after the application started, see the prefetcher write out a new copy of the file. Here is a capture of Notepad startup with an Include filter set to "prefetch" so that Process Monitor shows only accesses to the %SystemRoot%\Prefetch directory:

Time of Day	Process Name	Operation	Path	Result	Detail
11:05:26.8195632 PM	notepad.exe	CreateFile	C:\Windows\Prefetch\NOTEPAD.EXE-EB1B961A.pf	SUCCESS	Desired Access: Generic
11:05:26.8209631 PM	notepad.exe	QueryStandardInformationFile	C:\Windows\Prefetch\NOTEPAD.EXE-EB1B961A.pf	SUCCESS	AllocationSize: 16,384, E...
11:05:26.8212028 PM	notepad.exe	ReadFile	C:\Windows\Prefetch\NOTEPAD.EXE-EB1B961A.pf	SUCCESS	Offset: 0, Length: 12,962...
11:05:26.8217356 PM	notepad.exe	CloseFile	C:\Windows\Prefetch\NOTEPAD.EXE-EB1B961A.pf	SUCCESS	
11:05:36.8525758 PM	svchost.exe	CreateFile	C:\Windows\Prefetch\NOTEPAD.EXE-EB1B961A.pf	SUCCESS	Desired Access: Generic ...
11:05:36.8527032 PM	svchost.exe	QueryStandardInformationFile	C:\Windows\Prefetch\NOTEPAD.EXE-EB1B961A.pf	SUCCESS	AllocationSize: 16,384, E...
11:05:36.8527515 PM	svchost.exe	QueryStandardInformationFile	C:\Windows\Prefetch\NOTEPAD.EXE-EB1B961A.pf	SUCCESS	AllocationSize: 16,384, E...
11:05:36.8530815 PM	svchost.exe	CloseFile	C:\Windows\Prefetch\NOTEPAD.EXE-EB1B961A.pf	SUCCESS	
11:05:36.8535734 PM	svchost.exe	CreateFile	C:\Windows\Prefetch\NOTEPAD.EXE-EB1B961A.pf	SUCCESS	Desired Access: Generic ...
11:05:36.8595577 PM	svchost.exe	WriteFile	C:\Windows\Prefetch\NOTEPAD.EXE-EB1B961A.pf	SUCCESS	Offset: 0, Length: 13,166...
11:05:36.8641633 PM	svchost.exe	CloseFile	C:\Windows\Prefetch\NOTEPAD.EXE-EB1B961A.pf	SUCCESS	

Showing 11 of 30,186 events (0.036%)   Backed by page file

Lines 1 through 4 show the Notepad prefetch file being read in the context of the Notepad process during its startup. Lines 5 through 11, which have time stamps 10 seconds later than the first three lines, show the Superfetch service, which is running in the context of a Svchost process, write out the updated prefetch file.

To minimize seeking even further, every three days or so, during system idle periods, the Superfetch service organizes a list of files and directories in the order that they are referenced during a boot or application start and stores the list in a file named %SystemRoot%\Prefetch\Layout.ini, shown in Figure 10-49. This list also includes frequently accessed files tracked by Superfetch.

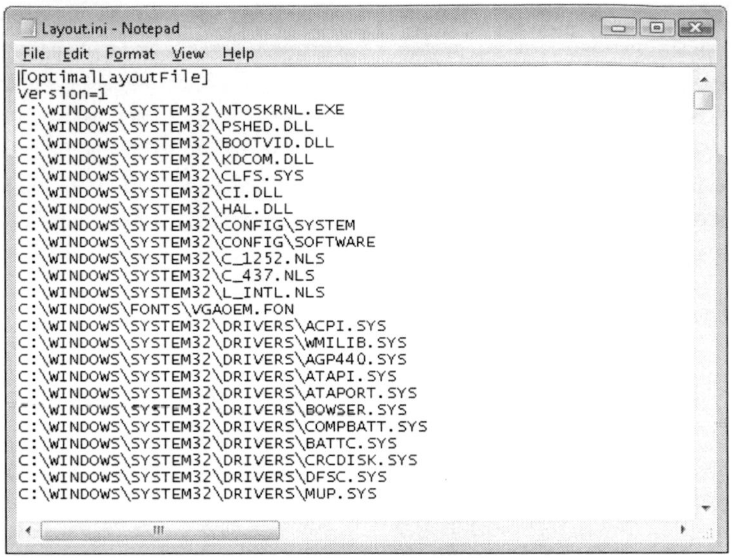

FIGURE 10-49 Prefetch defragmentation layout file

Then it launches the system defragmenter with a command-line option that tells the defragmenter to defragment based on the contents of the file instead of performing a full defrag. The defragmenter finds a contiguous area on each volume large enough to hold all the listed files and directories that reside on that volume and then moves them in their entirety into the area so that they are stored one after the other. Thus, future prefetch operations will even be more efficient because all the data read in is now stored physically on the disk in the order it will be read. Because the files defragmented for prefetching usually number only in the hundreds, this defragmentation is much faster than full volume defragmentations. (See Chapter 12 for more information on defragmentation.)

Placement Policy

When a thread receives a page fault, the memory manager must also determine where in physical memory to put the virtual page. The set of rules it uses to determine the best position is called a *placement policy*. Windows considers the size of CPU memory caches when choosing page frames to minimize unnecessary thrashing of the cache.

If physical memory is full when a page fault occurs, a *replacement policy* is used to determine which virtual page must be removed from memory to make room for the new page. Common replacement policies include *least recently used* (LRU) and *first in, first out* (FIFO). The LRU algorithm (also known as the *clock algorithm*, as implemented in most versions of UNIX) requires the virtual memory system to track when a page in memory is used. When a new page frame is required, the page that hasn't been used for the greatest amount of time is removed from the working set. The FIFO algorithm is somewhat simpler; it removes the page that has been in physical memory for the greatest amount of time, regardless of how often it's been used.

Replacement policies can be further characterized as either global or local. A global replacement policy allows a page fault to be satisfied by any page frame, whether or not that frame is owned by another process. For example, a global replacement policy using the FIFO algorithm would locate the page that has been in memory the longest and would free it to satisfy a page fault; a local replacement policy would limit its search for the oldest page to the set of pages already owned by the process that incurred the page fault. Global replacement policies make processes vulnerable to the behavior of other processes—an ill-behaved application can undermine the entire operating system by inducing excessive paging activity in all processes.

Windows implements a combination of local and global replacement policy. When a working set reaches its limit and/or needs to be trimmed because of demands for physical memory, the memory manager removes pages from working sets until it has determined there are enough free pages.

Working Set Management

Every process starts with a default working set minimum of 50 pages and a working set maximum of 345 pages. Although it has little effect, you can change the process working set limits with the Windows *SetProcessWorkingSetSize* function, though you must have the "increase scheduling priority" user right to do this. However, unless you have configured the process to use hard working set limits, these limits are ignored, in that the memory manager will permit a process to grow beyond its maximum if it is paging heavily and there is ample memory (and conversely, the memory manager will shrink a process below its working set minimum if it is not paging and there is a high demand for physical memory on the system). Hard working set limits can be set using the *SetProcessWorkingSetSizeEx* function along with the QUOTA_LIMITS_HARDWS_MIN_ENABLE flag, but it is almost always better to let the system manage your working set instead of setting your own hard working set minimums.

The maximum working set size can't exceed the systemwide maximum calculated at system initialization time and stored in the kernel variable *MiMaximumWorkingSet*, which is a hard upper limit based on the working set maximums listed in Table 10-21.

TABLE 10-21 Upper Limit for Working Set Maximums

Windows Version	Working Set Maximum
x86	2,047.9 MB
x86 versions of Windows booted with *increaseuserva*	2,047.9 MB+ user virtual address increase (MB)
IA64	7,152 GB
x64	8,192 GB

When a page fault occurs, the process's working set limits and the amount of free memory on the system are examined. If conditions permit, the memory manager allows a process to grow to its working set maximum (or beyond if the process does not have a hard working set limit and there are enough free pages available). However, if memory is tight, Windows replaces rather than adds pages in a working set when a fault occurs.

Although Windows attempts to keep memory available by writing modified pages to disk, when modified pages are being generated at a very high rate, more memory is required in order to meet memory demands. Therefore, when physical memory runs low, the *working set manager*, a routine that runs in the context of the balance set manager system thread (described in the next section), initiates automatic working set trimming to increase the amount of free memory available in the system. (With the Windows *SetProcessWorkingSetSizeEx* function mentioned earlier, you can also initiate working set trimming of your own process—for example, after process initialization.)

The working set manager examines available memory and decides which, if any, working sets need to be trimmed. If there is ample memory, the working set manager calculates how many pages could be removed from working sets if needed. If trimming is needed, it looks at working sets that are above their minimum setting. It also dynamically adjusts the rate at which it examines working sets as well as arranges the list of processes that are candidates to be trimmed into an optimal order. For example, processes with many pages that have not been accessed recently are examined first; larger processes that have been idle longer are considered before smaller processes that are running more often; the process running the foreground application is considered last; and so on.

When it finds processes using more than their minimums, the working set manager looks for pages to remove from their working sets, making the pages available for other uses. If the amount of free memory is still too low, the working set manager continues removing pages from processes' working sets until it achieves a minimum number of free pages on the system.

The working set manager tries to remove pages that haven't been accessed recently. It does this by checking the accessed bit in the hardware PTE to see whether the page has been accessed. If the bit is clear, the page is *aged*, that is, a count is incremented indicating that the page hasn't been referenced since the last working set trim scan. Later, the age of pages is used to locate candidate pages to remove from the working set.

If the hardware PTE accessed bit is set, the working set manager clears it and goes on to examine the next page in the working set. In this way, if the accessed bit is clear the next time the working set manager examines the page, it knows that the page hasn't been accessed since the last time it was examined. This scan for pages to remove continues through the working set list until either the number of desired pages has been removed or the scan has returned to the starting point. (The next time the working set is trimmed, the scan picks up where it left off last.)

EXPERIMENT: Viewing Process Working Set Sizes

You can use Performance Monitor to examine process working set sizes by looking at the performance counters shown in the following table.

Counter	Description
Process: Working Set	Current size of the selected process's working set in bytes
Process: Working Set Peak	Peak size of the selected process's working set in bytes
Process: Page Faults/sec	Number of page faults for the process that occur each second

Several other process viewer utilities (such as Task Manager and Process Explorer) also display the process working set size.

You can also get the total of all the process working sets by selecting the _Total process in the instance box in Performance Monitor. This process isn't real—it's simply a total of the process-specific counters for all processes currently running on the system. The total you see is larger than the actual RAM being used, however, because the size of each process working set includes pages being shared by other processes. Thus, if two or more processes share a page, the page is counted in each process's working set.

EXPERIMENT: Working Set vs. Virtual Size

Earlier in this chapter, we used the TestLimit utility to create two processes, one with a large amount of memory that was merely reserved, and the other in which the memory was private committed, and examined the difference between them with Process Explorer. Now we will create a third TestLimit process, one that not only commits the memory but also accesses it, thus bringing it into its working set:

```
C:\temp>testlimit -d 1 -c 800

Testlimit v5.2 - test Windows limits
Copyright (C) 2012 Mark Russinovich
Sysinternals - www.sysinternals.com

Process ID: 700

Leaking private bytes 1 MB at a time...
Leaked 800 MB of private memory (800 MB total leaked). Lasterror: 0
The operation completed successfully.
```

Now, invoke Process Explorer. Under View, Select Columns, choose the Process Memory tab and enable the Private Bytes, Virtual Size, Working Set Size, WS Shareable Bytes, and WS Private Bytes counters. Then find the three instances of TestLimit as shown in the display.

Process Explorer screenshot:

Process	PID	CPU	Private Bytes	Virtual Size	Working Set	WS Private	WS Shareable
svchost.exe	3792		29,240 K	124,332 K	14,352 K	7,784 K	6,568 K
System	4	0.31	56 K	7,040 K	1,888 K	48 K	1,840 K
System Idle Pr...	0	97.19	0 K	0 K	24 K	0 K	0 K
taskhost.exe	2084		2,384 K	41,772 K	5,324 K	1,388 K	3,936 K
taskmgr.exe	3048	0.20	2,344 K	69,324 K	8,396 K	2,080 K	6,316 K
Testlimit.exe	1544		2,868 K	844,620 K	1,932 K	436 K	1,496 K
Testlimit.exe	2828		822,068 K	844,620 K	1,928 K	436 K	1,492 K
Testlimit.exe	700		822,064 K	844,620 K	822,772 K	821,232 K	1,540 K

CPU Usage: 2.81%   Commit Charge: 34.82%   Processes: 49   Physical Usage: 44.00%

The new TestLimit process is the third one shown, PID 700. It is the only one of the three that actually referenced the memory allocated, so it is the only one with a working set that reflects the size of the test allocation.

Note that this result is possible only on a system with enough RAM to allow the process to grow to such a size. Even on this system, not quite all of the private bytes (822,064 K) are in the WS Private portion of the working set. A small number of the private pages have either been pushed out of the process working set due to replacement or have not been paged in yet.

EXPERIMENT: Viewing the Working Set List in the Debugger

You can view the individual entries in the working set by using the kernel debugger *!wsle* command. The following example shows a partial output of the working set list of WinDbg.

```
lkd> !wsle 7

Working Set @ c0802000
    FirstFree     209c  FirstDynamic     6
    LastEntry     242e  NextSlot         6  LastInitialized   24b9
    NonDirect        0  HashTable        0  HashTableSize        0

Reading the WSLE data ........................................................

Virtual Address       Age   Locked   ReferenceCount
        c0600203       0       1           1
        c0601203       0       1           1
        c0602203       0       1           1
        c0603203       0       1           1
        c0604213       0       1           1
        c0802203       0       1           1
        2865201        0       0           1
        1a6d201        0       0           1
          3f4201       0       0           1
        707ed101       0       0           1
        2d27201        0       0           1
        2d28201        0       0           1
```

772f5101	0	0	1
2d2a201	0	0	1
2d2b201	0	0	1
2d2c201	0	0	1
779c3101	0	0	1
c0002201	0	0	1
7794f101	0	0	1
7ffd1109	0	0	1
7ffd2109	0	0	1
7ffc0009	0	0	1
7ffb0009	0	0	1
77940101	0	0	1
77944101	0	0	1
112109	0	0	1
320109	0	0	1
322109	0	0	1
77949101	0	0	1
110109	0	0	1
77930101	0	0	1
111109	0	0	1

Notice that some entries in the working set list are page table pages (the ones with addresses greater than 0xC0000000), some are from system DLLs (the ones in the 0x7nnnnnnn range), and some are from the code of Windbg.exe itself.

Balance Set Manager and Swapper

Working set expansion and trimming take place in the context of a system thread called the *balance set manager* (routine *KeBalanceSetManager*). The balance set manager is created during system initialization. Although the balance set manager is technically part of the kernel, it calls the memory manager's working set manager (*MmWorkingSetManager*) to perform working set analysis and adjustment.

The balance set manager waits for two different event objects: an event that is signaled when a periodic timer set to fire once per second expires and an internal working set manager event that the memory manager signals at various points when it determines that working sets need to be adjusted. For example, if the system is experiencing a high page fault rate or the free list is too small, the memory manager wakes up the balance set manager so that it will call the working set manager to begin trimming working sets. When memory is more plentiful, the working set manager will permit faulting processes to gradually increase the size of their working sets by faulting pages back into memory, but the working sets will grow only as needed.

When the balance set manager wakes up as the result of its 1-second timer expiring, it takes the following five steps:

1. It queues a DPC associated to a 1-second timer. The DPC routine is the *KiScanReadyQueues* routine, which looks for threads that might warrant having their priority boosted because they are CPU starved. (See the section "Priority Boosts for CPU Starvation" in Chapter 5 in Part 1.)

2. Every fourth time the balance set manager wakes up because its 1-second timer has expired, it signals an event that wakes up another system thread called the swapper (*KiSwapperThread*) (routine *KeSwapProcessOrStack*).

3. The balance set manager then checks the look-aside lists and adjusts their depths if necessary (to improve access time and to reduce pool usage and pool fragmentation).

4. It adjusts IRP credits to optimize the usage of the per-processor look-aside lists used in IRP completion. This allows better scalability when certain processors are under heavy I/O load.

5. It calls the memory manager's working set manager. (The working set manager has its own internal counters that regulate when to perform working set trimming and how aggressively to trim.)

The swapper is also awakened by the scheduling code in the kernel if a thread that needs to run has its kernel stack swapped out or if the process has been swapped out. The swapper looks for threads that have been in a wait state for 15 seconds (or 3 seconds on a system with less than 12 MB of RAM). If it finds one, it puts the thread's kernel stack in transition (moving the pages to the modified or standby lists) so as to reclaim its physical memory, operating on the principle that if a thread's been waiting that long, it's going to be waiting even longer. When the last thread in a process has its kernel stack removed from memory, the process is marked to be entirely outswapped. That's why, for example, processes that have been idle for a long time (such as Winlogon is after you log on) can have a zero working set size.

System Working Sets

Just as processes have working sets that manage pageable portions of the process address space, the pageable code and data in the system address space is managed using three global working sets, collectively known as the *system working sets*:

- The system cache working set (*MmSystemCacheWs*) contains pages that are resident in the system cache.

- The paged pool working set (*MmPagedPoolWs*) contains pages that are resident in the paged pool.

- The system PTEs working set (*MmSystemPtesWs*) contains pageable code and data from loaded drivers and the kernel image, as well as pages from sections that have been mapped into the system space.

You can examine the sizes of these working sets or the sizes of the components that contribute to them with the performance counters or system variables shown in Table 10-22. Keep in mind that the performance counter values are in bytes, whereas the system variables are measured in terms of pages.

You can also examine the paging activity in the system cache working set by examining the Memory: Cache Faults/sec performance counter, which describes page faults that occur in the system cache working set (both hard and soft). *MmSystemCacheWs.PageFaultCount* is the system variable that contains the value for this counter.

TABLE 10-22 System Working Set Performance Counters

Performance Counter (in Bytes)	System Variable (in Pages)	Description
Memory: Cache Bytes, also Memory: System Cache Resident Bytes	MmSystemCacheWs. WorkingSetSize	Physical memory consumed by the file system cache.
Memory: Cache Bytes Peak	MmSystemCacheWs.Peak	Peak system working set size.
Memory: System Driver Resident Bytes	MmSystemDriverPage	Physical memory consumed by pageable device driver code.
Memory: Pool Paged Resident Bytes	MmPagedPoolWs. WorkingSetSize	Physical memory consumed by paged pool.

Memory Notification Events

Windows provides a way for user-mode processes and kernel-mode drivers to be notified when physical memory, paged pool, nonpaged pool, and commit charge are low and/or plentiful. This information can be used to determine memory usage as appropriate. For example, if available memory is low, the application can reduce memory consumption. If available paged pool is high, the driver can allocate more memory. Finally, the memory manager also provides an event that permits notification when corrupted pages have been detected.

User-mode processes can be notified only of low or high memory conditions. An application can call the *CreateMemoryResourceNotification* function, specifying whether low or high memory notification is desired. The returned handle can be provided to any of the wait functions. When memory is low (or high), the wait completes, thus notifying the thread of the condition. Alternatively, the *QueryMemoryResourceNotification* can be used to query the system memory condition at any time without blocking the calling thread.

Drivers, on the other hand, use the specific event name that the memory manager has set up in the \KernelObjects directory, since notification is implemented by the memory manager signaling one of the globally named event objects it defines, shown in Table 10-23.

TABLE 10-23 Memory Manager Notification Events

Event Name	Description
HighCommitCondition	This event is set when the commit charge is near the maximum commit limit. In other words, memory usage is very high, very little space is available in physical memory or paging files, and the operating system cannot increase the size of its paging files.
HighMemoryCondition	This event is set whenever the amount of free physical memory exceeds the defined amount.
HighNonPagedPoolCondition	This event is set whenever the amount of nonpaged pool exceeds the defined amount.
HighPagedPoolCondition	This event is set whenever the amount of paged pool exceeds the defined amount.
LowCommitCondition	This event is set when the commit charge is low, relative to the current commit limit. In other words, memory usage is low and a lot of space is available in physical memory or paging files.
LowMemoryCondition	This event is set whenever the amount of free physical memory falls below the defined amount.
LowNonPagedPoolCondition	This event is set whenever the amount of free nonpaged pool falls below the defined amount.
LowPagedPoolCondition	This event is set whenever the amount of free paged pool falls below the defined amount.
MaximumCommitCondition	This event is set when the commit charge is near the maximum commit limit. In other words, memory usage is very high, very little space is available in physical memory or paging files, and the operating system cannot increase the size or number of paging files.
MemoryErrors	A bad page (non-zeroed zero page) has been detected.

When a given memory condition is detected, the appropriate event is signaled, thus waking up any waiting threads.

> **Note** The high and low memory values can be overridden by adding a DWORD registry value, *LowMemoryThreshold* or *HighMemoryThreshold,* under HKLM\SYSTEM\ CurrentControlSet\Session Manager\Memory Management that specifies the number of megabytes to use as the low or high threshold. The system can also be configured to crash the system when a bad page is detected, instead of signaling a memory error event, by setting the *PageValidationAction* DWORD registry value in the same key.

EXPERIMENT: Viewing the Memory Resource Notification Events

To see the memory resource notification events, run Winobj from Sysinternals and click on the KernelObjects folder. You will see both the low and high memory condition events shown in the right pane:

Name	Type	SymLink
BootLoaderTraceReady	Event	
CritSecOutOfMemoryEvent	KeyedEvent	
HighCommitCondition	Event	
HighMemoryCondition	Event	
HighNonPagedPoolCondition	Event	
HighPagedPoolCondition	Event	
LowCommitCondition	Event	
LowMemoryCondition	Event	
LowNonPagedPoolCondition	Event	
LowPagedPoolCondition	Event	
MaximumCommitCondition	Event	
MemoryErrors	Event	
PrefetchTracesReady	Event	
Session0	Session	
Session1	Session	
Session2	Session	
SuperfetchParametersChanged	Event	
SuperfetchScenarioNotify	Event	
SuperfetchTracesReady	Event	
SystemErrorPortReady	Event	

\KernelObjects\LowMemoryCondition

If you double-click either event, you can see how many handles and/or references have been made to the objects.

To see whether any processes in the system have requested memory resource notification, search the handle table for references to "LowMemoryCondition" or "HighMemoryCondition." You can do this by using Process Explorer's Find menu and choosing the Handle capability or by using WinDbg. (For a description of the handle table, see the section "Object Manager" in Chapter 3 in Part 1.)

Proactive Memory Management (Superfetch)

Traditional memory management in operating systems has focused on the demand-paging model we've shown until now, with some advances in clustering and prefetching so that disk I/Os can be optimized at the time of the demand-page fault. Client versions of Windows, however, include a significant improvement in the management of physical memory with the implementation of Superfetch, a memory management scheme that enhances the least-recently accessed approach with historical file access information and proactive memory management.

The standby list management of previous Windows versions has had two limitations. First, the prioritization of pages relies only on the recent past behavior of processes and does not anticipate their future memory requirements. Second, the data used for prioritization is limited to the list of pages owned by a process at any given point in time. These shortcomings can result in scenarios in which the computer is left unattended for a brief period of time, during which a memory-intensive system application runs (doing work such as an antivirus scan or a disk defragmentation) and then causes subsequent interactive application use (or launch) to be sluggish. The same situation can happen when a user purposely runs a data and/or memory intensive application and then returns to use other programs, which appear to be significantly less responsive.

This decline in performance occurs because the memory-intensive application forces the code and data that active applications had cached in memory to be overwritten by the memory-intensive activities—applications perform sluggishly as they have to request their data and code from disk. Client versions of Windows take a big step toward resolving these limitations with Superfetch.

Components

Superfetch is composed of several components in the system that work hand in hand to proactively manage memory and limit the impact on user activity when Superfetch is performing its work. These components include:

- **Tracer** The tracer mechanisms are part of a kernel component (Pf) that allows Superfetch to query detailed page usage, session, and process information at any time. Superfetch also makes use of the FileInfo driver (%SystemRoot%\System32\Drivers\Fileinfo.sys) to track file usage.

- **Trace collector and processor** This collector works with the tracing components to provide a raw log based on the tracing data that has been acquired. This tracing data is kept in memory and handed off to the processor. The processor then hands the log entries in the trace to the agents, which maintain history files (described next) in memory and persist them to disk when the service stops (such as during a reboot).

- **Agents** Superfetch keeps file page access information in history files, which keep track of virtual offsets. Agents group pages by attributes, such as:

  - Page access while the user was active

  - Page access by a foreground process

  - Hard fault while the user was active

  - Page access during an application launch

  - Page access upon the user returning after a long idle period

- **Scenario manager** This component, also called the context agent, manages the three Superfetch scenario plans: hibernation, standby, and fast-user switching The kernel-mode part of the scenario manager provides APIs for initiating and terminating scenarios, managing current scenario state, and associating tracing information with these scenarios.

- **Rebalancer** Based on the information provided by the Superfetch agents, as well as the current state of the system (such as the state of the prioritized page lists), the rebalancer, a specialized agent that is located in the Superfetch user-mode service, queries the PFN database and reprioritizes it based on the associated score of each page, thus building the prioritized standby lists. The rebalancer can also issue commands to the memory manager that modify the working sets of processes on the system, and it is the only agent that actually takes action on the system—other agents merely filter information for the rebalancer to use in its decisions. Other than reprioritization, the rebalancer also initiates prefetching through the prefetcher thread, which makes use of FileInfo and kernel services to preload memory with useful pages.

Finally, all these components make use of facilities inside the memory manager that allow querying detailed information about the state of each page in the PFN database, the current page counts for each page list and prioritized list, and more. Figure 10-50 displays an architectural diagram of Superfetch's multiple components. Superfetch components also make use of prioritized I/O (see Chapter 8 for more information on I/O priority) to minimize user impact.

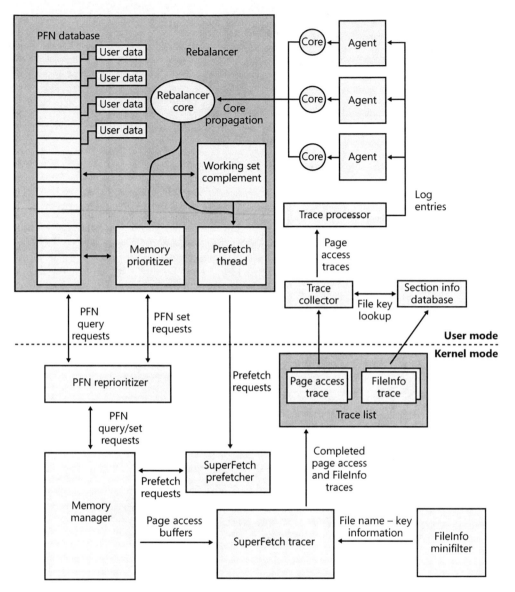

FIGURE 10-50 Superfetch architectural diagram

Tracing and Logging

Superfetch makes most of its decisions based on information that has been integrated, parsed, and post-processed from raw traces and logs, making these two components among the most critical. Tracing is similar to ETW in some ways because it makes use of certain triggers in code throughout the system to generate events, but it also works in conjunction with facilities already provided by the system, such as power manager notification, process callbacks, and file system filtering. The tracer also makes use of traditional page aging mechanisms that exist in the memory manager, as well as newer working set aging and access tracking implemented for Superfetch.

Superfetch always keeps a trace running and continuously queries trace data from the system, which tracks page usage and access through the memory manager's access bit tracking and working set aging. To track file-related information, which is as critical as page usage because it allows prioritization of file data in the cache, Superfetch leverages existing filtering functionality with the addition of the FileInfo driver. (See Chapter 8 for more information on filter drivers.) This driver sits on the file system device stack and monitors access and changes to files at the stream level (for more information on NTFS data streams, see Chapter 12), which provides it with fine-grained understanding of file access. The main job of the FileInfo driver is to associate streams (identified by a unique key, currently implemented as the *FsContext* field of the respective file object) with file names so that the user-mode Superfetch service can identify the specific file steam and offset with which a page in the standby list belonging to a memory mapped section is associated. It also provides the interface for prefetching file data transparently, without interfering with locked files and other file system state. The rest of the driver ensures that the information stays consistent by tracking deletions, renaming operations, truncations, and the reuse of file keys by implementing sequence numbers.

At any time during tracing, the rebalancer might be invoked to repopulate pages differently. These decisions are made by analyzing information such as the distribution of memory within working sets, the zero page list, the modified page list and the standby page lists, the number of faults, the state of PTE access bits, the per-page usage traces, current virtual address consumption, and working set size.

A given trace can be either a page access trace, in which the tracer keeps track (by using the access bit) of which pages were accessed by the process (both file page and private memory), or a name logging trace, which monitors the file-name-to-file-key-mapping updates (which allow Superfetch to map a page associated with a file object) to the actual file on disk.

Although a Superfetch trace only keeps track of page accesses, the Superfetch service processes this trace in user mode and goes much deeper, adding its own richer information such as where the page was loaded from (such as resident memory or a hard page fault), whether this was the initial access to that page, and what the rate of page access actually is. Additional information, such as the system state, is also kept, as well as information about in which recent scenarios each traced page was last referenced. The generated trace information is kept in memory through a logger into data structures, which identify, in the case of page access traces, a virtual-address-to-working-set pair or, in the case of a name logging trace, a file-to-offset pair. Superfetch can thus keep track of which range of virtual addresses for a given process have page-related events and which range of offsets for a given file have similar events.

Scenarios

One aspect of Superfetch that is distinct from its primary page repriorization and prefetching mechanisms (covered in more detail in the next section) is its support for scenarios, which are specific actions on the machine for which Superfetch strives to improve the user experience. These scenarios are standby and hibernation as well as fast user switching. Each of these scenarios has different goals, but all are centered around the main purpose of minimizing or removing hard faults.

- For hibernation, the goal is to intelligently decide which pages are saved in the hibernation file other than the existing working set pages. The goal is to minimize the amount of time that it takes for the system to become responsive after a resume.

- For standby, the goal is to completely remove hard faults after resume. Because a typical system can resume in less than 2 seconds, but can take 5 seconds to spin-up the hard drive after a long sleep, a single hard fault could cause such a delay in the resume cycle. Superfetch prioritizes pages needed after a standby to remove this chance.

- For fast user switching, the goal is to keep an accurate priority and understanding of each user's memory, so that switching to another user will cause the user's session to be immediately usable, and not require a large amount of lag time to allow pages to be faulted in.

Scenarios are hardcoded, and Superfetch manages them through the *NtSetSystemInformation* and *NtQuerySystemInformation* APIs that control system state. For Superfetch purposes, a special information class, *SystemSuperfetchInformation,* is used to control the kernel-mode components and to generate requests such as starting, ending, and querying a scenario or associating one or more traces with a scenario.

Each scenario is defined by a plan file, which contains, at minimum, a list of pages associated with the scenario. Page priority values are also assigned according to certain rules we'll describe next. When a scenario starts, the scenario manager is responsible for responding to the event by generating the list of pages that should be brought into memory and at which priority.

Page Priority and Rebalancing

We've already seen that the memory manager implements a system of page priorities to define from which standby list pages will be repurposed for a given operation and in which list a given page will be inserted. This mechanism provides benefits when processes and threads can have associated priorities—such that a defragmenter process doesn't pollute the standby page list and/or steal pages from an interactive, foreground process—but its real power is unleashed through Superfetch's page prioritization schemes and rebalancing, which don't require manual application input or hardcoded knowledge of process importance.

Superfetch assigns page priority based on an internal score it keeps for each page, part of which is based on frequency-based usage. This usage counts how many times a page was used in given relative time intervals, such as an hour, a day, or a week. Time of use is also kept track of, which records for how long a given page has not been accessed. Finally, data such as where this page comes from (which list) and other access patterns are used to compute this final score, which is then translated into a priority number, which can be anywhere from 1 to 6 (7 is used for another purpose described later). Going down each level, the lower standby page list priorities are repurposed first, as shown in the Experiment "Viewing the Prioritized Standby Lists." Priority 5 is typically used for normal applications, while priority 1 is meant for background applications that third-party developers can mark as such. Finally, priority 6 is used to keep a certain number of high-importance pages as far away as possible from repurposing. The other priorities are a result of the score associated with each page.

Because Superfetch "learns" a user's system, it can start from scratch with no existing historical data and slowly build up an understanding of the different page usage accesses associated with the user. However, this would result in a significant learning curve whenever a new application, user, or service pack was installed. Instead, by using an internal tool, Microsoft has the ability to pretrain Superfetch to capture Superfetch data and then turn it into prebuilt traces. Before Windows shipped, the Superfetch team traced common usages and patterns that all users will probably encounter, such as clicking the Start menu, opening Control Panel, or using the File Open/Save dialog box. This trace data was then saved to history files (which ship as resources in Sysmain.dll) and is used to prepopulate the special priority 7 list, which is where the most critical data is placed and which is very rarely repurposed. Pages at priority 7 are file pages kept in memory even after the process has exited and even across reboots (by being repopulated at the next boot). Finally, pages with priority 7 are static, in that they are never reprioritized, and Superfetch will never dynamically load pages at priority 7 other than the static pretrained set.

The prioritized list is loaded into memory (or prepopulated) by the rebalancer, but the actual act of rebalancing is actually handled by both Superfetch and the memory manager. As shown earlier, the prioritized standby page list mechanism is internal to the memory manager, and decisions as to which pages to throw out first and which to protect are innate, based on the priority number. The rebalancer actually does its job not by manually rebalancing memory but by reprioritizing it, which will cause the operation of the memory manager to perform the needed tasks. The rebalancer is also responsible for reading the actual pages from disk, if needed, so that they are present in memory (prefetching). It then assigns the priority that is mapped by each agent to the score for each page, and the memory manager will then ensure that the page is treated according to its importance.

The rebalancer can also take action without relying on other agents; for example, if it notices that the distribution of pages across paging lists is suboptimal or that the number of repurposed pages across different priority levels is detrimental. The rebalancer also has the ability to cause working set trimming if needed, which might be required for creating an appropriate budget of pages that will be used for Superfetch prepopulated cache data. The rebalancer will typically take low-utility pages—such as those that are already marked as low priority, pages that are zeroed, and pages with valid contents but not in any working set and have been unused—and build a more useful set of pages in memory, given the budget it has allocated itself.

Once the rebalancer has decided which pages to bring into memory and at which priority level they need to be loaded (as well as which pages can be thrown out), it performs the required disk reads to prefetch them. It also works in conjunction with the I/O manager's prioritization schemes so that the I/Os are performed with very low priority and do not interfere with the user. It is important to note that the actual memory consumption used by prefetching is all backed by standby pages—as described earlier in the discussion of page dynamics, standby memory is available memory because it can be repurposed as free memory for another allocator at any time. In other words, if Superfetch is prefetching the "wrong data," there is no real impact to the user, because that memory can be reused when needed and doesn't actually consume resources.

Finally, the rebalancer also runs periodically to ensure that pages it has marked as high priority have actually been recently used. Because these pages will rarely (sometimes never) be repurposed, it is important not to waste them on data that is rarely accessed but may have appeared to be frequently accessed during a certain time period. If such a situation is detected, the rebalancer runs again to push those pages down in the priority lists.

In addition to the rebalancer, a special agent called the application launch agent is also involved in a different kind of prefetching mechanism, which attempts to predict application launches and builds a Markov chain model that describes the probability of certain application launches given the existence of other application launches within a time segment. These time segments are divided across four different periods—morning, noon, evening, and night; roughly 6 hours each—and are also kept track of separately as weekdays or weekends. For example, if on Saturday and Sunday evening a user typically launches Outlook (to send email) after having launched Word (to write letters), the application launch agent will probably have prefetched Outlook based on the high probability of it running after Word during weekend evenings.

Because systems today have sufficiently large amounts of memory, on average more than 2 GB (although Superfetch works well on low-memory systems, too), the actual real amount of memory that frequently used processes on a machine need resident for optimal performance ends up being a manageable subset of their entire memory footprint, and Superfetch can often fit all the pages required into RAM. When it can't, technologies such as ReadyBoost and ReadyDrive can further avoid disk usage.

Robust Performance

A final performance enhancing functionality of Superfetch is called *robustness*, or *robust performance*. This component, managed by the user-mode Superfetch service, but ultimately implemented in the kernel (*Pf* routines), watches for specific file I/O access that might harm system performance by populating the standby lists with unneeded data. For example, if a process were to copy a large file across the file system, the standby list would be populated with the file's contents, even though that file might never be accessed again (or not for a long period of time). This would throw out any other data within that priority (and if this was an interactive and useful program, chances are its priority would've been at least 5).

Superfetch responds to two specific kinds of I/O access patterns: sequential file access (going through all the data in a file) and sequential directory access (going through every file in a directory). When Superfetch detects that a certain amount of data (past an internal threshold) has been populated in the standby list as a result of this kind of access, it applies aggressive deprioritization (robustion) to the pages being used to map this file, within the targeted process only (so as not to penalize other applications). These pages, so-called robusted, essentially become reprioritized to priority 2.

Because this component of Superfetch is reactive and not predictive, it does take some time for the robustion to kick in. Superfetch will therefore keep track of this process for the next time it runs. Once Superfetch has determined that it appears that this process always performs this kind of sequential access, Superfetch remembers it and robusts the file pages as soon as they're mapped, instead of waiting on the reactive behavior. At this point, the entire process is now considered robusted for future file access.

Just by applying this logic, however, Superfetch could potentially hurt many legitimate applications or user scenarios that perform sequential access in the future. For example, by using the Sysinternals Strings.exe utility, you can look for a string in all executables that are part of a directory. If there are many files, Superfetch would likely perform robustion. Now, next time you run Strings with a different search parameter, it would run just as slowly as it did the first time, even though you'd expect it to run much faster. To prevent this, Superfetch keeps a list of processes that it watches into the future, as well as an internal hard-coded list of exceptions. If a process is detected to later re-access robusted files, robustion is disabled on the process in order to restore expected behavior.

The main point to remember when thinking about robustion, and Superfetch optimizations in general, is that Superfetch constantly monitors usage patterns and updates its understanding of the system, so that it can avoid fetching useless data. Although changes in a user's daily activities or application startup behavior might cause Superfetch to incorrectly "pollute" the cache with irrelevant data or to throw out data that Superfetch might think is useless, it will quickly adapt to any pattern changes. If the user's actions are erratic and random, the worst that can happen is that the system behaves in a similar state as if Superfetch was not present at all. If Superfetch is ever in doubt or cannot track data reliably, it quiets itself and doesn't make changes to a given process or page.

RAM Optimization Software

While Superfetch provides valuable and realistic optimization of memory usage for the various scenarios it aims to support, many third-party software manufacturers are involved in the distribution of so-called "RAM Optimization" software, which aims to significantly increase available memory on a user's system. These memory optimizers typically present a user interface that shows a graph labeled "Available Memory," and a line typically shows the amount of memory that the optimizer will try to free when it runs. After the optimization job runs, the utility's available memory counter often goes up, sometimes dramatically, implying that the tool is actually freeing up memory for application use. RAM optimizers work by allocating and then freeing large amounts of virtual memory. The following illustration shows the effect a RAM optimizer has on a system.

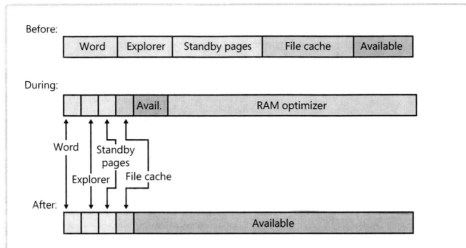

The Before bar depicts the process and system working sets, the pages in standby lists, and free memory before optimization. The During bar shows that the RAM optimizer creates a high memory demand, which it does by incurring many page faults in a short time. In response, the memory manager increases the RAM optimizer's working set. This working-set expansion occurs at the expense of free memory, followed by standby pages and—when available memory becomes low—at the expense of other process working sets. The After bar illustrates how, after the RAM optimizer frees its memory, the memory manager moves all the pages that were assigned to the RAM optimizer to the free page list (which ultimately get zeroed by the zero page thread and moved to the zeroed page list), thus contributing to the free memory value.

Although gaining more free memory might seem like a good thing, gaining free memory in this way is not. As RAM optimizers force the available memory counter up, they force other processes' data and code out of memory. If you're running Microsoft Word, for example, the text of open documents and the program code that was part of Word's working set before the optimization (and was therefore present in physical memory) must be reread from disk as you continue to edit your document. Additionally, by depleting the standby lists, valuable cached data is lost, including much of Superfetch's cache. The performance degradation can be especially severe on servers, where the trimming of the system working set causes cached file data in physical memory to be thrown out, causing hard faults the next time it is accessed.

ReadyBoost

Although RAM today is somewhat easily available and relatively cheap compared to a decade ago, it still doesn't beat the cost of secondary storage such as hard disk drives. Unfortunately, hard disks today contain many moving parts, are fragile, and, more importantly, relatively slow compared to RAM, especially during seeking, so storing active Superfetch data on the drive would be as bad as paging out a page and hard faulting it inside memory. (Solid state disks offset some of these disadvantages, but they are pricier and still slow compared to RAM.) On the other hand, portable solid state media such as USB flash disk (UFD), CompactFlash cards, and Secure Digital cards provide a useful compromise. (In practice, CompactFlash cards and Secure Digital cards are almost always interfaced through a USB adapter, so they all appear to the system as USB flash disks.) They are cheaper than RAM and available in larger sizes, but they also have seek times much shorter than hard drives because of the lack of moving parts.

Random disk I/O is especially expensive because disk head seek time plus rotational latency for typical desktop hard drives total about 13 milliseconds—an eternity for today's 3-GHz processors. Flash memory, however, can service random reads up to 10 times faster than a typical hard disk. Windows therefore includes a feature called ReadyBoost to take advantage of flash memory storage devices by creating an intermediate caching layer on them that logically sits between memory and disks.

ReadyBoost is implemented with the aid of a driver (%SystemRoot%\System32\Drivers\ Rdyboost.sys) that is responsible for writing the cached data to the NVRAM device. When you insert a USB flash disk into a system, ReadyBoost looks at the device to determine its performance characteristics and stores the results of its test in HKLM\SOFTWARE\Microsoft\Windows NT\CurrentVersion\ Emdmgmt, as shown in Figure 10-51. (Emd is short for External Memory Device, the working name for ReadyBoost during its development.)

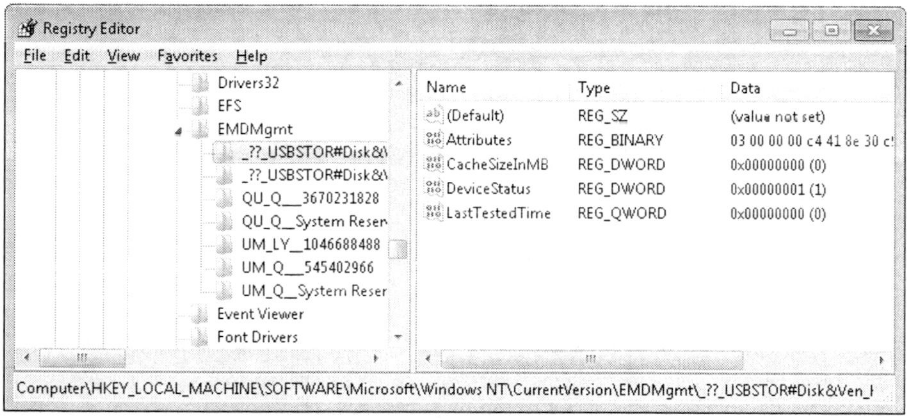

FIGURE 10-51 ReadyBoost device test results in the registry

If the new device is between 256 MB and 32 GB in size, has a transfer rate of 2.5 MB per second or higher for random 4-KB reads, and has a transfer rate of 1.75 MB per second or higher for random 512-KB writes, then ReadyBoost will ask if you'd like to dedicate some of the space for disk caching. If you agree, ReadyBoost creates a file named ReadyBoost.sfcache in the root of the device, which it will use to store cached pages.

After initializing caching, ReadyBoost intercepts all reads and writes to local hard disk volumes (C:\, for example) and copies any data being read or written into the caching file that the service created. There are exceptions such as data that hasn't been read in a long while, or data that belongs to Volume Snapshot requests. Data stored on the cached drive is compressed and typically achieves a 2:1 compression ratio, so a 4-GB cache file will usually contain 8 GB of data. Each block is encrypted as it is written using Advanced Encryption Standard (AES) encryption with a randomly generated per-boot session key in order to guarantee the privacy of the data in the cache if the device is removed from the system.

When ReadyBoost sees random reads that can be satisfied from the cache, it services them from there, but because hard disks have better sequential read access than flash memory, it lets reads that are part of sequential access patterns go directly to the disk even if the data is in the cache. Likewise, when reading the cache, if large I/Os have to be done, the on-disk cache will be read instead.

One disadvantage of depending on flash media is that the user can remove it at any time, which means the system can never solely store critical data on the media (as we've seen, writes always go to the secondary storage first). A related technology, ReadyDrive, covered in the next section, offers additional benefits and solves this problem.

ReadyDrive

ReadyDrive is a Windows feature that takes advantage of hybrid hard disk drives (H-HDDs). An H-HDD is a disk with embedded nonvolatile flash memory (also known as NVRAM). Typical H-HDDs include between 50 MB and 512 MB of cache, but the Windows cache limit is 2 TB.

Under ReadyDrive, the drive's flash memory does not simply act as an automatic, transparent cache, as does the RAM cache common on most hard drives. Instead, Windows uses ATA-8 commands to define the disk data to be held in the flash memory. For example, Windows will save boot data to the cache when the system shuts down, allowing for faster restarting. It also stores portions of hibernation file data in the cache when the system hibernates so that the subsequent resume is faster. Because the cache is enabled even when the disk is spun down, Windows can use the flash memory as a disk-write cache, which avoids spinning up the disk when the system is running on battery power. Keeping the disk spindle turned off can save much of the power consumed by the disk drive under normal usage.

Another consumer of ReadyDrive is Superfetch, since it offers the same advantages as ReadyBoost with some enhanced functionality, such as not requiring an external flash device and having the ability to work persistently. Because the cache is on the actual physical hard drive (which typically a user cannot remove while the computer is running), the hard drive controller typically doesn't have to worry about the data disappearing and can avoid making writes to the actual disk, using solely the cache.

Unified Caching

For simplicity, we have described the conceptual functionality of Superfetch, ReadyBoost, and ReadyDrive independently. Their storage allocation and content tracking functions, however, are implemented in unified code in the operating system and are integrated with each other. This unified caching mechanism is often referred to as the *Store Manager*, although the Store Manager is really only one component.

Unified caching was developed to take advantage of the characteristics of the various types of storage hardware that might exist on a system. For example, Superfetch can use either the flash memory of a hybrid hard disk drive (if available) or a USB flash disk (if available) instead of using system RAM. Since an H-HDD's flash memory can be better expected to be preserved across system shutdown and bootstrap cycles, it would be preferable for cache data that could help optimize boot times, while system RAM might be a better choice for other data. (In addition to optimizing boot times, a hybrid hard disk drive's NVRAM, if present, is generally preferred as a cache location to a UFD. A UFD may be unplugged at any time, hence disappearing; thus cache on a UFD must always be handled as write-through to the actual hard drive. The NVRAM in an H-HDD can be allowed to work in write-back mode because it is not going to disappear unless the hard drive itself also disappears.)

The overall architecture of the unified caching mechanism is shown in Figure 10-52.

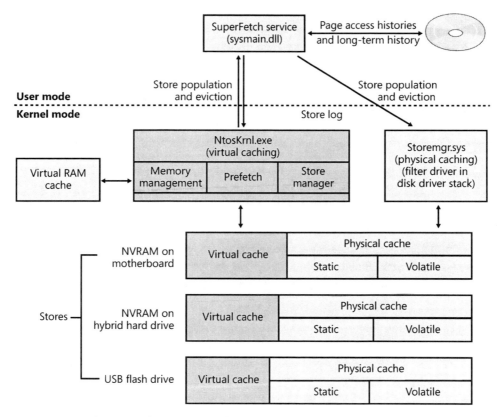

FIGURE 10-52 Architecture of the unified caching mechanism

The fundamental component that implements caching is called a "store." Each store implements the functions of adding data to the backing storage (which may be in system RAM or in NVRAM), reading data from it, or removing data from it.

All data in a store is managed in terms of *store pages* (often called simply *pages*). The size of a store page is the system's physical and virtual memory page size (4 KB, or 8KB on Itanium platforms), regardless of the "block size" (sometimes called "sector size") presented by the underlying storage device. This allows store pages to be mapped and moved efficiently between the store, system RAM, and page files (which have always been organized in blocks of the same size). The recent move toward "advanced format" hard drives, which export a block size of 4 KB, is a good fit for this approach. Store pages within a store are identified by "store keys," whose interpretation is up to the individual store.

When writing to a store, the store is responsible for buffering data so that the I/O to the actual storage device uses large buffers. This improves performance, as NVRAM devices as well as physical hard drives perform poorly with small random writes. The store may also perform compression and encryption before writing to the storage device.

The *Store Manager* component manages all of the stores and their contents. It is implemented as a component of the Superfetch service in Sysmain.dll, a set of executive services (*SmXxx*, such as *SmPageRead*) within Ntoskrnl.exe, and a filter driver in the disk storage stack, Storemgr.sys. Logically, it operates at the level just above all of the stores. Only the Store Manager communicates with stores; all other components interact with the Store Manager. Requests to the Store Manager look much like requests from the Store Manager to a store: requests to store data, retrieve data, or remove data from a store. Requests to the Store Manager to store data, however, include a parameter indicating which stores are to be written to.

The Store Manager keeps track of which stores contain each cached page. If a cached page is in one or more stores, requests to retrieve that page are routed by the Store Manager to one store or another according to which stores are the fastest or the least busy.

The Store Manager categorizes stores in the following ways. First, a store may reside in system RAM or in some form of nonvolatile RAM (either a UFD or the NVRAM of an H-HDD). Second, NVRAM stores are further divided into "virtual" and "physical" portions, while a store in system RAM acts only as a virtual store.

Virtual stores contain only page-file-backed information, including process-private memory and page-file-backed sections. Physical caches contain pages from disk, with the exception that physical caches never contain pages from page files. A store in system RAM can, however, contain pages from page files.

Physical caches are further divided into "static" and "volatile" (or "dynamic") regions. The contents of the static region are completely determined by the user-mode Store Manager service. The Store Manager uses logs of historical access to data to populate the static region. The volatile or dynamic region of each store, on the other hand, populates itself based on read and write requests that pass through the disk storage stack, much in the manner of the automatic RAM cache on a traditional hard drive. Stores that implement a dynamic region are responsible for reporting to the Store Manager any such automatically cached (and dropped) contents.

This section has provided a brief description of the organization and operation of the unified caching mechanism. As of this writing, there are no Performance Monitor counters or other means in the operating system to measure the mechanism's operation, other than the counters under the Cache object, which long predate the Store Manager.

Process Reflection

There are often cases where a process exhibits problematic behavior, but because it's still providing service, suspending it to generate a full memory dump or interactively debug it is undesirable. The length of time a process is suspended to generate a dump can be minimized by taking a minidump, which captures thread registers and stacks along with pages of memory referenced by registers, but that dump type has a very limited amount of information, which many times is sufficient for diagnosing crashes but not for troubleshooting general problems. With process reflection, the target process is suspended only long enough to generate a minidump and create a suspended cloned copy of the target, and then the larger dump that captures all of a process's valid user-mode memory can be generated from the clone while the target is allowed to continue executing.

Several Windows Diagnostic Infrastructure (WDI) components make use of process reflection to capture minimally intrusive memory dumps of processes their heuristics identify as exhibiting suspicious behavior. For example, the Memory Leak Diagnoser component of Windows Resource Exhaustion Detection and Resolution (also known as RADAR), generates a reflected memory dump of a process that appears to be leaking private virtual memory so that it can be sent to Microsoft via Windows Error Reporting (WER) for analysis. WDI's hung process detection heuristic does the same for processes that appear to be deadlocked with one another. Because these components use heuristics, they can't be certain the processes are faulty and therefore can't suspend them for long periods of time or terminate them.

Process reflection's implementation is driven by the *RtlCreateProcessReflection* function in Ntdll.dll. Its first step is to create a shared memory section, populate it with parameters, and map it into the current and target processes. It then creates two event objects and duplicates them into the target process so that the current process and target process can synchronize their operations. Next, it injects a thread into the target process via a call to *RtlpCreateUserThreadEx*. The thread is directed to begin execution in Ntdll's *RtlpProcessReflectionStartup* function. Because Ntdll.dll is mapped at the same address, randomly generated at boot, into every process's address space, the current process can simply pass the address of the function it obtains from its own Ntdll.dll mapping. If the caller of *RtlCreateProcessReflection* specified that it wants a handle to the cloned process, *RtlCreateProcessReflection* waits for the remote thread to terminate, otherwise it returns to the caller.

The injected thread in the target process allocates an additional event object that it will use to synchronize with the cloned process once it's created. Then it calls *RtlCloneUserProcess*, passing parameters it obtains from the memory mapping it shares with the initiating process. If the *RtlCreateProcessReflection* option that specifies the creation of the clone when the process is not executing in the loader, performing heap operations, modifying the process environment block (PEB), or modifying fiber-local storage is present, then *RtlCreateProcessReflection* acquires the associated locks before continuing. This can be useful for debugging because the memory dump's copy of the data structures will be in a consistent state.

RtlCloneUserProcess finishes by calling *RtlpCreateUserProcess*, the user-mode function responsible for general process creation, passing flags that indicate the new process should be a clone of the current one, and *RtlpCreateUserProcess* in turn calls *ZwCreateUserProcess* to request the kernel to create the process.

When creating a cloned process, *ZwCreateUserProcess* executes most of the same code paths as when it creates a new process, with the exception that *PspAllocateProcess*, which it calls to create the process object and initial thread, calls *MmInitializeProcessAddressSpace* with a flag specifying that the address should be a copy-on-write copy of the target process instead of an initial process address space. The memory manager uses the same support it provides for the Services for Unix Applications *fork* API to efficiently clone the address space. Once the target process continues execution, any changes it makes to its address space are seen only by it, not the clone, which enables the clone's address space to represent a consistent point-in-time view of the target process.

The clone's execution begins at the point just after the return from *RtlpCreateUserProcess*. If the clone's creation is successful, its thread receives the STATUS_PROCESS_CLONED return code, whereas the cloning thread receives STATUS_SUCCESS. The cloned process then synchronizes with the target and, as its final act, calls a function optionally passed to *RtlCreateProcessReflection*, which must be implemented in Ntdll.dll. RADAR, for instance, specifies *RtlDetectHeapLeaks*, which performs heuristic analysis of the process heaps and reports the results back to the thread that called *RtlCreateProcess-Reflection*. If no function was specified, the thread suspends itself or terminates, depending on the flags passed to *RtlCreateProcessReflection*.

When RADAR and WDI use process reflection, they call *RtlCreateProcessReflection*, asking for the function to return a handle to the cloned process and for the clone to suspend itself after it has initialized. Then they generate a minidump of the target process, which suspends the target for the duration of the dump generation, and next they generate a more comprehensive dump of the cloned process. After they finish generating the dump of the clone, they terminate the clone. The target process can execute during the time window between the minidump's completion and the creation of the clone, but for most scenarios any inconsistencies do not interfere with troubleshooting. The Procdump utility from Sysinternals also follows these steps when you specify the –r switch to have it create a reflected dump of a target process.

EXPERIMENT: Using Preflect to Observe the Behavior of Process Reflection

You can use the Preflect utility, which you can download from the *Windows Internals* book webpage, to see the effects of process reflection. First, launch Notepad.exe and obtain its process ID in a process management utility like Process Explorer or Task Manager. Next, open a command prompt and execute Preflect with the process ID as the command-line argument. This creates a cloned copy using process reflection. In Process Explorer, you will see two instances of Notepad: the one you launched and the cloned child instance that's highlighted in gray (gray indicates that all the process's threads are suspended):

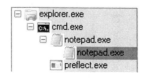

Open the process properties for each instance, switch to the Performance page, and put them side by side for comparison:

notepad.exe:748 Properties

TCP/IP	Security	Environment	Strings
Image	Performance	Performance Graph	Threads

CPU
		I/O	
Priority	8	I/O Priority	Normal
Kernel Time	0:00:00.015	Reads	1
User Time	0:00:00.000	Read Delta	0
Total Time	0:00:00.015	Read Bytes Delta	0
Cycles	110,875,171	Writes	0

Virtual Memory
		Write Delta	0
Private Bytes	964 K	Write Bytes Delta	0
Peak Private Bytes	1,048 K	Other	87
Virtual Size	60,004 K	Other Delta	0
Page Faults	1,160	Other Bytes Delta	0
Page Fault Delta	0	Handles	

Physical Memory
		Handles	56
Memory Priority	5	Peak Handles	60
Working Set	4,484 K	GDI Handles	23
WS Private	340 K	USER Handles	18
WS Shareable	4,144 K		
WS Shared	3,744 K		
Peak Working Set	4,500 K		

OK   Cancel

notepad.exe:2232 Properties

TCP/IP	Security	Environment	Strings
Image	Performance	Performance Graph	Threads

CPU
		I/O	
Priority	8	I/O Priority	Normal
Kernel Time	0:00:00.000	Reads	1
User Time	0:00:00.000	Read Delta	0
Total Time	0:00:00.000	Read Bytes Delta	0
Cycles	7,086,003	Writes	0

Virtual Memory
		Write Delta	0
Private Bytes	1,024 K	Write Bytes Delta	0
Peak Private Bytes	1,024 K	Other	156
Virtual Size	212 K	Other Delta	0
Page Faults	72	Other Bytes Delta	0
Page Fault Delta	0	Handles	

Physical Memory
		Handles	0
Memory Priority	5	Peak Handles	1
Working Set	312 K	GDI Handles	0
WS Private	128 K	USER Handles	0
WS Shareable	184 K		
WS Shared	152 K		
Peak Working Set	312 K		

OK   Cancel

The two instances are easily distinguishable because the target process has been executing and therefore has a significantly higher cycle count and larger working set, and the clone has no references to any kernel or window manager objects, as evidenced by its zero kernel handle, GDI handle, and USER handle counts. Further, if you look at the Threads tab and have configured the Process Explorer symbol options to obtain operating system symbols, you'll see that the target process's thread began executing in Notepad.exe code, whereas the clone's thread is the one injected by the target to execute *RtlpProcessReflectionStartup*.

notepad.exe:748 Properties

TCP/IP	Security	Environment	Strings
Image	Performance	Performance Graph	Threads

Count: 1

TID	CPU	Cycles Delta	Start Address
776			notepad.exe!WinMainCRTStartup

Thread ID:	776	Stack	Module
Start Time:	1:03:10 PM 1/13/2011		
State:	Wait:WrUserRequest	Base Priority:	8
Kernel Time:	0:00:00.015	Dynamic Priority:	12
User Time:	0:00:00.000	I/O Priority:	Normal
Context Switches:	130	Memory Priority:	5
Cycles:	109,290,807	Ideal Processor:	0

Permissions   Kill   Suspend

OK   Cancel

notepad.exe:2232 Properties

TCP/IP	Security	Environment	Strings
Image	Performance	Performance Graph	Threads

Count: 1

TID	CPU	Cycles Delta	Start Address
2268			rtdll.dll!RtlpProcessReflectionStartup

Thread ID:	2268	Stack	Module
Start Time:	1:03:53 PM 1/13/2011		
State:	Wait:Suspended	Base Priority:	8
Kernel Time:	0:00:00.000	Dynamic Priority:	10
User Time:	0:00:00.000	I/O Priority:	Normal
Context Switches:	4	Memory Priority:	5
Cycles:	7,092,215	Ideal Processor:	0

Permissions   Kill   Resume

OK   Cancel

Conclusion

In this chapter, we've examined how the Windows memory manager implements virtual memory management. As with most modern operating systems, each process is given access to a private address space, protecting one process's memory from another's but allowing processes to share memory efficiently and securely. Advanced capabilities, such as the inclusion of mapped files and the ability to sparsely allocate memory, are also available. The Windows environment subsystem makes most of the memory manager's capabilities available to applications through the Windows API.

The next chapter covers a component tightly integrated with the memory manager, the cache manager.

CHAPTER 11

Cache Manager

The cache manager is a set of kernel-mode functions and system threads that cooperate with the memory manager to provide data caching for all Windows file system drivers (both local and network). In this chapter, we'll explain how the cache manager, including its key internal data structures and functions, works; how it is sized at system initialization time; how it interacts with other elements of the operating system; and how you can observe its activity through performance counters. We'll also describe the five flags on the Windows *CreateFile* function that affect file caching.

> **Note** None of the cache manager's internal functions are outlined in this chapter beyond the depth required to explain how the cache manager works. The programming interfaces to the cache manager are documented in the Windows Driver Kit (WDK). For more information about the WDK, see *http://www.microsoft.com/whdc/devtools/wdk/default.mspx.*

Key Features of the Cache Manager

The cache manager has several key features:

- Supports all file system types (both local and network), thus removing the need for each file system to implement its own cache management code

- Uses the memory manager to control which parts of which files are in physical memory (trading off demands for physical memory between user processes and the operating system)

- Caches data on a virtual block basis (offsets within a file)—in contrast to many caching systems, which cache on a logical block basis (offsets within a disk volume)—allowing for intelligent read-ahead and high-speed access to the cache without involving file system drivers (This method of caching, called *fast I/O*, is described later in this chapter.)

- Supports "hints" passed by applications at file open time (such as random versus sequential access, temporary file creation, and so on)

- Supports recoverable file systems (for example, those that use transaction logging) to recover data after a system failure

Although we'll talk more throughout this chapter about how these features are used in the cache manager, in this section we'll introduce you to the concepts behind these features.

Single, Centralized System Cache

Some operating systems rely on each individual file system to cache data, a practice that results either in duplicated caching and memory management code in the operating system or in limitations on the kinds of data that can be cached. In contrast, Windows offers a centralized caching facility that caches all externally stored data, whether on local hard disks, floppy disks, network file servers, or CD-ROMs. Any data can be cached, whether it's user data streams (the contents of a file and the ongoing read and write activity to that file) or file *system metadata* (such as directory and file headers). As you'll discover in this chapter, the method Windows uses to access the cache depends on the type of data being cached.

The Memory Manager

One unusual aspect of the cache manager is that it never knows how much cached data is actually in physical memory. This statement might sound strange because the purpose of a cache is to keep a subset of frequently accessed data in physical memory as a way to improve I/O performance. The reason the cache manager doesn't know how much data is in physical memory is that it accesses data by mapping views of files into system virtual address spaces, using standard *section objects* (*file mapping objects* in Windows API terminology). (Section objects are the basic primitive of the memory manager and are explained in detail in Chapter 10, "Memory Management.") As addresses in these mapped views are accessed, the memory manager pages in blocks that aren't in physical memory. And when memory demands dictate, the memory manager unmaps these pages out of the cache and, if the data has changed, pages the data back to the files.

By caching on the basis of a virtual address space using mapped files, the cache manager avoids generating read or write I/O request packets (IRPs) to access the data for files it's caching. Instead, it simply copies data to or from the virtual addresses where the portion of the cached file is mapped and relies on the memory manager to fault in (or out) the data into (or out of) memory as needed. This process allows the memory manager to make global trade-offs on how much memory to give to the system cache versus how much to give to user processes. (The cache manager also initiates I/O, such as lazy writing, which is described later in this chapter; however, it calls the memory manager to write the pages.) Also, as you'll learn in the next section, this design makes it possible for processes that open cached files to see the same data as do processes that are mapping the same files into their user address spaces.

Cache Coherency

One important function of a cache manager is to ensure that any process accessing cached data will get the most recent version of that data. A problem can arise when one process opens a file (and hence the file is cached) while another process maps the file into its address space directly (using the Windows *MapViewOfFile* function). This potential problem doesn't occur under Windows because both the cache manager and the user applications that map files into their address spaces use the same memory management file mapping services. Because the memory manager guarantees that it has only one representation of each unique mapped file (regardless of the number of section objects or mapped views), it maps all views of a file (even if they overlap) to a single set of pages in physical memory, as shown in Figure 11-1. (For more information on how the memory manager works with mapped files, see Chapter 10.)

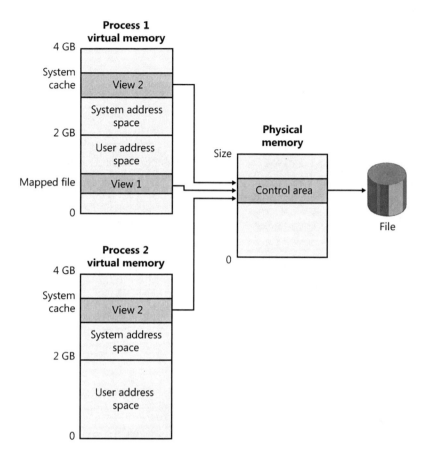

FIGURE 11-1 Coherent caching scheme

So, for example, if Process 1 has a view (View 1) of the file mapped into its user address space, and Process 2 is accessing the same view via the system cache, Process 2 will see any changes that Process 1 makes as they're made, not as they're flushed. The memory manager won't flush *all* user-mapped pages—only those that it knows have been written to (because they have the modified bit set). Therefore, any process accessing a file under Windows always sees the most up-to-date version of that file, even if some processes have the file open through the I/O system and others have the file mapped into their address space using the Windows file mapping functions.

Virtual Block Caching

The Windows cache manager uses a method known as *virtual block caching*, in which the cache manager keeps track of which parts of which *files* are in the cache. The cache manager is able to monitor these file portions by mapping 256-KB views of files into system virtual address spaces, using special system cache routines located in the memory manager. This approach has the following key benefits:

- It opens up the possibility of doing intelligent read-ahead; because the cache tracks which parts of which files are in the cache, it can predict where the caller might be going next.

- It allows the I/O system to bypass going to the file system for requests for data that is already in the cache (fast I/O). Because the cache manager knows which parts of which files are in the cache, it can return the address of cached data to satisfy an I/O request without having to call the file system.

Details of how intelligent read-ahead and fast I/O work are provided later in this chapter.

Stream-Based Caching

The cache manager is also designed to do *stream caching*, as opposed to file caching. A *stream* is a sequence of bytes within a file. Some file systems, such as NTFS, allow a file to contain more than one stream; the cache manager accommodates such file systems by caching each stream independently. NTFS can exploit this feature by organizing its master file table (described in Chapter 12) into streams and by caching these streams as well. In fact, although the cache manager might be said to cache files, it actually caches streams (all files have at least one stream of data) identified by both a file name and, if more than one stream exists in the file, a stream name.

Recoverable File System Support

Recoverable file systems such as NTFS are designed to reconstruct the disk volume structure after a system failure. This capability means that I/O operations in progress at the time of a system failure must be either entirely completed or entirely backed out from the disk when the system is restarted. Half-completed I/O operations can corrupt a disk volume and even render an entire volume inaccessible. To avoid this problem, a recoverable file system maintains a log file in which it records every update it intends to make to the file system structure (the file system's metadata) before it writes the change to the volume. If the system fails, interrupting volume modifications in progress, the recoverable file system uses information stored in the log to reissue the volume updates.

> **Note** The term *metadata* applies only to changes in the file system structure: file and directory creation, renaming, and deletion.

To guarantee a successful volume recovery, every log file record documenting a volume update must be completely written to disk before the update itself is applied to the volume. Because disk writes are cached, the cache manager and the file system must coordinate metadata updates by ensuring that the log file is flushed ahead of metadata updates. Overall, the following actions occur in sequence:

1. The file system writes a log file record documenting the metadata update it intends to make.

2. The file system calls the cache manager to flush the log file record to disk.

3. The file system writes the volume update to the cache—that is, it modifies its cached metadata.

4. The cache manager flushes the altered metadata to disk, updating the volume structure. (Actually, log file records are batched before being flushed to disk, as are volume modifications.)

When a file system writes data to the cache, it can supply a *logical sequence number* (LSN) that identifies the record in its log file, which corresponds to the cache update. The cache manager keeps track of these numbers, recording the lowest and highest LSNs (representing the oldest and newest log file records) associated with each page in the cache. In addition, data streams that are protected by transaction log records are marked as "no write" by NTFS so that the mapped page writer won't inadvertently write out these pages before the corresponding log records are written. (When the mapped page writer sees a page marked this way, it moves the page to a special list that the cache manager then flushes at the appropriate time, such as when lazy writer activity takes place.)

When it prepares to flush a group of dirty pages to disk, the cache manager determines the highest LSN associated with the pages to be flushed and reports that number to the file system. The file system can then call the cache manager back, directing it to flush log file data up to the point represented by the reported LSN. *After* the cache manager flushes the log file up to that LSN, it flushes the corresponding volume structure updates to disk, thus ensuring that it records what it's going to do before actually doing it. These interactions between the file system and the cache manager guarantee the recoverability of the disk volume after a system failure.

Cache Virtual Memory Management

Because the Windows system cache manager caches data on a virtual basis, it uses up regions of system virtual address space (instead of physical memory) and manages them in structures called *virtual address control blocks*, or VACBs. VACBs define these regions of address space into 256-KB slots called *views*. When the cache manager initializes during the bootup process, it allocates an initial array of VACBs to describe cached memory. As caching requirements grow and more memory is required, the cache manager allocates more VACB arrays, as needed. It can also shrink virtual address space as other demands put pressure on the system.

At a file's first I/O (read or write) operation, the cache manager maps a 256-KB view of the 256-KB-aligned region of the file that contains the requested data into a free slot in the system cache address space. For example, if 10 bytes starting at an offset of 300,000 bytes were read into a file, the view that would be mapped would begin at offset 262144 (the second 256-KB-aligned region of the file) and extend for 256 KB.

The cache manager maps views of files into slots in the cache's address space on a round-robin basis, mapping the first requested view into the first 256-KB slot, the second view into the second 256-KB slot, and so forth, as shown in Figure 11-2. In this example, File B was mapped first, File A second, and File C third, so File B's mapped chunk occupies the first slot in the cache. Notice that only the first 256-KB portion of File B has been mapped, which is due to the fact that only part of the file has been accessed and because although File C is only 100 KB (and thus smaller than one of the views in the system cache), it requires its own 256-KB slot in the cache.

The cache manager guarantees that a view is mapped as long as it's active (although views can remain mapped after they become inactive). A view is marked active, however, only during a read or write operation to or from the file. Unless a process opens a file by specifying the FILE_FLAG_RANDOM_ACCESS flag in the call to *CreateFile*, the cache manager unmaps inactive views of a file as it maps new views for the file if it detects that the file is being accessed sequentially. Pages for unmapped views are sent to the standby or modified lists (depending on whether they have been changed), and because the memory manager exports a special interface for the cache manager, the cache manager can direct the pages to be placed at the end or front of these lists. Pages that correspond to views of files opened with the FILE_FLAG_SEQUENTIAL_SCAN flag are moved to the front of the lists, whereas all others are moved to the end. This scheme encourages the reuse of pages belonging to sequentially read files and specifically prevents a large file copy operation from affecting more than a small part of physical memory. The flag also affects unmapping: the cache manager will aggressively unmap views when this flag is supplied.

If the cache manager needs to map a view of a file and there are no more free slots in the cache, it will unmap the least recently mapped inactive view and use that slot. If no views are available, an I/O error is returned, indicating that insufficient system resources are available to perform the operation. Given that views are marked active only during a read or write operation, however, this scenario is extremely unlikely because thousands of files would have to be accessed simultaneously for this situation to occur.

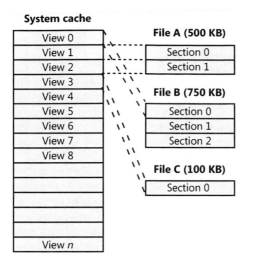

System cache

View 0
View 1
View 2
View 3
View 4
View 5
View 6
View 7
View 8
View *n*

File A (500 KB)

Section 0
Section 1

File B (750 KB)

Section 0
Section 1
Section 2

File C (100 KB)

Section 0

FIGURE 11-2 Files of varying sizes mapped into the system cache

Cache Size

In the following sections, we'll explain how Windows computes the size of the system cache, both virtually and physically. As with most calculations related to memory management, the size of the system cache depends on a number of factors.

Cache Virtual Size

On a 32-bit Windows system, the virtual size of the system cache is limited solely by the amount of kernel-mode virtual address space and the SystemCacheLimit registry key that can be optionally configured. (See Chapter 10 for more information on limiting the size of the kernel virtual address space.) This means that the cache size is capped by the 2-GB system address space, but it is typically significantly smaller because the system address space is shared with other resources, including system paged table entries (PTEs), nonpaged and paged pool, and page tables. The maximum virtual cache size is 1,024 GB (1 TB) on 64-bit Windows.

Cache Working Set Size

As mentioned earlier, one of the key differences in the design of the cache manager in Windows from that of other operating systems is the delegation of physical memory management to the global memory manager. Because of this, the existing code that handles working set expansion and trimming, as well as managing the modified and standby lists, is also used to control the size of the system cache, dynamically balancing demands for physical memory between processes and the operating system.

The system cache doesn't have its own working set but rather shares a single system set that includes cache data, paged pool, pageable Ntoskrnl code, and pageable driver code. As explained in the section "System Working Set" in Chapter 10, this single working set is called internally the *system cache working set* even though the system cache is just one of the components that contribute to it. For the purposes of this book, we'll refer to this working set simply as the *system working set*. Also explained in Chapter 10 is the fact that if the *LargeSystemCache* registry value is 1, the memory manager favors the system working set over that of processes running on the system.

EXPERIMENT: Looking at the Cache's Working Set

The *!filecache* debugger command dumps information about the physical memory the cache is using, the current and peak working set sizes, the number of valid pages associated with views, and the names of files mapped into views, where applicable, as you can see in the following output. (File system drivers cache metadata, such as directory structures and volume bitmaps, by using unnamed file streams.)

```
lkd> !filecache
***** Dump file cache******
   Reading and sorting 999 VACBs ...
ReadVirtual: 85b77038 not properly sign extended
ReadVirtual: 85ba7010 not properly sign extended
   Processing 998 active VACBs ...
File Cache Information
   Current size 30528 kb
   Peak size    65752 kb
   461 Control Areas
Skipping view @ 91980000 - no VACB, but PTE is a prototype!
   Loading file cache database (100% of 523264 PTEs)
   SkippedPageTableReads = 882
   File cache has 7668 valid pages

   Usage Summary (in Kb):
Control Valid Standby/Dirty Shared Locked FsContext Name
85fa5be0    0      4          0      0 add0dbf8 $Directory
85f971b8    0      8          0      0 ad9bc918 $Directory
87c489f0    4      4          0      0 93b390f8 $Directory
87c4a9c0    4      0          0      0 93b38c30 $Directory
87c451a8    0      4          0      0 93b35780 $Directory
86a83710 4512  45432          0      0 86a90168 $Mft
85f96770    0      8          0      0 ad9c00f8   No Name for File
85e90998    0    512          0      0 abb83510   No Name for File
88062008    4      0          0      0 9e6c40f8 $Directory
87c291e8   44    164          0      0 93b400f8 $Directory
87c27e10    0     16          0      0 93b4bd08 $Directory
87b4bc88  236     84          0      0 93b28d08 $Directory
86ce23a8   12      0          0      0 a2051528 $Directory
87c2bb20    4      0          0      0 93b3b850 $Directory
87d51480    0      4          0      0 824f9830 $Directory
87c8c900    0      4          0      0 825b06d0 utmpx
87c2aa30   44    216          0      0 93b3fc70 $Directory
86ecc168   12   4088          0      0 9c3c5c50 Microsoft-Windows-
                                               GroupPolicy%4Operational.evtx
...
```

Cache Physical Size

While the system working set includes the amount of physical memory that is mapped into views in the cache's virtual address space, it does not necessarily reflect the total amount of file data that is cached in physical memory. There can be a discrepancy between the two values because additional file data might be in the memory manager's standby or modified page lists.

Recall from Chapter 10 that during the course of working set trimming or page replacement the memory manager can move dirty pages from a working set to either the standby list or modified page list, depending on whether the page contains data that needs to be written to the paging file or another file before the page can be reused. If the memory manager didn't implement these lists, any time a process accessed data previously removed from its working set, the memory manager would have to hard-fault it in from disk. Instead, if the accessed data is present on either of these lists, the memory manager simply soft-faults the page back into the process's working set. Thus, the lists serve as in-memory caches of data that's stored in the paging file, executable images, or data files. Thus, the total amount of file data cached on a system includes not only the system working set but the combined sizes of the standby and modified page lists as well.

An example illustrates how the cache manager can cause much more file data than that containable in the system working set to be cached in physical memory. Consider a system that acts as a dedicated file server. A client application accesses file data from across the network, while a server, such as the file server driver (%SystemRoot%\System32\Drivers\Srv2.sys, described in Chapter 12), uses cache manager interfaces to read and write file data on behalf of the client. If the client reads through several thousand files of 1 MB each, the cache manager will have to start reusing views when it runs out of mapping space (and can't enlarge the VACB mapping area). For each file read thereafter, the cache manager unmaps views and remaps them for new files. When the cache manager unmaps a view, the memory manager doesn't discard the file data in the cache's working set that corresponds to the view, it moves the data to the standby list. In the absence of any other demand for physical memory, the standby list can consume almost all the physical memory that remains outside the system working set. In other words, virtually all the server's physical memory will be used to cache file data, as shown in Figure 11-3.

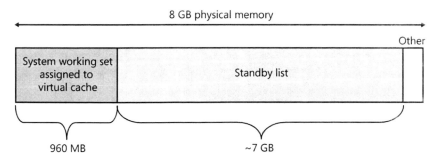

FIGURE 11-3 Example in which most of physical memory is being used by the file cache

Because the total amount of file data cached includes the system working set, modified page list, and standby list—the sizes of which are all controlled by the memory manager—it is in a sense the real cache manager. The cache manager subsystem simply provides convenient interfaces for accessing file data through the memory manager. It also plays an important role with its read-ahead and write-behind policies in influencing what data the memory manager keeps present in physical memory, as well as with managing system virtual address views of the space.

To try to accurately reflect the total amount of file data that's cached on a system, Task Manager shows a value named Cache in its performance view that reflects the combined size of the system working set, standby list, and modified page list. Process Explorer, on the other hand, breaks up these values into Cache WS (system cache working set), Standby, and Modified. Figure 11-4 shows the system information view in Process Explorer and the Cache WS value in the Physical Memory area in the lower left of the figure, as well as the size of the standby and modified lists in the Paging Lists area near the middle of the figure. Note that the Cache value in Task Manager also includes the Paged WS, Kernel WS, and Driver WS values shown in Process Explorer. When these values were chosen, the vast majority of System WS came from the Cache WS. This is no longer the case today, but the anachronism remains in Task Manager.

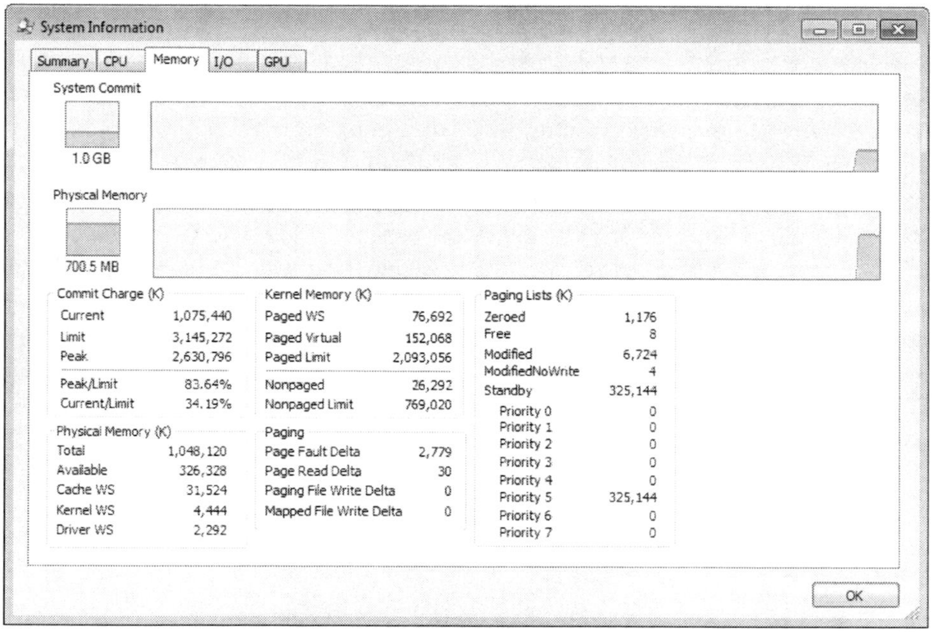

FIGURE 11-4 Process Explorer's System Information dialog box

Cache Data Structures

The cache manager uses the following data structures to keep track of cached files:

- Each 256-KB slot in the system cache is described by a VACB.

- Each separately opened cached file has a private cache map, which contains information used to control read-ahead (discussed later in the chapter).

- Each cached file has a single shared cache map structure, which points to slots in the system cache that contain mapped views of the file.

These structures and their relationships are described in the next sections.

Systemwide Cache Data Structures

As previously described, the cache manager keeps track of the state of the views in the system cache by using an array of data structures called *virtual address control block* (VACB) *arrays* that are stored in nonpaged pool. On a 32-bit system, each VACB is 32 bytes in size and a VACB array is 128 KB, resulting in 4,096 VACBs per array. On a 64-bit system, a VACB is 64 bytes, resulting in 2,048 VACBs per array. The cache manager allocates the initial VACB array during system initialization and links it into the systemwide list of VACB arrays called *CcVacbArrays*. Each VACB represents one 256-KB view in the system cache, as shown in Figure 11-5. The structure of a VACB is shown in Figure 11-6.

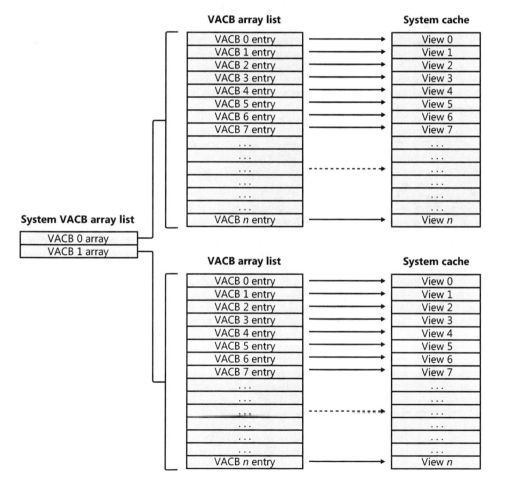

FIGURE 11-5 System VACB array

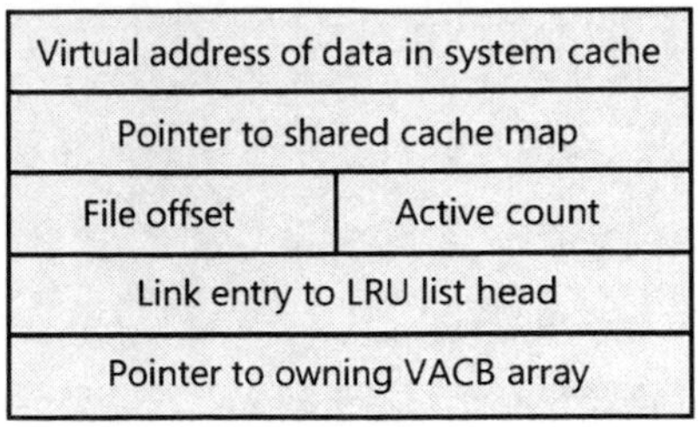

Virtual address of data in system cache
Pointer to shared cache map
File offset	Active count
Link entry to LRU list head
Pointer to owning VACB array

FIGURE 11-6 VACB structure

Additionally, each VACB array is composed of two kinds of VACB: *low priority mapping* VACBs and *high priority mapping* VACBs. The system allocates 64 initial high priority VACBs for each VACB array. High priority VACBs have the distinction of having their views preallocated from system address space. When the memory manager has no views to give to the cache manager at the time of mapping some data, and if the mapping request is marked as high priority, the cache manager will use one of the preallocated views present in a high priority VACB. It uses these high priority VACBs, for example, for critical file system metadata as well as for purging data from the cache. After high priority VACBs are gone, however, any operation requiring a VACB view will fail with insufficient resources. Typically, the mapping priority is set to the default of low, but by using the PIN_HIGH_PRIORITY flag when pinning (described later) cached data, file systems can request a high priority VACB to be used instead, if one is needed.

As you can see in Figure 11-6, the first field in a VACB is the virtual address of the data in the system cache. The second field is a pointer to the shared cache map structure, which identifies which file is cached. The third field identifies the offset within the file at which the view begins (always based on 256-KB granularity). Given this granularity, the bottom 16 bits of the file offset will always be zero, so those bits are reused to store the number of references to the view—that is, how many active reads or writes are accessing the view. The fourth field links the VACB into a list of least-recently-used (LRU) VACBs when the cache manager frees the VACB; the cache manager first checks this list when allocating a new VACB. Finally, the fifth field links this VACB to the VACB array header representing the array in which the VACB is stored.

During an I/O operation on a file, the file's VACB reference count is incremented, and then it's decremented when the I/O operation is over. When the reference count is nonzero the VACB is *active*. For access to file system metadata, the active count represents how many file system drivers have the pages in that view locked into memory.

EXPERIMENT: Looking at VACBs and VACB Statistics

The cache manager internally keeps track of various values that are useful to developers and support engineers when debugging crash dumps. All these debugging variables start with the *CcDbg* prefix, which makes it easy to see the whole list, thanks to the *x* command:

```
lkd> x nt!*ccdbg*
8194ba84        nt!CcDbgNumberOfCcUnmapInactiveViews = <no type information>
8197c740        nt!CcDbgNumberOfFailedMappingsDueToVacbSpace = <no type information>
8197c730        nt!CcDbgNumberOfFailedBitmapAllocations = <no type information>
8197c73c        nt!CcDbgNumberOfFailedHighPriorityMappingsDueToMmResources =
                    <no type information>
...
```

Some systems may show differences in variable names due to 32-bit versus 64-bit implementations. The exact variable names are irrelevant in this experiment—focus instead on the methodology that is explained. Using these variables and your knowledge of the VACB array header data structures, you can use the kernel debugger to list all the VACB array headers. The *CcVacbArrays* variable is an array of pointers to VACB array headers, which you dereference in order to dump the contents of the _VACB_ARRAY_HEADERs. First, obtain the highest array index:

```
lkd> dd nt!CcVacbArraysHighestUsedIndex 1 1
8194ba7c  00000000
```

And now you can dereference each index until the maximum index. On this system (and this is the norm), the highest index is 0, which means there's only one header to dereference:

```
lkd> ?? (*((nt!_VACB_ARRAY_HEADER***)@@(nt!CcVacbArrays)))[0]
struct _VACB_ARRAY_HEADER * 0x8315b000
   +0x000 VacbArrayIndex    : 0
   +0x004 MappingCount      : 0x5ab
   +0x008 HighestMappedIndex : 0x9a9
   +0x00c Reserved          : 0
```

If there were more, you could change the array index at the end of the command with a higher number, until you reached the highest used index. The output shows that the system has only one VACB array with 1,451 (0x5ab) active VACBs.

Finally, the *CcNumberOfFreeVacbs* variable stores the number of VACBs on the free VACB list. Dumping this variable on the system used for the experiment results in 2,645 (0xa55):

```
lkd> dd nt!CcNumberOfFreeVacbs 1 1
8197c768  00000a55
```

As expected, the sum of the free (0x5ab—1,451 decimal) and active VACBs (0xa55—2,645 decimal) on a 32-bit system with one VACB array equals 4,096, the number of VACBs in one VACB array. If the system were to run out of free VACBs, the cache manager would try to allocate a new VACB array. Because of the volatile nature of this experiment, your system may create and/or free additional VACBs between the two steps (dumping the active and then the free VACBs). This might cause your total of free and active VACBs to not match exactly 4,096. Try quickly repeating the experiment a couple of times if this happens, although you may never get stale numbers, especially if there is lots of file system activity on the system.

Per-File Cache Data Structures

Each open handle to a file has a corresponding file object. (File objects are explained in detail in Chapter 8, "I/O System.") If the file is cached, the file object points to a *private cache map* structure that contains the location of the last two reads so that the cache manager can perform intelligent read-ahead (described later, in the section "Intelligent Read-Ahead"). In addition, all the private cache maps for open instances of a file are linked together.

Each cached file (as opposed to file object) has a *shared cache map* structure that describes the state of the cached file, including its size and its valid data length. (The function of the valid data length field is explained in the section "Write-Back Caching and Lazy Writing.") The shared cache map also points to the *section object* (maintained by the memory manager and which describes the file's mapping into virtual memory), the list of private cache maps associated with that file, and any VACBs that describe currently mapped views of the file in the system cache. (See Chapter 10 for more about section object pointers.) The relationships among these per-file cache data structures are illustrated in Figure 11-7.

When asked to read from a particular file, the cache manager must determine the answers to two questions:

1. Is the file in the cache?

2. If so, which VACB, if any, refers to the requested location?

In other words, the cache manager must find out whether a view of the file at the desired address is mapped into the system cache. If no VACB contains the desired file offset, the requested data isn't currently mapped into the system cache.

To keep track of which views for a given file are mapped into the system cache, the cache manager maintains an array of pointers to VACBs, which is known as the *VACB index array*. The first entry in the VACB index array refers to the first 256 KB of the file, the second entry to the second 256 KB, and so on. The diagram in Figure 11-8 shows four different sections from three different files that are currently mapped into the system cache.

When a process accesses a particular file in a given location, the cache manager looks in the appropriate entry in the file's VACB index array to see whether the requested data has been mapped into the cache. If the array entry is nonzero (and hence contains a pointer to a VACB), the area of the file being referenced is in the cache. The VACB, in turn, points to the location in the system cache where the view of the file is mapped. If the entry is zero, the cache manager must find a free slot in the system cache (and therefore a free VACB) to map the required view.

As a size optimization, the shared cache map contains a VACB index array that is four entries in size. Because each VACB describes 256 KB, the entries in this small, fixed-size index array can point to VACB array entries that together describe a file of up to 1 MB. If a file is larger than 1 MB, a separate VACB index array is allocated from nonpaged pool, based on the size of the file divided by 256 KB and rounded up in the case of a remainder. The shared cache map then points to this separate structure.

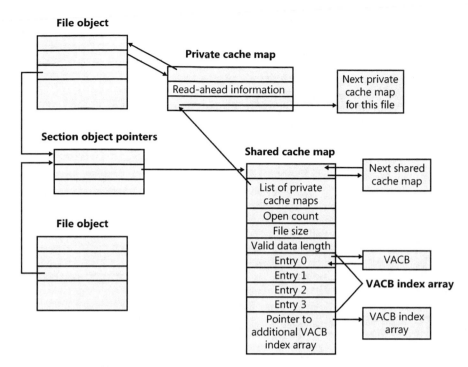

FIGURE 11-7 Per-file cache data structures

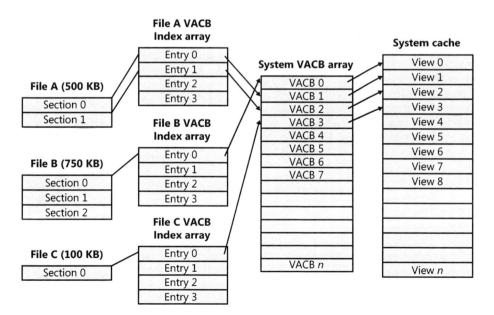

FIGURE 11-8 VACB index arrays

As a further optimization, the VACB index array allocated from nonpaged pool becomes a sparse multilevel index array if the file is larger than 32 MB, where each index array consists of 128 entries. You can calculate the number of levels required for a file with the following formula:

(Number of bits required to represent file size – 18) / 7

Round the result of the equation up to the next whole number. The value 18 in the equation comes from the fact that a VACB represents 256 KB, and 256 KB is 2^18. The value 7 comes from the fact that each level in the array has 128 entries and 2^7 is 128. Thus, a file that has a size that is the maximum that can be described with 63 bits (the largest size the cache manager supports) would require only seven levels. The array is sparse because the only branches that the cache manager allocates are ones for which there are active views at the lowest-level index array. Figure 11-9 shows an example of a multilevel VACB array for a sparse file that is large enough to require three levels.

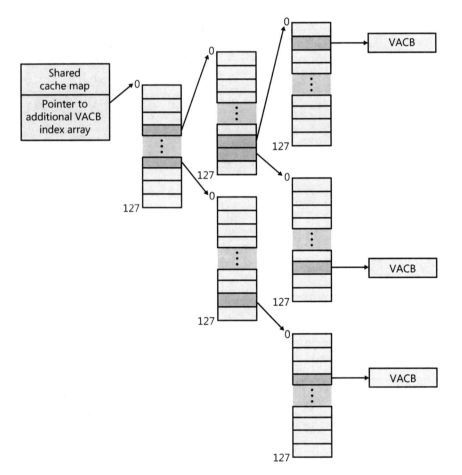

FIGURE 11-9 Multilevel VACB arrays

This scheme is required to efficiently handle sparse files that might have extremely large file sizes with only a small fraction of valid data because only enough of the array is allocated to handle the currently mapped views of a file. For example, a 32-GB sparse file for which only 256 KB is mapped into the cache's virtual address space would require a VACB array with three allocated index arrays because only one branch of the array has a mapping and a 32-GB (235 bytes) file requires a three-level array. If the cache manager didn't use the multilevel VACB index array optimization for this file, it would have to allocate a VACB index array with 128,000 entries, or the equivalent of 1,000 VACB index arrays.

EXPERIMENT: Looking at Shared and Private Cache Maps

You can use the kernel debugger's *dt* command to look at the shared and private cache map data structure definitions and examine the structures on a live system. First, execute the *!filecache* command and locate an entry in the VACB output with a file name you recognize. In this example, the file is the System event log:

```
8742a008  120  160   0    0 System.evtx
```

The first address is that of a control area data structure, which the memory manager uses to keep track of an address range. (See Chapter 10 for more information.) The control area stores the pointer to the file object that corresponds to the view in the cache. A file object identifies an instance of an open file. Execute the following command using the address of the control area of the entry you identified to see the control area structure:

```
lkd> !ca 8742a008
ControlArea  @ 87cd7248
  Segment       824157e0  Flink       00000000  Blink        00000000
  Section Ref          1  Pfn Ref         1117  Mapped Views        3
  User Ref             0  WaitForDel         0  Flush Count         0
  File Object   87bcab60  ModWriteCount      0  System Views        3
  WritableRefs         0
  Flags (c080) File WasPurged Accessed

    \Windows\System32\winevt\Logs\System.evtx
```

. . .

Next look at the file object referenced by the control area with this command:

```
lkd> dt nt!_FILE_OBJECT 87bcab60
   +0x000 Type            : 0n5
   +0x002 Size            : 0n128
   +0x004 DeviceObject    : 0x86a4c4d0 _DEVICE_OBJECT
   +0x008 Vpb             : 0x86a0c270 _VPB
   +0x00c FsContext       : 0x93b2a8e0 Void
   +0x010 FsContext2      : 0x93b2aa38 Void
   +0x014 SectionObjectPointer : 0x87c1b6f0 _SECTION_OBJECT_POINTERS
   +0x018 PrivateCacheMap : 0x87cd59e8 Void
   +0x01c FinalStatus     : 0n0
   +0x020 RelatedFileObject : (null)
   +0x024 LockOperation   : 0 ''
```

. . .

The private cache map is at offset 0x18:

```
lkd> dt nt!_PRIVATE_CACHE_MAP 0x87cd59e8
   +0x000 NodeTypeCode     : 0n766
   +0x000 Flags            : _PRIVATE_CACHE_MAP_FLAGS
   +0x000 UlongFlags       : 0x1402fe
   +0x004 ReadAheadMask    : 0xffff
   +0x008 FileObject       : 0x87bcab60 _FILE_OBJECT
   +0x010 FileOffset1      : _LARGE_INTEGER 0x1000
   +0x018 BeyondLastByte1  : _LARGE_INTEGER 0x1080
   +0x020 FileOffset2      : _LARGE_INTEGER 0x1000
   +0x028 BeyondLastByte2  : _LARGE_INTEGER 0x1080
...
```

Finally, you can locate the shared cache map in the *SectionObjectPointer* field of the file object and then view its contents:

```
lkd> dt nt!_SECTION_OBJECT_POINTERS  0x87c1b6f0
   +0x000 DataSectionObject : 0x87cd7248
   +0x004 SharedCacheMap    : 0x87cd58f8
   +0x008 ImageSectionObject : (null)

lkd> dt nt!_SHARED_CACHE_MAP 0x87cd58f8
   +0x000 NodeTypeCode     : 767
   +0x002 NodeByteSize     : 0n352
   +0x004 OpenCount        : 1
   +0x008 FileSize         : _LARGE_INTEGER 0x1211000
   +0x010 BcbList          : _LIST_ENTRY [ 0x87cd5908   - 0x87cd5908 ]
   +0x018 SectionSize      : _LARGE_INTEGER 0x1300000
   +0x020 ValidDataLength  : _LARGE_INTEGER 0x1116200
   +0x028 ValidDataGoal    : _LARGE_INTEGER 0x1116200
   +0x030 InitialVacbs     : [4] (null)
   +0x040 Vacbs            : 0x87dc3a20   -> 0x85ba9df0 _VACB
   +0x044 FileObjectFastRef : _EX_FAST_REF
   +0x048 VacbLock         : _EX_PUSH_LOCK
...
```

Alternatively, you can use the *!fileobj* command to look up and display much of this information automatically. For example, using this command on the same file object referenced earlier results in the following output:

```
lkd> !fileobj 87bcab60

\Windows\System32\winevt\Logs\System.evtx

Device Object: 0x86a4c4d0   \Driver\volmgr
Vpb: 0x86a0c270
Event signalled
Access: Read Write SharedRead
```

```
Flags:  0xc3042
        Synchronous IO
        Cache Supported
        Modified
        Size Changed
        Handle Created
        Fast IO Read

FsContext: 0x93b2a8e0    FsContext2: 0x93b2aa38
Private Cache Map: 0x87cd59e8
CurrentByteOffset: 1116180
Cache Data:
  Section Object Pointers: 87c1b6f0
  Shared Cache Map: 87cd58f8          File Offset: 1116180 in VACB number 44
  Vacb: 85ba9d90
  Your data is at: 82756180
```

File System Interfaces

The first time a file's data is accessed for a read or write operation, the file system driver is responsible for determining whether some part of the file is mapped in the system cache. If it's not, the file system driver must call the *CcInitializeCacheMap* function to set up the per-file data structures described in the preceding section.

Once a file is set up for cached access, the file system driver calls one of several functions to access the data in the file. There are three primary methods for accessing cached data, each intended for a specific situation:

- The copy method copies user data between cache buffers in system space and a process buffer in user space.

- The mapping and pinning method uses virtual addresses to read and write data directly from and to cache buffers.

- The physical memory access method uses physical addresses to read and write data directly from and to cache buffers.

File system drivers must provide two versions of the file read operation—cached and noncached—to prevent an infinite loop when the memory manager processes a page fault. When the memory manager resolves a page fault by calling the file system to retrieve data from the file (via the device driver, of course), it must specify this noncached read operation by setting the "no cache" flag in the IRP.

Figure 11-10 illustrates the typical interactions between the cache manager, the memory manager, and file system drivers in response to user read or write file I/O. The cache manager is invoked by a file system through the copy interfaces (the *CcCopyRead* and *CcCopyWrite* paths). To process a *CcFastCopyRead* or *CcCopyRead* read, for example, the cache manager creates a view in the cache to map a portion of the file being read and reads the file data into the user buffer by copying from the view. The copy operation generates page faults as it accesses each previously invalid page in the view, and in response the memory manager initiates noncached I/O into the file system driver to retrieve the data corresponding to the part of the file mapped to the page that faulted.

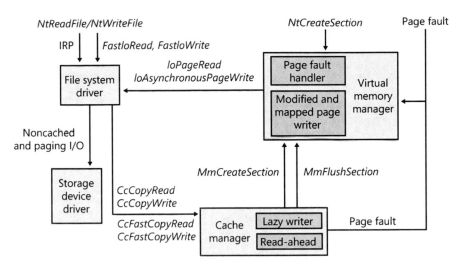

FIGURE 11-10 File system interaction with cache and memory managers

The next three sections explain these cache access mechanisms, their purpose, and how they're used.

Copying to and from the Cache

Because the system cache is in system space, it is mapped into the address space of every process. As with all system space pages, however, cache pages aren't accessible from user mode because that would be a potential security hole. (For example, a process might not have the rights to read a file whose data is currently contained in some part of the system cache.) Thus, user application file reads and writes to cached files must be serviced by kernel-mode routines that copy data between the cache's buffers in system space and the application's buffers residing in the process address space.

Caching with the Mapping and Pinning Interfaces

Just as user applications read and write data in files on a disk, file system drivers need to read and write the data that describes the files themselves (the metadata, or volume structure data). Because the file system drivers run in kernel mode, however, they could, if the cache manager were properly informed, modify data directly in the system cache. To permit this optimization, the cache manager provides functions that permit the file system drivers to find where in virtual memory the file system metadata resides, thus allowing direct modification without the use of intermediary buffers.

If a file system driver needs to read file system metadata in the cache, it calls the cache manager's mapping interface to obtain the virtual address of the desired data. The cache manager touches all the requested pages to bring them into memory and then returns control to the file system driver. The file system driver can then access the data directly.

If the file system driver needs to modify cache pages, it calls the cache manager's pinning services, which keep the pages active in virtual memory so that they cannot be reclaimed. The pages aren't actually locked into memory (such as when a device driver locks pages for direct memory access transfers). Most of the time, a file system driver will mark its metadata stream "no write", which instructs the memory manager's mapped page writer (explained in Chapter 10) to not write the pages to disk until explicitly told to do so. When the file system driver unpins (releases) them, the cache manager releases its resources so that it can lazily flush any changes to disk and release the cache view that the metadata occupied.

The mapping and pinning interfaces solve one thorny problem of implementing a file system: buffer management. Without directly manipulating cached metadata, a file system must predict the maximum number of buffers it will need when updating a volume's structure. By allowing the file system to access and update its metadata directly in the cache, the cache manager eliminates the need for buffers, simply updating the volume structure in the virtual memory the memory manager provides. The only limitation the file system encounters is the amount of available memory.

Caching with the Direct Memory Access Interfaces

In addition to the mapping and pinning interfaces used to access metadata directly in the cache, the cache manager provides a third interface to cached data: *direct memory access* (DMA). The DMA functions are used to read from or write to cache pages without intervening buffers, such as when a network file system is doing a transfer over the network.

The DMA interface returns to the file system the physical addresses of cached user data (rather than the virtual addresses, which the mapping and pinning interfaces return), which can then be used to transfer data directly from physical memory to a network device. Although small amounts of data (1 KB to 2 KB) can use the usual buffer-based copying interfaces, for larger transfers the DMA interface can result in significant performance improvements for a network server processing file requests from remote systems. To describe these references to physical memory, a *memory descriptor list* (MDL) is used. (MDLs are introduced in Chapter 10.)

Fast I/O

Whenever possible, reads and writes to cached files are handled by a high-speed mechanism named *fast I/O*. Fast I/O is a means of reading or writing a cached file without going through the work of generating an IRP, as described in Chapter 8. With fast I/O, the I/O manager calls the file system driver's fast I/O routine to see whether I/O can be satisfied directly from the cache manager without generating an IRP.

Because the cache manager is architected on top of the virtual memory subsystem, file system drivers can use the cache manager to access file data simply by copying to or from pages mapped to the actual file being referenced without going through the overhead of generating an IRP.

Fast I/O doesn't always occur. For example, the first read or write to a file requires setting up the file for caching (mapping the file into the cache and setting up the cache data structures, as explained earlier in the section "Cache Data Structures"). Also, if the caller specified an asynchronous read or write, fast I/O isn't used because the caller might be stalled during paging I/O operations required to satisfy the buffer copy to or from the system cache and thus not really providing the requested asynchronous I/O operation. But even on a synchronous I/O, the file system driver might decide that it can't process the I/O operation by using the fast I/O mechanism, say, for example, if the file in question has a locked range of bytes (as a result of calls to the Windows *LockFile* and *UnlockFile* functions). Because the cache manager doesn't know what parts of which files are locked, the file system driver must check the validity of the read or write, which requires generating an IRP. The decision tree for fast I/O is shown in Figure 11-11.

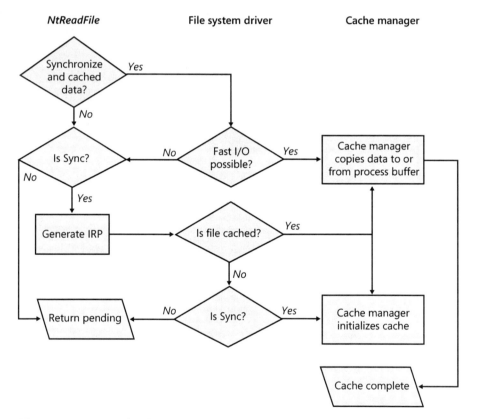

FIGURE 11-11 Fast I/O decision tree

These steps are involved in servicing a read or a write with fast I/O:

1. A thread performs a read or write operation.

2. If the file is cached and the I/O is synchronous, the request passes to the fast I/O entry point of the file system driver stack. If the file isn't cached, the file system driver sets up the file for caching so that the next time, fast I/O can be used to satisfy a read or write request.

3. If the file system driver's fast I/O routine determines that fast I/O is possible, it calls the cache manager's read or write routine to access the file data directly in the cache. (If fast I/O isn't possible, the file system driver returns to the I/O system, which then generates an IRP for the I/O and eventually calls the file system's regular read routine.)

4. The cache manager translates the supplied file offset into a virtual address in the cache.

5. For reads, the cache manager copies the data from the cache into the buffer of the process requesting it; for writes, it copies the data from the buffer to the cache.

6. One of the following actions occurs:

   • For reads where FILE_FLAG_RANDOM_ACCESS wasn't specified when the file was opened, the read-ahead information in the caller's private cache map is updated. Read-ahead may also be queued for files for which the FO_RANDOM_ACCESS flag is not specified.

   • For writes, the dirty bit of any modified page in the cache is set so that the lazy writer will know to flush it to disk.

   • For write-through files, any modifications are flushed to disk.

Read-Ahead and Write-Behind

In this section, you'll see how the cache manager implements reading and writing file data on behalf of file system drivers. Keep in mind that the cache manager is involved in file I/O only when a file is opened without the FILE_FLAG_NO_BUFFERING flag and then read from or written to using the Windows I/O functions (for example, using the Windows *ReadFile* and *WriteFile* functions). Mapped files don't go through the cache manager, nor do files opened with the FILE_FLAG_NO_BUFFERING flag set.

Note When an application uses the FILE_FLAG_NO_BUFFERING flag to open a file, its file I/O must start at device-aligned offsets and be of sizes that are a multiple of the alignment size; its input and output buffers must also be device-aligned virtual addresses. For file systems, this usually corresponds to the sector size (512 bytes on NTFS, typically, and 2,048 bytes on CDFS). One of the benefits of the cache manager, apart from the actual caching performance, is the fact that it performs intermediate buffering to allow arbitrarily aligned and sized I/O.

Intelligent Read-Ahead

The cache manager uses the principle of spatial locality to perform *intelligent read-ahead* by predicting what data the calling process is likely to read next based on the data that it is reading currently. Because the system cache is based on virtual addresses, which are contiguous for a particular file, it doesn't matter whether they're juxtaposed in physical memory. File read-ahead for logical block caching is more complex and requires tight cooperation between file system drivers and the block cache because that cache system is based on the relative positions of the accessed data on the disk, and, of course, files aren't necessarily stored contiguously on disk. You can examine read-ahead activity by using the Cache: Read Aheads/sec performance counter or the *CcReadAheadIos* system variable.

Reading the next block of a file that is being accessed sequentially provides an obvious performance improvement, with the disadvantage that it will cause head seeks. To extend read-ahead benefits to cases of strided data accesses (both forward and backward through a file), the cache manager maintains a history of the last two read requests in the private cache map for the file handle being accessed, a method known as *asynchronous read-ahead with history*. If a pattern can be determined from the caller's apparently random reads, the cache manager extrapolates it. For example, if the caller reads page 4000 and then page 3000, the cache manager assumes that the next page the caller will require is page 2000 and prereads it.

> **Note** Although a caller must issue a minimum of three read operations to establish a predictable sequence, only two are stored in the private cache map.

To make read-ahead even more efficient, the Win32 *CreateFile* function provides a flag indicating forward sequential file access: FILE_FLAG_SEQUENTIAL_SCAN. If this flag is set, the cache manager doesn't keep a read history for the caller for prediction but instead performs sequential read-ahead. However, as the file is read into the cache's working set, the cache manager unmaps views of the file that are no longer active and, if they are unmodified, directs the memory manager to place the pages belonging to the unmapped views at the front of the standby list so that they will be quickly reused. It also reads ahead two times as much data (2 MB instead of 1 MB, for example). As the caller continues reading, the cache manager prereads additional blocks of data, always staying about one read (of the size of the current read) ahead of the caller.

The cache manager's read-ahead is asynchronous because it is performed in a thread separate from the caller's thread and proceeds concurrently with the caller's execution. When called to retrieve cached data, the cache manager first accesses the requested virtual page to satisfy the request and then queues an additional I/O request to retrieve additional data to a system worker thread. The worker thread then executes in the background, reading additional data in anticipation of the caller's next read request. The preread pages are faulted into memory while the program continues executing so that when the caller requests the data it's already in memory.

For applications that have no predictable read pattern, the FILE_FLAG_RANDOM_ACCESS flag can be specified when the *CreateFile* function is called. This flag instructs the cache manager not to attempt to predict where the application is reading next and thus disables read-ahead. The flag also stops the cache manager from aggressively unmapping views of the file as the file is accessed so as to minimize the mapping/unmapping activity for the file when the application revisits portions of the file.

Write-Back Caching and Lazy Writing

The cache manager implements a write-back cache with lazy write. This means that data written to files is first stored in memory in cache pages and then written to disk later. Thus, write operations are allowed to accumulate for a short time and are then flushed to disk all at once, reducing the overall number of disk I/O operations.

The cache manager must explicitly call the memory manager to flush cache pages because otherwise the memory manager writes memory contents to disk only when demand for physical memory exceeds supply, as is appropriate for volatile data. Cached file data, however, represents nonvolatile disk data. If a process modifies cached data, the user expects the contents to be reflected on disk in a timely manner.

Additionally, the cache manager has the ability to veto the memory manager's mapped writer thread. Since the modified list (see Chapter 10 for more information) is not sorted in logical block address (LBA) order, the cache manager's attempts to cluster pages for larger sequential I/Os to the disk are not always successful and actually cause repeated seeks. To combat this effect, the cache manager has the ability to aggressively veto the mapped writer thread and stream out writes in virtual byte offset (VBO) order, which is much closer to the LBA order on disk. Since the cache manager now owns these writes, it can also apply its own scheduling and throttling algorithms to prefer read-ahead over write-behind and impact the system less.

The decision about how often to flush the cache is an important one. If the cache is flushed too frequently, system performance will be slowed by unnecessary I/O. If the cache is flushed too rarely, you risk losing modified file data in the cases of a system failure (a loss especially irritating to users who know that they asked the application to save the changes) and running out of physical memory (because it's being used by an excess of modified pages).

To balance these concerns, once per second the cache manager's *lazy writer* function executes on a system worker thread and queues one-eighth of the dirty pages in the system cache to be written to disk. If the rate at which dirty pages are being produced is greater than the amount the lazy writer had determined it should write, the lazy writer writes an additional number of dirty pages that it calculates are necessary to match that rate. System worker threads from the systemwide critical worker thread pool actually perform the I/O operations. The lazy writer is also aware of when the memory manager's mapped page writer is already performing a flush. In these cases, it delays its write-back capabilities to the same stream to avoid a situation where two flushers are writing to the same file.

Note The cache manager provides a means for file system drivers to track when and how much data has been written to a file. After the lazy writer flushes dirty pages to the disk, the cache manager notifies the file system, instructing it to update its view of the valid data length for the file. (The cache manager and file systems separately track in memory the valid data length for a file.)

EXPERIMENT: Watching the Cache Manager in Action

In this experiment, we'll use Process Monitor to view the underlying file system activity, including cache manager read-ahead and write-behind, when Windows Explorer copies a large file (in this example, a CD-ROM image) from one local directory to another.

First, configure Process Monitor's filter to include the source and destination file paths, the Explorer.exe and System processes, and the ReadFile and WriteFile operations. In this example, the C:\Users\Administrator\Downloads\dump.dmp file was copied to C:\dump.dmp, so the filter is configured as follows:

Column	Relation	Value	Action
☑ Process Name	is	explorer.exe	Include
☑ Process Name	is	System	Include
☑ Operation	is	ReadFile	Include
☑ Operation	is	WriteFile	Include
☑ Path	is	C:\Users\Administrator\Downloads\dump.dmp	Include
☑ Path	is	c:\dump.dmp	Include

You should see a Process Monitor trace like the one shown here after you copy the file:

The first few entries show the initial I/O processing performed by the copy engine and the first cache manager operations. Here are some of the things that you can see:

- The initial 1-MB cached read from Explorer at the first entry. The size of this read depends on an internal matrix calculation based on the file size and can vary from 128 KB to 1 MB. Because this file was large, the copy engine chose 1 MB.

- The 1-MB read is followed by another 1-MB noncached read. Noncached reads typically indicate activity due to page faults or cache manager access. A closer look at the stack trace for these events, which you can see by double-clicking an entry and choosing the Stack tab, reveals that indeed the *CcCopyRead* cache manager routine, which is called by the NTFS driver's read routine, causes the memory manager to fault the source data into physical memory:

- After this 1-MB page fault I/O, the cache manager's read-ahead mechanism starts reading the file, which includes the System process's subsequent noncached 1-MB read at the 1-MB offset. Because of the file size and Explorer's read I/O sizes, the cache manager chose 1 MB as the optimal read-ahead size. The stack trace for one of the read-ahead operations, shown next, confirms that one of the cache manager's worker threads is performing the read-ahead.

After this point, Explorer's 1-MB reads aren't followed by page faults, because the read-ahead thread stays ahead of Explorer, prefetching the file data with its 1-MB noncached reads. However, every once in a while, the read-ahead thread is not able to pick up enough data in time, and clustered page faults do occur, which appear as Synchronous Paging I/O.

If you look at the stack for these entries, you'll see that instead of *MmPrefetchForCache-Manager*, the *MmAccessFault/MiIssueHardFault* routines are called.

Frame	Module	Location	Address	Path
K 0	fltmgr.sys	FltRequestOperationStatusCallback + 0xeb5	0x81fc6aeb	C:\\
K 1	fltmgr.sys	FltGetIrpName + 0xc5c	0x81fc99f0	C:\\
K 2	fltmgr.sys	FltGetIrpName + 0x116d	0x81fc9f01	C:\\
K 3	fltmgr.sys	FltGetIrpName + 0x1626	0x81fca3ba	C:\\
K 4	ntkmlpa.exe	IofCallDriver + 0x63	0x8184b5be	C:\\
K 5	ntkmlpa.exe	IoPageRead + 0x1f5	0x818d8a1e	C:\\
K 6	ntkmlpa.exe	MiIssueHardFault + 0x28c	0x818bb5d0	C:\\
K 7	ntkmlpa.exe	MmAccessFault + 0x2656	0x818a495b	C:\\
K 8	ntkmlpa.exe	MmCheckCachedPageStates + 0x3f0	0x81870de1	C:\\
K 9	ntkmlpa.exe	CcFetchDataForRead + 0xb6	0x818c9717	C:\\
K 10	ntkmlpa.exe	CcMapAndCopyFromCache + 0x70	0x81a7cd23	C:\\
K 11	ntkmlpa.exe	CcPerformReadAhead + 0x24b	0x8184a2af	C:\\
K 12	ntkmlpa.exe	CcWorkerThread + 0x18d	0x818ae33d	C:\\
K 13	ntkmlpa.exe	ExpWorkerThread + 0x10d	0x81891aab	C:\\
K 14	ntkmlpa.exe	PspSystemThreadStartup + 0x9e	0x81a1d022	C:\\

As soon as it starts reading, Explorer also starts performing writes to the destination file. These are sequential, cached 64-KB writes. After about 132 MB of reads, the first *WriteFile* operation from the System process occurs, shown here:

Process Name	Operation	Path	Result	Detail
Explorer.EXE	WriteFile	C:\dump.dmp	SUCCESS	Offset: 132,907,008, Length: 65,536
Explorer.EXE	WriteFile	C:\dump.dmp	SUCCESS	Offset: 132,972,544, Length: 65,536
Explorer.EXE	WriteFile	C:\dump.dmp	SUCCESS	Offset: 133,038,080, Length: 65,536
Explorer.EXE	WriteFile	C:\dump.dmp	SUCCESS	Offset: 133,103,616, Length: 65,536
Explorer.EXE	ReadFile	C:\Users\Admi...	SUCCESS	Offset: 133,169,152, Length: 1,048,576
Explorer.EXE	ReadFile	C:\Users\Admi...	SUCCESS	Offset: 133,169,152, Length: 1,048,576, I/O Flags: Non-cached, Paging I/O, Pri...
System	WriteFile	C:\dump.dmp	SUCCESS	Offset: 0, Length: 2,097,152, I/O Flags: Non-cached, Paging I/O, Priority: Normal
Explorer.EXE	WriteFile	C:\dump.dmp	SUCCESS	Offset: 133,169,152, Length: 65,536
Explorer.EXE	WriteFile	C:\dump.dmp	SUCCESS	Offset: 133,234,688, Length: 65,536
Explorer.EXE	WriteFile	C:\dump.dmp	SUCCESS	Offset: 133,300,224, Length: 65,536
Explorer.EXE	WriteFile	C:\dump.dmp	SUCCESS	Offset: 133,365,760, Length: 65,536
Explorer.EXE	WriteFile	C:\dump.dmp	SUCCESS	Offset: 133,431,296, Length: 65,536
Explorer.EXE	WriteFile	C:\dump.dmp	SUCCESS	Offset: 133,496,832, Length: 65,536

Showing 19,226 of 106,847 events (17%)   Backed by virtual memory

The write operation's stack trace, shown here, indicates that the memory manager's *mapped page writer* thread was actually responsible for the write:

This occurs because for the first couple of megabytes of data, the cache manager hadn't started performing write-behind, so the memory manager's mapped page writer began flushing the modified destination file data. (See Chapter 10 for more information on the mapped page writer.)

To get a clearer view of the cache manager operations, remove Explorer from the Process Monitor's filter so that only the System process operations are visible, as shown next.

With this view, it's much easier to see the cache manager's 1-MB write-behind operations (the maximum write sizes are 1 MB on client versions of Windows and 32 MB on server versions; this experiment was performed on a client system). The stack trace for one of the write-behind operations, shown here, verifies that a cache manager worker thread is performing write-behind:

Frame	Module	Location	Address
K 0	fltmgr.sys	FltRequestOperationStatusCallback + 0xeb5	0x81fc6aeb
K 1	fltmgr.sys	FltGetIrpName + 0xc5c	0x81fc99f0
K 2	fltmgr.sys	FltGetIrpName + 0x116d	0x81fc9f01
K 3	fltmgr.sys	FltGetIrpName + 0x1626	0x81fca3ba
K 4	ntkmlpa.exe	IofCallDriver + 0x63	0x8184b5be
K 5	ntkmlpa.exe	IoSynchronousPageWrite + 0x19d	0x818adedf
K 6	ntkmlpa.exe	MiFlushSectionInternal + 0x81f	0x8189a8d3
K 7	ntkmlpa.exe	MmFlushSection + 0x78	0x818c7e77
K 8	ntkmlpa.exe	CcFlushCache + 0x329	0x8189c8e1
K 9	ntkmlpa.exe	CcWriteBehind + 0x105	0x8189f94e
K 10	ntkmlpa.exe	CcWorkerThread + 0x164	0x818ae314
K 11	ntkmlpa.exe	ExpWorkerThread + 0x10d	0x81891aab
K 12	ntkmlpa.exe	PspSystemThreadStartup + 0x9e	0x81a1d022

As an added experiment, try repeating this process with a remote copy instead (from one Windows system to another) and by copying files of varying sizes. You'll notice some different behaviors by the copy engine and the cache manager, both on the receiving and sending sides.

Disabling Lazy Writing for a File

If you create a temporary file by specifying the flag FILE_ATTRIBUTE_TEMPORARY in a call to the Windows *CreateFile* function, the lazy writer won't write dirty pages to the disk unless there is a severe shortage of physical memory or the file is explicitly flushed. This characteristic of the lazy writer improves system performance—the lazy writer doesn't immediately write data to a disk that might ultimately be discarded. Applications usually delete temporary files soon after closing them.

Forcing the Cache to Write Through to Disk

Because some applications can't tolerate even momentary delays between writing a file and seeing the updates on disk, the cache manager also supports write-through caching on a per–file object basis; changes are written to disk as soon as they're made. To turn on write-through caching, set the FILE_FLAG_WRITE_THROUGH flag in the call to the *CreateFile* function. Alternatively, a thread can explicitly flush an open file, by using the Windows *FlushFileBuffers* function, when it reaches a point at which the data needs to be written to disk.

Flushing Mapped Files

If the lazy writer must write data to disk from a view that's also mapped into another process's address space, the situation becomes a little more complicated, because the cache manager will only know about the pages it has modified. (Pages modified by another process are known only to that process because the modified bit in the page table entries for modified pages is kept in the process private page tables.) To address this situation, the memory manager informs the cache manager when a user maps a file. When such a file is flushed in the cache (for example, as a result of a call to the Windows *FlushFileBuffers* function), the cache manager writes the dirty pages in the cache and then checks to see whether the file is also mapped by another process. When the cache manager sees that the file is, the cache manager then flushes the entire view of the section to write out pages that the second process might have modified. If a user maps a view of a file that is also open in the cache, when the view is unmapped, the modified pages are marked as dirty so that when the lazy writer thread later flushes the view, those dirty pages will be written to disk. This procedure works as long as the sequence occurs in the following order:

1. A user unmaps the view.

2. A process flushes file buffers.

If this sequence isn't followed, you can't predict which pages will be written to disk.

EXPERIMENT: Watching Cache Flushes

You can see the cache manager map views into the system cache and flush pages to disk by running the Performance Monitor and adding the Data Maps/sec and Lazy Write Flushes/sec counters and then copying a large file from one location to another. The generally higher line in the following screen shot shows Data Maps/sec and the other shows Lazy Write Flushes/sec. During the file copy, Lazy Write Flushes/sec significantly increased.

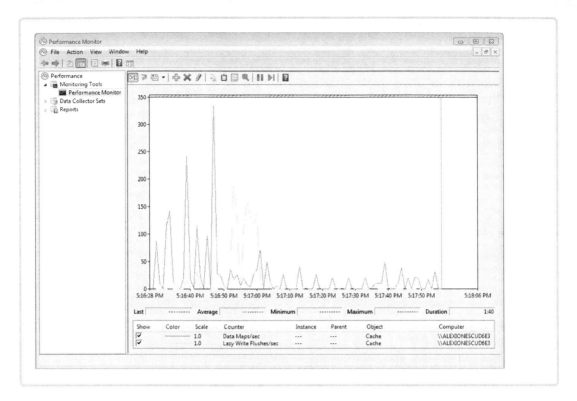

Write Throttling

The file system and cache manager must determine whether a cached write request will affect system performance and then schedule any delayed writes. First the file system asks the cache manager whether a certain number of bytes can be written right now without hurting performance by using the *CcCanIWrite* function and blocking that write if necessary. For asynchronous I/O, the file system sets up a callback with the cache manager for automatically writing the bytes when writes are again permitted by calling *CcDeferWrite*. Otherwise, it just blocks and waits on *CcCanIWrite* to continue. Once it's notified of an impending write operation, the cache manager determines how many dirty pages are in the cache and how much physical memory is available. If few physical pages are free, the cache manager momentarily blocks the file system thread that's requesting to write data to the cache. The cache manager's lazy writer flushes some of the dirty pages to disk and then allows the blocked file system thread to continue. This *write throttling* prevents system performance from degrading because of a lack of memory when a file system or network server issues a large write operation.

> **Note** The effects of write throttling are volume-aware, such that if a user is copying a large file on, say, a RAID-0 SSD while also transferring a document to a portable USB thumb drive, writes to the USB disk will not cause write throttling to occur on the SSD transfer.

The *dirty page threshold* is the number of pages that the system cache will allow to be dirty before throttling cached writers. This value is computed at system initialization time and depends on the product type (client or server). Two other values are also computed—the *top* dirty page threshold and the *bottom* dirty page threshold. Depending on memory consumption and the rate at which dirty pages are being processed, the lazy writer calls the internal function *CcAdjustThrottle*, which, on server systems, performs dynamic adjustment of the current threshold based on the calculated top and bottom values. This adjustment is made to preserve the read cache in cases of a heavy write load that will inevitably overrun the cache and become throttled. Table 11-1 lists the algorithms used to calculate the dirty page thresholds.

TABLE 11-1 Algorithms for Calculating the Dirty Page Thresholds

Product Type	Dirty Page Threshold	Top Dirty Page Threshold	Bottom Dirty Page Threshold
Client	Physical pages / 8	Physical pages / 8	Physical pages / 8
Server	Physical pages / 2	Physical pages / 2	Physical pages / 8

Write throttling is also useful for network redirectors transmitting data over slow communication lines. For example, suppose a local process writes a large amount of data to a remote file system over a 9600-baud line. The data isn't written to the remote disk until the cache manager's lazy writer flushes the cache. If the redirector has accumulated lots of dirty pages that are flushed to disk at once, the recipient could receive a network timeout before the data transfer completes. By using the *CcSetDirtyPageThreshold* function, the cache manager allows network redirectors to set a limit on the number of dirty cache pages they can tolerate (for each stream), thus preventing this scenario. By limiting the number of dirty pages, the redirector ensures that a cache flush operation won't cause a network timeout.

EXPERIMENT: Viewing the Write-Throttle Parameters

The *!defwrites* kernel debugger command dumps the values of the kernel variables the cache manager uses, including the number of dirty pages in the file cache (*CcTotalDirtyPages*), when determining whether it should throttle write operations:

```
lkd>
!defwrites
*** Cache Write Throttle Analysis ***

        CcTotalDirtyPages:              39 (     156 Kb)
        CcDirtyPageThreshold:        32753 (  131012 Kb)
        MmAvailablePages:            81569 (  326276 Kb)
        MmThrottleTop:                 450 (    1800 Kb)
        MmThrottleBottom:               80 (     320 Kb)
        MmModifiedPageListHead.Total:  4337 (   17348 Kb)


Write throttles not engaged
```

This output shows that the number of dirty pages is far from the number that triggers write throttling (*CcDirtyPageThreshold*), so the system has not engaged in any write throttling.

System Threads

As mentioned earlier, the cache manager performs lazy write and read-ahead I/O operations by submitting requests to the common critical system worker thread pool. However, it does limit the use of these threads to one less than the total number of critical system worker threads for small and medium memory systems (two less than the total for large memory systems).

Internally, the cache manager organizes its work requests into four lists (though these are serviced by the same set of executive worker threads):

- The express queue is used for read-ahead operations.

- The regular queue is used for lazy write scans (for dirty data to flush), write-behinds, and lazy closes.

- The fast teardown queue is used when the memory manager is waiting for the data section owned by the cache manager to be freed so that the file can be opened with an image section instead, which causes *CcWriteBehind* to flush the entire file and tear down the shared cache map.

- The post tick queue is used for the cache manager to internally register for a notification after each "tick" of the lazy writer thread—in other words, at the end of each pass.

To keep track of the work items the worker threads need to perform, the cache manager creates its own internal *per-processor look-aside list*, a fixed-length list—one for each processor—of worker queue item structures. (Look-aside lists are discussed in Chapter 10.) The number of worker queue items depends on system size: 32 for small-memory systems, 64 for medium-memory systems, 128 for large-memory client systems, and 256 for large-memory server systems. For cross-processor performance, the cache manager also allocates a *global look-aside list* at the same sizes as just described.

Conclusion

The cache manager provides a high-speed, intelligent mechanism for reducing disk I/O and increasing overall system throughput. By caching on the basis of virtual blocks, the cache manager can perform intelligent read-ahead. By relying on the global memory manager's mapped file primitive to access file data, the cache manager can provide the special fast I/O mechanism to reduce the CPU time required for read and write operations and also leave all matters related to physical memory management to the single Windows global memory manager, thus reducing code duplication and increasing efficiency.

CHAPTER 12

File Systems

In this chapter, we present an overview of the file system formats supported by Windows. We then describe the types of file system drivers and their basic operation, including how they interact with other system components, such as the memory manager and the cache manager. Following that is a description of how to use Process Monitor from Windows Sysinternals (at *http://www.microsoft.com/technet/sysinternals*) to troubleshoot a wide variety of file system access problems.

In the balance of the chapter, we first describe the Common Log File System (CLFS), a transactional logging virtual file system implemented on the native Windows file system format, NTFS. Then we focus on the on-disk layout of NTFS and its advanced features, such as compression, recoverability, quotas, symbolic links, transactions (which use the services provided by CLFS), and encryption.

To fully understand this chapter, you should be familiar with the terminology introduced in Chapter 9, "Storage Management," including the terms *volume* and *partition*. You'll also need to be acquainted with these additional terms:

- *Sectors* are hardware-addressable blocks on a storage medium. Hard disks usually define a 512-byte sector size, but they are moving to 4,096-byte sectors. (See Chapter 9.) Thus, if the sector size is 512 bytes and the operating system wants to modify the 632nd byte on a disk, it must write a 512-byte block of data to the second sector on the disk.

- *File system formats* define the way that file data is stored on storage media, and they affect a file system's features. For example, a format that doesn't allow user permissions to be associated with files and directories can't support security. A file system format can also impose limits on the sizes of files and storage devices that the file system supports. Finally, some file system formats efficiently implement support for either large or small files or for large or small disks. NTFS and exFAT are examples of file system formats that offer a different set of features and usage scenarios.

- *Clusters* are the addressable blocks that many file system formats use. Cluster size is always a multiple of the sector size, as shown in Figure 12-1. File system formats use clusters to manage disk space more efficiently; a cluster size that is larger than the sector size divides a disk into more manageable blocks. The potential trade-off of a larger cluster size is wasted disk space, or internal fragmentation, that results when file sizes aren't exact multiples of the cluster size.

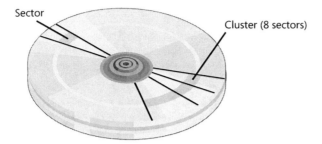

FIGURE 12-1 Sectors and a cluster on a disk

- *Metadata* is data stored on a volume in support of file system format management. It isn't typically made accessible to applications. Metadata includes the data that defines the placement of files and directories on a volume, for example.

Windows File System Formats

Windows includes support for the following file system formats:

- CDFS
- UDF
- FAT12, FAT16, and FAT32
- exFAT
- NTFS

Each of these formats is best suited for certain environments, as you'll see in the following sections.

CDFS

CDFS (%SystemRoot%\System32\Drivers\Cdfs.sys), or CD-ROM file system, is a read-only file system driver that supports a superset of the ISO-9660 format as well as a superset of the Joliet disk format. While the ISO-9660 format is relatively simple and has limitations such as ASCII uppercase names with a maximum length of 32 characters, Joliet is more flexible and supports Unicode names of arbitrary length. If structures for both formats are present on a disk (to offer maximum compatibility), CDFS uses the Joliet format. CDFS has a couple of restrictions:

- A maximum file size of 4 GB
- A maximum of 65,535 directories

CDFS is considered a legacy format because the industry has adopted the Universal Disk Format (UDF) as the standard for optical media.

UDF

The Windows UDF file system implementation is OSTA (Optical Storage Technology Association) UDF-compliant. (UDF is a subset of the ISO-13346 format with extensions for formats such as CD-R and DVD-R/RW.) OSTA defined UDF in 1995 as a format to replace the ISO-9660 format for magneto-optical storage media, mainly DVD-ROM. UDF is included in the DVD specification and is more flexible than CDFS. The UDF file system format has the following traits:

- Directory and file names can be 254 ASCII or 127 Unicode characters long.

- Files can be sparse. (Sparse files are defined later in this chapter.)

- File sizes are specified with 64 bits.

- Support for access control lists (ACLs).

- Support for alternate data streams.

The UDF driver supports UDF versions up to 2.60. The UDF format was designed with rewritable media in mind. The Windows UDF driver (%SystemRoot%\System32\Drivers\Udfs.sys) provides read-write support for Blu-ray, DVD-RAM, CD-R/RW, and DVD+-R/RW drives when using UDF 2.50 and read-only support when using UDF 2.60. However, Windows does not implement support for certain UDF features such as named streams and access control lists.

FAT12, FAT16, and FAT32

Windows supports the FAT file system primarily for compatibility with other operating systems in multiboot systems, and as a format for flash drives or memory cards. The Windows FAT file system driver is implemented in %SystemRoot%\System32\Drivers\Fastfat.sys.

The name of each FAT format includes a number that indicates the number of bits that the particular format uses to identify clusters on a disk. FAT12's 12-bit cluster identifier limits a partition to storing a maximum of 2^{12} (4,096) clusters. Windows permits cluster sizes from 512 bytes to 8 KB, which limits a FAT12 volume size to 32 MB.

> **Note** All FAT file system types reserve the first two clusters and the last 16 clusters of a volume, so the number of usable clusters for a FAT12 volume, for instance, is slightly less than 4,096.

FAT16, with a 16-bit cluster identifier, can address 2^{16} (65,536) clusters. On Windows, FAT16 cluster sizes range from 512 bytes (the sector size) to 64 KB (on disks with a 512-byte sector size), which limits FAT16 volume sizes to 4 GB. Disks with a sector size of 4,096 bytes allow for clusters of 256 KB. The cluster size Windows uses depends on the size of a volume. The various sizes are listed in Table 12-1. If you format a volume that is less than 16 MB as FAT by using the *format* command or the Disk Management snap-in, Windows uses the FAT12 format instead of FAT16.

TABLE 12-1 Default FAT16 Cluster Sizes in Windows

Volume Size	Default Cluster Size
<8 MB	Not supported
8 MB–32 MB	512 bytes
32 MB–64 MB	1 KB
64 MB–128 MB	2 KB
128 MB–256 MB	4 KB
256 MB–512 MB	8 KB
512 MB–1,024 MB	16 KB
1 GB–2 GB	32 KB
2 GB–4 GB	64 KB
>16 GB	Not supported

A FAT volume is divided into several regions, which are shown in Figure 12-2. The file allocation table, which gives the FAT file system format its name, has one entry for each cluster on a volume. Because the file allocation table is critical to the successful interpretation of a volume's contents, the FAT format maintains two copies of the table so that if a file system driver or consistency-checking program (such as Chkdsk) can't access one (because of a bad disk sector, for example), it can read from the other.

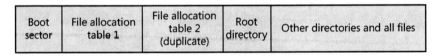

FIGURE 12-2 FAT format organization

Entries in the file allocation table define file-allocation chains (shown in Figure 12-3) for files and directories, where the links in the chain are indexes to the next cluster of a file's data. A file's directory entry stores the starting cluster of the file. The last entry of the file's allocation chain is the reserved value of 0xFFFF for FAT16 and 0xFFF for FAT12. The FAT entries for unused clusters have a value of 0. You can see in Figure 12-3 that FILE1 is assigned clusters 2, 3, and 4; FILE2 is fragmented and uses clusters 5, 6, and 8; and FILE3 uses only cluster 7. Reading a file from a FAT volume can involve reading large portions of a file allocation table to traverse the file's allocation chains.

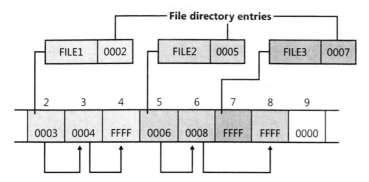

FIGURE 12-3 Sample FAT file-allocation chains

The root directory of FAT12 and FAT16 volumes is preassigned enough space at the start of a volume to store 256 directory entries, which places an upper limit on the number of files and directories that can be stored in the root directory. (There's no preassigned space or size limit on FAT32 root directories.) A FAT directory entry is 32 bytes and stores a file's name, size, starting cluster, and time stamp (last-accessed, created, and so on) information. If a file has a name that is Unicode or that doesn't follow the MS-DOS 8.3 naming convention, additional directory entries are allocated to store the long file name. The supplementary entries precede the file's main entry. Figure 12-4 shows a sample directory entry for a file named "The quick brown fox." The system has created a THEQUI~1.FOX 8.3 representation of the name (that is, you don't see a "." in the directory entry because it is assumed to come after the eighth character) and used two more directory entries to store the Unicode long file name. Each row in the figure is made up of 16 bytes.

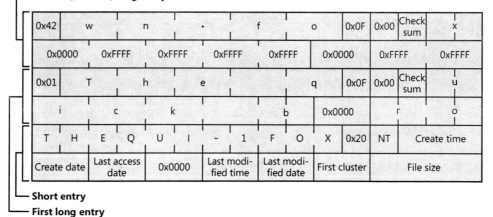

FIGURE 12-4 FAT directory entry

FAT32 uses 32-bit cluster identifiers but reserves the high 4 bits, so in effect it has 28-bit cluster identifiers. Because FAT32 cluster sizes can be as large as 64 KB, FAT32 has a theoretical ability to address 16-terabyte (TB) volumes. Although Windows works with existing FAT32 volumes of larger sizes (created in other operating systems), it limits new FAT32 volumes to a maximum of 32 GB. FAT32's higher potential cluster numbers let it manage disks more efficiently than FAT16; it can handle up to 128-GB volumes with 512-byte clusters. Table 12-2 shows default cluster sizes for FAT32 volumes.

TABLE 12-2 Default Cluster Sizes for FAT32 Volumes

Partition Size	Default Cluster Size
<32 MB	Not supported
32 MB–64 MB	512 bytes
64 MB–128 MB	1 KB
128 MB–256 MB	2 KB
256 MB–8 GB	4 KB
8 GB–16 GB	8 KB
16 GB–32 GB	16 KB
>32 GB	Not supported

Besides the higher limit on cluster numbers, other advantages FAT32 has over FAT12 and FAT16 include the fact that the FAT32 root directory isn't stored at a predefined location on the volume, the root directory doesn't have an upper limit on its size, and FAT32 stores a second copy of the boot sector for reliability. A limitation FAT32 shares with FAT16 is that the maximum file size is 4 GB because directories store file sizes as 32-bit values.

exFAT

Designed by Microsoft, the Extended File Allocation Table file system (exFAT, also called FAT64) is an improvement over the traditional FAT file systems and is specifically designed for flash drives. The main goal of exFAT is to provide some of the advanced functionality offered by NTFS, but without the metadata structure overhead and metadata logging that create write patterns not suited for many flash media devices. (See the description of flash media in Chapter 9). Table 12-3 lists the default cluster sizes for exFAT.

As the FAT64 name implies, the file size limit is increased to 2^{64}, allowing files up to 16 exabytes. This change is also matched by an increase in the maximum cluster size, which is currently implemented as 32 MB but can be as large as 2^{255} sectors. exFAT also adds a bitmap that tracks free clusters, which improves the performance of allocation and deletion operations. Finally, exFAT allows more than 1,000 files in a single directory. These characteristics result in increased scalability and support for large disk sizes.

TABLE 12-3 Default Cluster Sizes for exFAT Volumes

Volume Size	Default Cluster Size
<7 MB	Not supported
7 MB–256 MB	4 KB
256 MB–32 GB	32 KB
32 GB–256 TB	128 KB
>256 TB	Not supported

Additionally, exFAT implements certain features previously available only in NTFS, such as support for access control lists (ACLs) and transactions (called Transaction-Safe FAT, or TFAT). While the Windows Embedded CE implementation of exFAT includes these features, the version of exFAT in Windows does not.

> **Note** ReadyBoost (described in Chapter 10, "Memory Management") can work with exFAT-formatted flash drives to support cache files much larger than 4 GB.

NTFS

As noted at the beginning of the chapter, the NTFS file system is the native file system format of Windows. NTFS uses 64-bit cluster numbers. This capacity gives NTFS the ability to address volumes of up to 16 exaclusters; however, Windows limits the size of an NTFS volume to that addressable with 32-bit clusters, which is slightly less than 256 TB (using 64-KB clusters). Table 12-4 shows the default cluster sizes for NTFS volumes. (You can override the default when you format an NTFS volume.) NTFS also supports $2^{32}-1$ files per volume. The NTFS format allows for files that are 16 exabytes in size, but the implementation limits the maximum file size to 16 TB.

TABLE 12-4 Default Cluster Sizes for NTFS Volumes

Volume Size	Default Cluster Size
<7 MB	Not supported
7 MB–16 TB	4 KB
16 TB–32 TB	8 KB
32 TB–64 TB	16 KB
64 TB–128 TB	32 KB
128 TB–256 TB	64 KB

NTFS includes a number of advanced features, such as file and directory security, alternate data streams, disk quotas, sparse files, file compression, symbolic (soft) and hard links, support for transactional semantics, junction points, and encryption. One of its most significant features is *recoverability*. If a system is halted unexpectedly, the metadata of a FAT volume can be left in an inconsistent state, leading to the corruption of large amounts of file and directory data. NTFS logs changes to metadata in a transactional manner so that file system structures can be repaired to a consistent state with no loss of file or directory structure information. (File data can be lost unless the user is using TxF, which is covered later in this chapter.) Additionally, the NTFS driver in Windows also implements *self-healing*, a mechanism through which it makes most minor repairs to corruption of file system on-disk structures while Windows is running and without requiring a reboot.

We'll describe NTFS data structures and advanced features in detail later in this chapter.

File System Driver Architecture

File system drivers (FSDs) manage file system formats. Although FSDs run in kernel mode, they differ in a number of ways from standard kernel-mode drivers. Perhaps most significant, they must register as an FSD with the I/O manager and they interact more extensively with the memory manager. For enhanced performance, file system drivers also usually rely on the services of the cache manager. Thus, they use a superset of the exported Ntoskrnl.exe functions that standard drivers use. Just as for standard kernel-mode drivers, you must have the Windows Driver Kit (WDK) to build file system drivers. (See Chapter 1, "Concepts and Tools," in Part 1 and *http://www.microsoft.com/whdc/devtools/wdk* for more information on the WDK.)

Windows has two different types of file system drivers:

- *Local FSDs* manage volumes directly connected to the computer.

- *Network FSDs* allow users to access data volumes connected to remote computers.

Local FSDs

Local FSDs include Ntfs.sys, Fastfat.sys, Exfat.sys, Udfs.sys, Cdfs.sys, and the RAW FSD (integrated in Ntoskrnl.exe). Figure 12-5 shows a simplified view of how local FSDs interact with the I/O manager and storage device drivers. As we described in the section "Volume Mounting" in Chapter 9, a local FSD is responsible for registering with the I/O manager. Once the FSD is registered, the I/O manager can call on it to perform volume recognition when applications or the system initially access the volumes. Volume recognition involves an examination of a volume's boot sector and often, as a consistency check, the file system metadata. If none of the registered file systems recognizes the volume, the system assigns the RAW file system driver to the volume and then displays a dialog box to the user asking if the volume should be formatted. If the user chooses not to format the volume, the RAW file system driver provides access to the volume, but only at the sector level—in other words, the user can only read or write complete sectors.

The goal of file system recognition is to allow the system to have an additional option for a valid but unrecognized file system other than RAW. To achieve this, the system defines a fixed data structure type (FILE_SYSTEM_RECOGNITION_STRUCTURE) that is written to the first sector on the volume. This data structure, if present, would then be recognized by the operating system, which would then notify the user that the volume contains a valid but unrecognized file system. The system will still load the RAW file system on the volume, but it will not prompt the user to format the volume. A user application or kernel-mode driver might ask for a copy of the FILE_SYSTEM_RECOGNITION_STRUCTURE by using the new file system I/O control code FSCTL_QUERY_FILE_SYSTEM_RECOGNITION.

The first sector of every Windows-supported file system format is reserved as the volume's boot sector. A boot sector contains enough information so that a local FSD can both identify the volume on which the sector resides as containing a format that the FSD manages and locate any other metadata necessary to identify where metadata is stored on the volume.

When a local FSD recognizes a volume, it creates a device object that represents the mounted file system format. The I/O manager makes a connection through the volume parameter block (VPB) between the volume's device object (which is created by a storage device driver) and the device object that the FSD created. The VPB's connection results in the I/O manager redirecting I/O requests targeted at the volume device object to the FSD device object. (See Chapter 9 for more information on VPBs.)

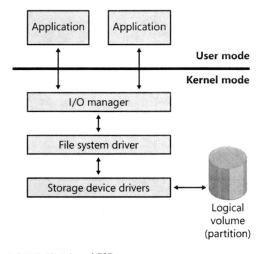

FIGURE 12-5 Local FSD

To improve performance, local FSDs usually use the cache manager to cache file system data, including metadata. (For more information, see Chapter 11, "Cache Manager.") FSDs also integrate with the memory manager so that mapped files are implemented correctly. For example, FSDs must query the memory manager whenever an application attempts to truncate a file in order to verify that no processes have mapped the part of the file beyond the truncation point. (See Chapter 10 for more information on the memory manager.) Windows doesn't permit file data that is mapped by an application to be deleted either through truncation or file deletion.

Local FSDs also support file system dismount operations, which permit the system to disconnect the FSD from the volume object. A dismount occurs whenever an application requires raw access to the on-disk contents of a volume or the media associated with a volume is changed. The first time an application accesses the media after a dismount, the I/O manager reinitiates a volume mount operation for the media.

Remote FSDs

Each remote FSD consists of two components: a client and a server. A client-side remote FSD allows applications to access remote files and directories. The client FSD component accepts I/O requests from applications and translates them into network file system protocol commands (such as SMB) that the FSD sends across the network to a server-side component, which is a remote FSD. A server-side FSD listens for commands coming from a network connection and fulfills them by issuing I/O requests to the local FSD that manages the volume on which the file or directory that the command is intended for resides.

Windows includes a client-side remote FSD named LANMan Redirector (usually referred to as just the *redirector*) and a server-side remote FSD named LANMan Server (%SystemRoot%\System32\Drivers\Srv2.sys). Figure 12-6 shows the relationship between a client accessing files remotely from a server through the redirector and server FSDs. See Chapter 7, "Networking," in Part 1 for more information on the redirectors and RDBSS.

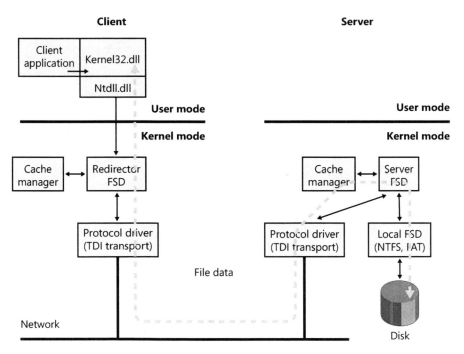

FIGURE 12-6 Common Internet File System file sharing

Windows relies on the Common Internet File System (CIFS) protocol to format messages exchanged between the redirector and the server.l CIFS is a version of Microsoft's Server Message Block (SMB) protocol. (For more information on SMB, go to *http://msdn.microsoft.com/en-us/library/windows/desktop/aa365233(v=vs.85).aspx.*)

Like local FSDs, client-side remote FSDs usually use cache manager services to locally cache file data belonging to remote files and directories, and in such cases both must implement a distributed locking mechanism on the client as well as the server. SMB client-side remote FSDs implement a distributed cache coherency protocol, called *oplock* (opportunistic locking), so that the data an application sees when it accesses a remote file is the same as the data applications running on other computers that are accessing the same file see. Third-party file systems may choose to use the oplock protocol, or they may implement their own protocol. Although server-side remote FSDs participate in maintaining cache coherency across their clients, they don't cache data from the local FSDs because local FSDs cache their own data.

Locking

It is fundamental that whenever a resource can be shared between multiple, simultaneous accessors, a serialization mechanism must be provided to arbitrate writes to that resource to ensure that only one accessor is writing to the resource at any given time. Without this mechanism, the resource may be corrupted. The locking mechanisms used by all file servers implementing the SMB protocol are the oplock and the lease. Which mechanism is used depends on the capabilities of both the server and the client, with the lease being the preferred mechanism.

Oplocks   The oplock functionality is implemented in the file system run-time library (*FsRtlXxx* functions) and may be used by any file system driver. The client of a remote file server uses an oplock to dynamically determine which client-side caching strategy to use to minimize network traffic. An oplock is requested on a file residing on a share, by the file system driver or redirector, on behalf of an application when it attempts to open a file. The granting of an oplock allows the client to cache the file rather than send every read or write to the file server across the network. For example, a client could open a file for exclusive access, allowing the client to cache all reads and writes to the file, and then copy the updates to the file server when the file is closed. In contrast, if the server does not grant an oplock to a client, all reads and writes must be sent to the server.

Once an oplock has been granted, a client may then start caching the file, with the type of oplock determining what type of caching is allowed. An oplock is not necessarily held until a client is finished with the file, and it may be broken at any time if the server receives an operation that is incompatible with the existing granted locks. This implies that the client must be able to quickly react to the break of the oplock and change its caching strategy dynamically.

Prior to SMB 2.1, there were four types of oplocks:

- **Level 1, exclusive access**   This lock allows a client to open a file for exclusive access. The client may perform read-ahead buffering and read or write caching.

- **Level 2, shared access**   This lock allows multiple, simultaneous readers of a file and no writers. The client may perform read-ahead buffering and read caching of file data and attributes. A write to the file will cause the holders of the lock to be notified that the lock has been broken.

- **Batch, exclusive access**   This lock takes its name from the locking used when processing batch (.bat) files, which are opened and closed to process each line within the file. The client may keep a file open on the server, even though the application has (perhaps temporarily) closed the file. This lock supports read, write, and handle caching.

- **Filter, exclusive access** This lock provides applications and file system filters with a mechanism to give up the lock when other clients try to access the same file, but unlike a Level 2 lock, the file cannot be opened for delete access, and the other client will not receive a sharing violation. This lock supports read and write caching.

In the simplest terms, if multiple client systems are all caching the same file shared by a server, then as long as every application accessing the file (from any client or the server) tries only to read the file, those reads can be satisfied from each system's local cache. This drastically reduces the network traffic because the contents of the file are not sent to each system from the server. Locking information must still be exchanged between the client systems and the server, but this requires very low network bandwidth. However, if even one of the clients opens the file for read *and* write access (or exclusive write), then none of the clients can use their local caches and all I/O to the file must go immediately to the server, *even if the file is never written.* (Lock modes are based upon how the file is opened, not individual I/O requests.)

An example, shown in Figure 12-7, will help illustrate oplock operation. The server automatically grants a Level 1 oplock to the first client to open a server file for access. The redirector on the client caches the file data for both reads and writes in the file cache of the client machine. If a second client opens the file, it too requests a Level 1 oplock. However, because there are now two clients accessing the same file, the server must take steps to present a consistent view of the file's data to both clients. If the first client has written to the file, as is the case in Figure 12-7, the server revokes its oplock and grants neither client an oplock. When the first client's oplock is revoked, or *broken*, the client flushes any data it has cached for the file back to the server.

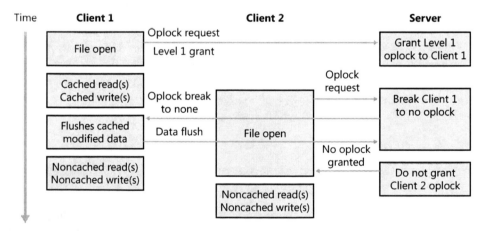

FIGURE 12-7 Oplock example

If the first client hadn't written to the file, the first client's oplock would have been broken to a Level 2 oplock, which is the same type of oplock the server would grant to the second client. Now both clients can cache reads, but if either writes to the file, the server revokes their oplocks so that noncached operation commences. Once oplocks are broken, they aren't granted again for the same open instance of a file. However, if a client closes a file and then reopens it, the server reassesses what level of oplock to grant the client based on which other clients have the file open and whether or not at least one of them has written to the file.

Note that just because a driver registers as a file system driver type doesn't mean that it is a local or remote FSD. For example, Npfs (Named Pipe File System) is a network API driver that supports named pipes but implements a private namespace, and therefore is in some ways like a file system driver. See Chapter 7 in Part 1 for an experiment that reveals the Npfs namespace.

Leases Prior to SMB 2.1, the SMB protocol assumed an error-free network connection between the client and the server and did not tolerate network disconnections caused by transient network failures, server reboot, or cluster failovers. When a network disconnect event was received by the client, it orphaned all handles opened to the affected server(s), and all subsequent I/O operations on the orphaned handles were failed. Similarly, the server would release all opened handles and resources associated with the disconnected user session. This behavior resulted in applications losing state and in unnecessary network traffic.

In SMB 2.1, the concept of a *lease* is introduced as a new type of client caching mechanism, similar to an oplock. The purpose of a lease and an oplock is the same, but a lease provides greater flexibility and much better performance.

- **Read (R), shared access**   Allows multiple simultaneous readers of a file, and no writers. This lease allows the client to perform read-ahead buffering and read caching.

- **Read-Handle (RH), shared access**   This is similar to the Level 2 oplock, with the added benefit of allowing the client to keep a file open on the server even though the accessor on the client has closed the file. (The cache manager will lazily flush the unwritten data and purge the unmodified cache pages based on memory availability.) This is superior to a Level 2 oplock because the lease does not need to be broken between opens and closes of the file handle. (In this respect, it provides semantics similar to the Batch oplock.) This type of lease is especially useful for files that are repeatedly opened and closed because the cache is not invalidated when the file is closed and refilled when the file is opened again, providing a big improvement in performance for complex I/O intensive applications.

- **Read-Write (RW), exclusive access**   This lease allows a client to open a file for exclusive access. This lock allows the client to perform read-ahead buffering and read or write caching.

- **Read-Write-Handle (RWH), exclusive access**   This lock allows a client to open a file for exclusive access. This lease supports read, write, and handle caching (similar to the Read-Handle lease).

Another advantage that a lease has over an oplock is that a file may be cached, even when there are multiple handles opened to the file on the client. (This is a common behavior in many applications.) This is implemented through the use of a lease *key* (implemented using a GUID), which is created by the client and associated with the File Control Block (FCB) for the cached file, allowing all handles to the same file to share the same lease state, which provides caching by file rather than caching by handle. Prior to the introduction of the lease, the oplock was broken whenever a new handle was opened to the file, even from the same client. Figure 12-8 shows the oplock behavior, and Figure 12-9 shows the new lease behavior.

Prior to SMB 2.1, oplocks could only be granted or broken, but leases can also be *converted*. For example, a Read lease may be converted to a Read-Write lease, which greatly reduces network traffic because the cache for a particular file does not need to be invalidated and refilled, as would be the case with an oplock break (of the Level 2 oplock), followed by the request and grant of a Level 1 oplock.

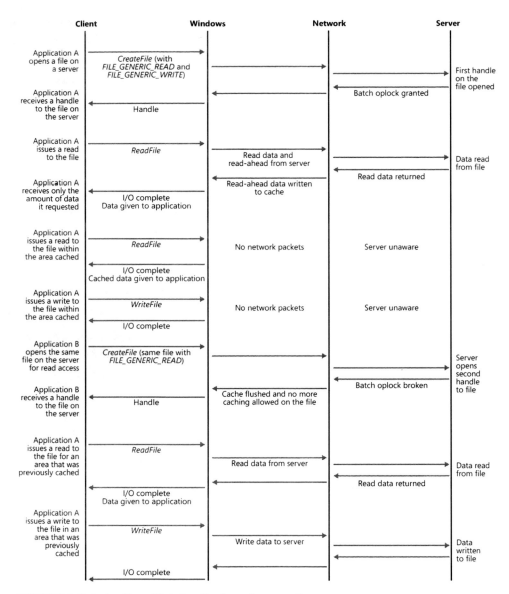

FIGURE 12-8 Oplock with multiple handles from the same client

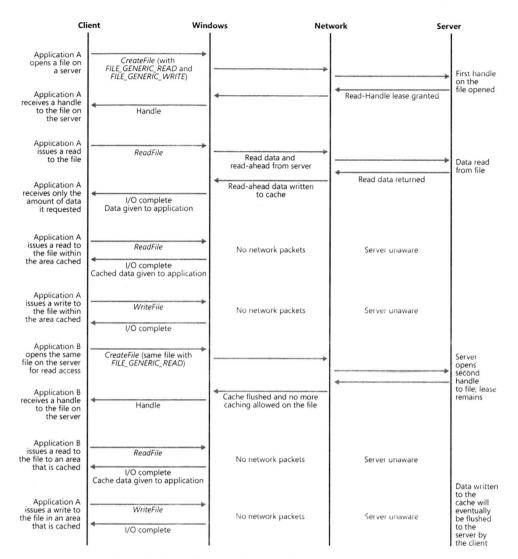

Client	Windows	Network	Server

Application A opens a file on a server → CreateFile (with FILE_GENERIC_READ and FILE_GENERIC_WRITE) → → First handle on the file opened

Application A receives a handle to the file on the server ← Handle ← Read-Handle lease granted

Application A issues a read to the file → ReadFile → Read data and read-ahead from server → Data read from file

Application A receives only the amount of data it requested ← I/O complete Data given to application ← Read-ahead data written to cache ← Read data returned

Application A issues a read to the file within the area cached → ReadFile → No network packets — Server unaware
← I/O complete Cached data given to application

Application A issues a write to the file within the area cached → WriteFile → No network packets — Server unaware
← I/O complete

Application B opens the same file on the server for read access → CreateFile (same file with FILE_GENERIC_READ) → → Server opens second handle to file; lease remains

Application B receives a handle to the file on the server ← Handle ← Cache flushed and no more caching allowed on the file

Application B issues a read to the file to an area that is cached → ReadFile → No network packets — Server unaware
← I/O complete Cache data given to application

Application A issues a write to the file in an area that is cached → WriteFile → No network packets — Server unaware — Data written to the cache will eventually be flushed to the server by the client
← I/O complete

FIGURE 12-9 Lease with multiple handles from the same client

File System Operation

Applications and the system access files in two ways: directly, via file I/O functions (such as *ReadFile* and *WriteFile*), and indirectly, by reading or writing a portion of their address space that represents a mapped file section. (See Chapter 10 for more information on mapped files.) Figure 12-10 is a simplified diagram that shows the components involved in these file system operations and the ways in which they interact. As you can see, an FSD can be invoked through several paths:

- From a user or system thread performing explicit file I/O

- From the memory manager's modified and mapped page writers

- Indirectly from the cache manager's lazy writer

- Indirectly from the cache manager's read-ahead thread

- From the memory manager's page fault handler

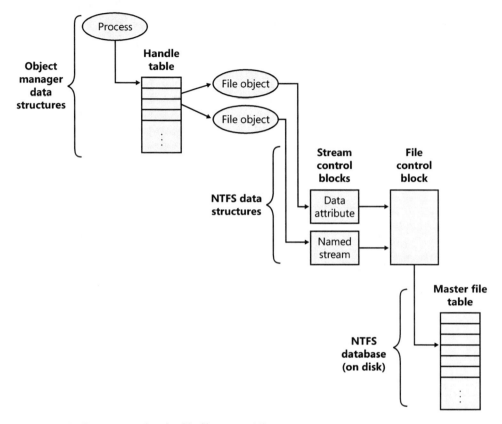

FIGURE 12-10 Components involved in file system I/O

The following sections describe the circumstances surrounding each of these scenarios and the steps FSDs typically take in response to each one. You'll see how much FSDs rely on the memory manager and the cache manager.

Explicit File I/O

The most obvious way an application accesses files is by calling Windows I/O functions such as *CreateFile*, *ReadFile*, and *WriteFile*. An application opens a file with *CreateFile* and then reads, writes, or deletes the file by passing the handle returned from *CreateFile* to other Windows functions. The *CreateFile* function, which is implemented in the Kernel32.dll Windows client-side DLL, invokes the native function *NtCreateFile*, forming a complete root-relative path name for the path that the application passed to it (processing "." and ".." symbols in the path name) and prefixing the path with "\??" (for example, \??\C:\Daryl\Todo.txt).

The *NtCreateFile* system service uses *ObOpenObjectByName* to open the file, which parses the name starting with the object manager root directory and the first component of the path name ("??"). Chapter 3, "System Mechanisms," in Part 1 includes a thorough description of object manager name resolution and its use of process device maps, but we'll review the steps it follows here with a focus on volume drive letter lookup.

The first step the object manager takes is to translate \?? to the process's per-session namespace directory that the *DosDevicesDirectory* field of the device map structure in the process object references (which was propagated from the first process in the logon session by using the logon session references field in the logon session's token). Only volume names for network shares and drive letters mapped by the Subst.exe utility are typically stored in the per-session directory, so on those systems when a name (C: in this example) is not present in the per-session directory, the object manager restarts its search in the directory referenced by the *GlobalDosDevicesDirectory* field of the device map associated with the per-session directory. The *GlobalDosDevicesDirectory* always points at the \Global?? directory, which is where Windows stores volume drive letters for local volumes. (See the section "Session Namespace" in Chapter 3 in Part 1 for more information.)

The symbolic link for a volume drive letter points to a volume device object under \Device, so when the object manager encounters the volume object, the object manager hands the rest of the path name to the parse function that the I/O manager has registered for device objects, *IopParseDevice*. (In volumes on dynamic disks, a symbolic link points to an intermediary symbolic link, which points to a volume device object.) Figure 12-11 shows how volume objects are accessed through the object manager namespace. The figure shows how the \GLOBAL??\C: symbolic link points to the \Device\HarddiskVolume1 volume device object.

After locking the caller's security context and obtaining security information from the caller's token, *IopParseDevice* creates an I/O request packet (IRP) of type IRP_MJ_CREATE, creates a file object that stores the name of the file being opened, follows the VPB of the volume device object to find the volume's mounted file system device object, and uses *IoCallDriver* to pass the IRP to the file system driver that owns the file system device object.

When an FSD receives an IRP_MJ_CREATE IRP, it looks up the specified file, performs security validation, and if the file exists and the user has permission to access the file in the way requested, returns a success status code. The object manager creates a handle for the file object in the process's handle table, and the handle propagates back through the calling chain, finally reaching the application as a return parameter from *CreateFile*. If the file system fails the create operation, the I/O manager deletes the file object it created for the file.

We've skipped over the details of how the FSD locates the file being opened on the volume, but a *ReadFile* function call operation shares many of the FSD's interactions with the cache manager and storage driver. Both *ReadFile* and *CreateFile* are system calls that map to I/O manager functions, but the *NtReadFile* system service doesn't need to perform a name lookup—it calls on the object manager to translate the handle passed from *ReadFile* into a file object pointer. If the handle indicates that the caller obtained permission to read the file when the file was opened, *NtReadFile* proceeds to create an IRP of type IRP_MJ_READ and sends it to the FSD for the volume on which the file resides.

NtReadFile obtains the FSD's device object, which is stored in the file object, and calls *IoCallDriver*, and the I/O manager locates the FSD from the device object and gives the IRP to the FSD.

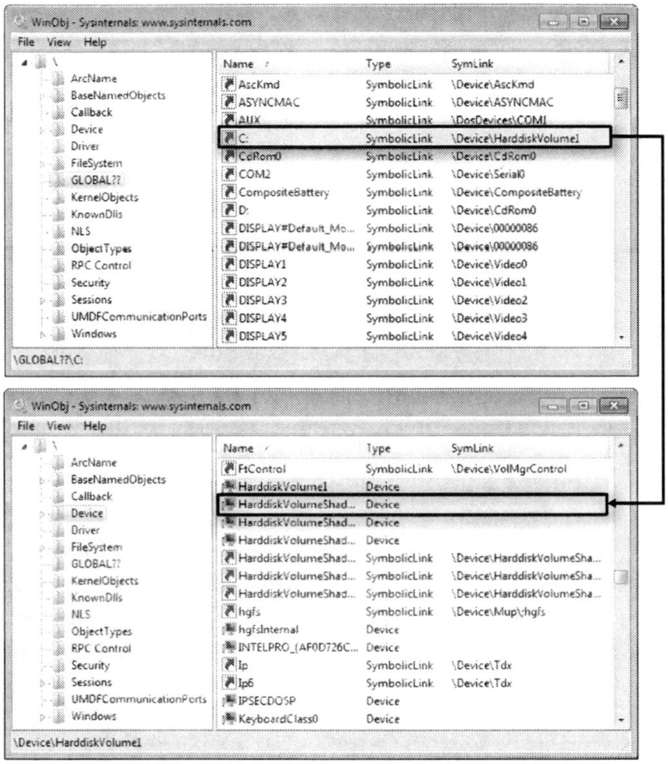

FIGURE 12-11 Drive-letter name resolution

If the file being read can be cached (that is, the FILE_FLAG_NO_BUFFERING flag wasn't passed to *CreateFile* when the file was opened), the FSD checks to see whether caching has already been initiated for the file object. The *PrivateCacheMap* field in a file object points to a private cache map data structure (which we described in Chapter 11) if caching is initiated for a file object. If the FSD hasn't initialized caching for the file object (which it does the first time a file object is read from or written to), the *PrivateCacheMap* field will be null. The FSD calls the cache manager's *CcInitializeCacheMap* function to initialize caching, which involves the cache manager creating a private cache map and, if another file object referring to the same file hasn't initiated caching, a shared cache map and a section object.

After it has verified that caching is enabled for the file, the FSD copies the requested file data from the cache manager's virtual memory to the buffer that the thread passed to the *ReadFile* function. The file system performs the copy within a try/except block so that it catches any faults that are the result of an invalid application buffer. The function the file system uses to perform the copy is the cache manager's *CcCopyRead* function. *CcCopyRead* takes as parameters a file object, file offset, and length.

When the cache manager executes *CcCopyRead*, it retrieves a pointer to a shared cache map, which is stored in the file object. Recall from Chapter 11 that a shared cache map stores pointers to virtual address control blocks (VACBs), with one VACB entry for each 256-KB block of the file. If the VACB pointer for a portion of a file being read is null, *CcCopyRead* allocates a VACB, reserving a 256-KB view in the cache manager's virtual address space, and maps (using *MmMapViewInSystemCache*) the specified portion of the file into the view. Then *CcCopyRead* simply copies the file data from the mapped view to the buffer it was passed (the buffer originally passed to *ReadFile*). If the file data isn't in physical memory, the copy operation generates page faults, which are serviced by *MmAccessFault*.

When a page fault occurs, *MmAccessFault* examines the virtual address that caused the fault and locates the virtual address descriptor (VAD) in the VAD tree of the process that caused the fault. (See Chapter 10 for more information on VAD trees.) In this scenario, the VAD describes the cache manager's mapped view of the file being read, so *MmAccessFault* calls *MiDispatchFault* to handle a page fault on a valid virtual memory address. *MiDispatchFault* locates the control area (which the VAD points to) and through the control area finds a file object representing the open file. (If the file has been opened more than once, there might be a list of file objects linked through pointers in their private cache maps.)

With the file object in hand, *MiDispatchFault* calls the I/O manager function *IoPageRead* to build an IRP (of type IRP_MJ_READ) and sends the IRP to the FSD that owns the device object the file object points to. Thus, the file system is reentered to read the data that it requested via *CcCopyRead*, but this time the IRP is marked as noncached and paging I/O. These flags signal the FSD that it should retrieve file data directly from disk, and it does so by determining which clusters on disk contain the requested data (the exact mechanism is file-system dependent) and sending IRPs to the volume manager that owns the volume device object on which the file resides. The volume parameter block (VPB) field in the FSD's device object points to the volume device object.

The memory manager waits for the FSD to complete the IRP read and then returns control to the cache manager, which continues the copy operation that was interrupted by a page fault. When *CcCopyRead* completes, the FSD returns control to the thread that called *NtReadFile*, having copied the requested file data—with the aid of the cache manager and the memory manager—to the thread's buffer.

The path for *WriteFile* is similar except that the *NtWriteFile* system service generates an IRP of type IRP_MJ_WRITE and the FSD calls *CcCopyWrite* instead of *CcCopyRead*. *CcCopyWrite*, like *CcCopyRead*, ensures that the portions of the file being written are mapped into the cache and then copies to the cache the buffer passed to *WriteFile*.

If a file's data is already cached (in the system's working set), there are several variants on the scenario we've just described. If a file's data is already stored in the cache, *CcCopyRead* doesn't incur page faults. Also, under certain conditions, *NtReadFile* and *NtWriteFile* call an FSD's fast I/O entry point instead of immediately building and sending an IRP to the FSD. Some of these conditions follow: the portion of the file being read must reside in the first 4 GB of the file, the file can have no locks, and the portion of the file being read or written must fall within the file's currently allocated size.

The fast I/O read and write entry points for most FSDs call the cache manager's *CcFastCopyRead* and *CcFastCopyWrite* functions. These variants on the standard copy routines ensure that the file's data is mapped in the file system cache before performing a copy operation. If this condition isn't met, *CcFastCopyRead* and *CcFastCopyWrite* indicate that fast I/O isn't possible. When fast I/O isn't possible, *NtReadFile* and *NtWriteFile* fall back on creating an IRP. (See the section "Fast I/O" in Chapter 11 for a more complete description of fast I/O.)

Memory Manager's Modified and Mapped Page Writer

The memory manager's modified and mapped page writer threads wake up periodically (and when available memory runs low) to flush modified pages to their backing store on disk. The threads call *IoAsynchronousPageWrite* to create IRPs of type IRP_MJ_WRITE and write pages to either a paging file or a file that was modified after being mapped. Like the IRPs that *MiDispatchFault* creates, these IRPs are flagged as noncached and paging I/O. Thus, an FSD bypasses the file system cache and issues IRPs directly to a storage driver to write the memory to disk.

Cache Manager's Lazy Writer

The cache manager's lazy writer thread also plays a role in writing modified pages because it periodically flushes views of file sections mapped in the cache that it knows are dirty. The flush operation, which the cache manager performs by calling *MmFlushSection*, triggers the memory manager to write any modified pages in the portion of the section being flushed to disk. Like the modified and mapped page writers, *MmFlushSection* uses *IoSynchronousPageWrite* to send the data to the FSD.

Cache Manager's Read-Ahead Thread

A cache utilizes two artifacts of how programs reference code and data: temporal locality and spatial locality. The underlying concept behind temporal locality is that if a memory location is referenced, it is likely to be referenced again soon. The idea behind spatial locality is that if a memory location is referenced, other nearby locations are also likely to be referenced soon. Thus a cache typically is very good at speeding up access to memory locations that have been accessed in the near past, but it is terrible at speeding up access to areas of memory that have not yet been accessed (it has zero lookahead capability). In an attempt to populate the cache with data that will likely be used soon, the cache manager implements two mechanisms: a read-ahead thread, and Superfetch.

The cache manager includes a thread that is responsible for attempting to read data from files before an application, a driver, or a system thread explicitly requests it. The read-ahead thread uses the history of read operations that were performed on a file, which are stored in a file object's private cache map, to determine how much data to read. When the thread performs a read-ahead, it simply maps the portion of the file it wants to read into the cache (allocating VACBs as necessary) and touches the mapped data. The page faults caused by the memory accesses invoke the page fault handler, which reads the pages into the system's working set.

A limitation of the read-ahead thread is that it works only on open files. Superfetch was added to Windows to proactively add files to the cache before they are even opened. Specifically, the memory manager sends page-usage information to the Superfetch service (%SystemRoot%\System32\Sysmain.dll), and a file system minifilter provides file name resolution data. The Superfetch service attempts to find file-usage patterns—for example, payroll is run every Friday at 12:00, or Outlook is run every morning at 8:00. When these patterns are derived, the information is stored in a database and timers are requested. Just prior to the time the file would most likely be used, a timer fires and wakes up the Superfetch service, which then tells the memory manager to read the file into low-priority memory (using low-priority disk I/O). If the file is then opened, the data is already in memory and there is no need to wait for the data to be read from disk. If the file is not opened, the low-priority memory will be reclaimed by the system.

Memory Manager's Page Fault Handler

We described how the page fault handler is used in the context of explicit file I/O and cache manager read-ahead, but it is also invoked whenever any application accesses virtual memory that is a view of a mapped file and encounters pages that represent portions of a file that are not yet in memory. The memory manager's *MmAccessFault* handler follows the same steps it does when the cache manager generates a page fault from *CcCopyRead* or *CcCopyWrite*, sending IRPs via *IoPageRead* to the file system on which the file is stored.

File System Filter Drivers

A filter driver that layers over a file system driver is called a *file system filter driver*. (See Chapter 8, "I/O System," for more information on filter drivers.) The ability to see all file system requests and optionally modify or complete them enables a range of applications, including remote file replication services, file encryption, efficient backup, and licensing. Every commercial on-access virus scanner includes a file system filter driver that intercepts IRPs that deliver IRP_MJ_CREATE commands that issue whenever an application opens a file. Before propagating the IRP to the file system driver to which the command is directed, the virus scanner examines the file being opened to ensure that it's clean of a virus. If the file is clean, the virus scanner passes the IRP on, but if the file is infected the virus scanner communicates with its associated Windows service process to quarantine or clean the file. If the file can't be cleaned, the driver fails the IRP (typically with an access-denied error) so that the virus cannot become active.

Process Monitor

Process Monitor (Procmon), a system activity monitoring utility from Sysinternals that has been used throughout this book, is an example of a passive filter driver, which is one that does not modify the flow of IRPs between applications and file system drivers. Windows includes the file system Filter Manager (%SystemRoot%\System32\Drivers\Fltmgr.sys) as part of a port/miniport model for file system filter drivers. The file system Filter Manager greatly simplifies the development of filter drivers by interfacing a filter miniport driver to the Windows I/O system and providing services for querying file names, attaching to volumes, and interacting with other filters. Process Monitor's file system monitoring is implemented as a *minifilter* driver.

Process Monitor works by extracting a file system filter device driver from its executable image (stored as a resource inside Procmon.exe) the first time you run it after a boot, installing the driver in memory, and then deleting the driver image from disk. Through the Process Monitor GUI, you can direct the driver to monitor file system activity on local volumes that have assigned drive letters, network shares, named pipes, and mail slots. When the driver receives a command to start monitoring a volume, it registers filtering callbacks with the Filter Manager, which is attached to the device object that represents a mounted file system on the volume. After an attach operation, the I/O manager redirects an IRP targeted at the underlying device object to the driver owning the attached device, in this case the Filter Manager, which sends the event to registered minifilter drivers, in this case Process Monitor.

When the Process Monitor driver intercepts an IRP, it records information about the IRP's command, including target file name and other parameters specific to the command (such as read and write lengths and offsets) to a nonpaged kernel buffer. Every 500 milliseconds, the Process Monitor GUI program sends an IRP to Process Monitor's interface device object, which requests a copy of the buffer containing the latest activity, and then displays the activity in its output window. Process Monitor's use is described further in the next section, "Troubleshooting File System Problems."

EXPERIMENT: Viewing Process Monitor's Filter Driver

To see which file system filter drivers are loaded, start an Administrative command prompt, and run the Filter Manager control program (%SystemRoot%\System32\Fltmc.exe). Start Process Monitor (ProcMon.exe) and run Fltmc again. You'll see that the Process Monitor's filter driver (PROCMON20) is loaded and has a nonzero value in the Instances column. Now, exit Process Monitor and run Fltmc again. This time, you'll see that the Process Monitor's filter driver is still loaded, but now its instance count is zero.

Troubleshooting File System Problems

Chapter 4, "Management Mechanisms," in Part 1 describes the way that the system and applications store data in the registry. Registry-related problems such as misconfigured security and missing registry values and keys are the source of many system and application failures. The system and applications also use files to store data, and they access executable and DLL image files. Misconfigured NTFS security and missing files or directories are therefore also a common source of system and application failures because the system and applications often make assumptions about what they should be able to access and then misbehave in unexpected ways when the assumptions are violated.

Process Monitor shows all file activity as it occurs, which makes it an ideal tool for troubleshooting file system–related system and application failures. To run Process Monitor the first time on a system, an account must have the Load Driver and Debug privileges. After loading, the driver remains resident, so subsequent executions require only the Debug privilege.

Process Monitor Basic vs. Advanced Modes

When you run Process Monitor, it starts in basic mode, which shows the file system activity most often useful for troubleshooting. When in basic mode, Process Monitor omits certain file system operations from being displayed, including:

- I/O to NTFS metadata files
- I/O to the paging file
- I/O generated by the System process
- I/O generated by the Process Monitor process

While in basic mode, Process Monitor also reports file I/O operations with friendly names rather than with the IRP types used to represent them. For example, both IRP_MJ_WRITE and FASTIO_WRITE operations display as WriteFile, and IRP_MJ_CREATE operations show as Open if they represent an open operation and as Create for the creation of new files.

EXPERIMENT: Viewing File System Activity on an Idle System

Windows file system drivers implement support for *file change notification*, which enables applications to request notifications of file system changes without polling for them. The Windows functions for doing so include *ReadDirectoryChangesW* and the *FindFirstChangeNotification*, *FindNextChangeNotification* pair. When you run Process Monitor on a system that's idle, you should therefore not see the repeated accesses to files or directories because that activity unnecessarily negatively affects a system's overall performance.

Run Process Monitor, and after several seconds examine the output log to see whether you can spot polling behavior. Right-click on an output line associated with polling, click Properties on the context menu, and then click the Process tab in the Properties dialog box to view details of the process performing the activity.

Process Monitor Troubleshooting Techniques

The two basic Process Monitor troubleshooting techniques for file system problems are identical to those for registry-related problems: look in a Process Monitor trace at the last thing an application did before it failed, or compare a Process Monitor trace of a failing application with a trace from a working system. See the section "Process Monitor Troubleshooting Techniques" in Chapter 4 in Part 1 for more information on these techniques.

Entries in a Process Monitor trace that have values of NAME NOT FOUND, NO SUCH FILE, PATH NOT FOUND, SHARING VIOLATION, and ACCESS DENIED in the Result column are ones that you should investigate. The first three are reported when an application or the system attempts to open a nonexistent file or directory. In many cases, these errors do not indicate a serious problem. When you execute a program from the Start menu's Run dialog box without specifying its full path, for instance, Windows Explorer will search the directories listed in the system PATH environment variable for the image file until it locates the file or has searched all the listed directories. Each attempt to find the image in a directory that does not contain it results in a Process Monitor output line similar to this:

```
25314    7:44:27.4180943 PM    Explorer.EXE    1640    CreateFile
C:\Program Files\Microsoft Windows Performance Toolkit\test.exe NAME NOT FOUND
Desired Access: Read Attributes, Disposition: Open, Options: Open    Reparse Point,
Attributes: n/a, ShareMode: Read, Write, Delete, AllocationSize: n/a
```

Access-denied errors are a common source of file system–related application failures, and they occur when an application does not have permission to open the file or directory for the access types it desires. Some applications do not check error codes or perform error recovery, and they fail by crashing or terminating; others often display misleading error messages that mask the root cause of the error.

Buffer-overflow exploits are a serious security concern, but a code result of BUFFER OVERFLOW is simply a file system driver's way to indicate to an application that the buffer it specified to store requested result data was too small to hold the data. Application developers use this behavior to determine how large a buffer should be because the file system driver also returns the size of the buffer required to store the data. Operations with a buffer overflow result are usually followed by the same operation with a successful result.

Process Monitor has been used extensively within Microsoft and other organizations to solve difficult or nearly impossible-to-diagnose problems.

Common Log File System

Transactional semantics for a database or a journaled file system often require keeping track of changes made to the data and metadata contained in the files or entries. Typically, these changes are stored in data structures called *log records* through an operation called *logging*. These log records can then be used to undo (roll back), redo, or validate the changes at a later time, even across system reboots.

Windows provides this kind of logging service through the Common Log File System (CLFS) to support the transactional features built into Windows, including transactional NTFS (TxF) and transactional registry (TxR), and to enable third-party developers to take advantage of similar technology. CLFS provides user-mode and kernel-mode APIs for creating, reading, and writing CLFS log files. The APIs are flexible and extensible, which allows the implementation details and structure of the log records stored in a log file to be defined by a caller. CLFS can be used by a variety of applications, such as databases; for store and forward message queues and replication agents; and for operations such as event logging, compliance logging, or even maintaining undo/redo history in an editor. The CLFS APIs provide a consistent view of a log and allow the sharing of a log between user-mode and kernel-mode components.

Although CLFS calls itself a file system, it actually provides a virtual abstraction layer on top of NTFS by using *streams* and *containers*, described later. What CLFS exposes as a single virtual log file could actually be a single physical log file, a single log file divided into multiple physical files, or even different log files each divided into multiple physical files. Later, we'll describe how NTFS interacts with CLFS to provide transactional support.

Marshalling

Internally, CLFS encapsulates the functionality of the Algorithm for Recovery and Isolation Exploiting Semantics (ARIES), which allows it to provide reliable recovery and replication of operations by using an industry-approved standard. However, CLFS is not limited to supporting ARIES; it is well suited to a variety of logging scenarios. You can find the full ARIES specification at *www.sai.msu.su/~megera/postgres/gist/papers/concurrency/p94-mohan.pdf*.

The primary job of any high-performance transactional log is to allow log clients to accurately repeat history. CLFS does this by marshalling client log records into memory buffers, forcing them to stable storage (a disk volume), and reading records back on request. After a record makes it to stable storage and the storage media is intact, CLFS is able to read the record across system failures.

Both user-mode and kernel-mode clients marshal data buffers into log records that are part of a *marshalling area* maintained in the client's address space. When creating a marshalling area, a client must specify the number and size of the log I/O buffers it wants to maintain in its marshaling area. The marshalling runtime implements policy on allocating log I/O buffers, appending them to the log internal queue and flushing them to disk. Clients can override the default marshalling code policy by forcing queue appends and flushes to disk via API calls.

One of the design goals of the CLFS marshalling runtime is to minimize kernel transitions, which it achieves, among other things, through log-space reservation, a requirement for supporting scenarios such as transaction rollbacks. Every time the log marshalling area talks to the CLFS driver (which implies a kernel transition for user-mode clients), the marshalling area tries to negotiate a desired amount of reserved space, usually larger than what is currently required. This means that if the client requires more space in the future, the marshalling area can immediately satisfy the new request without issuing a new kernel transition. Note, however, that if the amount of the reservation cannot be satisfied, the marshalling area will try to get just enough of the reservation to satisfy the user's request (without extra reserved space), which could potentially lead to additional kernel transitions.

Log Types

CLFS supports two types of logs: *dedicated* logs and *multiplexed* logs (also called *common logs*). A dedicated log has a single stream of log records that is used by all the log's clients. A multiplexed log has several streams: each stream has its own clients and its own memory buffers for marshalling log records, but the records from all those buffers are multiplexed into a single queue and written to a single log on stable storage. Multiplexing allows the I/O operations of several streams to be consolidated. When a log is created or opened, CLFS determines whether the log is dedicated or multiplexed depending on whether a dedicated log path or a multiplexed log path is specified.

If the request is for a client on a dedicated log (called a *physical client*), CLFS locates the physical file control block (FCB) object for the file proper and handles the request.

If the request is for a client on a multiplexed log (called a *virtual client*), CLFS locates the corresponding virtual FCB and context control block (CCB) objects to translate the request into an operation on the physical FCB object. CLFS then handles the operation on the CLFS physical FCB object as just described.

In either case, if the request is a cached read, CLFS uses the cache manager's services for accessing cached data. (For more information on the cache manager, see Chapter 11.) Just as it does for requests from other file system drivers, the cache manager maps a view of the file and references the view, which might cause the memory manager to issue noncached reads to CLFS against the physical log. For flushes and noncached reads, CLFS finds the target container object through the log metadata and issues IRPs to NTFS directly. Figure 12-12 shows the possible CLFS paths for a request coming from user mode or kernel mode.

Because each stream of a multiplexed log provides its clients with the illusion that their stream is the entire log, CLFS must include metadata in the physical log that identifies which client each data block belongs to. This data is called the *owner page* and is always exactly one page (4 KB) in size. Each 512 KB of client data results in an owner page to describe it. Since dedicated logs require no tracking of client and data mapping, they don't include owner pages. Figure 12-13 shows two clients writing log records to a multiplexed log and how the writes are kept together in a unified *flush queue* that can then be uniformly flushed to physical storage through a single I/O operation.

The flush queue will be emptied in the following conditions:

* The amount of data in the flush queue exceeds a certain threshold. (The default is 40,000 bytes.)

* The CLFS flush API is called.

* A restart area is being written, and the log needs to be flushed beyond the restart area. (For more information on the restart area, see the section "Log File Service" later in this chapter.)

When flushing, CLFS scans the flush queue and determines how many entries need to be flushed. It then issues IRPs to NTFS for the corresponding log files of each of the entries and waits for all the IRPs to complete. If some IRPs fail, CLFS may re-issue IRPs (failures such as low memory condition, lack of quota, and so on are subject to retry) to redo the work and wait again.

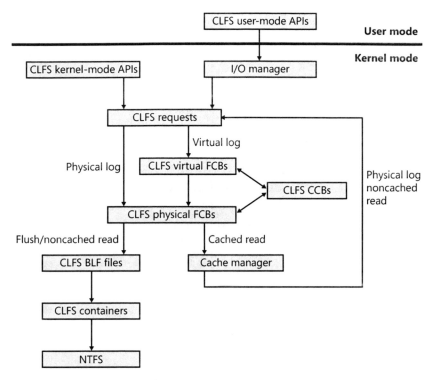

FIGURE 12-12 CLFS request paths

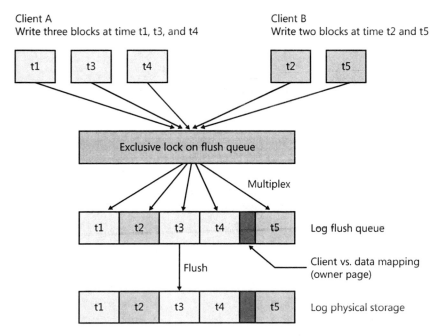

FIGURE 12-13 CLFS multiplexing

Log Layout

A log file is made up of a *base log file* (BLF) that contains metadata and up to 1,023 *containers* that hold the actual data. The base log file is initially 64 KB in size and grows as needed. The log metadata stores information about the log, including the beginning of the log, the container size, the container path, the location from which restart operations should be performed, the log state, the log name, and the log clients. For consistency in case a system failure occurs during a log update, the base log file stores two copies of the log metadata, and when it makes updates it overwrites the older copy. The BLF stores a value, the *dump count,* that indicates which copy is newer.

A container is the unit of allocation for an active physical log stream. All the containers in a log have the same size, which is a multiple of 512 KB with a 4-GB maximum size. A CLFS client grows or shrinks a log stream by adding or deleting containers from the log file. CLFS implements containers as contiguous files on the volume on which the BLF resides. Figure 12-14 shows the relationship between a base log file and the associated log data stored in containers.

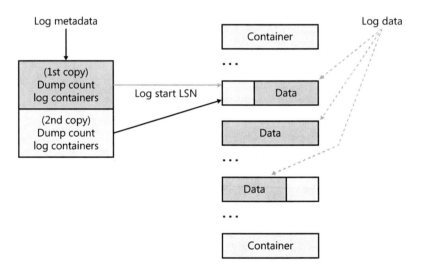

FIGURE 12-14 CLFS base log file and containers

Internally, the CLFS driver places the containers in a container queue to give clients a logical view of a single contiguous physical log stream; in doing so, the CLFS driver maps the *physical container identifier* to a *logical container identifier*. Containers are recycled when the tail of the active log migrates beyond the last sector of the container. Recycling a container involves moving it from the tail to the head of the container queue and appropriately updating its logical container identifier.

Log Sequence Numbers

When a client writes a record to a stream, CLFS returns a *log sequence number* (LSN) that identifies the log record for future reference. The LSNs assigned to the records that are written to a particular stream form an increasing sequence. That is, the LSN assigned to a record that is written to a stream is always greater than the LSN assigned to the previous record written to that same stream. Two critical

LSNs that the base log file keeps track of are the *log start LSN* and the *restart LSN*, which, as described earlier, are stored in the BLF metadata.

An LSN is 64 bits wide and consists of three parts, as shown in Figure 12-15:

- A 32-bit container index that identifies the log container where the log record resides
- A 23-bit block offset that identifies an offset within a container
- A 9-bit record offset that identifies a record within a block

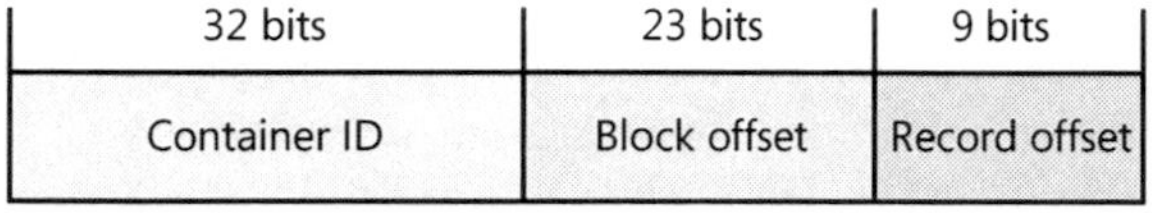

32 bits	23 bits	9 bits
Container ID	Block offset	Record offset

FIGURE 12-15 CLFS LSN structure

Log Blocks

Because it is possible that a write to a log might fail, which is called a *torn write*, CLFS uses *log blocks* to track whether log records are fully committed to storage. CLFS stores log records within log blocks, which correspond to 512-byte sectors, and reads and writes data to a log using log blocks. Each log block includes a 2-byte *sector signature* at the end of each sector in the block that stores a sequence number and flags, as well as a copy of the most recently committed signatures in a signature array at the end of the block, as shown in Figure 12-16. Only if all the sector signatures in a log block are valid and match the signatures in the array, does CLFS consider the block valid. If a log block is partially written and a system failure occurs, for example, the signatures won't match, and CLFS considers the log block invalid.

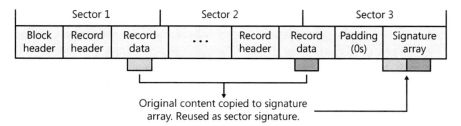

FIGURE 12-16 CLFS log blocks

Owner Pages

As mentioned previously, each 512-KB block of data in a multiplexed log (called a *region*) is corre- lated with its virtual log through an owner page. Each region consists of 4-KB *pages*, and each page contains one or more sectors, which contain log blocks. The owner page is the last page of a region, as shown in Figure 12-17. Because the owner page is itself a log block, CLFS can detect torn writes on the owner page, just as for a log record, by using the log block signature array.

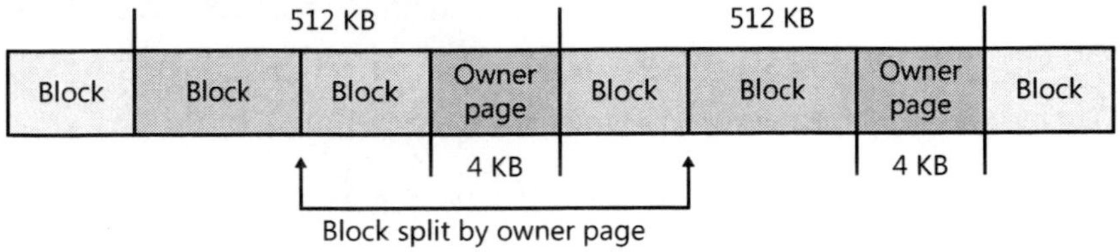

FIGURE 12-17 CLFS regions and owner pages

An owner page contains two kinds of information:

- For each sector in the region, the virtual log to which the sector belongs as well as the sector's serial number (starting from 0). There can be at most 1,024 sectors in a region.

- For each virtual log, the minimum and maximum virtual log LSN for the region. These values give the range of valid virtual LSNs for the region.

CLFS can tell by looking at the owner page of a virtual log LSN whether the record specified by the LSN resides in the current region or not. If the record does not reside in the current region, CLFS can decide whether it should search the previous region or the next region by comparing the virtual log LSN with the virtual log LSN range for the region.

When CLFS inserts log blocks into a multiplexed log's physical FCB flush queue, if it finds that the current log block will overlap the owner page of the current region, it splits the current log block and inserts an owner page log block after the first half of the split log block (as shown in Figure 12-17). In other words, the owner page is written to disk only after the region that it describes becomes full. When a client reopens a multiplexed log file, CLFS scans the regions and rebuilds an in-memory owner page describing the latest region for which it hasn't written an owner page log block.

Note that when reopening the log file, CLFS doesn't know exactly where the log end LSN is, so it must find the LSN to avoid losing data or using corrupted data. For a dedicated log, CLFS reads the log blocks sequentially until an invalid log block is found and then sets the end of the log there. For a multiplexed log, CLFS reads the last owner page (the base log file saves a copy of the last flushed owner page's LSN when the log metadata is last flushed) and verifies it is indeed valid. CLFS then reads the next region's owner page repeatedly until an invalid owner page is found. After that, CLFS scans backward to find the first region with only valid log data blocks. CLFS then assumes the end of the log must fall within the next region. It will scan log block by log block until an invalid log block is found and then set the end of the log there.

Translating Virtual LSNs to Physical LSNs

CLFS relies on physical LSNs to identify log blocks within a physical log. However, CLFS combines several virtual logs in a physical log for multiplexed logs and uses virtual LSNs to locate log blocks in a virtual log. Therefore, for a virtual log client, a log block can be addressed both by a physical LSN and by a virtual LSN.

To translate a virtual log LSN to a physical log LSN, CLFS follows these steps:

1. Reads the owner page for the region indicated by the virtual log LSN.

2. Checks the owner page's virtual LSN region to see whether the virtual LSN is actually in the region or not. Most of the time the log block will be in the region.

3. If the virtual LSN is in the region, CLFS refers to the *sector to client mapping* in the owner page to find the physical LSN's block offset. Given a client's virtual LSN and its size, CLFS can calculate the virtual LSN of the next log block. Applying this rule, CLFS can deterministically calculate the physical LSN of every virtual log block in the region, as shown in Figure 12-18.

4. If the virtual LSN is not in the region, CLFS searches either the previous region or the next region depending on whether the virtual LSN is smaller or larger than the current region's virtual LSN range.

Owner page
Sector 0: Client 1 1st sector of block
Sector 1: Client 1 2nd sector of block
Sector 2: Client 2 1st sector of block
Sector 3: Client 2 2nd sector of block
Sector 4: Client 2 3rd sector of block
Sector 5: Client 2 4th sector of block
Sector 6: Client 1 1st sector of block
Sector 7: Client 1 2nd sector of block
Sector 8: Client 1 1st sector of block
Sector 9: Client 1 2nd sector of block
Sector 10: Client 2 1st sector of block
Client 1 virtual LSN range (0.0.0 ~ 0.1400.0)
Client 2 virtual LSN range (0.0.0 ~ 0.1600.0)

To translate client 1 virtual LSN 0.1000.0:
1. Search owner page. The first sector that belongs to client 1 is physical LSN 0.0.0. This block's size is 2 sectors. So, its next virtual LSN must be 0.400.0.
2. Search owner page again. The next block that belongs to client 1 is physical LSN 0.C00.0. This block's size is 2 sectors. So, its next virtual LSN must be 0.1000.0. Find a match.
3. Search the owner page again. The next block that belongs to client 1 is physical LSN 0.1000.0. Done. Return 0.1000.0.

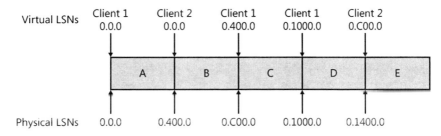

FIGURE 12-18 CLFS virtual to physical LSN translation

Management Policies

Each CLFS log can be defined by a set of management policies that are configurable by the client. Table 12-5 lists these policies and their usage.

TABLE 12-5 CLFS Management Policies

Policy Name	Description
ClfsMgmtPolicyMaximumSize	Specifies the maximum size of a log.
ClfsMgmtPolicyMinimumSize	Specifies the minimum size of a log.
ClfsMgmtPolicyNewContainerSize	Specifies the size of new containers that are created.
ClfsMgmtPolicyGrowthRate	Specifies how many new containers will be added to the log each time the log grows. Can be specified as either a relative percentage or an absolute number.
ClfsMgmtPolicyLogTail	Specifies how much free space will be requested when a client is notified to move its log tail. Can be specified as either a minimum percentage of free space or a minimum number of containers.
ClfsMgmtPolicyAutoShrink	Specifies when the log will shrink based on the percentage of the log that is free.
ClfsMgmtPolicyAutoGrow	Specifies whether the log should grow when fewer than two containers are free.
ClfsMgmtPolicyNewContainerPrefix	Specifies a prefix for the file name of each container, as well as the full path to the directory where the containers are located.

NTFS Design Goals and Features

In the following section, we'll look at the requirements that drove the design of NTFS. Then, in the subsequent section, we'll examine the advanced features of NTFS.

High-End File System Requirements

From the start, NTFS was designed to include features required of an enterprise-class file system. To minimize data loss in the face of an unexpected system outage or crash, a file system must ensure that the integrity of its metadata is guaranteed at all times; and to protect sensitive data from unauthorized access, a file system must have an integrated security model. Finally, a file system must allow for software-based data redundancy as a low-cost alternative to hardware-redundant solutions for protecting user data. In this section, you'll find out how NTFS implements each of these capabilities.

Recoverability

To address the requirement for reliable data storage and data access, NTFS provides file system recovery based on the concept of an *atomic transaction*. Atomic transactions are a technique for handling modifications to a database so that system failures don't affect the correctness or integrity of the database. The basic tenet of atomic transactions is that some database operations, called *transactions*, are all-or-nothing propositions. (A *transaction* is defined as an I/O operation that alters file system data or changes the volume's directory structure.) The separate disk updates that make up the transaction must be executed *atomically*—that is, once the transaction begins to execute, all its disk updates must be completed. If a system failure interrupts the transaction, the part that has been completed must be undone, or *rolled back*. The rollback operation returns the database to a previously known and consistent state, as if the transaction had never occurred.

NTFS uses atomic transactions to implement its file system recovery feature. If a program initiates an I/O operation that alters the structure of an NTFS volume—that is, changes the directory structure, extends a file, allocates space for a new file, and so on—NTFS treats that operation as an atomic transaction. It guarantees that the transaction is either completed or, if the system fails while executing the transaction, rolled back. The details of how NTFS does this are explained in the section "NTFS Recovery Support" later in the chapter. In addition, NTFS uses redundant storage for vital file system information so that if a sector on the disk goes bad, NTFS can still access the volume's critical file system data.

Security

Security in NTFS is derived directly from the Windows object model. Files and directories are protected from being accessed by unauthorized users. (For more information on Windows security, see Chapter 6, "Security," in Part 1.) An open file is implemented as a file object with a security descriptor stored on disk in the hidden $Secure metafile, in a stream named $SDS (Security Descriptor Stream). Before a process can open a handle to any object, including a file object, the Windows security system verifies that the process has appropriate authorization to do so. The security descriptor, combined with the requirement that a user log on to the system and provide an identifying password, ensures that no process can access a file unless it is given specific permission to do so by a system administrator or by the file's owner. (For more information about security descriptors, see the section "Security Descriptors and Access Control" in Chapter 6 in Part 1, and for more details about file objects, see the section "Opening Devices" in Chapter 8.)

Data Redundancy and Fault Tolerance

In addition to recoverability of file system data, some customers require that their own data not be endangered by a power outage or catastrophic disk failure. The NTFS recovery capabilities do ensure that the file system on a volume remains accessible, but they make no guarantees for complete recovery of user files. Protection for applications that can't risk losing file data is provided through data redundancy.

Data redundancy for user files is implemented via the Windows layered driver model (explained in Chapter 8), which provides fault-tolerant disk support. NTFS communicates with a volume manager, which in turn communicates with a disk driver to write data to a disk. A volume manager can *mirror*, or duplicate, data from one disk onto another disk so that a redundant copy can always be retrieved. This support is commonly called *RAID level 1*. Volume managers also allow data to be written in *stripes* across three or more disks, using the equivalent of one disk to maintain parity information. If the data on one disk is lost or becomes inaccessible, the driver can reconstruct the disk's contents by means of exclusive-OR operations. This support is called *RAID level 5*. (See Chapter 9 for more information on striped volumes, mirrored volumes, and RAID-5 volumes.)

Advanced Features of NTFS

In addition to NTFS being recoverable, secure, reliable, and efficient for mission-critical systems, it includes the following advanced features that allow it to support a broad range of applications. Some of these features are exposed as APIs for applications to leverage, and others are internal features:

- Multiple data streams

- Unicode-based names

- General indexing facility

- Dynamic bad-cluster remapping

- Hard links

- Symbolic (soft) links and junctions

- Compression and sparse files

- Change logging

- Per-user volume quotas

- Link tracking

- Encryption

- POSIX support

- Defragmentation

- Read-only support and dynamic partitioning

The following sections provide an overview of these features.

Multiple Data Streams

In NTFS, each unit of information associated with a file—including its name, its owner, its time stamps, its contents, and so on—is implemented as a file attribute (NTFS object attribute). Each attribute consists of a single *stream*—that is, a simple sequence of bytes. This generic implementation makes it easy to add more attributes (and therefore more streams) to a file. Because a file's data is "just another attribute" of the file and because new attributes can be added, NTFS files (and file directories) can contain multiple data streams.

An NTFS file has one default data stream, which has no name. An application can create additional, named data streams and access them by referring to their names. To avoid altering the Windows I/O APIs, which take a string as a file name argument, the name of the data stream is specified by appending a colon (:) to the file name. Because the colon is a reserved character, it can serve as a separator between the file name and the data stream name, as illustrated in this example:

```
myfile.dat:stream2
```

Each stream has a separate allocation size (which defines how much disk space has been reserved for it), actual size (which is how many bytes the caller has used), and valid data length (which is how much of the stream has been initialized). In addition, each stream is given a separate file lock that is used to lock byte ranges and to allow concurrent access.

One component in Windows that uses multiple data streams is the Attachment Execution Service, which is invoked whenever the standard Windows API for saving Internet-based attachments is used by applications such as Internet Explorer or Outlook. Depending on which *zone* the file was downloaded from (such as the My Computer zone, the Intranet zone, or the Untrusted zone), Windows Explorer might warn the user that the file came from a possibly untrusted location or even completely block access to the file. For example, Figure 12-19 shows the dialog box that's displayed when executing Process Explorer after it was downloaded from the Sysinternals site.

Note If you clear the check box for Always Ask Before Opening This File, the zone identifier data stream will be removed from the file.

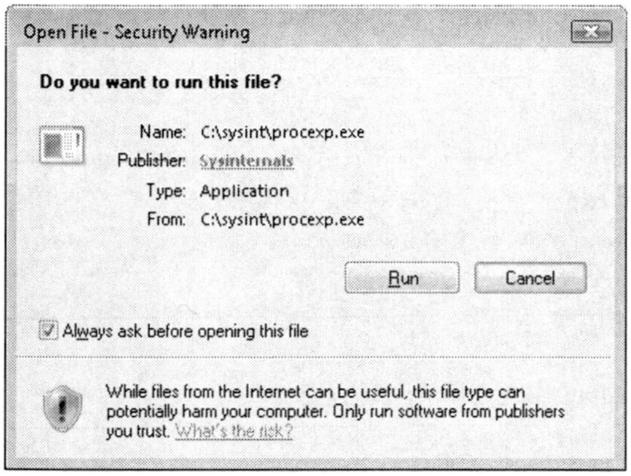

FIGURE 12-19 Security warning for files downloaded from the Internet

Other applications can use the multiple data stream feature as well. A backup utility, for example, might use an extra data stream to store backup-specific time stamps on files. Or an archival utility might implement hierarchical storage in which files that are older than a certain date or that haven't been accessed for a specified period of time are moved to offline storage. The utility could copy the file to offline storage, set the file's default data stream to 0, and add a data stream that specifies where the file is stored.

EXPERIMENT: Looking at Streams

Most Windows applications aren't designed to work with alternate named streams, but both the *echo* and *more* commands are. Thus, a simple way to view streams in action is to create a named stream using *echo* and then display it using *more*. The following command sequence creates a file named test with a stream named stream:

```
C:\>echo hello > test:stream
C:\>more < test:stream
hello
C:\>
```

If you perform a directory listing, Test's file size doesn't reflect the data stored in the alternate stream because NTFS returns the size of only the unnamed data stream for file query operations, including directory listings.

```
C:\>dir test
 Volume in drive C is WINDOWS
 Volume Serial Number is 3991-3040

 Directory of C:\

08/01/00  02:37p                     0 test
               1 File(s)             0 bytes
                         112,558,080 bytes free
```

You can determine what files and directories on your system have alternate data streams with the Streams utility from Sysinternals (see the following output) or by using the */r* switch in the *dir* command.

```
C:\>streams test

Streams v1.56 - Enumerate alternate NTFS data streams
Copyright (C) 1999-2007 Mark Russinovich
Sysinternals - www.sysinternals.com

 C:\test:
         :stream:$DATA 8
```

Unicode-Based Names

Like Windows as a whole, NTFS supports 16-bit Unicode 1.0/UTF-16 characters to store names of files, directories, and volumes. (The current version of the Unicode standard, version 6.1, from February 2012, supports up to 4 bytes per character and is not supported in kernel mode.) Unicode allows each character in each of the world's major languages to be uniquely represented, which aids in moving data easily from one country to another. Unicode is an improvement over the traditional representation of international characters—using a double-byte coding scheme that stores some characters in 8 bits and others in 16 bits, a technique that requires loading various code pages to establish the available characters. Because Unicode has a unique representation for each character, it doesn't depend on which code page is loaded. Each directory and file name in a path can be as many as 255 characters long and can contain Unicode characters, embedded spaces, and multiple periods.

General Indexing Facility

The NTFS architecture is structured to allow indexing of any file attribute on a disk volume using a B-tree structure. (Creating indexes on arbitrary attributes is not exported to users.) This structure enables the file system to efficiently locate files that match certain criteria—for example, all the files in a particular directory. In contrast, the FAT file system indexes file names but doesn't sort them, making lookups in large directories slow.

Several NTFS features take advantage of general indexing, including consolidated security descriptors, in which the security descriptors of a volume's files and directories are stored in a single internal stream, have duplicates removed, and are indexed using an internal security identifier that NTFS defines. The use of indexing by these features is described in the section "NTFS On-Disk Structure" later in this chapter.

Dynamic Bad-Cluster Remapping

Ordinarily, if a program tries to read data from a bad disk sector, the read operation fails and the data in the allocated cluster becomes inaccessible. If the disk is formatted as a fault-tolerant NTFS volume, however, the Windows volume manager dynamically retrieves a good copy of the data that was stored on the bad sector and then sends NTFS a warning that the sector is bad. NTFS will then allocate a new cluster, replacing the cluster in which the bad sector resides, and copies the data to the new cluster. It adds the bad cluster to the list of bad clusters on that volume (stored in the hidden metadata file $BadClus) and no longer uses it. This data recovery and dynamic bad-cluster remapping is an especially useful feature for file servers and fault-tolerant systems or for any application that can't afford to lose data. If the volume manager isn't loaded when a sector goes bad (such as early in the boot sequence), NTFS still replaces the cluster and doesn't reuse it, but it can't recover the data that was on the bad sector.

Hard Links

A hard link allows multiple paths to refer to the same file. (Hard links are not supported on directories.) If you create a hard link named C:\Documents\Spec.doc that refers to the existing file C:\Users\Administrator\Documents\Spec.doc, the two paths link to the same on-disk file, and you can make changes to the file using either path. Processes can create hard links with the Windows *CreateHardLink* function or the *ln* POSIX function.

NTFS implements hard links by keeping a reference count on the actual data, where each time a hard link is created for the file, an additional file name reference is made to the data. This means that if you have multiple hard links for a file, you can delete the original file name that referenced the data (C:\Users\Administrator\Documents\Spec.doc in our example), and the other hard links (C:\Documents\Spec.doc) will remain and point to the data. However, because hard links are on-disk local references to data (represented by a *file record number*), they can exist only within the same volume and can't span volumes or computers.

Symbolic (Soft) Links and Junctions

In addition to hard links, NTFS supports another type of file-name aliasing called *symbolic links* or *soft links*. Unlike hard links, symbolic links are strings that are interpreted dynamically and can be relative or absolute paths that refer to locations on any storage device, including ones on a different local volume or even a share on a different system. This means that symbolic links don't actually increase the reference count of the original file, so deleting the original file will result in the loss of the data, and a symbolic link that points to a nonexisting file will be left behind. Finally, unlike hard links, symbolic links can point to directories, not just files, which gives them an added advantage.

For example, if the path C:\Drivers is a directory symbolic link that redirects to %SystemRoot%\System32\Drivers, an application reading C:\Drivers\Ntfs.sys actually reads %SystemRoot%\System\Drivers\Ntfs.sys. Directory symbolic links are a useful way to lift directories that are deep in a directory tree to a more convenient depth without disturbing the original tree's structure or contents. The example just cited lifts the Drivers directory to the volume's root directory, reducing the directory depth of Ntfs.sys from three levels to one when Ntfs.sys is accessed through the directory symbolic link. File symbolic links work much the same way—you can think of them as shortcuts, except they are actually implemented on the file system instead of being .lnk files managed by Windows Explorer. Just like hard links, symbolic links can be created with the *mklink* utility (without the */H* option) or through the *CreateSymbolicLink* API.

Because certain legacy applications might not behave securely in the presence of symbolic links, especially across different machines, the creation of symbolic links requires the SeCreateSymbolicLink privilege, which is typically granted only to administrators. The file system also has a behavior option called *SymLinkEvaluation* that can be configured with the following command:

```
fsutil behavior set SymLinkEvaluation
```

By default, the Windows default symbolic link evaluation policy allows only local-to-local and local-to-remote symbolic links but not the opposite, as shown here:

```
C:\>fsutil behavior query SymLinkEvaluation
Local to local symbolic links are enabled
Local to remote symbolic links are enabled.
Remote to local symbolic links are disabled.
Remote to Remote symbolic links are disabled.
```

Symbolic links are implemented using an NTFS mechanism called *reparse points*. (Reparse points are discussed further in the section "Reparse Points" later in this chapter.) A reparse point is a file or directory that has a block of data called *reparse data* associated with it. Reparse data is user-defined data about the file or directory, such as its state or location that can be read from the reparse point by the application that created the data, a file system filter driver, or the I/O manager. When NTFS encounters a reparse point during a file or directory lookup, it returns the STATUS_REPARSE *status code*, which signals file system filter drivers that are attached to the volume and the I/O manager to examine the reparse data. Each reparse point type has a unique *reparse tag*. The reparse tag allows the component responsible for interpreting the reparse point's reparse data to recognize the reparse point without having to check the reparse data. A reparse tag owner, either a file system filter driver or the I/O manager, can choose one of the following options when it recognizes reparse data:

- The reparse tag owner can manipulate the path name specified in the file I/O operation that crosses the reparse point and let the I/O operation reissue with the altered path name. Junctions (described shortly) take this approach to redirect a directory lookup, for example.

- The reparse tag owner can remove the reparse point from the file, alter the file in some way, and then reissue the file I/O operation.

There are no Windows functions for creating reparse points. Instead, processes must use the FSCTL_SET_REPARSE_POINT file system control code with the Windows *DeviceIoControl* function. A process can query a reparse point's contents with the FSCTL_GET_REPARSE_POINT file system control code. The FILE_ATTRIBUTE_REPARSE_POINT flag is set in a reparse point's file attributes, so applications can check for reparse points by using the Windows *GetFileAttributes* function.

Another type of reparse point that NTFS supports is the *junction*. Junctions are a legacy NTFS concept and work almost identically to directory symbolic links, except they can only be local to a volume. There is no advantage to using a junction instead of a directory symbolic link, except that junctions are compatible with older versions of Windows, while directory symbolic links are not.

EXPERIMENT: Creating a Symbolic Link

This experiment shows you the main difference between a symbolic link and a hard link, even when dealing with files on the same volume. Create a symbolic link called soft.txt as shown here, pointing to the test.txt file created in the previous experiment:

```
C:\>mklink soft.txt test.txt
symbolic link created for soft.txt <<===>> test.txt
```

If you list the directory's contents, you'll notice that the symbolic link doesn't have a file size and is identified by the <SYMLINK> type. Furthermore, you'll note that the creation time is that of the symbolic link, not of the target file. The symbolic link can also have security permissions that are different from the permissions on the target file.

```
C:\>dir *.txt
 Volume in drive C is OS
 Volume Serial Number is 38D4-EA71

 Directory of C:\

05/12/2012  11:55 PM                     8 hard.txt
05/13/2012  12:28 AM    <SYMLINK>          soft.txt [test.txt]
05/12/2012  11:55 PM                     8 test.txt
               3 File(s)               16 bytes
               0 Dir(s)   10,636,480,512 bytes free
```

Finally, if you delete the original test.txt file, you can verify that both the hard link and symbolic link still exist but that the symbolic link does not point to a valid file anymore, while the hard link references the file data.

Compression and Sparse Files

NTFS supports compression of file data. Because NTFS performs compression and decompression procedures transparently, applications don't have to be modified to take advantage of this feature. Directories can also be compressed, which means that any files subsequently created in the directory are compressed.

Applications compress and decompress files by passing *DeviceIoControl* the FSCTL_SET_COMPRESSION file system control code. They query the compression state of a file or directory with the FSCTL_GET_COMPRESSION file system control code. A file or directory that is compressed has the FILE_ATTRIBUTE_COMPRESSED flag set in its attributes, so applications can also determine a file or directory's compression state with *GetFileAttributes*.

A second type of compression is known as *sparse files*. If a file is marked as sparse, NTFS doesn't allocate space on a volume for portions of the file that an application designates as empty. NTFS returns 0-filled buffers when an application reads from empty areas of a sparse file. This type of compression can be useful for client/server applications that implement circular-buffer logging, in which the server records information to a file and clients asynchronously read the information. Because the information that the server writes isn't needed after a client has read it, there's no need to store the information in the file. By making such a file sparse, the client can specify the portions of the file it reads as empty, freeing up space on the volume. The server can continue to append new information to the file without fear that the file will grow to consume all available space on the volume.

As with compressed files, NTFS manages sparse files transparently. Applications specify a file's sparseness state by passing the FSCTL_SET_SPARSE file system control code to *DeviceIoControl*. To set a range of a file to empty, applications use the FSCTL_SET_ZERO_DATA code, and they can ask NTFS for a description of what parts of a file are sparse by using the control code FSCTL_QUERY_ALLOCATED_RANGES. One application of sparse files is the NTFS *change journal*, described next.

Change Logging

Many types of applications need to monitor volumes for file and directory changes. For example, an automatic backup program might perform an initial full backup and then incremental backups based on file changes. An obvious way for an application to monitor a volume for changes is for it to scan the volume, recording the state of files and directories, and on a subsequent scan detect differences. This process can adversely affect system performance, however, especially on computers with thousands or tens of thousands of files.

An alternate approach is for an application to register a directory notification by using the *FindFirstChangeNotification* or *ReadDirectoryChangesW* Windows function. As an input parameter, the application specifies the name of a directory it wants to monitor, and the function returns whenever the contents of the directory change. Although this approach is more efficient than volume scanning, it requires the application to be running at all times. Using these functions can also require an application to scan directories because *FindFirstChangeNotification* doesn't indicate what changed—just that something in the directory has changed. An application can pass a buffer to *ReadDirectoryChangesW* that the FSD fills in with change records. If the buffer overflows, however, the application must be prepared to fall back on scanning the directory.

NTFS provides a third approach that overcomes the drawbacks of the first two: an application can configure the NTFS change journal facility by using the *DeviceIoControl* function's FSCTL_CREATE_USN_JOURNAL file system control code (USN is update sequence number) to have NTFS record information about file and directory changes to an internal file called the *change journal*. A change journal is usually large enough to virtually guarantee that applications get a chance to process changes without missing any. Applications use the FSCTL_QUERY_USN_JOURNAL file system control code to read records from a change journal, and they can specify that the *DeviceIoControl* function not complete until new records are available.

Per-User Volume Quotas

Systems administrators often need to track or limit user disk space usage on shared storage volumes, so NTFS includes quota-management support. NTFS quota-management support allows for per-user specification of quota enforcement, which is useful for usage tracking and tracking when a user reaches warning and limit thresholds. NTFS can be configured to log an event indicating the occurrence to the System event log if a user surpasses his warning limit. Similarly, if a user attempts to use more volume storage then her quota limit permits, NTFS can log an event to the System event log and fail the application file I/O that would have caused the quota violation with a "disk full" error code.

NTFS tracks a user's volume usage by relying on the fact that it tags files and directories with the security ID (SID) of the user who created them. (See Chapter 6 in Part 1 for a definition of SIDs.) The logical sizes of files and directories a user owns count against the user's administrator-defined quota limit. Thus, a user can't circumvent his or her quota limit by creating an empty sparse file that is larger than the quota would allow and then fill the file with nonzero data. Similarly, whereas a 50-KB file might compress to 10 KB, the full 50 KB is used for quota accounting.

By default, volumes don't have quota tracking enabled. You need to use the Quota tab of a volume's Properties dialog box, shown in Figure 12-20, to enable quotas, to specify default warning and limit thresholds, and to configure the NTFS behavior that occurs when a user hits the warning or limit threshold. The Quota Entries tool, which you can launch from this dialog box, enables an administrator to specify different limits and behavior for each user. Applications that want to interact with NTFS quota management use COM quota interfaces, including *IDiskQuotaControl*, *IDiskQuotaUser*, and *IDiskQuotaEvents*.

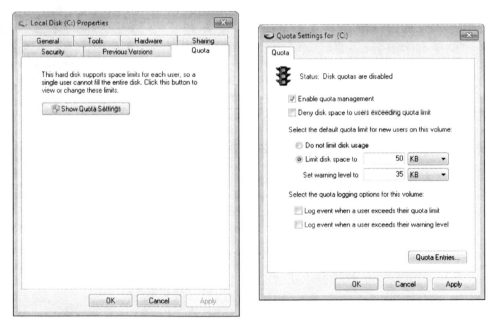

FIGURE 12-20 Volume Properties dialog box

Link Tracking

Shell shortcuts allow users to place files in their shell namespace (on their desktop, for example) that link to files located in the file system namespace. The Windows Start menu uses shell shortcuts extensively. Similarly, object linking and embedding (OLE) links allow documents from one application to be transparently embedded in the documents of other applications. The products of the Microsoft Office suite, including PowerPoint, Excel, and Word, use OLE linking.

Although shell and OLE links provide an easy way to connect files with one another and with the shell namespace, they can be difficult to manage if a user moves the source of a shell or OLE link (a link source is the file or directory to which a link points). NTFS in Windows includes support for a service application called *distributed link-tracking*, which maintains the integrity of shell and OLE links when link targets move. Using the NTFS link-tracking support, if a link target located on an NTFS volume moves to any other NTFS volume within the originating volume's domain, the link-tracking service can transparently follow the movement and update the link to reflect the change.

NTFS link-tracking support is based on an optional file attribute known as an *object ID*. An application can assign an object ID to a file by using the FSCTL_CREATE_OR_GET_OBJECT_ID (which assigns an ID if one isn't already assigned) and FSCTL_SET_OBJECT_ID file system control codes. Object IDs are queried with the FSCTL_CREATE_OR_GET_OBJECT_ID and FSCTL_GET_OBJECT_ID file system control codes. The FSCTL_DELETE_OBJECT_ID file system control code lets applications delete object IDs from files.

Encryption

Corporate users often store sensitive information on their computers. Although data stored on company servers is usually safely protected with proper network security settings and physical access control, data stored on laptops can be exposed when a laptop is lost or stolen. NTFS file permissions don't offer protection because NTFS volumes can be fully accessed without regard to security by using NTFS file-reading software that doesn't require Windows to be running. Furthermore, NTFS file permissions are rendered useless when an alternate Windows installation is used to access files from an administrator account. Recall from Chapter 6 in Part 1 that the administrator account has the take-ownership and backup privileges, both of which allow it to access any secured object by overriding the object's security settings.

NTFS includes a facility called Encrypting File System (EFS), which users can use to encrypt sensitive data. The operation of EFS, as that of file compression, is completely transparent to applications, which means that file data is automatically decrypted when an application running in the account of a user authorized to view the data reads it and is automatically encrypted when an authorized application changes the data.

> **Note** NTFS doesn't permit the encryption of files located in the system volume's root directory or in the \Windows directory because many files in these locations are required during the boot process and EFS isn't active during the boot process. BitLocker, described in Chapter 9, is a technology much better suited for environments in which this is a requirement because it supports full-volume encryption.

EFS relies on cryptographic services supplied by Windows in user mode, so it consists of both a kernel-mode component that tightly integrates with NTFS as well as user-mode DLLs that communicate with the Local Security Authority Subsystem (LSASS) and cryptographic DLLs.

Files that are encrypted can be accessed only by using the private key of an account's EFS private/ public key pair, and private keys are locked using an account's password. Thus, EFS-encrypted files on lost or stolen laptops can't be accessed using any means (other than a brute-force cryptographic attack) without the password of an account that is authorized to view the data.

Applications can use the *EncryptFile* and *DecryptFile* Windows API functions to encrypt and decrypt files, and *FileEncryptionStatus* to retrieve a file or directory's EFS-related attributes, such as whether the file or directory is encrypted. A file or directory that is encrypted has the FILE_ ATTRIBUTE_ENCRYPTED flag set in its attributes, so applications can also determine a file or directory's encryption state with *GetFileAttributes*.

POSIX Support

As explained in Chapter 2, "System Architecture," in Part 1, one of the mandates for Windows was to fully support the POSIX 1003.1 standard. In the file system area, the POSIX standard requires support for case-sensitive file and directory names, traversal permissions (where security for each directory of a path is used when determining whether a user has access to a file or directory), a "file-change-time" time stamp (which is different from the MS-DOS "time-last-modified" stamp), and hard links. NTFS implements each of these features.

Defragmentation

Even though NTFS makes efforts to keep files contiguous when allocating blocks to extend a file, a volume's files can still become fragmented over time, especially if the file is extended multiple times or when there is limited free space. A file is fragmented if its data occupies discontiguous clusters. For example, Figure 12-21 shows a fragmented file consisting of five fragments. However, like most file systems (including versions of FAT on Windows), NTFS makes no special efforts to keep files contiguous (this is handled by the built-in defragmenter), other than to reserve a region of disk space known as the *master file table* (MFT) zone for the MFT. (NTFS lets other files allocate from the MFT zone when volume free space runs low.) Keeping an area free for the MFT can help it stay contiguous, but it, too, can become fragmented. (See the section "Master File Table" later in this chapter for more information on MFTs.)

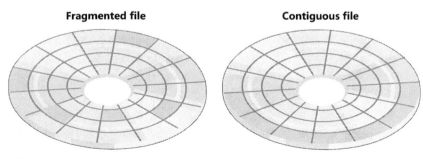

FIGURE 12-21 Fragmented and contiguous files

To facilitate the development of third-party disk defragmentation tools, Windows includes a defragmentation API that such tools can use to move file data so that files occupy contiguous clusters. The API consists of file system controls that let applications obtain a map of a volume's free and in-use clusters (FSCTL_GET_VOLUME_BITMAP), obtain a map of a file's cluster usage (FSCTL_GET_RETRIEVAL_POINTERS), and move a file (FSCTL_MOVE_FILE).

Windows includes a built-in defragmentation tool that is accessible by using the Disk Defragmenter utility (%SystemRoot%\System32\Dfrgui.exe), shown in Figure 12-22, as well as a command-line interface, %SystemRoot%\System32\Defrag.exe, that you can run interactively or schedule but that does not produce detailed reports or offer control—such as excluding files or directories—over the defragmentation process.

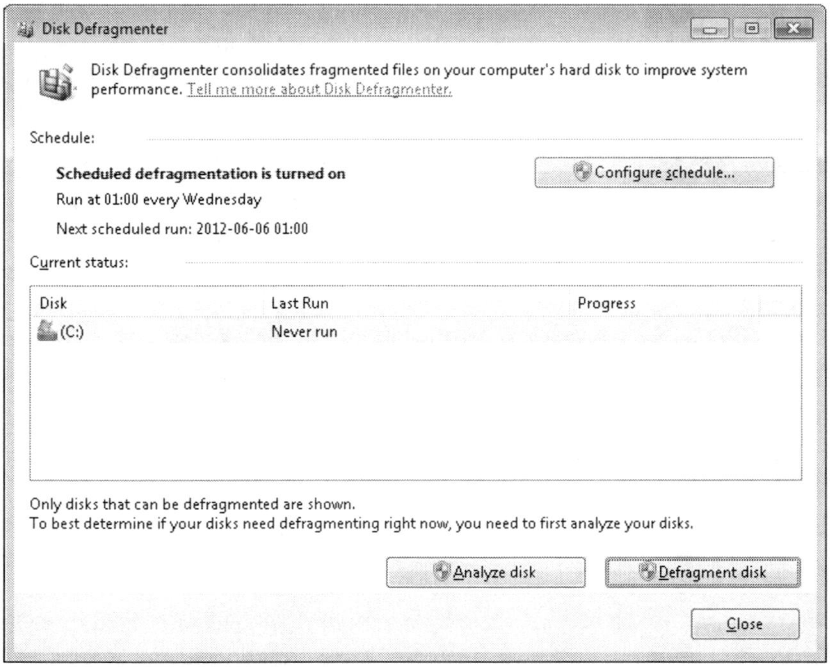

FIGURE 12-22 Disk Defragmenter

The only limitation imposed by the defragmentation implementation in NTFS is that paging files and NTFS log files cannot be defragmented.

Dynamic Partitioning

The NTFS driver allows users to dynamically resize any partition, including the system partition, either shrinking or expanding it (if enough space is available). Expanding a partition is easy if enough space exists on the disk and is performed through the FSCTL_EXPAND_VOLUME file system control code. Shrinking a partition is a more complicated process, because it requires moving any file system data that is currently in the area to be thrown away to the region that will still remain after the shrinking process (a mechanism similar to defragmentation). Shrinking is implemented by two components: the *shrinking engine* and the file system driver.

The shrinking engine is implemented in user mode. It communicates with NTFS to determine the maximum number of reclaimable bytes—that is, how much data can be moved from the region that will be resized into the region that will remain. The shrinking engine uses the standard defragmentation mechanism shown earlier, which doesn't support relocating page file fragments that are in use or any other files that have been marked as unmovable with the FSCTL_MARK_HANDLE file system control code (like the hibernation file). The master file table backup ($MftMirr), the NTFS metadata transaction log ($LogFile), and the volume label file ($Volume) cannot be moved, which limits the minimum size of the shrunk volume and causes wasted space.

The file system driver shrinking code is responsible for ensuring that the volume remains in a consistent state throughout the shrinking process. To do so, it exposes an interface that uses three requests that describe the current operation, which are sent through the FSCTL_SHRINK_VOLUME control code:

- The *ShrinkPrepare* request, which must be issued before any other operation. This request takes the desired size of the new volume in sectors and is used so that the file system can block further allocations outside the new volume boundary. The *ShrinkPrepare* request doesn't verify whether the volume can actually be shrunk by the specified amount, but it does ensure that the amount is numerically valid and that there aren't any other shrinking operations ongoing. Note that after a prepare operation, the file handle to the volume becomes associated with the shrink request. If the file handle is closed, the operation is assumed to be aborted.

- The *ShrinkCommit* request, which the shrinking engine issues after a *ShrinkPrepare* request. In this state, the file system attempts the removal of the requested number of clusters in the most recent prepare request. (If multiple prepare requests have been sent with different sizes, the last one is the determining one.) The *ShrinkCommit* request assumes that the shrinking engine has completed and will fail if any allocated blocks remain in the area to be shrunk.

- The *ShrinkAbort* request, which can be issued by the shrinking engine or caused by events such as the closure of the file handle to the volume. This request undoes the *ShrinkCommit* operation by returning the partition to its original size and allows new allocations outside the shrunk region to occur again. However, defragmentation changes made by the shrinking engine remain.

If a system is rebooted during a shrinking operation, NTFS restores the file system to a consistent state via its metadata recovery mechanism, explained later in the chapter. Because the actual shrink operation isn't executed until all other operations have been completed, the volume retains its original size and only defragmentation operations that had already been flushed out to disk persist.

Finally, shrinking a volume has several effects on the volume shadow copy mechanism (for more information on VSS, see Chapter 9). Recall that the copy-on-write mechanism allows VSS to simply retain parts of the file that were actually modified while still linking to the original file data. For deleted files, this file data will not be associated with visible files but appear as free space instead—free space that will likely be located in the area that is about to be shrunk. The shrinking engine therefore communicates with VSS to engage it in the shrinking process. In summary, the VSS mechanism's job is to copy deleted file data into its differencing area and to increase the differencing area as required to accommodate additional data. This detail is important because it poses another constraint on the size to which even volumes with ample free space can shrink.

NTFS File System Driver

As described in Chapter 8, in the framework of the Windows I/O system, NTFS and other file systems are loadable device drivers that run in kernel mode. They are invoked indirectly by applications that use Windows or other I/O APIs (such as POSIX). As Figure 12-23 shows, the Windows environment subsystems call Windows system services, which in turn locate the appropriate loaded drivers and call them. (For a description of system service dispatching, see the section "System Service Dispatching" in Chapter 3 in Part 1.)

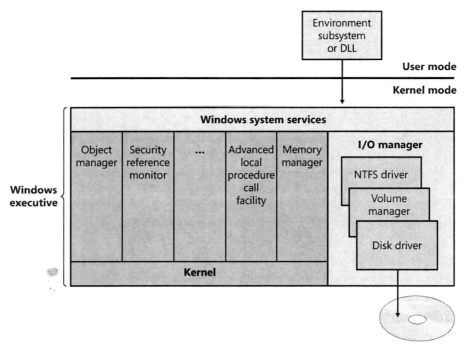

FIGURE 12-23 Components of the Windows I/O system

The layered drivers pass I/O requests to one another by calling the Windows executive's I/O manager. Relying on the I/O manager as an intermediary allows each driver to maintain independence so that it can be loaded or unloaded without affecting other drivers. In addition, the NTFS driver interacts with the three other Windows executive components, shown in the left side of Figure 12-24, that are closely related to file systems.

The log file service (LFS) is the part of NTFS that provides services for maintaining a log of disk writes. The log file that LFS writes is used to recover an NTFS-formatted volume in the case of a system failure. (See the section "Log File Service" later in the chapter.)

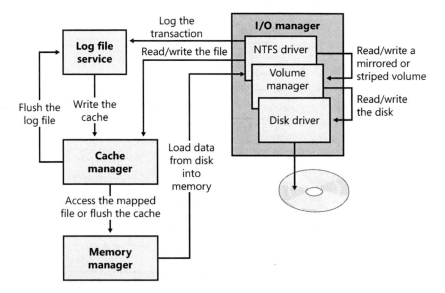

FIGURE 12-24 NTFS and related components

The cache manager is the component of the Windows executive that provides systemwide caching services for NTFS and other file system drivers, including network file system drivers (servers and redirectors). All file systems implemented for Windows access cached files by mapping them into system address space and then accessing the virtual memory. The cache manager provides a specialized file system interface to the Windows memory manager for this purpose. When a program tries to access a part of a file that isn't loaded into the cache (a *cache miss*), the memory manager calls NTFS to access the disk driver and obtain the file contents from disk. The cache manager optimizes disk I/O by using its lazy writer threads to call the memory manager to flush cache contents to disk as a background activity (asynchronous disk writing). (For a complete description of the cache manager, see Chapter 11.)

NTFS participates in the Windows object model by implementing files as objects. This implementation allows files to be shared and protected by the object manager, the component of Windows that manages all executive-level objects. (The object manager is described in the section "Object Manager" in Chapter 3 in Part 1.)

An application creates and accesses files just as it does other Windows objects: by means of object handles. By the time an I/O request reaches NTFS, the Windows object manager and security system have already verified that the calling process has the authority to access the file object in the way it is attempting to. The security system has compared the caller's access token to the entries in the access control list for the file object. (See Chapter 6 in Part 1 for more information about access control lists.) The I/O manager has also transformed the file handle into a pointer to a file object. NTFS uses the information in the file object to access the file on disk.

Figure 12-25 shows the data structures that link a file handle to the file system's on-disk structure.

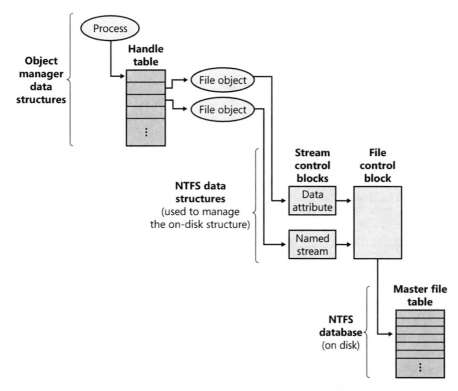

FIGURE 12-25 NTFS data structures

NTFS follows several pointers to get from the file object to the location of the file on disk. As Figure 12-25 shows, a file object, which represents a single call to the open-file system service, points to a *stream control block* (SCB) for the file attribute that the caller is trying to read or write. In Figure 12-25, a process has opened both the unnamed data attribute and a named stream (alternate data attribute) for the file. The SCBs represent individual file attributes and contain information about how to find specific attributes within a file. All the SCBs for a file point to a common data structure called a *file control block* (FCB). The FCB contains a pointer (actually, an index into the MFT, as explained in the section "File Record Numbers" later in this chapter) to the file's record in the disk-based master file table (MFT), which is described in detail in the following section.

NTFS On-Disk Structure

This section describes the on-disk structure of an NTFS volume, including how disk space is divided and organized into clusters, how files are organized into directories, how the actual file data and attribute information is stored on disk, and finally, how NTFS data compression works.

Volumes

The structure of NTFS begins with a volume. A *volume* corresponds to a logical partition on a disk, and it is created when you format a disk or part of a disk for NTFS. You can also create a RAID volume that spans multiple disks by using the Windows Disk Management MMC snap-in or the *diskpart* (%SystemRoot%\System32\Diskpart.exe) command available from the Windows command prompt.

A disk can have one volume or several. NTFS handles each volume independently of the others. Three sample disk configurations for a 150-GB hard disk are illustrated in Figure 12-26.

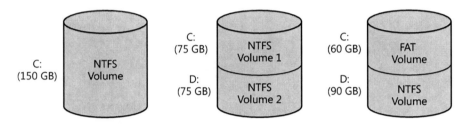

FIGURE 12-26 Sample disk configurations

A volume consists of a series of files plus any additional unallocated space remaining on the disk partition. In the FAT file system, a volume also contains areas specially formatted for use by the file system. An NTFS volume, however, stores all file system data, such as bitmaps and directories, and even the system bootstrap, as ordinary files.

> **Note** The on-disk format of NTFS volumes on Windows 7 and Windows Server 2008 R2 is version 3.1, the same as it has been since Windows XP and Windows Server 2003. The version number of a volume is stored in its $Volume metadata file.

Clusters

The cluster size on an NTFS volume, or the *cluster factor*, is established when a user formats the volume with either the *format* command or the Disk Management MMC snap-in. The default cluster factor varies with the size of the volume, but it is an integral number of physical sectors, always a power of 2 (1 sector, 2 sectors, 4 sectors, 8 sectors, and so on). The cluster factor is expressed as the number of bytes in the cluster, such as 512 bytes, 1 KB, 2 KB, and so on.

Internally, NTFS refers only to clusters. (However, NTFS forms low-level volume I/O operations such that clusters are sector-aligned and have a length that is a multiple of the sector size.) NTFS uses the cluster as its unit of allocation to maintain its independence from physical sector sizes. This independence allows NTFS to efficiently support very large disks by using a larger cluster factor or to support newer disks that have a sector size other than 512 bytes. (See Chapter 9 for more information on disks with sectors larger than 512 bytes.) On a larger volume, use of a larger cluster factor can reduce fragmentation and speed allocation, at the cost of wasted disk space. (If the cluster size is 4,096, and a file is only 1,024 bytes, then 3,072 bytes are wasted. See Chapter 9 for more information on default cluster sizes.) Both the *format* command available from the command prompt and the Format menu option under the All Tasks option on the Action menu in the Disk Management MMC snap-in choose a default cluster factor based on the volume size, but you can override this size.

NTFS refers to physical locations on a disk by means of *logical cluster numbers* (LCNs). LCNs are simply the numbering of all clusters from the beginning of the volume to the end. To convert an LCN to a physical disk address, NTFS multiplies the LCN by the cluster factor to get the physical byte offset on the volume, as the disk driver interface requires. NTFS refers to the data within a file by means of *virtual cluster numbers* (VCNs). VCNs number the clusters belonging to a particular file from 0 through *m*. VCNs aren't necessarily physically contiguous, however; they can be mapped to any number of LCNs on the volume.

Master File Table

In NTFS, all data stored on a volume is contained in files, including the data structures used to locate and retrieve files, the bootstrap data, and the bitmap that records the allocation state of the entire volume (the NTFS metadata). Storing everything in files allows the file system to easily locate and maintain the data, and each separate file can be protected by a security descriptor. In addition, if a particular part of the disk goes bad, NTFS can relocate the metadata files to prevent the disk from becoming inaccessible.

The MFT is the heart of the NTFS volume structure. The MFT is implemented as an array of file records. The size of each file record is fixed at 1 KB, regardless of cluster size. (The structure of a file record is described in the "File Records" section later in this chapter.) Logically, the MFT contains one record for each file on the volume, including a record for the MFT itself. In addition to the MFT, each NTFS volume includes a set of metadata files containing the information that is used to implement the file system structure. Each of these NTFS metadata files has a name that begins with a dollar sign ($), and is hidden. For example, the file name of the MFT is $MFT. The rest of the files on an NTFS volume are normal user files and directories, as shown in Figure 12-27.

Usually, each MFT record corresponds to a different file. If a file has a large number of attributes or becomes highly fragmented, however, more than one record might be needed for a single file. In such cases, the first MFT record, which stores the locations of the others, is called the *base file record*.

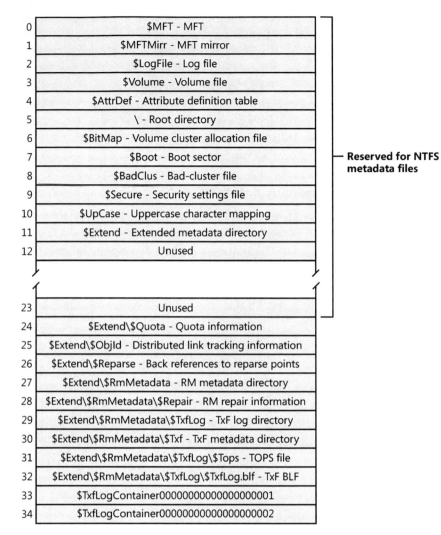

0	$MFT - MFT
1	$MFTMirr - MFT mirror
2	$LogFile - Log file
3	$Volume - Volume file
4	$AttrDef - Attribute definition table
5	\ - Root directory
6	$BitMap - Volume cluster allocation file
7	$Boot - Boot sector
8	$BadClus - Bad-cluster file
9	$Secure - Security settings file
10	$UpCase - Uppercase character mapping
11	$Extend - Extended metadata directory
12	Unused
23	Unused
24	$Extend\$Quota - Quota information
25	$Extend\$ObjId - Distributed link tracking information
26	$Extend\$Reparse - Back references to reparse points
27	$Extend\$RmMetadata - RM metadata directory
28	$Extend\$RmMetadata\$Repair - RM repair information
29	$Extend\$RmMetadata\$TxfLog - TxF log directory
30	$Extend\$RmMetadata\$Txf - TxF metadata directory
31	$Extend\$RmMetadata\$TxfLog\$Tops - TOPS file
32	$Extend\$RmMetadata\$TxfLog\$TxfLog.blf - TxF BLF
33	$TxfLogContainer00000000000000000001
34	$TxfLogContainer00000000000000000002

Reserved for NTFS metadata files

FIGURE 12-27 File records for NTFS metadata files in the MFT

When it first accesses a volume, NTFS must *mount* it—that is, read metadata from the disk and construct internal data structures so that it can process application file system accesses. To mount the volume, NTFS looks in the volume boot record (VBR) (located at LCN 0), which contains a data structure call the boot parameter block (BPB), to find the physical disk address of the MFT. The MFT's own file record is the first entry in the table; the second file record points to a file located in the middle of the disk called the *MFT mirror* (file name $MFTMirr) that contains a copy of the first four rows of the MFT. This partial copy of the MFT is used to locate metadata files if part of the MFT file can't be read for some reason.

Once NTFS finds the file record for the MFT, it obtains the VCN-to-LCN mapping information in the file record's data attribute and stores it into memory. Each run (runs are explained later in this chapter in the section "Resident and Nonresident Attributes") has a VCN-to-LCN mapping and a run length because that's all the information necessary to locate the LCN for any VCN. This mapping information tells NTFS where the runs containing the MFT are located on the disk. NTFS then processes the MFT records for several more metadata files and opens the files. Next, NTFS performs its file system recovery operation (described in the section "Recovery" later in this chapter), and finally, it opens its remaining metadata files. The volume is now ready for user access.

> **Note** For the sake of clarity, the text and diagrams in this chapter depict a run as including a VCN, an LCN, and a run length. NTFS actually compresses this information on disk into an LCN/next-VCN pair. Given a starting VCN, NTFS can determine the length of a run by subtracting the starting VCN from the next VCN.

As the system runs, NTFS writes to another important metadata file, the *log file* (file name $LogFile). NTFS uses the log file to record all operations that affect the NTFS volume structure, including file creation or any commands, such as *copy*, that alter the directory structure. The log file is used to recover an NTFS volume after a system failure and is also described in the "Recovery" section.

Another entry in the MFT is reserved for the *root directory* (also known as "\"; for example, C:\). Its file record contains an index of the files and directories stored in the root of the NTFS directory structure. When NTFS is first asked to open a file, it begins its search for the file in the root directory's file record. After opening a file, NTFS stores the file's MFT record number so that it can directly access the file's MFT record when it reads and writes the file later.

NTFS records the allocation state of the volume in the *bitmap file* (file name $BitMap). The data attribute for the bitmap file contains a bitmap, each of whose bits represents a cluster on the volume, identifying whether the cluster is free or has been allocated to a file.

The *security file* (file name $Secure) stores the volume-wide security descriptor database. NTFS files and directories have individually settable security descriptors, but to conserve space, NTFS stores the settings in a common file, which allows files and directories that have the same security settings to reference the same security descriptor. In most environments, entire directory trees have the same security settings, so this optimization provides a significant saving of disk space.

Another system file, the *boot file* (file name $Boot), stores the Windows bootstrap code if the volume is a system volume. On non-system volumes, there is code that displays an error message on the screen if an attempt is made to boot from that volume. For the system to boot, the bootstrap code must be located at a specific disk address so that the BIOS can find it. During formatting, the *format* command defines this area as a file by creating a file record for it. All files are in the MFT, and all clusters are either free or allocated to a file—there are no hidden files or clusters in NTFS, although some files (metadata) are not visible to users. The boot file as well as NTFS metadata files can be individually protected by means of the security descriptors that are applied to all Windows objects. Using this "everything on the disk is a file" model also means that the bootstrap can be modified by normal file I/O, although the boot file is protected from editing.

NTFS also maintains a *bad-cluster file* (file name $BadClus) for recording any bad spots on the disk volume and a file known as the *volume file* (file name $Volume), which contains the volume name, the version of NTFS for which the volume is formatted, and a number of flag bits that indicate the state and health of the volume, such as a bit that indicates that the volume is corrupt and must be repaired by the Chkdsk utility. (The Chkdsk utility is covered in more detail later in the chapter.) The *uppercase file* (file name $UpCase) includes a translation table between lowercase and uppercase characters. NTFS maintains a file containing an *attribute definition table* (file name $AttrDef) that defines the attribute types supported on the volume and indicates whether they can be indexed, recovered during a system recovery operation, and so on.

NTFS stores several metadata files in the *extensions* (directory name $Extend) metadata directory, including the *object identifier file* (file name $ObjId), the *quota file* (file name $Quota), the *change journal file* (file name $UsnJrnl), the *reparse point file* (file name $Reparse), and the *default resource manager directory* (directory name $RmMetadata). These files store information related to extended features of NTFS. The object identifier file stores file object IDs, the quota file stores quota limit and behavior information on volumes that have quotas enabled, the change journal file records file and directory changes, and the reparse point file stores information about which files and directories on the volume include reparse point data.

The default resource manager directory contains directories related to transactional NTFS (TxF) support, including the *transaction log directory* (directory name $TxfLog), the *transaction isolation directory* (directory name $Txf), and the *transaction repair directory* (file name $Repair). The transaction log directory contains the *TxF base log file* (file name $TxfLog.blf) and any number of log container files, depending on the size of the transaction log, but it always contains at least two: one for the Kernel Transaction Manager (KTM) log stream (file name $TxfLogContainer00000000000000000001), and one for the TxF log stream (file name $TxfLogContainer00000000000000000002). The transaction log directory also contains the *TxF old page stream* (file name $Tops), which we'll describe later.

EXPERIMENT: Viewing NTFS Information

You can use the built-in Fsutil.exe command-line program to view information about an NTFS volume, including the placement and size of the MFT and MFT zone:

```
C:\>fsutil fsinfo ntfsinfo c:
NTFS Volume Serial Number  :      0x9a38d50e38d4ea71
Version :                         3.1
Number Sectors :                  0x0000000015c82ff0
Total Clusters :                  0x0000000002b905fe
Free Clusters   :                 0x000000000013c332
Total Reserved :                  0x0000000000000780
Bytes Per Sector   :              512
Bytes Per Cluster :               4096
Bytes Per FileRecord Segment    : 1024
Clusters Per FileRecord Segment : 0
Mft Valid Data Length :           0x0000000023db0000
Mft Start Lcn  :                  0x00000000000c0000
Mft2 Start Lcn :                  0x00000000016082ff
Mft Zone Start :                  0x0000000002751f60
Mft Zone End   :                  0x000000000275cd60
RM Identifier:          CF7234E7-39E3-11DC-BDCE-00188BDD5F49
```

File Record Numbers

A file on an NTFS volume is identified by a 64-bit value called a *file record number,* which consists of a file number and a sequence number. The file number corresponds to the position of the file's file record in the MFT minus 1 (or to the position of the base file record minus 1 if the file has more than one file record). The sequence number, which is incremented each time an MFT file record position is reused, enables NTFS to perform internal consistency checks. A file record number is illustrated in Figure 12-28.

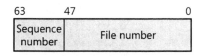

FIGURE 12-28 File record number

File Records

Instead of viewing a file as just a repository for textual or binary data, NTFS stores files as a collection of attribute/value pairs, one of which is the data it contains (called the *unnamed data attribute*). Other attributes that comprise a file include the file name, time stamp information, and possibly additional named data attributes. Figure 12-29 illustrates an MFT record for a small file.

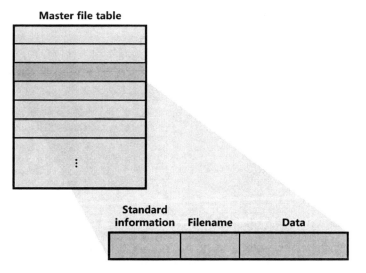

FIGURE 12-29 MFT record for a small file

Each file attribute is stored as a separate stream of bytes within a file. Strictly speaking, NTFS doesn't read and write files—it reads and writes attribute streams. NTFS supplies these attribute operations: create, delete, read (byte range), and write (byte range). The read and write services normally operate on the file's unnamed data attribute. However, a caller can specify a different data attribute by using the named data stream syntax.

Table 12-6 lists the attributes for files on an NTFS volume. (Not all attributes are present for every file.)

TABLE 12-6 Attributes for NTFS Files

Attribute	Attribute Type Name	Resident?	Description
Volume information	$VOLUME_INFORMATION, $VOLUME_NAME	Always, Always	These attributes are present only in the $Volume metadata file. They store volume version and label information.
Standard information	$STANDARD_INFORMATION	Always	File attributes such as read-only, archive, and so on; time stamps, including when the file was created or last modified.
Filename	$FILE_NAME	Maybe	The file's name in Unicode 1.0 characters. A file can have multiple filename attributes, as it does when a hard link to a file exists or when a file with a long name has an automatically generated "short name" for access by MS-DOS and 16-bit Windows applications.
Security descriptor	$SECURITY_DESCRIPTOR	Maybe	This attribute is present for backward compatibility with previous versions of NTFS and is rarely used in the current version of NTFS (3.1). NTFS stores almost all security descriptors in the $Secure metadata file, sharing descriptors among files and directories that have the same settings. Previous versions of NTFS stored private security descriptor information with each file and directory. Some files still include a $SECURITY_DESCRIPTOR attribute, such as $Boot.
Data	$DATA		The contents of the file. In NTFS, a file has one default unnamed data attribute and can have additional named data attributes—that is, a file can have multiple data streams. A directory has no default data attribute but can have optional named data attributes.
Index root, index allocation, and index bitmap	$INDEX_ROOT, $INDEX_ALLOCATION, $BITMAP	Always, Never, Maybe	Three attributes used to implement B-tree data structures used by directories, security, quota, and other metadata files.
Attribute list	$ATTRIBUTE_LIST	Maybe	A list of the attributes that make up the file and the file record number of the MFT entry where each attribute is located. This attribute is present when a file requires more than one MFT file record.
Object ID	$OBJECT_ID	Always	A 16-byte identifier (GUID) for a file or directory. The link-tracking service assigns object IDs to shell shortcut and OLE link source files. NTFS provides APIs so that files and directories can be opened with their object ID rather than their file name.
Reparse information	$REPARSE_POINT	Maybe	This attribute stores a file's reparse point data. NTFS junctions and mount points include this attribute.
Extended attributes	$EA, $EA_INFORMATION	Maybe, Always	Extended attributes are name/value pairs and aren't normally used but are provided for backward compatibility with OS/2 applications.

Attribute	Attribute Type Name	Resident?	Description
Logged utility stream	$LOGGED_UTILITY_STREAM	Maybe	EFS stores data in this attribute ($EFS) that's used to manage a file's encryption, such as the encrypted version of the key needed to decrypt the file and a list of users who are authorized to access the file. When a file or directory becomes part of a transaction, TxF also stores transaction data in the $TXF_DATA attribute, such as the file's unique transaction ID.

Table 12-6 shows attribute names; however, attributes actually correspond to numeric type codes, which NTFS uses to order the attributes within a file record. The file attributes in an MFT record are ordered by these type codes (numerically in ascending order), with some attribute types appearing more than once—if a file has multiple data attributes, for example, or multiple file names. All possible attribute types (and their names) are listed in the $AttrDef metadata file.

Each attribute in a file record is identified with its attribute type code and has a value and an optional name. An attribute's value is the byte stream composing the attribute. For example, the value of the $FILE_NAME attribute is the file's name; the value of the $DATA attribute is whatever bytes the user stored in the file.

Most attributes never have names, although the index-related attributes and the $DATA attribute often do. Names distinguish between multiple attributes of the same type that a file can include. For example, a file that has a named data stream has two $DATA attributes: an unnamed $DATA attribute storing the default unnamed data stream and a named $DATA attribute having the name of the alternate stream and storing the named stream's data.

File Names

Both NTFS and FAT allow each file name in a path to be as many as 255 characters long. File names can contain Unicode characters as well as multiple periods and embedded spaces. However, the FAT file system supplied with MS-DOS is limited to 8 (non-Unicode) characters for its file names, followed by a period and a 3-character extension. Figure 12-30 provides a visual representation of the different file namespaces Windows supports and shows how they intersect.

The POSIX subsystem requires the biggest namespace of all the application execution environments that Windows supports, and therefore the NTFS namespace is equivalent to the POSIX namespace. The POSIX subsystem can create names that aren't visible to Windows and MS-DOS applications, including names with trailing periods and trailing spaces. Ordinarily, creating a file using the large POSIX namespace isn't a problem because you would do that only if you intended the POSIX subsystem or POSIX client systems to use that file.

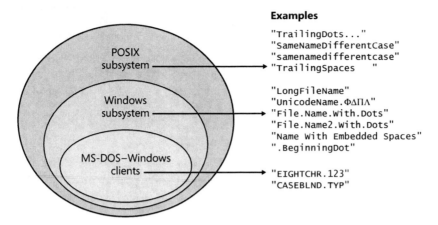

Examples

```
"TrailingDots..."
"SameNameDifferentCase"
"samenamedifferentcase"
"TrailingSpaces      "

"LongFileName"
"UnicodeName.ΦΔΠΛ"
"File.Name.With.Dots"
"File.Name2.With.Dots"
"Name With Embedded Spaces"
".BeginningDot"

"EIGHTCHR.123"
"CASEBLND.TYP"
```

FIGURE 12-30 Windows file namespaces

The relationship between 32-bit Windows (Windows) applications and MS-DOS and 16-bit Windows applications is a much closer one, however. The Windows area in Figure 12-30 represents file names that the Windows subsystem can create on an NTFS volume but that MS-DOS and 16-bit Windows applications can't see. This group includes file names longer than the 8.3 format of MS-DOS names, those containing Unicode (international) characters, those with multiple period characters or a beginning period, and those with embedded spaces. When a file is created with such a name, NTFS automatically generates an alternate, MS-DOS-style file name for the file. Windows displays these short names when you use the /x option with the *dir* command.

The MS-DOS file names are fully functional aliases for the NTFS files and are stored in the same directory as the long file names. The MFT record for a file with an autogenerated MS-DOS file name is shown in Figure 12-31.

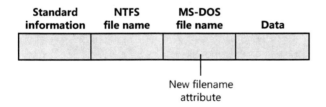

FIGURE 12-31 MFT file record with an MS-DOS filename attribute

The NTFS name and the generated MS-DOS name are stored in the same file record and therefore refer to the same file. The MS-DOS name can be used to open, read from, write to, or copy the file. If a user renames the file using either the long file name or the short file name, the new name replaces both the existing names. If the new name isn't a valid MS-DOS name, NTFS generates another MS-DOS name for the file (note that NTFS only generates MS-DOS-style file names for the first file name).

Here's the algorithm NTFS uses (the algorithm is actually implemented in the kernel function *RtlGenerate8dot3Name* and is also used by other drivers, such as CDFS, FAT, and third-party file systems) to generate an MS-DOS name from a long file name:

1. Remove from the long name any characters that are illegal in MS-DOS names, including spaces and Unicode characters. Remove preceding and trailing periods. Remove all other embedded periods, except the last one.

2. Truncate the string before the period (if present) to six characters (it may already be six or fewer because this algorithm is applied when any character that is illegal in MS-DOS is present in the name); if it is two or fewer characters, generate and concatenate a four-character hex checksum string. Append the string ~*n* (where *n* is a number, starting with 1, that is used to distinguish different files that truncate to the same name). Truncate the string after the period (if present) to three characters.

3. Put the result in uppercase letters. MS-DOS is case-insensitive, and this step guarantees that NTFS won't generate a new name that differs from the old only in case.

4. If the generated name duplicates an existing name in the directory, increment the ~*n* string. If *n* is greater than 4, and a checksum was not concatenated already, truncate the string before the period to two characters and generate and concatenate a four-character hex checksum string.

Table 12-7 shows the long Windows file names from Figure 12-30 and their NTFS-generated MS-DOS versions. The current algorithm and the examples in Figure 12-30 should give you an idea of what NTFS-generated MS-DOS-style file names look like.

Tunneling

NTFS uses the concept of *tunneling* to allow compatibility with older programs that depend on the file system to cache certain file metadata for a period of time even after the file is gone, such as when it has been deleted or renamed. With tunneling, any new file created with the same name as the original file, and within a certain period of time, will keep some of the same metadata. The idea is to replicate behavior expected by MS-DOS programs when using the *safe save* programming method, in which modified data is copied to a temporary file, the original file is deleted, and then the temporary file is renamed to the original name. The expected behavior in this case is that the renamed temporary file should appear to be the same as the original file, otherwise the creation time would continuously update itself with each modification (which is how the modified time is used).

NTFS uses tunneling so that when a file name is removed from a directory, its long name and short name, as well as its creation time, are saved into a cache. When a new file is added to a directory, the cache is searched to see whether there is any tunneled data to restore. Because these operations apply to directories, each directory instance has its own cache, which is deleted if the directory is removed. NTFS will use tunneling for the following series of operations if the names used result in the deletion and re-creation of the same file name:

- Delete + Create

- Delete + Rename

- Rename + Create

- Rename + Rename

By default, NTFS keeps the tunneling cache for 15 seconds, although you can modify this timeout by creating a new value called MaximumTunnelEntryAgeInSeconds in the HKLM\SYSTEM\CurrentControlSet\Control\FileSystem registry key. Tunneling can also be completely disabled by creating a new value called MaximumTunnelEntries and setting it to 0; however, this will cause older applications to break if they rely on the compatibility behavior.

You can see tunneling in action with the following simple experiment in the command prompt:

1. Create a file called file1.

2. Wait for more than 15 seconds (the default tunnel cache timeout).

3. Create a file called file2.

4. Perform a dir /TC. Note the creation times.

5. Rename file1 to file.

6. Rename file2 to file1.

7. Perform a dir /TC. Note that the creation times are identical.

TABLE 12-7 NTFS-Generated File Names

Windows Long Name	NTFS-Generated Short Name
LongFileName	LONGFI~1
UnicodeName.ΦΔΠΛ	UNICOD~1
File.Name.With.Dots	FILENA~1.DOT
File.Name2.With.Dots	FILENA~2.DOT
File.Name3.With.Dots	FILENA~3.DOT
File.Name4.With.Dots	FILENA~4.DOT
File.Name5.With.Dots	FIF596~1.DOT
Name With Embedded Spaces	NAMEWI~1
.BeginningDot	BEGINN~1
25¢.two characters	255440~1.TWO
©	6E2D~1

Resident and Nonresident Attributes

If a file is small, all its attributes and their values (its data, for example) fit within the file record that describes the file. When the value of an attribute is stored in the MFT (either in the file's main file record or an extension record located elsewhere within the MFT), the attribute is called a *resident attribute*. (In Figure 12-31, for example, all attributes are resident.) Several attributes are defined as always being resident so that NTFS can locate nonresident attributes. The standard information and index root attributes are always resident, for example.

Each attribute begins with a standard header containing information about the attribute, information that NTFS uses to manage the attributes in a generic way. The header, which is always resident, records whether the attribute's value is resident or nonresident. For resident attributes, the header also contains the offset from the header to the attribute's value and the length of the attribute's value, as Figure 12-32 illustrates for the filename attribute.

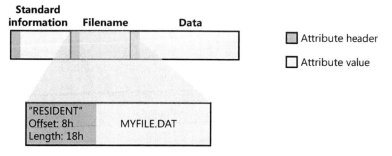

FIGURE 12-32 Resident attribute header and value

When an attribute's value is stored directly in the MFT, the time it takes NTFS to access the value is greatly reduced. Instead of looking up a file in a table and then reading a succession of allocation units to find the file's data (as the FAT file system does, for example), NTFS accesses the disk once and retrieves the data immediately.

The attributes for a small directory, as well as for a small file, can be resident in the MFT, as Figure 12-33 shows. For a small directory, the index root attribute contains an index (organized as a B-tree) of file record numbers for the files (and the subdirectories) within the directory.

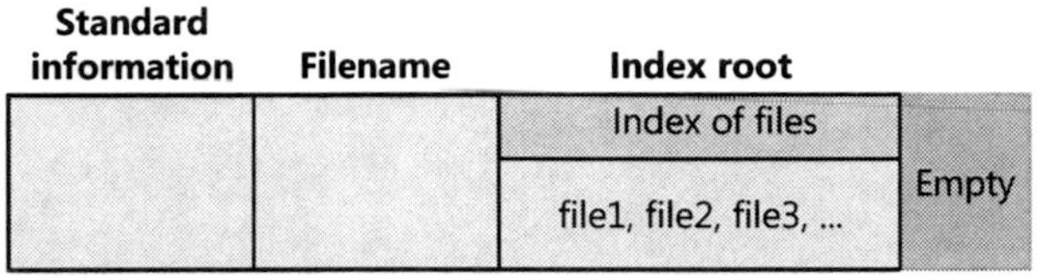

Standard information	Filename	Index root	
		Index of files	Empty
		file1, file2, file3, ...	

FIGURE 12-33 MFT file record for a small directory

Of course, many files and directories can't be squeezed into a 1-KB, fixed-size MFT record. If a particular attribute's value, such as a file's data attribute, is too large to be contained in an MFT file record, NTFS allocates clusters for the attribute's value outside the MFT. A contiguous group of clusters is called a *run* (or an *extent*). If the attribute's value later grows (if a user appends data to the file, for example), NTFS allocates another run for the additional data. Attributes whose values are stored in runs (rather than within the MFT) are called *nonresident attributes*. The file system decides whether a particular attribute is resident or nonresident; the location of the data is transparent to the process accessing it.

When an attribute is nonresident, as the data attribute for a large file will certainly be, its header contains the information NTFS needs to locate the attribute's value on the disk. Figure 12-34 shows a nonresident data attribute stored in two runs.

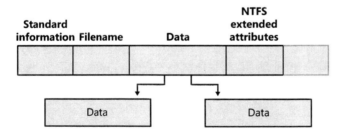

FIGURE 12-34 MFT file record for a large file with two data runs

Among the standard attributes, only those that can grow can be nonresident. For files, the attributes that can grow are the data and the attribute list (not shown in Figure 12-34). The standard information and filename attributes are always resident.

A large directory can also have nonresident attributes (or parts of attributes), as Figure 12-35 shows. In this example, the MFT file record doesn't have enough room to store the B-tree that contains the index of files that are within this large directory. A part of the index is stored in the index root attribute, and the rest of the index is stored in nonresident runs called *index allocations*. The index root, index allocation, and bitmap attributes are shown here in a simplified form. They are described in more detail in the next section. The standard information and filename attributes are always resident. The header and at least part of the value of the index root attribute are also resident for directories.

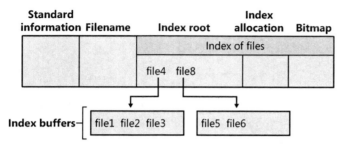

FIGURE 12-35 MFT file record for a large directory with a nonresident file name index

When an attribute's value can't fit in an MFT file record and separate allocations are needed, NTFS keeps track of the runs by means of VCN-to-LCN mapping pairs. LCNs represent the sequence of clusters on an entire volume from 0 through n. VCNs number the clusters belonging to a particular file from 0 through m. For example, the clusters in the runs of a nonresident data attribute are numbered as shown in Figure 12-36.

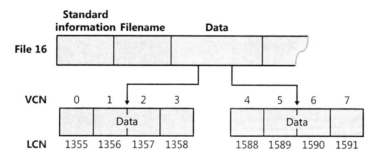

FIGURE 12-36 VCNs for a nonresident data attribute

If this file had more than two runs, the numbering of the third run would start with VCN 8. As Figure 12-37 shows, the data attribute header contains VCN-to-LCN mappings for the two runs here, which allows NTFS to easily find the allocations on the disk.

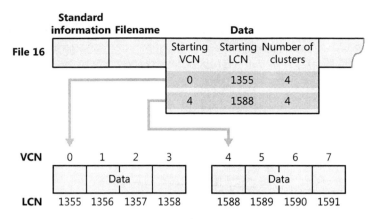

FIGURE 12-37 VCN-to-LCN mappings for a nonresident data attribute

Although Figure 12-36 shows just data runs, other attributes can be stored in runs if there isn't enough room in the MFT file record to contain them. And if a particular file has too many attributes to fit in the MFT record, a second MFT record is used to contain the additional attributes (or attribute headers for nonresident attributes). In this case, an attribute called the *attribute list* is added. The attribute list attribute contains the name and type code of each of the file's attributes and the file number of the MFT record where the attribute is located. The attribute list attribute is provided for those cases where all of a file's attributes will not fit within the file's file record or when a file grows so large or so fragmented that a single MFT record can't contain the multitude of VCN-to-LCN mappings needed to find all its runs. Files with more than 200 runs typically require an attribute list. In summary, attribute headers are always contained within file records in the MFT, but an attribute's value may be located outside the MFT in one or more extents.

Data Compression and Sparse Files

NTFS supports compression on a per-file, per-directory, or per-volume basis using a variant of the LZ77 algorithm, known as LZNT1. (NTFS compression is performed only on user data, not file system metadata.) You can tell whether a volume is compressed by using the Windows *GetVolumeInformation* function. To retrieve the actual compressed size of a file, use the Windows *GetCompressedFileSize* function. Finally, to examine or change the compression setting for a file or directory, use the Windows *DeviceIoControl* function. (See the FSCTL_GET_COMPRESSION and FSCTL_SET_COMPRESSION file system control codes.) Keep in mind that although setting a file's compression state compresses (or decompresses) the file right away, setting a directory's or volume's compression state doesn't cause any immediate compression or decompression. Instead, setting a directory's or volume's compression state sets a default compression state that will be given to all newly created files and subdirectories within that directory or volume (although, if you were to set directory compression using the directory's property page within Explorer, the contents of the entire directory tree will be compressed immediately).

The following section introduces NTFS compression by examining the simple case of compressing sparse data. The subsequent sections extend the discussion to the compression of ordinary files and sparse files.

Compressing Sparse Data

Sparse data is often large but contains only a small amount of nonzero data relative to its size. A sparse matrix is one example of sparse data. As described earlier, NTFS uses VCNs, from 0 through m, to enumerate the clusters of a file. Each VCN maps to a corresponding LCN, which identifies the disk location of the cluster. Figure 12-38 illustrates the runs (disk allocations) of a normal, noncompressed file, including its VCNs and the LCNs they map to.

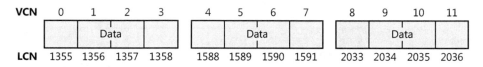

FIGURE 12-38 Runs of a noncompressed file

This file is stored in three runs, each of which is 4 clusters long, for a total of 12 clusters. Figure 12-39 shows the MFT record for this file. As described earlier, to save space the MFT record's data attribute, which contains VCN-to-LCN mappings, records only one mapping for each run, rather than one for each cluster. Notice, however, that each VCN from 0 through 11 has a corresponding LCN associated with it. The first entry starts at VCN 0 and covers 4 clusters, the second entry starts at VCN 4 and covers 4 clusters, and so on. This entry format is typical for a noncompressed file.

Standard information	Filename	Data			
		Starting VCN	Starting LCN	Number of clusters	
		0	1355	4	
		4	1588	4	
		8	2033	4	

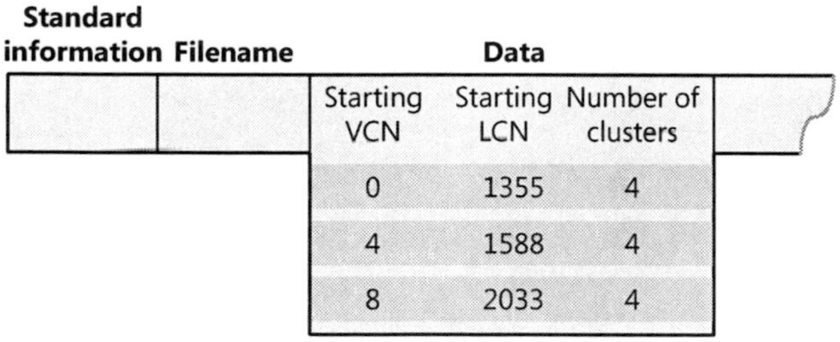

FIGURE 12-39 MFT record for a noncompressed file

When a user selects a file on an NTFS volume for compression, one NTFS compression technique is to remove long strings of zeros from the file. If the file's data is sparse, it typically shrinks to occupy a fraction of the disk space it would otherwise require. On subsequent writes to the file, NTFS allocates space only for runs that contain nonzero data.

Figure 12-40 depicts the runs of a compressed file containing sparse data. Notice that certain ranges of the file's VCNs (16–31 and 64–127) have no disk allocations.

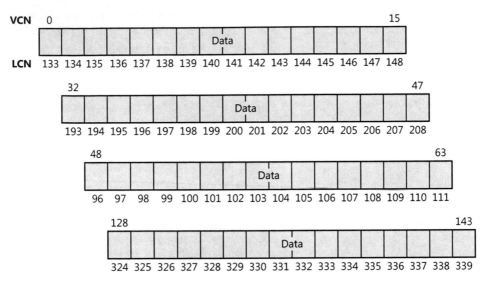

FIGURE 12-40 Runs of a compressed file containing sparse data

The MFT record for this compressed file omits blocks of VCNs that contain zeros and therefore have no physical storage allocated to them. The first data entry in Figure 12-41, for example, starts at VCN 0 and covers 16 clusters. The second entry jumps to VCN 32 and covers 16 clusters.

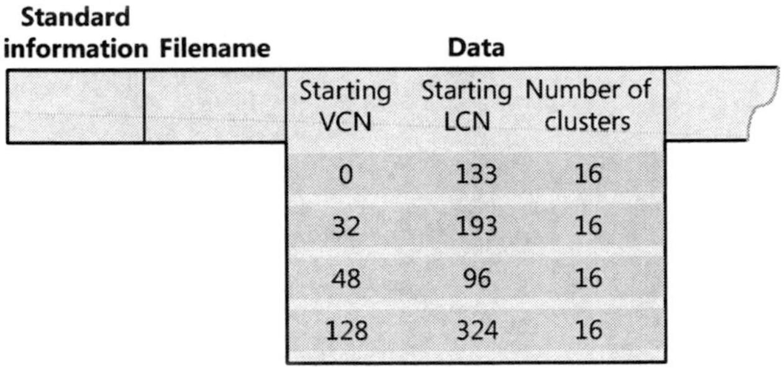

Standard information	Filename	Data		
		Starting VCN	Starting LCN	Number of clusters
		0	133	16
		32	193	16
		48	96	16
		128	324	16

FIGURE 12-41 MFT record for a compressed file containing sparse data

When a program reads data from a compressed file, NTFS checks the MFT record to determine whether a VCN-to-LCN mapping covers the location being read. If the program is reading from an unallocated "hole" in the file, it means that the data in that part of the file consists of zeros, so NTFS returns zeros without further accessing the disk. If a program writes nonzero data to a "hole," NTFS quietly allocates disk space and then writes the data. This technique is very efficient for sparse file data that contains a lot of zero data.

Compressing Nonsparse Data

The preceding example of compressing a sparse file is somewhat contrived. It describes "compression" for a case in which whole sections of a file were filled with zeros but the remaining data in the file wasn't affected by the compression. The data in most files isn't sparse, but it can still be compressed by the application of a compression algorithm.

In NTFS, users can specify compression for individual files or for all the files in a directory. (New files created in a directory marked for compression are automatically compressed—existing files must be compressed individually when programmatically enabling compression with FSCTL_SET_COMPRESSION.) When it compresses a file, NTFS divides the file's unprocessed data into *compression units* 16 clusters long (equal to 8 KB for a 512-byte cluster, for example). Certain sequences of data in a file might not compress much, if at all; so for each compression unit in the file, NTFS determines whether compressing the unit will save at least 1 cluster of storage. If compressing the unit won't free up at least 1 cluster, NTFS allocates a 16-cluster run and writes the data in that unit to disk without compressing it. If the data in a 16-cluster unit will compress to 15 or fewer clusters, NTFS allocates only the number of clusters needed to contain the compressed data and then writes it to disk. Figure 12-42 illustrates the compression of a file with four runs. The unshaded areas in this figure represent the actual storage locations that the file occupies after compression. The first, second, and fourth runs were compressed; the third run wasn't. Even with one noncompressed run, compressing this file saved 26 clusters of disk space, or 41 percent.

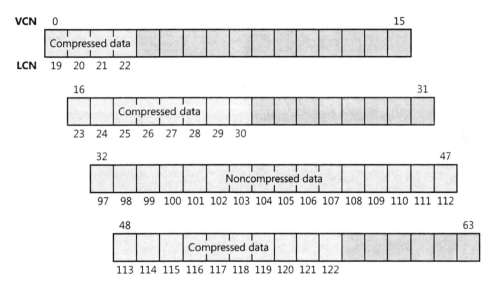

FIGURE 12-42 Data runs of a compressed file

> **Note** Although the diagrams in this chapter show contiguous LCNs, a compression unit need not be stored in physically contiguous clusters. Runs that occupy noncontiguous clusters produce slightly more complicated MFT records than the one shown in Figure 12-42.

When it writes data to a compressed file, NTFS ensures that each run begins on a virtual 16-cluster boundary. Thus the starting VCN of each run is a multiple of 16, and the runs are no longer than 16 clusters. NTFS reads and writes at least one compression unit at a time when it accesses compressed files. When it writes compressed data, however, NTFS tries to store compression units in physically contiguous locations so that it can read them all in a single I/O operation. The 16-cluster size of the NTFS compression unit was chosen to reduce internal fragmentation: the larger the compression unit, the less the overall disk space needed to store the data. This 16-cluster compression unit size represents a trade-off between producing smaller compressed files and slowing read operations for programs that randomly access files. The equivalent of 16 clusters must be decompressed for each cache miss. (A cache miss is more likely to occur during random file access.) Figure 12-43 shows the MFT record for the compressed file shown in Figure 12-42.

Standard information	Filename	Data		
		Starting VCN	Starting LCN	Number of clusters
		0	19	4
		16	23	8
		32	97	16
		48	113	10

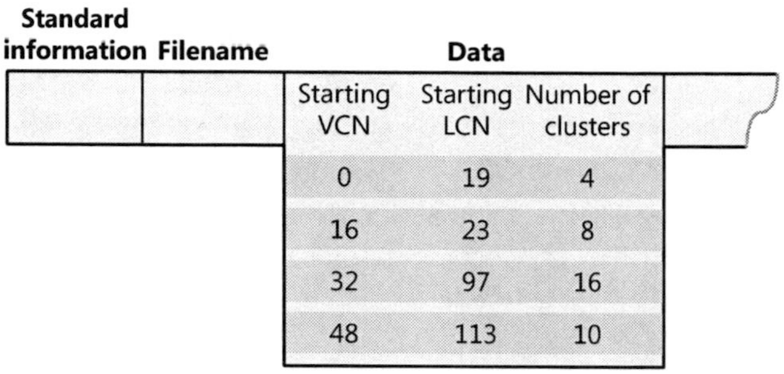

FIGURE 12-43 MFT record for a compressed file

One difference between this compressed file and the earlier example of a compressed file containing sparse data is that three of the compressed runs in this file are less than 16 clusters long. Reading this information from a file's MFT file record enables NTFS to know whether data in the file is compressed. Any run shorter than 16 clusters contains compressed data that NTFS must decompress when it first reads the data into the cache. A run that is exactly 16 clusters long doesn't contain compressed data and therefore requires no decompression.

If the data in a run has been compressed, NTFS decompresses the data into a scratch buffer and then copies it to the caller's buffer. NTFS also loads the decompressed data into the cache, which makes subsequent reads from the same run as fast as any other cached read. NTFS writes any updates to the file to the cache, leaving the lazy writer to compress and write the modified data to disk asynchronously. This strategy ensures that writing to a compressed file produces no more significant delay than writing to a noncompressed file would.

NTFS keeps disk allocations for a compressed file contiguous whenever possible. As the LCNs indicate, the first two runs of the compressed file shown in Figure 12-42 are physically contiguous, as are the last two. When two or more runs are contiguous, NTFS performs disk read-ahead, as it does with the data in other files. Because the reading and decompression of contiguous file data take place asynchronously before the program requests the data, subsequent read operations obtain the data directly from the cache, which greatly enhances read performance.

Sparse Files

Sparse files (the NTFS file type, as opposed to files that consist of sparse data, described earlier) are essentially compressed files for which NTFS doesn't apply compression to the file's nonsparse data.

However, NTFS manages the run data of a sparse file's MFT record the same way it does for compressed files that consist of sparse and nonsparse data.

The Change Journal File

The change journal file, \$Extend\$UsnJrnl, is a sparse file in which NTFS stores records of changes to files and directories. Applications like the Windows File Replication Service (FRS) and the Windows Search service make use of the journal to respond to file and directory changes as they occur.

The journal stores change entries in the $J data stream and the maximum size of the journal in the $Max data stream. Entries are versioned and include the following information about a file or directory change:

- The time of the change

- The reason for the change (see Table 12-8)

- The file or directory's attributes

- The file or directory's name

- The file or directory's MFT file record number

- The file record number of the file's parent directory

- The security ID

- The *update sequence number* (USN) of the record

- Additional information about the source of the change (a user, the FRS, and so on)

TABLE 12-8 Change Journal Change Reasons

Identifier	Reason
USN_REASON_DATA_OVERWRITE	The data in the file or directory was overwritten
USN_REASON_DATA_EXTEND	Data was added to the file or directory
USN_REASON_DATA_TRUNCATION	The data in the file or directory was truncated
USN_REASON_NAMED_DATA_OVERWRITE	The data in a file's data stream was overwritten
USN_REASON_NAMED_DATA_EXTEND	The data in a file's data stream was extended
USN_REASON_NAMED_DATA_TRUNCATION	The data in a file's data stream was truncated
USN_REASON_FILE_CREATE	A new file or directory was created
USN_REASON_FILE_DELETE	A file or directory was deleted
USN_REASON_EA_CHANGE	The extended attributes for a file or directory changed
USN_REASON_SECURITY_CHANGE	The security descriptor for a file or directory was changed
USN_REASON_RENAME_OLD_NAME	A file or directory was renamed; this is the old name
USN_REASON_RENAME_NEW_NAME	A file or directory was renamed; this is the new name

Identifier	Reason
USN_REASON_INDEXABLE_CHANGE	The indexing state for the file or directory was changed (whether or not the Indexing service will process this file or directory)
USN_REASON_BASIC_INFO_CHANGE	The file or directory attributes and/or the time stamps were changed
USN_REASON_HARD_LINK_CHANGE	A hard link was added or removed from the file or directory
USN_REASON_COMPRESSION_CHANGE	The compression state for the file or directory was changed
USN_REASON_ENCRYPTION_CHANGE	The encryption state (EFS) was enabled or disabled for this file or directory
USN_REASON_OBJECT_ID_CHANGE	The object ID for this file or directory was changed
USN_REASON_REPARSE_POINT_CHANGE	The reparse point for a file or directory was changed, or a new reparse point (such as a symbolic link) was added or deleted from a file or directory
USN_REASON_STREAM_CHANGE	A new data stream was added to or removed from a file or renamed
USN_REASON_TRANSACTED_CHANGE	This value is added (ORed) to the change reason to indicate that the change was the result of a recent commit of a TxF transaction
USN_REASON_CLOSE	The handle to a file or directory was closed, indicating that this is the final modification made to the file in this series of operations

EXPERIMENT: Reading the Change Journal

You can use the Usndump.exe command-line program from Winsider Seminars & Solutions (*www.winsiderss.com/tools/usndump/usndump.htm*) to dump the contents of the change journal if the current volume has one. You can also create, delete, or query journal information with the built-in Fsutil.exe utility, as shown here:

```
C:\>fsutil usn queryjournal c:
Usn Journal ID    : 0x01c89ddaec1b9648
First Usn         : 0x0000000038140000
Next Usn          : 0x000000003a22fa50
Lowest Valid Usn  : 0x0000000000000000
Max Usn           : 0x00000fffffff0000
Maximum Size      : 0x0000000002000000
Allocation Delta  : 0x0000000000400000
```

The output indicates the maximum size of the change journal on the volume and its current state. As a simple experiment to see how NTFS records changes in the journal, create a file called Usn.txt in the current directory, rename it to UsnNew.txt, and then dump the journal with Usndump, as shown here:

```
C:\>echo hello > Usn.txt
C:\>ren Usn.txt UsnNew.txt
C:\>Usndump.exe
...
```

```
File Ref#          : 0x4000000001be9
ParentFile Ref#    : 0x300000000a962
USN                : 0xfc54d8
SecurityId         : 0x00000000
Reason             : 0x00000100 (USN_REASON_FILE_CREATE)
Name (014)         : Usn.txt

File Ref#          : 0x4000000001be9
ParentFile Ref#    : 0x300000000a962
USN                : 0xfc5528
SecurityId         : 0x00000000
Reason             : 0x00000102 (USN_REASON_DATA_EXTEND USN_REASON_FILE_CREATE)
Name (014)         : Usn.txt

File Ref#          : 0x4000000001be9
ParentFile Ref#    : 0x300000000a962
USN                : 0xfc5578
SecurityId         : 0x00000000
Reason             : 0x80000102 (USN_REASON_DATA_EXTEND USN_REASON_FILE_CREATE)
Name (014)         : Usn.txt

File Ref#          : 0x4000000001be9
ParentFile Ref#    : 0x300000000a962
USN                : 0xfc55c8
SecurityId         : 0x00000000
Reason             : 0x00001000 (USN_REASON_RENAME_OLD_NAME)
Name (014)         : Usn.txt

File Ref#          : 0x4000000001be9
ParentFile Ref#    : 0x300000000a962
USN                : 0xfc5618
SecurityId         : 0x00000000
Reason             : 0x00002000 (USN_REASON_RENAME_NEW_NAME)
Name (020)         : UsnNew.txt

File Ref#          : 0x4000000001be9
ParentFile Ref#    : 0x300000000a962
USN                : 0xfc5668
SecurityId         : 0x00000000
Reason             : 0x80002000 (USN_REASON_RENAME_NEW_NAME)
Name (020)         : UsnNew.txt
```

The entries reflect the individual modification operations involved in the operations underlying the command-line operations.

The journal is sparse so that it never overflows; when the journal's on-disk size exceeds the maximum defined for the file, NTFS simply begins zeroing the file data that precedes the window of change information having a size equal to the maximum journal size, as shown in Figure 12-44. To prevent constant resizing when an application is continuously exceeding the journal's size, NTFS shrinks the journal only when its size is twice an application-defined value over the maximum configured size.

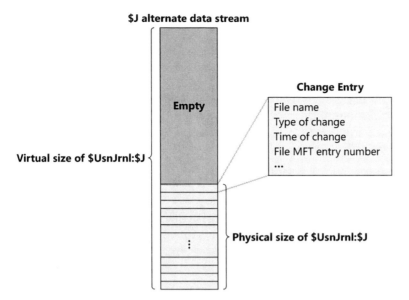

FIGURE 12-44 Change journal ($UsnJrnl) space allocation

Indexing

In NTFS, a file directory is simply an index of file names—that is, a collection of file names (along with their file record numbers) organized as a B-tree. To create a directory, NTFS indexes the filename attributes of the files in the directory. The MFT record for the root directory of a volume is shown in Figure 12-45.

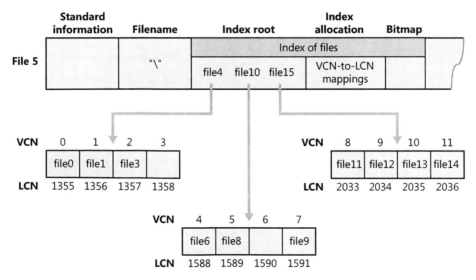

FIGURE 12-45 File name index for a volume's root directory

Conceptually, an MFT entry for a directory contains in its index root attribute a sorted list of the files in the directory. For large directories, however, the file names are actually stored in 4-KB, fixed-size index buffers (which are the nonresident value of the *index allocation* attribute) that contain and organize the file names. Index buffers implement a *B-tree* data structure, which minimizes the number of disk accesses needed to find a particular file, especially for large directories. The *index root* attribute contains the first level of the B-tree (root subdirectories) and points to index buffers containing the next level (more subdirectories, perhaps, or files).

Figure 12-45 shows only file names in the index root attribute and the index buffers (*file6*, for example), but each entry in an index also contains the record number in the MFT where the file is described and time stamp and file size information for the file. NTFS duplicates the time stamps and file size information from the file's MFT record. This technique, which is used by FAT and NTFS, requires updated information to be written in two places. Even so, it's a significant speed optimization for directory browsing because it enables the file system to display each file's time stamps and size without opening every file in the directory.

The index allocation attribute maps the VCNs of the index buffer runs to the LCNs that indicate where the index buffers reside on the disk, and the bitmap attribute keeps track of which VCNs in the index buffers are in use and which are free. Figure 12-45 shows one file entry per VCN (that is, per cluster), but file name entries are actually packed into each cluster. Each 4-KB index buffer will typically contain about 20 to 30 file name entries (depending on the lengths of the file names within the directory).

The B-tree data structure is a type of balanced tree that is ideal for organizing sorted data stored on a disk because it minimizes the number of disk accesses needed to find an entry. In the MFT, a directory's index root attribute contains several file names that act as indexes into the second level of the B-tree. Each file name in the index root attribute has an optional pointer associated with it that points to an index buffer. The index buffer it points to contains file names with lexicographic values less than its own. In Figure 12-45, for example, *file4* is a first-level entry in the B-tree. It points to an index buffer containing file names that are (lexicographically) less than itself—the file names *file0*, *file1*, and *file3*. Note that the names *file1*, *file3*, and so on that are used in this example are not literal file names but names intended to show the relative placement of files that are lexicographically ordered according to the displayed sequence.

Storing the file names in B-trees provides several benefits. Directory lookups are fast because the file names are stored in a sorted order. And when higher-level software enumerates the files in a directory, NTFS returns already-sorted names. Finally, because B-trees tend to grow wide rather than deep, NTFS's fast lookup times don't degrade as directories grow.

NTFS also provides general support for indexing data besides file names, and several NTFS features—including object IDs, quota tracking, and consolidated security—use indexing to manage internal data.

The B-tree indexes are a generic capability of NTFS and are used for organizing security descriptors, security IDs, object IDs, disk quota records, and reparse points. Directories are referred to as *file name indexes*, while other types of indexes are known as *view indexes*.

Object IDs

In addition to storing the object ID assigned to a file or directory in the $OBJECT_ID attribute of its MFT record, NTFS also keeps the correspondence between object IDs and their file record numbers in the $O index of the \$Extend\$ObjId metadata file. The index collates entries by object ID (which is a GUID), making it easy for NTFS to quickly locate a file based on its ID. This feature allows applications, using undocumented native API functionality, to open a file or directory using its object ID. Figure 12-46 demonstrates the correspondence of the $ObjId metadata file and $OBJECT_ID attributes in MFT records.

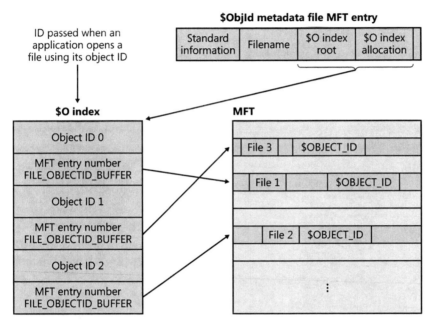

FIGURE 12-46 $ObjId and $OBJECT_ID relationships

Quota Tracking

NTFS stores quota information in the \$Extend\$Quota metadata file, which consists of the named index root attributes $O and $Q. Figure 12-47 shows the organization of these indexes. Just as NTFS assigns each security descriptor a unique internal security ID, NTFS assigns each user a unique user ID. When an administrator defines quota information for a user, NTFS allocates a user ID that corresponds to the user's SID. In the $O index, NTFS creates an entry that maps an SID to a user ID and sorts the index by SID; in the $Q index, NTFS creates a quota control entry. A quota control entry contains the value of the user's quota limits, as well as the amount of disk space the user consumes on the volume.

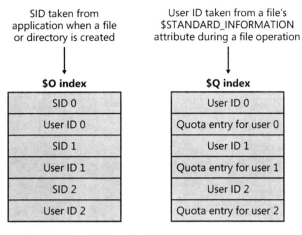

SID taken from application when a file or directory is created

User ID taken from a file's $STANDARD_INFORMATION attribute during a file operation

$O index

| SID 0 |
| User ID 0 |
| SID 1 |
| User ID 1 |
| SID 2 |
| User ID 2 |

$Q index

| User ID 0 |
| Quota entry for user 0 |
| User ID 1 |
| Quota entry for user 1 |
| User ID 2 |
| Quota entry for user 2 |

FIGURE 12-47 $Quota indexing

When an application creates a file or directory, NTFS obtains the application user's SID and looks up the associated user ID in the $O index. NTFS records the user ID in the new file or directory's $STANDARD_INFORMATION attribute, which counts all disk space allocated to the file or directory against that user's quota. Then NTFS looks up the quota entry in the $Q index and determines whether the new allocation causes the user to exceed his or her warning or limit threshold. When a new allocation causes the user to exceed a threshold, NTFS takes appropriate steps, such as logging an event to the System event log or not letting the user create the file or directory. As a file or directory changes size, NTFS updates the quota control entry associated with the user ID stored in the $STANDARD_INFORMATION attribute. NTFS uses the NTFS generic B-tree indexing to efficiently correlate user IDs with account SIDs and, given a user ID, to efficiently look up a user's quota control information.

Consolidated Security

NTFS has always supported security, which lets an administrator specify which users can and can't access individual files and directories. NTFS optimizes disk utilization for security descriptors by using a central metadata file named $Secure to store only one instance of each security descriptor on a volume.

The $Secure file contains two index attributes—$SDH (Security Descriptor Hash) and $SII (Security ID Index)—and a data-stream attribute named $SDS (Security Descriptor Stream), as Figure 12-48 shows. NTFS assigns every unique security descriptor on a volume an internal NTFS security ID (not to be confused with a Windows SID, which uniquely identifies computers and user accounts) and hashes the security descriptor according to a simple hash algorithm. A hash is a potentially nonunique shorthand representation of a descriptor. Entries in the $SDH index map the security descriptor hashes to the security descriptor's storage location within the $SDS data attribute, and the $SII index entries map NTFS security IDs to the security descriptor's location in the $SDS data attribute.

When you apply a security descriptor to a file or directory, NTFS obtains a hash of the descriptor and looks through the $SDH index for a match. NTFS sorts the $SDH index entries according to the hash of their corresponding security descriptor and stores the entries in a B-tree. If NTFS finds a match for the descriptor in the $SDH index, NTFS locates the offset of the entry's security descriptor from the entry's offset value and reads the security descriptor from the $SDS attribute. If the hashes match but the security descriptors don't, NTFS looks for another matching entry in the $SDH index. When NTFS finds a precise match, the file or directory to which you're applying the security descriptor can reference the existing security descriptor in the $SDS attribute. NTFS makes the reference by reading the NTFS security identifier from the $SDH entry and storing it in the file or directory's $STANDARD_INFORMATION attribute. The NTFS $STANDARD_INFORMATION attribute, which all files and directories have, stores basic information about a file, including its attributes, time stamp information, and security identifier.

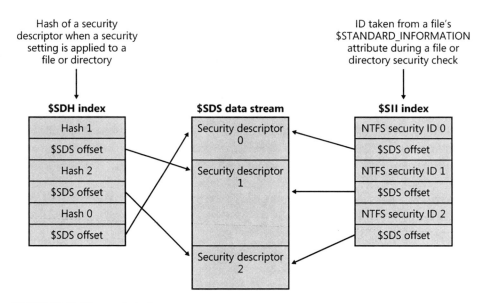

FIGURE 12-48 $Secure indexing

If NTFS doesn't find in the $SDH index an entry that has a security descriptor that matches the descriptor you're applying, the descriptor you're applying is unique to the volume and NTFS assigns the descriptor a new internal security ID. NTFS internal security IDs are 32-bit values, whereas SIDs are typically several times larger, so representing SIDs with NTFS security IDs saves space in the $STANDARD_INFORMATION attribute. NTFS then adds the security descriptor to the end of the $SDS data attribute, and it adds to the $SDH and $SII indexes entries that reference the descriptor's offset in the $SDS data.

When an application attempts to open a file or directory, NTFS uses the $SII index to look up the file or directory's security descriptor. NTFS reads the file or directory's internal security ID from the MFT entry's $STANDARD_INFORMATION attribute. It then uses the $Secure file's $SII index to locate the ID's entry in the $SDS data attribute. The offset into the $SDS attribute lets NTFS read the security descriptor and complete the security check. NTFS stores the 32 most recently accessed security descriptors with their $SII index entries in a cache so that it will access the $Secure file only when the $SII isn't cached.

NTFS doesn't delete entries in the $Secure file, even if no file or directory on a volume references the entry. Not deleting these entries doesn't significantly decrease disk space because most volumes, even those used for long periods, have relatively few unique security descriptors.

NTFS's use of generic B-tree indexing lets files and directories that have the same security settings efficiently share security descriptors. The $SII index lets NTFS quickly look up a security descriptor in the $Secure file while performing security checks, and the $SDH index lets NTFS quickly determine whether a security descriptor being applied to a file or directory is already stored in the $Secure file and can be shared.

Reparse Points

As described earlier in the chapter, a *reparse point* is a block of up to 16 KB of application-defined reparse data and a 32-bit reparse tag that are stored in the $REPARSE_POINT attribute of a file or directory. Whenever an application creates or deletes a reparse point, NTFS updates the \$Extend\ $Reparse metadata file, in which NTFS stores entries that identify the file record numbers of files and directories that contain reparse points. Storing the records in a central location enables NTFS to provide interfaces for applications to enumerate all a volume's reparse points or just specific types of reparse points, such as mount points. (See Chapter 9 for more information on mount points.) The \$Extend\$Reparse file uses the generic B-tree indexing facility of NTFS by collating the file's entries (in an index named $R) by reparse point tags and file record numbers.

Transaction Support

By leveraging the Kernel Transaction Manager (KTM) support in the kernel, as well as the facilities provided by the Common Log File System that were described earlier, NTFS implements a transactional model called *transactional NTFS* or *TxF*. TxF provides a set of user-mode APIs that applications can use for transacted operations on their files and directories and also a file system control (FSCTL) interface for managing its resource managers.

> **Note** Support for TxF was added to the NTFS driver without actually changing the format of the NTFS data structures, which is why the NTFS format version number, 3.1, is the same as it has been since Windows XP and Windows Server 2003. TxF achieves backward compatibility by reusing the attribute type ($LOGGED_UTILITY_STREAM) that was previously used only for EFS support instead of adding a new one.

The overall architecture for TxF, shown in Figure 12-49, uses several components:

- *Transacted* APIs implemented in the Kernel32.dll library

- A library for reading TxF logs (%SystemRoot%\System32\Txfw32.dll)

- A COM component for TxF logging functionality (%SystemRoot%\System32\Txflog.dll)

- The transactional NTFS library inside the NTFS driver

- The CLFS infrastructure for reading and writing log records

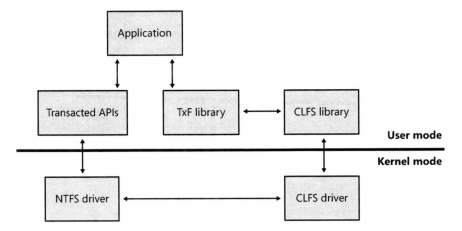

FIGURE 12-49 TxF architecture

Isolation

Although transactional file operations are opt-in, just like the transactional registry (TxR) operations described in Chapter 4 in Part 1, TxF has an impact on regular applications that are not transaction-aware because it ensures that the transactional operations are *isolated*. For example, if an antivirus program is scanning a file that's currently being modified by another application via a transacted operation, TxF must ensure that the scanner reads the pretransaction data, while applications that access the file within the transaction work with the modified data. This model is called *read-committed isolation*.

Read-committed isolation involves the concept of *transacted writers* and *transacted readers*. The former always view the most up-to-date version of a file, including all changes made by the transaction that is currently associated with the file. At any given time, there can be only one transacted writer for a file, which means that its write access is exclusive. Transacted readers, on the other hand, have access only to the committed version of the file at the time they open the file. They are therefore isolated from changes made by transacted writers. This allows for readers to have a consistent view of a file, even when a transacted writer commits its changes. To see the updated data, the transacted reader must open a new handle to the modified file.

Nontransacted writers, on the other hand, are prevented from opening the file by both transacted writers and transacted readers, so they cannot make changes to the file without being part of the transaction. Nontransacted readers act similarly to transacted readers in that they see only the file contents that were last committed when the file handle was open. Unlike transacted readers, however, they do not receive read-committed isolation, and as such they always receive the updated view of the latest committed version of a transacted file without having to open a new file handle. This allows non-transaction-aware applications to behave as expected.

To summarize, TxF's read-committed isolation model has the following characteristics:

- Changes are isolated from transacted readers

- Changes are rolled back (undone) if the associated transaction is rolled back, if the machine crashes, or if the volume is forcibly dismounted.

- Changes are flushed to disk if the associated transaction is committed.

EXPERIMENT: Understanding and Managing Transactions

In this experiment we'll use the Transactdemo.exe tool to create a new file, add some data to it as part of a transaction, and see how nontransacted clients interact with the file while the transaction is active. First, open a Command Prompt window and run Transactdemo.exe:

```
C:\>Transactdemo.exe

Transaction Demo v1.0
by Mark Russinovich

Transaction created: {5CD5E900-9DA8-11DD-8379-005056C00008}

Created C:\TransactionDemo.txt.
Pass TransDemo the GUID listed above to see the transacted file.

Rollback or commit transaction? (r/c):
```

Transactdemo creates C:\TransactionDemo.txt within a transaction that it has not committed. Open a second Command Prompt window, and use the *dir* command to look for the presence of the TransactionDemo.txt file:

```
C:\>dir transactiondemo.txt
 Volume in drive C is OS
 Volume Serial Number is 0C30-686E

 Directory of C:\
File Not Found
```

According to this second command prompt, the file doesn't even exist. Now simulate a non-transacted writer by trying to add data to the file via the *echo* command:

```
C:\>echo Hello > TransactionDemo.txt
The function attempted to use a name that is reserved for use by another transaction.
```

As expected, nontransacted writers are blocked from modifying the file.

The %SystemRoot%\System32\Ktmutil.exe and %SystemRoot%\System32\Fsutil.exe built-in applications can be very useful for dealing with transactional operations on the file system. For example, you can get a list of all current transactions on the system with the following command:

```
C:\>ktmutil tx list
TxGuid                                  Description
--------------------------------------  -------------------------------------------
{5cd5e900-9da8-11dd-8379-005056c00008}  Demo Transaction?
```

Note that the GUID matches what Transactdemo returned. With the GUID, you can now use the Fsutil command to query information about the transaction and to commit it or roll it back. For example, here's how to list the files part of the transaction and the owner account:

```
C:\>fsutil transaction query all {5cd5e900-9da8-11dd-8379-005056c00008}
dwOutcome:        1
dwIsolationLevel: 0
dwIsolationFlags: 0
dwTimeout:        -1
Owner:            BUILTIN\Administrators
Number of Files:  1
---- \TransactionDemo.txt
```

Although the Transactdemo tool presents you with the option to roll back or commit the current transaction, the Fsutil utility allows commits or rollbacks to any ongoing transaction your account has access to. Go back to the command prompt where you ran Transactdemo and press C to commit the transaction, after which the file becomes a standard nontransacted file.

Transactional APIs

TxF implements transacted versions of the Windows file I/O APIs, which use the suffix *Transacted*:

- **Create APIs**   *CreateDirectoryTransacted, CreateFileTransacted, CreateHardLinkTransacted, CreateSymbolicLinkTransacted*

- **Find APIs**   *FindFirstFileNameTransacted, FindFirstFileTransacted, FindFirstStreamTransacted*

- **Query APIs**   *GetCompressedFileSizeTransacted, GetFileAttributesTransacted, GetFullPathNameTransacted, GetLongPathNameTransacted*

- **Delete APIs**   *DeleteFileTransacted, RemoveDirectoryTransacted*

- **Copy and Move/Rename APIs**   *CopyFileTransacted, MoveFileTransacted*

- **Set APIs**   *SetFileAttributesTransacted*

In addition, some APIs automatically participate in transacted operations when the file handle they are passed is part of a transaction, like one created by the *CreateFileTransacted* API. Table 12-9 lists Windows APIs that have modified behavior when dealing with a transacted file handle.

TABLE 12-9 API Behavior Changed by TxF

API Name	Change
CloseHandle	Transactions will not be committed until all applications close transacted handles to the file.
CreateFileMapping, MapViewOfFile	Modifications to mapped views of a file part of a transaction will be associated with the transaction themselves.
FindNextFile, ReadDirectoryChanges, GetInformationByHandle, GetFileSize	If the file handle is part of a transaction, read-isolation rules will be applied to these operations.
GetVolumeInformation	Function will return FILE_SUPPORTS_TRANSACTIONS if the volume supports TxF.
ReadFile, WriteFile	Read and write operations to a transacted file handle will be part of the transaction.
SetFileInformationByHandle	Changes to the *FileBasicInfo, FileRenameInfo, FileAllocationInfo, FileEndOfFileInfo*, and *FileDispositionInfo* classes will be transacted if the file handle is part of a transaction.
SetEndOfFile, SetFileShortName, SetFileTime	Changes will be transacted if the file handle is part of a transaction.

Resource Managers

Just like TxR uses a resource manager (RM) to keep track of transactional metadata and log files, TxF uses a *default resource manager*, one for each volume, to keep track of its transactional state. TxF, however, also supports additional resource managers called *secondary resource managers*. These resource managers can be defined by application writers and have their metadata located in any directory of the application's choosing, defining their own transactional work units for undo, backup, restore, and redo operations. TxF uses the default resource manager for transacted APIs, and applications that use transactions with the *Distributed Transaction Coordinator* or the .NET Framework's *System.Transaction* classes create and manage secondary TxF resource managers with TxF resource manager file system control commands. Applications can create and manage secondary RMs by using file system control codes defined for TxF, such as FSCTL_TXFS_CREATE_SECONDARY_RM, FSCTL_TXFS_START_RM, and FSCTL_TXFS_SHUTDOWN_RM. When a secondary RM is created, it must be made consistent by one or more FSCTL_TXFS_ROLLFORWARD_REDO calls followed by FSCTL_TXFS_ROLLFORWARD_UNDO, which redo and/or undo operations that were stored in the log but never committed (such as in the case of a machine crash). We'll cover the recovery procedure for resource managers shortly. Both the default resource manager and secondary resource managers contain a number of metadata files and directories that describe their current state:

- The $Txf directory, which is where files are linked when they are deleted or overwritten by transactional operations. If a file is deleted in a transaction, read-isolation rules specify that nontransacted readers should still be able to access the file before the delete operation is actually committed. This isolation is achieved by moving the transaction-deleted file into the $Txf directory. The NTFS driver will then keep track of the isolation by inserting a temporary structure in the SCB of the parent directory where the deleted file was originally located. In this way, the file will continue to show up if the parent is enumerated, and it will store the file record number, allowing the file to be opened. When the transaction is committed, NTFS deletes the temporary structure and deletes the file from the $Txf directory. On the other hand, if the transaction is rolled back, NTFS moves the file back to its original directory.

- The $Tops, or TxF Old Page Stream (TOPS) file, which contains a default data stream and an alternate data stream called $T. The default stream for the TOPS file contains metadata about the resource manager, such as its GUID, its CLFS log policy, and the LSN at which recovery should start. The $T stream contains file data that is partially overwritten by a transactional writer (as opposed to a full overwrite, which would move the file into the $Txf directory). NTFS keeps a structure in memory that keeps track of which parts of a file are being modified under a transaction so that nontransacted readers can still access the noncommitted data by having their reads forwarded to $Tops:$T. When the transaction is committed or aborted, the pages are either moved from the $T stream into the original file or simply thrown out in the case of an abort.

- The TxF log files, which are CLFS log files storing transaction records. For the default resource manager, these files are part of the $TxfLog directory, but secondary resource managers can store them anywhere. TxF uses a multiplexed base log file called $TxfLog.blf. The file \$Extend\$RmMetadata\$TxfLog\$TxfLog contains two streams: the KtmLog stream used for Kernel Transaction Manager metadata records, and the TxfLog stream, which contains the TxF log records. Each stream is stored in CLFS log containers that start with $TxfLogContainer and are followed by a unique, increasing ID, such as 00000000000000000001. As the TxF log grows, more container files are created.

As described earlier, the default resource manager stores its files in the \$Extend\$RmMetadata directory on each NTFS-formatted volume on the machine.

EXPERIMENT: Querying Resource Manager Information

You can use the built-in %SystemRoot%\System32\Fsutil.exe command-line program to query information about the default resource manager, as well as to create, start, and stop secondary resource managers and configure their logging policies and behaviors. The following command queries information about the default resource manager, which is identified by the root directory (\):

```
C:\>fsutil resource info \
RM Identifier:          CF7234E7-39E3-11DC-BDCE-00188BDD5F49
KTM Log Path for RM:    \Device\HarddiskVolume3\$Extend\$RmMetadata\$TxfLog\
                        $TxfLog::KtmLog
Space used by TOPS:     79 Mb
TOPS free space:        100%
RM State:               Active
Running transactions: 0
One phase commits:      0
Two phase commits:      1
System initiated rollbacks: 0
Age of oldest transaction:  00:00:00
Logging Mode:           Simple
Number of containers: 2
Container size:         10 Mb
Total log capacity:     20 Mb
Total free log space: 14 Mb
```

```
Minimum containers:     2
Maximum containers:     20
Log growth increment: 2 container(s)
Auto shrink:            Not enabled

RM prefers availability over consistency.
```

As mentioned, the *fsutil resource* command has many options for configuring TxF resource managers, including the ability to create a secondary resource manager in any directory of your choice. For example, you can use the *fsutil resource create c:\rmtest* command to create a secondary resource manager in the Rmtest directory, followed by the *fsutil resource start c:\rmtest* command to initiate it. Note the presence of the $Tops and $TxfLogContainer* files and of the TxfLog and $Txf directories in this folder.

On-Disk Implementation

As shown earlier in Table 12-6, TxF uses the $LOGGED_UTILITY_STREAM attribute type to store additional data for files and directories that are or have been part of a transaction. This attribute is called $TXF_DATA and contains important information that allows TxF to keep active offline data for a file part of a transaction. The attribute is permanently stored in the MFT; that is, even after the file is not part of a transaction anymore, the stream remains, for reasons we'll explain shortly. The major components of the attribute are shown in Figure 12-50.

File record number of RM root
Flags
TxF file ID (TxID)
LSN for NTFS metadata
LSN for user data
LSN for directory index
USN index

FIGURE 12-50 $TXF_DATA attribute

The first field shown is the file record number of the root of the resource manager responsible for the transaction associated with this file. For the default resource manager, the file record number is 5, which is the file record number for the root directory (\) in the MFT, as shown earlier in Figure 12-27. TxF needs this information when it creates an FCB for the file so that it can link it to the correct resource manager, which in turn needs to create an enlistment for the transaction when a transacted file request is received by NTFS. (For more information on enlistments and transactions, see the KTM section in Chapter 3 in Part 1.)

Another important piece of data stored in the $TXF_DATA attribute is the TxF file ID, or TxID, and this explains why $TXF_DATA attributes are never deleted. Because NTFS writes file names to its records when writing to the transaction log, it needs a way to uniquely identify files in the same directory that may have had the same name. For example, if sample.txt is deleted from a directory in a transaction and later a new file with the same name is created in the same directory (and as part of the same transaction), TxF needs a way to uniquely identify the two instances of sample.txt. This identification is provided by a 64-bit unique number, the TxID, that TxF increments when a new file (or an instance of a file) becomes part of a transaction. Because they can never be reused, TxIDs are permanent, so the $TXF_DATA attribute will never be removed from a file.

Last but not least, three CLFS LSNs are stored for each file part of a transaction. Whenever a transaction is active, such as during create, rename, or write operations, TxF writes a log record to its CLFS log. Each record is assigned an LSN, and that LSN gets written to the appropriate field in the $TXF_DATA attribute. The first LSN is used to store the log record that identifies the changes to NTFS metadata in relation to this file. For example, if the standard attributes of a file are changed as part of a transacted operation, TxF must update the relevant MFT file record, and the LSN for the log record describing the change is stored. TxF uses the second LSN when the file's data is modified. Finally, TxF uses the third LSN when the file name index for the directory requires a change related to a transaction the file took part in, or when a directory was part of a transaction and received a TxID.

The $TXF_DATA attribute also stores internal flags that describe the state information to TxF and the index of the USN record that was applied to the file on commit. A TxF transaction can span multiple USN records that may have been partly updated by NTFS's recovery mechanism (described shortly), so the index tells TxF how many more USN records must be applied after a recovery.

Logging Implementation

As mentioned earlier, each time a change is made to the disk because of an ongoing transaction, TxF writes a record of the change to its log. TxF uses a variety of log record types to keep track of transactional changes, but regardless of the record type, all TxF log records have a generic header that contains information identifying the type of the record, the action related to the record, the TxID that the record applies to, and the GUID of the KTM transaction that the record is associated with.

A *redo record* specifies how to reapply a change part of a transaction that's already been committed to the volume if the transaction has actually never been flushed from cache to disk. An *undo record*, on the other hand, specifies how to reverse a change part of a transaction that hasn't been committed at the time of a rollback. Some records are redo-only, meaning they don't contain any equivalent undo data, while other records contain both redo and undo information.

Through the TOPS file, TxF maintains two critical pieces of data, the *base LSN* and the *restart LSN*. The base LSN determines the LSN of the first valid record in the log, while the restart LSN indicates at which LSN recovery should begin when starting the resource manager. When TxF writes a *restart record*, it updates these two values, indicating that changes have been made to the volume and flushed out to disk—meaning that the file system is fully consistent up to the new restart LSN.

TxF also writes *compensating log records*, or CLRs. These records store the actions that are being performed during transaction rollback (explained next). They're primarily used to store the *undo-next LSN*, which allows the recovery process to avoid repeated undo operations by bypassing undo records that have already been processed, a situation that can happen if the system fails during the recovery phase and has already performed part of the undo pass. Finally, TxF also deals with *prepare records*, *abort records*, and *commit records*, which describe the state of the KTM transactions related to TxF.

Recovery Implementation

When a resource manager starts because of an FSCTL_TXFS_START_RM call (or, for the default resource manager, as soon as the volume is mounted), TxF runs the recovery process. It reads the TOPS file to determine the restart LSN, where the recovery process should start, and then reads each record forward through the log (called the *redo pass*). As each record is being processed, TxF opens the file referenced by the record and compares the LSN in the $TXF_DATA attribute with the LSN in the record. If the LSN stored in the attribute is greater than or equal to the LSN of the log record, the action is not applied because the on-disk copy of the file is as new or newer than that of the log record action. If the LSN is not greater than or equal to the LSN in the record, the log contains information about the file that was never written to the file itself. In this case, TxF applies whichever action was recorded in the log record and updates the LSN in the $TXF_DATA attribute with the LSN from the record.

As TxF is processing its redo pass, it builds its *transaction table,* which describes the operations that it has completed; if it encounters an abort or commit record along the way, TxF discards the related transactions. By the end of the redo pass, TxF parses the final transaction table and connects to the KTM to see whether the KTM recorded a commit or an abort for the transactions. (KTM stores this information in the KtmLog stream of the TxF multiplexed log, as explained earlier.)

After TxF has finished communicating with the KTM, it looks at any leftover transactions in the transaction table and begins the *undo pass*. In the undo pass, TxF aborts all the remaining transactions in the transaction table by traversing each transaction's undo LSN chain and applying the undo action for each log record. At the end of the undo pass, the resource manager is consistent and initialized.

This process is very similar to the log file service's recovery procedure, which is described later in more detail. You should refer to this description for a complete picture of the standard transactional recovery mechanisms.

NTFS Recovery Support

NTFS recovery support ensures that if a power failure or a system failure occurs, no file system operations (transactions) will be left incomplete and the structure of the disk volume will remain intact without the need to run a disk repair utility. The NTFS Chkdsk utility is used to repair catastrophic disk corruption caused by I/O errors (bad disk sectors, electrical anomalies, or disk failures, for example) or software bugs. But with the NTFS recovery capabilities in place, Chkdsk is rarely needed.

As mentioned earlier (in the section "Recoverability"), NTFS uses a transaction-processing scheme to implement recoverability. This strategy ensures a full disk recovery that is also extremely fast (on the order of seconds) for even the largest disks. NTFS limits its recovery procedures to file system data to ensure that at the very least the user will never lose a volume because of a corrupted file system;

however, unless an application takes specific action (such as flushing cached files to disk), NTFS's recovery support doesn't guarantee user data to be fully updated if a crash occurs. This is the job of transactional NTFS (TxF).

The following sections detail the transaction-logging scheme NTFS uses to record modifications to file system data structures and explain how NTFS recovers a volume if the system fails.

Design

NTFS implements the design of a *recoverable file system*. These file systems ensure volume consistency by using logging techniques (sometimes called *journaling*) originally developed for transaction processing. If the operating system crashes, the recoverable file system restores consistency by executing a recovery procedure that accesses information that has been stored in a log file. Because the file system has logged its disk writes, the recovery procedure takes only seconds, regardless of the size of the volume (unlike in the FAT file system, where the repair time is related to the volume size). The recovery procedure for a recoverable file system is exact, guaranteeing that the volume will be restored to a consistent state.

A recoverable file system incurs some costs for the safety it provides. Every transaction that alters the volume structure requires that one record be written to the log file for each of the transaction's suboperations. This logging overhead is ameliorated by the file system's *batching* of log records—writing many records to the log file in a single I/O operation. In addition, the recoverable file system can employ the optimization techniques of a lazy write file system. It can even increase the length of the intervals between cache flushes because the file system metadata can be recovered if the system crashes before the cache changes have been flushed to disk. This gain over the caching performance of lazy write file systems makes up for, and often exceeds, the overhead of the recoverable file system's logging activity.

Neither careful write nor lazy write file systems guarantee protection of user file data. If the system crashes while an application is writing a file, the file can be lost or corrupted. Worse, the crash can corrupt a lazy write file system, destroying existing files or even rendering an entire volume inaccessible.

The NTFS recoverable file system implements several strategies that improve its reliability over that of the traditional file systems. First, NTFS recoverability guarantees that the volume structure won't be corrupted, so all files will remain accessible after a system failure. Second, although NTFS doesn't guarantee protection of user data in the event of a system crash—some changes can be lost from the cache—applications can take advantage of the NTFS write-through and cache-flushing capabilities to ensure that file modifications are recorded on disk at appropriate intervals.

Both *cache write-through*—forcing write operations to be immediately recorded on disk—and *cache flushing*—forcing cache contents to be written to disk—are efficient operations. NTFS doesn't have to do extra disk I/O to flush modifications to several different file system data structures because changes to the data structures are recorded—in a single write operation—in the log file; if a failure occurs and cache contents are lost, the file system modifications can be recovered from the log.

Furthermore, unlike the FAT file system, NTFS guarantees that user data will be consistent and available immediately after a write-through operation or a cache flush, even if the system subsequently fails.

Metadata Logging

NTFS provides file system recoverability by using the same logging technique used by TxF, which consists of recording all operations that modify file system metadata to a log file. Unlike TxF, however, NTFS's built-in file system recovery support doesn't make use of CLFS but uses an internal logging implementation called the *log file service* (which is not a background service process as described in Chapter 4 in Part 1). Another difference is that while TxF is used only when callers opt in for transacted operations, NTFS records all metadata changes so that the file system can be made consistent in the face of a system failure.

Log File Service

The log file service (LFS) is a series of kernel-mode routines inside the NTFS driver that NTFS uses to access the log file. NTFS passes the LFS a pointer to an open file object, which specifies a log file to be accessed. The LFS either initializes a new log file or calls the Windows cache manager to access the existing log file through the cache, as shown in Figure 12-51. Note that although LFS and CLFS have similar sounding names, they are separate logging implementations used for different purposes, although their operation is similar in many ways.

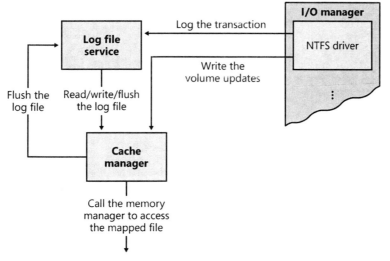

FIGURE 12-51 Log file service (LFS)

The LFS divides the log file into two regions: a *restart area* and an "infinite" *logging area*, as shown in Figure 12-52.

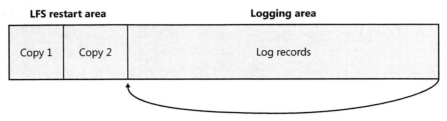

FIGURE 12-52 Log file regions

NTFS calls the LFS to read and write the restart area. NTFS uses the restart area to store context information such as the location in the logging area at which NTFS will begin to read during recovery after a system failure. The LFS maintains a second copy of the restart data in case the first becomes corrupted or otherwise inaccessible. The remainder of the log file is the logging area, which contains transaction records NTFS writes to recover a volume in the event of a system failure. The LFS makes the log file appear infinite by reusing it circularly (while guaranteeing that it doesn't overwrite information it needs). Just like CLFS, the LFS uses LSNs to identify records written to the log file. As the LFS cycles through the file, it increases the values of the LSNs. NTFS uses 64 bits to represent LSNs, so the number of possible LSNs is so large as to be virtually infinite.

NTFS never reads transactions from or writes transactions to the log file directly. The LFS provides services that NTFS calls to open the log file, write log records, read log records in forward or backward order, flush log records up to a specified LSN, or set the beginning of the log file to a higher LSN. During recovery, NTFS calls the LFS to perform the same actions as described in the TxF recovery section: a redo pass for nonflushed committed changes, followed by an undo pass for noncommitted changes.

Here's how the system guarantees that the volume can be recovered:

1. NTFS first calls the LFS to record in the (cached) log file any transactions that will modify the volume structure.

2. NTFS modifies the volume (also in the cache).

3. The cache manager prompts the LFS to flush the log file to disk. (The LFS implements the flush by calling the cache manager back, telling it which pages of memory to flush. Refer back to the calling sequence shown in Figure 12-51.)

4. After the cache manager flushes the log file to disk, it flushes the volume changes (the meta-data operations themselves) to disk.

These steps ensure that if the file system modifications are ultimately unsuccessful, the corresponding transactions can be retrieved from the log file and can be either redone or undone as part of the file system recovery procedure.

File system recovery begins automatically the first time the volume is used after the system is rebooted. NTFS checks whether the transactions that were recorded in the log file before the crash were applied to the volume, and if they weren't, it redoes them. NTFS also guarantees that transactions not completely logged before the crash are undone so that they don't appear on the volume.

Log Record Types

The NTFS recovery mechanism uses similar log record types as the TxF recovery mechanism: *update records*, which correspond to the redo and undo records that TxF uses, and *checkpoint records*, which are similar to the restart records used by TxF. Figure 12-53 shows three update records in the log file. Each record represents one suboperation of a transaction, creating a new file. The redo entry in each update record tells NTFS how to reapply the suboperation to the volume, and the undo entry tells NTFS how to roll back (undo) the suboperation.

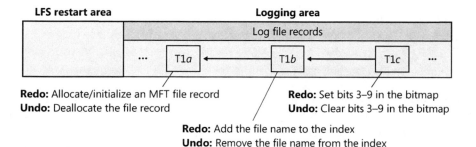

Redo: Allocate/initialize an MFT file record
Undo: Deallocate the file record

Redo: Set bits 3–9 in the bitmap
Undo: Clear bits 3–9 in the bitmap

Redo: Add the file name to the index
Undo: Remove the file name from the index

FIGURE 12-53 Update records in the log file

After logging a transaction (in this example, by calling the LFS to write the three update records to the log file), NTFS performs the suboperations on the volume itself, in the cache. When it has finished updating the cache, NTFS writes another record to the log file, recording the entire transaction as complete—a suboperation known as *committing* a transaction. Once a transaction is committed, NTFS guarantees that the entire transaction will appear on the volume, even if the operating system subsequently fails.

When recovering after a system failure, NTFS reads through the log file and redoes each committed transaction. Although NTFS completed the committed transactions from before the system failure, it doesn't know whether the cache manager flushed the volume modifications to disk in time. The updates might have been lost from the cache when the system failed. Therefore, NTFS executes the committed transactions again just to be sure that the disk is up to date.

After redoing the committed transactions during a file system recovery, NTFS locates all the transactions in the log file that weren't committed at failure and rolls back each suboperation that had been logged. In Figure 12-53, NTFS would first undo the T1*c* suboperation and then follow the backward pointer to T1*b* and undo that suboperation. It would continue to follow the backward pointers, undoing suboperations, until it reached the first suboperation in the transaction. By following the pointers, NTFS knows how many and which update records it must undo to roll back a transaction.

Redo and undo information can be expressed either physically or logically. As the lowest layer of software maintaining the file system structure, NTFS writes update records with *physical descriptions* that specify volume updates in terms of particular byte ranges on the disk that are to be changed, moved, and so on, unlike TxF, which uses *logical descriptions* that express updates in terms of operations such as "delete file A.dat." NTFS writes update records (usually several) for each of the following transactions:

- Creating a file

- Deleting a file

- Extending a file

- Truncating a file

- Setting file information

- Renaming a file

- Changing the security applied to a file

The redo and undo information in an update record must be carefully designed because although NTFS undoes a transaction, recovers from a system failure, or even operates normally, it might try to redo a transaction that has already been done or, conversely, to undo a transaction that never occurred or that has already been undone. Similarly, NTFS might try to redo or undo a transaction consisting of several update records, only some of which are complete on disk. The format of the update records must ensure that executing redundant redo or undo operations is *idempotent*, that is, has a neutral effect. For example, setting a bit that is already set has no effect, but toggling a bit that has already been toggled does. The file system must also handle intermediate volume states correctly.

In addition to update records, NTFS periodically writes a checkpoint record to the log file, as illustrated in Figure 12-54.

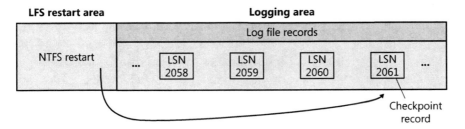

FIGURE 12-54 Checkpoint record in the log file

A checkpoint record helps NTFS determine what processing would be needed to recover a volume if a crash were to occur immediately. Using information stored in the checkpoint record, NTFS knows, for example, how far back in the log file it must go to begin its recovery. After writing a checkpoint record, NTFS stores the LSN of the record in the restart area so that it can quickly find its most recently written checkpoint record when it begins file system recovery after a crash occurs—this is similar to the restart LSN used by TxF for the same reason.

Although the LFS presents the log file to NTFS as if it were infinitely large, it isn't. The generous size of the log file and the frequent writing of checkpoint records (an operation that usually frees up space in the log file) make the possibility of the log file filling up a remote one. Nevertheless, the LFS, just like CLFS, accounts for this possibility by tracking several operational parameters:

- The available log space

- The amount of space needed to write an incoming log record and to undo the write, should that be necessary

- The amount of space needed to roll back all active (noncommitted) transactions, should that be necessary

If the log file doesn't contain enough available space to accommodate the total of the last two items, the LFS returns a "log file full" error, and NTFS raises an exception. The NTFS exception handler rolls back the current transaction and places it in a queue to be restarted later.

To free up space in the log file, NTFS must momentarily prevent further transactions on files. To do so, NTFS blocks file creation and deletion and then requests exclusive access to all system files and shared access to all user files. Gradually, active transactions either are completed successfully or receive the "log file full" exception. NTFS rolls back and queues the transactions that receive the exception.

Once it has blocked transaction activity on files as just described, NTFS calls the cache manager to flush unwritten data to disk, including unwritten log file data. After everything is safely flushed to disk, NTFS no longer needs the data in the log file. It resets the beginning of the log file to the current position, making the log file "empty." Then it restarts the queued transactions. Beyond the short pause in I/O processing, the "log file full" error has no effect on executing programs.

This scenario is one example of how NTFS uses the log file not only for file system recovery but also for error recovery during normal operation. You'll find out more about error recovery in the following section.

Recovery

NTFS automatically performs a disk recovery the first time a program accesses an NTFS volume after the system has been booted. (If no recovery is needed, the process is trivial.) Recovery depends on two tables NTFS maintains in memory: a transaction table, which behaves just like the one TxF maintains, and a *dirty page table*, which records which pages in the cache contain modifications to the file system structure that haven't yet been written to disk. This data must be flushed to disk during recovery.

NTFS writes a checkpoint record to the log file once every 5 seconds. Just before it does, it calls the LFS to store a current copy of the transaction table and of the dirty page table in the log file. NTFS then records in the checkpoint record the LSNs of the log records containing the copied tables. When recovery begins after a system failure, NTFS calls the LFS to locate the log records containing the most recent checkpoint record and the most recent copies of the transaction and dirty page tables. It then copies the tables to memory.

The log file usually contains more update records following the last checkpoint record. These update records represent volume modifications that occurred after the last checkpoint record was written. NTFS must update the transaction and dirty page tables to include these operations. After updating the tables, NTFS uses the tables and the contents of the log file to update the volume itself.

To perform its volume recovery, NTFS scans the log file three times, loading the file into memory during the first pass to minimize disk I/O. Each pass has a particular purpose:

1. Analysis

2. Redoing transactions

3. Undoing transactions

Analysis Pass

During the *analysis pass*, as shown in Figure 12-55, NTFS scans forward in the log file from the beginning of the last checkpoint operation to find update records and use them to update the transaction and dirty page tables it copied to memory. Notice in the figure that the checkpoint operation stores three records in the log file and that update records might be interspersed among these records. NTFS therefore must start its scan at the beginning of the checkpoint operation.

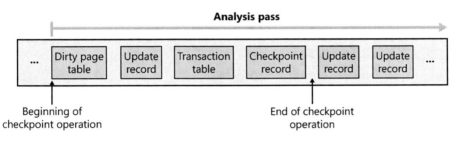

FIGURE 12-55 Analysis pass

Most update records that appear in the log file after the checkpoint operation begins represent a modification to either the transaction table or the dirty page table. If an update record is a "transaction committed" record, for example, the transaction the record represents must be removed from the transaction table. Similarly, if the update record is a "page update" record that modifies a file system data structure, the dirty page table must be updated to reflect that change.

Once the tables are up to date in memory, NTFS scans the tables to determine the LSN of the oldest update record that logs an operation that hasn't been carried out on disk. The transaction table contains the LSNs of the noncommitted (incomplete) transactions, and the dirty page table contains the LSNs of records in the cache that haven't been flushed to disk. The LSN of the oldest update record that NTFS finds in these two tables determines where the redo pass will begin. If the last checkpoint record is older, however, NTFS will start the redo pass there instead.

Note In the TxF recovery model, there is no distinct analysis pass. Instead, as described in the TxF recovery section, TxF performs the equivalent work in the redo pass.

Redo Pass

During the *redo pass*, as shown in Figure 12-56, NTFS scans forward in the log file from the LSN of the oldest update record, which it found during the analysis pass. It looks for "page update" records, which contain volume modifications that were written before the system failure but that might not have been flushed to disk. NTFS redoes these updates in the cache.

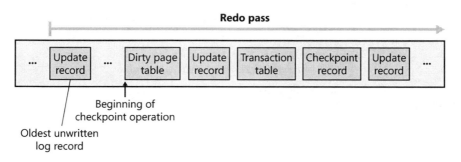

FIGURE 12-56 Redo pass

When NTFS reaches the end of the log file, it has updated the cache with the necessary volume modifications, and the cache manager's lazy writer can begin writing cache contents to disk in the background.

Undo Pass

After it completes the redo pass, NTFS begins its *undo pass*, in which it rolls back any transactions that weren't committed when the system failed. Figure 12-57 shows two transactions in the log file; transaction 1 was committed before the power failure, but transaction 2 wasn't. NTFS must undo transaction 2.

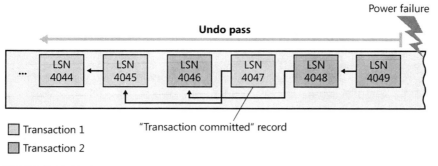

FIGURE 12-57 Undo pass

Suppose that transaction 2 created a file, an operation that comprises three suboperations, each with its own update record. The update records of a transaction are linked by backward pointers in the log file because they are usually not contiguous.

The NTFS transaction table lists the LSN of the last-logged update record for each noncommitted transaction. In this example, the transaction table identifies LSN 4049 as the last update record logged for transaction 2. As shown from right to left in Figure 12-58, NTFS rolls back transaction 2.

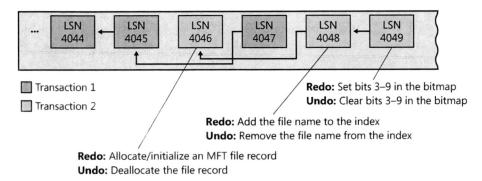

FIGURE 12-58 Undoing a transaction

After locating LSN 4049, NTFS finds the undo information and executes it, clearing bits 3 through 9 in its allocation bitmap. NTFS then follows the backward pointer to LSN 4048, which directs it to remove the new file name from the appropriate file name index. Finally, it follows the last backward pointer and deallocates the MFT file record reserved for the file, as the update record with LSN 4046 specifies. Transaction 2 is now rolled back. If there are other noncommitted transactions to undo, NTFS follows the same procedure to roll them back. Because undoing transactions affects the volume's file system structure, NTFS must log the undo operations in the log file. After all, the power might fail again during the recovery, and NTFS would have to redo its undo operations!

When the undo pass of the recovery is finished, the volume has been restored to a consistent state. At this point, NTFS is prepared to flush the cache changes to disk to ensure that the volume is up to date. Before doing so, however, it executes a callback that TxF registers for notifications of LFS flushes. Because TxF and NTFS both use write-ahead logging, TxF must flush its log through CLFS before the NTFS log is flushed to ensure consistency of its own metadata. (And similarly, the TOPS file must be flushed before the CLFS-managed log files.) NTFS then writes an "empty" LFS restart area to indicate that the volume is consistent and that no recovery need be done if the system should fail again immediately. Recovery is complete.

NTFS guarantees that recovery will return the volume to some preexisting consistent state, but not necessarily to the state that existed just before the system crash. NTFS can't make that guarantee because, for performance, it uses a "lazy commit" algorithm, which means that the log file isn't immediately flushed to disk each time a "transaction committed" record is written. Instead, numerous "transaction committed" records are batched and written together, either when the cache manager calls the LFS to flush the log file to disk or when the LFS writes a checkpoint record (once every 5 seconds) to the log file. Another reason the recovered volume might not be completely up to date is that several parallel transactions might be active when the system crashes and some of their "transaction committed" records might make it to disk whereas others might not. The consistent volume that recovery produces includes all the volume updates whose "transaction committed" records made it to disk and none of the updates whose "transaction committed" records didn't make it to disk.

NTFS uses the log file to recover a volume after the system fails, but it also takes advantage of an important "freebie" it gets from logging transactions. File systems necessarily contain a lot of code devoted to recovering from file system errors that occur during the course of normal file I/O. Because NTFS logs each transaction that modifies the volume structure, it can use the log file to recover when a file system error occurs and thus can greatly simplify its error handling code. The "log file full" error described earlier is one example of using the log file for error recovery.

Most I/O errors that a program receives aren't file system errors and therefore can't be resolved entirely by NTFS. When called to create a file, for example, NTFS might begin by creating a file record in the MFT and then enter the new file's name in a directory index. When it tries to allocate space for the file in its bitmap, however, it could discover that the disk is full and the create request can't be completed. In such a case, NTFS uses the information in the log file to undo the part of the operation it has already completed and to deallocate the data structures it reserved for the file. Then it returns a "disk full" error to the caller, which in turn must respond appropriately to the error.

NTFS Bad-Cluster Recovery

The volume manager included with Windows (VolMgr) can recover data from a bad sector on a fault-tolerant volume, but if the hard disk doesn't perform bad-sector remapping or runs out of spare sectors, the volume manager can't perform bad-sector replacement to replace the bad sector. (See Chapter 9 for more information on the volume manager.) When the file system reads from the sector, the volume manager instead recovers the data and returns the warning to the file system that there is only one copy of the data.

The FAT file system doesn't respond to this volume manager warning. Moreover, neither FAT nor the volume manager keeps track of the bad sectors, so a user must run the Chkdsk or Format utility to prevent the volume manager from repeatedly recovering data for the file system. Both Chkdsk and Format are less than ideal for removing bad sectors from use. Chkdsk can take a long time to find and remove bad sectors, and Format wipes all the data off the partition it's formatting.

In the file system equivalent of a volume manager's bad-sector replacement, NTFS dynamically replaces the cluster containing a bad sector and keeps track of the bad cluster so that it won't be reused. (Recall that NTFS maintains portability by addressing logical clusters rather than physical sectors.) NTFS performs these functions when the volume manager can't perform bad-sector replacement. When a volume manager returns a bad-sector warning or when the hard disk driver returns a bad-sector error, NTFS allocates a new cluster to replace the one containing the bad sector. NTFS copies the data that the volume manager has recovered into the new cluster to reestablish data redundancy.

Figure 12-59 shows an MFT record for a user file with a bad cluster in one of its data runs as it existed before the cluster went bad. When it receives a bad-sector error, NTFS reassigns the cluster containing the sector to its bad-cluster file, $BadClus. This prevents the bad cluster from being allocated to another file. NTFS then allocates a new cluster for the file and changes the file's VCN-to-LCN mappings to point to the new cluster. This bad-cluster remapping (introduced earlier in this chapter) is illustrated in Figure 12-59. Cluster number 1357, which contains the bad sector, must be replaced by a good cluster.

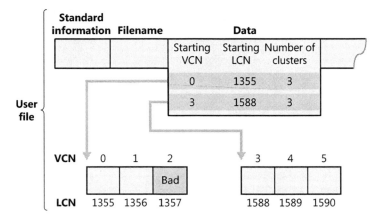

FIGURE 12-59 MFT record for a user file with a bad cluster

Bad-sector errors are undesirable, but when they do occur, the combination of NTFS and the volume manager provides the best possible solution. If the bad sector is on a redundant volume, the volume manager recovers the data and replaces the sector if it can. If it can't replace the sector, it returns a warning to NTFS, and NTFS replaces the cluster containing the bad sector.

If the volume isn't configured as a redundant volume, the data in the bad sector can't be recovered. When the volume is formatted as a FAT volume and the volume manager can't recover the data, reading from the bad sector yields indeterminate results. If some of the file system's control structures reside in the bad sector, an entire file or group of files (or potentially, the whole disk) can be lost. At best, some data in the affected file (often, all the data in the file beyond the bad sector) is lost. Moreover, the FAT file system is likely to reallocate the bad sector to the same or another file on the volume, causing the problem to resurface.

Like the other file systems, NTFS can't recover data from a bad sector without help from a volume manager. However, NTFS greatly contains the damage a bad sector can cause. If NTFS discovers the bad sector during a read operation, it remaps the cluster the sector is in, as shown in Figure 12-60. If the volume isn't configured as a redundant volume, NTFS returns a "data read" error to the calling program. Although the data that was in that cluster is lost, the rest of the file—and the file system—remains intact; the calling program can respond appropriately to the data loss, and the bad cluster won't be reused in future allocations. If NTFS discovers the bad cluster on a write operation rather than a read, NTFS remaps the cluster before writing and thus loses no data and generates no error.

The same recovery procedures are followed if file system data is stored in a sector that goes bad. If the bad sector is on a redundant volume, NTFS replaces the cluster dynamically, using the data recovered by the volume manager. If the volume isn't redundant, the data can't be recovered, so NTFS sets a bit in the $Volume metadata file that indicates corruption on the volume. The NTFS Chkdsk utility checks this bit when the system is next rebooted, and if the bit is set, Chkdsk executes, repairing the file system corruption by reconstructing the NTFS metadata.

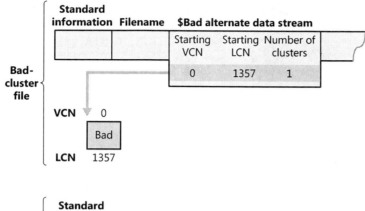

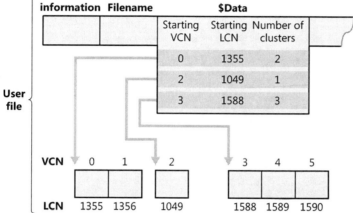

FIGURE 12-60 Bad-cluster remapping

In rare instances, file system corruption can occur even on a fault-tolerant disk configuration. A double error can destroy both file system data and the means to reconstruct it. If the system crashes while NTFS is writing the mirror copy of an MFT file record—of a file name index or of the log file, for example—the mirror copy of such file system data might not be fully updated. If the system were rebooted and a bad-sector error occurred on the primary disk at exactly the same location as the incomplete write on the disk mirror, NTFS would be unable to recover the correct data from the disk mirror. NTFS implements a special scheme for detecting such corruptions in file system data. If it ever finds an inconsistency, it sets the corruption bit in the volume file, which causes Chkdsk to reconstruct the NTFS metadata when the system is next rebooted. Because file system corruption is rare on a fault-tolerant disk configuration, Chkdsk is seldom needed. It is supplied as a safety precaution rather than as a first-line data recovery strategy.

The use of Chkdsk on NTFS is vastly different from its use on the FAT file system. Before writing anything to disk, FAT sets the volume's dirty bit and then resets the bit after the modification is complete. If any I/O operation is in progress when the system crashes, the dirty bit is left set and Chkdsk runs when the system is rebooted. On NTFS, Chkdsk runs only when unexpected or unreadable file system data is found and NTFS can't recover the data from a redundant volume or from redundant file system structures on a single volume. (The system boot sector is duplicated—in the last sector of a volume—as are the parts of the MFT [$MftMirr] required for booting the system and running the NTFS recovery procedure. This redundancy ensures that NTFS will always be able to boot and recover itself.)

Table 12-10 summarizes what happens when a sector goes bad on a disk volume formatted for one of the Windows-supported file systems according to various conditions we've described in this section.

TABLE 12-10 Summary of NTFS Data Recovery Scenarios

Scenario	With a Disk That Supports Bad-Sector Remapping and Has Spare Sectors	With a Disk That Does Not Perform Bad-Sector Remapping or Has No Spare Sectors
Fault-tolerant volume[1]	1. Volume manager recovers the data. 2. Volume manager performs bad-sector replacement. 3. File system remains unaware of the error.	1. Volume manager recovers the data. 2. Volume manager sends the data and a bad-sector error to the file system. 3. NTFS performs cluster remapping.
Non-fault-tolerant volume	1. Volume manager can't recover the data. 2. Volume manager sends a bad-sector error to the file system. 3. NTFS performs cluster remapping. Data is lost.[2]	1. Volume manager can't recover the data. 2. Volume manager sends a bad-sector error to the file system. 3. NTFS performs cluster remapping. Data is lost.

[1] A fault-tolerant volume is one of the following: a mirror set (RAID-1) or a RAID-5 set.

[2] In a write operation, no data is lost: NTFS remaps the cluster before the write.

If the volume on which the bad sector appears is a fault-tolerant volume—a mirrored (RAID-1) or RAID-5 volume—and if the hard disk is one that supports bad-sector replacement (and that hasn't run out of spare sectors), it doesn't matter which file system you're using (FAT or NTFS). The volume manager replaces the bad sector without the need for user or file system intervention.

If a bad sector is located on a hard disk that doesn't support bad sector replacement, the file system is responsible for replacing (remapping) the bad sector or—in the case of NTFS—the cluster in which the bad sector resides. The FAT file system doesn't provide sector or cluster remapping. The benefits of NTFS cluster remapping are that bad spots in a file can be fixed without harm to the file (or harm to the file system, as the case may be) and that the bad cluster will not be used ever again.

Self-Healing

With today's multiterabyte storage devices, taking a volume offline for a consistency check can result in a service outage of many hours. Recognizing that many disk corruptions are localized to a single file or portion of metadata, NTFS implements a self-healing feature to repair damage while a volume remains online. When NTFS detects corruption, it prevents access to the damaged file or files and creates a system worker thread that performs Chkdsk-like corrections to the corrupted data structures, allowing access to the repaired files when it has finished. Access to other files continues normally during this operation, minimizing service disruption.

You can use the *fsutil repair set* command to view and set a volume's repair options, which are summarized in Table 12-11. The Fsutil utility uses the FSCTL_SET_REPAIR file system control code to set these settings, which are saved in the VCB for the volume.

TABLE 12-11 NTFS Self-Healing Behaviors

Flag	Behavior
SET_REPAIR_ENABLED	Enable self-healing for the volume.
SET_REPAIR_WARN_ABOUT_DATA_LOSS	If the self-healing process is unable to fully recover a file, specifies whether the user should be visually warned.
SET_REPAIR_DISABLED_AND_BUGCHECK_ON_CORRUPTION	If the NtfsBugCheckOnCorrupt NTFS registry value was set by using *fsutil* behavior set *NtfsBugCheckOnCorrupt 1* and this flag is set, the system will crash with a STOP error 0x24, indicating file system corruption. This setting is automatically cleared during boot time to avoid repeated reboot cycles.

In all cases, including when the visual warning is disabled (the default), NTFS will log any self-healing operation it undertook in the System event log.

Apart from periodic automatic self-healing, NTFS also supports manually initiated self-healing cycles through the FSCTL_INITIATE_REPAIR and FSCTL_WAIT_FOR_REPAIR control codes, which can be initiated with the *fsutil repair initiate* and *fsutil repair wait* commands. This allows the user to force the repair of a specific file and to wait until repair of that file is complete.

To check the status of the self-healing mechanism, the FSCTL_QUERY_REPAIR control code or the *fsutil repair query* command can be used, as shown here:

```
C:\>fsutil repair query c:
Self healing is enabled for volume c: with flags 0x1.
 flags: 0x01 - enable general repair
        0x08 - warn about potential data loss
        0x10 - disable general repair and bugcheck once on first corruption
```

Encrypting File System Security

As covered in Chapter 9, BitLocker encrypts and protects volumes from offline attacks, but once a system is booted BitLocker's job is done. The Encrypting File System (EFS) protects individual files and directories from other authenticated users on a system. When choosing how to protect your data, it is not an "either/or" choice between BitLocker and EFS; each provides protection from specific—and nonoverlapping—threats. Together BitLocker and EFS provide a "defense in depth" for the data on your system.

The paradigm used by EFS is to encrypt files and directories using symmetric encryption (a single key that is used for encrypting and decrypting the file). The symmetric encryption key is then encrypted using asymmetric encryption (one key for encryption—often referred to as the "public" key—and a different key for decryption—often referred to as the "private" key) for each user who is granted access to the file. The details and theory behind these encryption methods is beyond the scope of this book; however, a good primer is available at *http://msdn.microsoft.com/en-us/library/windows/desktop/aa380251(v=vs.85).aspx*.

EFS works with the Windows Cryptography Next Generation (CNG) APIs, and thus may be configured to use any algorithm supported by (or added to) CNG. By default, EFS will use the Advanced Encryption Standard (AES) for symmetric encryption (256-bit key) and the Rivest-Shamir-Adleman (RSA) public key algorithm for asymmetric encryption (2,048-bit keys).

Users can encrypt files via Windows Explorer by opening a file's Properties dialog box, clicking Advanced, and then selecting the Encrypt Contents To Secure Data option, as shown in Figure 12-61. (A file may be encrypted or compressed, but not both.) Users can also encrypt files via a command-line utility named Cipher (%SystemRoot%\System32\Cipher.exe) or programmatically using Windows APIs such as *EncryptFile* and *AddUsersToEncryptedFile*.

Windows automatically encrypts files that reside in directories that are designated as encrypted directories. When a file is encrypted, EFS generates a random number for the file that EFS calls the file's *File Encryption Key* (FEK). EFS uses the FEK to encrypt the file's contents using symmetric encryption. EFS then encrypts the FEK using the user's asymmetric public key and stores the encrypted FEK in the $EFS alternate data stream for the file. The source of the public key may be administratively specified to come from an assigned X.509 certificate or a smartcard or randomly generated (which would then be added to the user's certificate store, which can be viewed using the Certificate Manager (%SystemRoot%\System32\Certmgr.msc). After EFS completes these steps, the file is secure: other users can't decrypt the data without the file's decrypted FEK, and they can't decrypt the FEK without the private key.

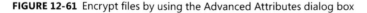

FIGURE 12-61 Encrypt files by using the Advanced Attributes dialog box

Symmetric encryption algorithms are typically very fast, which makes them suitable for encrypting large amounts of data, such as file data. However, symmetric encryption algorithms have a weakness: you can bypass their security if you obtain the key. If multiple users want to share one encrypted file protected only using symmetric encryption, each user would require access to the file's FEK. Leaving the FEK unencrypted would obviously be a security problem, but encrypting the FEK once would require all the users to share the same FEK decryption key—another potential security problem.

Keeping the FEK secure is a difficult problem, which EFS addresses with the public key–based half of its encryption architecture. Encrypting a file's FEK for individual users who access the file lets multiple users share an encrypted file. EFS can encrypt a file's FEK with each user's public key and can store each user's encrypted FEK in the file's $EFS data stream. Anyone can access a user's public key, but no one can use a public key to decrypt the data that the public key encrypted. The only way users can decrypt a file is with their private key, which the operating system must access. A user's private key decrypts the user's encrypted copy of a file's FEK. Public key–based algorithms are usually slow, but EFS uses these algorithms only to encrypt FEKs. Splitting key management between a publicly available key and a private key makes key management a little easier than symmetric encryption algorithms do and solves the dilemma of keeping the FEK secure.

Several components work together to make EFS work, as the diagram of EFS architecture in Figure 12-62 shows. EFS support is merged into the NTFS driver. Whenever NTFS encounters an encrypted file, NTFS executes EFS functions that it contains. The EFS functions encrypt and decrypt file data as applications access encrypted files. Although EFS stores an FEK with a file's data, users' public keys encrypt the FEK. To encrypt or decrypt file data, EFS must decrypt the file's FEK with the aid of CNG key management services that reside in user mode.

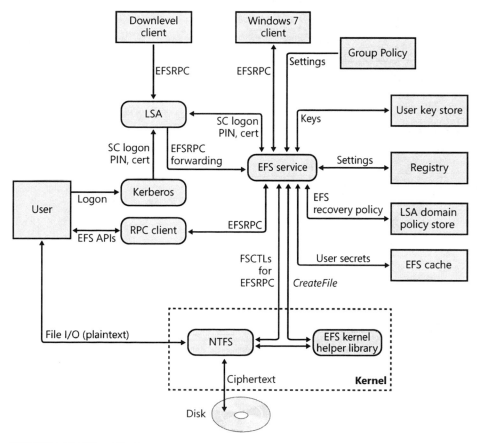

FIGURE 12-62 EFS architecture

The Local Security Authority Subsystem (LSASS; %SystemRoot%\System32\Lsass.exe) manages logon sessions but also hosts the EFS service. For example, when EFS needs to decrypt an FEK to decrypt file data a user wants to access, NTFS sends a request to the EFS service inside LSASS.

Encrypting a File for the First Time

The NTFS driver calls its EFS helper functions when it encounters an encrypted file. A file's attributes record that the file is encrypted in the same way that a file records that it is compressed (discussed earlier in this chapter). NTFS has specific interfaces for converting a file from nonencrypted to encrypted form, but user-mode components primarily drive the process. As described earlier, Windows lets you encrypt a file in two ways: by using the *cipher* command-line utility or by checking the Encrypt Contents To Secure Data check box in the Advanced Attributes dialog box for a file in Windows Explorer. Both Windows Explorer and the *cipher* command rely on the *EncryptFile* Windows API that Advapi32.dll (Advanced Windows APIs DLL) exports.

EFS stores only one block of information in an encrypted file, and that block contains an entry for each user sharing the file. These entries are called *key entries*, and EFS stores them in the data decryption field (DDF) portion of the file's EFS data. A collection of multiple key entries is called a *key ring* because, as mentioned earlier, EFS lets multiple users share encrypted files.

Figure 12-63 shows a file's EFS information format and key entry format. EFS stores enough information in the first part of a key entry to precisely describe a user's public key. This data includes the user's security ID (SID) (note that the SID is not guaranteed to be present), the container name in which the key is stored, the cryptographic provider name, and the asymmetric key pair certificate hash. Only the asymmetric key pair certificate hash is used by the decryption process. The second part of the key entry contains an encrypted version of the FEK. EFS uses the CNG to encrypt the FEK with the selected asymmetric encryption algorithm and the user's public key.

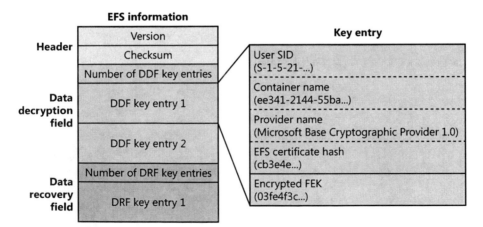

FIGURE 12-63 Format of EFS information and key entries

EFS stores information about recovery key entries in a file's data recovery field (DRF). The format of DRF entries is identical to the format of DDF entries. The DRF's purpose is to let designated accounts, or recovery agents, decrypt a user's file when administrative authority must have access to the user's data. For example, suppose a company employee forgot his or her logon password. An administrator can reset the user's password, but without recovery agents, no one can recover the user's encrypted data.

Recovery agents are defined with the Encrypted Data Recovery Agents security policy of the local computer or domain. This policy is available from the Local Security Policy MMC snap-in, as shown in Figure 12-64. When you use the Add Recovery Agent Wizard (by right-clicking Encrypting File System and then clicking Add Data Recovery Agent), you can add recovery agents and specify which private/public key pairs (designated by their certificates) the recovery agents use for EFS recovery. Lsasrv interprets the recovery policy when it initializes and when it receives notification that the recovery policy has changed. EFS creates a DRF key entry for each recovery agent by using the cryptographic provider registered for EFS recovery.

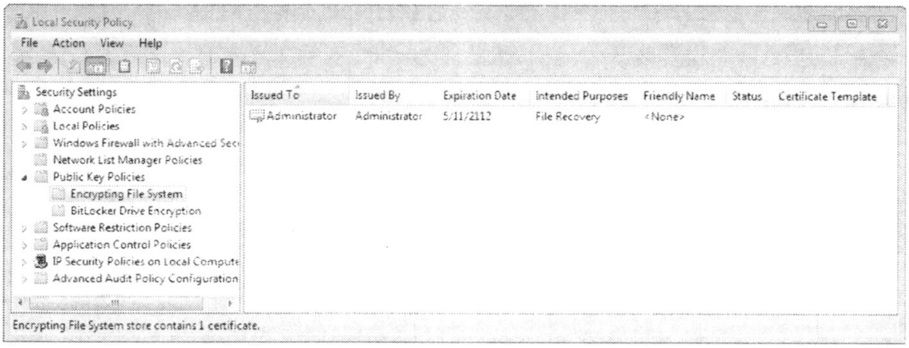

FIGURE 12-64 Encrypted Data Recovery Agents group policy

In the final step in creating EFS information for a file, Lsasrv calculates a checksum for the DDF and DRF by using the MD5 hash facility of Base Cryptographic Provider 1.0. Lsasrv stores the checksum's result in the EFS information header. EFS references this checksum during decryption to ensure that the contents of a file's EFS information haven't become corrupted or been tampered with.

Encrypting File Data

When a user encrypts an existing file, the following process occurs:

1. The EFS service opens the file for exclusive access.

2. All data streams in the file are copied to a plaintext temporary file in the system's temporary directory.

3. An FEK is randomly generated and used to encrypt the file by using DESX or 3DES, depending on the effective security policy.

4. A DDF is created to contain the FEK encrypted by using the user's public key. EFS automatically obtains the user's public key from the user's X.509 version 3 file encryption certificate.

5. If a recovery agent has been designated through Group Policy, a DRF is created to contain the FEK encrypted by using RSA and the recovery agent's public key.

EFS automatically obtains the recovery agent's public key for file recovery from the recovery agent's X.509 version 3 certificate, which is stored in the EFS recovery policy. If there are multiple recovery agents, a copy of the FEK is encrypted by using each agent's public key, and a DRF is created to store each encrypted FEK.

> **Note** The file recovery property in the certificate is an example of an enhanced key usage (EKU) field. An EKU extension and extended property specify and limit the valid uses of a certificate. File Recovery is one of the EKU fields defined by Microsoft as part of the Microsoft public key infrastructure (PKI).

6. EFS writes the encrypted data, along with the DDF and the DRF, back to the file. Because symmetric encryption does not add additional data, file size increase is minimal after encryption. The metadata, consisting primarily of encrypted FEKs, is usually less than 1 KB. File size in bytes before and after encryption is normally reported to be the same.

7. The plaintext temporary file is deleted.

When a user saves a file to a folder that has been configured for encryption, the process is similar except that no temporary file is created.

The Decryption Process

When an application accesses an encrypted file, decryption proceeds as follows:

1. NTFS recognizes that the file is encrypted and sends a request to the EFS driver.

2. The EFS driver retrieves the DDF and passes it to the EFS service.

3. The EFS service retrieves the user's private key from the user's profile and uses it to decrypt the DDF and obtain the FEK.

4. The EFS service passes the FEK back to the EFS driver.

5. The EFS driver uses the FEK to decrypt sections of the file as needed for the application.

> **Note** When an application opens a file, only those sections of the file that the application is using are decrypted because EFS uses cipher block chaining. The behavior is different if the user removes the encryption attribute from the file. In this case, the entire file is decrypted and rewritten as plaintext.

6. The EFS driver returns the decrypted data to NTFS, which then sends the data to the requesting application.

Backing Up Encrypted Files

An important aspect of any file encryption facility's design is that file data is never available in un-encrypted form except to applications that access the file via the encryption facility. This restriction particularly affects backup utilities, in which archival media store files. EFS addresses this problem by providing a facility for backup utilities so that the utilities can back up and restore files in their encrypted states. Thus, backup utilities don't have to be able to decrypt file data, nor do they need to encrypt file data in their backup procedures.

Backup utilities use the EFS API functions *OpenEncryptedFileRaw*, *ReadEncryptedFileRaw*, *WriteEncryptedFileRaw*, and *CloseEncryptedFileRaw* in Windows to access a file's encrypted contents. After a backup utility opens a file for raw access during a backup operation, the utility calls *ReadEncryptedFileRaw* to obtain the file data.

EXPERIMENT: Viewing EFS Information

EFS has a handful of other API functions that applications can use to manipulate encrypted files. For example, applications use the *AddUsersToEncryptedFile* API function to give additional users access to an encrypted file and *RemoveUsersFromEncryptedFile* to revoke users' access to an encrypted file. Applications use the *QueryUsersOnEncryptedFile* function to obtain information about a file's associated DDF and DRF key fields. *QueryUsersOnEncryptedFile* returns the SID, certificate hash value, and display information that each DDF and DRF key field contains. The following output is from the EFSDump utility, from Sysinternals, when an encrypted file is specified as a command-line argument:

```
C:\>efsdump test.txt
EFS Information Dumper v1.02
Copyright (C) 1999 Mark Russinovich
Systems Internals - http://www.sysinternals.com

test.txt:
DDF Entry:
    DARYL\Mark:
        CN=Mark,L=EFS,OU=EFS File Encryption Certificate
DRF Entry:
    Unknown user:
        EFS Data Recovery
```

You can see that the file test.txt has one DDF entry for user Mark and one DRF entry for the EFS Data Recovery agent, which is the only recovery agent currently registered on the system.

Copying Encrypted Files

When an encrypted file is copied, the system does not decrypt the file and re-encrypt it at its destination; it just copies the encrypted data and the EFS alternate data streams to the specified destination. However, if the destination does not support alternate data streams—if it is not an NTFS volume (such as a FAT volume) or is a network share (even if the network share is an NTFS volume)—the copy cannot proceed normally because the alternate data streams would be lost. If the copy is done with Explorer, a dialog box informs the user that the destination volume does not support encryption and asks the user whether the file should be copied to the destination unencrypted. If the user agrees, the file will be decrypted and copied to the specified destination. If the copy is done from a command prompt, the copy command will fail and return the error message "The specified file could not be encrypted".

Conclusion

Windows supports a wide variety of file system formats accessible to both the local system and remote clients. The file system filter driver architecture provides a clean way to extend and augment file system access, and NTFS provides a reliable, secure, scalable file system format for local file system storage. In the next chapter, we'll look at startup and shutdown in Windows.

CHAPTER 13

Startup and Shutdown

I n this chapter, we'll describe the steps required to boot Windows and the options that can affect system startup. Understanding the details of the boot process will help you diagnose problems that can arise during a boot. Then we'll explain the kinds of things that can go wrong during the boot process and how to resolve them. Finally, we'll explain what occurs on an orderly system shutdown.

Boot Process

In describing the Windows boot process, we'll start with the installation of Windows and proceed through the execution of boot support files. Device drivers are a crucial part of the boot process, so we'll explain the way that they control the point in the boot process at which they load and initialize. Then we'll describe how the executive subsystems initialize and how the kernel launches the user-mode portion of Windows by starting the Session Manager process (Smss.exe), which starts the initial two sessions (session 0 and session 1). Along the way, we'll highlight the points at which various on-screen messages appear to help you correlate the internal process with what you see when you watch Windows boot.

The early phases of the boot process differ significantly on systems with a BIOS (basic input output system) versus systems with an EFI (Extensible Firmware Interface). EFI is a newer standard that does away with much of the legacy 16-bit code that BIOS systems use and allows the loading of preboot programs and drivers to support the operating system loading phase. The next sections describe the portions of the boot process specific to BIOS-based systems and are followed with a section describing the EFI-specific portions of the boot process.

To support these different firmware implementations (as well as EFI 2.0, which is known as Unified EFI, or UEFI), Windows provides a boot architecture that abstracts many of the differences away from users and developers in order to provide a consistent environment and experience regardless of the type of firmware used on the installed system.

BIOS Preboot

The Windows boot process doesn't begin when you power on your computer or press the reset button. It begins when you install Windows on your computer. At some point during the execution of the Windows Setup program, the system's primary hard disk is prepared with code that takes part in the boot process. Before we get into what this code does, let's look at how and where Windows places the code on a disk. Since the early days of MS-DOS, a standard has existed on x86 systems for the way physical hard disks are divided into volumes.

Microsoft operating systems split hard disks into discrete areas known as *partitions* and use file systems (such as FAT and NTFS) to format each partition into a volume. A hard disk can contain up to four primary partitions. Because this apportioning scheme would limit a disk to four volumes, a special partition type, called an *extended partition*, further allocates up to four additional partitions within each extended partition. Extended partitions can contain extended partitions, which can contain extended partitions, and so on, making the number of volumes an operating system can place on a disk effectively infinite. Figure 13-1 shows an example of a hard disk layout, and Table 13-1 summarizes the files involved in the BIOS boot process. (You can learn more about Windows partitioning in Chapter 9, "Storage Management.")

TABLE 13-1 BIOS Boot Process Components

Component	Processor Execution	Responsibilities	Location
Master Boot Record (MBR)	16-bit real mode	Reads and loads the volume boot record (VBR)	Per storage device
Boot sector (also called volume boot record)	16-bit real mode	Understands the file system on the partition and locates Bootmgr by name, loading it into memory	Per active (bootable) partition
Bootmgr	16-bit real mode and 32-bit without paging	Reads the Boot Configuration Database (BCD), presents boot menu, and allows execution of preboot programs such as the Memory Test application (Memtest.exe). If a 64-bit installation is booted, switches to 64-bit long mode before loading Winload.	Per system
Winload.exe	32-bit protected mode with paging, 64-bit protected mode if booting a Win64 installation	Loads Ntoskrnl.exe and its dependencies (Bootvid.dll on 32-bit systems, Hal.dll, Kdcom.dll, Ci.dll, Clfs.sys, Pshed.dll) and boot-start device drivers.	Per Windows installation
Winresume.exe	32-bit protected mode, 64-bit protected mode if resuming a Win64 installation	If resuming after a hibernation state, resumes from the hibernation file (Hiberfil.sys) instead of typical Windows loading.	Per Windows installation
Memtest.exe	32-bit protected mode	If selected from the Boot Manager, starts up and provides a graphical interface for scanning memory and detecting damaged RAM.	Per system
Ntoskrnl.exe	Protected mode with paging	Initializes executive subsystems and boot and system-start device drivers, prepares the system for running native applications, and runs Smss.exe.	Per Windows installation
Hal.dll	Protected mode with paging	Kernel-mode DLL that interfaces Ntoskrnl and drivers to the hardware. It also acts as a driver for the motherboard itself, supporting soldered components that are not otherwise managed by another driver.	Per Windows installation

Component	Processor Execution	Responsibilities	Location
Smss.exe	Native application	Initial instance starts a copy of itself to initialize each session. The session 0 instance loads the Windows subsystem driver (Win32k.sys) and starts the Windows subsystem process (Csrss.exe) and Windows initialization process (Wininit.exe). All other per-session instances start a Csrss and Winlogon process.	Per Windows installation
Wininit.exe	Windows application	Starts the service control manager (SCM), the Local Security Authority process (LSASS), and the local session manager (LSM). Initializes the rest of the registry and performs user-mode initialization tasks.	Per Windows installation
Winlogon.exe	Windows application	Coordinates logon and user security, launches LogonUI.	Per Windows installation
Logonui.exe	Windows application	Presents interactive logon dialog box.	Per Windows installation
Services.exe	Windows application	Loads and initializes auto-start device drivers and Windows services.	Per Windows installation

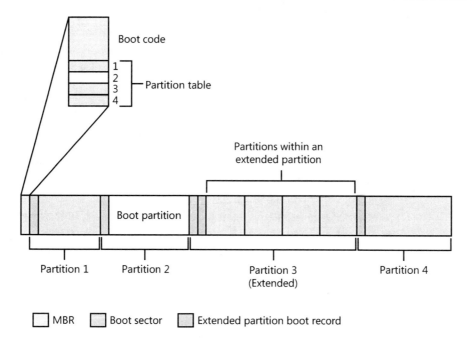

FIGURE 13-1 Sample hard disk layout

Physical disks are addressed in units known as *sectors*. A hard disk sector on a BIOS PC is typically 512 bytes (but moving to 4,096 bytes; see Chapter 9 for more information). Utilities that prepare hard disks for the definition of volumes, such as the Windows Setup program, write a sector of data called a Master Boot Record (MBR) to the first sector on a hard disk. (MBR partitioning is described in Chapter 9.) The MBR includes a fixed amount of space that contains executable instructions (called *boot code*) and a table (called a *partition table*) with four entries that define the locations of the primary partitions on the disk. When a BIOS-based computer boots, the first code it executes is called the BIOS, which is encoded into the computer's flash memory. The BIOS selects a boot device, reads that device's MBR into memory, and transfers control to the code in the MBR.

The MBRs written by Microsoft partitioning tools, such as the one integrated into Windows Setup and the Disk Management MMC snap-in, go through a similar process of reading and transferring control. First, an MBR's code scans the primary partition table until it locates a partition containing a flag (Active) that signals the partition is bootable. When the MBR finds at least one such flag, it reads the first sector from the flagged partition into memory and transfers control to code within the partition. This type of partition is called a *system partition*, and the first sector of such a partition is called a *boot sector* or *volume boot record* (VBR). The volume defined for this partition is called the *system volume*.

Operating systems generally write boot sectors to disk without a user's involvement. For example, when Windows Setup writes the MBR to a hard disk, it also writes the file system boot code (part of the boot sector) to a 100-MB bootable partition of the disk, marked as hidden to prevent accidental modification after the operating system has loaded. This is the system volume described earlier.

Before writing to a partition's boot sector, Windows Setup ensures that the boot partition (the *boot partition* is the partition on which Windows is installed, which is typically not the same as the system partition, where the boot files are located) is formatted with NTFS, the only supported file system that Windows can boot from when installed on a fixed disk, or formats the boot partition (and any other partition) with NTFS. Note that the format of the system partition can be any format that Windows supports (such as FAT32). If partitions are already formatted appropriately, you can instruct Setup to skip this step. After Setup formats the system partition, Setup copies the Boot Manager program (Bootmgr) that Windows uses to the system partition (the system volume).

Another of Setup's roles is to prepare the Boot Configuration Database (BCD), which on BIOS systems is stored in the \Boot\BCD file on the root directory of the system volume. This file contains options for starting the version of Windows that Setup installs and any preexisting Windows installations. If the BCD already exists, the Setup program simply adds new entries relevant to the new installation. For more information on the BCD, see Chapter 3, "System Mechanisms," in Part 1.

The BIOS Boot Sector and Bootmgr

Setup must know the partition format before it writes a boot sector because the contents of the boot sector vary depending on the format. For a partition that is in NTFS format, Windows writes NTFS-capable code. The role of the boot-sector code is to give Windows information about the structure and format of a volume and to read in the Bootmgr file from the root directory of the volume. Thus, the boot-sector code contains just enough read-only file system code to accomplish this task. After the boot-sector code loads Bootmgr into memory, it transfers control to Bootmgr's entry point. If the boot-sector code can't find Bootmgr in the volume's root directory, it displays the error message "BOOTMGR is missing".

Bootmgr is actually a concatenation of a .com file (Startup.com) and an .exe file (Bootmgr.exe), so it begins its existence while a system is executing in an x86 operating mode called *real mode*, associated with .com files. In real mode, no virtual-to-physical translation of memory addresses occurs, which means that programs that use the memory addresses interpret them as physical addresses and that only the first 1 MB of the computer's physical memory is accessible. Simple MS-DOS programs execute in a real-mode environment. However, the first action Bootmgr takes is to switch the system to *protected mode*. Still no virtual-to-physical translation occurs at this point in the boot process, but a full 32 bits of memory becomes accessible. After the system is in protected mode, Bootmgr can access all of physical memory. After creating enough page tables to make memory below 16 MB accessible with paging turned on, Bootmgr enables paging. Protected mode with paging enabled is the mode in which Windows executes in normal operation.

After Bootmgr enables protected mode, it is fully operational. However, it still relies on functions supplied by BIOS to access IDE-based system and boot disks as well as the display. Bootmgr's BIOS-interfacing functions briefly switch the processor back to real mode so that services provided by the BIOS can be executed. Bootmgr next reads the BCD file from the \Boot directory using built-in file system code. Like the boot sector's code, Bootmgr contains a lightweight NTFS file system library (Bootmgr also supports other file systems, such as FAT, El Torito CDFS, and UDFS, as well as WIM and VHD files); unlike the boot sector's code, Bootmgr's file system code can also read subdirectories.

Note Bootmgr and other boot applications can still write to preallocated files on NTFS volumes, because only the data needs to be written, instead of performing all the complex allocation work that is typically required on an NTFS volume. This is how these applications can write to bootsect.dat, for example.

Bootmgr next clears the screen. If Windows enabled the BCD setting to inform Bootmgr of a hibernation resume, this shortcuts the boot process by launching Winresume.exe, which will read the contents of the hibernation file into memory and transfer control to code in the kernel that resumes a hibernated system. That code is responsible for restarting drivers that were active when the system was shut down. Hiberfil.sys is only valid if the last computer shutdown was hibernation, since the hibernation file is invalidated after a resume, to avoid multiple resumes from the same point. (See the section "The Power Manager" in Chapter 8, "I/O System," for information on hibernation.)

If there is more than one boot-selection entry in the BCD, Bootmgr presents the user with the boot-selection menu (if there is only one entry, Bootmgr bypasses the menu and proceeds to launch Winload.exe). Selection entries in the BCD direct Bootmgr to the partition on which the Windows system directory (typically \Windows) of the selected installation resides. If Windows was upgraded from an older version, this partition might be the same as the system partition, or, on a clean install, it will always be the 100-MB hidden partition described earlier.

Entries in the BCD can include optional arguments that Bootmgr, Winload, and other components involved in the boot process interpret. Table 13-2 contains a list of these options and their effects for Bootmgr, Table 13-3 shows a list of BCD options for boot applications, and Table 13-4 shows BCD options for the Windows boot loader.

The Bcdedit.exe tool provides a convenient interface for setting a number of the switches. Some options that are included in the BCD are stored as command-line switches ("/DEBUG", for example) to the registry value HKLM\SYSTEM\CurrentControlSet\Control\SystemStartOptions; otherwise, they are stored only in the BCD binary format in the BCD hive.

TABLE 13-2 BCD Options for the Windows Boot Manager (Bootmgr)

BCD Element	Values	Meaning
bcdfilepath	Path	Points to the Boot Configuration Database (usually \Boot\BCD) file on the disk.
displaybootmenu	Boolean	Determines whether the Boot Manager shows the boot menu or picks the default entry automatically.
keyringaddress	Physical address	Specifies the physical address where the BitLocker key ring is located.
noerrordisplay	Boolean	Silences the output of errors encountered by the Boot Manager.
Resume	Boolean	Specifies whether or not resuming from hibernation should be attempted. This option is automatically set when Windows hibernates.
Timeout	Seconds	Number of seconds that the Boot Manager should wait before choosing the default entry.
resumeobject	GUID	Identifier for which boot application should be used to resume the system after hibernation.
displayorder	List	Definition of the Boot Manager's display order list.
toolsdisplayorder	List	Definition of the Boot Manager's tool display order list.
bootsequence	List	Definition of the one-time boot sequence.
Default	GUID	The default boot entry to launch.
customactions	List	Definition of custom actions to take when a specific keyboard sequence has been entered.
bcddevice	GUID	Device ID of where the BCD store is located.

TABLE 13-3 BCD Options for Boot Applications

BCD Element	Values	Meaning
avoidlowmemory	Integer	Forces physical addresses below the specified value to be avoided by the boot loader as much as possible. Sometimes required on legacy devices (such as ISA) where only memory below 16 MB is usable or visible.
badmemoryaccess	Boolean	Forces usage of memory pages in the Bad Page List (see Chapter 10, "Memory Management," for more information on the page lists).
badmemorylist	Array of page frame numbers (PFNs)	Specifies a list of physical pages on the system that are known to be bad because of faulty RAM.
baudrate	Baud rate in bps	Specifies an override for the default baud rate (19200) at which a remote kernel debugger host will connect through a serial port.
bootdebug	Boolean	Enables remote boot debugging for the boot loader. With this option enabled, you can use Kd.exe or Windbg.exe to connect to the boot loader.

BCD Element	Values	Meaning
bootems	Boolean	Used to cause Windows to enable Emergency Management Services (EMS) for boot applications, which reports boot information and accepts system management commands through a serial port.
busparams	String	If a physical PCI debugging device is used to provide FireWire or serial debugging, specifies the PCI bus, function, and device number for the device.
channel	Channel between 0 and 62	Used in conjunction with {debugtype, 1394} to specify the IEEE 1394 channel through which kernel debugging communications will flow.
configaccesspolicy	Default, DisallowMmConfig	Configures whether the system uses memory mapped I/O to access the PCI manufacturer's configuration space or falls back to using the HAL's I/O port access routines. Can sometimes be helpful in solving platform device problems.
debugaddress	Hardware address	Specifies the hardware address of the serial (COM) port used for debugging.
debugport	COM port number	Specifies an override for the default serial port (usually COM2 on systems with at least two serial ports) to which a remote kernel debugger host is connected.
debugstart	Active, AutoEnable, Disable	Specifies settings for the debugger when kernel debugging is enabled. AutoEnable enables the debugger when a breakpoint or kernel exception, including kernel crashes, occurs.
debugtype	Serial, 1394, USB	Specifies whether kernel debugging will be communicated through a serial, FireWire (IEEE 1394), or USB 2.0 port. (The default is serial.)
emsbaudrate	Baud rate in bps	Specifies the baud rate to use for EMS.
emsport	COM port number	Specifies the serial (COM) port to use for EMS.
extendedinput	Boolean	Enables boot applications to leverage BIOS support for extended console input.
firstmegabytepolicy	UseNone, UseAll, UsePrivate	Specifies how the low 1 MB of physical memory is consumed by the HAL to mitigate corruptions by the BIOS during power transitions.
fontpath	String	Specifies the path of the OEM font that should be used by the boot application.
graphicsmodedisabled	Boolean	Disables graphics mode for boot applications.
graphicsresolution	Resolution	Sets the graphics resolution for boot applications.
initialconsoleinput	Boolean	Specifies an initial character that the system inserts into the PC/AT keyboard input buffer.
integrityservices	Default, Disable, Enable	Enables or disables code integrity services, which are used by Kernel Mode Code Signing. Default is Enabled.
locale	Localization string	Sets the locale for the boot application (such as EN-US).
noumex	Boolean	Disables user-mode exceptions when kernel debugging is enabled. If you experience system hangs (freezes) when booting in debugging mode, try enabling this option.
novesa	Boolean	Disables the usage of VESA display modes.

BCD Element	Values	Meaning
recoveryenabled	Boolean	Enables the recovery sequence, if any. Used by fresh installations of Windows to present the Windows PE-based Startup And Recovery interface.
recoverysequence	List	Defines the recovery sequence (described above).
relocatephysical	Physical address	Relocates an automatically selected NUMA node's physical memory to the specified physical address.
targetname	String	Defines the target name for the USB debugger when used with USB2 debugging {debugtype, usb}.
testsigning	Boolean	Enables test-signing mode, which allows driver developers to load locally signed 64-bit drivers. This option results in a watermarked desktop.
traditionalksegmappings	Boolean	Determines whether the kernel will honor the traditional KSEG0 mapping that was originally required for MIPS support. With KSEG0 mappings, the bottom 24 bits of the kernel's initial virtual address space will map to the same physical address (that is, 0x80800000 virtual is 0x800000 in RAM). Disabling this requirement allows more low memory to be available, which can help with some hardware.
truncatememory	Address in bytes	Disregards physical memory above the specified physical address.

TABLE 13-4 BCD Options for the Windows Boot Loader (Winload)

BCD Element	Values	Meaning
advancedoptions	Boolean	If false, executes the default behavior of launching the auto-recovery command boot entry when the boot fails; otherwise, displays the boot error and offers the user the advanced boot option menu associated with the boot entry. This is equivalent to pressing F8.
bootlog	Boolean	Causes Windows to write a log of the boot to the file %SystemRoot%\Ntbtlog.txt.
bootstatuspolicy	DisplayAllFailures, IgnoreAllFailures, IgnoreShutdownFailures, IgnoreBootFailures	Overrides the system's default behavior of offering the user a troubleshooting boot menu if the system did not complete the previous boot or shutdown.
bootux	Disabled, Basic, Standard	Defines the boot graphics user experience that the user will see. Disabled means that no graphics will be seen during boot time (only a black screen), while Basic will display only a progress bar during load. Standard displays the usual Windows logo animation during boot.
clustermodeaddressing	Number of processors	Defines the maximum number of processors to include in a single Advanced Programmable Interrupt Controller (APIC) cluster.
configflags	Flags	Specifies processor-specific configuration flags.
dbgtransport	Transport image name	Overrides using one of the default kernel debugging transports (Kdcom.dll, Kd1394, Kdusb.dll) and instead uses the given file, permitting specialized debugging transports to be used that are not typically supported by Windows.
debug	Boolean	Enables kernel-mode debugging.

BCD Element	Values	Meaning
detecthal	Boolean	Enables the dynamic detection of the HAL.
driverloadfailurepolicy	Fatal, UseErrorControl	Describes the loader behavior to use when a boot driver has failed to load. Fatal will prevent booting, while UseErrorControl causes the system to honor a driver's default error behavior, specified in its service key.
ems	Boolean	Instructs the kernel to use EMS as well. (If only *bootems* is used, only the boot loader will use EMS.)
evstore	String	Stores the location of a boot preloaded hive.
exportascd	Boolean	If this option is set, the kernel will treat the ramdisk file specified as an ISO image and not a Windows Installation Media (WIM) or System Deployment Image (SDI) file.
groupaware	Boolean	Forces the system to use groups other than zero when associating the group seed to new processes. Used only on 64-bit Windows.
groupsize	Integer	Forces the maximum number of logical processors that can be part of a group (maximum of 64). Can be used to force groups to be created on a system that would normally not require them to exist. Must be a power of 2, and is used only on 64-bit Windows.
hal	HAL image name	Overrides the default file name for the HAL image (hal.dll). This option can be useful when booting a combination of a checked HAL and checked kernel (requires specifying the *kernel* element as well).
halbreakpoint	Boolean	Causes the HAL to stop at a breakpoint early in HAL initialization. The first thing the Windows kernel does when it initializes is to initialize the HAL, so this breakpoint is the earliest one possible (unless boot debugging is used). If the switch is used without the /DEBUG switch, the system will elicit a blue screen with a STOP code of 0x00000078 (PHASE0_ EXCEPTION).
hypervisorbaudrate	Baud rate in bps	If using serial hypervisor debugging, specifies the baud rate to use.
hypervisorchannel	Channel number from 0 to 62	If using FireWire (IEEE 1394) hypervisor debugging, specifies the channel number to use.
hypervisordebug	Boolean	Enables debugging the hypervisor.
hypervisordebugport	COM port number	If using serial hypervisor debugging, specifies the COM port to use.
hypervisordebugtype	Serial, 1394	Specifies which hardware port to use for hypervisor debugging.
hypervisordisableslat	Boolean	Forces the hypervisor to ignore the presence of the Second Layer Address Translation (SLAT) feature if supported by the processor.
hypervisorlaunchtype	Off, Auto	Enables loading of the hypervisor on a Hyper-V system, or forces it to be disabled.
hypervisorpath	Hypervisor binary image name	Specifies the path of the hypervisor binary.
hypervisoruselargevtlb	Boolean	Enables the hypervisor to use a larger amount of virtual TLB entries.

BCD Element	Values	Meaning
increaseuserva	Size in MB	Increases the size of the user process address space from 2 GB to the specified size, up to 3 GB (and therefore reduces the size of system space). Giving virtual-memory-intensive applications such as database servers a larger address space can improve their performance. (See the section "Address Space Layout" in Chapter 9 for more information.)
kernel	Kernel image name	Overrides the default file name for the kernel image (Ntoskrnl.exe). This option can be useful when booting a combination of a checked HAL and checked kernel (requires specifying the *hal* element to be used as well).
lastknowngood	Boolean	Boots the last known good configuration, instead of the current control set.
loadoptions	Extra command-line parameters	This option is used to add other command-line parameters that are not defined by BCD elements. These parameters could be used to configure or define the operation of other components on the system that might not be able to use the BCD (such as legacy components).
maxgroup	Boolean	Maximizes the number of processor groups that are created during processor topology configuration. See Chapter 3 in Part 1 for more information about group selection and its relationship to NUMA.
maxproc	Boolean	Forces the maximum number of supported processors that Windows will report to drivers and applications to accommodate the arrival of additional CPUs via dynamic processor support.
msi	Default, ForceDisable	Allows disabling support for message signaled interrupts.
nocrashautoreboot	Boolean	Disables the automatic reboot after a system crash (blue screen).
nointegritychecks	Boolean	Disables integrity checks performed by Windows when loading drivers. Automatically removed at the next reboot.
nolowmem	Boolean	Requires that PAE be enabled and that the system have more than 4 GB of physical memory. If these conditions are met, the PAE-enabled version of the Windows kernel, Ntkrnlpa.exe, won't use the first 4 GB of physical memory. Instead, it will load all applications and device drivers and allocate all memory pools from above that boundary. This switch is useful only to test device-driver compatibility with large memory systems.
numproc	Number of processors	Specifies the number of CPUs that can be used on a multiprocessor system. Example: /NUMPROC=2 on a four-way system will prevent Windows from using two of the four processors.
nx	OptIn, OptOut, AlwaysOff, AlwaysOn	This option is available only on 32-bit versions of Windows when running on processors that support no-execute memory and only when PAE (explained further in the *pae* entry) is also enabled. It enables no-execute protection. No-execute protection is always enabled on 64-bit versions of Windows on x64 processors. See Chapter 9 for a description of this behavior.
onecpu	Boolean	Causes Windows to use only one CPU on a multiprocessor system.

BCD Element	Values	Meaning
optionsedit	Boolean	Enables the options editor in the Boot Manager. With this option, Boot Manager allows the user to interactively set on-demand command-line options and switches for the current boot. This is equivalent to pressing F10.
osdevice	GUID	Specifies the device on which the operating system is installed.
pae	Default, ForceEnable, ForceDisable	Default allows the boot loader to determine whether the system supports PAE and loads the PAE kernel. ForceEnable forces this behavior, while ForceDisable forces the loader to load the non–PAE version of the Windows kernel, even if the system is detected as supporting x86 PAEs and has more than 4 GB of physical memory.
pciexpress	Default, ForceDisable	Can be used to disable support for PCI Express buses and devices.
perfmem	Size in MB	Size of the buffer to allocate for performance data logging. This option acts similarly to the *removememory* element, since it prevents Windows from seeing the size specified as available memory.
quietboot	Boolean	Instructs Windows not to initialize the VGA video driver responsible for presenting bitmapped graphics during the boot process. The driver is used to display boot progress information, so disabling it will disable the ability of Windows to show this information.
ramdiskimagelength	Length in bytes	Size of the ramdisk specified.
ramdiskimageoffset	Offset in bytes	If the ramdisk contains other data (such as a header) before the virtual file system, instructs the boot loader where to start reading the ramdisk file from.
ramdisksdipath	Image file name	Specifies the name of the SDI ramdisk to load.
ramdisktftpblocksize	Block size	If loading a WIM ramdisk from a network Trivial FTP (TFTP) server, specifies the block size to use.
ramdisktftpclientport	Port number	If loading a WIM ramdisk from a network TFTP server, specifies the port.
ramdisktftpwindowsize	Window size	If loading a WIM ramdisk from a network TFTP server, specifies the window size to use.
removememory	Size in bytes	Specifies an amount of memory Windows won't use.
restrictapiccluster	Cluster number	Defines the largest APIC cluster number to be used by the system.
resumeobject	Object GUID	Describes which application to use for resuming from hibernation, typically Winresume.exe.
safeboot	Minimal, Network, DsRepair	Specifies options for a safe-mode boot. Minimal corresponds to safe mode without networking, Network to safe mode with networking, and DsRepair to safe mode with Directory Services Restore mode. (Safe mode is described later in this chapter.)
safebootalternateshell	Boolean	Tells Windows to use the program specified by the HKLM\SYSTEM\CurrentControlSet\Control\SafeBoot\AlternateShell value as the graphical shell rather than the default, which is Windows Explorer. This option is referred to as Safe Mode With Command Prompt in the alternate boot menu.

BCD Element	Values	Meaning
sos	Boolean	Causes Windows to list the device drivers marked to load at boot time and then to display the system version number (including the build number), amount of physical memory, and number of processors.
stampdisks	Boolean	Specifies that Winload will write an MBR disk signature to a RAW disk when booting Windows PE (Preinstallation Environment). This can be required in deployment environments in order to create a mapping from operating system–enumerated hard disks to BIOS-enumerated hard disks to know which disk should be the system disk.
systemroot	String	Specifies the path, relative to osdevice, in which the operating system is installed.
targetname	Name	For USB 2.0 debugging, assigns a name to the machine that is being debugged.
tpmbootentropy	Default, ForceDisable, ForceEnable	Forces a specific TPM Boot Entropy policy to be selected by the boot loader and passed on to the kernel. TPM Boot Entropy, when used, seeds the kernel's random number generator (RNG) with data obtained from the TPM (if present).
usefirmwarepcisettings	Boolean	Stops Windows from dynamically assigning IO/IRQ resources to PCI devices and leaves the devices configured by the BIOS. See Microsoft Knowledge Base article 148501 for more information.
uselegacyapicmode	Boolean	Forces usage of basic APIC functionality even though the chipset reports extended APIC functionality as present. Used in cases of hardware errata and/or incompatibility.
usephysicaldestination	Boolean	Forces the use of the APIC in physical destination mode.
useplatformclock	Boolean	Forces usage of the platforms's clock source as the system's performance counter.
vga	Boolean	Forces Windows to use the VGA display driver instead of the third-party high-performance driver.
winpe	Boolean	Used by Windows PE, this option causes the configuration manager to load the registry SYSTEM hive as a volatile hive such that changes made to it in memory are not saved back to the hive image.
x2apicpolicy	Disabled, Enabled, Default	Specifies whether extended APIC functionality should be used if the chipset supports it. Disabled is equivalent to setting uselegacyapicmode, while Enabled forces ACPI functionality on even if errata are detected. Default uses the chipset's reported capabilities (unless errata are present).
xsavepolicy	Integer	Forces the given XSAVE policy to be loaded from the XSAVE Policy Resource Driver (Hwpolicy.sys).
xsaveaddfeature0-7	Integer	Used while testing support for XSAVE on modern Intel processors; allows for faking that certain processor features are present when, in fact, they are not. This helps increase the size of the CONTEXT structure and confirms that applications work correctly with extended features that might appear in the future. No actual extra functionality will be present, however.
xsaveremovefeature	Integer	Forces the entered XSAVE feature not to be reported to the kernel, even though the processor supports it.

BCD Element	Values	Meaning
xsaveprocessorsmask	Integer	Bitmask of which processors the XSAVE policy should apply to.
xsavedisable	Boolean	Turns off support for the XSAVE functionality even though the processor supports it.

If the user doesn't select an entry from the selection menu within the timeout period the BCD specifies, Bootmgr chooses the default selection specified in the BCD (if there is only one entry, it immediately chooses this one). Once the boot selection has been made, Bootmgr loads the boot loader associated with that entry, which will be Winload.exe for Windows installations.

Winload.exe also contains code that queries the system's ACPI BIOS to retrieve basic device and configuration information. This information includes the following:

- The time and date information stored in the system's CMOS (nonvolatile memory)

- The number, size, and type of disk drives on the system

- Legacy device information, such as buses (for example, ISA, PCI, EISA, Micro Channel Architecture [MCA]), mice, parallel ports, and video adapters are not queried and instead faked out

This information is gathered into internal data structures that will be stored under the HKLM\ HARDWARE\DESCRIPTION registry key later in the boot. This is mostly a legacy key as CMOS settings and BIOS-detected disk drive configuration settings, as well as legacy buses, are no longer supported by Windows, and this information is mainly stored for compatibility reasons. Today, it is the Plug and Play manager database that stores the true information on hardware.

Next, Winload begins loading the files from the *boot volume* needed to start the kernel initialization. The boot volume is the volume that corresponds to the partition on which the system directory (usually \Windows) of the installation being booted is located. The steps Winload follows here include:

1. Loads the appropriate kernel and HAL images (Ntoskrnl.exe and Hal.dll by default) as well as any of their dependencies. If Winload fails to load either of these files, it prints the message "Windows could not start because the following file was missing or corrupt", followed by the name of the file.

2. Reads in the VGA font file (by default, vgaoem.fon). If this file fails, the same error message as described in step 1 will be shown.

3. Reads in the NLS (National Language System) files used for internationalization. By default, these are l_intl.nls, c_1252.nls, and c_437.nls.

4. Reads in the SYSTEM registry hive, \Windows\System32\Config\System, so that it can determine which device drivers need to be loaded to accomplish the boot. (A hive is a file that contains a registry subtree. You'll find more details about the registry in Chapter 4, "Management Mechanisms," in Part 1.)

5. Scans the in-memory SYSTEM registry hive and locates all the *boot device drivers*. Boot device drivers are drivers necessary to boot the system. These drivers are indicated in the registry

by a start value of SERVICE_BOOT_START (0). Every device driver has a registry subkey under HKLM\SYSTEM\CurrentControlSet\Services. For example, Services has a subkey named fvevol for the BitLocker driver, which you can see in Figure 13-2. (For a detailed description of the Services registry entries, see the section "Services" in Chapter 4 in Part 1.)

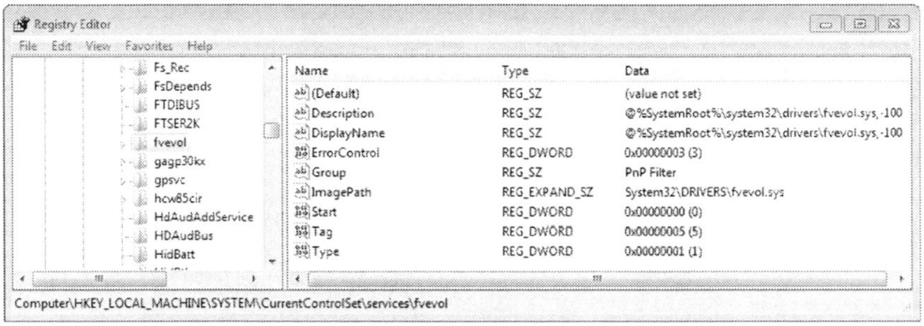

FIGURE 13-2 BitLocker driver service settings

6. Adds the file system driver that's responsible for implementing the code for the type of partition (NTFS) on which the installation directory resides to the list of boot drivers to load. Winload must load this driver at this time; if it didn't, the kernel would require the drivers to load themselves, a requirement that would introduce a circular dependency.

7. Loads the boot drivers, which should only be drivers that, like the file system driver for the boot volume, would introduce a circular dependency if the kernel was required to load them. To indicate the progress of the loading, Winload updates a progress bar displayed below the text "Starting Windows". If the *sos* option is specified in the BCD, Winload doesn't display the progress bar but instead displays the file names of each boot driver. Keep in mind that the drivers are loaded but not initialized at this time—they initialize later in the boot sequence.

8. Prepares CPU registers for the execution of Ntoskrnl.exe.

For steps 1 and 8, Winload also implements part of the Kernel Mode Code Signing (KMCS) infrastructure, which was described in Chapter 3 in Part 1, by enforcing that all boot drivers are signed on 64-bit Windows. Additionally, the system will crash if the signature of the early boot files is incorrect.

This action is the end of Winload's role in the boot process. At this point, Winload calls the main function in Ntoskrnl.exe (*KiSystemStartup*) to perform the rest of the system initialization.

The UEFI Boot Process

A UEFI-compliant system has firmware that runs boot loader code that's been programmed into the system's nonvolatile RAM (NVRAM) by Windows Setup. The boot code reads the BCD's contents, which are also stored in NVRAM. The Bcdedit.exe tool mentioned earlier also has the ability to abstract the firmware's NVRAM variables in the BCD, allowing for full transparency of this mechanism.

The UEFI standard defines the ability to prompt the user with an EFI Boot Manager that can be used to select an operating system or additional applications to load. However, to provide a consistent user interface between BIOS systems and UEFI systems, Windows sets a 2-second timeout for selecting the EFI Boot Manager, after which the EFI-version of Bootmgr (Bootmgfw.efi) loads instead.

Hardware detection occurs next, where the boot loader uses UEFI interfaces to determine the number and type of the following devices:

- Network adapters
- Video adapters
- Keyboards
- Disk controllers
- Storage devices

On UEFI systems, all operations and programs execute in the native CPU mode with paging enabled and no part of the Windows boot process executes in 16-bit mode. Note that although EFI is supported on both 32-bit and 64-bit systems, Windows provides support for EFI only on 64-bit platforms.

Just as Bootmgr does on x86 and x64 systems, the EFI Boot Manager presents a menu of boot selections with an optional timeout. Once a boot selection is made, the loader navigates to the subdirectory on the EFI System partition corresponding to the selection and loads the EFI version of the Windows boot loader (Winload.efi).

The UEFI specification requires that the system have a partition designated as the EFI System partition that is formatted with the FAT file system and is between 100 MB and 1 GB in size or up to 1 percent of the size of the disk, and each Windows installation has a subdirectory on the EFI System partition under EFI\Microsoft.

Note that thanks to the unified boot process and model present in Windows, the components in Table 13-1 apply almost identically to UEFI systems, except that those ending in *.exe* end in *.efi*, and they use EFI APIs and services instead of BIOS interrupts. Another difference is that to avoid limitations of the MBR partition format (including a maximum of four partitions per disk), UEFI systems use the GPT (GUID Partition Table) format, which uses GUIDs to identify different partitions and their roles on the system.

> **Note** Although the EFI standard has been available since early 2001, and UEFI since 2005, very few computer manufacturers have started using this technology because of backward compatibility concerns and the difficulty of moving from an entrenched 20-year-old technology to a new one. Two notable exceptions are Itanium machines and Apple's Intel Macintosh computers.

Booting from iSCSI

Internet SCSI (iSCSI) devices are a kind of network-attached storage, in that remote physical disks are connected to an iSCSI Host Bus Adapter (HBA) or through Ethernet. These devices, however, are different from traditional network-attached storage (NAS) because they provide block-level access to disks, unlike the logical-based access over a network file system that NAS employs. Therefore, an iSCSI-connected disk appears as any other disk drive, both to the boot loader as well as to the OS, as long as the Microsoft iSCSI Initiator is used to provide access over an Ethernet connection. By using iSCSI-enabled disks instead of local storage, companies can save on space, power consumption, and cooling.

Although Windows has traditionally supported booting only from locally connected disks, or network booting through PXE, modern versions of Windows are also capable of natively booting from iSCSI devices through a mechanism called *iSCSI Boot*. The boot loader (Winload.exe) contains a minimalistic network stack conforming to the Universal Network Device Interface (UNDI) standard, which allows compatible NIC ROMs to respond to Interrupt 13h (the legacy BIOS disk I/O interrupt) and convert the requests to network I/O. On EFI systems, the network interface driver provided by the manufacturer is used instead, and EFI Device APIs are used instead of interrupts.

Finally, to know the location, path, and authentication information for the remote disk, the boot loader also reads an iSCSI Boot Firmware Table (iBFT) that must be present in physical memory (typically exposed through ACPI). Additionally, Windows Setup also has the capability of reading this table to determine bootable iSCSI devices and allow direct installation on such a device, such that no imaging is required. Combined with the Microsoft iSCSI Initiator, this is all that's required for Windows to boot from iSCSI, as shown in Figure 13-3.

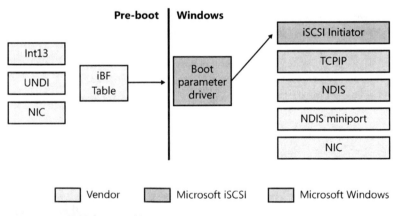

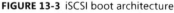

FIGURE 13-3 iSCSI boot architecture

Initializing the Kernel and Executive Subsystems

When Winload calls Ntoskrnl, it passes a data structure called the loader parameter block that contains the system and boot partition paths, a pointer to the memory tables Winload generated to describe the physical memory on the system, a physical hardware tree that is later used to build the volatile HARDWARE registry hive, an in-memory copy of the SYSTEM registry hive, and a pointer to the list of boot drivers Winload loaded, as well as various other information related to the boot processing performed until this point.

EXPERIMENT: Loader Parameter Block

While booting, the kernel keeps a pointer to the loader parameter block in the *KeLoaderBlock* variable. The kernel discards the parameter block after the first boot phase, so the only way to see the contents of the structure is to attach a kernel debugger before booting and break at the initial kernel debugger breakpoint. If you are able to do so, you can use the *dt* command to dump the block, as shown:

```
0: kd> dt poi(nt!KeLoaderBlock) nt!_LOADER_PARAMETER_BLOCK
   +0x000 OsMajorVersion         : 6
   +0x004 OsMinorVersion         : 1
   +0x008 Size                   : 0x88
   +0x00c Reserved               : 0
   +0x010 LoadOrderListHead      : _LIST_ENTRY [ 0x8085b4c8 - 0x80869c70 ]
   +0x018 MemoryDescriptorListHead : _LIST_ENTRY [ 0x80a00000 - 0x80a00de8 ]
   +0x020 BootDriverListHead     : _LIST_ENTRY [ 0x80860d10 - 0x8085eba0 ]
   +0x028 KernelStack            : 0x88e7c000
   +0x02c Prcb                   : 0
   +0x030 Process                : 0
   +0x034 Thread                 : 0x88e64800
   +0x038 RegistryLength         : 0x2940000
   +0x03c RegistryBase           : 0x80adf000 Void
   +0x040 ConfigurationRoot      : 0x8082d450 _CONFIGURATION_COMPONENT_DATA
   +0x044 ArcBootDeviceName      : 0x8082d9a0  "multi(0)disk(0)rdisk(0)partition(4)"
   +0x048 ArcHalDeviceName       : 0x8082d788  "multi(0)disk(0)rdisk(0)partition(4)"
   +0x04c NtBootPathName         : 0x8082d828  "\Windows\"
   +0x050 NtHalPathName          : 0x80826358  "\"
   +0x054 LoadOptions            : 0x8080e1b0  "NOEXECUTE=ALWAYSON DEBUGPORT=COM1
                                                BAUDRATE=115200"
   +0x058 NlsData                : 0x808691e0 _NLS_DATA_BLOCK
   +0x05c ArcDiskInformation     : 0x80821408 _ARC_DISK_INFORMATION
   +0x060 OemFontFile            : 0x84a551d0 Void
   +0x064 Extension              : 0x8082d9d8 _LOADER_PARAMETER_EXTENSION
   +0x068 u                      : <unnamed-tag>
   +0x074 FirmwareInformation    : _FIRMWARE_INFORMATION_LOADER_BLOCK
```

Additionally, the *!loadermemorylist* command can be used on the *MemoryDescriptorListHead* field to dump the physical memory ranges:

```
0: kd> !loadermemorylist 0x80a00000
Base Length     Type
1    00000001   HALCachedMemory
2    00000004   HALCachedMemory
...
4a32 00000023   NlsData
4a55 00000002   BootDriver
4a57 00000026   BootDriver
4a7d 00000014   BootDriver
4a91 0000016f   Free
```

```
4c00      0001b3f0      Free
1fff0     00000001      FirmwarePermanent
1fff1     00000002      FirmwarePermanent
1fff3     00000001      FirmwarePermanent
1fff4     0000000b      FirmwarePermanent
1ffff     00000001      FirmwarePermanent
fd000     00000800      FirmwarePermanent
fec00     00000001      FirmwarePermanent
fee00     00000001      FirmwarePermanent
ffc00     00000400      FirmwarePermanent

Summary
Memory Type         Pages
Free                0001bc50    (  113744)
LoadedProgram       0000013d    (     317)
FirmwareTemporary   000006dd    (    1757)
FirmwarePermanent   00000c37    (    3127)
OsloaderHeap        0000022a    (     554)
SystemCode          000005dc    (    1500)
BootDriver          00000968    (    2408)
RegistryData        00002940    (   10560)
MemoryData          00000035    (      53)
NlsData             00000023    (      35)
HALCachedMemory     0000001e    (      30)
                    ========    ========
Total               00020bc5    (  134085)  = ~523MB
```

Ntoskrnl then begins *phase 0*, the first of its two-phase initialization process (*phase 1* is the second). Most executive subsystems have an initialization function that takes a parameter that identifies which phase is executing.

During phase 0, interrupts are disabled. The purpose of this phase is to build the rudimentary structures required to allow the services needed in phase 1 to be invoked. Ntoskrnl's main function calls *KiSystemStartup*, which in turn calls *HalInitializeProcessor* and *KiInitializeKernel* for each CPU. *KiInitializeKernel*, if running on the boot CPU, performs systemwide kernel initialization, such as initializing internal lists and other data structures that all CPUs share. It also checks whether virtualization was specified as a BCD option (*hypervisorlaunchtype*), and whether the CPU supports hardware virtualization technology. The first instance of *KiInitializeKernel* then calls the function responsible for orchestrating phase 0, *InitBootProcessor*, while subsequent processors only call *HalInitSystem*.

InitBootProcessor starts by initializing the pool look-aside pointers for the initial CPU and by checking for and honoring the BCD *burnmemory* boot option, where it discards the amount of physical memory the value specifies. It then performs enough initialization of the NLS files that were loaded by Winload (described earlier) to allow Unicode to ANSI and OEM translation to work. Next, it continues by calling the HAL function *HalInitSystem*, which gives the HAL a chance to gain system control before Windows performs significant further initialization. One responsibility of *HalInitSystem* is to prepare the system interrupt controller of each CPU for interrupts and to configure the interval clock timer interrupt, which is used for CPU time accounting. (See the section "Quantum Accounting" in Chapter 5, "Processes, Threads, and Jobs," in Part 1 for more on CPU time accounting.)

When *HalInitSystem* returns control, *InitBootProcessor* proceeds by computing the reciprocal for timer expiration. Reciprocals are used for optimizing divisions on most modern processors. They can perform multiplications faster, and because Windows must divide the current 64-bit time value in order to find out which timers need to expire, this static calculation reduces interrupt latency when the clock interval fires. *InitBootProcessor* then continues by setting up the system root path and searching the kernel image for the location of the crash message strings it displays on blue screens, caching their location to avoid looking up the strings during a crash, which could be dangerous and unreliable. Next, *InitBootProcessor* initializes the quota functionality part of the process manager and reads the *control vector*. This data structure contains more than 150 kernel-tuning options that are part of the HKLM\SYSTEM\CurrentControlSet\Control registry key, including information such as the licensing data and version information for the installation.

InitBootProcessor is now ready to call the phase 0 initialization routines for the executive, Driver Verifier, and the memory manager. These components perform the following initialization steps:

1. The executive initializes various internal locks, resources, lists, and variables and validates that the product suite type in the registry is valid, discouraging casual modification of the registry in order to "upgrade" to an SKU of Windows that was not actually purchased. This is only one of the many such checks in the kernel.

2. Driver Verifier, if enabled, initializes various settings and behaviors based on the current state of the system (such as whether safe mode is enabled) and verification options. It also picks which drivers to target for tests that target randomly chosen drivers.

3. The memory manager constructs page tables and internal data structures that are necessary to provide basic memory services. It also builds and reserves an area for the system file cache and creates memory areas for the paged and nonpaged pools (described in Chapter 10). The other executive subsystems, the kernel, and device drivers use these two memory pools for allocating their data structures.

Next, *InitBootProcessor* calls *HalInitializeBios* to set up the BIOS emulation code part of the HAL. This code is used both on real BIOS systems as well as on EFI systems to allow access (or to emulate access) to 16-bit real mode interrupts and memory, which are used mainly by Bootvid to display the early VGA boot screen and bugcheck screen. After the function returns, the kernel initializes the Bootvid library and displays early boot status messages by calling *InbvEnableBootDriver* and *InbvDriverInitailize*.

At this point, *InitBootProcessor* enumerates the boot-start drivers that were loaded by Winload and calls *DbgLoadImageSymbols* to inform the kernel debugger (if attached) to load symbols for each of these drivers. If the host debugger has configured the *break on symbol load* option, this will be the earliest point for a kernel debugger to gain control of the system. *InitBootProcessor* now calls *HvlInitSystem*, which attempts to connect to the hypervisor in case Windows might be running inside a Hyper-V host system's child partition. When the function returns, it calls *HeadlessInit* to initialize the serial console if the machine was configured for Emergency Management Services (EMS).

Next, *InitBootProcessor* builds the versioning information that will be used later in the boot process, such as the build number, service pack version, and beta version status. Then it copies the NLS tables that Winload previously loaded into paged pool, re-initializes them, and creates the kernel stack trace database if the global flags specify creating one. (For more information on the global flags, see Chapter 3 in Part 1.)

Finally, *InitBootProcessor* calls the object manager, security reference monitor, process manager, user-mode debugging framework, and the Plug and Play manager. These components perform the following initialization steps:

1. During the object manager initialization, the objects that are necessary to construct the object manager namespace are defined so that other subsystems can insert objects into it. A handle table is created so that resource tracking can begin.

2. The security reference monitor initializes the token type object and then uses the object to create and prepare the first local system account token for assignment to the initial process. (See Chapter 6, "Security," in Part 1 for a description of the local system account.)

3. The process manager performs most of its initialization in phase 0, defining the process and thread object types and setting up lists to track active processes and threads. The process manager also creates a process object for the initial process and names it *Idle*. As its last step, the process manager creates the System process and a system thread to execute the routine *Phase1Initialization*. This thread doesn't start running right away because interrupts are still disabled.

4. The user-mode debugging framework creates the definition of the debug object type that is used for attaching a debugger to a process and receiving debugger events. For more information on user-mode debugging, see Chapter 3 in Part 1.

5. The Plug and Play manager's phase 0 initialization then takes place, which involves simply initializing an executive resource used to synchronize access to bus resources.

When control returns to *KiInitializeKernel*, the last step is to allocate the DPC stack for the current processor and the I/O privilege map save area (on x86 systems only), after which control proceeds to the *Idle* loop, which then causes the system thread created in step 3 of the previous process description to begin executing phase 1. (Secondary processors wait to begin their initialization until step 8 of phase 1, described in the following list.)

Phase 1 consists of the following steps:

1. *Phase1InitializationDiscard*, which, as the name implies, discards the code that is part of the INIT section of the kernel image in order to preserve memory.

2. The initialization thread sets its priority to 31, the highest possible, in order to prevent preemption.

3. The NUMA/group topology relationships are created, in which the system tries to come up with the most optimized mapping between logical processors and processor groups, taking into account NUMA localities and distances, unless overridden by the relevant BCD settings.

4. *HalInitSystem* prepares the system to accept interrupts from devices and to enable interrupts.

5. The boot video driver is called, which in turn displays the Windows startup screen, which by default consists of a black screen and a progress bar. If the *quietboot* boot option was used, this step will not occur.

6. The kernel builds various strings and version information, which are displayed on the boot screen through Bootvid if the *sos* boot option was enabled. This includes the full version information, number of processors supported, and amount of memory supported.

7. The power manager's initialization is called.

8. The system time is initialized (by calling *HalQueryRealTimeClock*) and then stored as the time the system booted.

9. On a multiprocessor system, the remaining processors are initialized by *KeStartAllProcessors* and *HalAllProcessorsStarted*. The number of processors that will be initialized and supported depends on a combination of the actual physical count, the licensing information for the installed SKU of Windows, boot options such as *numproc* and *onecpu*, and whether dynamic partitioning is enabled (server systems only). After all the available processors have initialized, the affinity of the system process is updated to include all processors.

10. The object manager creates the namespace root directory (\), \ObjectTypes directory, and the DOS device name mapping directory (\Global??). It then creates the \DosDevices symbolic link that points at the Windows subsystem device name mapping directory.

11. The executive is called to create the executive object types, including semaphore, mutex, event, and timer.

12. The I/O manager is called to create the I/O manager object types, including device, driver, controller, adapter, and file objects.

13. The kernel debugger library finalizes initialization of debugging settings and parameters if the debugger has not been triggered prior to this point.

14. The transaction manager also creates its object types, such as the enlistment, resource manager, and transaction manager types.

15. The kernel initializes scheduler (dispatcher) data structures and the system service dispatch table.

16. The user-mode debugging library (Dbgk) data structures are initialized.

17. If Driver Verifier is enabled and, depending on verification options, pool verification is enabled, object handle tracing is started for the system process.

18. The security reference monitor creates the \Security directory in the object manager namespace and initializes auditing data structures if auditing is enabled.

19. The \SystemRoot symbolic link is created.

20. The memory manager is called to create the \Device\PhysicalMemory section object and the memory manager's system worker threads (which are explained in Chapter 10).

21. NLS tables are mapped into system space so that they can be easily mapped by user-mode processes.

22. Ntdll.dll is mapped into the system address space.

23. The cache manager initializes the file system cache data structures and creates its worker threads.

24. The configuration manager creates the \Registry key object in the object manager namespace and opens the in-memory SYSTEM hive as a proper hive file. It then copies the initial hardware tree data passed by Winload into the volatile HARDWARE hive.

25. The high-resolution boot graphics library initializes, unless it has been disabled through the BCD or the system is booting headless.

26. The errata manager initializes and scans the registry for errata information, as well as the INF (driver installation file, described in Chapter 8) database containing errata for various drivers.

27. Superfetch and the prefetcher are initialized.

28. The Store Manager is initialized.

29. The current time zone information is initialized.

30. Global file system driver data structures are initialized.

31. Phase 1 of debugger-transport-specific information is performed by calling the *KdDebugger-Initialize1* routine in the registered transport, such as Kdcom.dll.

32. The Plug and Play manager calls the Plug and Play BIOS.

33. The advanced local procedure call (ALPC) subsystem initializes the ALPC port type and ALPC waitable port type objects. The older LPC objects are set as aliases.

34. If the system was booted with boot logging (with the BCD *bootlog* option), the boot log file is initialized. If the system was booted in safe mode, a string is displayed on the boot screen with the current safe mode boot type.

35. The executive is called to execute its second initialization phase, where it configures part of the Windows licensing functionality in the kernel, such as validating the registry settings that hold license data. Also, if persistent data from boot applications is present (such as memory diagnostic results or resume from hibernation information), the relevant log files and information are written to disk or to the registry.

36. The MiniNT/WinPE registry keys are created if this is such a boot, and the NLS object directory is created in the namespace, which will be used later to host the section objects for the various memory-mapped NLS files.

37. The power manager is called to initialize again. This time it sets up support for power requests, the ALPC channel for brightness notifications, and profile callback support.

38. The I/O manager initialization now takes place. This stage is a complex phase of system startup that accounts for most of the boot time.

    The I/O manager first initializes various internal structures and creates the driver and device object types. It then calls the Plug and Play manager, power manager, and HAL to begin the various stages of dynamic device enumeration and initialization. (Because this process is complex and specific to the I/O system, we cover the details in Chapter 8.) Then the Windows Management Instrumentation (WMI) subsystem is initialized, which provides WMI support for device drivers. (See the section "Windows Management Instrumentation" in Chapter 4 in Part 1 for more information.) This also initializes Event Tracing for Windows (ETW). Next, all the boot-start drivers are called to perform their driver-specific initialization, and then the system-start device drivers are loaded and initialized. (Details on the processing of the driver load control information on the registry are also covered in Chapter 8.) Finally, the Windows subsystem device names are created as symbolic links in the object manager's namespace.

39. The transaction manager sets up the Windows software trace preprocessor (WPP) and ETW and initializes with WMI. (ETW and WMI are described in Chapter 4 in Part 1.)

40. Now that boot-start and system-start drivers are loaded, the errata manager loads the INF database with the driver errata and begins parsing it, which includes applying registry PCI configuration workarounds.

41. If the computer is booting in safe mode, this fact is recorded in the registry.

42. Unless explicitly disabled in the registry, paging of kernel-mode code (in Ntoskrnl and drivers) is enabled.

43. The configuration manager makes sure that all processors on an SMP system are identical in terms of the features that they support; otherwise, it crashes the system.

44. On 32-bit systems, VDM (Virtual Dos Machine) support is initialized, which includes determining whether the processor supports Virtual Machine Extensions (VME).

45. The process manager is called to set up rate limiting for jobs, initialize the static environment for protected processes, and look up the various system-defined entry points in the user-mode system library (Ntdll.dll).

46. The power manager is called to finalize its initialization.

47. The rest of the licensing information for the system is initialized, including caching the current policy settings stored in the registry.

48. The security reference monitor is called to create the Command Server Thread that communicates with LSASS. (See the section "Security System Components" in Chapter 6 in Part 1 for more on how security is enforced in Windows.)

49. The Session Manager (Smss) process (introduced in Chapter 2, "System Architecture," in Part 1) is started. Smss is responsible for creating the user-mode environment that provides the visible interface to Windows—its initialization steps are covered in the next section.

50. The TPM boot entropy values are queried. These values can be queried only once per boot, and normally, the TPM system driver should have queried them by now, but if this driver had not been running for some reason (perhaps the user disabled it), the unqueried values would still be available. Therefore, the kernel manually queries them too to avoid this situation, and in normal scenarios, the kernel's own query should fail.

51. All the memory used up by the loader parameter block and all its references is now freed.

As a final step before considering the executive and kernel initialization complete, the phase 1 initialization thread waits for the handle to the Session Manager process with a timeout value of 5 seconds. If the Session Manager process exits before the 5 seconds elapse, the system crashes with a SESSION5_INITIALIZATION_FAILED stop code.

If the 5-second wait times out (that is, if 5 seconds elapse), the Session Manager is assumed to have started successfully, and the phase 1 initialization function calls the memory manager's zero page thread function (explained in Chapter 10). Thus, this system thread becomes the zero page thread for the remainder of the life of the system.

Smss, Csrss, and Wininit

Smss is like any other user-mode process except for two differences. First, Windows considers Smss a trusted part of the operating system. Second, Smss is a *native* application. Because it's a trusted operating system component, Smss can perform actions few other processes can perform, such as creating security tokens. Because it's a native application, Smss doesn't use Windows APIs—it uses only core executive APIs known collectively as the Windows native API. Smss doesn't use the Win32 APIs because the Windows subsystem isn't executing when Smss launches. In fact, one of Smss's first tasks is to start the Windows subsystem.

Smss then calls the configuration manager executive subsystem to finish initializing the registry, fleshing the registry out to include all its keys. The configuration manager is programmed to know where the core registry hives are stored on disk (excluding hives corresponding to user profiles), and it records the paths to the hives it loads in the HKLM\SYSTEM\CurrentControlSet\Control\hivelist key.

The main thread of Smss performs the following initialization steps:

1. Marks itself as a critical process and its main thread as a critical thread. As discussed in Chapter 5 in Part 1, this will cause the kernel to crash the system if Smss quits unexpectedly. Smss

also enables the automatic affinity update mode to support dynamic processor addition. (See Chapter 5 in Part 1 for more information.)

2. Creates *protected prefixes* for the mailslot and named pipe file system drivers, creating privileged paths for administrators and service accounts to communicate through those paths. See Chapter 7, "Networking," in Part 1 for more information.

3. Calls *SmpInit*, which tunes the maximum concurrency level for Smss, meaning the maximum number of parallel sessions that will be created by spawning copies of Smss into other sessions. This is at least four and at most the number of active CPUs.

4. *SmpInit* then creates an ALPC port object (*SmApiPort*) to receive client requests (such as to load a new subsystem or create a session).

5. *SmpInit* calls *SmpLoadDataFromRegistry*, which starts by setting up the default environment variables for the system, and sets the SAFEBOOT variable if the system was booted in safe mode.

6. *SmpLoadDataFromRegistry* calls *SmpInitializeDosDevices* to define the symbolic links for MS-DOS device names (such as COM1 and LPT1).

7. *SmpLoadDataFromRegistry* creates the \Sessions directory in the object manager's namespace (for multiple sessions).

8. *SmpLoadDataFromRegistry* runs any programs defined in HKLM\SYSTEM\CurrentControlSet\Control\Session Manager\BootExecute with *SmpExecuteCommand*. Typically, this value contains one command to run Autochk (the boot-time version of Chkdsk).

9. *SmpLoadDataFromRegistry* calls *SmpProcessFileRenames* to perform delayed file rename and delete operations as directed by HKLM\SYSTEM\CurrentControlSet\Control\Session Manager\PendingFileRenameOperations and HKLM\SYSTEM\CurrentControlSet\Control\Session Manager\PendingFileRenameOperations2.

10. *SmpLoadDataFromRegistry* calls *SmpCreatePagingFiles* to create additional paging files. Paging file configuration is stored under HKLM\SYSTEM\CurrentControlSet\Control\Session Manager\Memory Management\PagingFiles.

11. *SmpLoadDataFromRegistry* initializes the registry by calling the native function *NtInitializeRegistry*. The configuration manager builds the rest of the registry by loading the registry hives for the HKLM\SAM, HKLM\SECURITY, and HKLM\SOFTWARE keys. Although HKLM\SYSTEM\CurrentControlSet\Control\hivelist locates the hive files on disk, the configuration manager is coded to look for them in \Windows\System32\Config.

12. *SmpLoadDataFromRegistry* calls *SmpCreateDynamicEnvironmentVariables* to add system environment variables that are defined in HKLM\SYSTEM\CurrentControlSet\Session Manager\Environment, as well as processor-specific environment variables such as NUMBER_PROCESSORS, PROCESSOR_ARCHITECTURE, and PROCESSOR_LEVEL.

13. *SmpLoadDataFromRegistry* runs any programs defined in HKLM\SYSTEM\CurrentControlSet\ Control\Session Manager\SetupExecute with *SmpExecuteCommand*. Typically, this value is set only if Windows is being booted as part of the second stage of installation and Setupcl.exe is the default value.

14. *SmpLoadDataFromRegistry* calls *SmpConfigureSharedSessionData* to initialize the list of sub-systems that will be started in each session (both immediately and deferred) as well as the Session 0 initialization command (which, by default, is to launch the Wininit.exe process). The initialization command can be overridden by creating a string value called S0InitialCommand in HKLM\SYSTEM\CurrentControlSet\Control\Session Manager and setting it as the path to another program.

15. *SmpLoadDataFromRegistry* calls *SmpInitializeKnownDlls* to open known DLLs, and creates section objects for them in the \Knowndlls directory of the object manager namespace. The list of DLLs considered known is located in HKLM\SYSTEM\CurrentControlSet\Control\Session Manager\KnownDLLs, and the path to the directory in which the DLLs are located is stored in the DllDirectory value of the key. On 64-bit systems, 32-bit DLLs used as part of Wow64 are stored in the DllDirectory32 value.

16. Finally, *SmpLoadDataFromRegistry* calls *SmpTranslateSystemPartitionInformation* to convert the SystemPartition value stored in HKLM\SYSTEM\Setup, which is stored in native NT object manager path format, to a volume drive letter stored in the BootDir value. Among other components, Windows Update uses this registry key to figure out what the system volume is.

17. At this point, *SmpLoadDataFromRegistry* returns to *SmpInit*, which returns to the main thread entry point. Smss then creates the number of initial sessions that were defined (typically, only one, session 0, but you can change this number through the NumberOfInitialSessions registry value in the Smss registry key mentioned earlier) by calling *SmpCreateInitialSession*, which creates an Smss process for each user session. This function's main job is to call *SmpStartCsr* to start Csrss in each session.

18. As part of Csrss's initialization, it loads the kernel-mode part of the Windows subsystem (Win32k.sys). The initialization code in Win32k.sys uses the video driver to switch the screen to the resolution defined by the default profile, so this is the point at which the screen changes from the VGA mode the boot video driver uses to the default resolution chosen for the system.

19. Meanwhile, each spawned Smss in a different user session starts the other subsystem pro-cesses, such as Psxss if the Subsystem for Unix-based Applications feature was installed. (See Chapter 3 in Part 1 for more information on subsystem processes.)

20. The first Smss from session 0 executes the Session 0 initialization command (described in step 14), by default launching the Windows initialization process (Wininit). Other Smss instances start the interactive logon manager process (Winlogon), which, unlike Wininit, is hardcoded. The startup steps of Wininit and Winlogon are described shortly.

Pending File Rename Operations

The fact that executable images and DLLs are memory-mapped when they are used makes it impossible to update core system files after Windows has finished booting (unless hotpatching technology is used, which is only for Microsoft patches to the operating system). The *Move-FileEx* Windows API has an option to specify that a file move be delayed until the next boot. Service packs and hotfixes that must update in-use memory-mapped files install replacement files onto a system in temporary locations and use the *MoveFileEx* API to have them replace otherwise in-use files. When used with that option, *MoveFileEx* simply records commands in the PendingFileRenameOperations and PendingFileRenameOperations2 keys under HKLM\SYSTEM\CurrentControlSet\Control\Session Manager. These registry values are of type MULTI_SZ, where each operation is specified in pairs of file names: the first file name is the source location, and the second is the target location. Delete operations use an empty string as their target path. You can use the Pendmoves utility from Windows Sysinternals (*http://www.microsoft.com/technet/sysinternals*) to view registered delayed rename and delete commands.

After performing these initialization steps, the main thread in Smss waits forever on the process handle of Winlogon, while the other ALPC threads wait for messages to create new sessions or subsystems. If either Wininit or Csrss terminate unexpectedly, the kernel crashes the system because these processes are marked as *critical*. If Winlogon terminates unexpectedly, the session associated with it is logged off.

Wininit then performs its startup steps, such as creating the initial window station and desktop objects. It also configures the Session 0 window hook, which is used by the Interactive Services Detection service (UI0Detect.exe) to provide backward compatibility with interactive services. (See Chapter 4 in Part 1 for more information on services.) Wininit then creates the service control manager (SCM) process (%SystemRoot%\System32\Services.exe), which loads all services and device drivers marked for auto-start, and the Local Security Authority subsystem (LSASS) process (%SystemRoot%\System32\Lsass.exe). Finally, it loads the local session manager (%SystemRoot%\System32\Lsm.exe). On session 1 and beyond, Winlogon runs instead and loads the registered credential providers for the system (by default, the Microsoft credential provider supports password-based and smartcard-based logons) into a child process called LogonUI (%SystemRoot%\System32\Logonui.exe), which is responsible for displaying the logon interface. (For more details on the startup sequence for Wininit, Winlogon, and LSASS, see the section "Winlogon Initialization" in Chapter 6 in Part 1.)

After the SCM initializes the auto-start services and drivers and a user has successfully logged on at the console, the SCM deems the boot successful. The registry's last known good control set (as indicated by HKLM\SYSTEM\Select\LastKnownGood) is updated to match \CurrentControlSet.

After launching the SCM, Winlogon waits for an interactive logon notification from the credential provider. When it receives a logon and validates the logon (a process for which you can find more information in the section "User Logon Steps" in Chapter 6 in Part 1), Winlogon loads the registry hive from the profile of the user logging on and maps it to HKCU. It then sets the user's environment variables that are stored in HKCU\Environment and notifies the Winlogon notification packages registered in HKLM\SOFTWARE\Microsoft\Windows NT\CurrentVersion\Winlogon\Notify that a logon has occurred.

Winlogon next starts the shell by launching the executable or executables specified in HKLM\ SOFTWARE\Microsoft\Windows NT\CurrentVersion\WinLogon\Userinit (with multiple executables separated by commas) that by default points at \Windows\System32\Userinit.exe. Userinit.exe performs the following steps:

1. Processes the user scripts specified in HKCU\Software\Policies\Microsoft\Windows\System\ Scripts and the machine logon scripts in HKLM\SOFTWARE\Policies\Microsoft\Windows\ System\Scripts. (Because machine scripts run after user scripts, they can override user settings.)

2. If Group Policy specifies a user profile quota, starts %SystemRoot%\System32\Proquota.exe to enforce the quota for the current user.

3. Launches the comma-separated shell or shells specified in HKCU\Software\Microsoft\Windows NT\CurrentVersion\Winlogon\Shell. If that value doesn't exist, Userinit.exe launches the shell or shells specified in HKLM\SOFTWARE\Microsoft\Windows NT\CurrentVersion\Winlogon\ Shell, which is by default Explorer.exe.

Winlogon then notifies registered network providers that a user has logged on. The Microsoft network provider, Multiple Provider Router (%SystemRoot%\System32\Mpr.dll), restores the user's persistent drive letter and printer mappings stored in HKCU\Network and HKCU\Printers, respectively. Figure 13-4 shows the process tree as seen in Process Monitor after a logon (using its boot logging capability). Note the Smss processes that are dimmed (meaning that they have since exited). These refer to the spawned copies that initialized each session.

FIGURE 13-4 Process tree during logon

ReadyBoot

Windows uses the standard logical boot-time prefetcher (described in Chapter 10) if the system has less than 700 MB of memory, but if the system has 700 MB or more of RAM, it uses an in-RAM cache to optimize the boot process. The size of the cache depends on the total RAM available, but it is large enough to create a reasonable cache and yet allow the system the memory It needs to boot smoothly.

After every boot, the ReadyBoost service (see Chapter 10 for information on ReadyBoost) uses idle CPU time to calculate a boot-time caching plan for the next boot. It analyzes file trace information from the five previous boots and identifies which files were accessed and where they are located on disk. It stores the processed traces in %SystemRoot%\Prefetch\Readyboot as .fx files and saves the caching plan under HKLM\SYSTEM\CurrentControlSet\Services\Rdyboost\Parameters in REG_BINARY values named for internal disk volumes they refer to.

The cache is implemented by the same device driver that implements ReadyBoost caching (Ecache.sys), but the cache's population is guided by the boot plan previously stored in the registry. Although the boot cache is compressed like the ReadyBoost cache, another difference between ReadyBoost and ReadyBoot cache management is that while in ReadyBoot mode, the cache is not encrypted. The ReadyBoost service deletes the cache 50 seconds after the service starts, or if other memory demands warrant it, and records the cache's statistics in HKLM\SYSTEM\CurrentControlSet\Services\Ecache\Parameters\ReadyBootStats, as shown in Figure 13-5.

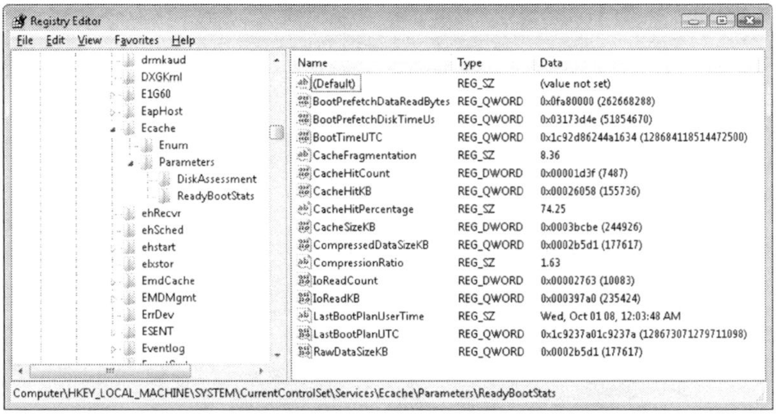

FIGURE 13-5 ReadyBoot statistics

Images That Start Automatically

In addition to the Userinit and Shell registry values in Winlogon's key, there are many other registry locations and directories that default system components check and process for automatic process startup during the boot and logon processes. The Msconfig utility (%SystemRoot%\System32\Msconfig.exe) displays the images configured by several of the locations. The Autoruns tool, which you can download from Sysinternals and that is shown in Figure 13-6, examines more locations than Msconfig and displays more information about the images configured to automatically run. By default, Autoruns shows only the locations that are configured to automatically execute at least one image, but selecting the Include Empty Locations entry on the Options menu causes Autoruns to show all the locations it inspects. The Options menu also has selections to direct Autoruns to hide Microsoft entries, but you should always combine this option with Verify Image Signatures; otherwise, you risk hiding malicious programs that include false information about their company name information.

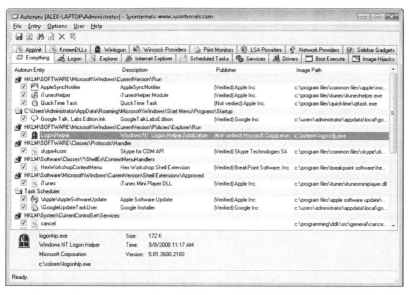

FIGURE 13-6 The Autoruns tool available from Sysinternals

EXPERIMENT: Autoruns

Many users are unaware of how many programs execute as part of their logon. Original equipment manufacturers (OEMs) often configure their systems with add-on utilities that execute in the background using registry values or file system directories processed for automatic execution and so are not normally visible. See what programs are configured to start automatically on your computer by running the Autoruns utility from Sysinternals. Compare the list shown in Autoruns with that shown in Msconfig and identify any differences. Then ensure that you understand the purpose of each program.

Troubleshooting Boot and Startup Problems

This section presents approaches to solving problems that can occur during the Windows startup process as a result of hard disk corruption, file corruption, missing files, and third-party driver bugs. First we describe three Windows boot-problem recovery modes: last known good, safe mode, and Windows Recovery Environment (WinRE). Then we present common boot problems, their causes, and approaches to solving them. The solutions refer to last known good, safe mode, WinRE, and other tools that ship with Windows.

Last Known Good

Last known good (LKG) is a useful mechanism for getting a system that crashes during the boot process back to a bootable state. Because the system's configuration settings are stored in HKLM\ SYSTEM\CurrentControlSet\Control and driver and service configuration is stored in HKLM\SYSTEM\ CurrentControlSet\Services, changes to these parts of the registry can render a system unbootable. For example, if you install a device driver that has a bug that crashes the system during the boot, you can press the F8 key during the boot and select last known good from the resulting menu. The system marks the control set that it was using to boot the system as failed by setting the Failed value of HKLM\SYSTEM\Select and then changes HKLM\SYSTEM\Select\Current to the value stored in HKLM\ SYSTEM\Select\LastKnownGood. It also updates the symbolic link HKLM\SYSTEM\CurrentControlSet to point at the LastKnownGood control set. Because the new driver's key is not present in the Services subkey of the LastKnownGood control set, the system will boot successfully.

Safe Mode

Perhaps the most common reason Windows systems become unbootable is that a device driver crashes the machine during the boot sequence. Because software or hardware configurations can change over time, latent bugs can surface in drivers at any time. Windows offers a way for an administrator to attack the problem: booting in *safe mode*. Safe mode is a boot configuration that consists of the minimal set of device drivers and services. By relying on only the drivers and services that are necessary for booting, Windows avoids loading third-party and other nonessential drivers that might crash.

When Windows boots, you press the F8 key to enter a special boot menu that contains the safe-mode boot options. You typically choose from three safe-mode variations: Safe Mode, Safe Mode With Networking, and Safe Mode With Command Prompt. Standard safe mode includes the minimum number of device drivers and services necessary to boot successfully. Networking-enabled safe mode adds network drivers and services to the drivers and services that standard safe mode includes. Finally, safe mode with command prompt is identical to standard safe mode except that Windows runs the Command Prompt application (Cmd.exe) instead of Windows Explorer as the shell when the system enables GUI mode.

Windows includes a fourth safe mode—Directory Services Restore mode—which is different from the standard and networking-enabled safe modes. You use Directory Services Restore mode to boot the system into a mode where the Active Directory service of a domain controller is offline and unopened. This allows you to perform repair operations on the database or restore it from backup media. All drivers and services, with the exception of the Active Directory service, load during a Directory Services Restore mode boot. In cases where you can't log on to a system because of Active Directory database corruption, this mode enables you to repair the corruption.

Driver Loading in Safe Mode

How does Windows know which device drivers and services are part of standard and networking-enabled safe mode? The answer lies in the HKLM\SYSTEM\CurrentControlSet\Control\SafeBoot registry key. This key contains the Minimal and Network subkeys. Each subkey contains more subkeys that specify the names of device drivers or services or of groups of drivers. For example, the vga.sys subkey identifies the VGA display device driver that the startup configuration includes. The VGA display driver provides basic graphics services for any PC-compatible display adapter. The system uses this driver as the safe-mode display driver in lieu of a driver that might take advantage of an adapter's advanced hardware features but that might also prevent the system from booting. Each subkey under the SafeBoot key has a default value that describes what the subkey identifies; the vga.sys subkey's default value is "Driver".

The Boot file system subkey has as its default value "Driver Group". When developers design a device driver's installation script (.inf file), they can specify that the device driver belongs to a driver group. The driver groups that a system defines are listed in the List value of the HKLM\SYSTEM\CurrentControlSet\Control\ServiceGroupOrder key. A developer specifies a driver as a member of a group to indicate to Windows at what point during the boot process the driver should start. The ServiceGroupOrder key's primary purpose is to define the order in which driver groups load; some driver types must load either before or after other driver types. The Group value beneath a driver's configuration registry key associates the driver with a group.

Driver and service configuration keys reside beneath HKLM\SYSTEM\CurrentControlSet\Services. If you look under this key, you'll find the VgaSave key for the VGA display device driver, which you can see in the registry is a member of the Video Save group. Any file system drivers that Windows requires for access to the Windows system drive are automatically loaded as if part of the Boot file system group. Other file system drivers are part of the File system group, which the standard and networking-enabled safe-mode configurations also include.

When you boot into a safe-mode configuration, the boot loader (Winload) passes an associated switch to the kernel (Ntoskrnl.exe) as a command-line parameter, along with any switches you've specified in the BCD for the installation you're booting. If you boot into any safe mode, Winload sets the *safeboot* BCD option with a value describing the type of safe mode you select. For standard safe mode, Winload sets *minimal*, and for networking-enabled safe mode, it adds *network*. Winload adds *minimal* and sets *safebootalternateshell* for safe mode with command prompt and *dsrepair* for Directory Services Restore mode.

The Windows kernel scans boot parameters in search of the safe-mode switches early during the boot, during the *InitSafeBoot* function, and sets the internal variable *InitSafeBootMode* to a value that reflects the switches the kernel finds. The kernel writes the *InitSafeBootMode* value to the registry value HKLM\SYSTEM\CurrentControlSet\Control\SafeBoot\Option\OptionValue so that user-mode components, such as the SCM, can determine what boot mode the system is in. In addition, if the system is booting in safe mode with command prompt, the kernel sets the HKLM\SYSTEM\CurrentControlSet\Control\SafeBoot\Option\UseAlternateShell value to 1. The kernel records the parameters that Winload passes to it in the value HKLM\SYSTEM\CurrentControlSet\Control\SystemStartOptions.

When the I/O manager kernel subsystem loads device drivers that HKLM\SYSTEM\CurrentControlSet\Services specifies, the I/O manager executes the function *IopLoadDriver*. When the Plug and Play manager detects a new device and wants to dynamically load the device driver for the detected device, the Plug and Play manager executes the function *PipCallDriverAddDevice*. Both these functions call the function *IopSafebootDriverLoad* before they load the driver in question.

IopSafebootDriverLoad checks the value of *InitSafeBootMode* and determines whether the driver should load. For example, if the system boots in standard safe mode, *IopSafebootDriverLoad* looks for the driver's group, if the driver has one, under the Minimal subkey. If *IopSafebootDriverLoad* finds the driver's group listed, *IopSafebootDriverLoad* indicates to its caller that the driver can load. Otherwise, *IopSafebootDriverLoad* looks for the driver's name under the Minimal subkey. If the driver's name is listed as a subkey, the driver can load. If *IopSafebootDriverLoad* can't find the driver group or driver name subkeys, the driver will not be loaded. If the system boots in networking-enabled safe mode, *IopSafebootDriverLoad* performs the searches on the Network subkey. If the system doesn't boot in safe mode, *IopSafebootDriverLoad* lets all drivers load.

> **Note** An exception exists regarding the drivers that safe mode excludes from a boot: Winload, rather than the kernel, loads any drivers with a Start value of 0 in their registry key, which specifies loading the drivers at boot time. Winload doesn't check the SafeBoot registry key because it assumes that any driver with a Start value of 0 is required for the system to boot successfully. Because Winload doesn't check the SafeBoot registry key to identify which drivers to load, Winload loads all boot-start drivers (and later Ntoskrnl starts them).

Safe-Mode-Aware User Programs

When the service control manager (SCM) user-mode component (which Services.exe implements) initializes during the boot process, the SCM checks the value of HKLM\SYSTEM\CurrentControlSet\ Control\SafeBoot\Option\OptionValue to determine whether the system is performing a safe-mode boot. If so, the SCM mirrors the actions of *IopSafebootDriverLoad*. Although the SCM processes the services listed under HKLM\SYSTEM\CurrentControlSet\Services, it loads only services that the appropriate safe-mode subkey specifies by name. You can find more information on the SCM initialization process in the section "Services" in Chapter 4 in Part 1.

Userinit, the component that initializes a user's environment when the user logs on (%SystemRoot%\System32\Userinit.exe), is another user-mode component that needs to know whether the system is booting in safe mode. It checks the value of HKLM\SYSTEM\CurrentControlSet\ Control\SafeBoot\Option\UseAlternateShell. If this value is set, Userinit runs the program specified as the user's shell in the value HKLM\SYSTEM\CurrentControlSet\Control\SafeBoot\AlternateShell rather than executing Explorer.exe. Windows writes the program name Cmd.exe to the AlternateShell value during installation, making the Windows command prompt the default shell for safe mode with command prompt. Even though the command prompt is the shell, you can type **Explorer.exe** at the command prompt to start Windows Explorer, and you can run any other GUI program from the command prompt as well.

How does an application determine whether the system is booting in safe mode? By calling the Windows *GetSystemMetrics(SM_CLEANBOOT)* function. Batch scripts that need to perform certain operations when the system boots in safe mode look for the SAFEBOOT_OPTION environment variable because the system defines this environment variable only when booting in safe mode.

Boot Logging in Safe Mode

When you direct the system to boot into safe mode, Winload hands the string specified by the *bootlog* option to the Windows kernel as a parameter, together with the parameter that requests safe mode. When the kernel initializes, it checks for the presence of the *bootlog* parameter whether or not any safe-mode parameter is present. If the kernel detects a boot log string, the kernel records the action the kernel takes on every device driver it considers for loading. For example, if *IopSafeboot-DriverLoad* tells the I/O manager not to load a driver, the I/O manager calls *IopBootLog* to record that the driver wasn't loaded. Likewise, after *IopLoadDriver* successfully loads a driver that is part of the safe-mode configuration, *IopLoadDriver* calls *IopBootLog* to record that the driver loaded. You can examine boot logs to see which device drivers are part of a boot configuration.

Because the kernel wants to avoid modifying the disk until Chkdsk executes, late in the boot process, *IopBootLog* can't simply dump messages into a log file. Instead, *IopBootLog* records messages in the HKLM\SYSTEM\CurrentControlSet\BootLog registry value. As the first user-mode component to load during a boot, the Session Manager (%SystemRoot%\System32\Smss.exe) executes Chkdsk to ensure the system drives' consistency and then completes registry initialization by executing the *NtInitializeRegistry* system call. The kernel takes this action as a cue that it can safely open a log file on the disk, which it does, invoking the function *IopCopyBootLogRegistryToFile*. This function creates the file Ntbtlog.txt in the Windows system directory (%SystemRoot%) and copies the contents of the BootLog registry value to the file. *IopCopyBootLogRegistryToFile* also sets a flag for *IopBootLog* that lets *IopBootLog* know that writing directly to the log file, rather than recording messages in the registry, is now OK. The following output shows the partial contents of a sample boot log:

```
Microsoft (R) Windows (R) Version 6.1 (Build 7601)
10   4 2012 09:04:53.375
Loaded driver \SystemRoot\system32\ntkrnlpa.exe
Loaded driver \SystemRoot\system32\hal.dll
Loaded driver \SystemRoot\system32\kdcom.dll
Loaded driver \SystemRoot\system32\mcupdate_GenuineIntel.dll
Loaded driver \SystemRoot\system32\PSHED.dll
Loaded driver \SystemRoot\system32\BOOTVID.dll
Loaded driver \SystemRoot\system32\CLFS.SYS
Loaded driver \SystemRoot\system32\CI.dll
Loaded driver \SystemRoot\system32\drivers\Wdf01000.sys
Loaded driver \SystemRoot\system32\drivers\WDFLDR.SYS
Loaded driver \SystemRoot\system32\drivers\acpi.sys
Loaded driver \SystemRoot\system32\drivers\WMILIB.SYS
Loaded driver \SystemRoot\system32\drivers\msisadrv.sys
Loaded driver \SystemRoot\system32\drivers\pci.sys
Loaded driver \SystemRoot\system32\drivers\volmgr.sys
Loaded driver \SystemRoot\system32\DRIVERS\compbatt.sys
Loaded driver \SystemRoot\system32\DRIVERS\BATTC.SYS
Loaded driver \SystemRoot\System32\drivers\mountmgr.sys
Loaded driver \SystemRoot\System32\drivers\intelide.sys
Loaded driver \SystemRoot\System32\drivers\PCIIDEX.SYS
Loaded driver \SystemRoot\System32\DRIVERS\pciide.sys
Loaded driver \SystemRoot\System32\drivers\volmgrx.sys
Loaded driver \SystemRoot\System32\drivers\atapi.sys
Loaded driver \SystemRoot\System32\drivers\ataport.SYS
Loaded driver \SystemRoot\System32\drivers\fltmgr.sys
```

```
Loaded driver \SystemRoot\system32\drivers\fileinfo.sys
...
Did not load driver @battery.inf,%acpi\acpi0003.devicedesc%;Microsoft AC Adapter
Did not load driver @battery.inf,%acpi\pnp0c0a.devicedesc%;Microsoft ACPI-Compliant
Control Method Battery
Did not load driver @oem46.inf,%nvidia_g71.dev_0297.1%;NVIDIA GeForce Go 7950 GTX
Did not load driver @oem5.inf,%nic_mpciex%;Intel(R) PRO/Wireless 3945ABG Network Connection
Did not load driver @netb57vx.inf,%bcm5750a1clnahkd%;Broadcom NetXtreme 57xx Gigabit Controller
Did not load driver @sdbus.inf,%pci\cc_080501.devicedesc%;SDA Standard Compliant
SD Host Controller
...
```

Windows Recovery Environment (WinRE)

Safe mode is a satisfactory fallback for systems that become unbootable because a device driver crashes during the boot sequence, but in some situations a safe-mode boot won't help the system boot. For example, if a driver that prevents the system from booting is a member of a Safe group, safe-mode boots will fail. Another example of a situation in which safe mode won't help the system boot is when a third-party driver, such as a virus scanner driver, that loads at the boot prevents the system from booting. (Boot-start drivers load whether or not the system is in safe mode.) Other situations in which safe-mode boots will fail are when a system module or critical device driver file that is part of a safe-mode configuration becomes corrupt or when the system drive's Master Boot Record (MBR) is damaged.

You can get around these problems by using the Windows Recovery Environment. The Windows Recovery Environment provides an assortment of tools and automated repair technologies to automatically fix the most common startup problems. It includes five main tools:

- **Startup Repair** An automated tool that detects the most common Windows startup problems and automatically attempts to repair them.

- **System Restore** Allows restoring to a previous restore point in cases in which you cannot boot the Windows installation to do so, even in safe mode.

- **System Image Recover** Called Complete PC Restore, as well as ASR (Automated System Recovery), in previous versions of Windows, this restores a Windows installation from a complete backup, not just a system restore point, which might not contain all damaged files and lost data.

- **Windows Memory Diagnostic Tool** Performs memory diagnostic tests that check for signs of faulty RAM. Faulty RAM can be the reason for random kernel and application crashes and erratic system behavior.

- **Command Prompt** For cases where troubleshooting or repair requires manual intervention (such as copying files from another drive or manipulating the BCD), you can use the command prompt to have a full Windows shell that can launch almost any Windows program (as long as the required dependencies can be satisfied)—unlike the Recovery Console on earlier versions of Windows, which only supported a limited set of specialized commands.

When you boot a system from the Windows CD or boot disks, Windows Setup gives you the choice of installing Windows or repairing an existing installation. If you choose to repair an installation, the system displays a dialog box called System Recovery Options, shown in Figure 13-7.

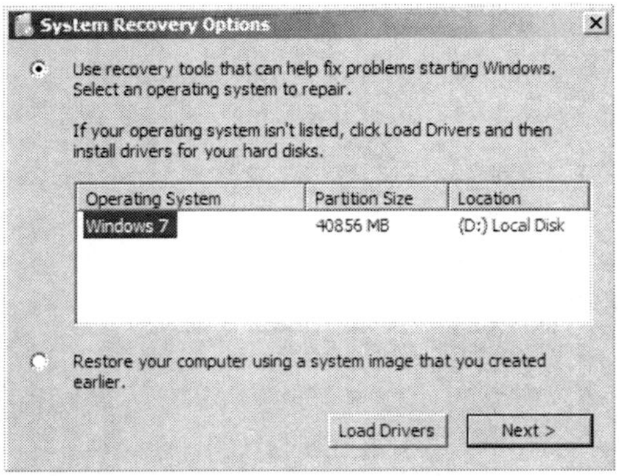

FIGURE 13-7 The System Recovery Options dialog box

Newer versions of Windows also install WinRE to a recovery partition on a clean system installation. On these systems, you can access WinRE by using the F8 option to access advanced boot options during Bootmgr execution. If you see an option Repair Your Computer, your machine has a local hard disk copy. If for some reason yours does not, you can follow the instructions at the Microsoft WinRE blog (*http://blogs.msdn.com/winre*) to install WinRE on the hard disk yourself from your Windows installation media and Windows Automated Installation Kit (AIK).

If you select the first option, WinRE will then display the dialog box in Figure 13-8, which has the various recovery options. Choosing the second option, on the other hand, is equivalent to the System Image Recovery option shown in Figure 13-8.

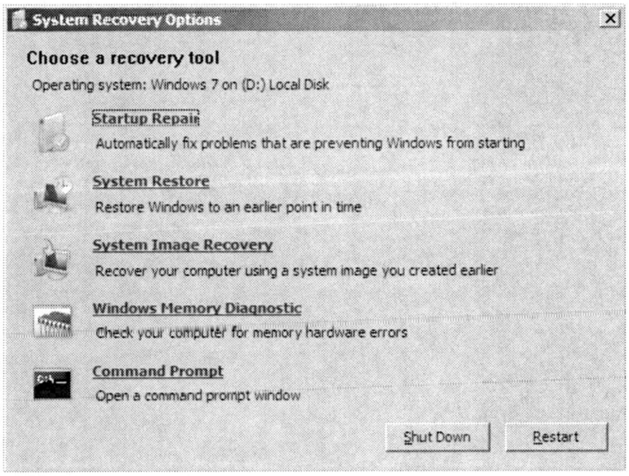

FIGURE 13-8 The Advanced System Recovery Options dialog box

Additionally, if your system failed to boot as the result of damaged files or for any other reason that Winload can understand, it instructs Bootmgr to automatically start WinRE at the next reboot cycle. Instead of the dialog box shown in Figure 13-8, the recovery environment will automatically launch the Startup Repair tool, shown in Figure 13-9.

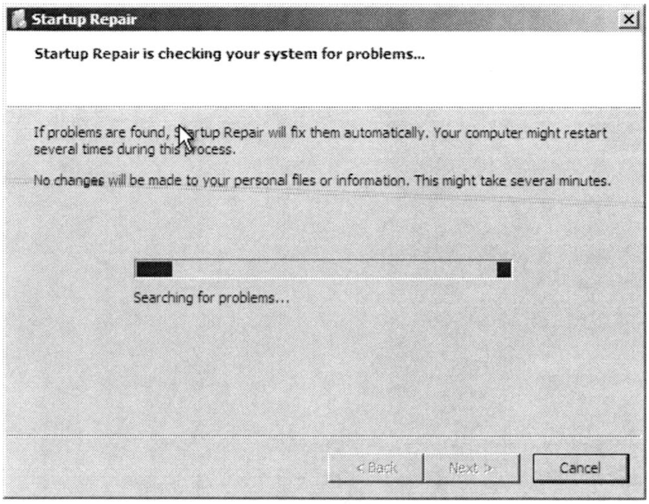

FIGURE 13-9 The Startup Repair tool

At the end of the scan and repair cycle, the tool will automatically attempt to fix any damage found, including replacing system files from the installation media. You can click the details link to see information about the damage that was fixed. For example, in Figure 13-10, the Startup Repair tool fixed a damaged boot sector.

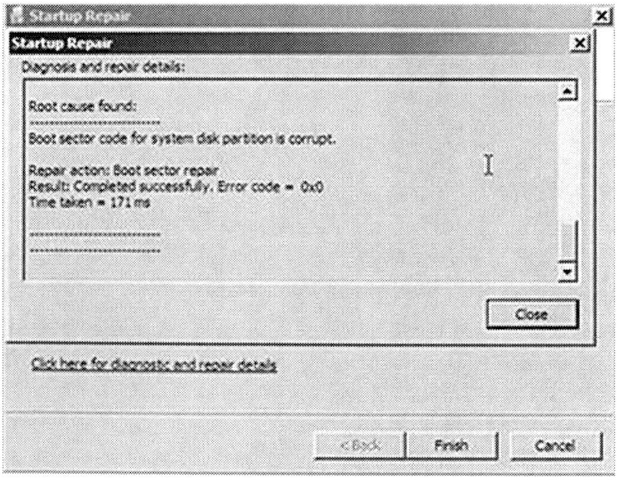

FIGURE 13-10 Details view of the Startup Repair tool

If the Startup Repair tool cannot automatically fix the damage, or if you cancel the operation, you'll get a chance to try other methods and the System Recovery Options dialog box will be displayed.

Boot Status File

Windows uses a *boot status file* (%SystemRoot%\Bootstat.dat) to record the fact that it has progressed through various stages of the system life cycle, including boot and shutdown. This allows the Boot Manager, Windows loader, and the Startup Repair tool to detect abnormal shutdown or a failure to shut down cleanly and offer the user recovery and diagnostic boot options, like Last Known Good and Safe Mode. This binary file contains information through which the system reports the success of the following phases of the system life cycle:

- Boot (the definition of a successful boot is the same as the one used for determining Last Known Good status, which was described earlier)

- Shutdown

- Resume from hibernate or suspend

The boot status file also indicates whether a problem was detected the last time the user attempted to boot the operating system and the recovery options shown, indicating that the user has been made aware of the problem and taken action. Runtime Library APIs (Rtl) in Ntdll.dll contain the private interfaces that Windows uses to read from and write to the file. Like the BCD, it cannot be edited by users.

Solving Common Boot Problems

This section describes problems that can occur during the boot process, describing their symptoms, what caused them, and approaches to solving them. To help you locate a problem that you might encounter, they are organized according to the place in the boot at which they occur. Note that for most of these problems, you should be able to simply boot into the Windows Recovery Environment and allow the Startup Repair tool to scan your system and perform any automated repair tasks.

MBR Corruption

- **Symptoms**   A system that has Master Boot Record (MBR) corruption will execute the BIOS power-on self test (POST), display BIOS version information or OEM branding, switch to a black screen, and then hang. Depending on the type of corruption the MBR has experienced, you might see one of the following messages: "Invalid partition table", "Error loading operating system", or "Missing operating system".

- **Cause**   The MBR can become corrupt because of hard-disk errors, disk corruption as a result of a driver bug while Windows is running, or intentional scrambling as a result of a virus.

- **Resolution**   Boot into the Windows Recovery Environment, choose the Command Prompt option, and then execute the *bootrec /fixmbr* command. This command replaces the executable code in the MBR.

Boot Sector Corruption

■ **Symptoms**   Boot sector corruption can look like MBR corruption, where the system hangs after BIOS POST at a black screen, or you might see the messages "A disk read error occurred", "BOOTMGR is missing", or " BOOTMGR is compressed" displayed on a black screen.

■ **Cause**   The boot sector can become corrupt because of hard-disk errors, disk corruption as a result of a driver bug while Windows is running, or intentional scrambling as a result of a virus.

■ **Resolution**   Boot into the Windows Recovery Environment, choose the Command Prompt option, and then execute the *bootrec /fixboot* command. This command rewrites the boot sector of the volume that you specify. You should execute the command on both the system and boot volumes if they are different.

BCD Misconfiguration

■ **Symptom**   After BIOS POST, you'll see a message that begins "Windows could not start because of a computer disk hardware configuration problem", "Could not read from selected boot disk", or "Check boot path and disk hardware".

■ **Cause**   The BCD has been deleted, become corrupt, or no longer references the boot volume because the addition of a partition has changed the name of the volume.

■ **Resolution**   Boot into the Windows Recovery Environment, choose the Command Prompt option, and then execute the *bootrec /scanos* and *bootrec /rebuildbcd* commands. These commands will scan each volume looking for Windows installations. When they discover an installation, they will ask you whether they should add it to the BCD as a boot option and what name should be displayed for the installation in the boot menu. For other kinds of BCD-related damage, you can also use Bcdedit.exe to perform tasks such as building a new BCD from scratch or cloning an existing good copy.

System File Corruption

■ **Symptoms**   There are several ways the corruption of system files—which include executables, drivers, or DLLs—can manifest. One way is with a message on a black screen after BIOS POST that says, "Windows could not start because the following file is missing or corrupt", followed by the name of a file and a request to reinstall the file. Another way is with a blue screen crash during the boot with the text, "STOP: 0xC0000135 {Unable to Locate Component}".

■ **Causes**   The volume on which a system file is located is corrupt or one or more system files have been deleted or become corrupt.

■ **Resolution**   Boot into the Windows Recovery Environment, choose the Command Prompt option, and then execute the *chkdsk* command. Chkdsk will attempt to repair volume corruption. If Chkdsk does not report any problems, obtain a backup copy of the system file in question. One place to check is in the %SystemRoot%\winsxs\Backup directory, in which Windows places copies of many system files for access by Windows Resource Protection. (See the "Windows Resource Protection" sidebar.) If you cannot find a copy of the file there, see if you can locate a copy from another system in the network. Note that the backup file must be from the same service pack or hotfix as the file that you are replacing.

In some cases, multiple system files are deleted or become corrupt, so the repair process can involve multiple reboots and boot failures as you repair the files one by one. If you believe the system file corruption to be extensive, you should consider restoring the system from a backup image, such as one generated by Windows Backup and Restore or from a system restore point.

When you run Backup and Restore (located in the Maintenance folder on the Start menu), you can generate a System Image Recovery image, which includes all the files on the system and boot volumes, plus a floppy disk on which it stores information about the system's disks and volumes. To restore a system from such an image, boot from the Windows setup media and select the appropriate option when prompted (or use the recovery environment shown earlier).

If you do not have a backup from which to restore, a last resort is to execute a Windows repair install: boot from the Windows setup media, and follow the wizard as if you were going to perform a new installation. The wizard will ask you whether you want to perform a repair or fresh install. When you tell it that you want to repair, Setup reinstalls all system files, leaving your application data and registry settings intact.

Windows Resource Protection

To preserve the integrity of the many components involved in the boot process, as well as other critical Windows files, libraries, and applications, Windows implements a technology called *Windows Resource Protection* (WRP). WRP is implemented through access control lists (ACLs) that protect critical system files on the machine. It is also exposed through an API (located in %SystemRoot%\System32\Sfc.dll and %SystemRoot%\System32\Sfc_os.dll) that can be accessed by the Sfc.exe utility to manually check a file for corruption and restore it.

WRP will also protect entire critical folders if required, even locking down the folder so that it is inaccessible by administrators (without modifying the access control list on the folder). The only supported way to modify WRP-protected files is through the Windows Modules Installer service, which can run under the TrustedInstaller account. This service is used for the installation of patches, service packs, hotfixes, and Windows Update. This account has access to the various protected files and is trusted by the system (as its name implies) to modify critical files and replace them. WRP also protects critical registry keys, and it may even lock entire registry trees if all the values and subkeys are considered to be critical.

WRP sets the ACL on protected files, directories, or registry keys such that only the TrustedInstaller account is able to modify or delete these files. Application developers can use the *SfcIsFileProtected* or *SfcIsKeyProtected* APIs to check whether a file or registry key is locked down.

For backward compatibility, certain installers are considered *well-known*—an application compatibility shim exists that will suppress the "access denied" error that certain installers would receive while attempting to modify WRP-protected resources. Instead, the installer receives a fake "success" code, but the modification isn't made. This virtualization is similar to the User

Access Control (UAC) virtualization technology discussed in Chapter 6 in Part 1, but it applies to write operations as well. It applies if the following are true:

- The application is a *legacy* application, meaning that it does not contain a manifest file compatible with the *requestedExecutionLevel* value set.

- The application is trying to modify a WRP-protected resource (the file or registry key contains the TrustedInstaller SID).

- The application is being run under an administrator account (always true on systems with UAC enabled because of automatic installer program detection).

WRP copies files that are needed to restart Windows to the *cache directory* located at %SystemRoot%\winsxs\Backup. Critical files that are not needed to restart Windows are not copied to the cache directory. The size of the cache directory and the list of files copied to the cache cannot be modified. To recover a file from the cache directory, you can use the System File Checker (Sfc.exe) tool, which can scan your system for modified protected files and restore them from a good copy.

System Hive Corruption

- **Symptoms** If the System registry hive (which is discussed along with hive files in the section "The Registry" in Chapter 4 in Part 1) is missing or corrupted, Winload will display the message "Windows could not start because the following file is missing or corrupt: \WINDOWS\SYSTEM32\CONFIG\SYSTEM", on a black screen after the BIOS POST.

- **Causes** The System registry hive, which contains configuration information necessary for the system to boot, has become corrupt or has been deleted.

- **Resolution** Boot into the Windows Recovery Environment, choose the Command Prompt option, and then execute the *chkdsk* command. If the problem is not corrected, obtain a backup of the System registry hive. Windows makes copies of the registry hives every 12 hours (keeping the immediately previous copy with a .OLD extension) in a folder called %SystemRoot%\System32\Config\RegBack, so copy the file named System to %SystemRoot%\System32\Config.

If System Restore is enabled (System Restore is discussed in Chapter 12, "File System"), you can often obtain a more recent backup of the registry hives, including the System hive, from the most recent restore point. You can choose System Restore from the Windows Recovery Environment to restore your registry from the last restore point.

Post–Splash Screen Crash or Hang

- **Symptoms** Problems that occur after the Windows splash screen displays, the desktop appears, or you log on fall into this category and can appear as a blue screen crash or a hang, where the entire system is frozen or the mouse cursor tracks the mouse but the system is otherwise unresponsive.

- **Causes** These problems are almost always a result of a bug in a device driver, but they can sometimes be the result of corruption of a registry hive other than the System hive.

- **Resolution** You can take several steps to try and correct the problem. The first thing you should try is the last known good configuration. Last known good (LKG), which is described earlier in this chapter and in the "Services" section of Chapter 4 in Part 1, consists of the registry control set that was last used to boot the system successfully. Because a control set includes core system configuration and the device driver and services registration database, using a version that does not reflect changes or newly installed drivers or services might avoid the source of the problem. You access last known good by pressing the F8 key early in the boot process to access the same menu from which you can boot into safe mode.

As stated earlier in the chapter, when you boot into LKG, the system saves the control set that you are avoiding and labels it as the *failed* control set. You can leverage the failed control set in cases where LKG makes a system bootable to determine what was causing the system to fail to boot by exporting the contents of the current control set of the successful boot and the failed control set to .reg files. You do this by using Regedit's export functionality, which you access under the File menu:

1. Run Regedit, and select HKLM\SYSTEM\CurrentControlSet.

2. Select Export from the File menu, and save to a file named good.reg.

3. Open HKLM\SYSTEM\Select, read the value of Failed, and select the subkey named HKLM\SYSTEM\Control*XXX*, where *XXX* is the value of Failed.

4. Export the contents of the control set to bad.reg.

5. Use WordPad (which is found under Accessories on the Start menu) to globally replace all instances of CurrentControlSet in good.reg with ControlSet.

6. Use WordPad to change all instances of Control*XXX* (replacing *XXX* with the value of the Failed control set) in bad.reg with ControlSet.

7. Run Windiff from the Support Tools, and compare the two files.

The differences between a failed control set and a good one can be numerous, so you should focus your examination on changes beneath the Control subkey as well as under the Parameters subkeys of drivers and services registered in the Services subkey. Ignore changes made to Enum subkeys of driver registry keys in the Services branch of the control set.

If the problem you're experiencing is caused by a driver or service that was present on the system since before the last successful boot, LKG will not make the system bootable. Similarly, if a problematic configuration setting changed outside the control set or was made before the last successful boot, LKG will not help. In those cases, the next option to try is safe mode (described earlier in this section). If the system boots successfully in safe mode and you know what particular driver was causing the normal boot to fail, you can disable the driver by using the Device Manager (accessible from the System Control Panel item). To do so, select the driver in question and choose Disable from the Action menu. If you recently updated the driver, and believe that the update introduced a bug, you can choose to roll back the driver to its previous version instead, also with the Device Manager. To restore a driver to its previous version, double-click on the device to open its Properties dialog box and click Roll Back Driver on the Driver tab.

On systems with System Restore enabled, an option when LKG fails is to roll back all system state (as defined by System Restore) to a previous point in time. Safe mode detects the existence of restore points, and when they are present it will ask you whether you want to log on to the installation to perform a manual diagnosis and repair or launch the System Restore Wizard. Using System Restore to make a system bootable again is attractive when you know the cause of a problem and want the repair to be automatic or when you don't know the cause but do not want to invest time to determine the cause.

If System Restore is not an option or you want to determine the cause of a crash during the normal boot and the system boots successfully in safe mode, attempt to obtain a boot log from the unsuccessful boot by pressing F8 to access the special boot menu and choosing the boot logging option. As described earlier in this chapter, Session Manager (%SystemRoot%\System32\Smss.exe) saves a log of the boot that includes a record of device drivers that the system loaded and chose not to load to %SystemRoot%\ntbtlog.txt, so you'll obtain a boot log if the crash or hang occurs after Session Manager initializes. When you reboot into safe mode, the system appends new entries to the existing boot log. Extract the portions of the log file that refer to the failed attempt and safe-mode boots into separate files. Strip out lines that contain the text "Did not load driver", and then compare them with a text comparison tool such as Windiff. One by one, disable the drivers that loaded during the normal boot but not in the safe-mode boot until the system boots successfully again. (Then reenable the drivers that were not responsible for the problem.)

If you cannot obtain a boot log from the normal boot (for instance, because the system is crashing before Session Manager initializes), if the system also crashes during the safe-mode boot, or if a comparison of boot logs from the normal and safe-mode boots do not reveal any significant differences (for example, when the driver that's crashing the normal boot starts after Session Manager initializes), the next tool to try is Driver Verifier combined with crash dump analysis. (See Chapter 14, "Crash Dump Analysis," for more information on both these topics.)

Shutdown

If someone is logged on and a process initiates a shutdown by calling the Windows *ExitWindowsEx* function, a message is sent to that session's Csrss instructing it to perform the shutdown. Csrss in turn impersonates the caller and sends an RPC message to Winlogon, telling it to perform a system shutdown. Winlogon then impersonates the currently logged-on user (who might or might not have the same security context as the user who initiated the system shutdown) and calls *ExitWindowsEx* with some special internal flags. Again this call causes a message to be sent to the Csrss process inside that session, requesting a system shutdown.

This time, Csrss sees that the request is from Winlogon and loops through all the processes in the logon session of the interactive user (again, not the user who requested a shutdown) in reverse order of their *shutdown level*. A process can specify a shutdown level, which indicates to the system when it wants to exit with respect to other processes, by calling *SetProcessShutdownParameters*. Valid shutdown levels are in the range 0 through 1023, and the default level is 640. Explorer, for example, sets its shutdown level to 2 and Task Manager specifies 1. For each process that owns a top-level window, Csrss sends the WM_QUERYENDSESSION message to each thread in the process that has a Windows message loop. If the thread returns TRUE, the system shutdown can proceed. Csrss then sends the WM_ENDSESSION Windows message to the thread to request it to exit. Csrss waits the number of seconds defined in HKCU\Control Panel\Desktop\HungAppTimeout for the thread to exit. (The default is 5,000 milliseconds.)

If the thread doesn't exit before the timeout, Csrss fades out the screen and displays the hung-program screen shown in Figure 13-11. (You can disable this screen by creating the registry value HKCU\Control Panel\Desktop\AutoEndTasks and setting it to 1.) This screen indicates which programs are currently running and, if available, their current state. Windows indicates which program isn't shutting down in a timely manner and gives the user a choice of either killing the process or aborting the shutdown. (There is no timeout on this screen, which means that a shutdown request could wait forever at this point.) Additionally, third-party applications can add their own specific information regarding state—for example, a virtualization product could display the number of actively running virtual machines.

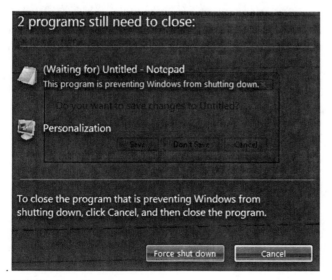

FIGURE 13-11 Hung program screen

EXPERIMENT: Witnessing the HungAppTimeout

You can see the use of the HungAppTimeout registry value by running Notepad, entering text into its editor, and then logging off. After the amount of time specified by the HungAppTimeout registry value has expired, Csrss.exe presents a prompt that asks you whether or not you want to end the Notepad process, which has not exited because it's waiting for you to tell it whether or not to save the entered text to a file. If you click the Cancel button, Csrss.exe aborts the shutdown.

As a second experiment, if you try shutting down again (with Notepad's query dialog box still open), Notepad will display its own message box to inform you that shutdown cannot cleanly proceed. However, this dialog box is merely an informational message to help users—Csrss.exe will still consider that Notepad is "hung" and display the user interface to terminate unresponsive processes.

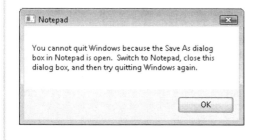

If the thread does exit before the timeout, Csrss continues sending the WM_QUERYENDSESSION/WM_ENDSESSION message pairs to the other threads in the process that own windows. Once all the threads that own windows in the process have exited, Csrss terminates the process and goes on to the next process in the interactive session.

If Csrss finds a console application, it invokes the console control handler by sending the CTRL_LOGOFF_EVENT event. (Only service processes receive the CTRL_SHUTDOWN_EVENT event on shutdown.) If the handler returns FALSE, Csrss kills the process. If the handler returns TRUE or doesn't respond by the number of seconds defined by HKCU\Control Panel\Desktop\WaitToKillAppTimeout (the default is 20,000 milliseconds), Csrss displays the hung-program screen shown in Figure 13-11.

Next, Winlogon calls *ExitWindowsEx* to have Csrss terminate any COM processes that are part of the interactive user's session.

At this point, all the processes in the interactive user's session have been terminated. Wininit next calls *ExitWindowsEx*, which this time executes within the system process context. This causes Wininit to send a message to the Csrss part of session 0, where the services live. Csrss then looks at all the processes belonging to the system context and performs and sends the WM_QUERYENDSESSION/WM_ENDSESSION messages to GUI threads (as before). Instead of sending CTRL_LOGOFF_EVENT, however, it sends CTRL_SHUTDOWN_EVENT to console applications that have registered control handlers. Note that the SCM is a console program that does register a control handler. When it receives the shutdown request, it in turn sends the service shutdown control message to all services that registered for shutdown notification. For more details on service shutdown (such as the shutdown timeout Csrss uses for the SCM), see the "Services" section in Chapter 4 in Part 1.

Although Csrss performs the same timeouts as when it was terminating the user processes, it doesn't display any dialog boxes and doesn't kill any processes. (The registry values for the system process timeouts are taken from the default user profile.) These timeouts simply allow system processes a chance to clean up and exit before the system shuts down. Therefore, many system processes are in fact still running when the system shuts down, such as Smss, Wininit, Services, and LSASS.

Once Csrss has finished its pass notifying system processes that the system is shutting down, Winlogon finishes the shutdown process by calling the executive subsystem function *NtShutdownSystem*. This function calls the function *PoSetSystemPowerState* to orchestrate the shutdown of drivers and the rest of the executive subsystems (Plug and Play manager, power manager, executive, I/O manager, configuration manager, and memory manager).

For example, *PoSetSystemPowerState* calls the I/O manager to send shutdown I/O packets to all device drivers that have requested shutdown notification. This action gives device drivers a chance to perform any special processing their device might require before Windows exits. The stacks of worker threads are swapped in, the configuration manager flushes any modified registry data to disk, and the memory manager writes all modified pages containing file data back to their respective files. If the option to clear the paging file at shutdown is enabled, the memory manager clears the paging file at this time. The I/O manager is called a second time to inform the file system drivers that the system is shutting down. System shutdown ends in the power manager. The action the power manager takes depends on whether the user specified a shutdown, a reboot, or a power down.

Conclusion

In this chapter, we've examined the detailed steps involved in starting and shutting down Windows (both normally and in error cases). We've examined the overall structure of Windows and the core system mechanisms that get the system going, keep it running, and eventually shut it down. The final chapter of this book explains how to deal with an unusual type of shutdown: system crashes.

CHAPTER 14

Crash Dump Analysis

Almost every Windows user has heard of, if not experienced, the infamous "blue screen of death." This ominous term refers to the blue screen that is displayed when Windows crashes, or stops executing, because of a catastrophic fault or an internal condition that prevents the system from continuing to run.

In this chapter, we'll cover the basic problems that cause Windows to crash, describe the information presented on the blue screen, and explain the various configuration options available to create a *crash dump*, a record of system memory at the time of a crash that can help you figure out which component caused the crash and why. This section is *not* intended to provide detailed troubleshooting information on how to analyze a Windows system crash. This section will also show you how to analyze a crash dump to identify a faulty driver or component. The effort required to perform basic crash dump analysis is minimal and takes a few minutes. Even if an analysis ascertains the problematic driver for only one out of every five or ten crash dumps, it's still worth doing: one successful analysis can avoid future data loss, system downtime, and frustration.

Why Does Windows Crash?

Windows crashes (stops execution and displays the blue screen) for many possible reasons. A common source is a reference to a memory address that causes an access violation, either a write operation to read-only memory or a read operation on an address that is not mapped. Another common cause is an unexpected exception or trap. Crashes also occur when a kernel subsystem (such as the memory manager or power manager) or a driver (such as a USB or display driver) detect inconsistencies in their operation.

When a kernel-mode device driver or subsystem causes an illegal exception, Windows faces a difficult dilemma. It has detected that a part of the operating system with the ability to access any hardware device and any valid memory has done something it wasn't supposed to do.

But why does that mean Windows has to crash? Couldn't it just ignore the exception and let the device driver or subsystem continue as if nothing had happened? The possibility exists that the error was isolated and that the component will somehow recover. But what's more likely is that the detected exception resulted from deeper problems—for example, from a general corruption of memory or from a hardware device that's not functioning properly. Permitting the system to continue operating would probably result in more exceptions, and data stored on disk or other peripherals could become corrupt—a risk that's too high to take. So Windows adopts a *fail fast* policy in attempting to prevent the corruption in RAM from spreading to disk.

The Blue Screen

Regardless of the reason for a system crash, the function that actually performs the crash is *KeBugCheckEx,* documented in the Windows Driver Kit (WDK). This function takes a *stop code* (sometimes called a *bugcheck code*) and four parameters that are interpreted on a per–stop code basis. After *KeBugCheckEx* masks out all interrupts on all processors of the system, it switches the display into a low-resolution VGA graphics mode (one implemented by all Windows-supported video cards), paints a blue background, and then displays the stop code, followed by some text suggesting what the user can do. Finally, *KeBugCheckEx* calls any registered device driver bugcheck callbacks (registered by calling the *KeRegisterBugCheckCallback* function), allowing drivers an opportunity to stop their devices. It then calls registered reason callbacks (registered with *KeRegisterBugCheckReasonCallback),* which allow drivers to append data to the crash dump or write crash dump information to alternate devices.

The first line in the Technical information section in the sample Windows blue screen shown in Figure 14-1 lists the stop code and the four additional parameters passed to *KeBugCheckEx.* A text line near the top of the screen provides the text equivalent of the stop code's numeric identifier. According to the example in Figure 14-1, the stop code 0x000000D1 is a DRIVER_IRQL_NOT_LESS_OR_ EQUAL crash. When a parameter contains an address of a piece of operating system or device driver code (as in Figure 14-1), Windows displays the base address of the module the address falls in, the date stamp, and the file name of the device driver. This information alone might help you pinpoint the faulty component.

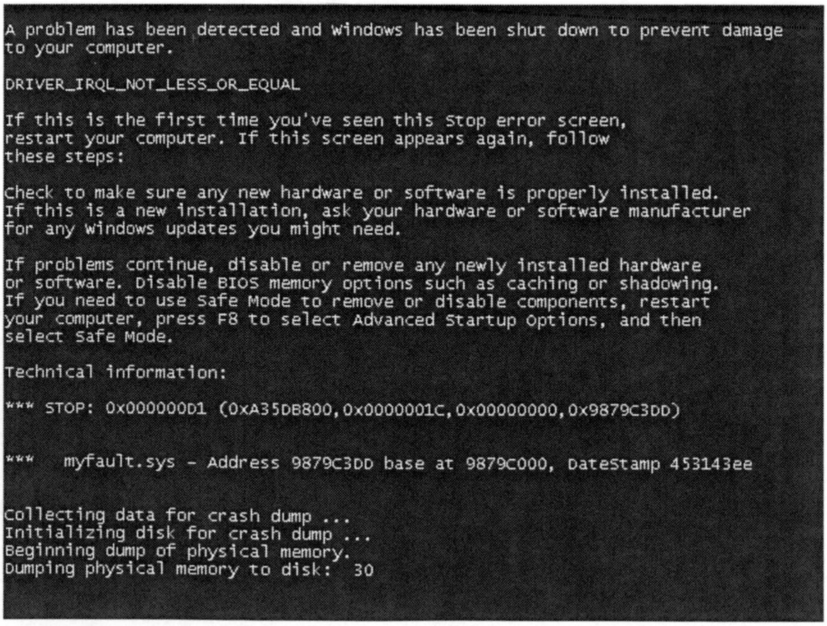

```
A problem has been detected and windows has been shut down to prevent damage
to your computer.

DRIVER_IRQL_NOT_LESS_OR_EQUAL

If this is the first time you've seen this Stop error screen,
restart your computer. If this screen appears again, follow
these steps:

Check to make sure any new hardware or software is properly installed.
If this is a new installation, ask your hardware or software manufacturer
for any Windows updates you might need.

If problems continue, disable or remove any newly installed hardware
or software. Disable BIOS memory options such as caching or shadowing.
If you need to use Safe Mode to remove or disable components, restart
your computer, press F8 to select Advanced Startup Options, and then
select Safe Mode.

Technical information:

*** STOP: 0x000000D1 (0xA35DB800,0x0000001C,0x00000000,0x9879C3DD)


*** myfault.sys - Address 9879C3DD base at 9879C000, DateStamp 453143ee


Collecting data for crash dump ...
Initializing disk for crash dump ...
Beginning dump of physical memory.
Dumping physical memory to disk: 30
```

FIGURE 14-1 Example of a blue screen

Although there are more than 300 unique stop codes, most are rarely, if ever, seen on production systems. Instead, just a few common stop codes represent the majority of Windows system crashes. Also, the meaning of the four additional parameters depends on the stop code (and not all stop codes have extended parameter information). Nevertheless, looking up the stop code and the meaning of the parameters (if applicable) might at least assist you in diagnosing the component that is failing (or the hardware device that is causing the crash).

You can find stop code information in the section "Bug Checks (Blue Screens)" in the Debugging Tools for Windows help file. (For information on the Debugging Tools for Windows, see Chapter 1, "Concepts and Tools," in Part 1.) You can also search Microsoft's Knowledge Base (*http://support.microsoft.com*) for the stop code and the name of the suspect hardware or driver. You might find information about a workaround, an update, or a service pack that fixes the problem you're having. The Bugcodes.h file in the WDK contains a complete list of the 300 or so stop codes, with some additional details on the reasons for some of them. Last but not least, these stop codes are listed and documented at *http://msdn.microsoft.com/en-us/library/windows/hardware/hh406232(v=vs.85).aspx*.

Causes of Windows Crashes

Based on data collected from the release of Windows 7 through the release of Windows 7 SP1, the top 20 stop codes account for 91 percent of crashes and can be grouped into the following categories:

- **Page fault** A page fault on memory backed by data in a paging file or a memory-mapped file occurs at an IRQL of DPC/dispatch level or above, which would require the memory manager to have to wait for an I/O operation to occur. The kernel cannot wait or reschedule threads at an IRQL of DPC/dispatch level or higher. (See Chapter 3, "System Mechanisms," in Part 1 for details on IRQLs.) The common stop codes are:

  - 0xA - IRQL_NOT_LESS_OR_EQUAL

  - 0xD1 - DRIVER_IRQL_NOT_LESS_OR_EQUAL

- **Power management** A device driver or an operating system function running in kernel mode is in an inconsistent or invalid power state. Most frequently, some component has failed to complete a power management I/O request operation within the default period of 10 minutes. The common stop code is:

  - 0x9F - DRIVER_POWER_STATE_FAILURE

- **Exceptions and traps** A device driver or an operating system function running in kernel mode incurs an unexpected exception or trap. The common stop codes are:

  - 0x1E - KMODE_EXCEPTION_NOT_HANDLED

  - 0x3B - SYSTEM_SERVICE_EXCEPTION

  - 0x7E - SYSTEM_THREAD_EXCEPTION_NOT_HANDLED

  - 0x7F - UNEXPECTED_KERNEL_MODE_TRAP

- 0x8E - KERNEL_MODE_EXCEPTION_NOT_HANDLED with P1 != 0xC0000005 STATUS_ACCESS_VIOLATION

■ **Access violations**   A device driver or an operating system function running in kernel mode incurs a memory access violation, which is caused either by attempting to write to a read-only page or by attempting to read an address that isn't currently mapped and therefore is not a valid memory location. The common stop codes are:

- 0x50 - PAGE_FAULT_IN_NONPAGED_AREA

- 0x8E - KERNEL_MODE_EXCEPTION_NOT_HANDLED with P1 = 0xC0000005 STATUS_ACCESS_VIOLATION

■ **Display**   The display device driver detects that it can no longer control the graphics processing unit. This indicates that an attempt to reset the display driver failed. The common stop code is:

- 0x116 - VIDEO_TDR_FAILURE

■ **Pool**   The kernel pool manager detects a corrupt pool header or an improper pool reference. The common stop codes are:

- 0x19 - BAD_POOL_HEADER

- 0xC2 - BAD_POOL_CALLER

- 0xC5 - DRIVER_CORRUPTED_EXPOOL

■ **Memory management**   The kernel memory manager detects a corruption of memory management data structures or an improper memory management request. The common stop codes are:

- 0x1A - MEMORY_MANAGEMENT

- 0x4E - PFN_LIST_CORRUPT

■ **Hardware**   A hardware error, such as a machine check or a nonmaskable interrupt (NMI), occurs. This category also includes disk failures when the memory manager is attempting to read data to satisfy page faults. The common stop codes are:

- 0x7A - KERNEL_DATA_INPAGE_ERROR

- 0x124 - WHEA_UNCORRECTABLE_ERROR

■ **USB**   An unrecoverable error occurs in a universal serial bus operation. The common stop code is:

- 0xFE - BUGCODE_USB_DRIVER

■ **Critical object**   A fatal error occurs in a critical object without which Windows cannot continue to run. The common stop code is:

- 0xF4 - CRITICAL_OBJECT_TERMINATION

■ **NTFS file system** A fatal error is detected by the NTFS file system. The common stop code is:

- 0x24 - NTFS_FILE_SYSTEM

Figure 14-2 shows the distribution of these categories for Windows 7 and Windows 7 SP1 in May 2012:

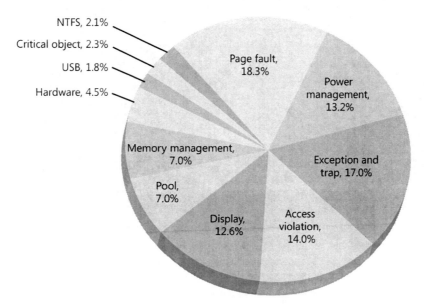

FIGURE 14-2 Distribution of top 20 stop codes by category for Windows 7 and Windows 7 SP1 in May 2012.

Troubleshooting Crashes

You often begin seeing blue screens after you install a new software product or piece of hardware. If you've just added a driver, rebooted, and gotten a blue screen early in system initialization, you can reset the machine, press the F8 key when instructed, and then select Last Known Good Configuration. Enabling last known good causes Windows to revert to a copy of the registry's device driver registration key (HKLM\SYSTEM\CurrentControlSet\Services) from the last successful boot (before you installed the driver). From the perspective of last known good, a successful boot is one in which all services and drivers have finished loading and at least one logon has succeeded. (Last known good is further described in Chapter 13, "Startup and Shutdown.")

During the reboot after a crash, the Boot Manager (Bootmgr) will automatically detect that Windows did not shut down properly and display a Windows Error Recovery message similar to the one shown in Figure 14-3. This screen gives you the option to attempt booting into safe mode so that you can disable or uninstall the software component that might be broken.

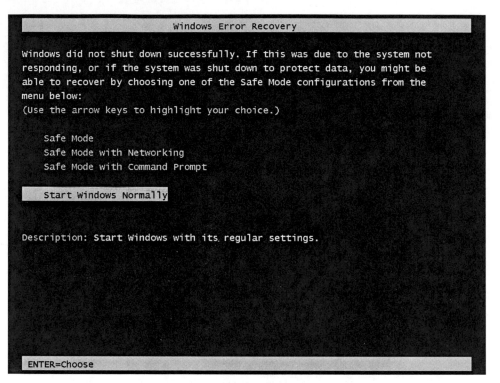

FIGURE 14-3 An example of a Windows Error Recovery message

If you keep getting blue screens, an obvious approach is to uninstall the components you added just before the first blue screen appeared. If some time has passed since you added something new or you added several things at about the same time, you need to note the names of the device drivers referenced in any of the parameters. If you recognize any of the names as being related to something you just added (such as Storport.sys if you installed a new SCSI drive), you've possibly found your culprit.

Many device drivers have cryptic names, but one approach you can take to figure out which application or hardware device is associated with a name is to find out the name of the service in the registry associated with a device driver by searching for the name of the device driver under the HKLM\SYSTEM\CurrentControlSet\Services key. This branch of the registry is where Windows stores registration information for every device driver in the system. If you find a match, look for values named DisplayName and Description. Some drivers fill in these values to describe the device driver's purpose. For example, you might find the string "Virus Scanner" in the DisplayName value, which can implicate the antivirus software you have running. The list of drivers can be displayed in the System Information tool (from the Start menu, select All Programs, Accessories, System Tools, System Information). In System Information, expand Software Environment, and then select System Drivers. Process Explorer also lists the currently loaded drivers, including their version numbers and load addresses, in the DLL view of the System process. Another option is to open the Properties dialog box for the driver file and examine the information on the Details tab, which often contains the description and company information for the driver. Keep in mind that the registry information and file description are provided by the driver manufacturer, and there is nothing to guarantee their accuracy.

More often than not, however, the stop code and the four associated parameters aren't enough information to troubleshoot a system crash. For example, you might need to examine the kernel-mode call stack to pinpoint the driver or system component that triggered the crash. Also, because the default behavior on Windows systems is to automatically reboot after a system crash, it's unlikely that you would have time to record the information displayed on the blue screen. That is why, by default, Windows attempts to record information about the system crash to the disk for later analysis, which takes us to our next topic, crash dump files.

Crash Dump Files

By default, all Windows systems are configured to attempt to record information about the state of the system when the system crashes. You can see these settings by opening the System Properties tool in Control Panel (under System, Advanced System Settings), clicking the Advanced tab, and then clicking the Settings button under Startup And Recovery. The default settings for a Windows system are shown in Figure 14-4.

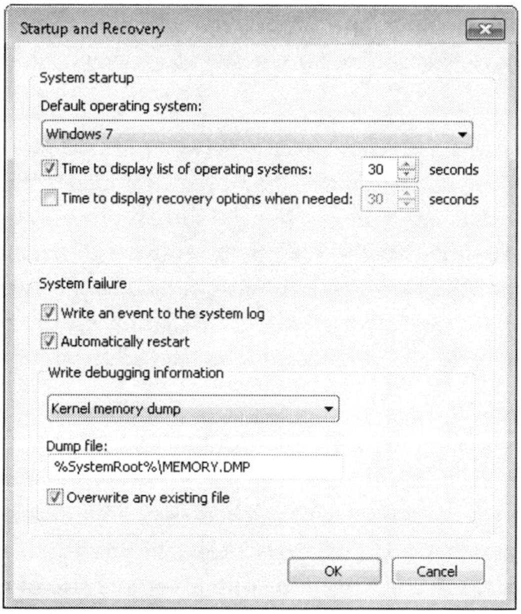

FIGURE 14-4 Crash dump settings

Three levels of information can be recorded on a system crash:

- **Complete memory dump** A complete memory dump contains all physical memory accessible by Windows at the time of the crash. This type of dump requires that a page file be at least the size of physical memory plus 1 MB for the header. Device drivers can add up to

256 MB for secondary crash dump data, so to be safe, it's recommended to increase the size of the page file by an additional 256 MB. Because it can require an inordinately large page file on large memory systems, this type of dump file is the least common setting. If the system has more than 2 GB of RAM, this option will be disabled in the UI, but you can manually enable it by running the following command from an elevated command prompt:

```
wmic recoveros set DebugInfoType=1
```

When using Wmic.exe to enable a complete dump, the WMI Win32 Provider sets the Crash-DumpEnabled value to 1 in the HKLM\SYSTEM\CurrentControlSet\Control\CrashControl registry key. At initialization time, Windows will check whether the page-file size is large enough for a complete dump and automatically switch to creating a small memory dump if not.

- **Kernel memory dump** A kernel memory dump contains only the kernel-mode pages allocated by the operating system and device drivers that are present in physical memory at the time of the crash. This type of dump doesn't contain pages belonging to user processes. Because only kernel-mode code can directly cause Windows to crash, however, it's unlikely that user process pages are necessary to debug a crash. In addition, all data structures relevant for crash dump analysis—including the list of running processes, the kernel-mode stack of the current thread, and list of loaded drivers—are stored in nonpaged memory that saves in a *kernel memory dump*. There is no way to predict the size of a kernel memory dump because its size depends on the amount of kernel-mode memory allocated by the operating system and drivers present on the machine. This is the default setting for both Windows client and server systems.

- **Small memory dump** A small memory dump, which is typically between 128 KB and 1 MB in size and is also called a *minidump* or *triage dump*, contains the stop code and parameters, the list of loaded device drivers, the data structures that describe the current process and thread (called the EPROCESS and ETHREAD—described in Chapter 5, "Processes, Threads, and Jobs," in Part 1), the kernel stack for the thread that caused the crash, and additional memory considered potentially relevant by crash dump heuristics, such as the pages referenced by processor registers that contain memory addresses and secondary dump data added by drivers.

> **Note** Device drivers can register a secondary dump data callback routine by calling *KeRegisterBugCheckReasonCallback*. The kernel invokes these callbacks after a crash and a callback routine can add additional data to a crash dump file, such as device hardware memory or device information for easier debugging. Up to 256 MB can be added system-wide by all drivers, depending on the space required to store the dump and the size of the file into which the dump is written, and each callback can add at most one-eighth of the available additional space. Once the additional space is consumed, drivers subsequently called are not offered the chance to add data.

The debugger indicates that it has limited information available to it when it loads a minidump, and basic commands like *!process*, which lists active processes, don't have the data they need. Here is an example of *!process* executed on a minidump:

```
Microsoft (R) Windows Debugger Version 6.12.0002.633 AMD64
Copyright (c) Microsoft Corporation. All rights reserved.

Loading Dump File [C:\Windows\Minidump\100911-22965-01.dmp]
Mini Kernel Dump File: Only registers and stack trace are available
...
0: kd> !process 0 0
**** NT ACTIVE PROCESS DUMP ****
GetPointerFromAddress: unable to read from fffff800030c5000
Error in reading nt!_EPROCESS at 0000000000000000
```

A kernel memory dump includes more information, but switching to a different process's address space mappings won't work because required data isn't in the dump file. Here is an example of the debugger loading a kernel memory dump, followed by an attempt to switch process address spaces:

```
Microsoft (R) Windows Debugger Version 6.12.0002.633 AMD64
Copyright (c) Microsoft Corporation. All rights reserved.

Loading Dump File [C:\Windows\MEMORY.DMP]
Kernel Summary Dump File: Only kernel address space is available
...
0: kd> !process 0 0 explorer.exe
PROCESS fffffa8009b47540 ...

0: kd> .process fffffa8009b47540
Process fffffa80`09b47540 has invalid page directories
```

While a complete memory dump is a superset of the other options, it has the drawback that its size tracks the amount of physical memory on a system and can therefore become unwieldy. Because user-mode code and data are not used during the analysis of most crashes (because crashes originate as a result of problems in kernel memory, and system data structures reside in kernel memory), much of the data stored in a complete memory dump is not relevant to crash analysis and therefore contributes wastefully to the size of a dump file. A final disadvantage is that the paging file must be at least as large as the amount of physical memory on the system plus 1 MB for the dump header, plus up to an additional 256 MB for secondary crash dump data. Because the size of the paging files required, in general, inversely tracks the amount of physical memory present, this requirement can force the paging file to be unnecessarily large. You should therefore consider the advantages offered by the small and kernel memory dump options.

An advantage of a minidump is its small size, which makes it convenient for exchange via e-mail, for example. In addition, each crash generates a file in the directory %SystemRoot%\Minidump with a unique file name consisting of the date, the number of milliseconds that have elapsed since the system was started, and a sequence number (for example, 040712-24835-01.dmp). If there's a conflict, the system will attempt to create additional unique file names by calling the Windows *GetTickCount* function to return an updated system tick count, and it will also increment the sequence number. By default, Windows saves the last 50 minidumps. The number of minidumps saved is configurable by modifying the MinidumpsCount value under the HKLM\SYSTEM\CurrentControlSet\Control\ CrashControl registry key.

A disadvantage of minidumps is that to analyze them, you must have access to the exact images used on the system that generated the dump at the time of analysis. (At a minimum, a copy of the matching Ntoskrnl.exe is needed to perform the most basic analysis.) This can be problematic if you want to analyze a dump on a system different from the system that generated the dump. However, the Microsoft symbol server contains images (and symbols) for all recent Windows versions, so you can set the symbol path in the debugger to point to the symbol server, and the debugger will automatically download the needed images. (Of course, the Microsoft symbol server won't have images for third-party drivers you have installed.)

A more significant disadvantage is that the limited amount of data stored in the dump can hamper effective analysis. You can also get the advantages of minidumps even when you configure a system to generate kernel or complete crash dumps by opening the larger crash with WinDbg and using the *.dump /m* command to extract a minidump. Note that a minidump is automatically created even if the system is set for full or kernel dumps.

> **Note** You can use the *.dump* command from within LiveKd to generate a memory image of a live system that you can analyze offline without stopping the system. This approach is useful when a system is exhibiting a problem but is still delivering services, and you want to troubleshoot the problem without interrupting service. To prevent creating crash images that aren't necessarily fully consistent because the contents of different regions of memory reflect different points in time, LiveKd supports the *–m* flag. The mirror dump option produces a consistent snapshot of kernel-mode memory by leveraging the memory manager's *memory mirroring* APIs, which give a point-in-time view of the system. For information about using LiveKd with Hyper-V guests, refer to the "Dumping Hyper-V Guests Using LiveKd" experiment later in the chapter.

The kernel memory dump option offers a practical middle ground. Because it contains all of kernel-mode-owned physical memory, it has the same level of analysis-related data as a complete memory dump, but it omits the usually irrelevant user-mode data and code, and therefore can be significantly smaller. As an example, on a system running a 64-bit version of Windows with 4 GB of RAM, a kernel memory dump was 294 MB in size.

When you configure kernel memory dumps, the system checks whether the paging file is large enough, as described earlier. Some general recommendations follow in Table 14-1, but these are only estimated sizes because there is no way to predict the size of a kernel memory dump. The reason you can't predict the size of a kernel memory dump is that its size depends on the amount of kernel-mode memory in use by the operating system and drivers present on the machine at the time of the crash.

Therefore, it is possible that at the time of the crash, the paging file is too small to hold a kernel dump, in which case the system will switch to generating a minidump. If you want to see the size of a kernel dump on your system, force a manual crash either by configuring the option to allow you to initiate a manual system crash from the console or by using the Notmyfault tool. (Both Notmyfault and initiating a crash are described later in the chapter.) When you reboot, you can check to make sure that a kernel dump was generated and check its size to gauge how large to make your paging file. To be conservative, on 32-bit systems you can choose a page file size of 2 GB plus up to 256 MB, because 2 GB is the maximum kernel-mode address space available (unless you are booting with the *increaseuserva* boot option, in which case this can be as low as 1 GB). If you do not have enough space on the boot volume for saving the Memory.dmp file, you can choose a location on any other local hard disk through the dialog box shown earlier in Figure 14-4.

TABLE 14-1 Default Minimum Paging File Sizes for Kernel Dumps

System Memory Size	Minimum Page File Size for Kernel Dumps
< 4 GB	200 MB
< 8 GB	400 MB
>= 8 GB	800 MB

To limit the amount of disk space that is taken up by crash dumps, Windows needs to determine whether it should maintain a copy of the last kernel or complete dump. After reporting the kernel fault (described later), Windows uses the following algorithm to decide if it should keep the Memory.dmp file. If the system is a server, Windows will always store the dump file. On a Windows client system, only domain-joined machines will store a crash dump by default. For a non-domain-joined machine, Windows will maintain a copy of the crash dump only if there is more than 25 GB of free disk space on the destination volume—that is, the volume where the system is configured to write the Memory.dmp file. If the system, due to disk space constraints, is unable to keep a copy of the crash dump file, an event is written to the System event log indicating that the dump file was deleted, as shown in Figure 14-5. This behavior can be overridden by creating the DWORD registry value HKLM\SYSTEM\CurrentControlSet\Control\CrashControl\AlwaysKeepMemoryDump and setting it to 1, in which case Windows will always keep a crash dump, regardless of the amount of free disk space.

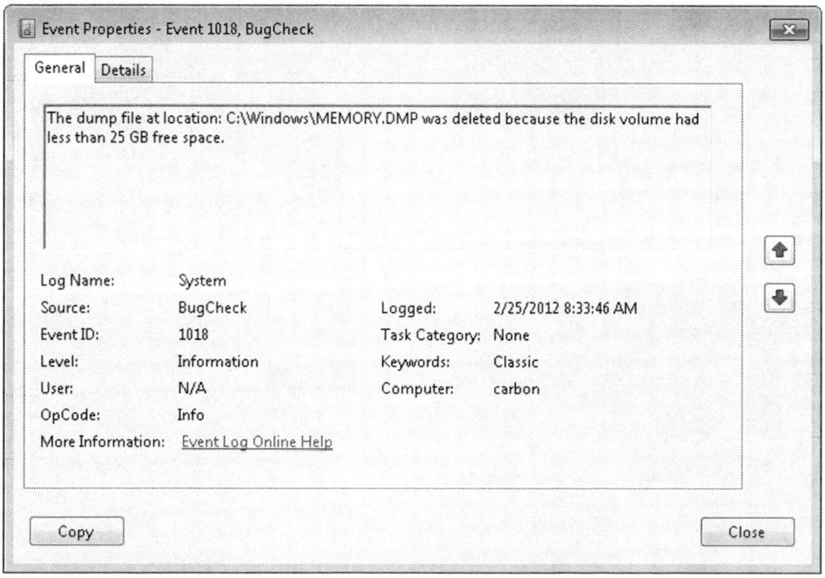

FIGURE 14-5 Dump file deletion event log entry

EXPERIMENT: Viewing Dump File Information

Each crash dump file contains a dump header that describes the stop code and its parameters, the type of system the crash occurred on (including version information), and a list of pointers to important kernel-mode structures required during analysis. The dump header also contains the type of crash dump that was written and any information specific to that type of dump. The *.dumpdebug* debugger command can be used to display the dump header of a crash dump file. For example, the following output is from a crash of a system that was configured for a kernel (or summary) dump:

```
0: kd> .dumpdebug
----- 64 bit Kernel Summary Dump Analysis

DUMP_HEADER64:
MajorVersion        0000000f
MinorVersion        00001db1
KdSecondaryVersion  00000000
DirectoryTableBase  00000001`ad6a2000
PfnDataBase         fffffa80`00000000
PsLoadedModuleList  fffff800`02a47670
PsActiveProcessHead fffff800`02a29350
MachineImageType    00008664
NumberProcessors    00000002
BugCheckCode        000000d1
BugCheckParameter1  fffff8a0`027475c0
BugCheckParameter2  00000000`00000002
BugCheckParameter3  00000000`00000000
BugCheckParameter4  fffff880`0343a361
KdDebuggerDataBlock fffff800`029f30a0
SecondaryDataState  00000000
ProductType         00000001
SuiteMask           00000110

SUMMARY_DUMP64:
DumpOptions         504d4453
HeaderSize          00049000
BitmapSize          00230000
Pages               000151f0
Bitmap.SizeOfBitMap 00230000

KiProcessorBlock at fffff800`02ab1c40
  2 KiProcessorBlock entries:
  fffff800`029f4e80 fffff880`009ec180
```

The *.enumtag* command displays all secondary dump data stored within a crash dump. For each callback of secondary data, the tag, the length of the data, and the data itself (in byte and ASCII format) are displayed. Developers can utilize Debugger Extension APIs to create custom debugger extensions to also read secondary dump data. (See the Debugging Tools for Windows help file for more information.)

```
0: kd> .enumtag
{270A33FD-3DA6-460D-BA893C1BAE21E39B} - 0xfc8 bytes
   09 00 00 00 00 00 00 00 48 00 00 00 13 00 00 00   ........H.......
   48 08 00 00 14 00 00 00 C8 0F 00 00 15 00 00 00   H...............
   C8 0F 00 00 17 00 00 00 00 00 00 00 00 00 00 00   ................
   00 00 00 00 00 00 00 00 00 00 00 00 00 00 00 00   ................
   00 00 00 00 00 00 00 00 EF B2 01 00 00 00 00 00   ................
...
```

Crash Dump Generation

When the system boots, it checks the crash dump options configured by reading the HKLM\SYSTEM\CurrentControlSet\Control\CrashControl registry key. If a dump is configured, it makes a copy of the disk miniport driver used to write to the volume in memory and gives it the same name as the miniport with the word "dump_" prefixed. The system also queries the DumpFilters value for any filter drivers that are required for writing to the volume, an example being Dumpfve.sys, the BitLocker Drive Encryption Crashdump Filter driver. (See Chapter 9, "Storage Management," for more details on BitLocker Drive Encryption.) It also collects information related to the components involved with writing a crash dump—including the name of the disk miniport driver, the I/O manager structures that are necessary to write the dump, and the map of where the paging file is on disk—and saves two copies of the data in dump-context structures.

When the system crashes, the crash dump driver (%SystemRoot%\System32\Drivers\Crashdmp.sys) verifies the integrity of the two dump-context structures obtained at boot by performing a memory comparison. If there's not a match, it does not write a crash dump, because doing so would likely fail or corrupt the disk. Upon a successful verification match, Crashdmp.sys, with support from the disk miniport driver and any required filter drivers, writes the dump information directly to the sectors on disk occupied by the paging file, bypassing the file system driver and storage driver stack (which might be corrupted or even have caused the crash).

During the boot process, the Session Manager (Smss.exe) checks the registry value HKLM\SYSTEM\CurrentControlSet\Control\Session Manager\Memory Management\ExistingPageFiles for a list of existing page files from the previous boot. (See Chapter 10, "Memory Management," for more information on page files.) It then cycles through the list, calling the function *SmpCheckForCrashDump* on each file present, looking to see whether it contains crash dump data. It checks by searching the header at the top of each paging file for the signature *PAGEDUMP* or *PAGEDU64* on 32-bit or 64-bit systems, respectively. (A match indicates that the paging file contains crash dump information.) If crash dump data is present, the Session Manager then reads a set of crash parameters from the HKLM\SYSTEM\CurrentControlSet\Control\CrashControl registry key, one of which contains the name of the target dump file (typically %SystemRoot%\Memory.dmp, unless configured otherwise).

Smss.exe then checks whether the target dump file is on a different volume than the paging file. If so, it checks whether the target volume has enough free disk space (the size required for the crash dump is stored in the dump header of the page file) before truncating the paging file to the size of the crash data and renaming it to a temporary dump file name. (A new page file will be created later when the Session Manager calls the *NtCreatePagingFile* function.) The temporary dump file name takes the format DUMPxxxx.tmp, where xxxx is the current low-word value of the system's tick count. (The system will attempt 100 times to find a nonconflicting value.) After renaming the page file, the system removes both the hidden and system attributes from the file and sets the appropriate security descriptors to secure the crash dump.

Next the Session Manager creates the volatile registry key HKLM\SYSTEM\CurrentControlSet\Control\CrashControl\MachineCrash and stores the temporary dump file name in the value DumpFile. It then writes a DWORD to the TempDestination value indicating whether the dump file location is only a temporary destination. If the paging file is on the same volume as the destination dump file, a temporary dump file isn't used, because the paging file is truncated and directly renamed to the target dump file name. In this case, the DumpFile value will be that of the target dump file and TempDestination will be 0.

Later in the boot, Wininit checks for the presence of the MachineCrash key, and if it exists, Wininit launches WerFault (described in the next section), which reads the TempDestination and DumpFile values. If the TempDestination value is set to 1, which indicates a temporary file was used, WerFault moves the temporary file to its target location and secures the target file by allowing only the System account and the local Administrators group access. WerFault then writes the final dump file name to the FinalDumpFileLocation value in the MachineCrash key. These steps are shown in Figure 14-6.

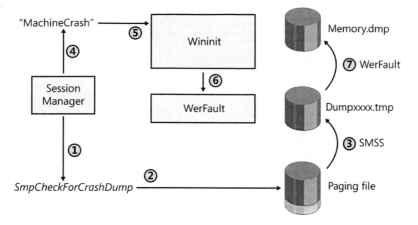

FIGURE 14-6 Crash dump file generation

To provide more control over where the dump file data is written to, for example on systems that boot from a SAN or systems with insufficient disk space on the volume where the paging file is configured, Windows also supports the use of a *dedicated dump file* that is configured in the DedicatedDumpFile and DumpFileSize values under the HKLM\SYSTEM\CurrentControlSet\Control\CrashControl registry key. When a dedicated dump file is specified, the crash dump driver creates the dump file of the specified size and writes the crash data there instead of to the paging file. If no DumpFileSize value is given, Windows creates a dedicated dump file using the largest file size that would be required to store a complete dump. Windows calculates the required size as the size of the total number of physical pages of memory present in the system plus the size required for the dump header (one page on 32-bit systems, and two pages on 64-bit), plus the maximum value for secondary crash dump data, which is 256 MB. If a full or kernel dump is configured but there is not enough space on the target volume to create the dedicated dump file of the required size, the system falls back to writing a minidump.

Windows Error Reporting

As mentioned in Chapter 3 in Part 1, Windows includes a facility called Windows Error Reporting (WER), which facilitates the automatic submission of process and system failures (such as crashes and/or hangs) to Microsoft (or an internal error reporting server) for analysis. This feature is enabled by default, but it can be modified by changing WER's behavior since WER takes the additional step of determining whether the system is configured to send a crash dump to Microsoft (or a private server, explained further in the "Online Crash Analysis" section later in the chapter) for analysis on a reboot following a crash. The main Problem Reporting Settings page, which you access from the Control Panel's Action Center applet by following the Change Action Center Settings link, is shown in Figure 14-7. This page allows you to configure the system's error reporting settings.

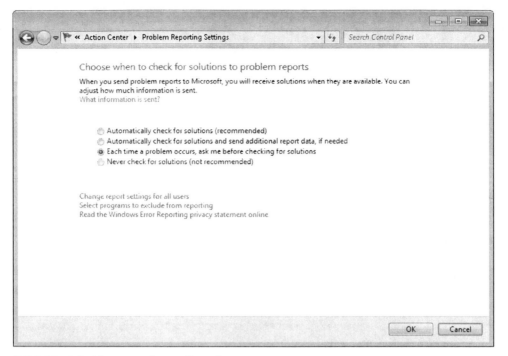

FIGURE 14-7 Problem reporting configuration page

As mentioned earlier, if Wininit.exe finds the HKLM\SYSTEM\CurrentControlSet\Control\Crash-Control\MachineCrash key, it executes WerFault.exe with the *–k –c* flags (the *k* flag indicates kernel error reporting, and the *c* flag indicates that the full or kernel dump should be converted to a mini-dump) to have WerFault.exe check for the kernel-mode crash dump file. WerFault takes the following steps in preparing to send a crash dump report to the Microsoft Online Crash Analysis (OCA) site (or, if configured, an internal error reporting server):

1. If the type of dump generated was not a minidump, it extracts a minidump from the dump file and stores it in the default location of %SystemRoot%\Minidump, unless otherwise configured through the MinidumpDir value in the HKLM\SYSTEM\CurrentControlSet\Control\Crash-Control key.

2. It writes the name of the minidump files to HKLM\SOFTWARE\Microsoft\Windows\Windows Error Reporting\KernelFaults\Queue.

3. It adds a command to execute WerFault.exe (%SystemRoot%\System32\WerFault.exe) with the *–k –qr* flags (the *qr* flag specifies to use queued reporting mode and that WerFault should be restarted) to HKLM\SOFTWARE\Microsoft\Windows\CurrentVersion\RunOnce so that Wer-Fault is executed during the first user's logon to the system for purposes of actually sending the error report.

Online Crash Analysis

When the WerFault utility executes during logon, as a result of having configured itself to start, it launches itself again using the *−k −q* flags (the *q* flag on its own specifies queued reporting mode) and terminates the previous instance. It does this to prevent the Windows shell from waiting on Wer-Fault by returning control to RunOnce as quickly as possible. The newly launched WerFault.exe checks the HKLM\SOFTWARE\Microsoft\Windows\Windows Error Reporting\KernelFaults\Queue key to look for queued reports that may have been added in the previous dump conversion phase. It also checks whether there are previously unsent crash reports from previous sessions. If there are, WerFault.exe generates two XML-formatted files:

- The first contains a basic description of the system, including the operating system version, a list of drivers installed on the machine, and the list of devices present in the system.

- The second contains metadata used by the OCA service, including the event type that triggered WER and additional configuration information such as the system manufacturer.

If configured to ask for user input (which is the default), it then presents the dialog box shown in Figure 14-8, which prompts the user whether he or she wants to check online for a solution to the problem. If the user chooses to check for a solution, and unless overridden by Group Policy, WerFault sends a copy of the two XML files and the minidump to *https://oca.microsoft.com*, which forwards the data to a server farm for automated analysis, described in the next section.

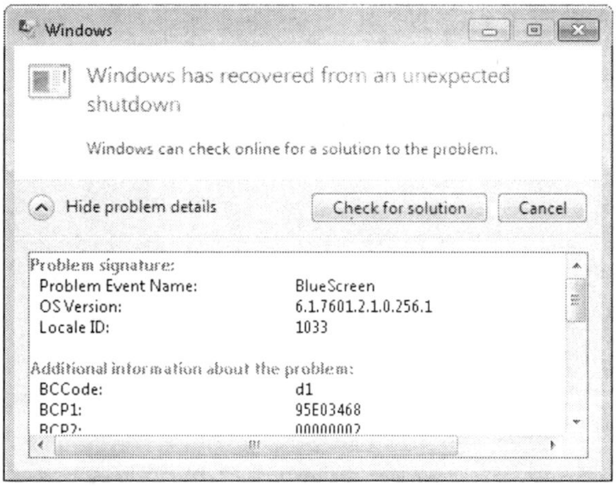

FIGURE 14-8 Crash dump error reporting dialog box

The server farm's automated analysis uses the same analysis engine that the Microsoft kernel debuggers use when you load a crash dump file into them (described shortly). The analysis generates a *bucket ID*, which is a signature that identifies a particular crash type. The server farm queries a database using the bucket ID to see whether a resolution has been found for the crash, and it sends a URL back to WerFault that refers it to the WER website (*https://wer.microsoft.com*). Any solutions are made available on the main Action Center page of Control Panel under System And Security. When browsing for solutions, the Action Center contains an Internet browser frame to open the page on the

WER website that reports the preliminary crash analysis. If a resolution is available, the page instructs the user where to obtain a hotfix, service pack, or third-party driver update.

Basic Crash Dump Analysis

If OCA fails to identify a resolution or you are unable to submit the crash to OCA, an alternative is analyzing crashes yourself. As mentioned earlier, WinDbg and Kd both execute the same analysis engine used by OCA when you load a crash dump file, and the basic analysis can sometimes pinpoint the problem. As a result, you might be fortunate and have the crash dump solved by the automatic analysis. If not, there are some straightforward techniques to try to solve the crash.

This section explains how to perform basic crash analysis steps, followed by tips on leveraging Driver Verifier (which is introduced in Chapter 8, "I/O System") to catch buggy drivers when they corrupt the system so that a crash dump analysis pinpoints them.

Note OCA's automated analysis may occasionally identify a highly likely cause of a crash but not be able to inform you of the suspected driver. This happens because it only reports the cause for crashes that have their bucket ID entry populated in the OCA database, and entries are created only when Microsoft crash-analysis engineers have verified the cause. If there's no bucket ID entry, OCA reports that the crash was caused by *"unknown driver."*

Notmyfault

You can use the Notmyfault utility from Windows Sysinternals (*http://technet.microsoft.com/en-us/sysinternals/bb963901*) to generate the crashes described here. Notmyfault consists of an executable named Notmyfault.exe and a driver named Myfault.sys. When you run the Notmyfault executable, it loads the driver and presents the dialog box shown in Figure 14-9, which allows you to crash or hang the system in various ways or to cause the driver to leak paged or nonpaged pool. The crash types offered represent the ones most commonly seen by Microsoft's Customer Service and Support group. Selecting an option and clicking the Crash, Hang, Leak Paged, or Leak Nonpaged button causes the executable to tell the driver, by using the *DeviceIoControl* Windows API, which type of bug to trigger.

Note You should execute Notmyfault crashes on a test system or on a virtual machine because there is a small risk that memory it corrupts will be written to disk and result in file or disk corruption.

Note The names of the Notmyfault executable and driver highlight the fact that user mode cannot directly cause the system to crash. The Notmyfault executable can cause a crash only by loading a driver to perform an illegal operation for it in kernel mode.

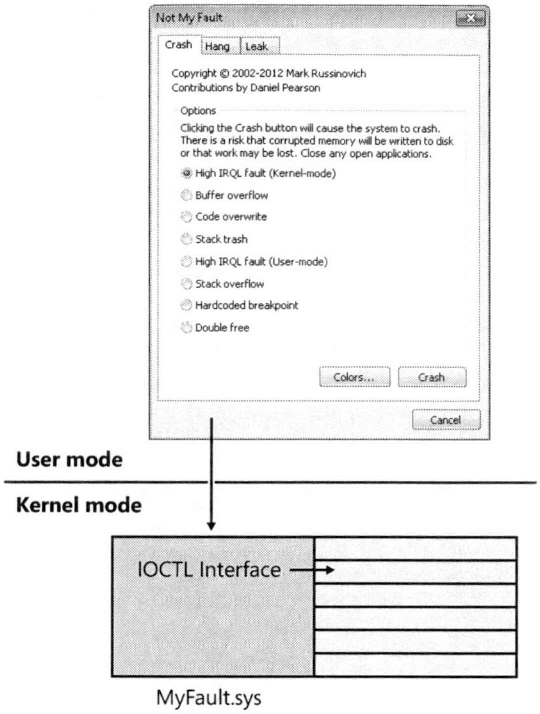

FIGURE 14-9 Notmyfault

Basic Crash Dump Analysis

The most straightforward Notmyfault crash to debug is the one caused by selecting the High IRQL Fault (Kernel-Mode) option and clicking the Crash button. This causes the driver to allocate a page of paged pool, free the pool, raise the IRQL to DPC/dispatch level, and then touch the page it has freed. (See Chapter 3 in Part 1 for more information on IRQLs.) If that doesn't cause a crash, the process continues by reading memory past the end of the page until it causes a crash by accessing invalid pages. The driver performs several illegal operations as a result:

1. It references memory that doesn't belong to it.

2. It references paged pool at an IRQL that's DPC/dispatch level or higher, which is illegal because page faults are not permitted when the processor IRQL is DPC/dispatch level or higher.

3. When it goes past the end of the memory that it had allocated, it tries to reference memory that is potentially invalid.

The reason the first page reference might not cause a crash is that it won't generate a page fault if the page that the driver frees remains in the system working set. (See Chapter 10 for information on the system working set.)

When you load a crash generated with this bug into WinDbg, the tool's analysis displays something like this:

```
Microsoft (R) Windows Debugger Version 6.12.0002.633 AMD64
Copyright (c) Microsoft Corporation. All rights reserved.

Loading Dump File [C:\Windows\MEMORY.DMP]
Kernel Complete Dump File: Full address space is available

Symbol search path is: srv*c:\symbols*http://msdl.microsoft.com/download/symbols
Executable search path is:
Windows 7 Kernel Version 7601 (Service Pack 1) MP (2 procs) Free x86 compatible
Product: WinNt, suite: TerminalServer SingleUserTS
Built by: 7601.17514.x86fre.win7sp1_rtm.101119-1850
Machine Name:
Kernel base = 0x82814000 PsLoadedModuleList = 0x8295e850
Debug session time: Wed Mar 21 08:12:50.194 2012 (UTC - 7:00)
System Uptime: 8 days 8:54:38.580
Loading Kernel Symbols
...............................................................
...........
Loading User Symbols
......................
Loading unloaded module list
.....
*******************************************************************************
*                                                                             *
*                        Bugcheck Analysis                                    *
*                                                                             *
*******************************************************************************

Use !analyze -v to get detailed debugging information.

BugCheck D1, {946ae800, 2, 0, 91df15ab}

*** ERROR: Module load completed but symbols could not be loaded for myfault.sys
Probably caused by : myfault.sys ( myfault+5ab )

Followup: MachineOwner
---------
```

The first thing to note is that WinDbg reports errors trying to load symbols for Myfault.sys. This is expected because the symbol file for Myfault.sys is not stored in the symbol-file path (which is configured to point at the Microsoft symbol server). You'll see similar errors for third-party drivers that do not ship with the operating system.

The analysis text itself is terse, showing the numeric stop code and bug-check parameters followed by a "Probably caused by" line that shows the analysis engine's best guess at the offending driver. In this case it's on the mark and points directly at Myfault.sys, so there's no need for manual analysis.

The "Followup" line is not generally useful except within Microsoft, where the debugger looks for the module name in the Triage.ini file that's located within the Triage directory of the Debugging Tools for Windows installation directory. The Microsoft-internal version of that file lists the developer or group responsible for handling crashes in a specific driver, and the debugger displays the developer's or group's name in the Followup line when appropriate.

Verbose Analysis

Even though the basic analysis of the Notmyfault crash identifies the faulty driver, you should always have the debugger execute a verbose analysis by entering the command:

!analyze –v

The first obvious difference between the verbose and default analysis is the description of the stop code and its parameters. Following is the output of the command when executed on the same dump:

```
DRIVER_IRQL_NOT_LESS_OR_EQUAL (d1)
An attempt was made to access a pageable (or completely invalid) address at an
interrupt request level (IRQL) that is too high.  This is usually
caused by drivers using improper addresses.
If kernel debugger is available get stack backtrace.
Arguments:
Arg1: 946ae800, memory referenced
Arg2: 00000002, IRQL
Arg3: 00000000, value 0 = read operation, 1 = write operation
Arg4: 91df15ab, address which referenced memory
```

This saves you the trouble of opening the help file to find the same information, and the text sometimes suggests troubleshooting steps, an example of which you'll see in the next section on advanced crash dump analysis.

The other potentially useful information in a verbose analysis is the stack trace of the thread that was executing on the processor that crashed at the time of the crash. Here's what it looks like for the same complete dump:

```
STACK_TEXT:
93cdbb3c 91df15ab badb0d00 84f3e380 946ad800 nt!KiTrap0E+0x2cf
WARNING: Stack unwind information not available. Following frames may be wrong.
93cdbbb8 91df19db 86d77900 93cdbbfc 91df1b26 myfault+0x5ab
93cdbbc4 91df1b26 85e38488 00000001 00000000 myfault+0x9db
93cdbbfc 8284b593 86c9a510 86d77900 86d77900 myfault+0xb26
93cdbc14 82a3f99f 85e38488 86d77900 86d77970 nt!IofCallDriver+0x63
93cdbc34 82a42b71 86c9a510 85e38488 00000000 nt!IopSynchronousServiceTail+0x1f8
93cdbcd0 82a893f4 86c9a510 86d77900 00000000 nt!IopXxxControlFile+0x6aa
93cdbd04 828521ea 000000c4 00000000 00000000 nt!NtDeviceIoControlFile+0x2a
93cdbd04 77af70b4 000000c4 00000000 00000000 nt!KiFastCallEntry+0x12a
0009f370 77af5864 75cb989d 000000c4 00000000 ntdll!KiFastSystemCallRet
0009f374 75cb989d 000000c4 00000000 00000000 ntdll!NtDeviceIoControlFile+0xc
0009f3d4 77a1a671 000000c4 83360018 00000000 KERNELBASE!DeviceIoControl+0xf6
0009f400 00c421f9 000000c4 83360018 00000000 kernel32!DeviceIoControlImplementation+0x80
0009f4a0 7749c4e7 000201ec 00000111 000003f9 NotMyfault+0x21f9
```

The preceding stack shows that the Notmyfault executable image, shown at the bottom, invoked the *DeviceIoControlImplementation* function in Kernel32.dll, which in turn invoked *DeviceIoControl* in Kernelbase.dll, and so on, until finally the system crashed with the execution of an instruction in the

Myfault image. A stack trace like this can be useful because crashes sometimes occur as the result of one driver passing another one data that is improperly formatted or corrupt or contains illegal parameters. The driver that's passed the invalid data might cause a crash and get the blame in an analysis, when the stack reveals that another driver was involved. In this sample trace, no driver other than Myfault is listed. (The module "nt" is Ntoskrnl.)

If the driver singled out by an analysis is unfamiliar to you, use the *lm* (list modules) command to look at the driver's version information. Add the *k* (kernel modules) and *v* (verbose) options along with the *m* (match) option followed by the name of the driver:

```
0: kd> lm kv m myfault
start       end         module name
91df1000 91df2880    myfault    (no symbols)
    Loaded symbol image file: myfault.sys
    Image path: \??\C:\Windows\system32\drivers\myfault.sys
    Image name: myfault.sys
    Timestamp:        Sat Apr 07 09:34:40 2012 (4F806CA0)
    CheckSum:         00003871
    ImageSize:        00001880
    File version:     4.0.0.0
    Product version:  4.0.0.0
    File flags:       0 (Mask 3F)
    File OS:          40004 NT Win32
    File type:        3.7 Driver
    File date:        00000000.00000000
    Translations:     0409.04b0
    CompanyName:      Sysinternals
    ProductName:      Sysinternals Myfault
    InternalName:     myfault.sys
    OriginalFilename: myfault.sys
    ProductVersion:   4.0
    FileVersion:      4.0 (sysinternals.com)
    FileDescription:  Crash Test Driver
    LegalCopyright:   Copyright © 2002-2012 Mark Russinovich
```

Before you spend additional time and energy further analyzing crashes, you should ensure that your system's kernel and drivers are the most recent available by using the services of Windows Update and third-party driver support sites.

In addition to using the description to identify the purpose of a driver, you can also use the file and product version numbers to see whether the version installed is the most up-to-date version available. If version information isn't present (because it might have been paged out of physical memory at the time of the crash), look at the driver image file's properties in Windows Explorer on the system that crashed.

To use Windows Update to check for a newer version of a driver, open Device Manager and locate the device that the driver is associated with. Right-click on the device, and select Update Driver Software. If Windows Update reports that no newer version of the driver is available for download, it may be worthwhile checking the website of the original equipment manufacturer (OEM) for the system. Finally, since both Windows Update and the OEM may not have the latest drivers, also check the website of the actual driver author for a newer version.

Using Crash Troubleshooting Tools

The crash generated in the preceding section with Notmyfault's High IRQL Fault (Kernel-Mode) option poses no challenge for the debugger's automated analysis. Unfortunately, most crashes are not so easy and sometimes are impossible to debug. There are several levels of increasing severity in terms of system performance degradation that might help turn system crashes that cannot be analyzed into ones that can be. If the crashes generated after you configure a level and reboot aren't revealing the cause, try the next level.

1. If there are one or more drivers you consider likely sources of the crashes—because they were introduced into the system relatively recently, they were recently updated, or the circumstances of the crash implicate them—enable them for verification using Driver Verifier and check all the verification options except for low resources simulation. (See Chapter 8 for more information on Driver Verifier.)

2. If the computer is running a 32-bit version of Windows, enable the same level of verification as in level 1 on all unsigned drivers in the system. (All drivers on a 64-bit system must be signed unless this restriction is disabled manually at boot time by pressing F8 and choosing the advanced boot option Disable Driver Signature Enforcement.)

3. Enable the same verification as in level 1 on all drivers in the system. To maintain reasonable performance, you may want to divide the drivers into groups, enabling Driver Verifier on one group at a time between reboots.

> **Note** If your system becomes unbootable because Driver Verifier detects a driver error and crashes the system, start in safe mode (where verification is disabled), run Driver Verifier, and delete the verification settings.

The following sections demonstrate how Driver Verifier can make impossible-to-debug crashes into ones that you can solve.

Buffer Overruns, Memory Corruption, and Special Pool

One of the most common sources of crashes on Windows is pool corruption. Pool corruption usually occurs when a driver suffers from a buffer overrun or buffer underrun bug that causes it to overwrite data past either the end or start of a buffer it has allocated from paged or nonpaged pool. The Executive's pool-tracking structures reside on either side of a pool buffer and separate buffers from each other. These bugs, therefore, cause corruption to the pool tracking structures, to buffers owned by other drivers, or to both. You can often catch the culprit of a pool overrun by using the *!pool* command to examine the surrounding pool tags. Find the address at which the corruption occurred, and use *!pool address_of_corruption*. This command will display all the pool allocations that are on the same page as the corruption. Looking in the left column, find the range of the corrupted address and then look at the allocation just previous to it and find its pool tag. This will likely be the culprit in a buffer overrun. You can use the Pooltag.txt file in the Triage folder of the Debugging Tools for

Windows installation directory to find the driver that owns the pool tag, or use the Strings utility from Sysinternals.

Pool corruption can also occur when a driver writes to pool it had previously owned but subsequently freed. This is called a *use after free* bug and is usually caused by a race condition in a driver. These bugs are particularly hard to debug because the driver that corrupts memory no longer has any traceable ties to the memory, such as a neighboring pool tag as in a buffer overrun. Another fairly common cause of pool corruption is *direct memory access* (DMA). DMA occurs when hardware writes directly to RAM instead of going through a driver; however, the driver is still responsible for coordinating the whole process by allocating the memory that the hardware will write to and programming the hardware registers of the device with the details of the operation. If a driver has a bug that releases the memory it is using for DMA before the hardware writes to it, the memory can be given to another driver or even to a user-mode application, which will certainly not expect to have hardware writing to it.

The crashes caused by pool corruption are virtually impossible to debug because the system crashes when corrupted data is referenced, not when the corruption occurs. However, sometimes you can take steps to at least obtain a clue about what corrupted the memory. The first step is to try to determine the size of the corruption by looking at the corrupted data. If the corruption is a single bit, it was likely caused by bad RAM or a faulty processor. If the corruption is fairly small, it could be caused by hardware or software, and finding a root cause will be nearly impossible. In the case of large corruptions, you can look for patterns in the corruption, like strings (for example, HTTP packet payloads, file contents of text-based files, and so on).

> **Note** To assist in catching pool corruptions, Windows checks the consistency of a buffer's pool-tracking structures, and those of the buffer's immediate neighbors, on every pool allocation and free operation. Thus, buffer overruns are likely to be detected shortly after the corruption and identified with a crash that has the BAD_POOL_HEADER (0x19) stop code.

You can generate a pool corruption crash by running Notmyfault and selecting the Buffer Overflow bug. This causes Myfault to allocate a buffer and then overwrite the 48 bytes following the buffer. There can be a significant delay between the time you click the Crash button and when a crash occurs, and you might even have to generate pool usage by exercising applications before a crash occurs, which highlights the distance between a corruption and its effect on system stability. An analysis of the resultant crash almost always reports Ntoskrnl or another driver as being the likely cause, which demonstrates the usefulness of a verbose analysis with its description of the stop code:

```
DRIVER_CORRUPTED_EXPOOL (c5)
An attempt was made to access a pageable (or completely invalid) address at an
interrupt request level (IRQL) that is too high.  This is
caused by drivers that have corrupted the system pool.  Run the driver
verifier against any new (or suspect) drivers, and if that doesn't turn up
the culprit, then use gflags to enable special pool.
```

```
Arguments:
Arg1: 4f4f4f53, memory referenced
Arg2: 00000002, IRQL
Arg3: 00000000, value 0 = read operation, 1 = write operation
Arg4: 829234a7, address which referenced memory
```

The advice in the description is to run Driver Verifier against any new or suspect drivers or to use Gflags to enable special pool. Both accomplish the same thing: to have the system detect a potential corruption when it occurs and crash the system in a way that makes the automated analysis point at the driver causing the corruption.

If Driver Verifier's special pool option is enabled, verified drivers use special pool, rather than paged or nonpaged pool, for any allocations they make for buffers slightly less than a page in size. A buffer allocated from special pool is sandwiched between two invalid pages and by default is aligned against the top of the page. The special pool routines also fill the unused portions of the page in which the buffer resides with a random pattern (based on the system's tick count). See Chapter 10 for more information on special pool.

The system detects any buffer overruns of under a page in size at the time of the overrun because they cause a page fault on the invalid page following the buffer. The signature serves to catch buffer underruns at the time the driver frees a buffer because the integrity of the pattern placed there at the time of allocation will have been compromised.

EXPERIMENT: Enabling Special Pool with Driver Verifier

To see how the use of special pool causes a crash that the analysis engine easily diagnoses, run the Driver Verifier Manager to configure the special pool option. The Driver Verifier Manager provides the ability to activate most verification features without having to restart the system. The following steps show how to use the Driver Verifier Manager to enable the special pool feature, without requiring a restart:

1. From the Start menu, type **verifier**, and then press Enter to run the Driver Verifier Manager.

2. Select the option Display Information About The Currently Verified Drivers, and then click Next.

3. Click the Change button, select Special Pool, and click OK to enable the special pool option. (The Enabled? option will read No until you select a driver for verification.)

4. Next, click the Add button, type **myfault.sys** in the File Name field, and then click Open. (You do not have to find Myfault.sys in the dialog box; just enter its name.)

5. Click the Next button to progress to where the Driver Verifier Manager displays a list of global counters for any currently verified drivers. Clicking the Next button again shows you a list of counters specific to each verified driver. You should see Myfault.sys in the list.

6. Finally, click the Finish button to complete the wizard.

Drivers that are verified using the No Reboot feature of Driver Verifier are not monitored as thoroughly as drivers that are loaded after a reboot. Whenever possible, enable the driver for verification, and then restart the system. Running the following command from an elevated command prompt causes Driver Verifier to preserve verification settings across reboots:

```
C:\>verifier /flags 0x1 /driver myfault.sys

New verifier settings:

Special pool: Enabled
Pool tracking: Disabled
Force IRQL checking: Disabled
I/O verification: Disabled
Deadlock detection: Disabled
DMA checking: Disabled
Security checks: Disabled
Force pending I/O requests: Disabled
Low resources simulation: Disabled
IRP Logging: Disabled
Miscellaneous checks: Disabled

Verified drivers:

myfault.sys

You must restart this computer for the changes to take effect.
```

When you run Notmyfault and cause a buffer overflow, the system will immediately crash and the analysis of the dump reports this:

```
Probably caused by : myfault.sys ( myfault+61d )
```

A verbose analysis describes the stop code like this:

```
DRIVER_PAGE_FAULT_BEYOND_END_OF_ALLOCATION (d6)
N bytes of memory was allocated and more than N bytes are being referenced.
This cannot be protected by try-except.
When possible, the guilty driver's name (Unicode string) is printed on
the bugcheck screen and saved in KiBugCheckDriver.
Arguments:
Arg1: beb50000, memory referenced
Arg2: 00000001, value 0 = read operation, 1 = write operation
Arg3: 9201161d, if non-zero, the address which referenced memory.
Arg4: 00000000, (reserved)
```

Special pool made an elusive bug into one that instantly reveals itself and makes the analysis trivial.

Code Overwrite and System Code Write Protection

A driver with a bug that causes corruption or misinterpretation of its own data structures can reference memory the driver doesn't own when it interprets corrupted data as a memory pointer value. The target of the pointer can be anything in the virtual address space, including data belonging to other drivers, invalid memory, or the code of other drivers or the kernel. As with buffer overruns, by the time that corruption is detected and the system crashes, it's usually impossible to identify the driver that caused the corruption. Enabling special pool increases the chance of catching wild-pointer bugs, but it does not catch code corruption.

When you run Notmyfault and select the Code Overwrite option, the Myfault driver corrupts the entry point to the *NtReadFile* kernel function. One of two things will happen at this point: if your system has 2 GB or less of physical memory, you'll get a crash for which an analysis points at Myfault.sys. The stop code description that a verbose analysis displays tells you that Myfault attempted to write to read-only memory:

```
ATTEMPTED_WRITE_TO_READONLY_MEMORY (be)
An attempt was made to write to readonly memory.  The guilty driver is on the
stack trace (and is typically the current instruction pointer).
When possible, the guilty driver's name (Unicode string) is printed on
the bugcheck screen and saved in KiBugCheckDriver.
Arguments:
Arg1: 826a023c, Virtual address for the attempted write.
Arg2: 026a0121, PTE contents.
Arg3: 90f83b4c, (reserved)
Arg4: 0000000b, (reserved)
```

However, if you have more than 2 GB of memory, you'll get a different type of crash because the attempt to corrupt the memory isn't caught. Because *NtReadFile* is a commonly executed system service that is used by Windows, the system will almost immediately crash as a thread attempts to execute the corrupted code and generates an illegal instruction fault. The analysis of crashes generated with this bug is always wrong, but it might vary, with Win32k.sys and Ntoskrnl.exe commonly being the analyzer's best guess as to what's responsible. The bugcheck description for these crashes is:

```
KERNEL_MODE_EXCEPTION_NOT_HANDLED (8e)
This is a very common bugcheck.  Usually the exception address pinpoints
the driver/function that caused the problem.  Always note this address
as well as the link date of the driver/image that contains this address.
Some common problems are exception code 0x80000003.  This means a hard
coded breakpoint or assertion was hit, but this system was booted
/NODEBUG.  This is not supposed to happen as developers should never have
hardcoded breakpoints in retail code, but ...
If this happens, make sure a debugger gets connected, and the
system is booted /DEBUG.  This will let us see why this breakpoint is
happening.
Arguments:
Arg1: c0000005, The exception code that was not handled
Arg2: 826a0240, The address that the exception occurred at
Arg3: 978eb9c4, Trap Frame
Arg4: 00000000
```

The reason for the different behaviors on different configurations relates to a mechanism called *system code write protection*. If system code write protection is enabled, the memory manager maps Ntoskrnl.exe, the HAL, and boot drivers using standard physical pages (4 KB on x86 and x64, and 8 KB on IA64). Because the granularity of protection in an image is the standard page size, the memory manager can write-protect code pages so that an attempt to modify them generates an access fault (as seen in the first crash). However, when system code write protection is disabled on systems with more than 2 GB of RAM, the memory manager uses large pages (4 MB on x86, and 16 MB on IA64 and x64) to map Ntoskrnl.exe and the HAL.

If system code write protection is off and crash analysis reports unlikely causes for a crash or you suspect code corruption, you should enable it. Verifying at least one driver with Driver Verifier is the easiest way to enable it. You can also enable it manually by adding a registry value under HKLM\ SYSTEM\CurrentControlSet\Control\Session Manager\Memory Management. You need to specify the amount of RAM at which the memory manager uses large pages instead of standard pages to map Ntoskrnl.exe as an effectively infinite value. You do this by creating a DWORD value called Large-PageMinimum and setting it to 0xFFFFFFFF. You must reboot for the changes to take effect.

Advanced Crash Dump Analysis

The preceding section leverages Driver Verifier to create crashes that the debugger's automated analysis engine can resolve. You might still encounter cases where you cannot get a system to produce easily analyzable crashes, and, if so, you will need to execute manual analysis to try to determine what the problem is. Here are some examples of basic commands that can provide clues during crash analysis. The Debugging Tools for Windows help file provides complete documentation on these and other commands as well as examples of how to use them during crash analysis:

■ Use the *!cpuinfo* command to display a list of processors the system is configured to use.

■ Use the processor ID with the *k* command to display the stack trace of each processor in the system—for example, *1k*. Be sure you recognize each of the modules listed in the stack trace and that you have the most recent versions.

■ Use the *!thread* command to display information about the current thread on each processor. The ~s command can be used with the processor ID to change the current processor (such as ~1s). Look for any pending I/O request packets (explained in the next section).

■ Use the *.time* command to display information about the system time, including when the system crashed and for how long it had been running. A short uptime value can indicate frequent problems.

■ Use the *lm* command with the *k t* option (the *t* flag specifies to display time stamp information—that is, when the file was compiled, not what appears on the file system, which might differ) to list the loaded kernel-mode drivers. Be sure you understand the purpose of any third-party drivers and that you have the most recent versions.

■ Use the *!vm* command to see whether the system has exhausted virtual memory, paged pool, or nonpaged pool. If virtual memory is exhausted, the committed pages will be close to the commit limit, so try to identify a potential memory leak by examining the list of processes to see which one reports high commit usage. If nonpaged pool or paged pool is exhausted (that is, the usage is close to the maximum), see the "Troubleshooting a Pool Leak" experiment in Chapter 10.

- Use the *!process 0 0* debugger command to look at the processes running, and be sure that you understand the purpose of each one. Try disabling or uninstalling unnecessary applications and services.

There are other debugging commands that can prove useful, but more advanced knowledge is required to apply them. The *!irp* command is one of them. The next section shows the use of this command to identify a suspect driver.

Stack Trashes

Stack overruns or stack trashing typically results from a buffer overrun or underrun or when a driver passes a buffer address located on the stack to a lower driver on the device stack, which then performs the work asynchronously.

In the case of a stack overrun or underrun, instead of residing in pool, as you saw with Notmyfault's buffer overrun bug, the target buffer is on the stack of the thread that executes the bug. This type of bug is another one that's difficult to debug because the stack is the foundation for any crash dump analysis.

In the case of passing buffers on the stack to lower drivers, if the lower driver returns to the caller immediately because it used a completion routine to perform the work, instead of returning synchronously, when the completion routine is called, it will use the stack address that was passed previously, which could now correspond to a different state on the caller's stack and result in corruption.

When you run Notmyfault and select Stack Trash, the Myfault driver overruns a buffer it allocates on the kernel stack of the thread that executes it. When Myfault tries to return control to the Ntoskrnl function that was invoked, it reads the return address, which is the address at which it should continue executing, from the stack. The address was corrupted by the stack-buffer overrun, so the thread continues execution at some different address in memory—an address that might not even contain code. An illegal exception and crash occur when the thread executes an illegal CPU instruction or it references invalid memory.

The driver that the crash dump analysis of a stack overrun points the blame at will vary from crash to crash, but the stop code will almost always be KERNEL_MODE_EXCEPTION_NOT_HANDLED (0x8E) on a 32-bit system and KMODE_EXCEPTION_NOT_HANDLED (0x1E) on a 64-bit one. If you execute a verbose analysis, the stack trace looks like this:

```
STACK_TEXT:
9569b6b4 828c108c 0000008e c0000005 00000000 nt!KeBugCheckEx+0x1e
9569badc 8284add6 9569baf8 00000000 9569bb4c nt!KiDispatchException+0x1ac
9569bb44 8284ad8a 00000000 00000000 badb0d00 nt!CommonDispatchException+0x4a
9569bbfc 82843593 853422b0 86b99278 86b99278 nt!Kei386EoiHelper+0x192
00000000 00000000 00000000 00000000 00000000 nt!IofCallDriver+0x63
```

Notice how the call to *IofCallDriver* leads immediately to *Kei386EoiHelper* and into an exception, instead of a driver's IRP dispatch routine. This is consistent with the stack having been corrupted and the IRP dispatch routine causing an exception when attempting to return to its caller by referencing a corrupted return address. Unfortunately, mechanisms like special pool and system code write protection can't catch this type of bug. Instead, you must take some manual analysis steps to determine indirectly which driver was operating at the time of the corruption. One way is to examine the IRPs that are in progress for the thread that was executing at the time of the stack trash. When a thread issues an I/O request, the I/O manager stores a pointer to the outstanding IRP on the IRP list of the ETHREAD structure for the thread. The *!thread* debugger command dumps the IRP list of the target thread. (If you don't specify a thread object address, *!thread* dumps the processor's current thread.) Then you can look at the IRP with the *!irp* command:

```
0: kd> !thread
THREAD 8527fa58  Cid 0d0c.0d10  Teb: 7ffdf000 Win32Thread: fe4ec4f8 RUNNING on processor 0
IRP List:
    86b99278: (0006,0094) Flags: 00060000  Mdl: 00000000
Not impersonating
...

0: kd> !irp 86b99278
Irp is active with 1 stacks 1 is current (= 0x86b992e8)
 No Mdl: No System Buffer: Thread 8527fa58:  Irp stack trace.
    cmd  flg cl Device   File     Completion-Context
>[  e, 0]   5  0 853422b0 85e3aed8 00000000-00000000
             \Driver\MYFAULT
               Args: 00000000 00000000 83360010 00000000
```

The output shows that the IRP's current and only stack location (designated with the ">" prefix) is owned by the Myfault driver. If this were a real crash, the next steps would be to ensure that the driver version installed is the most recent available, install the new version if it isn't, and if it is, to enable Driver Verifier on the driver (with all settings except low memory simulation).

> **Note** Most newer drivers built using the WDK are compiled by default to use the */GS* (Buffer Security Check) compiler flag. When the Buffer Security Check option is enabled, the compiler reserves space before the return address on the stack, which, when the function executes, is filled with a *security cookie*. On function exit, the security cookie is verified. A mismatch indicates that a stack overwrite may have occurred, in which case, the compiler-generated code will call *KeBugCheckEx*, passing the DRIVER_OVERRAN_STACK_BUFFER (0xF7) stop code.

Manually analyzing the stack is often the most powerful technique when dealing with crashes such as these. Typically, this involves dumping the current *stack pointer* register (for example, *esp* and *rsp* on x86 and x64 processors, respectively). However, because the code responsible for crashing the system itself might modify the stack in ways that make analysis difficult, the processor responsible for crashing the system provides a backing store for the current data in the stack, called *KiPreBugcheckStackSaveArea,* which contains a copy of the stack before any code in *KeBugCheckEx* executes.

By using the *dps* (dump pointer with symbols) command in the debugger, you can dump this area (instead of the CPU's stack pointer register) and resolve symbols in an attempt to discover any potential stack traces. In this crash, here's what dumping the stack area eventually revealed on a 32-bit system:

```
0: kd> dps KiPreBugcheckStackSaveArea KiPreBugcheckStackSaveArea+3000
81d7dd20  881fcc44
81d7dd24  98fcf406 myfault+0x406
81d7dd28  badb0d00
```

Although this data was located among many other different functions, it is of special interest because it mentions a function in the Myfault driver, which as we've seen was currently executing an IRP, that doesn't show on the stack. For more information on manual stack analysis, see the Debugging Tools for Windows help file and the additional resources referenced later in this chapter.

Hung or Unresponsive Systems

If a system becomes unresponsive (that is, you are receiving no response to keyboard or mouse input), the mouse freezes, or you can move the mouse but the system doesn't respond to clicks, the system is said to have *hung*. A number of things can cause the system to hang:

- A device driver does not return from its interrupt service (ISR) routine or deferred procedure call (DPC) routine

- A high priority real-time thread preempts the windowing system driver's input threads

- A deadlock (when two threads or processors hold resources each other wants and neither will yield what they have) occurs in kernel mode

You can check for deadlocks by using the Driver Verifier option called *deadlock detection*. Deadlock detection monitors the use of spinlocks, mutexes, and fast mutexes, looking for patterns that could result in a deadlock. (For more information on these and other synchronization primitives, see Chapter 3 in Part 1.) If one is found, Driver Verifier crashes the system with an indication of which driver causes the deadlock. The simplest form of deadlock occurs when two threads hold resources each other thread wants and neither will yield what they have or give up waiting for the one they want. The first step to troubleshooting hung systems is therefore to enable deadlock detection on suspect drivers, then unsigned drivers, and then all drivers, until you get a crash that pinpoints the driver causing the deadlock.

There are two ways to approach a hanging system so that you can apply the manual crash troubleshooting techniques described in this chapter to determine what driver or component is causing the hang: the first is to crash the hung system and hope that you get a dump that you can analyze, and the second is to break into the system with a kernel debugger and analyze the system's activity. Both approaches require prior setup and a reboot. You use the same exploration of system state with both approaches to try to determine the cause of the hang.

To manually crash a hung system, you must first add the DWORD registry value HKLM\SYSTEM\ CurrentControlSet\Services\i8042prt\Parameters\CrashOnCtrlScroll and set it to 1. After rebooting, the i8042 port driver, which is the port driver for PS/2 keyboard input, monitors keystrokes in its

ISR (discussed further in Chapter 3 in Part 1) looking for two presses of the Scroll Lock key while the right Control key is depressed. When the driver sees that sequence, it calls *KeBugCheckEx* with the MANUALLY_INITIATED_CRASH (0xE2) stop code that indicates a manually initiated crash. When the system reboots, open the crash dump file and apply the techniques mentioned earlier to try to determine why the system was hung (for example, determining what thread was running when the system hung, what the kernel stack indicates was happening, and so on). Note that this works for most hung system scenarios, but it won't work if the i8042 port driver's ISR doesn't execute. (The i8042 port driver's ISR won't execute if all processors are hung as a result of their IRQL being higher than the ISR's IRQL, or if corruption of system data structures extends to interrupt-related code or data.)

> **Note** Manually crashing a hung system by using the support provided in the i8042 port driver does not work with USB keyboards. It works with PS/2 keyboards only. See *http://msdn.microsoft.com/en-us/library/windows/hardware/ff545499.aspx* for information about enabling USB keyboard support.

You can also trigger a crash if your hardware has a built-in "crash" button. (Some high-end servers have these embedded on their motherboards or exposed via remote management interfaces.) In this case, the crash is initiated by signaling the nonmaskable interrupt (NMI) pin of the system's motherboard. To enable this, set the registry DWORD value HKLM\SYSTEM\CurrentControlSet\Control\CrashControl\NMICrashDump to 1. Then, when you press the dump switch, an NMI is delivered to the system and the kernel's NMI interrupt handler calls *KeBugCheckEx*. This works in more cases than the i8042 port driver mechanism because the NMI IRQL is always higher than that of the i8042 port driver interrupt. See *http://support.microsoft.com/kb/927069* for more information.

If you are unable to manually generate a crash dump, you can attempt to break into the hung system by first making the system boot into debugging mode. You do this in one of two ways. You can press the F8 key during the boot and select Debugging Mode, or you can create a debugging-mode boot option in the BCD by copying an existing boot entry and adding the *debug* option. When using the F8 approach, the system will use the default connection (serial port COM1 and 115200 baud), but you can use the F10 key to display the Edit Boot Options screen to edit debug-related boot options. With the *debug* option enabled, you must also configure the connection mechanism to be used between the host system running the kernel debugger and the target system booting in debugging mode and then configure the transport parameters appropriately for the connection type. The three connection types are a null modem cable using a serial port, an IEEE 1394 (FireWire) cable using 1394 ports on each system, or a USB 2.0 host-to-host dongle using USB ports on each system. For details on configuring the host and target system for kernel debugging, see the Debugging Tools for Windows help file and the "Attaching a Kernel Debugger" experiment later in the chapter.

When booting in debugging mode, the system loads the kernel debugger at boot time and makes it ready for a connection from a kernel debugger running on a different computer connected through a serial cable, IEEE 1394 cable, or USB 2.0 host-to-host dongle. Note that the kernel debugger's presence does not affect performance. When the system hangs, run the WinDbg or Kd debugger on the connected system, establish a kernel debugging connection, and break into the hung system. This approach will not work if interrupts are disabled or the kernel debugger has become corrupted.

Note Booting a system in debugging mode does not affect performance if it's not connected to another system. Also, if a system booted in debugging mode is configured to automatically reboot after a crash, it will not wait for a connection from another system if a debugger isn't already connected.

Instead of leaving the system in its halted state while you perform analysis, you can also use the debugger *.dump* command to create a crash dump file on the host debugger machine. Then you can reboot the hung system and analyze the crash dump offline (or submit it to Microsoft). Note that this can take a long time if you are connected using a serial null modem cable or USB 2.0 connection (versus a higher speed 1394 connection), so you might want to just capture a minidump using the *.dump /m* command. Alternatively, if the target machine is capable of writing a crash dump, you can force it to do so by issuing the *.crash* command from the debugger. This will cause the target machine to create a dump on its local hard drive that you can examine after the system reboots.

EXPERIMENT: Dumping Hyper-V Guests Using LiveKd

The LiveKd tool, in addition to allowing the use of the *.dump* command on a live system, also permits a crash dump of a running Hyper-V guest to be created. To query the list of running guests on a Hyper-V host, the *–hvl* option can be specified. LiveKd will display both the name of the guest virtual machine and its partition GUID:

```
C:\Users\Administrator>livekd -hvl

LiveKd v5.2 - Execute kd/windbg on a live system
Sysinternals - www.sysinternals.com
Copyright (C) 2000-2012 Mark Russinovich and Ken Johnson

Partition GUID                          Name
7EB669F2-EB6E-405D-94EA-21CB2ABD0A52    Windows Server 2008
D57D7601-D154-473B-847D-C3C77413AD0B    Windows Server 2003
```

Once the name or the partition GUID of the target Hyper-V guest has been obtained, it can be passed to LiveKd using the *–hv* option, along with the *–o* switch, specifying where to write the crash dump file. LiveKd will write a complete dump, which requires enough free disk space on the destination volume equal to the amount of memory assigned to the virtual machine. Because the Hyper-V guest is still running, LiveKd might run into situations in which data structures are in the middle of being changed by the system and are inconsistent. To prevent such an event from occurring, LiveKd is able to pause the Hyper-V guest before writing the crash dump by specifying the *–p* option.

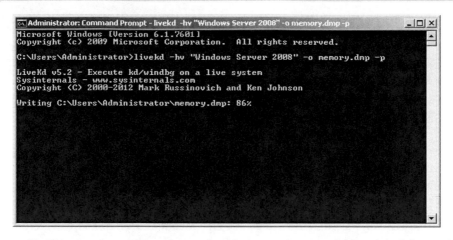

LiveKd takes the additional step of writing a comment to the header of the crash dump file, specifying that a live system view was taken—notifying the user performing analysis of any possible inconsistencies. After LiveKd finishes writing the crash dump file, the file can then be analyzed using any of the kernel debuggers and techniques described earlier in the chapter. If the Hyper-V guest was previously in the running state, LiveKd will automatically resume the target system.

You can cause a hang by running Notmyfault and selecting the Hang With DPC option. This causes the Myfault driver to queue a DPC on each processor of the system that executes an infinite loop. Because the IRQL of the processor while executing DPC functions is DPC/dispatch level, the keyboard ISR will respond to the special keyboard crashing sequence.

Once you've broken into a hung system or loaded a manually generated dump from a hung system into a debugger, you should execute the *!analyze* command with the *–hang* option. This causes the debugger to examine the locks on the system and try to determine whether there's a deadlock and, if so, what driver or drivers are involved. However, for a hang like the one that Notmyfault's Hang With DPC option generates, the *!analyze* analysis command will report nothing useful.

If the *!analyze* command doesn't pinpoint the problem, execute *!thread* and *!process* in each of the dump's CPU contexts to see what each processor is doing. (Switch CPU contexts with the ~s command—for example, use ~1s to switch to processor 1's context.) If a thread has hung the system by executing in an infinite loop at an IRQL of DPC/dispatch level or higher, you'll see the driver module in which it has become stuck in the stack trace of the *!thread* command. The stack trace of the crash dump you get when you crash a system experiencing the Notmyfault hang bug looks like this:

```
STACK_TEXT:
8078ae30 8cb49160 000000e2 00000000 00000000 nt!KeBugCheckEx+0x1e
8078ae60 8cb49768 00527658 010001c6 00000000 i8042prt!I8xProcessCrashDump+0x251
8078aeac 8287c7ad 851c8780 855275a0 8078aed8 i8042prt!I8042KeyboardInterruptService+0x2ce
8078aeac 91d924ca 851c8780 855275a0 8078aed8 nt!KiInterruptDispatch+0x6d
WARNING: Stack unwind information not available. Following frames may be wrong.
8078afa4 828a5218 82966d20 86659780 00000000 myfault+0x4ca
...
```

The top few lines of the stack trace reference the routines that execute when you type the i8042 port driver's crash key sequence. The presence of the Myfault driver indicates that it might be responsible for the hang. Another command that might be revealing is *!locks*, which dumps the status of all executive resource locks. By default, the command lists only resources that are under *contention*, which means that they are both owned and have at least one thread waiting to acquire them. Examine the thread stacks of the owners with the *!thread* command to see what driver they might be executing in. Sometimes you will find that the owner of one of the locks is waiting for an IRP to complete (a list of IRPs related to a thread is displayed in the *!thread* output). In these cases it is very hard to tell why an IRP is not making forward progress. (IRPs are usually queued to privately managed driver queues before they are completed). One thing you can do is examine the IRP with the *!irp* command and find the driver that pended the IRP (it will have the word "pending" displayed in its stack location from the *!irp* output). Once you have the driver name, you can use the *!stacks* command to look for other threads that the driver might be running on, which often provides clues about what the lock-owning driver is doing. Much of the time you will find the driver is deadlocked or waiting on some other resource that is blocked waiting for the driver.

When There Is No Crash Dump

In this section, we'll address how to troubleshoot systems that for some reason are not recording a crash dump. One reason why a crash dump might not be recorded is if no paging file is configured to hold the dump. This can easily be remedied by creating a paging file of the required size. A second reason why there might not be a crash dump recorded is because the kernel code and data structures needed to write the crash dump have been corrupted at the time of the crash. As described earlier, this data is captured when the system boots, and if the integrity verification check made at the time of the crash does not match, the system does not even attempt to save the crash dump (so as not to risk corrupting data on the disk). So in this case, you need to catch the system as it crashes and then try to determine the reason for the crash.

Another reason occurs when the disk subsystem for the system disk is not able to process disk write requests (a condition that might have triggered the system failure itself). One such condition would be a hardware failure in the disk controller or maybe a cabling issue near the hard disk.

Yet another possibility occurs when the system has drivers that have registered callbacks that are invoked before the crash dump is written. When the driver callbacks are called, they might incorrectly access data structures located in paged memory (for example), which will lead to a second crash. In the case of a crash inside of a secondary dump callback, the system should still have a valid crash dump file but any secondary crash dump data may be missing or incomplete.

One simple option is to turn off the Automatically Restart option in the Startup And Recovery settings so that if the system crashes, you can examine the blue screen on the console. However, only the most straightforward crashes can be solved from just the blue-screen text.

To perform more in-depth analysis, you need to use the kernel debugger to look at the system at the time of the crash. This can be done by booting the system in debugging mode, which is described in the previous section. When a system is booted in debugging mode (with a debugger attached) and crashes, instead of painting the blue screen and attempting to record the dump, it will break into the host kernel debugger. In this way, you can see the reason for the crash and perhaps perform some basic analysis using the kernel debugger commands described earlier. As mentioned in the previous section, you can use the *.dump* command in the debugger to save a copy of the crashed system's memory space for later debugging, thus allowing you to reboot the crashed system and debug the problem offline.

EXPERIMENT: Attaching a Kernel Debugger

Connecting a kernel debugger to a live, running system requires two computers—a target and a host. The target, the system being debugged, must be booted in debugging mode by pressing F8 during the boot process and selecting Debugging Mode or by modifying the boot configuration database from within an elevated command prompt using the BCDEdit tool:

```
bcdedit /debug on
```

The system will use the default settings of serial port COM1 and baud rate 115200 if no other settings are specified. On the host system—the computer running the debugger—the symbol path option needs to be set so that the debugger can locate the required symbol files. One option for configuring the symbol path is to use the systemwide environment variable _NT_SYMBOL_PATH. Setting the systemwide variable allows for other applications, such as Process Explorer and Process Monitor, to take advantage of the symbol path without requiring additional configuration. The symbol path can be set via an elevated command prompt by using the following command:

```
setx _NT_SYMBOL_PATH srv*c:\symbols*http://msdl.microsoft.com/download/symbols /m
```

The */m* switch specifies that the variable should be set system wide. Without it, the default option is to set it only for the current user. One final step that's required is to configure the transport layer. If two physical computers are being used, this is done by connecting the serial ports of the computers to each other by using a null modem cable.

In the following example, a Hyper-V guest has been selected as the target. Hyper-V (as is the case with other virtual-machine technologies) supports the option of configuring a virtual serial port to communicate with a physical computer through a named pipe. If you are using multiple named pipes, each pipe name should be unique to avoid a conflict.

Before restarting the target system, the debugger on the host needs to be configured to specify the named pipe that should be used as a transport. Both the *resets=0* and *reconnect* options specified in the following command are required when connecting to Hyper-V guests. (For other virtual-machine technologies, refer to the Debugging Tools for Windows help file.) The command shown here will start a debugging session on a virtual machine, which is running on the same physical computer as the debugger:

```
windbg -k com:pipe,port=\\.\pipe\debugger,resets=0,reconnect
```

The WinDbg command window should appear with a prompt that the debugger is waiting to connect:

```
Microsoft (R) Windows Debugger Version 6.12.0002.633 AMD64
Copyright (c) Microsoft Corporation. All rights reserved.

Waiting for pipe \\.\pipe\debugger
Waiting to reconnect...
```

At this point, the target system should be restarted. After a brief period, the two systems should connect via the named pipe. The following output confirms that the host is now connected to the target system through the kernel debugger:

```
Connected to Windows 7 7601 x86 compatible target at
    (Mon Mar 12 19:34:01.295 2012 (UTC - 7:00)), ptr64 FALSE
Kernel Debugger connection established.
Symbol search path is: srv*c:\symbols*http://msdl.microsoft.com/download/symbols
```

```
Executable search path is:
Windows 7 Kernel Version 7601 (Service Pack 1) MP (1 procs) Free x86 compatible
Built by: 7601.17514.x86fre.win7sp1_rtm.101119-1850
Machine Name:
Kernel base = 0x82813000 PsLoadedModuleList = 0x8295d850
System Uptime: not available
```

To verify that the system will break into the debugger when a crash occurs, the /bugcheck option of Notmyfault can be used to crash the system. As is the case with other Notmyfault functions, a control code is sent to the Myfault.sys driver. The control code specifies that the *KeBugCheckEx* routine should be called, passing it a reference to the stop code. Here is an example of using a user-defined stop code:

```
notmyfault /bugcheck 0xdeaddead
```

When a debugger is connected to the system and a crash occurs, control is given to the debugger before painting the blue screen and any bugcheck callbacks have been called. This allows for further analysis to be performed or for breakpoints to be set:

```
*** Fatal System Error: 0xdeaddead
                        (0x00000000,0x00000000,0x00000000,0x00000000)

Break instruction exception - code 80000003 (first chance)

A fatal system error has occurred.
Debugger entered on first try; Bugcheck callbacks have not been invoked.

A fatal system error has occurred.
...
```

The operating system code and data structures that handle processor exceptions can become corrupted such that a series of recursive faults occur. One example of this would be if the operating system trap handler got corrupted and caused a page fault. This would invoke the page fault handler, which would fault again, and so on. If such a situation occurred, the system would be hopelessly stuck. To prevent such a situation from occurring, CPUs have a built-in recursive fault protection mechanism, which sets a hard limit on the depth of a recursive fault. On most x86 processors, a fault can nest to two levels deep. When the third recursive fault occurs, the processor resets itself and the machine reboots. This is called a *triple fault*. This can happen when there's a faulty hardware component as well. Even a kernel debugger won't be invoked in a triple fault situation. However, sometimes the mere fact that the kernel debugger doesn't activate can confirm that there's a problem with newly added hardware or drivers.

Note You can use the kernel debugger to trigger a triple fault on a machine by setting a breakpoint on the kernel debugger dispatch routine *KiDispatchException*. This happens because the exception dispatcher now causes a breakpoint exception, which invokes the exception dispatcher, and so on.

Analysis of Common Stop Codes

The following sections provide a walkthrough of common stop codes reported to Microsoft's Online Crash Analysis service. For each stop code presented, the analysis begins with the verbose output of the analysis engine's *!analyze –v* command.

The reasons for each type of crash may vary, as will the commands and techniques used to analyze them. For more information on analyzing common stop codes, see the Debugging Tools for Windows help file and the additional resources referenced later in this chapter.

0xD1 - DRIVER_IRQL_NOT_LESS_OR_EQUAL

The DRIVER_IRQL_NOT_LESS_OR_EQUAL (0xD1) stop code is the result of a device driver attempting to access a pageable or invalid address at an interrupt request level that is too high. This stop code is usually the result of device drivers using improper addresses.

```
DRIVER_IRQL_NOT_LESS_OR_EQUAL (d1)
An attempt was made to access a pageable (or completely invalid) address at an
interrupt request level (IRQL) that is too high.  This is usually
caused by drivers using improper addresses.
If kernel debugger is available get stack backtrace.
Arguments:
Arg1: a0a91660, memory referenced
Arg2: 00000002, IRQL
Arg3: 00000000, value 0 = read operation, 1 = write operation
Arg4: 85701579, address which referenced memory
```

In analyzing a stop DRIVER_IRQL_NOT_LESS_OR_EQUAL (0xD1), viewing the stack trace of the thread that was executing at the time of the crash will reveal the device driver that was referencing pageable or invalid memory:

```
STACK_TEXT:
8b94bb3c 85701579 badb0d00 84f40600 a0a4f660 nt!KiTrap0E+0x2cf
WARNING: Stack unwind information not available. Following frames may be wrong.
8b94bbb8 85701849 86ffe5d8 8b94bbfc 857018ac myfault+0x579
8b94bbc4 857018ac 850d6890 00000001 00000000 myfault+0x849
8b94bbfc 8283e593 86efaa98 86ffe5d8 86ffe5d8 myfault+0x8ac
8b94bc14 82a3299f 850d6890 86ffe5d8 86ffe648 nt!IofCallDriver+0x63
8b94bc34 82a35b71 86efaa98 850d6890 00000000 nt!IopSynchronousServiceTail+0x1f8
8b94bcd0 82a7c3f4 86efaa98 86ffe5d8 00000000 nt!IopXxxControlFile+0x6aa
8b94bd04 828451ea 000000b8 00000000 00000000 nt!NtDeviceIoControlFile+0x2a
8b94bd04 776f70b4 000000b8 00000000 00000000 nt!KiFastCallEntry+0x12a
0012f994 00000000 00000000 00000000 00000000 0x776f70b4
```

The debugger's analysis engine is able to locate and display the trap frame that was created when the exception that caused the crash occurred. The trap frame contains the kernel thread's machine state, which includes the register values of the CPU that the thread was executing on. The instruction pointer register (*eip* on an x86 processor and *rip* on an x64) contains the address of the instruction that, when executed, generated the trap. The lower line of the output from the *.trap* command in the debugger lists the address of the instruction that caused the crash, its binary code, assembly language mnemonic, and assembly language details:

```
TRAP_FRAME:  8b94bb3c -- (.trap 0xffffffff8b94bb3c)
ErrCode = 00000000
eax=a0a91660 ebx=86ffe5f0 ecx=00200073 edx=84f40600 esi=a0a4f660 edi=00000000
eip=85701579 esp=8b94bbb0 ebp=8b94bbb8 iopl=0         nv up ei ng nz na pe nc
cs=0008  ss=0010  ds=0023  es=0023  fs=0030  gs=0000          efl=00010286
myfault+0x579:
85701579 8b08           mov     ecx,dword ptr [eax]  ds:0023:a0a91660=????????
```

The first bugcheck parameter of a stop DRIVER_IRQL_NOT_LESS_OR_EQUAL (0xD1) points to the memory address that was being referenced by the device driver. If the debugger is unable to display an address (because it is invalid or not present in the dump file), a series of question marks is displayed. In the trap frame just shown, the debugger has been unable to resolve the address of the memory referenced by the device driver.

Viewing the output of the *!pte* command for the address that was referenced confirms that the *valid* bit for the page table entry is not set, which indicates that the address does not map to a page in physical memory:

```
0: kd> !pte a0a91660
                      VA a0a91660
PDE at C0602828          PTE at C0505488
contains 0000000010BE6863  contains 00007A1800000000
pfn 10be6     ---DA--KWEV   not valid
                           PageFile:  0
                           Offset:  7a18
                           Protect:  0
```

0x8E - KERNEL_MODE_EXCEPTION_NOT_HANDLED

The KERNEL_MODE_EXCEPTION_NOT_HANDLED (0x8E) stop message is caused by a kernel-mode thread generating an exception that was not handled. The first bugcheck parameter identifies the exception code for which a handler was not found. Common exception codes are STATUS_BREAKPOINT (0x80000003) and STATUS_ACCESS_VIOLATION (0xC0000005).

```
KERNEL_MODE_EXCEPTION_NOT_HANDLED (8e)
This is a very common bugcheck.  Usually the exception address pinpoints
the driver/function that caused the problem.  Always note this address
as well as the link date of the driver/image that contains this address.
Some common problems are exception code 0x80000003.  This means a
hard coded breakpoint or assertion was hit, but this system was booted
/NODEBUG.  This is not supposed to happen as developers should never have
hardcoded breakpoints in retail code, but ...
If this happens, make sure a debugger gets connected, and the
system is booted /DEBUG.  This will let us see why this breakpoint is
happening.Arguments:
Arg1: 80000003, The exception code that was not handled
Arg2: 92c70a78, The address that the exception occurred at
Arg3: 9444fb4c, Trap Frame
Arg4: 00000000
```

Viewing the stack trace of the crashed thread can give an indication of the driver or function that caused the problem. If there's nothing that looks suspicious, viewing the address where the exception occurred should provide more details. The stack trace from a crashed system looks like this:

```
STACK_TEXT:
9444f6b4 828ba08c 0000008e 80000003 92c70a78 nt!KeBugCheckEx+0x1e
9444fadc 82843dd6 9444faf8 00000000 9444fb4c nt!KiDispatchException+0x1ac
9444fb44 82844678 9444fbc4 92c70a79 badb0d00 nt!CommonDispatchException+0x4a
9444fb44 92c70a79 9444fbc4 92c70a79 badb0d00 nt!KiTrap03+0xb8
WARNING: Stack unwind information not available. Following frames may be wrong.
9444fbc4 92c70b1c 8730f980 00000001 00000000 myfault+0xa79
9444fbfc 8283c593 87314a08 87279950 87279950 myfault+0xb1c
9444fc14 82a3099f 8730f980 87279950 872799c0 nt!IofCallDriver+0x63
9444fc34 82a33b71 87314a08 8730f980 00000000 nt!IopSynchronousServiceTail+0x1f8
9444fcd0 82a7a3f4 87314a08 87279950 00000000 nt!IopXxxControlFile+0x6aa
9444fd04 828431ea 000000c4 00000000 00000000 nt!NtDeviceIoControlFile+0x2a
9444fd04 772c70b4 000000c4 00000000 00000000 nt!KiFastCallEntry+0x12a
0012f2ac 00000000 00000000 00000000 00000000 0x772c70b4
```

The second bugcheck parameter contains the location in memory that the exception occurred at. In the case of a STATUS_BREAKPOINT exception, unassembling the address will confirm the presence of a breakpoint instruction. The processor instruction INT 3 is called the *trap to debugger* instruction. An INT 3 instruction, when executed, causes the system to call the kernel's debugger exception handler. If a debugger is attached to the computer, the system will break in.

```
0: kd> u 92c70a78
myfault+0xa78:
92c70a78 cc              int     3
...
```

Breakpoints shouldn't usually appear in retail versions of device drivers. Using the *lm* command, it's sometimes possible to determine which environment a device driver was targeted for. When compiling a driver for release (and unless overridden by the developer), a flag is set indicating the release type. When viewing the *File flags* property, the presence of the word *Debug* indicates that the driver was built using a checked (or debug) environment:

```
0: kd> lm kv m myfault
start    end           module name
92c70000 92c71880   myfault    (no symbols)
    Loaded symbol image file: myfault.sys
    Image path: \??\C:\Windows\system32\drivers\myfault.sys
    Image name: myfault.sys
    Timestamp:        Sat Apr 07 09:34:40 2012 (4F806CA0)
    CheckSum:         00004227
    ImageSize:        00001880
    File version:     4.0.0.0
    Product version:  4.0.0.0
    File flags:       1 (Mask 3F) Debug
    File OS:          40004 NT Win32
...
```

A breakpoint in a debug version of a driver could also indicate the failure of an ASSERT macro. If a kernel debugger is attached to the system, a message would be displayed followed by a prompt asking the user what to do about the assertion failure.

0x7F - UNEXPECTED_KERNEL_MODE_TRAP

An UNEXPECTED_KERNEL_MODE_TRAP (0x7F) stop code indicates that the CPU generated a trap that the Windows kernel failed to handle. The trap could be the result of a *bound trap* (which the kernel is not permitted to catch) or a *double fault* (a fault that occurs while the kernel is processing an earlier fault). The first bugcheck parameter defines the type of trap.

```
UNEXPECTED_KERNEL_MODE_TRAP (7f)
This means a trap occurred in kernel mode, and it's a trap of a kind
that the kernel isn't allowed to have/catch (bound trap) or that
is always instant death (double fault).  The first number in the
bugcheck params is the number of the trap (8 = double fault, etc)
Consult an Intel x86 family manual to learn more about what these
traps are. Here is a *portion* of those codes:
If kv shows a taskGate
        use .tss on the part before the colon, then kv.
Else if kv shows a trapframe
        use .trap on that value
Else
        .trap on the appropriate frame will show where the trap was taken
        (on x86, this will be the ebp that goes with the procedure KiTrap)
Endif
kb will then show the corrected stack.
Arguments:
Arg1: 00000008, EXCEPTION_DOUBLE_FAULT
Arg2: 801db000
Arg3: 00000000
Arg4: 00000000
```

Most traps in this category are the result of faulty or failed hardware. If you recently added new hardware to the computer, try removing it to see whether the problem no longer occurs. Remove any existing hardware that may have failed and have it replaced. It's also recommended to run any manufacturer-supplied hardware-diagnostic tools to determine which components may have failed.

There are, however, certain traps that are the result of software errors. Viewing the trap frame that was generated or the task gate (depending on the type of trap) displays the instruction that generated the trap:

```
TSS:  00000028 -- (.tss 0x28)
eax=8336001c ebx=86d57388 ecx=83360044 edx=00000000 esi=86d57388 edi=00000000
eip=96890918 esp=92985000 ebp=92987bc4 iopl=0         nv up ei pl zr na pe nc
cs=0008  ss=0010  ds=0023  es=0023  fs=0030  gs=0000             efl=00010246
myfault+0x918:
96890918 e8f9ffffff     call    myfault+0x916 (96890916)
```

The type of trap described earlier, an EXCEPTION_DOUBLE_FAULT, is usually the result of one of two common causes—a kernel stack overflow or faulty hardware. A kernel stack overflow occurs when a kernel thread's guard page is hit, as a result of having exhausted all of the current thread's stack allocation. The kernel attempts to push a trap frame onto the stack—for which no more space exists—causing a double fault.

Using the *!thread* command to verify the stack limits of the thread that was executing confirms whether the double fault was caused by a kernel stack overflow:

```
0: kd> !thread
THREAD 850e3918  Cid 0fb8.0fbc  Teb: 7ffde000 Win32Thread: fe4f0dd8 RUNNING on processor 0
IRP List:
    86d57370: (0006,0094) Flags: 00060000  Mdl: 00000000
Not impersonating
DeviceMap                8fa3b8e8
Owning Process           85100670       Image:          NotMyfault.exe
Attached Process         N/A            Image:          N/A
Wait Start TickCount     21664          Ticks: 0
Context Switch Count     461
UserTime                 00:00:00.000
KernelTime               00:00:00.046
Win32 Start Address 0x00fe27ff
Stack Init 92987fd0 Current 92987af8 Base 92988000 Limit 92985000 Call 0
Priority 12 BasePriority 8 UnusualBoost 0 ForegroundBoost 2 IoPriority 2 PagePriority 5
ChildEBP RetAddr  Args to Child
00000000 96890918 00000000 00000000 00000000 nt!KiTrap08+0x75 (FPO: TSS 28:0)
WARNING: Stack unwind information not available. Following frames may be wrong.
92987bc4 96890b1c 87015038 00000001 00000000 myfault+0x918
92987bfc 82845593 85154158 86d57370 86d57370 myfault+0xb1c
92987c14 82a3999f 87015038 86d57370 86d573e0 nt!IofCallDriver+0x63
92987c34 82a3cb71 85154158 87015038 00000000 nt!IopSynchronousServiceTail+0x1f8
92987cd0 82a833f4 85154158 86d57370 00000000 nt!IopXxxControlFile+0x6aa
92987d04 8284c1ea 000000c4 00000000 00000000 nt!NtDeviceIoControlFile+0x2a
92987d04 779a70b4 000000c4 00000000 00000000 nt!KiFastCallEntry+0x12a (FPO: [0,3]
    TrapFrame @ 92987d34)
0012f424 00000000 00000000 00000000 00000000 0x779a70b4
```

The two values of interest are the stack base and the stack limit. Comparing the value of the stack limit with the value stored in the stack pointer register (*esp* in this case) of the task state segment shown earlier confirms that the lower limit of the stack has been reached. (Both locations contain the same value.)

To understand what component has used all of the kernel thread's stack allocation requires the two values obtained earlier—the stack base and the stack limit. Using the *dps* command with both values displays the thread's stack, using symbols to resolve any function names:

```
0: kd> dps 92985000 92988000
92985000  9689091d myfault+0x91d
92985004  9689091d myfault+0x91d
92985008  9689091d myfault+0x91d
...
```

In this output, a repeating address is shown for the Myfault.sys driver. This is consistent with a device driver that is recursively calling into itself. Each call to a function pushes the return address onto the stack—growing the stack and contributing to the thread's overall stack limit. The return address is popped off the stack only when the function returns. In the case of a driver or function recursively calling itself, each function called never returns.

0xC5 - DRIVER_CORRUPTED_EXPOOL

Diagnosing the cause of pool corruption can be difficult, if not virtually impossible, without the use of additional tools. The recommended course of action for troubleshooting any type of pool corruption issue is to enable the special pool option of Driver Verifier against any new or suspect drivers. Before you enable Driver Verifier, spending a few extra minutes analyzing the crash may yield some interesting results.

The cause of a DRIVER_CORRUPTED_EXPOOL (0xC5) stop code is the result of an attempt to access a pageable or invalid address at an IRQL that is too high. The stop code originates from the kernel as a stop IRQL_NOT_LESS_OR_EQUAL (0xA). Inside the kernel's *KeBugCheck2* function (for which *KeBugCheckEx* is just a stub), the system checks the value of the stop code. If the stop code's value is equal to IRQL_NOT_LESS_OR_EQUAL (0xA), the system queries the fourth bugcheck parameter, which is the address that referenced the memory that led to the crash. If the address lies between the regions of memory that contain the Windows executive's pool functions, the system changes the stop code to DRIVER_CORRUPTED_EXPOOL (0xC5). The reason for modifying the stop code is to highlight that it's not the fault of the pool routines, but rather that one of the pool structures they manage has been corrupted.

```
DRIVER_CORRUPTED_EXPOOL (c5)
An attempt was made to access a pageable (or completely invalid) address at an
interrupt request level (IRQL) that is too high.  This is
caused by drivers that have corrupted the system pool.  Run the driver
verifier against any new (or suspect) drivers, and if that doesn't turn up
the culprit, then use gflags to enable special pool.
Arguments:
Arg1: 4f4f4f53, memory referenced
Arg2: 00000002, IRQL
Arg3: 00000000, value 0 = read operation, 1 = write operation
Arg4: 829234a7, address which referenced memory
```

In the case of pool corruption, a stack trace almost always points to Ntoskrnl or another device driver as being the likely cause of the crash. In the following example, the stack trace of the thread that was executing when the system crashed lists only Windows operating system functions:

```
STACK_TEXT:
8b8e3554 829234a7 badb0d00 00000000 91470d90 nt!KiTrap0E+0x2cf
8b8e3610 8288d2c6 00000000 00000280 76615358 nt!ExAllocatePoolWithTag+0x49d
8b8e3620 8288d19d 00000001 00000053 8b8e38a8 nt!KeAllocateXStateContext+0x25
8b8e3644 8288d6b5 00000003 00000000 8b8e37b4 nt!KeSaveExtendedProcessorState+0x104
8b8e3658 9139b443 8b8e37b4 fe7b8010 8288d038 nt!KeSaveFloatingPointState+0x14
8b8e3864 9139bfdb fe8af408 ffbbd540 00000000 win32k!EngAlphaBlend+0x230
8b8e38d0 9139c394 fe7b8010 fe989010 fe1c0010 win32k!SURFREFDC::vUnlock+0x1e5
8b8e3974 913a4a2f fe7b8010 fe989010 00000000 win32k!SURFREFDC::vUnlock+0x59e
8b8e39d4 913a4981 fe7b8010 fe989010 00000000 win32k!EngNineGrid+0x6e
```

```
8b8e3a34 913a4847 fe7b8010 fe989010 00000000 win32k!EngDrawStream+0x109
8b8e3aa8 913a13a3 8b8e3ba4 00000000 fe989000 win32k!NtGdiDrawStreamInternal+0x232
8b8e3bd4 913a0e09 3a010231 00000000 fe9ef140 win32k!GreDrawStream+0x557
8b8e3d20 828401ea 3a010231 00000060 0012f628 win32k!NtGdiDrawStream+0x8c
8b8e3d20 774570b4 3a010231 00000060 0012f628 nt!KiFastCallEntry+0x12a
0012f49c 75c973a5 75c9738f 3a010231 00000060 ntdll!KiFastSystemCallRet
0012f4a0 75c9738f 3a010231 00000060 0012f628 GDI32!NtGdiDrawStream+0xc
0012f5a4 74243efa 3a010231 00000060 0012f628 GDI32!GdiDrawStream+0x432
```

The trap frame that was generated when the attempt to access pageable or invalid memory was made displays the processor instruction that was executed and the register values of the CPU the thread was executing on. The debugger, with the assistance of the symbol file for the kernel image, is able to display the name of the function that crashed, using the instruction pointer as a reference:

```
TRAP_FRAME:  8b8e3554 -- (.trap 0xffffffff8b8e3554)
eax=8b8e35f8 ebx=82939940 ecx=4f4f4f4f edx=00000000 esi=82939da8 edi=82939944
eip=829234a7 esp=8b8e35c8 ebp=8b8e3610 iopl=0         ov up ei ng nz na po cy
cs=0008  ss=0010  ds=0023  es=0023  fs=0030  gs=0000              efl=00010a83
nt!ExAllocatePoolWithTag+0x49d:
829234a7 8b4104          mov     eax,dword ptr [ecx+4] ds:0023:4f4f4f53=????????
```

As with previous examples, the series of question marks is used to represent invalid addresses that were unable to be displayed by the debugger. In the case of the preceding instruction, the processor read the address stored in the *ecx* register, added a value of four to it, and then attempted to reference the memory pointed to by that address (for storage into the *eax* register). The resulting address to be fetched was invalid, causing an exception to be raised by the processor.

To understand why the invalid value was stored in the *ecx* register, analyzing the set of instructions that executed prior to the crash may give an indication. The following output shows the results of unassembling the instruction stream of the crashed thread, backward from the current instruction pointer:

```
0: kd> ub 829234a7
nt!ExAllocatePoolWithTag+0x479:
...
829234a5 8b0e            mov     ecx,dword ptr [esi]
```

Analysis reveals that the address in the *ecx* register was written to by an instruction that read the value pointed to by the *esi* register. Using the *dc* command with the address stored in the *esi* register of the trap frame shows from where the value *4f4f4f4f* originated. What is of interest in the output of the command is that each of the addresses listed appears as a pair and that the first value—the one that contains the invalid address—doesn't match the value adjacent to it:

```
0: kd> dc 82939da8
82939da8  4f4f4f4f 85045810 82939db0 82939db0  OOOO.X..........
82939db8  82939db8 82939db8 86f749f8 86f749f8  .........I...I..
82939dc8  82939dc8 82939dc8 82939dd0 82939dd0  ...............
82939dd8  82939dd8 82939dd8 82939de0 82939de0  ...............
82939de8  82939de8 82939de8 82939df0 82939df0  ...............
...
```

Following the suspicion that these values are address pairs and that the first value is invalid, displaying the address next to the corrupted value leads toward determining the cause of the corruption. The value *4f4f4f4f* is *OOOO* in ASCII, which is apparent in the output shown here:

```
0: kd> dc 85045810
85045810  4f4f4f4f 4f4f4f4f 4f4f4f4f 4f4f4f4f  OOOOOOOOOOOOOOOO
85045820  4f4f4f4f 4f4f4f4f 4f4f4f4f 4f4f4f4f  OOOOOOOOOOOOOOOO
85045830  46524556 00574f4c 00000000 00000000  VERFLOW.........
85045840  00000000 00000000 00000000 00000000  ................
85045850  00000000 00000000 00000000 00000000  ................
...
```

Checking the pool allocation with the *!pool* command confirms that the allocation, along with its pool headers, have been corrupted:

```
0: kd> !pool 85045810
Pool page 85045810 region is Nonpaged pool
 85045000 size:  808 previous size:   0 (Allocated) None
85045808 is not a valid large pool allocation, checking large session pool...
85045808 is freed (or corrupt) pool
Bad previous allocation size @85045808, last size was 101
```

It's important to note that although corruption has been identified, it may or may not have directly caused the crash currently being analyzed. Any pool corruption that has been discovered requires further investigation. Pool corruption left undiagnosed risks further crashes to the system or corruption of data stored on disk.

Of further interest in the output of the corrupted pool allocation is a reference to the string *OVERFLOW*. Using the *!for_each_module* command, it's possible to search each loaded module for any occurrences of the suspect string. The following debugger command displays the name of any loaded drivers that contain a match for the search phrase:

```
0: kd> !for_each_module .foreach (address {s -[1]a @#Base @#End "OVERFLOW"}) {lm 1m a address}
BTHUSB
CLASSPNP
CLASSPNP
rfcomm
rfcomm
rfcomm
...
myfault
```

Further analysis of a crash dump that appears at first to be virtually impossible to diagnose has narrowed down the list of suspect drivers. The next step would be to enable the special pool option of Driver Verifier with the device drivers listed.

Hardware Malfunctions

Another type of stop message is the hardware malfunction screen. This type of screen is displayed when the processor detects a hardware condition. Figure 14-10 shows a sample hardware malfunction screen. Depending on the type of condition that generated the hardware malfunction, the system might display additional information indicating the cause of the error. When displaying the hardware malfunction screen, the system ignores the AutoReboot value of the HKLM\SYSTEM\CurrentControl-Set\Control\CrashControl registry key and will display the screen indefinitely.

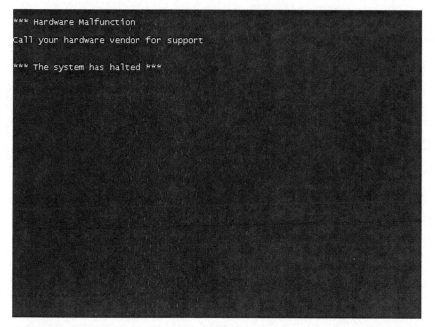

FIGURE 14-10 Example of a hardware malfunction screen

As you should with any stop messages that are suspected to be caused by hardware failures, run any manufacturer-supplied hardware-diagnostic tools to determine which components, if any, may have failed. If you recently added new hardware to the computer, try removing it to see whether the problem no longer occurs. Remove any existing hardware that may have failed, and have it replaced.

Signaling the nonmaskable interrupt (NMI) pin of the system's motherboard when the HKLM\SYSTEM\CurrentControlSet\Control\CrashControl\NMICrashDump registry value isn't set will also generate a hardware malfunction screen. If the intention was to generate a manual crash dump using an NMI button for offline analysis, verify that the NMICrashDump value is configured correctly.

EXPERIMENT: The Blue Screen Screen Saver

A great way to remind yourself of what a blue screen looks like or to fool your office workers and friends is to run the Sysinternals Blue Screen screen saver from Sysinternals. The screen saver simulates authentic looking blue screens that reflect the version of Windows on which you run it, generating all blue screen text using actual system information, such as the list of loaded drivers. It also mimics an automatic reboot, complete with the Windows startup splash screen. Note that unlike other screen savers, where a mouse movement dismisses them, the Blue Screen screen saver requires a key press.

By using the following syntax for the Psexec tool from Sysinternals, you can even run the screen saver on another system:

```
psexec \\computername -c -f -i -d "SysInternalsBluescreen.scr" -s -accepteula
```

The command requires that you have administrative privilege on the remote system. (You can use the *-u* and *-p* Psexec switches to specify alternate credentials.) Make sure that your coworker has a sense of humor!

Conclusion

Although many crashes can be analyzed with some of the techniques described in this chapter, many require analysis that goes beyond the scope of this book. Here are some additional resources that may be useful if you want to learn more advanced crash analysis techniques and information:

- The Microsoft Platforms Global Escalation Services team blog, at *http://blogs.msdn.com/ ntdebugging*, provides various tips and tricks and real-life scenarios encountered by the team.

- The website *http://www.dumpanalysis.org* provides hundreds of patterns and advanced analysis scenarios and hints.

Contents of
Windows Internals, Sixth Edition, Part 1

Chapter 4 Management Mechanisms

Chapter 5   Processes, Threads, and Jobs

Chapter 6 Security

Chapter 7   Networking

Index

Symbols and Numbers

P

X

Z

About the Authors

Mark Russinovich is a Technical Fellow in Windows Azure at Microsoft, working on Microsoft's cloud operating system. He is the author of the cyberthriller *Zero Day* (Thomas Dunne Books, 2011) and coauthor of *Windows Sysinternals Administrator's Reference* (Microsoft Press, 2011). Mark joined Microsoft in 2006 when Microsoft acquired Winternals Software, the company he cofounded in 1996, as well as Sysinternals, where he still authors and publishes dozens of popular Windows administration and diagnostic utilities. He is a featured speaker at major industry conferences. Follow Mark on Twitter at @markrussinovich and on Facebook at *http://facebook.com/markrussinovich*.

David Solomon, president of David Solomon Expert Seminars (*www.solsem.com*), has focused on explaining the internals of the Microsoft Windows NT operating system line since 1992. He has taught his world-renowned Windows internals classes to thousands of developers and IT professionals worldwide. His clients include all the major software and hardware companies, including Microsoft. He was nominated a Microsoft Most Valuable Professional in 1993 and from 2005 to 2008.

Prior to starting his own company, David worked for nine years as a project leader and developer in the VMS operating system development group at Digital Equipment Corporation. His first book was entitled *Windows NT for Open VMS Professionals* (Digital Press/Butterworth Heinemann, 1996). It explained Windows NT to VMS-knowledgeable programmers and system administrators. His second book, *Inside Windows NT, Second Edition* (Microsoft Press, 1998), covered the internals of Windows NT 4.0. Since the third edition (*Inside Windows 2000*) David has coauthored this book series with Mark Russinovich.

In addition to organizing and teaching seminars, David is a regular speaker at technical conferences such as Microsoft TechEd and Microsoft PDC. He has also served as technical chair for several past Windows NT conferences. When he's not researching Windows, David enjoys sailing, reading, and watching *Star Trek*.

 **Alex Ionescu** is the founder of Winsider Seminars & Solutions Inc., specializing in low-level system software for administrators and developers as well as reverse engineering and security training for government and infosec clients. He also teaches Windows internals courses for David Solomon Expert Seminars, including at Microsoft. From 2003 to 2007, Alex was the lead kernel developer for ReactOS, an open source clone of Windows XP/Server 2003 written from scratch, for which he wrote most of the Windows NT-based kernel. While in school and part-time in summers, Alex worked as an intern at Apple on the iOS kernel, boot loader, firmware, and drivers on the original core platform team behind the iPhone, iPad, and AppleTV. Returning to his Windows security roots, Alex is now chief architect at CrowdStrike, a startup based in Seattle and San Francisco.

Alex continues to be very active in the security research community, discovering and reporting several vulnerabilities related to the Windows kernel, and presenting talks at conferences such as Blackhat, SyScan, and Recon. His work has led to the fixing of many critical kernel vulnerabilities, as well as to fixing over a few dozen nonsecurity bugs. Previous to his work in the security field, Alex's early efforts led to the publishing of nearly complete NTFS data structure documentation, as well as the Visual Basic metadata and pseudo-code format specifications.

SIT DOWN WITH THE EXPERTS
who literally wrote the book on Windows internals!

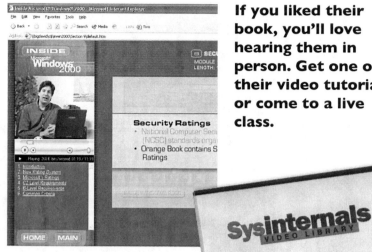

If you liked their book, you'll love hearing them in person. Get one of their video tutorials or come to a live class.

LIVE, INSTRUCTOR LED CLASSES

If you're an IT professional deploying and supporting Windows servers and workstations, you need to be able to dig beneath the surface when things go wrong. In our classes, you'll gain a deep understanding of the internals of the operating system and how to leverage advanced troubleshooting tools to solve system and application problems and understand performance issues more effectively. Attend a public class or schedule a private on site seminar at your location. For dates, course details, pricing, and registration information, see www.solsem.com.

> "The information given in this class should be required for all Windows engineers/administrators."
>
> "This course holds the key to understanding Windows."
>
> "Should be required training for anyone responsible for Windows software development, administration, or design."

INTERACTIVE DVD TUTORIAL

Sit down with the experts who literally wrote the book on Windows internals. Windows Internals COMPLETE consists of 12 hours of interactive training taking you under the hood of the operating system to learn how the kernel components work. As the ultimate compliment, Microsoft Corporation licensed these videos for their corporate training worldwide.

The Sysinternals Video Library (also 12 hours) covers essential Windows troubleshooting topics such as crash dump analysis and memory troubleshooting as well as how to leverage key Sysinternals tools.

> "These videos drill into the core of the platform, capture its technical essence and present it in a powerful interactive video format."–Rob Short, Vice President Core Technologies, Microsoft Corporation

To view video samples or for a detailed outline, visit www.solsem.com or email videos@solsem.com

What do you think of this book?

We want to hear from you!

To participate in a brief online survey, please visit:

microsoft.com/learning/booksurvey

Tell us how well this book meets your needs—what works effectively, and what we can do better. Your feedback will help us continually improve our books and learning resources for you.

Thank you in advance for your input!

CPSIA information can be obtained at www.ICGtesting.com
Printed in the USA
BVOW060944080213

312695BV00008B/8/P